CARTA'S ILLUSTRATED THE JEWISH WAR

JOSEPHUS

CARTA'S ILLUSTRATED THE JEWISH WAR

Translated from the Greek by
William Whiston

*

Introduced by
R. Steven Notley

carta Jerusalem

First published in 2016 by
CARTA Jerusalem

Arranged & edited by Barbara Laurel Ball

Maps: Carta Jerusalem
Cover design: Mike Horton
Frontispiece: Aerial view of Masada (photo by Samuel Magal)

ISBN: 978-965-220-877-4

Great care has been taken to cite all sources of illustrations whenever known. If inadvertently such mention has been omitted but is called to our attention, due amends will be made in the following edition. We shall also be grateful for pointing out any errors, omissions or incomplete information. Please address all comments to Carta Jerusalem.

Carta Jerusalem, Ltd.
11 Rivka Street, POB 2500
Jerusalem 9102401, Israel
E-mail: carta@carta.co.il
Website: www.carta-jerusalem.com

Printed in Israel

INTRODUCTION

R. Steven Notley

The revolt against Rome in A.D. 66–70 proved to be a watershed in the history of the Jewish people. It brought with it the destruction of the holy city, its legendary temple and the loss of any national independence—a political reality that continued for almost two millennia. Sixty years after the revolt, a second uprising (A.D. 132–135) led by Shimon bar Kokhba (Simeon bar Kosevah) likewise ended in devastating defeat. The second insurrection, in fact, presented a much greater challenge to the empire. An entire Roman legion disappeared from the pages of history, apparently the casualty of the Jewish conflict. The outcome of the struggle was in question, and so the emperor Hadrian visited his troops to encourage them. In his report to the Senate, the emperor failed to open with the traditional greeting, "I and the legions are in health," signaling that all was not going well (Dio Cassius, 69.14.3). In spite of the severity of this second determined Jewish rebellion that brought Rome to the brink of defeat, we have very little firsthand information about the Bar Kokhba Revolt.

So, it is one of history's ironies that the reason we have such an abundance of detail about the earlier, first Jewish revolt against Rome is because of the writings of Flavius Josephus, a turncoat, who was an eyewitness to the events. Josephus was born Joseph ben Mattathias in A.D. 37, the first year of the reign of Gaius Caligula (*Life* 1 §5). He descended from priestly lineage and claimed that his mother belonged to the family of the Hasmoneans (*Life* 1 §2), priest-kings who had ruled a century before Josephus was born. He was educated in Jerusalem, and in his early years he explored the varieties of contemporary Jewish thought (*Life* 2 §10: Sadducees, Pharisees, Essenes), including three years with the hermit Bannus (*Life* 2 §11). In the end he decided in favor of the approach of the Pharisees, likely because of their widespread popularity (*Ant.* 18.1.3 §15).

At the young age of 26, Josephus was selected to lead a delegation in A.D. 64 to Rome to appeal to the emperor Nero to release Jewish priests who had been imprisoned there (*Life* 3 §13). Perhaps on account of the successful completion of his mission to Rome, two years later, Josephus was chosen by the Jewish leadership in Jerusalem to take responsibility for the preparation of the defenses in Galilee against Rome's anticipated assault on Judea. In *The Jewish War* he lists the cities that benefited from his efforts (*J.W.* 2.19.6 §573). For such an important task, it is remarkable that we have no record of Josephus' previous military experience.

There is some question how fervent Josephus' support for the revolt actually was. In his autobiography written shortly before his death he indicates that he was chosen, not because of his military expertise but because the Jerusalem leadership hoped he could convince the rebels to fight only in their self-defense (*Life* 4 §17). In other words, his primary task was to dampen the embers of the rebellion. Whatever his own disposition towards the revolt against Rome, archaeological remains from Josephus' efforts indicate that they presented a minimal defense at best.

According to his account, Josephus personally led the defense of Jotapata (*J.W.* 3.7.3–30 §§141–288; 3.7.33–8.1 §§316–344). In the face of sure defeat, the fighters at Jotapata chose death over surrender (*J.W.* 3.8.6–7 §§383–391). Rather than each man taking his own life, Josephus appealed to them to draw lots to determine who would kill the others before taking his own life. He manipulated the outcome and was one of two at the end left alive. He then convinced his fellow survivor that they could serve better purposes, if they lived. The veracity of the details of this episode has been questioned, in no small part because of Josephus' repeated accounts of glorified Jewish suicide (Arbel: *J.W.* 1.16.4 §§309–313; Gamala: *J.W.* 4.1.10 §§70–83; Masada: *J.W.* 7.8.1–9.2 §§252–406)—an act at odds with the Jewish faith.

For our interests what is important is that out of the defeat at Jotapata, Josephus fell into the hands of the general Vespasian. When he discovered that Vespasian intended to send him as a prisoner to Nero, he asked for a private meeting. Alone with Vespasian and his son Titus, Josephus proceeded to predict that the general would soon be declared the emperor, and that after his death his son would follow him on the throne (*J.W.* 3.8.9 §§399–408; see Suetonius, *Vesp.* 5.6; Appian, *Fragment* 17; Dio Cassius, 66:1). Fortune smiled upon Josephus. A few days later word arrived informing Vespasian that Nero had died and that he had been chosen to be Caesar. Rather than send his prisoner away, the new ruler opted to keep this intriguing Jewish figure in his entourage.

Modern historians have looked askance at the report of Josephus' prediction. A nearly identical story is told in the rabbinic sources about Johanan ben Zakkai (*b. Git.* 56a–b), who made a similar prophecy to Vespasian during the siege of Jerusalem. Yet, rather than suggest that either Josephus or the rabbis adopted the other's story for their own purposes, it may be that these prognostications reflect the rumors of succession that were widespread and well-known (see also *J.W.* 6.5.4 §312; Suetonius, *Vesp.* 4; Tacitus, *Hist.* 5:13).

When Vespasian traveled to Rome from Alexandria, Titus returned to Judea to prosecute the siege of Jerusalem with Josephus at his side. The Jewish prisoner-now-ally proved to be an asset, at times appealing to his countrymen to abandon the folly of their resistance to Rome (*J.W.* 7.2.1–2 §96-117). According to his own reports, these appeals were only partly successful, but they underscore his shift in loyalties to Rome. At the conclusion of the war, Josephus was rewarded with land in Judea, Roman citizenship, a residence in Rome and a pension (*Life* 76 §422–423). It was from his new home in Rome that he penned four works that have come down to us today: *The Jewish War*, *Jewish Antiquities*, *Life*, and *Against Apion*.

The writings of Josephus likely would have been lost, except for the efforts to preserve them by the Church. Christian interest was doubtless because of Josephus' testimony concerning three figures from the New Testament: John the Baptist (*Ant.* 18.1.2 §§116–119); James the brother of Jesus (*Ant.* 20.9.1 §§197–203); and the famous *Testimonium Flavium* concerning Jesus of Nazareth (*Ant.* 18.3.3 §63–64).

We have no record of Josephus' death, but scholars assume that he died in Rome during the reign of Trajan sometime after A.D. 100. In the space remaining we will consider briefly each of his works in the order that they were written.

The Jewish War. Josephus' history of the first Jewish revolt was probably written within ten years of the end of the conflict (c. 79), although, there is a question whether the final Book 7 was a later addition composed during the reign of Domitian (A.D. 81–96). The perspective of *The Jewish War* is Roman, and is in the style of other Roman military histories. Josephus presents the insurrection as a misguided effort instigated by extremist elements that the writer calls the Fourth Philosophy (*Ant.* 18.1.1 §9). By contrast in *The Jewish War* Josephus minimizes his description of Roman excesses, and even reports that Titus had no desire for the destruction of the temple in Jerusalem (*J.W.* 6.4.3 §241), an assertion that agrees with the opinion of the rabbinic sources (*b. Git.* 56b) and Roman history (Dio Cassius, 6.65). However, this picture of Titus does not square with Josephus' statement in his later report found in Book 7: "(Titus) gave orders that they should now demolish the entire city and temple" (*J.W.* 7.1.1 §1). The shift in culpability for the temple's destruction is also witnessed in *Jewish Antiquities* 20.10.5 §250 (see Sulpicius Severus, *Chronica* 2.30.6–7).

For the content of his history Josephus augments his own firsthand information with the memoirs of Vespasian and Titus (*Life* 65 §342). To these he added details gleaned from his communications with King Agrippa II (*Life* 65 §364), the Jewish client king who ruled Judea on behalf of the Romans during the revolt. Josephus claims that he originally wrote *The Jewish War* in his ancestral language (*J.W.* 1.1.1 §3), which modern scholars have assumed to be Aramaic, because he states that the original account was first sent to the Aramaic-speaking Jewish community in Babylonia. The question of the original audience notwithstanding, there are unmistakable examples of Hebraisms perserved in Josephus' Greek text that can not have been Aramaic (e.g., *J.W.* 5.6.3 §272). Whatever the language of the original, the Greek text that has come to us is the most refined of his four works, and it presents his finest command of the Greek language, likely an indication of the editorial assitance given to him in Rome.

Jewish Antiquities. His history of the Jewish people is the longest and most complex of Josephus' compositions. It was intended to convince non-Jews of the antiquity of the Jewish people and is patterned after *Antiquitates Romanae* by Dionysius of Halicarnassus. Josephus' work traces the history of the Jewish people from their biblical beginnings to the days of the Jewish revolt against Rome in A.D. 66–70. In the preface the author claims that he will give precise details, and neither add nor omit anything (*Ant.* Proem 3 §17). Nevertheless, the accounts found in the biblical narrative often part company in detail with the traditions of the Hebrew Bible. While there is no reason to assume that Josephus was unable to read the Hebrew Bible, the text he preserves more often approximates the textual tradition of the Greek Bible (Septuagint). One of the important contributions of Books 1–11 in Josephus' *Jewish Antiquities* is the insight they provide on the state of the biblical text in the first century A.D., and the ways in which scripture was interpreted.

The historical details given in Josephus' treatise are a study in contrasts, which is likely a consequence of the number and the quality of his sources. The period from Ezra to Alexander the Great (*Ant.* Book 11) provides us the least information about any of the periods he recounts, either because there was not much to relate in terms of significant Jewish history or because of the lack of written sources available to the author. Only a slight increase in information can be seen in the Ptolemaic period (*Ant.* 12.1.1–3.2 §§1–128) for which Josephus relies heavily upon the Letter of Aristeas.

Perhaps because of his own Hasmonean heritage, Josephus writes extensively about the Jewish struggle for freedom against the Seleucids led by Judas Maccabaeus and his brothers. One of the historian's main sources for the account of the military struggle and the early decades of the Hasmonean rule (*Ant.* 12.5.3–13.16.6 §§12.246–13.432) is the Book of First Maccabees. Following upon this the historian writes in great detail about the man who unseated the Hasmoneans—Herod the Great (37–4 B.C.; *Ant.* Books 15–17). It seems that Josephus had access to the archives of Herod's court historian, Nicolaus of Damascus, whom he cites regularly (*Ant.* 1.2.6 §94; 1.7.2 §159; 7.5.2 §101; 12.3.2 §§126–127, etc.). Herod's great-grandson, King Agrippa II, may have also proven a valuable source for Herodian family history (*Life* 65 §§362–366). While Josephus strongly criticized Herod's excesses, he recognized the important role Herod played in forging the Jewish nation's political alliance with the Roman empire.

Life. Josephus' life story is the first autobiography to be preserved in antiquity. It was written in answer to attacks on him by Justus of Tiberias, who accused Josephus of misconduct in Galilee before the arrival of Vespasian. In his defense the historian drew from testimony by his friend King Agrippa II (*Life* 65 §§365–366). *Life* first appeared as an appendix to the second edition of *Jewish Antiquities* and likely was published in A.D. 93/94.

Against Apion. The last of Josephus' literary works, this short treatise follows in the genre of the Greek apologists. It consists of two parts in which Josephus refutes the growing antisemitism of his day. The first book draws largely from works that are no longer extant in a defense of the Jewish people. The second part is an affirmation of the positive value of Judaism in comparison to Hellenism. In *Apion* 2:14–41 §§145–295 it seems that Josephus has modelled his argument after the first-century Jewish philosopher, Philo's *Hypothetica*.

Select Bibliography

Beall, Todd S. *Josephus' Description of the Essenes Illustrated by the Dead Sea Scrolls*. Cambridge, UK: Cambridge University Press, 2004.

Bentwich, Norman. *Josephus*. Philadelphia, PA: Jewish Publication Society, 1914.

Bilde, Per. *Flavius Josephus between Jerusalem and Rome: His Life, His Works and Their Importance*. Sheffield: *Journal for the Study of the Old Testament*, 1988.

Cohen, Shaye J. D. *Josephus in Galilee and Rome: His Vita and Development as a Historian*. Leiden: Brill, 1979.

Edmondson, J. C., Steve Mason, and J. B. Rives, eds. *Flavius Josephus and Flavian Rome*. Oxford: Oxford University Press, 2005.

Feldman, Louis H. *Josephus's Interpretation of the Bible*. Berkeley: University of California Press, 1998.

—. *Studies in Josephus' Rewritten Bible*. Atlanta: Society of Biblical Literature, 2005.

Feldman, Louis H., and Gohei Hata, eds. *Josephus, the Bible, and History*. Leiden: Brill, 1989.

Josephus, Flavius. *Flavius Josephus: Translation and Commentary*. Edited by Steve Mason. 8 Vols. Leiden: Brill, 2001–2013.

Mason, Steve. *Flavius Josephus on the Pharisees: A Composition-critical Study*. Leiden: Brill, 1991.

—. *Josephus and the New Testament*. Peabody, MA: Hendrickson, 1993.

Rajak, Tessa. *Josephus: The Historian and His Society*. Philadelphia: Fortress Press, 1984.

Rappaport, Uriel. *Yosef ben Matityahu: Historyon shel Erets-Yiśra'el ba-tekufah ha-Helenistit veha-Romit: kovets mehkarim*. Jerusalem: Yad Yitshak Ben-Tsevi, 1982.

Rengstorf, Karl Heinrich, and Flavius Josephus. *A Complete Concordance to Flavius Josephus*. 4 Vols. Leiden: Brill, 1973–1983.

Schwartz, Seth. *Josephus and Judaean Politics*. Leiden: Brill, 1990.

Shahar, Yuval. *Josephus Geographicus: The Classical Context of Geography in Josephus*. Tübingen: Mohr Siebeck, 2004.

Sievers, Joseph, and Gaia Lembi, eds. *Josephus and Jewish History in Flavian Rome and Beyond*. Leiden: Brill, 2005.

TABLE OF CONTENTS

Users' Guide

Maps: To facilitate comparison of Josephus' account with the latest scholarly research, the map numbers follow those appearing in *The Carta Bible Atlas*, 5th edition (duotone; Jerusalem 2011). These maps and their text can also be accessed in *The Sacred Bridge: Carta's Atlas of the Biblical World* (Jerusalem 2006, 2014), as follows:

Josephus: Carta's Illustrated The Jewish War (page number)	The Carta Bible Atlas (map number)	The Sacred Bridge (page number)
1	207	306
2	216	313
2	218	315
3	229	323
6	237	332
9	239	335
10	240	336
13	241	337
18	242	338
23	243	339
28	244	343
50	263	344
52	246	347
55	249	340
59	281	384
60	282	385
71	283	387
91	285	389
119	286	391
130	287	392
136	288	393
201	290	395
212	291	395

JOSEPHUS: CARTA'S ILLUSTRATED THE JEWISH WAR

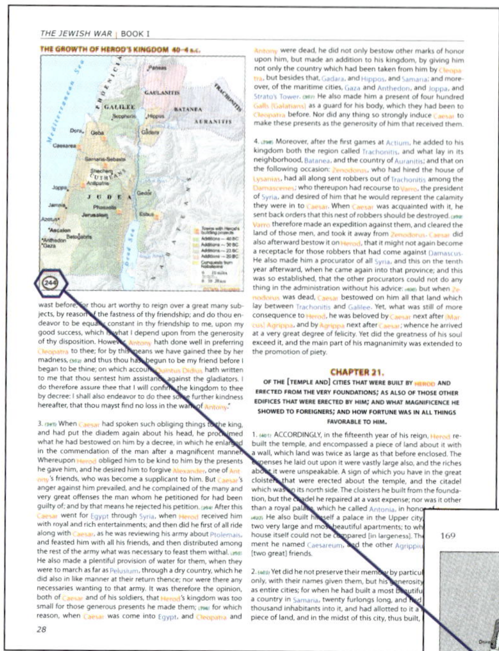

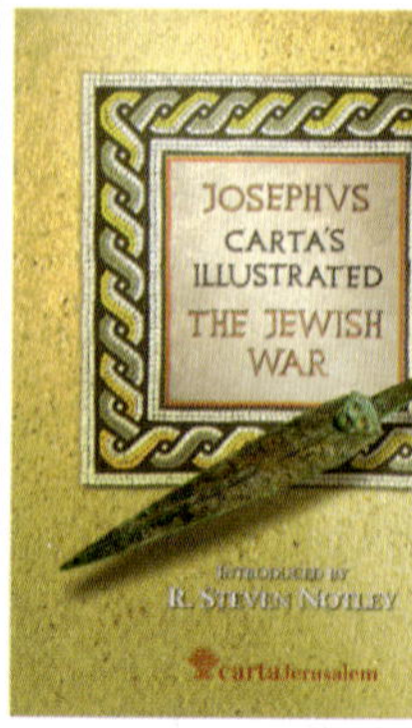

THE CARTA BIBLE ATLAS (TCBA)

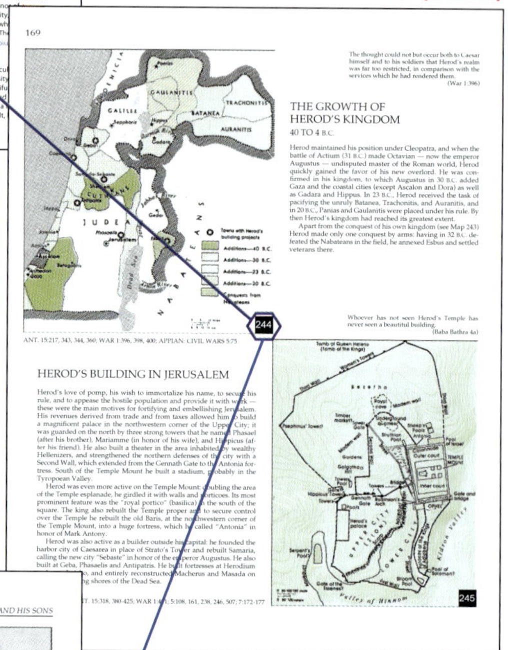

THE SACRED BRIDGE (TSB)

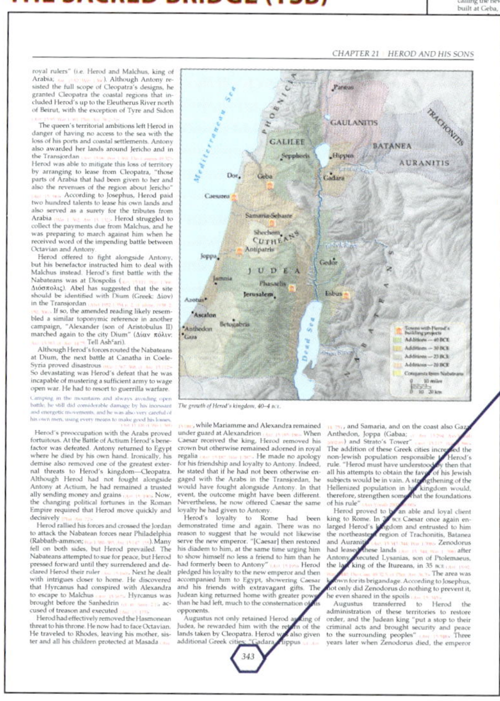

TCBA	TSB
244	343

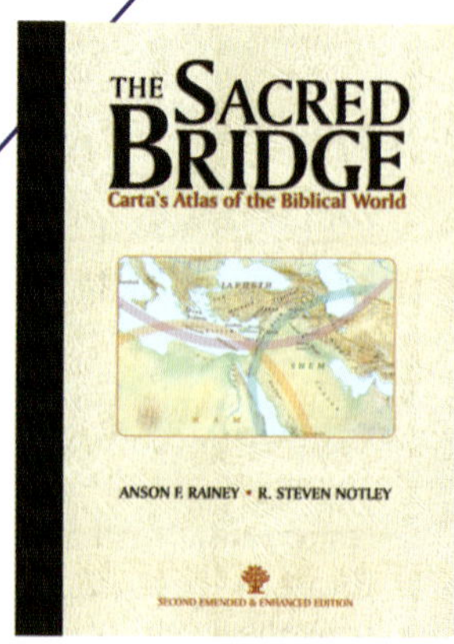

Maps and plans derived from other sources are referenced adjacent to each item.

Illustrations: The archaeological treasures discovered over long years make it possible to illustrate Josephus' story with contemporary remains and relics; we have endeavored to include a decent sampling of enlightening details. An additional feature is the landscapes. Some are as pristine today as they were then; others illustrate the scene as it is today.

Name search: For quick and easy location, names in the text have been color coded as follows:

Persons/Peoples (red): e.g., Vespasian
Places (blue): e.g., Jerusalem
References (green): e.g., **(35)**

A note on references: One of the challenges for modern readers of Josephus' works is that the current English translations are based on either one of two completely different referencing systems. Most popular editions of Josephus use William Whiston's English translation (1737) that divided the Jewish author's writings according to book, chapter, and paragraph (e.g., *Jewish War* 3.10.7–8). A decidedly different referencing system was created a century later by Benedictus Niese, who published the standard Greek edition of Josephus (1885–1895). His small-unit numbering system (e.g., *Jewish War* 3.506–521 for the same passage cited above according to Whiston) was adopted by Henry St. John Thackeray for the Loeb Classical Library edition that is used by most students and scholars in the academic world. *Carta's Illustrated The Jewish War* has sought to bridge these differences by providing the reader a combined referencing system. The primary division is according to Whiston's book, chapter, and paragraph; but the reader will also find included the Loeb small-unit reference numbers in parentheses and highlighted in green font. If the reader needs to find a passage in *The Jewish War* cited in a book or article reference, with Carta's combined referencing system no matter which system has been used by the author, the reader will be able to find it with ease.

PREFACE by JOSEPHUS

THE WARS OF THE JEWS, OR, THE HISTORY OF THE DESTRUCTION OF JERUSALEM

1. (1) WHEREAS the war which the Jews made with the Romans hath been the greatest of all those, not only that have been in our times, but, in a manner, of those that ever were heard of; both of those wherein cities have fought against cities, or nations against nations; while some men who were not concerned in the affairs themselves have gotten together vain and contradictory stories by hearsay, and have written them down after a sophistical manner; (2) and while those that were there present have given false accounts of things, and this either out of a humor of flattery to the Romans, or of hatred towards the Jews; and while their writings contain sometimes accusations, and sometimes encomiums, but no where the accurate truth of the facts; (3) I have proposed to myself, for the sake of such as live under the government of the Romans, to translate those books into the Greek tongue, which I formerly composed in the language of our country, and sent to the Upper Barbarians; Joseph, the son of Matthias, by birth a Hebrew, a priest also, and one who at first fought against the Romans myself, and was forced to be present at what was done afterwards, [am the author of this work].

2. (4) Now at the time when this great concussion of affairs happened, the affairs of the Romans were themselves in great disorder. Those Jews also who were for innovations, then arose when the times were disturbed; they were also in a flourishing condition for strength and riches, insomuch that the affairs of the East were then exceeding tumultuous, while some hoped for gain, and others were afraid of loss in such troubles; (5) for the Jews hoped that all of their nation which were beyond Euphrates would have raised an insurrection together with them. The Gauls also, in the neighborhood of the Romans, were in motion, and the Geltin were not quiet; but all was in disorder after the death of Nero. And the opportunity now offered induced many to aim at the royal power; and the soldiery affected change, out of the hopes of getting money. (6) I thought it therefore an absurd thing to see the truth falsified in affairs of such great consequence, and to take no notice of it; but to suffer those Greeks and Romans that were not in the wars to be ignorant of these things, and to read either flatteries or fictions, while the Parthians, and the Babylonians, and the remotest Arabians, and those of our nation beyond Euphrates, with the Adiabeni, by my means, knew accurately both whence the war begun, what miseries it brought upon us, and after what manner it ended.

3. (7) It is true, these writers have the confidence to call their accounts histories; wherein yet they seem to me to fail of their own purpose, as well as to relate nothing that is sound. For they have a mind to demonstrate the greatness of the Romans, while they still diminish and lessen the actions of the Jews, (8) as not discerning how it cannot be that those must appear to be great who have only conquered those that were little. Nor are they ashamed to overlook the length of the war, the multitude of the Roman forces who so greatly suffered in it, or the might of the commanders, whose great labors about Jerusalem will be deemed inglorious, if what they achieved be reckoned but a small matter.

4. (9) However, I will not go to the other extreme, out of opposition to those men who extol the Romans nor will I determine to raise the actions of my countrymen too high; but I will prosecute the actions of both parties with accuracy. Yet shall I suit my language to the passions I am under, as to the affairs I describe, and must be allowed to indulge some lamentations upon the miseries undergone by my own country. (10) For that it was a seditious temper of our own that destroyed it, and that they were the tyrants among the Jews who brought the Roman power upon us, who unwillingly attacked us, and occasioned the burning of our holy temple, Titus Caesar, who destroyed it, is himself a witness, who, daring the entire war, pitied the people who were kept under by the seditious, and did often voluntarily delay the taking of the city, and allowed time to the siege, in order to let the authors have opportunity for repentance. (11) But if any one makes an unjust accusation against us, when we speak so passionately about the tyrants, or the robbers, or sorely bewail the misfortunes of our country, let him indulge my affections herein, though it be contrary to the rules for writing history; because it had so come to pass, that our city Jerusalem had arrived at a higher degree of felicity than any other city under the Roman government, and yet at last fell into the sorest of calamities again. (12) Accordingly, it appears to me that the misfortunes of all men, from the beginning of the world, if they be compared to these of the Jews are not so considerable as they were; while the authors of them were not foreigners neither. This makes it impossible for me to contain my lamentations. But if any one be inflexible in his censures of me, let him attribute the facts themselves to the historical part, and the lamentations to the writer himself only.

5. (13) However, I may justly blame the learned men among the Greeks, who, when such great actions have been done in their own times, which, upon the comparison, quite eclipse the old wars, do yet sit as judges of those affairs, and pass bitter censures upon the labors of the best writers of antiquity; which moderns, although they may be superior to the old writers in eloquence, yet are they inferior to them in the execution of what they intended to do. While these also write new histories about the Assyrians and Medes, as if the ancient writers had not described their affairs as they ought to have done; (14) although these be as far inferior to them in abilities as they are different in their notions from them. For of old every one took upon them to write what happened in his own time; where their immediate concern in the actions made their promises of value; and where it must be reproachful to write lies, when they must be known by the readers to be such. (15) But then, an undertaking to preserve the memory of what hath not been before recorded, and to represent the affairs of one's own time to those that come afterwards, is really worthy of praise and commendation. Now he is to be esteemed to have taken good pains in earnest, not who does no more than change the disposition and order of other men's works, but he who not only relates what had not been related before, but composes an entire body of history of his own: (16) accordingly, I have been at great charges, and have taken very great pains [about this history], though I be a foreigner; and do dedicate this work, as a memorial of great actions, both to the Greeks and to the Barbarians. But for some of our own principal men, their mouths are wide open, and their

tongues loosed presently, for gain and law-suits, but quite muzzled up when they are to write history, where they must speak truth and gather facts together with a great deal of pains; and so they leave the writing such histories to weaker people, and to such as are not acquainted with the actions of princes. Yet shall the real truth of historical facts be preferred by us, how much soever it be neglected among the Greek historians.

6. (17) To write concerning the Antiquities of the Jews, who they were [originally], and how they revolted from the Egyptians, and what country they traveled over, and what countries they seized upon afterward, and how they were removed out of them, I think this not to be a fit opportunity, and, on other accounts, also superfluous; and this because many Jews before me have composed the histories of our ancestors very exactly; as have some of the Greeks done it also, and have translated our histories into their own tongue, and have not much mistaken the truth in their histories. (18) But then, where the writers of these affairs and our prophets leave off, thence shall I take my rise, and begin my history. Now as to what concerns that war which happened in my own time, I will go over it very largely, and with all the diligence I am able; but for what preceded mine own age, that I shall run over briefly.

7. (19) [For example, I shall relate] how Antiochus, who was named Epiphanes, took Jerusalem by force, and held it three years and three months, and was then ejected out of the country by the sons of Asamoneus: after that, how their posterity quarreled about the government, and brought upon their settlement the Romans and Pompey; how Herod also, the son of Antipater, dissolved their government, and brought Sosius upon them; (20) as also how our people made a sedition upon Herod's death, while Augustus was the Roman emperor, and Quintilius Varus was in that country; and how the war broke out in the twelfth year of Nero, with what happened to Cestius; and what places the Jews assaulted in a hostile manner in the first sallies of the war.

8. (21) As also [I shall relate] how they built walls about the neighboring cities; and how Nero, upon Cestius's defeat, was in fear of the entire event of the war, and thereupon made Vespasian general in this war; and how this Vespasian, with the elder of his sons made an expedition into the country of Judea; what was the number of the Roman army that he made use of; and how many of his auxiliaries were cut off in all Galilee; and how he took some of its cities entirely, and by force, and others of them by treaty, and on terms. (22) Now, when I am come so far, I shall describe the good order of the Romans in war, and the discipline of their legions; the amplitude of both the Galilees, with its nature, and the limits of Judea. And, besides this, I shall particularly go over what is peculiar to the country, the lakes and fountains that are in them, and what miseries happened to every city as they were taken; and all this with accuracy, as I saw the things done, or suffered in them. For I shall not conceal any of the calamities I myself endured, since I shall relate them to such as know the truth of them.

9. (23) After this, [I shall relate] how, When the Jews' affairs were become very bad, Nero died, and Vespasian, when he was going to attack Jerusalem, was called back to take the government upon him; what signs happened to him relating to his gaining that government, and what mutations of government then happened at Rome, (24) and how he was unwillingly made emperor by his soldiers; and how, upon his departure to Egypt, to take upon him the government of the empire, the affairs of the Jews became very tumultuous; as also how the tyrants rose up against them, and fell into dissensions among themselves.

10. (25) Moreover, [I shall relate] how Titus marched out of Egypt into Judea the second time; as also how, and where, and how many forces he got together; and in what state the city was, by the means of the seditious, at his coming; what attacks he made, and how many ramparts he cast up; of the three walls that encompassed the city, and of their measures; of the strength of the city, and the structure of the temple and holy house; (26) and besides, the measures of those edifices, and of the altar, and all accurately determined. A description also of certain of their festivals, and seven purifications of purity, and the sacred ministrations of the priests, with the garments of the priests, and of the high priests; and of the nature of the most holy place of the temple; without concealing any thing, or adding any thing to the known truth of things.

11. (27) After this, I shall relate the barbarity of the tyrants towards the people of their own nation, as well as the indulgence of the Romans in sparing foreigners; and how often Titus, out of his desire to preserve the city and the temple, invited the seditious to come to terms of accommodation. I shall also distinguish the sufferings of the people, and their calamities; how far they were afflicted by the sedition, and how far by the famine, and at length were taken. (28) Nor shall I omit to mention the misfortunes of the deserters, nor the punishments inflicted on the captives; as also how the temple was burnt, against the consent of Caesar; and how many sacred things that had been laid up in the temple were snatched out of the fire; the destruction also of the entire city, with the signs and wonders that went before it; and the taking the tyrants captives, and the multitude of those that were made slaves, and into what different misfortunes they were every one distributed. (29) Moreover, what the Romans did to the remains of the wall; and how they demolished the strong holds that were in the country; and how Titus went over the whole country, and settled its affairs; together with his return into Italy, and his triumph.

12. (30) I have comprehended all these things in seven books, and have left no occasion for complaint or accusation to such as have been acquainted with this war; and I have written it down for the sake of those that love truth, but not for those that please themselves [with fictitious relations]. And I will begin my account of these things with what I call my First Chapter.

BOOK I

FROM THE TAKING OF JERUSALEM BY ANTIOCHUS EPIPHANES, TO THE DEATH OF HEROD THE GREAT

CHAPTER 1

HOW THE CITY JERUSALEM WAS TAKEN, AND THE TEMPLE PILLAGED [BY ANTIOCHUS EPIPHANES]. AS ALSO CONCERNING THE ACTIONS OF THE MACCABEES, MATTHIAS AND JUDAS; AND CONCERNING THE DEATH OF JUDAS.

1. (31) AT the same time that Antiochus [IV], who was called Epiphanes, had a quarrel with the sixth Ptolemy about his right to the whole country of Syria, a great sedition fell among the men of power in Judea, and they had a contention about obtaining the government; while each of those that were of dignity could not endure to be subject to their equals. However, Onias, one of the high priests, got the better, and cast the sons of Tobias out of the city; (32) who fled to Antiochus, and besought him to make use of them for his leaders, and to make an expedition into Judea. The king being thereto disposed beforehand, complied with them, and came upon the Jews with a great army, and took their city by force, and slew a great multitude of those that favored Ptolemy, and sent out his soldiers to plunder them without mercy. He also spoiled the temple, and put a stop to the constant practice of offering a daily sacrifice of expiation for three years and six months. (33) But Onias, the high priest, fled to Ptolemy, and received a place from him in the Nomus of Heliopolis, where he built a city resembling Jerusalem, and a temple that was like its temple concerning which we shall speak more in its proper place hereafter.

2. (34) Now Antiochus was not satisfied either with his unexpected taking the city, or with its pillage, or with the great slaughter he had made there; but being overcome with his violent passions, and remembering what he had suffered during the siege, he compelled the Jews to dissolve the laws of their country, and to keep their infants uncircumcised, and to sacrifice swine's flesh upon the altar; (35) against which they all opposed themselves, and the most approved among them were put to death. Bacchides also, who was sent to keep the fortresses, having these wicked commands, joined to his own natural barbarity, indulged all sorts of the extremest wickedness, and tormented the worthiest of the inhabitants, man by man, and threatened their city every day with open destruction, till at length he provoked the poor sufferers by the extremity of his wicked doings to avenge themselves.

3. (36) Accordingly Matthias, the son of Asamoneus, one of the priests who lived in a village called Modin, armed himself, together with his own family, which had five sons of his in it, and slew Bacchides with daggers; and thereupon, out of the fear of the many garrisons [of the enemy], he fled to the mountains; (37) and so many of the people followed him, that he was encouraged to come down from the mountains, and to give battle to Antiochus's generals, when he beat them, and drove them out of Judea. So he came to the government by this his success, and became the prince of his own people by their own free consent, and then died, leaving the government to Judas, his eldest son.

4. (38) Now Judas, supposing that Antiochus would not lie still, gathered an army out of his own countrymen, and was the first that made a league of friendship with the Romans, and drove Epiphanes out of the country when he had made a second expedition into it, and this by giving him a great defeat there; (39) and when he was warmed by this great success, he made an assault upon the garrison that was in the city, for it had not been cut off hitherto; so he ejected them out of the upper city, and drove the soldiers into the lower, which part of the city was called the Citadel. He then got the temple under his power, and cleansed the whole place, and walled it round about, and made new vessels for

EGYPTIAN CAMPAIGNS OF ANTIOCHUS IV 170–167 B.C.

Coin of Antiochus IV Epiphanes. (Carta archives)

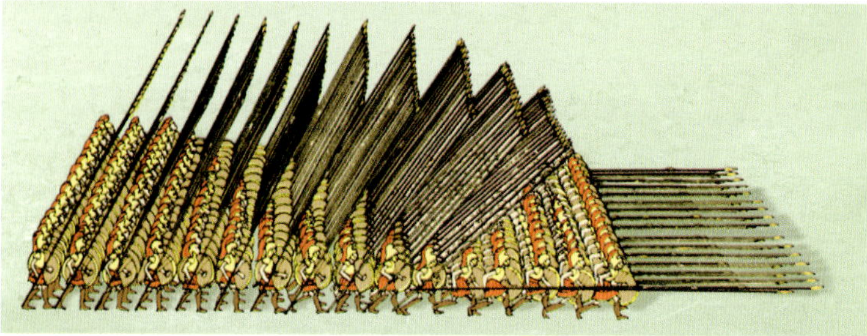

Macedonian phalanx. (Carta collection)

sacred ministrations, and brought them into the temple, because the former vessels had been profaned. He also built another altar, and began to offer the sacrifices; (40) and when the city had already received its sacred constitution again, Antiochus [IV] died; whose son Antiochus [V] succeeded him in the kingdom, and in his hatred to the Jews also.

5. (41) So this Antiochus got together fifty thousand footmen, and five thousand horsemen, and fourscore elephants, and marched through Judea into the mountainous parts. He then took Bethsura, which was a small city; but at a place called Bethzacharis, where the passage was narrow, Judas met him with his army. (42) However, before the forces joined battle, Judas's brother Eleazar, seeing the very highest of the elephants adorned with a large tower, and with military trappings of gold to guard him, and supposing that Antiochus himself was upon him, he ran a great way before his own army, and cutting his way through the enemy's troops, he got up to the elephant; (43) yet could he not reach him who seemed to be the king, by reason of his being so high; but still he ran his weapon into the belly of the beast, and brought him down upon himself, and was crushed to death, having done no more than attempted great things, and showed that he preferred glory before life. (44) Now he that governed the elephant was but a private man; and had he proved to be Antiochus, Eleazar had performed nothing more by this bold stroke than that it might appear he chose to die, when he had the bare hope of thereby doing a glorious action; (45) nay, this disappointment proved an omen to his brother [Judas] how the entire battle would end. It is true that the Jews fought it out bravely for a long time, but the king's forces, being superior in number, and having fortune on their side, obtained the victory. And when a great many of his men were slain, Judas took the rest with him, and fled to the toparchy of Gophna. (46) So Antiochus went to Jerusalem, and staid there but a few days, for he wanted provisions, and so he went his way. He left indeed a garrison behind him, such as he thought sufficient to keep the place, but drew the rest of his army off, to take their winter-quarters in Syria.

THE BATTLE OF BETH-ZACHARIS/BETH-ZECHARIAH 162 B.C.

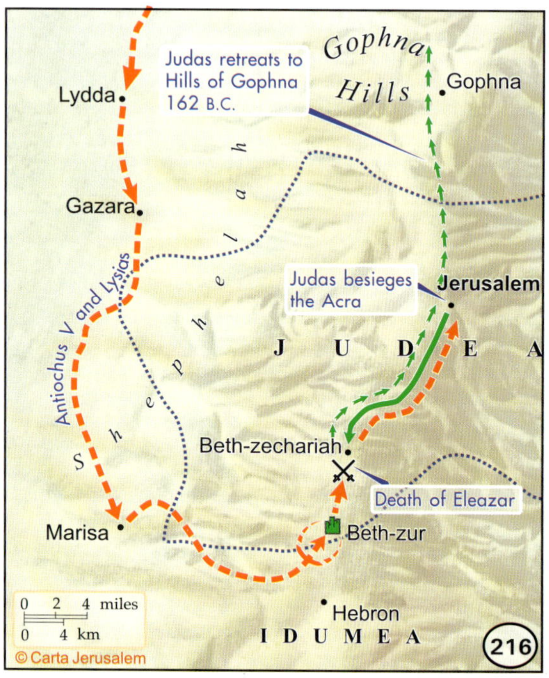

6. (47) Now, after the king was departed, Judas was not idle; for as many of his own nation came to him, so did he gather those that had escaped out of the battle together, and gave battle again to Antiochus's generals at a village called Adasa; and being too hard for his enemies in the battle, and killing a great number of them, he was at last himself slain also. Nor was it many days afterward that his brother John had a plot laid against him by Antiochus's party, and was slain by them.

THE BATTLE OF ADASA 161 B.C.

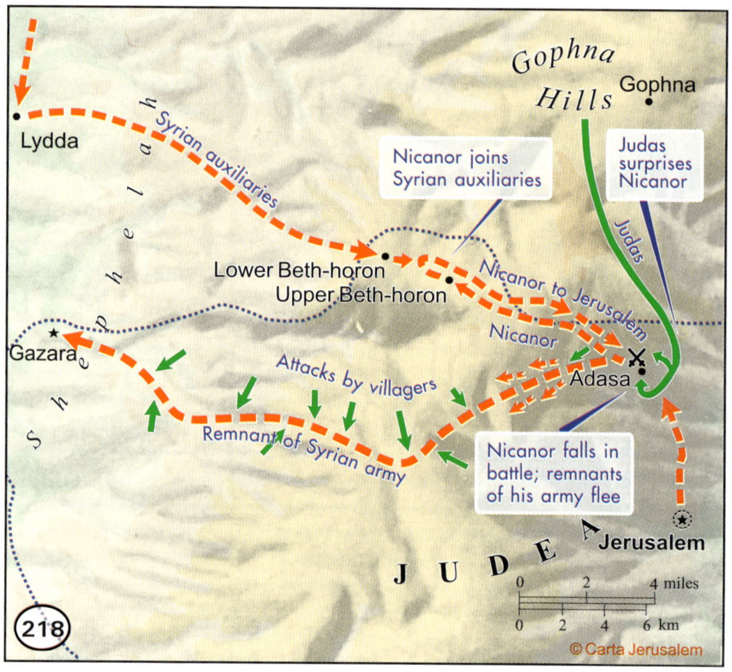

CHAPTER 2.

CONCERNING THE SUCCESSORS OF JUDAS, WHO WERE JONATHAN AND SIMON, AND JOHN HYRCANUS.

1. (48) WHEN Jonathan, who was Judas's brother, succeeded him, he behaved himself with great circumspection in other respects, with relation to his own people; and he corroborated his authority by preserving his friendship with the Romans. He also made a league with Antiochus [VI] the son. Yet was not all this sufficient for his security; (49) for the tyrant Trypho, who was guardian to Antiochus's son, laid a plot against him; and besides that, endeavored to take off his friends, and caught Jonathan by a wile, as he was going to Ptolemais to Antiochus, with a few persons in his company, and put him in bonds, and then made an expedition against the Jews; but when he was afterward driven away by Simon, who was Jonathan's brother, and was enraged at his defeat, he put Jonathan to death.

2. (50) However, Simon managed the public affairs after a courageous manner, and took Gazara, and Joppa, and Jamnia, which were cities in his neighborhood. He also got the garrison under, and demolished the citadel. He was afterward an auxiliary to Antiochus, against Trypho, whom he besieged in Dora, before he went on

TRYPHO'S CAMPAIGN AGAINST JONATHAN 143–142 B.C.

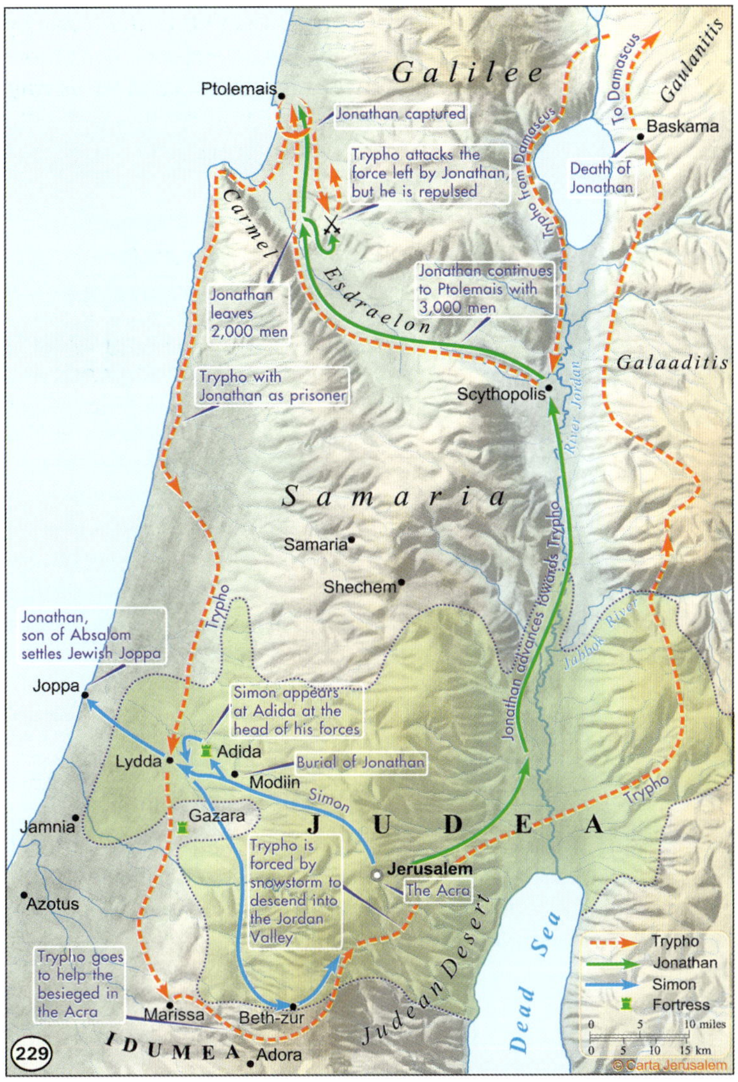

his expedition against the Medes; (51) yet could not he make the king ashamed of his ambition, though he had assisted him in killing Trypho; for it was not long ere Antiochus sent Cendebeus his general with an army to lay waste Judea, and to subdue Simon; (52) yet he, though he was now in years, conducted the war as if he were a much younger man. He also sent his sons with a band of strong men against Antiochus, while he took part of the army himself with him, and fell upon him from another quarter. (53) He also laid a great many men in ambush in many places of the mountains, and was superior in all his attacks upon them; and when he had been conqueror after so glorious a manner, he was made high priest, and also freed the Jews from the dominion of the Macedonians, after one hundred and seventy years of the empire [of Seleucus].

3. (54) This Simon also had a plot laid against him, and was slain at a feast by his son-in-law Ptolemy, who put his wife and two sons into prison, and sent some persons to kill John, who was also called Hyrcanus. (55) But when the young man was informed of their coming beforehand, he made haste to get to the city, as having a very great confidence in the people there, both on account of the memory of the glorious actions of his father, and of the hatred they could not but bear to the injustice of Ptolemy. Ptolemy also made an attempt to get into the city by another gate; but was repelled by the people, who had just then admitted of Hyrcanus; (56) so he retired presently to one of the fortresses that were about Jericho, which was called Dagon. Now when Hyrcanus had received the high priesthood, which his father had held before, and had offered sacrifice to God, he made great haste to attack Ptolemy, that he might afford relief to his mother and brethren.

4. (57) So he laid siege to the fortress, and was superior to Ptolemy in other respects, but was overcome by him as to the just affection [he had for his relations]; for when Ptolemy was distressed, he brought forth his mother, and his brethren, and set them upon the wall, and beat them with rods in every body's sight, and threatened, that unless he would go away immediately, he would throw them down headlong; (58) at which sight Hyrcanus's commiseration and concern were too hard for his anger. But his mother was not dismayed, neither at the stripes she received, nor at the death with which she was threatened; but stretched out her hands, and prayed her son not to be moved with the injuries that she suffered to spare the wretch; since it was to her better to die by the means of Ptolemy, than to live ever so long, provided he might be punished for the injuries he done to their family. (59) Now John's case was this: When he considered the courage of his mother, and heard her entreaty, he set about his attacks; but when he saw her beaten, and torn to pieces with the stripes, he grew feeble, and was entirely overcome by his affections. (60) And as the siege was delayed by this means, the year of rest came on, upon which the Jews rest every seventh year as they do on every seventh day. On this year, therefore, Ptolemy was freed from being besieged, and slew the brethren of John, with their mother, and fled to Zeno, who was also called Cotylas, who was tyrant of Philadelphia.

5. (61) And now Antiochus was so angry at what he had suffered from Simon, that he made an expedition into Judea, and sat down before Jerusalem and besieged Hyrcanus; but Hyrcanus opened the sepulcher of David, who was the richest of all kings, and took thence about three thousand talents in money, and induced Antiochus, by the promise of three thousand talents, to raise the siege. Moreover, he was the first of the Jews that had money enough, and began to hire foreign auxiliaries also.

6. (62) However, at another time, when Antiochus was gone upon an expedition against the Medes, and so gave Hyrcanus an opportunity of being revenged upon him, he immediately made an attack upon the cities of Syria, as thinking, what proved to be the case with them, that he should find them empty of god troops. (63) So he took Medaba and Samea, with the towns in their neighborhood, as also Shechem, and Gerizzim; and besides these, [he subdued] the nation of the Cutheans, who dwelt round about that temple which was built in imitation of the temple at Jerusalem; he also took a great many other cities of Idumea, with Adoreon and Marissa.

Hasmonean coin of John Hyrcanus. (Carta archives)

7. (64) He also proceeded as far as Samaria, where is now the city Sebaste, which was built by Herod the king, and encompassed it all round with a wall, and set his sons, Aristobulus and Antigonus, over the siege; who pushed it on so hard, that a famine so far prevailed within the city, that they were forced to eat what never was esteemed food. (65) They also invited Antiochus [IX],

Ruins of the colonnaded street at Sebaste. (photo Samuel Magal)

who was called Cyzicenus, to come to their assistance; whereupon he got ready, and complied with their invitation, but was beaten by Aristobulus and Antigonus; and indeed he was pursued as far as Scythopolis by these brethren, and fled away from them. So they returned back to Samaria, and shut the multitude again within the wall; and when they had taken the city, they demolished it, and made slaves of its inhabitants. (66) And as they had still great success in their undertakings, they did not suffer their zeal to cool, but marched with an army as far as Scythopolis, and made an incursion upon it, and laid waste all the country that lay within Mount Carmel.

8. (67) But then these successes of John and of his sons made them be envied, and occasioned a sedition in the country; and many there were who got together, and would not be at rest till they brake out into open war, in which war they were beaten. (68) So John lived the rest of his life very happily, and administered the government after a most extraordinary manner, and this for thirty-three entire years together. He died, leaving five sons behind him. He was certainly a very happy man, and afforded no occasion to have any complaint made of fortune on his account. He it was who alone had three of the most desirable things in the world,—the government of his nation, and the high priesthood, and the gift of prophecy. (69) For the Deity conversed with him, and he was not ignorant of any thing that was to come afterward; insomuch that he foresaw and foretold that his two eldest sons would not continue masters of the government; and it will highly deserve our narration to describe their catastrophe, and how far inferior these men were to their father in felicity.

CHAPTER 3.

HOW ARISTOBULUS WAS THE FIRST THAT PUT A DIADEM ABOUT HIS HEAD; AND AFTER HE HAD PUT HIS MOTHER AND BROTHER TO DEATH, DIED HIMSELF, WHEN HE HAD REIGNED NO MORE THAN A YEAR.

1. (70) FOR after the death of their father, the elder of them, Aristobulus, changed the government into a kingdom, and was the first that put a diadem upon his head, four hundred seventy and one years and three months after our people came down into this country, when they were set free from the Babylonian slavery. (71) Now, of his brethren, he appeared to have an affection for Antigonus, who was next to him, and made him his equal; but for the rest, he bound them, and put them in prison. He also put his mother in bonds, for her contesting the government with him; for John had left her to be the governess of public affairs. He also proceeded to that degree of barbarity as to cause her to be pined to death in prison.

2. (72) But vengeance circumvented him in the affair of his brother Antigonus, whom he loved, and whom he made his partner in the kingdom; for he slew him by the means of the calumnies which ill men about the palace contrived against him. At first, indeed, Aristobulus would not believe their reports, partly out of the affection he had for his brother, and partly because he thought that a great part of these tales were owing to the envy of their relaters: (73) however, as Antigonus came once in a splendid manner from the army to that festival, wherein our ancient custom is to make tabernacles for God, it happened, in those days, that Aristobulus was sick, and that, at the conclusion of the feast, Antigonus came up to it, with his armed men about him; and this when he was adorned in the finest manner possible; and that, in a great measure, to pray to God on the behalf of his brother. (74) Now at this very time it was that these ill men came to the king, and told him in what a pompous manner the armed men came, and with what insolence Antigonus marched, and that such his insolence was too great for a private person, and that accordingly he was come with a great band of men to kill him; for that he could not endure this bare enjoyment of royal honor, when it was in his power to take the kingdom himself.

3. (75) Now Aristobulus, by degrees, and unwillingly, gave credit to these accusations; and accordingly he took care not to discover his suspicion openly, though he provided to be secure against any accidents; so he placed the guards of his body in a certain dark subterranean passage; for he lay sick in a place called formerly the Citadel, though afterwards its name was changed to Antonia; and he gave orders that if Antigonus came unarmed, they should let him alone; but if he came to him in his armor, they should kill him. He also sent

General view of the Greco-Roman remains at Scythopolis. (photo Samuel Magal)

some to let him know beforehand that he should come unarmed. (76) But, upon this occasion, the queen very cunningly contrived the matter with those that plotted his ruin, for she persuaded those that were sent to conceal the king's message; but to tell Antigonus how his brother had heard he had got a very the suit of armor made with fine martial ornaments, in Galilee; and because his present sickness hindered him from coming and seeing all that finery, he very much desired to see him now in his armor; because, said he, in a little time thou art going away from me.

4. (77) As soon as Antigonus heard this, the good temper of his brother not allowing him to suspect any harm from him, he came along with his armor on, to show it to his brother; but when he was going along that dark passage which was called Strato's Tower, he was slain by the body guards, and became an eminent instance how calumny destroys all good-will and natural affection, and how none of our good affections are strong enough to resist envy perpetually.

5. (78) And truly any one would be surprised at Judas upon this occasion. He was of the sect of the Essens, and had never failed or deceived men in his predictions before. Now this man saw Antigonus as he was passing along by the temple, and cried out to his acquaintance, (they were not a few who attended upon him as his scholars,) (79) "O strange!" said he, "it is good for me to die now, since truth is dead before me, and somewhat that I have foretold hath proved false; for this Antigonus is this day alive, who ought to have died this day; and the place where he ought to be slain, according to that fatal decree, was Strato's Tower, which is at the distance of six hundred furlongs from this place; and yet four hours of this day are over already; which point of time renders the prediction impossible to be fulfilled." (80) And when the old man had said this, he was dejected in his mind, and so continued. But in a little time news came that Antigonus was slain in a subterraneous place, which was itself also called Strato's Tower, by the same name with that Cesarea which lay by the sea-side; and this ambiguity it was which caused the prophet's disorder.

6. (81) Hereupon Aristobulus repented of the great crime he had been guilty of, and this gave occasion to the increase of his distemper. He also grew worse and worse, and his soul was constantly disturbed at the thoughts of what he had done, till his very bowels being torn to pieces by the intolerable grief he was under, he threw up a great quantity of blood. (82) And as one of those servants that attended him carried out that blood, he, by some supernatural providence, slipped and fell down in the very place where Antigonus had been slain; and so he spilt some of the murderer's blood upon the spots of the blood of him that had been murdered, which still appeared. Hereupon a lamentable cry arose among the spectators, as if the servant had spilled the blood on purpose in that place; (83) and as the king heard that cry, he inquired what was the cause of it; and while nobody durst tell him, he pressed them so much the more to let him know what was the matter; so at length, when he had threatened them, and forced them to speak out, they told; whereupon he burst into tears, and groaned, and said, (84) "So I perceive I am not like to escape the all-seeing eye of God, as to the great crimes I have committed; but the vengeance of the blood of my kinsman pursues me hastily. O thou most impudent body! how long wilt thou retain a soul that ought to die on account of that punishment it ought to suffer for a mother and a brother slain! How long shall I myself spend my blood drop by drop? let them take it all at once; and let their ghosts no longer be disappointed by a few parcels of my bowels offered to them." As soon as he had said these words, he presently died, when he had reigned no longer than a year.

CHAPTER 4.

WHAT ACTIONS WERE DONE BY ALEXANDER JANNEUS, WHO REIGNED TWENTY-SEVEN YEARS.

1. (85) AND now the king's wife loosed the king's brethren, and made Alexander king, who appeared both elder in age, and more moderate in his temper than the rest; who, when he came to the government, slew one of his brethren, as affecting to govern himself; but had the other of them in great esteem, as loving a quiet life, without meddling with public affairs.

Coin of Alexander Janneus. (PHG at the English language Wikipedia)

2. (86) Now it happened that there was a battle between him and Ptolemy, who was called Lathyrus, who had taken the city Asochis. He indeed slew a great many of his enemies, but the victory rather inclined to Ptolemy. But when this Ptolemy was pursued by his mother Cleopatra [III], and retired into Egypt, Alexander besieged Gadara, and took it; as also he did Amathus, which was the strongest of all the fortresses that were about Jordan [River], and therein were the most precious of all the possessions of Theodorus, the son of Zeno. (87) Whereupon Theodorus marched against him, and took what belonged to himself as well as the king's baggage, and slew ten thousand of the Jews. However, Alexander recovered this blow, and turned his force towards the maritime parts, and took Raphia and Gaza, with Anthedon also, which was afterwards called Agrippias by king Herod.

3. (88) But when he had made slaves of the citizens of all these cities, the nation of the Jews made an insurrection against him at a festival; for at those feasts seditions are generally begun; and it looked as if he should not be able to escape the plot they had laid for him, had not his foreign auxiliaries, the Pisidians and Cilicians, assisted him; for as to the Syrians, he never admitted them among his mercenary troops, on account of their innate enmity against the Jewish nation. (89) And when he had slain more than six thousand of the rebels, he made an incursion into Arabia; and when he had taken that country, together with the Gileadites and Moabites, he enjoined them to pay him tribute, and returned to Areathus; and as Theodorus was surprised at his great success, he took the fortress, and demolished it.

4. (90) However, when he fought with Obodas, king of the Arabians, who had laid an ambush for him near Golan, and a plot against him, he lost his entire army, which was crowded together in a deep valley, and broken to pieces by the multitude of camels. And when he had made his escape to Jerusalem, he provoked the multitude, which hated him before, to make an insurrection against him, and this on account of the greatness of the calamity that he was under. (91) However, he was then too hard for them; and, in the several battles that were fought on both sides, he slew not fewer than fifty thousand of the Jews in the interval of six years. Yet had he no reason to rejoice in these victories, since he did but consume his

THE KINGDOM OF ALEXANDER JANNEUS 103–76 B.C.

own kingdom; till at length he left off fighting, and endeavored to come to a composition with them, by talking with his subjects. (92) But this mutability and irregularity of his conduct made them hate him still more. And when he asked them why they so hated him, and what he should do in order to appease them, they said, by killing himself; for that it would be then all they could do to be reconciled to him, who had done such tragical things to them, even when he was dead. At the same time they invited Demetrius [III], who was called Eucerus, to assist them; and as he readily complied with their requests, in hopes of great advantages, and came with his army, the Jews joined with those their auxiliaries about Shechem.

5. (93) Yet did Alexander meet both these forces with one thousand horsemen, and eight thousand mercenaries that were on foot. He had also with him that part of the Jews which favored him, to the number of ten thousand; while the adverse party had three thousand horsemen, and fourteen thousand footmen. Now, before they joined battle, the kings made proclamation, and endeavored to draw off each other's soldiers, and make them revolt; while Demetrius hoped to induce Alexander's mercenaries to leave him, and Alexander hoped to induce the Jews that were with Demetrius to leave him. (94) But since neither the Jews would leave off their rage, nor the Greeks prove unfaithful, they came to an engagement, and to a close fight with their weapons. (95) In which battle Demetrius was the conqueror, although Alexander's mercenaries showed the greatest exploits, both in soul and body. Yet did the upshot of this battle prove different from what was expected, as to both of them; for neither did those that invited Demetrius to come to them continue firm to him, though he was conqueror; and six thousand Jews, out of pity to the change of Alexander's condition, when he was fled to the mountains, came over to him. Yet could not Demetrius bear this turn of affairs; but supposing that Alexander was already become a match for him again, and that all the nation would [at length] run to him, he left the country, and went his way.

6. (96) However, the rest of the [Jewish] multitude did not lay aside their quarrels with him, when the [foreign] auxiliaries were gone; but they had a perpetual war with Alexander, until he had slain the greatest part of them, and driven the rest into the city Berneselis; and when he had demolished that city, he carried the captives to Jerusalem. (97) Nay, his rage was grown so extravagant, that his barbarity proceeded to the degree of impiety; for when he had ordered eight hundred to be hung upon crosses in the midst of the city, he had the throats of their wives and children cut before their eyes; and these executions he saw as he was drinking and lying down with his concubines. (98) Upon which so deep a surprise seized on the people, that eight thousand of his opposers fled away the very next night, out of all Judea, whose flight was only terminated by Alexander's death; so at last, though not till late, and with great difficulty, he, by such actions, procured quiet to his kingdom, and left off fighting any more.

7. (99) Yet did that Antiochus [XII], who was also called Dionysius, become an origin of troubles again. This man was the brother of Demetrius, and the last of the race of the Seleucids. Alexander was afraid of him, when he was marching against the Arabians; so he cut a deep trench between Antipatris, which was near the mountains, and the shores of Joppa; he also erected a high wall before the trench, and built wooden towers, in order to hinder any sudden approaches. (100) But still he was not able to exclude Antiochus, for he burnt the towers, and filled up the trenches, and marched on with his army. And as he looked upon taking his revenge on Alexander, for endeavoring to stop him, as a thing of less consequence, he marched directly against the Arabians, (101) whose king retired into such parts of the country as were fittest for engaging the enemy, and then on the sudden made his horse turn back, which were in number ten thousand, and fell upon Antiochus's army while they were in disorder, and a terrible battle ensued. Antiochus's troops, so long as he was alive, fought it out, although a mighty slaughter was made among them by the Arabians; (102) but when he fell, for he was in the forefront, in the utmost danger, in rallying his troops, they all gave ground, and the greatest part of his army were destroyed, either in the action or the flight; and for the rest, who fled to the village of Cana, it happened that they were all consumed by want of necessaries, a few only excepted.

8. (103) About this time it was that the people of Damascus, out of their hatred to Ptolemy, the son of Menhens, invited Aretas [to take the government], and made him king of Celesyria. This man also made an expedition against Judea, and beat Alexander in battle; but afterwards retired by mutual agreement. (104) But Alex-

ander, when he had taken Pella, marched to Gerasa again, out of the covetous desire he had of Theodorus's possessions; and when he had built a triple wall about the garrison, he took the place by force. (105) He also demolished Golan, and Seleucia, and what was called the Valley of Antiochus; besides which, he took the strong fortress of Gamala, and stripped Demetrius, who was governor therein, of what he had, on account of the many crimes laid to his charge, and then returned into Judea, after he had been three whole years in this expedition. And now he was kindly received of the nation, because of the good success he had. So when he was at rest from war, he fell into a distemper; (106) for he was afflicted with a quartan ague, and supposed that, by exercising himself again in martial affairs, he should get rid of this distemper; but by making such expeditions at unseasonable times, and forcing his body to undergo greater hardships than it was able to bear, he brought himself to his end. He died, therefore, in the midst of his troubles, after he had reigned seven and twenty years.

CHAPTER 5.

ALEXANDRA REIGNS NINE YEARS, DURING WHICH TIME THE PHARISEES WERE THE REAL RULERS OF THE NATION.

1. (107) NOW Alexander left the kingdom to Alexandra his wife, and depended upon it that the Jews would now very readily submit to her, because she had been very averse to such cruelty as he had treated them with, and had opposed his violation of their laws, and had thereby got the good-will of the people. (108) Nor was he mistaken as to his expectations; for this woman kept the dominion, by the opinion that the people had of her piety; for she chiefly studied the ancient customs of her country, and cast those men out of the government that offended against their holy laws. (109) And as she had two sons by Alexander, she made Hyrcanus [II] the elder high priest, on account of his age, as also, besides that, on account of his inactive temper, no way disposing him to disturb the public. But she retained the younger, Aristobulus [II], with her as a private person, by reason of the warmth of his temper.

2. (110) And now the Pharisees joined themselves to her, to assist her in the government. These are a certain sect of the Jews that appear more religious than others, and seem to interpret the laws more accurately. (111) Alexandra hearkened to them to an extraordinary degree, as being herself a woman of great piety towards God. But these Pharisees artfully insinuated themselves into her favor by little and little, and became themselves the real administrators of the public affairs: they banished and reduced whom they pleased; they bound and loosed [men] at their pleasure; (Matthew 16:19; 18:18) and, to say all at once, they had the enjoyment of the royal authority, whilst the expenses and the difficulties of it belonged to Alexandra. (112) She was a sagacious woman in the management of great affairs, and intent always upon gathering soldiers together; so that she increased the army the one half, and procured a great body of foreign troops, till her own nation became not only very powerful at home, but terrible also to foreign potentates, while she governed other people, and the Pharisees governed her.

3. (113) Accordingly, they themselves slew Diogenes, a person of figure, and one that had been a friend to Alexander; and accused him as having assisted the king with his advice, for crucifying the eight hundred men [before mentioned.] They also prevailed with Alexandra to put to death the rest of those who had irritated him against them. Now she was so superstitious as to comply with their desires, and accordingly they slew whom they pleased them-

Salome Alexandra, wife of Aristobulus I. (From "Promptuarii Iconum Insigniorum" pub. by Guillaume Rouille [1518?–1589])

selves. (114) But the principal of those that were in danger fled to Aristobulus, who persuaded his mother to spare the men on account of their dignity, but to expel them out of the city, unless she took them to be innocent; so they were suffered to go unpunished, and were dispersed all over the country. (115) But when Alexandra sent out her army to Damascus, under pretense that Ptolemy was always oppressing that city, she got possession of it; nor did it make any considerable resistance. (116) She also prevailed with Tigranes, king of Armenia, who lay with his troops about Ptolemais, and besieged Cleopatra, by agreements and presents, to go away. Accordingly, Tigranes soon arose from the siege, by reason of those domestic tumults which happened upon Lucullus's expedition into Armenia.

4. (117) In the mean time, Alexandra fell sick, and Aristobulus, her younger son, took hold of this opportunity, with his domestics, of which he had a great many, who were all of them his friends, on account of the warmth of their youth, and got possession of all the fortresses. He also used the sums of money he found in them to get together a number of mercenary soldiers, and made himself king; (118) and besides this, upon Hyrcanus's complaint to his mother, she compassionated his case, and put Aristobulus's wife and sons under restraint in Antonia, which was a fortress that joined to the north part of the temple. It was, as I have already said, of old called the Citadel; but afterwards got the name of Antonia, when Antony was [lord of the East], just as the other cities, Sebaste and Agrippias, had their names changed, and these given them from Sebastus and Agrippa. (119) But Alexandra died before she could punish Aristobulus for his disinheriting his brother, after she had reigned nine years.

CHAPTER 6.

WHEN HYRCANUS WHO WAS ALEXANDER'S HEIR, RECEDED FROM HIS CLAIM TO THE CROWN ARISTOBULUS IS MADE KING; AND AFTERWARD THE SAME HYRCANUS BY THE MEANS OF ANTIPATER, IS BROUGHT BACK BY ARETAS. AT LAST POMPEY IS MADE THE ARBITRATOR OF THE DISPUTE BETWEEN THE BROTHERS.

1. (120) NOW Hyrcanus was heir to the kingdom, and to him did his mother commit it before she died; but Aristobulus was superior to him in power and magnanimity; and when there was a battle between them, to decide the dispute about the kingdom, near Jericho, the greatest part deserted Hyrcanus, and went over to Aristobulus; (121) but Hyrcanus, with those of his party who staid with him, fled to Antonia, and got into his power the hostages that might he for his preservation (which were Aristobulus's wife, with her children); but they came to an agreement before things should come to extremities, that Aristobulus should be king, and Hyrcanus should resign that up, but retain all the rest of his dignities, as being the king's brother. (122) Hereupon they were reconciled to each other in the temple, and embraced one another in a very kind manner, while the people stood round about them; they also changed their houses, while Aristobulus went to the royal palace, and Hyrcanus retired to the house of Aristobulus.

2. (123) Now those other people which were at variance with Aristobulus were afraid upon his unexpected obtaining the government; and especially this concerned Antipater whom Aristobulus

View of Petra's monastery (ed-Deir) from a nearby cave. (photo David Bjorgen, via Wikimedia Commons)

hated of old. He was by birth an Idumean, and one of the principal of that nation, on account of his ancestors and riches, and other authority to him belonging: (124) he also persuaded Hyrcanus to fly to Aretas, the king of Arabia, and to lay claim to the kingdom; as also he persuaded Aretas to receive Hyrcanus, and to bring him back to his kingdom: he also cast great reproaches upon Aristobulus, as to his morals, and gave great commendations to Hyrcanus, and exhorted Aretas to receive him, and told him how becoming a filing it would be for him, who ruled so great a kingdom, to afford his assistance to such as are injured; alleging that Hyrcanus was treated unjustly, by being deprived of that dominion which belonged to him by the prerogative of his birth. (125) And when he had predisposed them both to do what he would have them, he took Hyrcanus by night, and ran away from the city, and, continuing his flight with great swiftness, he escaped to the place called Petra, which is the royal seat of the king of Arabia, (126) where he put Hyrcanus into Aretas's hand; and by discoursing much with him, and gaining upon him with many presents, he prevailed with him to give him an army that might restore him to his kingdom. This army consisted of fifty thousand footmen and horsemen, against which Aristobulus was not able to make resistance, but was deserted in his first onset, and was driven to Jerusalem; (127) he also had been taken at first by force, if Scaurus, the Roman general, had not come and seasonably interposed himself, and raised the siege. This Scaurus was sent into Syria from Armenia by Pompey the Great, when he fought against Tigranes; so Scaurus came to Damascus, which had been lately taken by Metellus and Lollius, and caused them to leave the place; and, upon his hearing how the affairs of Judea stood, he made haste thither as to a certain booty.

3. (128) As soon, therefore, as he was come into the country, there came ambassadors from both the brothers, each of them desiring his assistance; but Aristobulus's three hundred talents had more weight with him than the justice of the cause; which sum, when Scaurus had received, he sent a herald to Hyrcanus and the Arabians, and threatened them with the resentment of the Romans and of Pompey, unless they would raise the siege. (129) So Aretas was terrified, and retired out of Judea to Philadelphia, as did Scaurus return to Damascus again; (130) nor was Aristobulus satisfied with escaping [out of his brother's hands,] but gathered all his forces together, and pursued his enemies, and fought them at a place called Papyron, and slew about six thousand of them, and, together with them Antipater's brother Phalion.

4. (131) When Hyrcanus and Antipater were thus deprived of their hopes from the Arabians, they transferred the same to their adversaries; and because Pompey had passed through Syria, and was come to Damascus, they fled to him for assistance; and, without any bribes, they made the same equitable pleas that they had used to Aretas, and besought him to hate the violent behavior of Aristobulus, and to bestow the kingdom on him to whom it justly belonged, both on account of his good character and on account of his superiority in age. (132) However, neither was Aristobulus wanting to himself in this case, as relying on the bribes that Scaurus had received: he was also there himself, and adorned himself after a manner the most agreeable to royalty that he was able. But he soon thought it beneath him to come in such a servile manner, and could not endure to serve his own ends in a way so much more abject than he was used to; so he departed from Diospolis.

5. (133) At this his behavior Pompey had great indignation; Hyrcanus also and his friends made great intercessions to Pompey; so he took not only his Roman forces, but many of his Syrian auxiliaries, and marched against Aristobulus. (134) But when he had passed by Pella and Scythopolis, and was come to Corea, where you enter into the country of Judea, when you go up to it through the Mediterranean parts, he heard that Aristobulus was fled to Alexandrium, which is a strong hold fortified with the utmost magnificence, and situated upon a high mountain; and he sent to

Remains of the Temple of Jupiter in Damascus. (photo Sean Leatherbury/Manar al-Athar)

him, and commanded him to come down. (135) Now his inclination was to try his fortune in a battle, since he was called in such an imperious manner, rather than to comply with that call. However, he saw the multitude were in great fear, and his friends exhorted him to consider what the power of the Romans was, and how it was irresistible; so he complied with their advice, and came down to Pompey; and when he had made a long apology for himself, and for the justness of his cause in taking the government, he returned to the fortress. (136) And when his brother invited him again [to plead his cause], he came down and spake about the justice of it, and then went away without any hinderance from Pompey; so he was between hope and fear. And when he came down, it was to prevail with Pompey to allow him the government entirely; and when he went up to the citadel, it was that he might not appear to debase himself too low. (137) However, Pompey commanded him to give up his fortified places, and forced him to write to every one of their governors to yield them up; they having had this charge given them, to obey no letters but what were of his own handwriting. Accordingly he did what he was ordered to do; but had still an indignation at what was done, and retired to Jerusalem, and prepared to fight with Pompey.

6. (138) But Pompey did not give him time to make any preparations [for a siege], but followed him at his heels; he was also obliged to make haste in his attempt, by the death of Mithridates, of which he was informed about Jericho. Now here is the most fruitful country of Judea, which bears a vast number of palm trees besides the balsam tree, whose sprouts they cut with sharp stones, and at the incisions they gather the juice, which drops down like tears. (139) So Pompey pitched his camp in that place one night, and then hasted away the next morning to Jerusalem; but Aristobulus was so aftrighted at his approach, that he came and met him by way of supplication. He also promised him money, and that he would deliver up both himself and the city into his disposal, and thereby mitigated the anger of Pompey. (140) Yet did not he perform any of the conditions he had agreed to; for Aristobulus's party would not so much as admit Gabinius into the city, who was sent to receive the money that he had promised.

CHAPTER 7.

HOW POMPEY HAD THE CITY OF JERUSALEM DELIVERED UP TO HIM BUT TOOK THE TEMPLE BY FORCE. HOW HE WENT INTO THE HOLY OF HOLIES; AS ALSO WHAT WERE HIS OTHER EXPLOITS IN JUDEA.

1. (141) At this treatment Pompey was very angry, and took Aristobulus into custody. And when he was come to the city, he looked about where he might make his attack; for he saw the walls were so firm, that it would be hard to overcome them; and that the valley before the walls was terrible; and that the temple, which was within that valley, was itself encompassed with a very strong wall, insomuch that if the city were taken, that temple would be a second place of refuge for the enemy to retire to.

2. (142) Now as be was long in deliberating about this matter, a sedition arose among the people within the city; Aristobulus's party being willing to fight, and to set their king at liberty, while the party of Hyrcanus were for opening the gates to Pompey; and the dread people were in occasioned these last to be a very numerous party, when they looked upon the excellent order the Roman soldiers were in. (143) So Aristobulus's party was worsted, and retired into the temple, and cut off the communication between the temple and the city, by breaking down the bridge that joined them together, and prepared to make an opposition to the utmost; but as the others had received the Romans into the city, and had delivered up the palace to him, Pompey sent Piso, one of his great officers, into that palace with an army, (144) who distributed a garrison about the city, because he could not persuade any one of those that had fled to the temple to come to terms of accommodation; he then disposed all things that were round about them so as might favor their attacks, as having Hyrcanus's party very ready to afford them both counsel and assistance.

3. (145) But Pompey himself filled up the ditch that was on the north side of the temple, and the entire valley also, the army itself being obliged to carry the materials for that purpose. And indeed it was a hard thing to fill up that valley, by reason of its immense depth, especially as the Jews used all the means possible to repel them from their superior situation; (146) nor had the Romans succeeded in their endeavors, had not Pompey taken notice of the seventh days, on which the Jews abstain from all sorts of work on a religious account, and raised his bank, but restrained his soldiers from fighting on those days; for the Jews only acted defensively on sabbath days. (147) But as soon as Pompey had filled up the valley, he erected high towers upon the bank, and brought those engines which they had fetched from Tyre near to the wall, and tried to batter it down; and the slingers of stones beat off those that stood above them, and drove them away; but the towers on this side of the city made very great resistance, and were indeed extraordinary both for largeness and magnificence.

4. (148) Now here it was that, upon the many hardships which the Romans underwent, Pompey could not but admire not only at the other instances of the Jews' fortitude, but especially that they did not at all intermit their religious services, even when they were encompassed with darts on all sides; for, as if the city were in full

POMPEY'S SIEGE OF JERUSALEM 63 B.C.

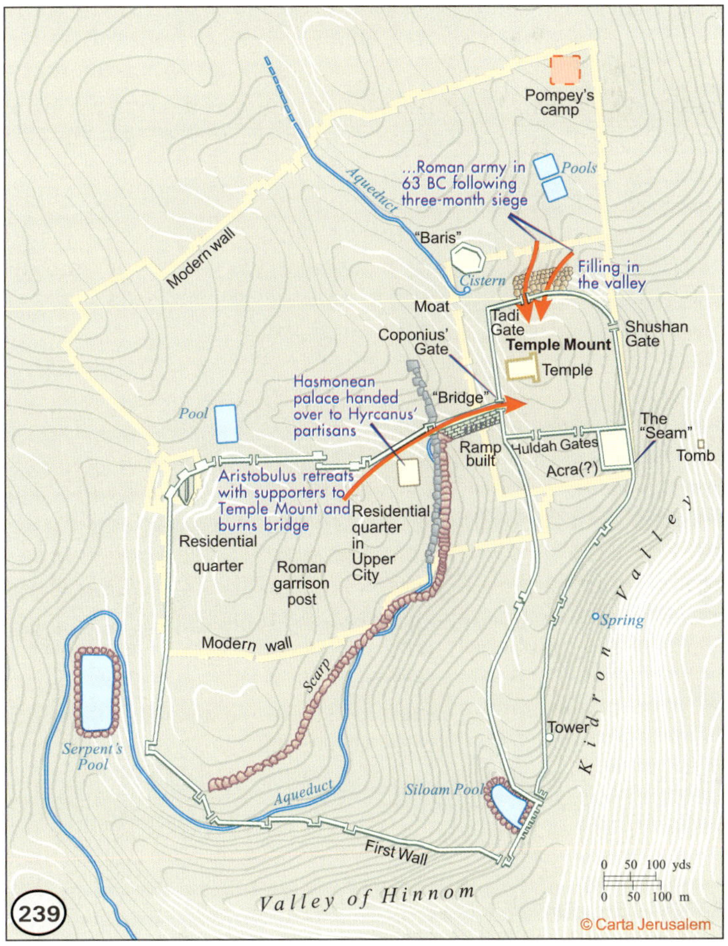

peace, their daily sacrifices and purifications, and every branch of their religious worship, was still performed to God with the utmost exactness. Nor indeed when the temple was actually taken, and they were every day slain about the altar, did they leave off the instances of their Divine worship that were appointed by their law; (149) for it was in the third month of the siege before the Romans could even with great difficulty overthrow one of the towers, and get into the temple. Now he that first of all ventured to get over the wall, was Faustus Cornelius the son of Sylla; and next after him were two centurions, Furius and Fabius; and every one of these was followed by a cohort of his own, who encompassed the Jews on all sides, and slew them, some of them as they were running for shelter to the temple, and others as they, for a while, fought in their own defense.

POMPEY'S TERRITORIAL ARRANGEMENTS 63–55 B.C.

5. (150) And now did many of the priests, even when they saw their enemies assailing them with swords in their hands, without any disturbance, go on with their Divine worship, and were slain while they were offering their drink-offerings, and burning their incense, as preferring the duties about their worship to God before their own preservation. The greatest part of them were slain by their own countrymen, of the adverse faction, and an innumerable multitude threw themselves down precipices; nay, some there were who were so distracted among the insuperable difficulties they were under, that they set fire to the buildings that were near to the wall, and were burnt together with them. (151) Now of the Jews were slain twelve thousand; but of the Romans very few were slain, but a greater number was wounded.

6. (152) But there was nothing that affected the nation so much, in the calamities they were then under, as that their holy place, which had been hitherto seen by none, should be laid open to strangers; for Pompey, and those that were about him, went into the temple itself whither it was not lawful for any to enter but the high priest, and saw what was reposited therein, the candlestick with its lamps, and the table, and the pouring vessels, and the censers, all made entirely of gold, as also a great quantity of spices heaped together, with two thousand talents of sacred money. (153) Yet did not he touch that money, nor any thing else that was there reposited; but he commanded the ministers about the temple, the very next day after he had taken it, to cleanse it, and to perform their accustomed sacrifices. Moreover, he made Hyrcanus high priest, as one that not only in other respects had showed great alacrity, on his side, during the siege, but as he had been the means of hindering the multitude that was in the country from fighting for Aristobulus, which they were otherwise very ready to have done; by which means he acted the part of a good general, and reconciled the people to him more by benevolence than by terror. (154) Now, among the captives, Aristobulus's father-in-law was taken, who was also his uncle: so those that were the most guilty he punished with decollation; but rewarded Faustus, and those with him that had fought so bravely, with glorious presents, and laid a tribute upon the country, and upon Jerusalem itself.

7. (155) He also took away from the nation all those cities that they had formerly taken, and that belonged to Celesyria, and made them subject to him that was at that time appointed to be the Roman president there; and reduced Judea within its proper bounds. He also rebuilt Gadara, that had been demolished by the Jews, in order to gratify one Demetrius, who was of Gadara, (156) and was one of his own freedmen. He also made other cities free from their dominion, that lay in the midst of the country, such, I mean, as they had not demolished before that time; Hippos, and Scythopolis, as also Pella, and Samaria, and Marissa; and besides these Ashdod, and Jamnia, and Arethusa; and in like manner dealt he with the maritime cities, Gaza, and Joppa, and Dora, and that which was anciently called Strato's Tower, but was afterward rebuilt with the most magnificent edifices, and had its name changed to Cesarea, by king Herod. (157) All which he restored to their own citizens, and put them under the province of Syria; which province, together with Judea, and the countries as far as Egypt and Euphrates, he committed to Scaurus as their governor, and gave him two legions to support him; while he made all the haste he could himself to go through Cilicia, in his way to Rome, having Aristobulus and his children along with him as his captives. (158) They were two daughters and two sons; the one of which sons, Alexander, ran away as he was going; but the younger, Antigonus, with his sisters, were carried to Rome.

CHAPTER 8.

ALEXANDER, THE SON OF ARISTOBULUS, WHO RAN AWAY FROM POMPEY, MAKES AN EXPEDITION AGAINST HYRCANUS; BUT BEING OVERCOME BY GABINIUS HE DELIVERS UP THE FORTRESSES TO HIM. AFTER THIS ARISTOBULUS ESCAPES FROM ROME AND GATHERS AN ARMY TOGETHER; BUT BEING BEATEN BY THE ROMANS, HE IS BROUGHT BACK TO ROME; WITH OTHER THINGS RELATING TO GABINIUS, CRASSUS AND CASSIUS.

1. (159) IN the meantime, Scaurus made an expedition into Arabia, but was stopped by the difficulty of the places about Petra. However, he laid waste the country about Pella, though even there he was under great hardship; for his army was afflicted with famine. In order to supply which want, Hyrcanus afforded him some assistance, and sent him provisions by the means of Antipater; whom also Scaurus sent to Aretas, as one well acquainted with him, to induce him to pay him money to buy his peace. The king of Arabia complied with the proposal, and gave him three hundred talents; upon which Scaurus drew his army out of Arabia.

2. (160) But as for Alexander, that son of Aristobulus who ran away from Pompey, in some time he got a considerable band of men together, and lay heavy upon Hyrcanus, and overran Judea, and was likely to overturn him quickly; and indeed he had come to Jerusalem, and had ventured to rebuild its wall that was thrown down by Pompey, had not Gabinius, who was sent as successor to Scaurus into Syria, showed his bravery, as in many other points, so in making an expedition against Alexander; (161) who, as he was afraid that he would attack him, so he got together a large army, composed of ten thousand armed footmen, and fifteen hundred horsemen. He also built walls about proper places; Alexandrium, and Hyrcanium, and Macherus, that lay upon the mountains of Arabia.

3. (162) However, Gabinius sent before him Marcus Antonius, and followed himself with his whole army; but for the select body of soldiers that were about Antipater, and another body of Jews under the command of Malichus and Pitholaus, these joined themselves to those captains that were about Marcus Antonius, and met Alexander; to which body came Gabinius with his main army soon afterward; (163) and as Alexander was not able to sustain the charge of the enemies' forces, now they were joined, he retired. But when he was come near to Jerusalem, he was forced to fight, and lost six thousand men in the battle; three thousand of which

Wall of the Hasmonean fortress at Alexandrium (Sartaba). (photo Tamarah, via Wikimedia Commons)

Macherus, looking west. (photo Thomas Bantle, via Wikimedia Commons)

fell down dead, and three thousand were taken alive; so he fled with the remainder to Alexandrium.

4. (164) Now when Gabinius was come to Alexandrium, because he found a great many there encamped, he tried, by promising them pardon for their former offenses, to induce them to come over to him before it came to a fight; but when they would hearken to no terms of accommodation, he slew a great number of them, and shut up a great number of them in the citadel. (165) Now Marcus Antonius, their leader, signalized himself in this battle, who, as he always showed great courage, so did he never show it so much as now; but Gabinius, leaving forces to take the citadel, went away himself, and settled the cities that had not been demolished, and rebuilt those that had been destroyed. (166) Accordingly, upon his injunctions, the following cities were restored: Scythopolis, and Samaria, and Anthedon, and Apollonia, and Jamnia, and Raphia, and Marissa, and Adoreus, and Gamala, and Ashdod, and many others; while a great number of men readily ran to each of them, and became their inhabitants.

5. (167) When Gabinius had taken care of these cities, he returned to Alexandrium, and pressed on the siege. So when Alexander despaired of ever obtaining the government, he sent ambassadors to him, and prayed him to forgive what he had offended him in, and gave up to him the remaining fortresses, Hyrcanium and Macherus, as he put Alexandrium into his hands afterwards; (168) all which Gabinius demolished, at the persuasion of Alexander's mother, that they might not be receptacles of men in a second war. She was now there in order to mollify Gabinius, out of her concern for her relations that were captives at Rome, which were her husband and her other children. (169) After this Gabinius brought Hyrcanus to Jerusalem, and committed the care of the temple to him; but ordained the other political government to be by an aristocracy. (170) He also parted the whole nation into five conventions, assigning one portion to Jerusalem, another to Gadara, that another should belong to Amathus, a fourth to Jericho, and to the fifth division was allotted Sepphoris, a city of Galilee. So the people were glad to be thus freed from monarchical government, and were governed for the future by all aristocracy.

6. (171) Yet did Aristobulus afford another foundation for new disturbances. He fled away from Rome, and got together again many of the Jews that were desirous of a change, such as had borne an affection to him of old; and when he had taken Alexandrium in the first place, he attempted to build a wall about it; but as soon as Gabinius had sent an army against him under Siscuria, and Anto-

Aerial view of Mount Tabor. (photo Itamar Grinberg, via Wikimedia Commons)

nius, and Servilius, he was aware of it, and retreated to Macherus. (172) And as for the unprofitable multitude, he dismissed them, and only marched on with those that were armed, being to the number of eight thousand, among whom was Pitholaus, who had been the lieutenant at Jerusalem, but deserted to Aristobulus with a thousand of his men; so the Romans followed him, and when it came to a battle, Aristobulus's party for a long time fought courageously; but at length they were overborne by the Romans, and of them five thousand fell down dead, and about two thousand fled to a certain little hill, but the thousand that remained with Aristobulus brake through the Roman army, and marched together to Macherus; (173) and when the king had lodged the first night upon its ruins, he was in hopes of raising another army, if the war would but cease a while; accordingly, he fortified that strong hold, though it was done after a poor manner. But the Romans falling upon him, he resisted, even beyond his abilities, for two days, and then was taken, and brought a prisoner to Gabinius, with Antigonus his son, who had fled away together with him from Rome; and from Gabinius he was carried to Rome again. (174) Wherefore the senate put him under confinement, but returned his children back to Judea, because Gabinius informed them by letters that he had promised Aristobulus's mother to do so, for her delivering the fortresses up to him.

7. (175) But now as Gabinius was marching to the war against the Parthians, he was hindered by Ptolemy [XII], whom, upon his return from Euphrates, he brought back into Egypt, making use of Hyrcanus and Antipater to provide every thing that was necessary for this expedition; for Antipater furnished him with money, and weapons, and corn, and auxiliaries; he also prevailed with the Jews that were there, and guarded the avenues at Pelusium, to let them pass. (176) But now, upon Gabinius's absence, the other part of Syria was in motion, and Alexander, the son of Aristobulus, brought the Jews to revolt again. Accordingly, he got together a very great army, and set about killing all the Romans that were in the country; (177) hereupon Gabinius was afraid, (for he was come back already out of Egypt, and obliged to come back quickly by these tumults,) and sent Antipater, who prevailed with some of the revolters to be quiet. However, thirty thousand still continued with Alexander, who was himself eager to fight also; accordingly, Gabinius went out to fight, when the Jews met him; and as the battle was fought near Mount Tabor, ten thousand of them were slain, and the rest of the multitude dispersed themselves, and fled away. (178) So Gabinius came to Jerusalem, and settled the government as Antipater would have it; thence he marched, and fought and beat the Nabateans: as for Mithridates and Orsanes, who fled out of Parthin, he sent them away privately, but gave it out among the soldiers that they had run away.

8. (179) In the mean time, Crassus came as successor to Gabinius in Syria. He took away all the rest of the gold belonging to the temple of Jerusalem, in order to furnish himself for his expedition against the Parthians. He also took away the two thousand talents which Pompey had not touched; but when he had passed over Euphrates, he perished himself, and his army with him; concerning which affairs this is not a proper time to speak [more largely].

9. (180) But now Cassius, after Crassus, put a stop to the Parthians, who were marching in order to enter Syria. Cassius had fled into that province, and when he had taken possession of the same, he made a hasty march into Judea; and, upon his taking Taricheae, he carried thirty thousand Jews into slavery. He also slew Pitholaus, who had supported the seditious followers of Aristobulus; and it was Antipater who advised him so to do. (181) Now this Antipater married a wife of an eminent family among the Arabians, whose name was Cypros, and had four sons born to him by her, Phasaelus and Herod, who was afterwards king, and, besides these, Joseph and Pheroras; and he had a daughter whose name was Salome. Now as he made himself friends among the men of power every where, by the kind offices he did them, and the hospitable manner that he treated them; so did he contract the greatest friendship with the king of Arabia, by marrying his relation; insomuch that when he made war with Aristobulus, he sent and intrusted his children with him. (182) So when Cassius had forced Alexander to come to terms and to be quiet, he returned to Euphrates, in order to prevent the Parthians from repassing it; concerning which matter we shall speak elsewhere.

CHAPTER 9.

ARISTOBULUS IS TAKEN OFF BY POMPEY'S FRIENDS, AS IS HIS SON ALEXANDER BY SCIPIO. ANTIPATER CULTIVATES A FRIENDSHIP WITH CAESAR, AFTER POMPEY'S DEATH; HE ALSO PERFORMS GREAT ACTIONS IN THAT WAR, WHEREIN HE ASSISTED MITHRIDATES.

1. (183) NOW, upon the flight of Pompey and of the senate beyond the Ionian Sea, [Julius] Caesar got Rome and the empire under his power, and released Aristobulus from his bonds. He also committed two legions to him, and sent him in haste into Syria, as hoping that by his means he should easily conquer that country, and the parts adjoining to Judea. (184) But envy prevented any effect of Aristobulus's alacrity, and the hopes of Caesar; for he was taken off by poison given him by those of Pompey's party; and, for a long while, he had not so much as a burial vouchsafed him in his own country; but his dead body lay [above ground], preserved in honey, until it was sent to the Jews by Antony, in order to be buried in the royal sepulchers.

JULIUS CAESAR AND JUDEA 47 B.C.

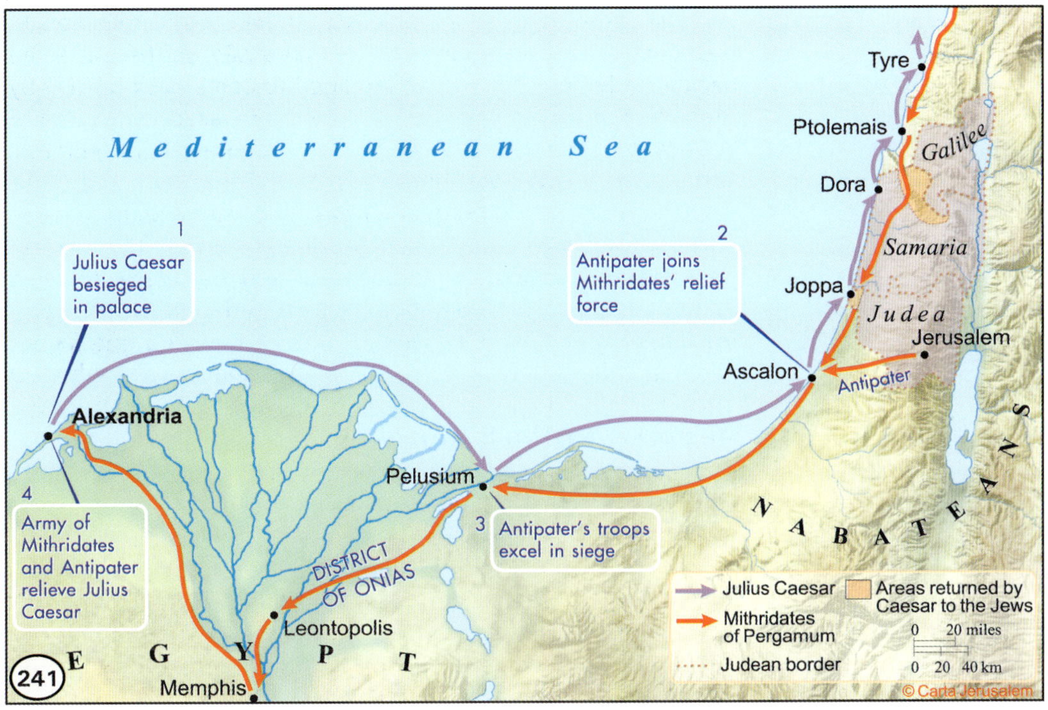

Julius Caesar. (Remastered from Alfred von Domaszewski, *Geschichte der Romischen Kaiser*, Leipzig 1914)

2. (185) His son Alexander also was beheaded by Scipio at Antioch, and that by the command of Pompey, and upon an accusation laid against him before his tribunal, for the mischiefs he had done to the Romans. But Ptolemy, the son of Menneus, who was then ruler of Chalcis, under Libanus, took his brethren to him by sending his son Philippio for them to Ascalon, (186) who took Antigonus, as well as his sisters, away from Aristobulus's wife, and brought them to his father; and falling in love with the younger daughter, he married her, and was afterwards slain by his father on her account; for Ptolemy himself, after he had slain his son, married her, whose name was Alexandra; on the account of which marriage he took the greater care of her brother and sister.

3. (187) Now, after Pompey was dead, Antipater changed sides, and cultivated a friendship with Caesar. And since Mithridates of Pergamus, with the forces he led against Egypt, was excluded from the avenues about Pelusium, and was forced to stay at Ascalon, he persuaded the Arabians, among whom he had lived, to assist him, and came himself to him, at the head of three thousand armed men. (188) He also encouraged the men of power in Syria to come to his assistance, as also of the inhabitants of Libanus, Ptolemy, and Jamblicus, and another Ptolemy; by which means the cities of that country came readily into this war; (189) insomuch that Mithridates ventured now, in dependence upon the additional strength that he had gotten by Antipater, to march forward to Pelusium; and when they refused him a passage through it, he besieged the city; in the attack of which place Antipater principally signalized himself, for he brought down that part of the wall which was over against him, and leaped first of all into the city, with the men that were about him.

4. (190) Thus was Pelusium taken. But still, as they were marching on, those Egyptian Jews that inhabited the country called the country of Onias stopped them. Then did Antipater not only persuade them not to stop them, but to afford provisions for their army; on which account even the people about Memphis would not fight against them, but of their own accord joined Mithridates. (191) Whereupon he went round about Delta, and fought the rest of the Egyptians at a place called the Jews' Camp; nay, when he was in danger in the battle with all his right wing, Antipater wheeled about, and came along the bank of the river to him; (192) for he had beaten those that opposed him as he led the left wing. After which success he fell upon those that pursued Mithridates, and slew a great many of them, and pursued the remainder so far that he took their camp, while he lost no more than fourscore of his own men; as Mithridates lost, during the pursuit that was made after him, about eight hundred. He was also himself saved unexpectedly, and became an unreproachable witness to Caesar of the great actions of Antipater.

5. (193) Whereupon Caesar encouraged Antipater to undertake other hazardous enterprises for him, and that by giving him great commendations and hopes of reward. In all which enterprises he readily exposed himself to many dangers, and became a most courageous warrior; and had many wounds almost all over his body, as demonstrations of his valor. (194) And when Caesar had settled the affairs of Egypt, and was returning into Syria again, he gave him the privilege of a Roman citizen, and freedom from taxes, and rendered him an object of admiration by the honors and marks of friendship he bestowed upon him. On this account it was that he also confirmed Hyrcanus in the high priesthood.

CHAPTER 10.

CAESAR MAKES ANTIPATER PROCURATOR OF JUDEA; AS DOES ANTIPATER APPOINT PHASAELUS TO BE GOVERNOR OF JERUSALEM, AND HEROD GOVERNOR OF GALILEE; WHO, IN SOME TIME, WAS CALLED TO ANSWER FOR HIMSELF [BEFORE THE SANHEDRIN], WHERE HE IS ACQUITTED. SEXTUS CAESAR IS TREACHEROUSLY KILLED BY BASSUS AND IS SUCCEEDED BY MARCUS.

1. (195) ABOUT this time it was that Antigonus, the son of Aristobulus, came to Caesar, and became, in a surprising manner, the occasion of Antipater's further advancement; for whereas he ought to have lamented that his father appeared to have been poisoned on account of his quarrels with Pompey, and to have complained of Scipio's barbarity towards his brother, and not to mix any invidious passion when he was suing for mercy; besides those things, he came before Caesar, and accused Hyrcanus and Antipater, (196)

how they had driven him and his brethren entirely out of their native country, and had acted in a great many instances unjustly and extravagantly with relation to their nation; and that as to the assistance they had sent him into Egypt, it was not done out of good-will to him, but out of the fear they were in from former quarrels, and in order to gain pardon for their friendship to [his enemy] Pompey.

2. (197) Hereupon Antipater threw away his garments, and showed the multitude of the wounds he had, and said, that as to his good-will to Caesar, he had no occasion to say a word, because his body cried aloud, though he said nothing himself; (198) that he wondered at Antigonus's boldness, while he was himself no other than the son of an enemy to the Romans, and of a fugitive, and had it by inheritance from his father to be fond of innovations and seditions, that he should undertake to accuse other men before the Roman governor, and endeavor to gain some advantages to himself, when he ought to be contented that he was suffered to live; for that the reason of his desire of governing public affairs was not so much because he was in want of it, but because, if he could once obtain the same, he might stir up a sedition among the Jews, and use what he should gain from the Romans to the disservice of those that gave it him.

3. (199) When Caesar heard this, he declared Hyrcanus to be the most worthy of the high priesthood, and gave leave to Antipater to choose what authority he pleased; but he left the determination of such dignity to him that bestowed the dignity upon him; so he was constituted procurator of all Judea, and obtained leave, moreover, to rebuild those walls of his country that had been thrown down. (200) These honorary grants Caesar sent orders to have engraved in the Capitol, that they might stand there as indications of his own justice, and of the virtue of Antipater.

Hyrcanus II, high priest and king of Judea. (from "Promptuarii Iconum Insigniorum" pub. by Guillaume Rouille [1518?–1589])

4. (201) But as soon as Antipater had conducted Caesar out of Syria he returned to Judea, and the first thing he did was to rebuild that wall of his own country [Jerusalem] which Pompey had overthrown, and then to go over the country, and to quiet the tumults that were therein; where he partly threatened, and partly advised, every one, and told them that in case they would submit to Hyrcanus, they would live happily and peaceably, and enjoy what they possessed, and that with universal peace and quietness; (202) but that in case they hearkened to such as had some frigid hopes by raising new troubles to get themselves some gain, they should then find him to be their lord instead of their procurator; and find Hyrcanus to be a tyrant instead of a king; and both the Romans and Caesar to be their enemies, instead of rulers; for that they would not suffer him to be removed from the government, whom they had made their governor. (203) And, at the same time that he said this, he settled the affairs of the country by himself, because he saw that Hyrcanus was inactive, and not fit to manage the affairs of the kingdom. So he constituted his eldest son, Phasaelus, governor of Jerusalem, and of the parts about it; he also sent his next son, Herod, who was very young, with equal authority into Galilee.

5. (204) Now Herod was an active man, and soon found proper materials for his active spirit to work upon. As therefore he found that Hezekias, the head of the robbers, ran over the neighboring parts of Syria with a great band of men, he caught him and slew him, and many more of the robbers with him; (205) which exploit was chiefly grateful to the Syrians, insomuch that hymns were sung in Herod's commendation, both in the villages and in the cities, as having procured their quietness, and having preserved what they possessed to them; on which occasion he became acquainted with Sextus Caesar, a kinsman of the great Caesar, and president of Syria. (206) A just emulation of his glorious actions excited Phasaelus also to imitate him. Accordingly, he procured the good-will of the inhabitants of Jerusalem, by his own management of the city affairs, and did not abuse his power in any disagreeable manner; (207) whence it came to pass that the nation paid Antipater the respects that were due only to a king, and the honors they all yielded him were equal to the honors due to an absolute lord; yet did he not abate any part of that good-will or fidelity which he owed to Hyrcanus.

6. (208) However, he found it impossible to escape envy in such his prosperity; for the glory of these young men affected even Hyrcanus himself already privately, though he said nothing of it to any body; but what he principally was grieved at was the great actions of Herod, and that so many messengers came one before another, and informed him of the great reputation he got in all his undertakings. There were also many people in the royal palace itself who inflamed his envy at him; those, I mean, who were obstructed in their designs by the prudence either of the young men, or of Antipater. (209) These men said, that by committing the public affairs to the management of Antipater and of his sons, he sat down with nothing but the bare name of a king, without any of its authority; and they asked him how long he would so far mistake himself, as to breed up kings against his own interest; for that they did not now conceal their government of affairs any longer, but were plainly lords of the nation, and had thrust him out of his authority; that this was the case when Herod slew so many men without his giving him any command to do it, either by word of mouth, or by his letter, and this in contradiction to the law of the Jews; who therefore, in case he be not a king, but a private man, still ought to come to his trial, and answer it to him, and to the laws of his country, which do not permit any one to be killed till he hath been condemned in judgment.

7. (210) Now Hyrcanus was, by degrees, inflamed with these discourses, and at length could bear no longer, but he summoned Herod to take his trial. Accordingly, by his father's advice, and as soon as the affairs of Galilee would give him leave, he came up to [Jerusalem], when he had first placed garrisons in Galilee; however, he came with a sufficient body of soldiers, so many indeed that he might not appear to have with him an army able to overthrow Hyrcanus's government, nor yet so few as to expose him to the insults of those that envied him. (211) However, Sextus Caesar was in fear for the young man, lest he should be taken by his enemies, and brought to punishment; so he sent some to denounce expressly to Hyrcanus that he should acquit Herod of the capital charge against him; who acquitted him accordingly, as being otherwise inclined also so to do, for he loved Herod.

8. (212) But Herod, supposing that he had escaped punishment without the consent of the king, retired to Sextus, to Damascus, and got every thing ready, in order not to obey him if he should summon him again; whereupon those that were evil-disposed irritated Hyrcanus, and told him that Herod was gone away in anger, and was prepared to make war upon him; and as the king believed

what they said, he knew not what to do, since he saw his antagonist was stronger than he was himself. (213) And now, since Herod was made general of Coelesyria and Samaria by Sextus Caesar, he was formidable, not only from the good-will which the nation bore him, but by the power he himself had; insomuch that Hyrcanus fell into the utmost degree of terror, and expected he would presently march against him with his army.

9. (214) Nor was he mistaken in the conjecture he made; for Herod got his army together, out of the anger he bare him for his threatening him with the accusation in a public court, and led it to Jerusalem, in order to throw Hyrcanus down from his kingdom; and this he had soon done, unless his father and brother had gone out together and broken the force of his fury, and this by exhorting him to carry his revenge no further than to threatening and affrighting, but to spare the king, under whom he had been advanced to such a degree of power; and that he ought not to be so much provoked at his being tried, as to forget to be thankful that he was acquitted; nor so long to think upon what was of a melancholy nature, as to be ungrateful for his deliverance; (215) and if we ought to reckon that God is the arbitrator of success in war, an unjust cause is of more disadvantage than an army can be of advantage; and that therefore he ought not to be entirely confident of success in a case where he is to fight against his king, his supporter, and one that had often been his benefactor, and that had never been severe to him, any otherwise than as he had hearkened to evil counselors, and this no further than by bringing a shadow of injustice upon him. So Herod was prevailed upon by these arguments, and supposed that what he had already done was sufficient for his future hopes, and that he had enough shown his power to the nation.

10. (216) In the mean time, there was a disturbance among the Romans about Apamia, and a civil war occasioned by the treacherous slaughter of Sextus Caesar, by Cecilius Bassus, which he perpetrated out of his good-will to Pompey; he also took the authority over his forces; but as the rest of Caesar's commanders attacked Bassus with their whole army, in order to punish him for the murder of Caesar, (217) Antipater also sent them assistance by his sons, both on account of him that was murdered, and on account of that Caesar who was still alive, both of which were their friends; and as this war grew to be of a considerable length, Marcus came out of Italy as successor to Sextus.

CHAPTER 11.

HEROD IS MADE PROCURATOR OF ALL SYRIA; MALICHUS IS AFRAID OF HIM, AND TAKES ANTIPATER OFF BY POISON; WHEREUPON THE TRIBUNES OF THE SOLDIERS ARE PREVAILED WITH TO KILL HIM.

1. (218) THERE, was at this time a mighty war raised among the Romans upon the sudden and treacherous slaughter of Caesar by Cassius and Brutus, after he had held the government for three years and seven months. Upon this murder there were very great agitations, and the great men were mightily at difference one with another, and every one betook himself to that party where they had the greatest hopes of their own, of advancing themselves. Accordingly, Cassius came into Syria, in order to receive the forces that were at Apamia, (219) where he procured a reconciliation between Bassus and Marcus, and the legions which were at difference with him; so he raised the siege of Apamia, and took upon him the command of the army, and went about exacting tribute of the cities, and demanding their money to such a degree as they were not able to bear.

Marble bust of Brutus (Palazzo Massimo alle Terme in the National Museum of Rome)

(below) Denarius (42 B.C.) issued by Cassius Longinus and Lentulus Spinther, depicting the crowned head of Liberty and on the reverse a sacrificial jug and lituus. (Classical Numismatic Group, Inc. http://www.cngcoins.com)

2. (220) So he gave command that the Jews should bring in seven hundred talents; whereupon Antipater, out of his dread of Cassius's threats, parted the raising of this sum among his sons, and among others of his acquaintance, and to be done immediately; and among them he required one Malichus, who was at enmity with him, to do his part also, which necessity forced him to do. (221) Now Herod, in the first place, mitigated the passion of Cassius, by bringing his share out of Galilee, which was a hundred talents, on which account he was in the highest favor with him; and when he reproached the rest for being tardy, he was angry at the cities themselves; (222) so he made slaves of Gophna and Emmaus, and two others of less note; nay, he proceeded as if he would kill Malichus, because he had not made greater haste in exacting his tribute; but Antipater prevented the ruin of this man, and of the other cities, and got into Cassius's favor by bringing in a hundred talents immediately.

3. (223) However, when Cassius was gone Malichus forgot the kindness that Antipater had done him, and laid frequent plots against him that had saved him, as making haste to get him out of the way, who was an obstacle to his wicked practices; but Antipater was so much afraid of the power and cunning of the man, that he went beyond Jordan, in order to get an army to guard himself against his treacherous designs; (224) but when Malichus was caught in his plot, he put upon Antipater's sons by his impudence, for he thoroughly deluded Phasaelus, who was the guardian of Jerusalem, and Herod who was intrusted with the weapons of war, and this by a great many excuses and oaths, and persuaded them to procure his reconciliation to his father. Thus was he preserved again by Antipater, who dissuaded Marcus, the then president of Syria, from his resolution of killing Malichus, on account of his attempts for innovation.

4. (225) Upon the war between Cassius and Brutus on one side, against the younger Caesar [Augustus] and Antony on the other, Cassius and Marcus got together an army out of Syria; and because Herod was likely to have a great share in providing necessaries, they then made him procurator of all Syria, and gave him an army of foot and horse. Cassius premised him also, that after the war was over, he would make him king of Judea. (226) But it so happened that the power and hopes of his son became the cause of his perdition; for as Malichus was afraid of this, he corrupted one of the king's cup-bearers with money to give a poisoned potion to Antipater; so he became a sacrifice to Malichus's wickedness, and died at a feast. He was a man in other respects active in the management of affairs, and one that recovered the government to Hyrcanus, and preserved it in his hands.

5. (227) However, Malichus, when he was suspected of poisoning Antipater, and when the multitude was angry with him for it, denied it, and made the people believe he was not guilty. He also prepared to make a greater figure, and raised soldiers; for he did not suppose that Herod would be quiet, who indeed came upon him with an army presently, in order to revenge his father's death; (228) but, upon hearing the advice of his brother Phasaelus, not to punish him in an open manner, lest the multitude should fall into a sedition, he admitted of Malichus's apology, and professed that he cleared him of that suspicion; he also made a pompous funeral for his father.

6. (229) So Herod went to Samaria, which was then in a tumult, and settled the city in peace; after which at the [Pentecost] festival, he returned to Jerusalem, having his armed men with him: hereupon Hyrcanus, at the request of Malichus, who feared his reproach, forbade them to introduce foreigners to mix themselves with the people of the country while they were purifying themselves; but Herod despised the pretense, and him that gave that command, and came in by night. (230) Upon which Malichus came to him, and bewailed Antipater; Herod also made him believe [he admitted of his lamentations as real], although he had much ado to restrain his passion at him; however, he did himself bewail the murder of his father in his letters to Cassius, who, on other accounts, also hated Malichus. Cassius sent him word back that he should avenge his father's death upon him, and privately gave order to the tribunes that were under him, that they should assist Herod in a righteous action he was about.

7. (231) And because, upon the taking of Laodicea by Cassius, the men of power were gotten together from all quarters, with presents and crowns in their hands, Herod allotted this time for the punishment of Malichus. When Malichus suspected that, and was at Tyre, he resolved to withdraw his son privately from among the Tyrians, who was a hostage there, while he got ready to fly away into Judea; (232) the despair he was in of escaping excited him to think of greater things; for he hoped that he should raise the nation to a revolt from the Romans, while Cassius was busy about the war against Antony, and that he should easily depose Hyrcanus, and get the crown for himself.

8. (233) But fate laughed at the hopes he had; for Herod foresaw what he was so zealous about, and invited both Hyrcanus and him to supper; but calling one of the principal servants that stood by him to him, he sent him out, as though it were to get things ready for supper, but in reality to give notice beforehand about the plot that was laid against him; (234) accordingly they called to mind what orders Cassius had given them, and went out of the city with their swords in their hands upon the sea-shore, where they encompassed Malichus round about, and killed him with many wounds. Upon which Hyrcanus was immediately aftrighted, till he swooned away and fell down at the surprise he was in; and it was with difficulty that he was recovered, when he asked who it was that had killed Malichus. (235) And when one of the tribunes replied that it was done by the command of Cassius, "Then," said he, "Cassius hath saved both me and my country, by cutting off one that was laying plots against them both." Whether he spake according to his own sentiments, or whether his fear was such that he was obliged to commend the action by saying so, is uncertain; however, by this method Herod inflicted punishment upon Malichus.

Aerial view of Masada. (photo Andrew Shiva, via Wikimedia Commons)

CHAPTER 12.

PHASAELUS IS TOO HARD FOR FELIX; HEROD ALSO OVERCOMES ANTIGONUS IN BATTLE; AND THE JEWS ACCUSE BOTH HEROD AND PHASAELUS BUT ANTONIUS ACQUITS THEM, AND MAKES THEM TETRARCHS.

1. (236) WHEN Cassius was gone out of Syria, another sedition arose at Jerusalem, wherein Felix assaulted Phasaelus with an army, that he might revenge the death of Malichus upon Herod, by falling upon his brother. Now Herod happened then to be with Fabius, the governor of Damascus, and as he was going to his brother's assistance, he was detained by sickness; (237) in the meantime, Phasaelus was by himself too hard for Felix, and reproached Hyrcanus on account of his ingratitude, both for what assistance he had afforded Malichus, and for overlooking Malichus's brother, when he possessed himself of the fortresses; for he had gotten a great many of them already, and among them the strongest of them all, Masada.

2. (238) However, nothing could be sufficient for him against the force of Herod, who, as soon as he was recovered, took the other fortresses again, and drove him out of Masada in the posture of a supplicant; he also drove away Marion, the tyrant of the Tyrians, out of Galilee, when he had already possessed himself of three fortified places; but as to those Tyrians whom he had caught, he preserved them all alive; nay, some of them he gave presents to, and so sent them away, and thereby procured good-will to himself from the city, and hatred to the tyrant. (239) Marion had indeed obtained that tyrannical power of Cassius, who set tyrants over all Syria and out of hatred to Herod it was that he assisted Antigonus,

the son of Aristobulus, and principally on Fabius's account, whom Antigonus had made his assistant by money, and had him accordingly on his side when he made his descent; but it was Ptolemy, the kinsman of Antigonus, that supplied all that he wanted.

3. (240) When Herod had fought against these in the avenues of Judea, he was conqueror in the battle, and drove away Antigonus, and returned to Jerusalem, beloved by every body for the glorious action he had done; for those who did not before favor him did join themselves to him now, because of his marriage into the family of Hyrcanus; (241) for as he had formerly married a wife out of his own country of no ignoble blood, who was called Doris, of whom he begat Antipater; so did he now marry Mariamne, the daughter of Alexander, the son of Aristobulus, and the granddaughter of Hyrcanus, and was become thereby a relation of the king.

4. (242) But when Caesar [Augustus] and Antony had slain Cassius near Philippi, and Caesar was gone to Italy, and Antony to Asia, amongst the rest of the cities which sent ambassadors to Antony unto Bithynia, the great men of the Jews came also, and accused Phasaelus and Herod, that they kept the government by force, and that Hyrcanus had no more than an honorable name. Herod appeared ready to answer this accusation; and having made Antony his friend by the large sums of money which he gave him, he brought him to such a temper as not to hear the others speak against him; and thus did they part at this time.

5. (243) However, after this, there came a hundred of the principal men among the Jews to Daphne by Antioch to Antony, who was already in love with Cleopatra [VII] to the degree of slavery; these Jews put those men that were the most potent, both in dignity and eloquence, foremost, and accused the brethren. But Messala opposed them, and defended the brethren, and that while Hyrcanus stood by him, on account of his relation to them. (244) When Antony had heard both sides, he asked Hyrcanus which party was the fittest to govern, who replied that Herod and his party were the fittest. Antony was glad of that answer, for he had been formerly treated in an hospitable and obliging manner by his father Antipater, when he marched into Judea with Gabinius; so he constituted the brethren tetrarchs, and committed to them the government of Judea.

6. (245) But when the ambassadors had indignation at this procedure, Antony took fifteen of them, and put them into custody, whom he was also going to kill presently, and the rest he drove away with disgrace; on which occasion a still greater tumult arose at Jerusalem; so they sent again a thousand ambassadors to Tyre, where Antony now abode, as he was marching to Jerusalem; upon these men who made a clamor he sent out the governor of Tyre, and ordered him to punish all that he could catch of them, and to settle those in the administration whom he had made tetrarchs.

7. (246) But before this Herod, and Hyrcanus went out upon the sea-shore, and earnestly desired of these ambassadors that they would neither bring ruin upon themselves, nor war upon their native country, by their rash contentions; and when they grew still more outrageous, Antony sent out armed men, and slew a great many, and wounded more of them; of whom those that were slain were buried by Hyrcanus, as were the wounded put under the care of physicians by him; (247) yet would not those that had escaped be quiet still, but put the affairs of the city into such disorder, and so provoked Antony, that he slew those whom he had in bonds also.

Antony and Cleopatra on a silver denarius minted in 32 B.C. (Classical Numismatic Group, Inc. http://www.cngcoins.com)

CHAPTER 13.

THE PARTHIANS BRING ANTIGONUS BACK INTO JUDEA, AND CAST HYRCANUS AND PHASAELUS INTO PRISON. THE FLIGHT OF HEROD, AND THE TAKING OF JERUSALEM AND WHAT HYRCANUS AND PHASAELUS SUFFERED.

1. (248) Now two years afterward, when Barzapharnes, a governor among the Parthians, and Pacorus, the king's son, had possessed themselves of Syria, and when Lysanias had already succeeded upon the death of his father Ptolemy, the son of Menneus, in the government [of Chalcis], he prevailed with the governor, by a promise of a thousand talents, and five hundred women, to bring back Antigonus to his kingdom, and to turn Hyrcanus out of it. (249) Pacorus was by these means induced so to do, and marched along the sea-coast, while he ordered Barzapharnes to fall upon the Jews as he went along the Mediterranean part of the country; but of the maritime people, the Tyrians would not receive Pacorus, although those of Ptolemais and Sidon had received him; so he committed a troop of his horse to a certain cup-bearer belonging to the royal family, of his own name [Pacorus], and gave him orders to march into Judea, in order to learn the state of affairs among their enemies, and to help Antigonus when he should want his assistance.

2. (250) Now as these men were ravaging Carmel, many of the Jews ran together to Antigonus, and showed themselves ready to make an incursion into the country; so he sent them before into that place called Drymus, [the woodland **(cf. 2 Kings 19:23; Isaiah 37:24)**] to seize upon the place; whereupon a battle was fought between them, and they drove the enemy away, and pursued them, and ran after them as far as Jerusalem, and as their numbers increased, they proceeded as far as the king's palace; (251) but as Hyrcanus and Phasaelus received them with a strong body of men, there happened a battle in the market-place, in which Herod's party beat the enemy, and shut them up in the temple, and set sixty men in the houses adjoining as a guard to them. (252) But the people that were tumultuous against the brethren came in, and burnt those men; while Herod, in his rage for killing them, attacked and slew many of the people, till one party made incursions on the other by turns, day by day, in the way of ambushes, and slaughters were made continually among them.

3. (253) Now when that festival which we call Pentecost was at hand, all the places about the temple, and the whole city, was full of a multitude of people that were come out of the country, and which were the greatest part of them armed also, at which time Phasaelus guarded the wall, and Herod, with a few, guarded the royal palace; and when he made an assault upon his enemies, as they were out of their ranks, on the north quarter of the city, he slew a very great number of them, and put them all to flight; and some of them he shut up within the city, and others within the outward

THE PARTHIAN INVASION AND THE ESCAPE OF HEROD
40 B.C.

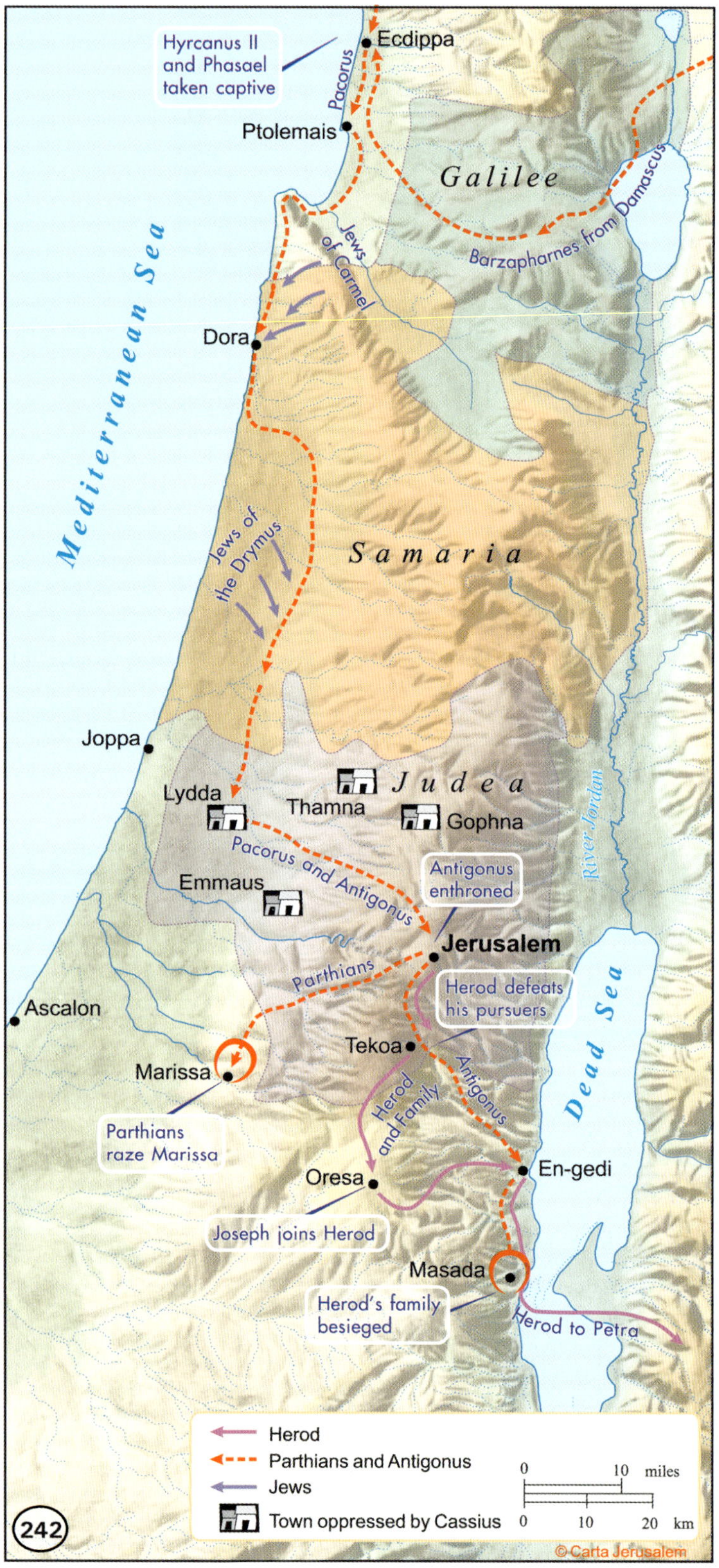

rampart. (254) In the meantime, Antigonus desired that Pacorus might be admitted to be a reconciler between them; and Phasaelus was prevailed upon to admit the Parthian into the city with five hundred horses, and to treat him in an hospitable manner, who pretended that he came to quell the tumult, but in reality he came to assist Antigonus; (255) however, he laid a plot for Phasaelus, and persuaded him to go as an ambassador to Barzapharnes, in order to put an end to the war, although Herod was very earnest with him to the contrary, and exhorted him to kill the plotter, but not expose himself to the snares he had laid for him, because the barbarians are naturally perfidious. However, Pacorus went out and took Hyrcanus with him, that he might be the less suspected; he also left some of the horsemen, called the Freemen, with Herod, and conducted Phasaelus with the rest.

4. (256) But now, when they were come to Galilee, they found that the people of that country had revolted, and were in arms, who came very cunningly to their leader, and besought him to conceal his treacherous intentions by an obliging behavior to them; accordingly, he at first made them presents; and afterward, as they went away, laid ambushes for them; (257) and when they were come to one of the maritime cities called Ecdippon, they perceived that a plot was laid for them; for they were there informed of the promise of a thousand talents, and how Antigonus had devoted the greatest number of the women that were there with them, among the five hundred, to the Parthians; (258) they also perceived that an ambush was always laid for them by the barbarians in the night time; they had also been seized on before this, unless they had waited for the seizure of Herod first at Jerusalem, because if he were once informed of this treachery of theirs, he would take care of himself; nor was this a mere report, but they saw the guards already not far off them.

5. (259) Nor would Phasaelus think of forsaking Hyrcanus and flying away, although Ophellius earnestly persuaded him to it; for this man had learned the whole scheme of the plot from Saramalla, the richest of all the Syrians. But Phasaelus went up to the Parthian governor, and reproached him to his face for laying this treacherous plot against them, and chiefly because he had done it for money; and he promised him that he would give him more money for their preservation, than Antigonus had promised to give for the kingdom. (260) But the sly Parthian endeavored to remove all this suspicion by apologies and by oaths, and then went [to the other] Pacorus; immediately after which those Parthians who were left, and had it in charge, seized upon Phasaelus and Hyrcanus, who could do no more than curse their perfidiousness and their perjury.

6. (261) In the mean time, the cup-bearer was sent [back], and laid a plot how to seize upon Herod, by deluding him, and getting him out of the city, as he was commanded to do. But Herod suspected the barbarians from the beginning; and having then received intelligence that a messenger, who was to bring him the letters that informed him of the treachery intended, had fallen among the enemy, he would not go out of the city; though Pacorus said very positively that he ought to go out, and meet the messengers that brought the letters, for that the enemy had not taken them, and that the contents of them were not accounts of any plots upon them, but of what Phasaelus had done; (262) yet had he heard from others that his brother was seized; and Alexandra the shrewdest woman in the world, Hyrcanus's daughter, begged of him that he would not go out, nor trust himself to those barbarians, who now were come to make an attempt upon him openly.

7. (263) Now as Pacorus and his friends were considering how they might bring their plot to bear privately, because it was not possible to circumvent a man of so great prudence by openly attacking him, Herod prevented them, and went off with the persons that were the most nearly related to him by night, and this without their enemies being apprized of it. (264) But as soon as the Parthians perceived it, they pursued after them; and as he gave orders for his mother, and sister, and the young woman who was betrothed to him, with her mother, and his youngest brother, to

make the best of their way, he himself, with his servants, took all the care they could to keep off the barbarians; and when at every assault he had slain a great many of them, he came to the strong hold of Masada.

8. (265) Nay, he found by experience that the Jews fell more heavily upon him than did the Parthians, and created him troubles perpetually, and this ever since he was gotten sixty furlongs from the city; these sometimes brought it to a sort of a regular battle. Now in the place where Herod beat them, and killed a great number of them, there he afterward built a citadel, in memory of the great actions he did there, and adorned it with the most costly palaces, and erected very strong fortifications, and called it, from his own name, Herodium. (266) Now as they were in their flight, many joined themselves to him every day; and at a place called Thressa of Idumea his brother Joseph met him, and advised him to ease himself of a great number of his followers, because Masada would not contain so great a multitude, which were above nine thousand. (267) Herod complied with this advice, and sent away the most cumbersome part of his retinue, that they might go into Idumea, and gave them provisions for their journey; but he got safe to the fortress with his nearest relations, and retained with him only the stoutest of his followers; and there it was that he left eight hundred of his men as a guard for the women, and provisions sufficient for a siege; but he made haste himself to Petra of Arabia.

9. (268) As for the Parthians in Jerusalem, they betook themselves to plundering, and fell upon the houses of those that were fled, and upon the king's palace, and spared nothing but Hyrcanus's money, which was not above three hundred talents. They lighted on other men's money also, but not so much as they hoped for; for Herod having a long while had a suspicion of the perfidiousness of the barbarians, had taken care to have what was most splendid among his treasures conveyed into Idumea, as every one belonging to him had in like manner done also. (269) But the Parthians proceeded to that degree of injustice, as to fill all the country with war without denouncing it, and to demolish the city Marissa, and not only to set up Antigonus for king, but to deliver Phasaelus and Hyrcanus bound into his hands, in order to their being tormented by him. (270) Antigonus himself also bit off Hyrcanus's ears with his own teeth, as he fell down upon his knees to him, that so he might never be able upon any mutation of affairs to take the high priesthood again, for the high priests that officiated were to be complete, and without blemish.

10. (271) However, he failed in his purpose of abusing Phasaelus, by reason of his courage; for though he neither had the command of his sword nor of his hands, he prevented all abuses by dashing his head against a stone; so he demonstrated himself to be Herod's own brother, and Hyrcanus a most degenerate relation, and died with great bravery, and made the end of his life agreeable to the actions of it. (272) There is also another report about his end, viz. that he recovered of that stroke, and that a surgeon, who was sent by Antigonus to heal him, filled the wound with poisonous ingredients, and so killed him; whichsoever of these deaths he came to, the beginning of it was glorious. It is also reported that before he expired he was informed by a certain poor woman how Herod had escaped out of their hands, and that he said thereupon, "I now die with comfort, since I leave behind me one alive that will avenge me of mine enemies."

11. (273) This was the death of Phasaelus; but the Parthians, al-

PLAN OF MARISSA

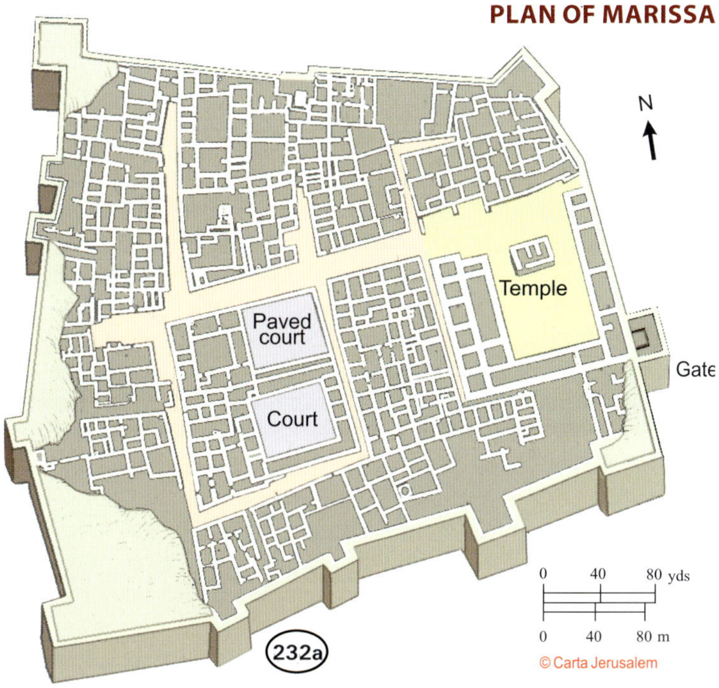

though they had failed of the women they chiefly desired, yet did they put the government of Jerusalem into the hands of Antigonus, and took away Hyrcanus, and bound him, and carried him to Parthia.

CHAPTER 14.

WHEN HEROD IS REJECTED IN ARABIA, HE MAKES HASTE TO ROME WHERE ANTONY AND CAESAR JOIN THEIR INTEREST TO MAKE HIM KING.

1. (274) NOW Herod did the more zealously pursue his journey into Arabia, as making haste to get money of the king, while his brother was yet alive; by which money alone it was that he hoped to prevail upon the covetous temper of the barbarians to spare Phasaelus; for he reasoned thus with himself,:—that if the Arabian king was too forgetful of his father's friendship with him, and was too covetous to make him a free gift, he would however borrow of him as much as might redeem his brother, and put into his hands, as a pledge, the son of him that was to be redeemed. (275) Accordingly he led his brother's son along with him, who was of the age of seven years. Now he was ready to give three hundred talents for his brother, and intended to desire the intercession of the Tyrians, to get them accepted; however, fate had been too quick for his diligence; and since Phasaelus was dead, Herod's brotherly love was now in vain. Moreover, he was not able to find any lasting friendship among the Arabians; (276) for their king, Malichus, sent to him immediately, and commanded him to return back out of his country, and used the name of the Parthians as a pretense for so doing, as though these had denounced to him by their ambassadors to cast Herod out of Arabia; while in reality they had a mind to keep back what they owed to Antipater, and not be obliged to make requitals to his sons for the free gifts the father had made them. He also took the impudent advice of those who, equally with himself, were willing to deprive Herod of what Antipater had deposited among them; and these men were the most potent of all whom he had in his kingdom.

2. (277) So when Herod had found that the Arabians were his enemies, and this for those very reasons whence he hoped they would have been the most friendly, and had given them such an answer as his passion suggested, he returned back, and went for

Egypt. Now he lodged the first evening at one of the temples of that country, in order to meet with those whom he left behind; but on the next day word was brought him, as he was going to Rhinocurura, that his brother was dead, and how he came by his death; (278) and when he had lamented him as much as his present circumstances could bear, he soon laid aside such cares, and proceeded on his journey. But now, after some time, the king of Arabia repented of what he had done, and sent presently away messengers to call him back: Herod had prevented them, and was come to Pelusium, where he could not obtain a passage from those that lay with the fleet, so he besought their captains to let him go by them; accordingly, out of the reverence they bore to the fame and dignity of the man, they conducted him to Alexandria; (279) and when he came into the city, he was received by Cleopatra with great splendor, who hoped he might be persuaded to be commander of her forces in the expedition she was now about; but he rejected the queen's solicitations, and being neither affrighted at the height of that storm which. then happened, nor at the tumults that were now in Italy, he sailed for Rome.

3. (280) But as he was in peril about Pamphylia, and obliged to cast out the greatest part of the ship's lading, he with difficulty got safe to Rhodes, a place which had been grievously harassed in the war with Cassius. He was there received by his friends, Ptolemy and Sappinius; and although he was then in want of money, he fitted up a three-decked ship of very great magnitude, (281) wherein he and his friends sailed to Brundusium, and went thence to Rome with all speed; where he first of all went to Antony, on account of the friendship his father had with him, and laid before him the calamities of himself and his family; and that he had left his nearest relations besieged in a fortress, and had sailed to him through a storm, to make supplication to him for assistance.

4. (282) Hereupon Antony was moved to compassion at the change that had been made in Herod's affairs, and this both upon his calling to mind how hospitably he had been treated by Antipater, but more especially on account of Herod's own virtue; so he then resolved to get him made king of the Jews, whom he had himself formerly made tetrarch. The contest also that he had with Antigonus was another inducement, and that of no less weight than the great regard he had for Herod; for he looked upon Antigonus as a seditious person, and an enemy of the Romans; (283) and as for Caesar, Herod found him better prepared than Antony, as remembering very fresh the wars he had gone through together with his father, the hospitable treatment he had met with from him, and the entire good-will he had showed to him; besides the activity which he saw in Herod himself. (284) So he called the senate together, wherein Messala, and after him Atratinus, produced Herod before them, and gave a full account of the merits of his father, and his own good-will to the Romans. At the same time they demonstrated that Antigonus was their enemy, not only because he

Coin of Herod the Great. (Carta archives)

soon quarreled with them, but because he now overlooked the Romans, and took the government by the means of the Parthians. These reasons greatly moved the senate; at which juncture Antony came in, and told them that it was for their advantage in the Parthian war that Herod should be king; so they all gave their votes for it. (285) And when the senate was separated, Antony and Caesar went out, with Herod between them; while the consul and the rest of the magistrates went before them, in order to offer sacrifices, and to lay the decree in the Capitol. Antony also made a feast for Herod on the first day of his reign.

CHAPTER 15.

ANTIGONUS BESIEGES THOSE THAT WERE IN MASADA, WHOM HEROD FREES FROM CONFINEMENT WHEN HE CAME BACK FROM ROME, AND PRESENTLY MARCHES TO JERUSALEM WHERE HE FINDS SILO CORRUPTED BY BRIBES.

1. (286) NOW during this time Antigonus besieged those that were in Masada, who had all other necessaries in sufficient quantity, but were in want of water; on which account Joseph, Herod's brother, was disposed to run away to the Arabians, with two hundred of his own friends, because he had heard that Malichus repented of his offenses with regard to Herod; (287) and he had been so quick as to have been gone out of the fortress already, unless, on that very night when he was going away, there had fallen a great deal of rain, insomuch that his reservoirs were full of water, and so he was under no necessity of running away. After which, therefore, they made an irruption upon Antigonus's party, and slew a great many of them, some in open battles, and some in private ambush; nor had they always success in their attempts, for sometimes they were beaten, and ran away.

2. (288) In the mean time Ventidius, the Roman general, was sent out of Syria, to restrain the incursions of the Parthians; and after he had done that, he came into Judea, in pretense indeed to assist Joseph and his party, but in reality to get money of Antigonus; (289) and when he had pitched his camp very near to Jerusalem, as soon as he had got money enough, he went away with the greatest part of his forces; yet still did he leave Silo with some part of them, lest if he had taken them all away, his taking of bribes might have been too openly discovered. Now Antigonus hoped that the Parthians would come again to his assistance, and therefore cultivated a good understanding with Silo in the mean time, lest any interruption should be given to his hopes.

3. (290) Now by this time Herod had sailed out of Italy, and was come to Ptolemais; and as soon as he had gotten together no small army of foreigners, and of his own countrymen, he marched through Galilee against Antigonus, wherein he was assisted by Ventidius and Silo, both whom Dellius, a person sent by Antony, persuaded to bring Herod [into his kingdom]. (291) Now Ventidius was at this time among the cities, and composing the disturbances which had happened by means of the Parthians, as was Silo in Judea corrupted by the bribes that Antigonus had given him; yet was not Herod himself destitute of power, but the number of his forces increased every day as he went along, and all Galilee, with few exceptions, joined themselves to him. (292) So he proposed to himself to set about his most necessary enterprise, and that was Masada, in order to deliver his relations from the siege they endured. But still Joppa stood in his way, and hindered his going thither; for it was necessary to take that city first, which was in the enemies' hands, that when he should go to Jerusalem, no fortress might be left in the enemies' power behind him. Silo also willingly

Remains of the Hasmonean palace at ancient Jericho (Tulul Abu el-Alayiq) (photo: Bukvoed, via Wikimedia Commons)

joined him, as having now a plausible occasion of drawing off his forces [from Jerusalem]; and when the Jews pursued him, and pressed upon him, [in his retreat,] Herod made all excursion upon them with a small body of his men, and soon put them to flight, and saved Silo when he was in distress.

4. (293) After this Herod took Joppa, and then made haste to Masada to free his relations. Now, as he was marching, many came in to him, induced by their friendship to his father, some by the reputation he had already gained himself, and some in order to repay the benefits they had received from them both; but still what engaged the greatest number on his side, was the hopes from him when he should be established in his kingdom; so that he had gotten together already an army hard to be conquered. (294) But Antigonus laid an ambush for him as he marched out, in which he did little or no harm to his enemies. However, he easily recovered his relations again that were in Masada, as well as the fortress Ressa [i.e., Oresa], and then marched to Jerusalem, where the soldiers that were with Silo joined themselves to his own, as did many out of the city, from a dread of his power.

5. (295) Now when he had pitched his camp on the west side of the city, the guards that were there shot their arrows and threw their darts at them, while others ran out in companies, and attacked those in the forefront; but Herod commanded proclamation to be made at the wall, that he was come for the good of the people and the preservation of the city, without any design to be revenged on his open enemies, but to grant oblivion to them, though they had been the most obstinate against him. (296) Now the soldiers that were for Antigonus made a contrary clamor, and did neither permit any body to hear that proclamation, nor to change their party; so Antigonus gave order to his forces to beat the enemy from the walls; accordingly, they soon threw their darts at them from the towers, and put them to flight.

6. (297) And here it was that Silo discovered he had taken bribes; for he set many of the soldiers to clamor about their want of necessaries, and to require their pay, in order to buy themselves food, and to demand that he would lead them into places convenient for their winter quarters; because all the parts about the city were laid waste by the means of Antigonus's army, which had taken all things away. By this he moved the army, and attempted to get them off the siege; (298) but Herod went to the captains that were under Silo, and to a great many of the soldiers, and begged of them not to leave him, who was sent thither by Caesar, and Antony, and the senate; for that he would take care to have their wants supplied that very day. (299) After the making of which entreaty, he went hastily into the country, and brought thither so great an abundance of necessaries, that he cut off all Silo's pretenses; and in order to provide that for the following days they should not want supplies, he sent to the people that were about Samaria (which city had joined itself to him) to bring corn, and wine, and oil, and cattle to Jericho. (300) When Antigonus heard of this, be sent some of his party with orders to hinder, and lay ambushes for these collectors of corn. This command was obeyed, and a great multitude of armed men were gathered together about Jericho, and lay upon the mountains, to watch those that brought the provisions. (301) Yet was Herod not idle, but took with him ten cohorts, five of them were Romans, and five were Jewish cohorts, together with some mercenary troops intermixed among them, and besides those a few horsemen, and came to Jericho; and when he came, he found the city deserted, but that there were five hundred men, with their wives and children, who had taken possession of the tops of the mountains; these he took, and dismissed them, (302) while the Romans fell upon the rest of the city, and plundered it, having found the houses full of all sorts of good things. So the king left a garrison at Jericho, and came back, and sent the Roman army into those cities which were come over to him, to take their winter quarters there, viz. into Judea, [or Idumea,] and Galilee, and Samaria. Antigonus also by bribes obtained of Silo to let a part of his army be received at Lydda, as a compliment to Antonius.

CHAPTER 16.

HEROD TAKES SEPPHORIS AND SUBDUES THE ROBBERS THAT WERE IN THE CAVES; HE AFTER THAT AVENGES HIMSELF UPON MACHERAS, AS UPON AN ENEMY OF HIS AND GOES TO ANTONY AS HE WAS BESIEGING SAMOSATA.

1. (303) SO the Romans lived in plenty of all things, and rested from war. However, Herod did not lie at rest, but seized upon Idumea, and kept it, with two thousand footmen, and four hundred horsemen; and this he did by sending his brother Joseph thither, that no innovation might be made by Antigonus. He also removed his mother, and all his relations, who had been in Masada, to Samaria; and when he had settled them securely, he marched to take the remaining parts of Galilee, and to drive away the garrisons placed there by Antigonus.

2. (304) But when Herod had reached Sepphoris, in a very great snow, he took the city without any difficulty; the guards that should have kept it flying away before it was assaulted; where he gave an opportunity to his followers that had been in distress to refresh themselves, there being in that city a great abundance of necessaries. After which he hasted away to the robbers that were in the caves, who overran a great part of the country, and did as great mischief to its inhabitants as a war itself could have done. (305) Accordingly, he sent beforehand three cohorts of footmen, and one troop of horsemen, to the village Arbela, and came himself forty days afterwards with the rest of his forces. Yet were not the enemy aftrighted at his assault but met him in arms; for their skill was that of warriors, but their boldness was the boldness of robbers: (306) when therefore it came to a pitched battle, they put to flight Herod's left wing with their right one; but Herod, wheeling about on the sudden from his own right wing, came to their assistance, and both made his own left wing return back from its flight, and fell upon the pursuers, and cooled their courage, till

Remains of the Roman theater at Sepphoris. (photo Samuel Magal)

they could not bear the attempts that were made directly upon them, and so turned back and ran away.

3. (307) But Herod followed them, and slew them as he followed them, and destroyed a great part of them, till those that remained were scattered beyond the river [Jordan;] and Galilee was freed from the terrors they had been under, excepting from those that remained, and lay concealed in caves, which required longer time ere they could be conquered. (308) In order to which Herod, in the first place, distributed the fruits of their former labors to the soldiers, and gave every one of them a hundred and fifty drachmae of silver, and a great deal more to their commanders, and sent them into their winter quarters. He also sent to his youngest brother Pheroras, to take care of a good market for them, where they might buy themselves provisions, and to build a wall about Alexandrium; who took care of both those injunctions accordingly.

4. (309) In the mean time Antony abode at Athens, while Ventidius called for Silo and Herod to come to the war against the Parthians, but ordered them first to settle the affairs of Judea; so Herod willingly dismissed Silo to go to Ventidius, but he made an expedition himself against those that lay in the caves. (310) Now these caves were in the precipices of craggy mountains, and could not be come at from any side, since they had only some winding pathways, very narrow, by which they got up to them; but the rock that lay on their front had beneath it valleys of a vast depth, and of an almost perpendicular declivity; insomuch that the king was doubtful for a long time what to do, by reason of a kind of impossibility there was of attacking the place. Yet did he at length make use of a contrivance that was subject to the utmost hazard; (311) for he let down the most hardy of his men in chests, and set them at the mouths of the dens. Now these men slew the robbers and their families, and when they made resistance, they sent in fire upon them [and burnt them]; and as Herod was desirous of saving some of them, he had proclamation made, that they should come and deliver themselves up to him; but not one of them came willingly to him; and of those that were compelled to come, many preferred death to captivity. (312) And here a certain old man, the father of seven children, whose children, together with their mother, desired him to give them leave to go out, upon the assurance and right hand that was offered them, slew them after the following manner: He ordered every one of them to go out, while he stood himself at the cave's mouth, and slew that son of his perpetually who went out. Herod was near enough to see this sight, and his bowels of compassion were moved at it, and he stretched out his right hand to the old man, and besought him to spare his children; (313) yet did not he relent at all upon what he said, but over and above reproached Herod on the lowness of his descent, and slew his wife as well as his children; and when he had thrown their dead bodies down the precipice, he at last threw himself down after them.

5. (314) By this means Herod subdued these caves, and the robbers that were in them. He then left there a part of his army, as many as he thought sufficient to prevent any sedition, and made Ptolemy their general, and returned to Samaria; he led also with him three thousand armed footmen, and six hundred horsemen, against Antigonus. (315) Now here those that used to raise tumults in Galilee, having liberty so to do upon his departure, fell unexpectedly upon Ptolemy, the general of his forces, and slew him; they also laid the country waste, and then retired to the bogs, and to places not easily to be found. (316) But when Herod was informed of this insurrection, he came to the assistance of the country immediately, and destroyed a great number of the seditions, and raised the sieges of all those fortresses they had besieged; he also exacted the tribute of a hundred talents of his enemies, as a penalty for the mutations they had made in the country.

6. (317) By this time (the Parthians being already driven out of the country, and Pacorus slain), Ventidius, by Antony's command, sent a thousand horsemen, and two legions, as auxiliaries to Herod, against Antigonus. Now Antigonus besought Macheras, who was their general, by letter, to come to his assistance, and made a great many mournful complaints about Herod's violence, and about the injuries he did to the kingdom; and promised to give him money for such his assistance; (318) but he complied not with his invitation to betray his trust, for he did not condemn him that sent him, especially while Herod gave him more money [than the other offered]. So he pretended friendship to Antigonus, but came as a spy to discover his affairs; although he did not herein comply with Herod, who dissuaded him from so doing. (319) But Antigonus perceived what his intentions were beforehand, and excluded him out of the city, and defended himself against him as against an enemy, from the walls; till Macheras was ashamed of what he had done, and retired to Emmaus to Herod; and as he was in a rage at his disappointment, he slew all the Jews whom he met with, without sparing those that were for Herod, but using them all as if they were for Antigonus.

7. (320) Hereupon Herod was very angry at him, and was going to fight against Macheras as his enemy; but he restrained his indignation, and marched to Antony to accuse Macheras of maladministration. But Macheras was made sensible of his offenses, and followed after the king immediately, and earnestly begged and obtained that he would be reconciled to him. (321) However, Herod did not desist from his resolution of going to Antony; but when he heard that he was besieging Samosata with a great army, which is a strong city near to Euphrates, he made the greater haste; as observing that this was a proper opportunity for showing at once his courage, and for doing what would greatly oblige Antony. (322) Indeed, when he came, he soon made an end of that siege,

Coin of Samosata, 31 B.C. to A.D. 38, depicting laureate head of Zeus (left) and lion walking (right), with inscription ΣΑΜΟ(ΣΑΤΩΝ). (Classical Numismatic Group, Inc. http://www.cngcoins.com)

and slew a great number of the barbarians, and took from them a large prey; insomuch that Antony, who admired his courage formerly, did now admire it still more. Accordingly, he heaped many more honors upon him, and gave him more assured hopes that he should gain his kingdom; and now king Antiochus was forced to deliver up Samosata.

CHAPTER 17.

THE DEATH OF JOSEPH [HEROD'S BROTHER] WHICH HAD BEEN SIGNIFIED TO HEROD IN DREAMS. HOW HEROD WAS PRESERVED TWICE AFTER A WONDERFUL MANNER. HE CUTS OFF THE HEAD OF PAPPUS, WHO WAS THE MURDERER OF HIS BROTHER AND SENDS THAT HEAD TO [HIS OTHER BROTHER] PHERORAS, AND IN NO LONG TIME HE BESIEGES JERUSALEM AND MARRIES MARIAMNE.

1. (323) IN the meantime, Herod's affairs in Judea were in an ill state. He had left his brother Joseph with full power, but had charged him to make no attempts against Antigonus till his return; for that Macheras would not be such an assistant as he could depend on, as it appeared by what he had done already; but as soon as Joseph heard that his brother was at a very great distance, he neglected the charge he had received, and marched towards Jericho with five cohorts, which Macheras sent with him. This movement was intended for seizing on the corn, as it was now in the midst of summer; (324) but when his enemies attacked him in the mountains, and in places which were difficult to pass, he was both killed himself, as he was very bravely fighting in the battle, and the entire Roman cohorts were destroyed; for these cohorts were new-raised men, gathered out of Syria, and here was no mixture of those called veteran soldiers among them, who might have supported those that were unskillful in war.

2. (325) This victory was not sufficient for Antigonus; but he proceeded to that degree of rage, as to treat the dead body of Joseph barbarously; for when he had got possession of the bodies of those that were slain, he cut off his head, although his brother Pheroras would have given fifty talents as a price of redemption for it. (326) And now the affairs of Galilee were put in such disorder after this victory of Antigonus's, that those of Antigonus's party brought the principal men that were on Herod's side to the lake, and there drowned them. There was a great change made also in Idumea, where Macheras was building a wall about one of the fortresses, which was called Gittha. (327) But Herod had not yet been informed of these things; for after the taking of Samosata, and when Antony had set Sosius over the affairs of Syria, and had given him orders to assist Herod against Antigonus, he departed into Egypt; but Sosius sent two legions before him into Judea to assist Herod, and followed himself soon after with the rest of his army.

3. (328) Now when Herod was at Daphne, by Antioch, he had some dreams which clearly foreboded his brother's death; and as he leaped out of his bed in a disturbed manner, there came messengers that acquainted him with that calamity. So when he had lamented this misfortune for a while, he put off the main part of his mourning, and made haste to march against his enemies; (329) and when he had performed a march that was above his strength, and was gone as far as Libanus, he got him eight hundred men of those that lived near to that mountain as his assistants, and joined with them one Roman legion, with which, before it was day, he made an irruption into Galilee, and met his enemies, and drove them back to the place which they had left. (330) He also made an immediate and continual attack upon the fortress. Yet was he forced by a most terrible storm to pitch his camp in the neighboring villages before he could take it. But when, after a few days' time, the second legion, that came from Antony, joined themselves to him, the enemy were aftrighted at his power, and left their fortifications ill the night time.

THE RISE OF HEROD 40–37 B.C.

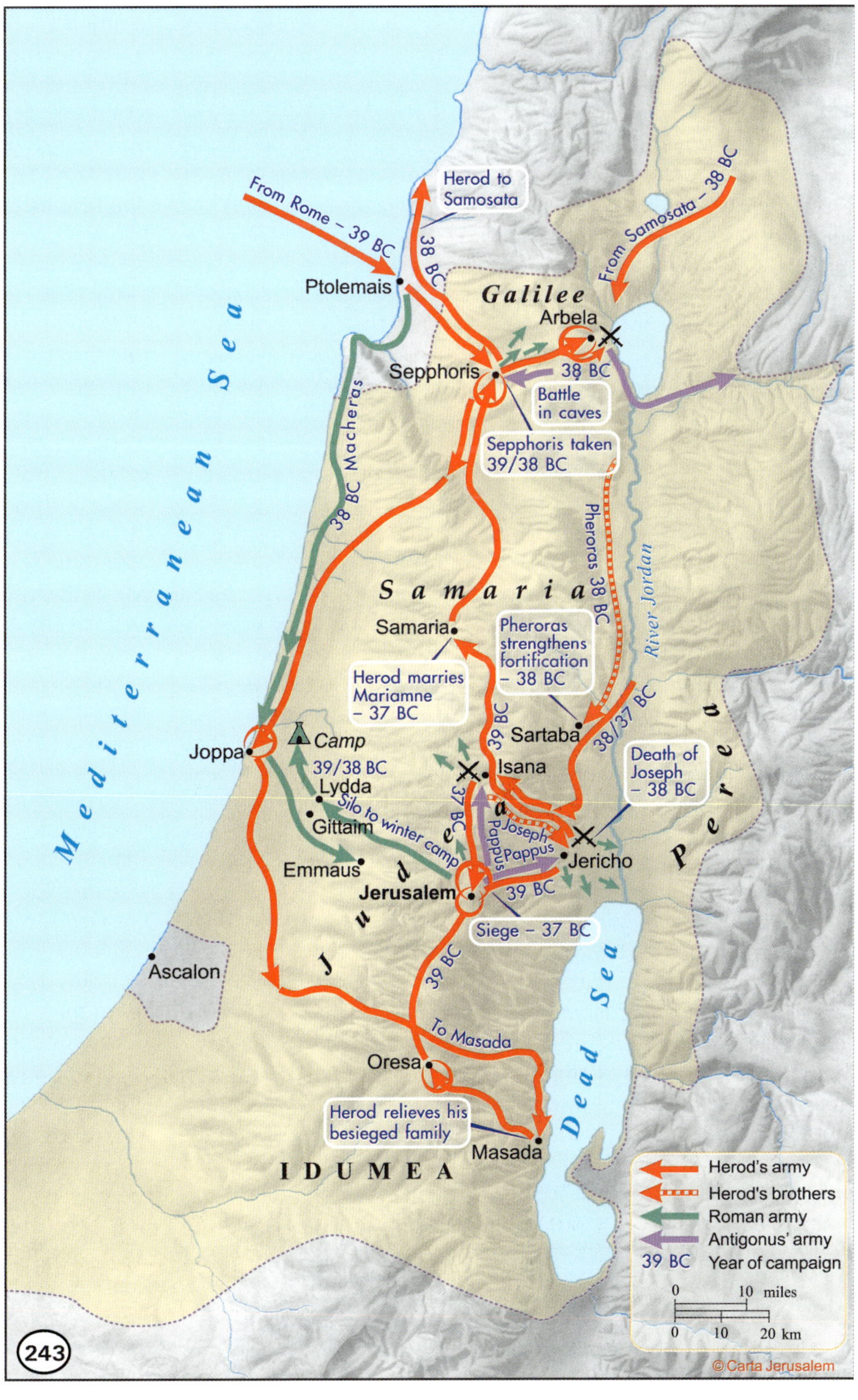

4. (331) After this he marched through Jericho, as making what haste he could to be avenged on his brother's murderers; where happened to him a providential sign, out of which, when he had unexpectedly escaped, he had the reputation of being very dear to God; for that evening there feasted with him many of the principal men; and after that feast was over, and all the guests were gone out, the house fell down immediately. (332) And as he judged this to be a common signal of what dangers he should undergo, and how he should escape them in the war that he was going about, he, in the morning, set forward with his army, when about six thousand of his enemies came running down from the mountains, and began to fight with those in his forefront; yet durst they not be so very bold as to engage the Romans hand to hand, but threw stones and darts at them at a distance; by which means they wounded a considerable number; in which action Herod's own side was wounded with a dart.

5. (333) Now as Antigonus had a mind to appear to exceed Herod, not only in the courage, but in the number of his men, he sent Pappus, one of his companions, with an army against Samaria, (334) whose fortune it was to oppose Macheras; but Herod overran the enemy's country, and demolished five little cities, and destroyed two thousand men that were in them, and burned their houses, and then returned to his camp; but his head-quarters were at the village called Cana.

6. (335) Now a great multitude of Jews resorted to him every day, both out of Jericho and the other parts of the country. Some were moved so to do out of their hatred to Antigonus, and some out of regard to the glorious actions Herod had done; but others were led on by an unreasonable desire of change; so he fell upon them immediately. As for Pappus and his party, they were not terrified either at their number or at their zeal, but marched out with great alacrity to fight them; and it came to a close fight. (336) Now other parts of their army made resistance for a while; but Herod, running the utmost hazard, out of the rage he was in at the murder of his brother, that he might be avenged on those that had been the authors of it, soon beat those that opposed him; and after he had beaten them, he always turned his force against those that stood to it still, and pursued them all; (337) so that a great slaughter was made, while some were forced back into that village whence they came out; he also pressed hard upon the hindermost, and slew a vast number of them; he also fell into the village with the enemy, where every house was filled with armed men, and the upper rooms were crowded above with soldiers for their defense; (338) and when he had beaten those that were on the outside, he pulled the houses to pieces, and plucked out those that were within; upon many he had the roofs shaken down, whereby they perished by heaps; and as for those that fled out of the ruins, the soldiers received them with their swords in their hands; and the multitude of those slain and lying on heaps was so great, that the conquerors could not pass along the roads. (339) Now the enemy could not bear this blow, so that when the multitude of them which was gathered together saw that those in the village were slain, they dispersed themselves, and fled away; upon the confidence of which victory, Herod had marched immediately to Jerusalem, unless he had been hindered by the depth of winter's [coming on]. This was the impediment that lay in the way of this his entire glorious progress, and was what hindered Antigonus from being now conquered, who was already disposed to forsake the city.

7. (340) Now when at the evening Herod had already dismissed his friends to refresh themselves after their fatigue, and when he was gone himself, while he was still hot in his armor, like a common soldier, to bathe himself, and had but one servant that attended him, and before he was gotten into the bath, one of the enemies met him in the face with a sword in his hand, and then a second, and then a third, and after that more of them; (341) these were men who had run away out of the battle into the bath in their armor, and they had lain there for some time in, great terror, and in privacy; and when they saw the king, they trembled for fear, and ran by him in a flight, although he was naked, and endeavored to get off into the public road. Now there was by chance nobody else at hand that might seize upon these men; and for Herod, he was contented to have come to no harm himself, so that they all got away in safety.

8. (342) But on the next day Herod had Pappus's head cut off, who was the general for Antigonus, and was slain in the battle, and sent it to his brother Pheroras, by way of punishment for their slain brother; for he was the man that slew Joseph. (343) Now as winter was going off, Herod marched to Jerusalem, and brought his army to the wall of it; this was the third year since he had been made king at Rome; so he pitched his camp before the temple, for on that side it might be besieged, and there it was that Pompey took the city. (344) So he parted the work among the army, and demolished the suburbs, and raised three banks, and gave orders to have towers built upon those banks, and left the most laborious of his acquaintance at the works. But he went himself to Samaria, to take the daughter of Alexander, the son of Aristobulus, to wife, who had been betrothed to him before, as we have already said; and thus he accomplished this by the by, during the siege of the city, for he had his enemies in great contempt already.

9. (345) When he had thus married Mariamne, he came back to Jerusalem with a greater army. Sosius also joined him with a large army, both of horsemen and footmen, which he sent before him through the midland parts, while he marched himself along Phoenicia; (346) and when the whole army was gotten together, which were eleven regiments of footmen, and six thousand horsemen, besides the Syrian auxiliaries, which were no small part of the army, they pitched their camp near to the north wall. Herod's dependence was upon the decree of the senate, by which he was made king; and Sosius relied upon Antony, who sent the army that was under him to Herod's assistance.

CHAPTER 18.

HOW HEROD AND SOSIUS TOOK JERUSALEM BY FORCE; AND WHAT DEATH ANTIGONUS CAME TO. ALSO CONCERNING CLEOPATRA'S AVARICIOUS TEMPER.

1. (347) NOW the multitude of the Jews that were in the city were divided into several factions; for the people that crowded about the temple, being the weaker part of them, gave it out that, as the times were, he was the happiest and most religious man who should die first. But as to the more bold and hardy men, they got together in bodies, and fell a robbing others after various manners, and these particularly plundered the places that were about the city, and this because there was no food left either for the horses or the men; (348) yet some of the warlike men, who were used to fight regularly, were appointed to defend the city during the siege, and these drove those that raised the banks away from the wall; and these were always inventing some engine or another to be a hinderance to the engines of the enemy; nor had they so much success any way as in the mines under ground.

2. (349) Now as for the robberies which were committed, the king contrived that ambushes should be so laid, that they might restrain their excursions; and as for the want of provisions, he provided that they should be brought to them from great distances. He was also too hard for the Jews, by the Romans' skill in the art of war; (350) although they were bold to the utmost degree, now they durst not come to a plain battle with the Romans, which was certain death; but through their mines under ground they would appear in the midst of them on the sudden, and before they could batter down one wall, they built them another in its stead; and to sum up all at once, they did not show any want either of painstaking or of contrivances, as having resolved to hold out to the very last. (351) Indeed, though they had so great an army lying round about them, they bore a siege of five months, till some of Herod's chosen men ventured to get upon the wall, and fell into the city, as did Sosius's centurions after them; and now they first of all seized upon what was about the temple; and upon the pouring in of the army, there was slaughter of vast multitudes every where, by reason of the rage the Romans were in at the length of this siege, and by reason that the Jews who were about Herod earnestly endeavored that none of their adversaries might remain; (352) so they were cut to pieces by great multitudes, as they were crowded together in narrow streets, and in houses, or were running away to the temple; nor was there any mercy showed either to infants, or to the aged, or to the weaker sex; insomuch that although the king sent about and desired them to spare the people, nobody could be persuaded to withhold their right hand from slaughter, but they slew people of all ages, like madmen. (353) Then it was that Antigonus, without any regard to his former or to his present fortune, came down from the citadel, and fell at Sosius's feet, who without pitying him at all, upon the change of his condition, laughed at him beyond measure, and called him Antigona. Yet did he not treat him like a woman, or let him go free, but put him into bonds, and kept him in custody.

3. (354) But Herod's concern at present, now he had gotten his enemies under his power, was to restrain the zeal of his foreign auxiliaries; for the multitude of the strange people were very eager to see the temple, and what was sacred in the holy house itself; but the king endeavored to restrain them, partly by his exhortations, partly by his threatenings, nay, partly by force, as thinking the victory worse than a defeat to him, if any thing that ought not to be seen were seen by them. (355) He also forbade, at the same time, the spoiling of the city, asking Sosius in the most earnest manner, whether the Romans, by thus emptying the city of money and men, had a mind to leave him king of a desert, and told him that he judged the dominion of the habitable earth too small a compensation for the slaughter of so many citizens. (356) And when Sosius said that it was but just to allow the soldiers this plunder as a reward for what they suffered during the siege, Herod made answer, that he would give every one of the soldiers a reward out of his own money. So he purchased the deliverance of his country, and performed his promises to them, and made presents after a magnificent manner to each soldier, and proportionably to their commanders, and with a most royal bounty to Sosius himself, whereby nobody went away but in a wealthy condition. (357) Hereupon Sosius dedicated a crown of gold to God, and then went away from Jerusalem, leading Antigonus away in bonds to Antony; then did the axe bring him to his end, who still had a fond desire of life, and some frigid hopes of it to the last, but by his cowardly behavior well deserved to die by it.

4. (358) Hereupon king Herod distinguished the multitude that

Jericho, the city of palms. (photo Deror_avi, via Wikimedia Commons)

was in the city; and for those that were of his side, he made them still more his friends by the honors he conferred on them; but for those of Antigonus's party, he slew them; and as his money ran low, he turned all the ornaments he had into money, and sent it to Antony, and to those about him. (359) Yet could he not hereby purchase an exemption from all sufferings; for Antony was now bewitched by his love to Cleopatra, and was entirely conquered by her charms. Now Cleopatra had put to death all her kindred, till no one near her in blood remained alive, and after that she fell a slaying those no way related to her. (360) So she calumniated the principal men among the Syrians to Antony, and persuaded him to have them slain, that so she might easily gain to be mistress of what they had; nay, she extended her avaricious humor to the Jews and Arabians, and secretly labored to have Herod and Malichus, the kings of both those nations, slain by his order.

5. (361) Now is to these her injunctions to Antony, he complied in part; for though he esteemed it too abominable a thing to kill such good and great kings, yet was he thereby alienated from the friendship he had for them. He also took away a great deal of their country; nay, even the plantation of palm trees at Jericho, where also grows the balsam tree, and bestowed them upon her; as also all the cities on this side the river Eleutherus, Tyre and Sidon excepted. (362) And when she was become mistress of these, and had conducted Antony in his expedition against the Parthians as far as Euphrates, she came by Apamia and Damascus into Judea and there did Herod pacify her indignation at him by large presents. He also hired of her those places that had been torn away from his kingdom, at the yearly rent of two hundred talents. He conducted her also as far as Pelusium, and paid her all the respects possible. (363) Now it was not long after this that Antony was come back from Parthia, and led with him Artabazes, Tigranes's son, captive, as a present for Cleopatra; for this Parthian was presently given her, with his money, and all the prey that was taken with him.

CHAPTER 19.

HOW ANTONY AT THE PERSUASION OF CLEOPATRA SENT HEROD TO FIGHT AGAINST THE ARABIANS; AND NOW AFTER SEVERAL BATTLES, HE AT LENGTH GOT THE VICTORY. AS ALSO CONCERNING A GREAT EARTHQUAKE.

1. (364) NOW when the war about Actium was begun, Herod pre-

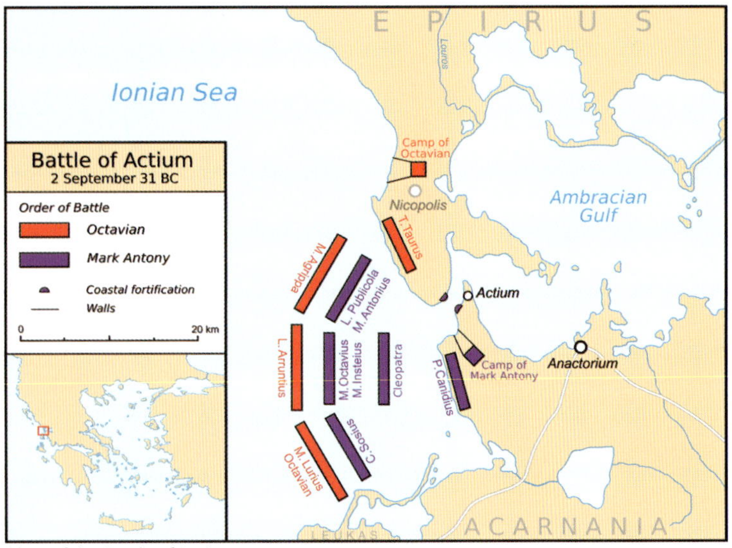

Map of the Battle of Actium. (By Future Perfect at Sunrise, on the basis of work by User:Lencer and User:Leo2004 [translated from File:Schlacht bei Actium.svg], via Wikimedia Commons)

pared to come to the assistance of Antony, as being already freed from his troubles in Judea, and having gained Hyrcania, which was a place that was held by Antigonus's sister. (365) However, he was cunningly hindered from partaking of the hazards that Antony went through by Cleopatra; for since, as we have already noted, she had laid a plot against the kings [of Judea and Arabia], she prevailed with Antony to commit the war against the Arabians to Herod; that so, if he got the better, she might become mistress of Arabia, or, if he were worsted, of Judea; and that she might destroy one of those kings by the other.

2. (366) However, this contrivance tended to the advantage of Herod; for at the very first he took hostages from the enemy, and got together a great body of horse, and ordered them to march against them about Diespous; and he conquered that army, although it fought resolutely against him. After which defeat, the Arabians were in great motion, and assembled themselves together at Kanatha, a city of Celesyria, in vast multitudes, and waited for the Jews. (367) And when Herod was come thither, he tried to manage this war with particular prudence, and gave orders that they should build a wall about their camp; yet did not the multitude comply with those orders, but were so emboldened by their foregoing victory, that they presently attacked the Arabians, and beat them at the first onset, and then pursued them; yet were there snares laid for Herod in that pursuit; while Athenio, who was one of Cleopatra's generals, and always an antagonist to Herod, sent out of Kanatha the men of that country against him; (368) for, upon this fresh onset, the Arabians took courage, and returned back, and both joined their numerous forces about stony places, that were hard to be gone over, and there put Herod's men to the rout, and made a great slaughter of them; but those that escaped out of the battle fled to Ormiza, where the Arabians surrounded their camp, and took it, with all the men in it.

3. (369) In a little time after this calamity, Herod came to bring them succors; but he came too late. Now the occasion of that blow was this, that the officers would not obey orders; for had not the fight begun so suddenly, Athenio had not found a proper season for the snares he laid for Herod: however, he was even with the Arabians afterward, and overran their country, and did them more harm than their single victory could compensate. (370) But as he was avenging himself on his enemies, there fell upon him another providential calamity; for in the seventh year of his reign, when the war about Actium was at the height, at the beginning of the spring, the earth was shaken, and destroyed an immense number of cattle, with thirty thousand men; but the army received no harm, because it lay in the open air. (371) In the meantime, the fame of this earthquake elevated the Arabians to greater courage, and this by augmenting it to a fabulous height, as is constantly the case in melancholy accidents, and pretending that all Judea was overthrown. Upon this supposal, therefore, that they should easily get a land that was destitute of inhabitants into their power, they first sacrificed those ambassadors who were come to them from the Jews, and then marched into Judea immediately. (372) Now the Jewish nation were affrighted at this invasion, and quite dispirited at the greatness of their calamities one after another; whom yet Herod got together, and endeavored to encourage to defend themselves by the following speech which he made to them:

4. (373) "The present dread you are under seems to me to have seized upon you very unreasonably. It is true, you might justly be dismayed at that providential chastisement which hath befallen you; but to suffer yourselves to be equally terrified at the invasion of men is unmanly. As for myself, I am so far from being affrighted at our enemies after this earthquake, that I imagine that God hath thereby laid a bait for the Arabians, that we may be avenged on them; for their present invasion proceeds more from our accidental misfortunes, than that they have any great dependence on their weapons, or their own fitness for action. Now that hope which depends not on men's own power, but on others' ill success, is a very ticklish thing; for there is no certainty among men, either in their bad or good fortunes; (374) but we may easily observe that fortune is mutable, and goes from one side to another; and this you may readily learn from examples among yourselves; for when you were once victors in the former fight, your enemies overcame you at last; and very likely it will now happen so, that these who think themselves sure of beating you will themselves be beaten. For when men are very confident, they are not upon their guard, while fear teaches men to act with caution; insomuch that I venture to prove from your very timorousness that you ought to take courage; (375) for when you were more bold than you ought to have been, and than I would have had you, and marched on, Athenio's treachery took place; but your present slowness and seeming dejection of mind is to me a pledge and assurance of victory. (376) And indeed it is proper beforehand to be thus provident; but when we come to action, we ought to erect our minds, and to make our enemies, be they ever so wicked, believe that neither any human, no, nor any providential misfortune, can ever depress the courage of Jews while they are alive; nor will any of them ever overlook an Arabian, or suffer such a one to become lord of his good things, whom he has in a manner taken captive, and that many times also. (377) And do not you disturb yourselves at the quaking of inanimate creatures, nor do you imagine that this earthquake is a sign of another calamity; for such affections of the elements are according to the course of nature, nor does it import any thing further to men, than what mischief it does immediately of itself. Perhaps there may come some short sign beforehand in the case of pestilences, and famines, and earthquakes; but these calamities themselves have their force limited by themselves [without foreboding any other calamity]. And indeed what greater mischief can the war, though it should be a violent one, do to us than the earthquake hath done? (378) Nay, there is a signal of our enemies' destruction visible, and that a very great one also; and this is not a natural one, nor derived from the hand of foreigners neither, but it is this, that they have barbarously murdered our ambas-

sadors, contrary to the common law of mankind; and they have destroyed so many, as if they esteemed them sacrifices for God, in relation to this war. But they will not avoid his great eye, nor his invincible right hand; and we shall be revenged of them presently, in case we still retain any of the courage of our forefathers, and rise up boldly to punish these covenant-breakers. (379) Let every one therefore go on and fight, not so much for his wife or his children, or for the danger his country is in, as for these ambassadors of ours; those dead ambassadors will conduct this war of ours better than we ourselves who are alive. And if you will be ruled by me, I will myself go before you into danger; for you know this well enough, that your courage is irresistible, unless you hurt yourselves by acting rashly."

Remains of Roman Philadelphia (Rabbath-ammon). (photo Ken and Nyetta, via Wikimedia Commons)

5. (380) When Herod had encouraged them by this speech, and he saw with what alacrity they went, he offered sacrifice to God; and after that sacrifice, he passed over the river Jordan with his army, and pitched his camp about Philadelphia, near the enemy, and about a fortification that lay between them. He then shot at them at a distance, and was desirous to come to an engagement presently; (381) for some of them had been sent beforehand to seize upon that fortification: but the king sent some who immediately beat them out of the fortification, while he himself went in the forefront of the army, which he put in battle-array every day, and invited the Arabians to fight. But as none of them came out of their camp, for they were in a terrible fright, and their general, Elthemus, was not able to say a word for fear,—so Herod came upon them, and pulled their fortification to pieces, (382) by which means they were compelled to come out to fight, which they did in disorder, and so that the horsemen and foot-men were mixed together. They were indeed superior to the Jews in number, but inferior in their alacrity, although they were obliged to expose themselves to danger by their very despair of victory.

6. (383) Now while they made opposition, they had not a great number slain; but as soon as they turned their backs, a great many were trodden to pieces by the Jews, and a great many by themselves, and so perished, till five thousand were fallen down dead in their flight, while the rest of the multitude prevented their immediate death, by crowding into the fortification. Herod encompassed these around, and besieged them; and while they were ready to be taken by their enemies in arms, they had another additional distress upon them, which was thirst and want of water; (384) for the king was above hearkening to their ambassadors; and when they offered five hundred talents, as the price of their redemption, he pressed still harder upon them. And as they were burnt up by their thirst, they came out and voluntarily delivered themselves up by multitudes to the Jews, till in five days' time four thousand of them were put into bonds; and on the sixth day the multitude that were left despaired of saving themselves, and came out to fight: with these Herod fought, and slew again about seven thousand, (385) insomuch that he punished Arabia so severely, and so far extinguished the spirits of the men, that he was chosen by the nation for their ruler.

CHAPTER 20.

HEROD IS CONFIRMED IN HIS KINGDOM BY CAESAR, AND CULTIVATES A FRIENDSHIP WITH THE EMPEROR BY MAGNIFICENT PRESENTS; WHILE CAESAR RETURNS HIS KINDNESS BY BESTOWING ON HIM THAT PART OF HIS KINGDOM WHICH HAD BEEN TAKEN AWAY FROM IT BY CLEOPATRA WITH THE ADDITION OF ZENODORUS'S COUNTRY ALSO.

1. (386) BUT now Herod was under immediate concern about a most important affair, on account of his friendship with Antony, who was already overcome at Actium by Caesar; yet he was more afraid than hurt; for Caesar did not think he had quite undone Antony, while Herod continued his assistance to him. (387) However, the king resolved to expose himself to dangers: accordingly he sailed to Rhodes, where Caesar then abode, and came to him without his diadem, and in the habit and appearance of a private person, but in his behavior as a king. So he concealed nothing of the truth, but spoke thus before his face: (388) "O Caesar, as I was made king of the Jews by Antony, so do I profess that I have used my royal authority in the best manner, and entirely for his advantage; nor will I conceal this further, that thou hadst certainly found me in arms, and an inseparable companion of his, had not the Arabians hindered me. However, I sent him as many auxiliaries as I was able, and many ten thousand [cori] of corn. Nay, indeed, I did not desert my benefactor after the bow that was given him at Actium; but I gave him the best advice I was able, (389) when I was no longer able to assist him in the war; and I told him that there was but one way of recovering his affairs, and that was to kill Cleopatra; and I promised him that, if she were once dead, I would afford him money and walls for his security, with an army and myself to assist him in his war against thee: (390) but his affections for Cleopatra stopped his ears, as did God himself also who hath bestowed the government on thee. I own myself also to be overcome together with him; and with his last fortune I have laid aside my diadem, and am come hither to thee, having my hopes of safety in thy virtue; and I desire that thou wilt first consider how faithful a friend, and not whose friend, I have been."

2. (391) Caesar replied to him thus: "Nay, thou shalt not only be in safety, but thou shalt be a king; and that more firmly than thou

THE GROWTH OF HEROD'S KINGDOM 40–4 B.C.

wast before; for thou art worthy to reign over a great many subjects, by reason of the fastness of thy friendship; and do thou endeavor to be equally constant in thy friendship to me, upon my good success, which is what I depend upon from the generosity of thy disposition. However, Antony hath done well in preferring Cleopatra to thee; for by this means we have gained thee by her madness, (392) and thus thou hast begun to be my friend before I began to be thine; on which account Quintus Didius hath written to me that thou sentest him assistance against the gladiators. I do therefore assure thee that I will confirm the kingdom to thee by decree: I shall also endeavor to do thee some further kindness hereafter, that thou mayst find no loss in the want of Antony."

3. (393) When Caesar had spoken such obliging things to the king, and had put the diadem again about his head, he proclaimed what he had bestowed on him by a decree, in which he enlarged in the commendation of the man after a magnificent manner. Whereupon Herod obliged him to be kind to him by the presents he gave him, and he desired him to forgive Alexander, one of Antony's friends, who was become a supplicant to him. But Caesar's anger against him prevailed, and he complained of the many and very great offenses the man whom he petitioned for had been guilty of; and by that means he rejected his petition. (394) After this Caesar went for Egypt through Syria, when Herod received him with royal and rich entertainments; and then did he first of all ride along with Caesar, as he was reviewing his army about Ptolemais, and feasted him with all his friends, and then distributed among the rest of the army what was necessary to feast them withal. (395) He also made a plentiful provision of water for them, when they were to march as far as Pelusium, through a dry country, which he did also in like manner at their return thence; nor were there any necessaries wanting to that army. It was therefore the opinion, both of Caesar and of his soldiers, that Herod's kingdom was too small for those generous presents he made them; (396) for which reason, when Caesar was come into Egypt, and Cleopatra and Antony were dead, he did not only bestow other marks of honor upon him, but made an addition to his kingdom, by giving him not only the country which had been taken from him by Cleopatra, but besides that, Gadara, and Hippos, and Samaria; and moreover, of the maritime cities, Gaza and Anthedon, and Joppa, and Strato's Tower. (397) He also made him a present of four hundred Galls [Galatians] as a guard for his body, which they had been to Cleopatra before. Nor did any thing so strongly induce Caesar to make these presents as the generosity of him that received them.

4. (398) Moreover, after the first games at Actium, he added to his kingdom both the region called Trachonitis, and what lay in its neighborhood, Batanea, and the country of Auranitis; and that on the following occasion: Zenodorus, who had hired the house of Lysanias, had all along sent robbers out of Trachonitis among the Damascenes; who thereupon had recourse to Varro, the president of Syria, and desired of him that he would represent the calamity they were in to Caesar. When Caesar was acquainted with it, he sent back orders that this nest of robbers should be destroyed. (399) Varro therefore made an expedition against them, and cleared the land of those men, and took it away from Zenodorus. Caesar did also afterward bestow it on Herod, that it might not again become a receptacle for those robbers that had come against Damascus. He also made him a procurator of all Syria, and this on the tenth year afterward, when he came again into that province; and this was so established, that the other procurators could not do any thing in the administration without his advice: (400) but when Zenodorus was dead, Caesar bestowed on him all that land which lay between Trachonitis and Galilee. Yet, what was still of more consequence to Herod, he was beloved by Caesar next after [Marcus] Agrippa, and by Agrippa next after Caesar; whence he arrived at a very great degree of felicity. Yet did the greatness of his soul exceed it, and the main part of his magnanimity was extended to the promotion of piety.

CHAPTER 21.

OF THE [TEMPLE AND] CITIES THAT WERE BUILT BY HEROD AND ERECTED FROM THE VERY FOUNDATIONS; AS ALSO OF THOSE OTHER EDIFICES THAT WERE ERECTED BY HIM; AND WHAT MAGNIFICENCE HE SHOWED TO FOREIGNERS; AND HOW FORTUNE WAS IN ALL THINGS FAVORABLE TO HIM.

1. (401) ACCORDINGLY, in the fifteenth year of his reign, Herod rebuilt the temple, and encompassed a piece of land about it with a wall, which land was twice as large as that before enclosed. The expenses he laid out upon it were vastly large also, and the riches about it were unspeakable. A sign of which you have in the great cloisters that were erected about the temple, and the citadel which was on its north side. The cloisters he built from the foundation, but the citadel he repaired at a vast expense; nor was it other than a royal palace, which he called Antonia, in honor of Antony. (402) He also built himself a palace in the Upper city, containing two very large and most beautiful apartments; to which the holy house itself could not be compared [in largeness]. The one apartment he named Caesareum, and the other Agrippium, from his [two great] friends.

2. (403) Yet did he not preserve their memory by particular buildings only, with their names given them, but his generosity went as far as entire cities; for when he had built a most beautiful wall round a country in Samaria, twenty furlongs long, and had brought six thousand inhabitants into it, and had allotted to it a most fruitful piece of land, and in the midst of this city, thus built, had erected

a very large temple to Caesar, and had laid round about it a portion of sacred land of three furlongs and a half, he called the city Sebaste, from Sebastus, or Augustus, and settled the affairs of the city after a most regular manner.

3. (404) And when Caesar had further bestowed upon him another additional country, he built there also a temple of white marble, hard by the fountains of Jordan: the place is called Panium, (405) where is a top of a mountain that is raised to an immense height, and at its side, beneath, or at its bottom, a dark cave opens itself; within which there is a horrible precipice, that descends abruptly to a vast depth; it contains a mighty quantity of water, which is immovable; and when any body lets down any thing to measure the depth of the earth beneath the water, no length of cord is sufficient to reach it. (406) Now the fountains of Jordan rise at the roots of this cavity outwardly; and, as some think, this is the utmost origin of Jordan: but we shall speak of that matter more accurately in our following history.

4. (407) But the king erected other places at Jericho also, between the citadel Cypros and the former palace, such as were better and more useful than the former for travelers, and named them from the same friends of his. To say all at once, there was not any place of his kingdom fit for the purpose that was permitted to be without somewhat that was for Caesar's honor; and when he had filled his own country with temples, he poured out the like plentiful marks of his esteem into his province, and built many cities which he called Cesareas.

5. (408) And when he observed that there was a city by the sea-side that was much decayed, (its name was Strato's Tower,) but that the place, by the happiness of its situation, was capable of great improvements from his liberality, he rebuilt it all with white stone, and adorned it with several most splendid palaces, wherein he especially demonstrated his magnanimity; (409) for the case was this, that all the sea-shore between Dora and Joppa, in the middle,

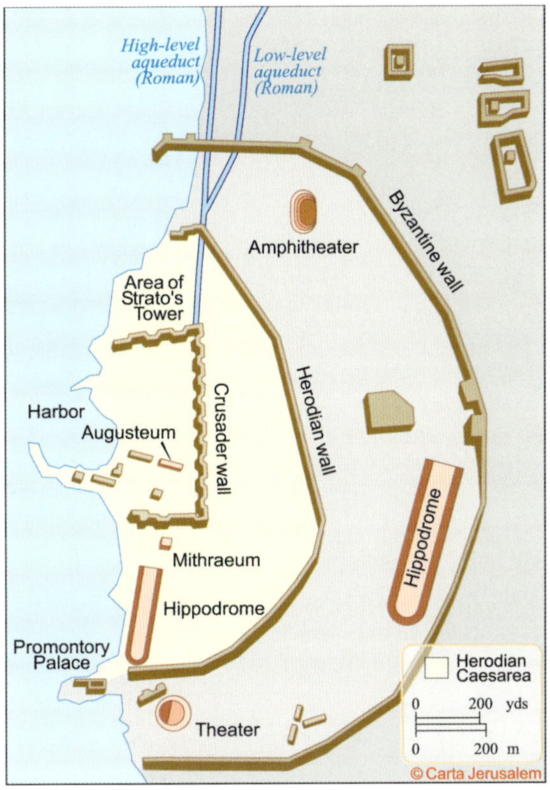

CAESAREA—PLAN OF THE CITY

(from Carta's *Atlas of the Bible*)

between which this city is situated, had no good haven, insomuch that every one that sailed from Phoenicia for Egypt was obliged to lie in the stormy sea, by reason of the south winds that threatened them; which wind, if it blew but a little fresh, such vast waves are raised, and dash upon the rocks, that upon their retreat the sea is in a great ferment for a long way. (410) But the king, by the expenses he was at, and the liberal disposal of them, overcame nature, and built a haven larger than was the Pyrecum [at Athens]; and in the inner retirements of the water he built other deep stations [for the ships also].

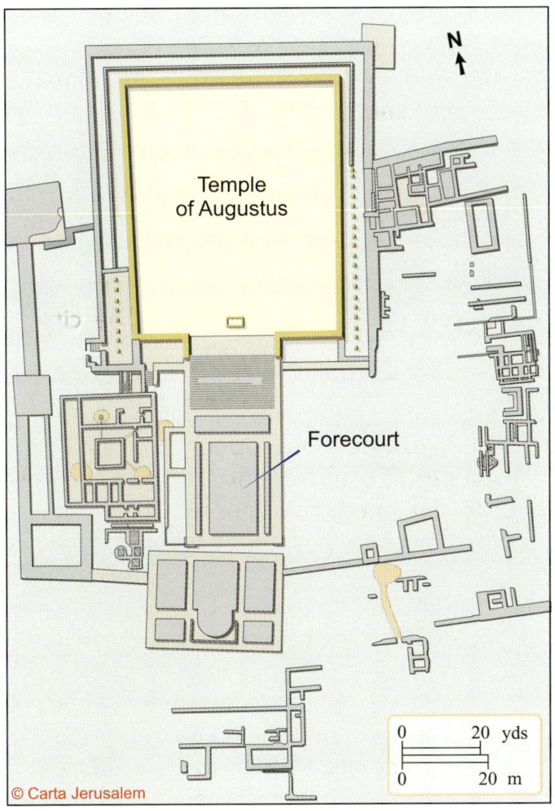

SEBASTE—PLAN OF THE TEMPLE OF AUGUSTUS ENCLOSURE

(from *The Sacred Bridge: Carta's Atlas of the Biblical World*)

6. (411) Now although the place where he built was greatly opposite to his purposes, yet did he so fully struggle with that difficulty, that the firmness of his building could not easily be conquered by the sea; and the beauty and ornament of the works were such, as though he had not had any difficulty in the operation; for when he had measured out as large a space as we have before mentioned, he let down stones into twenty fathom water, the greatest part of which were fifty feet in length, and nine in depth, and ten in breadth, and some still larger. (412) But when the haven was filled up to that depth, he enlarged that wall which was thus already extant above the sea, till it was two hundred feet wide; one hundred of which had buildings before it, in order to break the force of the waves, whence it was called Procumatia, or the first breaker of the waves; but the rest of the space was under a stone wall that ran round it. On this wall were very large towers, the principal and most beautiful of which was called Drusium, from Drusus, who was son-in-law to Caesar.

7. (413) There were also a great number of arches, where the mariners dwelt; and all the places before them round about was a large valley, or walk, for a quay [or landing-place] to those that came on shore; but the entrance was on the north, because the north wind was there the most gentle of all the winds. At the mouth of the haven were on each side three great Colossi, supported by pillars, where those Colossi that are on your left hand as you sail into the port are supported by a solid tower; but those on the right

Remains of Herod's palace at Cesarea. (photo Samuel Magal)

HERODIUM—PLAN OF THE PALACE-FORTRESS

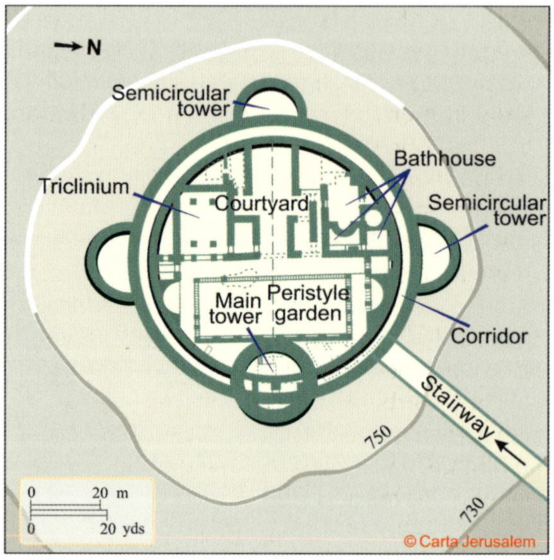

(from *The Basilica of the Nativity in Bethlehem* / G.S.P. Freeman-Grenville)

hand are supported by two upright stones joined together, which stones were larger than that tower which was on the other side of the entrance. (414) Now there were continual edifices joined to the haven, which were also themselves of white stone; and to this haven did the narrow streets of the city lead, and were built at equal distances one from another. And over against the mouth of the haven, upon an elevation, there was a temple for Caesar, which was excellent both in beauty and largeness; and therein was a Colossus of Caesar, not less than that of Jupiter Olympius, which it was made to resemble. The other Colossus of Rome was equal to that of Juno at Argos. So he dedicated the city to the province, and the haven to the sailors there; but the honor of the building he ascribed to Caesar, and named it Cesarea accordingly.

8. (415) He also built the other edifices, the amphitheater, and theater, and market-place, in a manner agreeable to that denomination; and appointed games every fifth year, and called them, in like manner, Caesar's Games; and he first himself proposed the largest prizes upon the hundred ninety-second olympiad; in which not only the victors themselves, but those that came next to them, and even those that came in the third place, were partakers of his royal bounty. (416) He also rebuilt Anthedon, a city that lay on the coast, and had been demolished in the wars, and named it Agrippeum. Moreover, he had so very great a kindness for his friend Agrippa, that he had his name engraved upon that gate which he had himself erected in the temple.

9. (417) Herod was also a lover of his father, if any other person ever was so; for he made a monument for his father, even that city which he built in the finest plain that was in his kingdom, and which had rivers and trees in abundance, and named it Antipatris. He also built a wall about a citadel that lay above Jericho, and was a very strong and very fine building, and dedicated it to his mother, and called it Cypros. (418) Moreover, he dedicated a tower that was at Jerusalem, and called it by the name of his brother Phasaelus, whose structure, largeness, and magnificence we shall describe hereafter. He also built another city in the valley that leads northward from Jericho, and named it Phasaelis.

10. (419) And as he transmitted to eternity his family and friends, so did he not neglect a memorial for himself, but built a fortress upon a mountain towards Arabia, and named it from himself, Herodium and he called that hill that was of the shape of a woman's breast, and was sixty furlongs distant from Jerusalem, by the same name. He also bestowed much curious art upon it, with great ambition, (420) and built round towers all about the top of it, and filled up the remaining space with the most costly palaces round about, insomuch that not only the sight of the inner apartments was splendid, but great wealth was laid out on the outward walls, and partitions, and roofs also. Besides this, he brought a mighty quantity of water from a great distance, and at vast charges, and raised an ascent to it of two hundred steps of the whitest marble, for the hill was itself moderately high, and entirely factitious. (421) He also built other palaces about the roots of the hill, sufficient to receive the furniture that was put into them, with his friends also, insomuch that, on account of its containing all necessaries, the fortress might seem to be a city, but, by the bounds it had, a palace only.

11. (422) And when he had built so much, he showed the greatness of his soul to no small number of foreign cities. He built palaces for exercise at Tripoli, and Damascus, and Ptolemais; he built a wall about Byblus, as also large rooms, and cloisters, and temples, and market-places at Berytus and Tyre, with theatres at Sidon and Damascus. He also built aqueducts for those Laodiceans who lived by the sea-side; and for those of Ascalon he built baths and costly fountains, as also cloisters round a court, that were admirable both for their workmanship and largeness. Moreover, he dedicated groves and meadows to some people; (423) nay, not a few cities there were who had lands of his donation, as if they were parts of his own kingdom. (424) He also bestowed annual revenues, and those for ever also, on the settlements for exercises, and appoint-

The fortress of Cypros. (photo Liadmalone, via Wikimedia Commons)

ed for them, as well as for the people of Cos, that such rewards should never be wanting. He also gave corn to all such as wanted it, and conferred upon Rhodes large sums of money for building ships; and this he did in many places, and frequently also. And when Apollo's temple had been burnt down, he rebuilt it at his own charges, after a better manner than it was before. (425) What need I speak of the presents he made to the Lycians and Samnians? or of his great liberality through all Ionia? and that according to every body's wants of them. And are not the Athenians, and Lacedemonians, and Nicopolitans, and that Pergamus which is in Mysia, full of donations that Herod presented them withal? And as for that large open place belonging to Antioch in Syria, did not he pave it with polished marble, though it were twenty furlongs long? and this when it was shunned by all men before, because it was full of dirt and filthiness, when he besides adorned the same place with a cloister of the same length.

12. (426) It is true, a man may say, these were favors peculiar to those particular places on which he bestowed his benefits; but then what favors he bestowed on the Eleans was a donation not only in common to all Greece, but to all the habitable earth, as far as the glory of the Olympic games reached. (427) For when he perceived that they were come to nothing, for want of money, and that the only remains of ancient Greece were in a manner gone, he not only became one of the combatants in that return of the fifth-year games, which in his sailing to Rome he happened to be present at, but he settled upon them revenues of money for perpetuity, insomuch that his memorial as a combatant there can never fail. (428) It would be an infinite task if I should go over his payments of people's debts, or tributes, for them, as he eased the people of Phasaelis, of Batanea, and of the small cities about Cilicia, of those annual pensions they before paid. However, the fear he was in much disturbed the greatness of his soul, lest he should be exposed to envy, or seem to hunt after greater filings than he ought, while he bestowed more liberal gifts upon these cities than did their owners themselves.

13. (429) Now Herod had a body suited to his soul, and was ever a most excellent hunter, where he generally had good success, by the means of his great skill in riding horses; for in one day he caught forty wild beasts: that country breeds also bears, and the greatest part of it is replenished with stags and wild asses. (430) He was also such a warrior as could not be withstood: many men, therefore, there are who have stood amazed at his readiness in his exercises, when they saw him throw the javelin directly forward, and shoot the arrow upon the mark. And then, besides these performances of his depending on his own strength of mind and body, fortune was also very favorable to him; for he seldom failed of success in his wars; and when he failed, he was not himself the occasion of such failings, but he either was betrayed by some, or the rashness of his own soldiers procured his defeat.

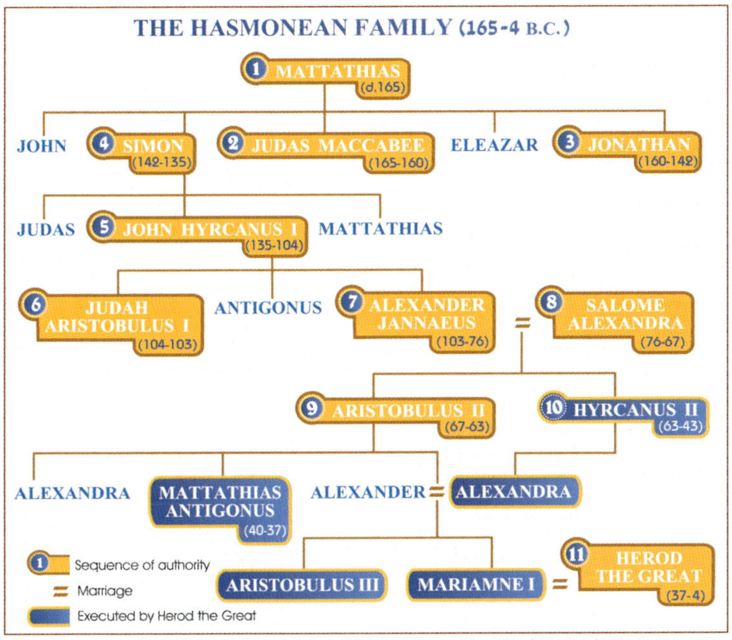

(from *Greatness Grace & Glory: Carta's Atlas of Biblical Biography* / Paul H. Wright; © Carta Jerusalem)

CHAPTER 22.

THE MURDER OF ARISTOBULUS AND HYRCANUS, THE HIGH PRIESTS, AS ALSO OF MARIAMNE THE QUEEN.

1. (431) HOWEVER, fortune was avenged on Herod in his external great successes, by raising him up domestical troubles; and he began to have wild disorders in his family, on account of his wife, of whom he was so very fond. (432) For when he came to the government, he sent away her whom he had before married when he was a private person, and who was born at Jerusalem, whose name was Doris, and married Mariamne, the daughter of Alexander, the son of Aristobulus; on whose account disturbances arose in his family, and that in part very soon, but chiefly after his return from Rome. (433) For, first of all, he expelled Antipater the son of Doris, for the sake of his sons by Mariamne, out of the city, and permitted him to come thither at no other times than at the festivals. After this he slew his wife's grandfather, Hyrcanus, when he was returned out of Parthin to him, under this pretense, that he suspected him of plotting against him. Now this Hyrcanus had been carried captive to Barzapharnes, when he overran Syria; but those of his own country beyond Euphrates were desirous he would stay with them, and this out of the commiseration they had for his condition; (434) and had he complied with their desires, when they exhorted him not to go over the river to lierod, he had not perished: but the marriage of his granddaughter [to Herod] was his temptation; for as he relied upon him, and was over-fond of his own country, he came back to it. Herod's provocation was this,—not that Hyrcanus made any attempt to gain the kingdom, but that it was fitter for him to be their king than for Herod.

2. (435) Now of the five children which Herod had by Mariamne, two of them were daughters, and three were sons; and the youngest of these sons was educated at Rome, and there died; but the two eldest he treated as those of royal blood, on account of the nobility of their mother, and because they were not born till he was king. (436) But then what was stronger than all this was the love that he bare to Mariamne, and which inflamed him every day to a great degree, and so far conspired with the other motives, that he felt no other troubles, on account of her he loved so entirely. But Mariamne's hatred to him was not inferior to his love to her. (437) She had indeed but too just a cause of indignation from what he had done, while her boldness proceeded from his affection to her; so she openly reproached him with what he had done to her grandfather Hyrcanus, and to her brother Aristobulus; for he had not spared this Aristobulus [III], though he were but a child; for when he had given him the high priesthood at the age of seventeen, he slew him quickly after he had conferred that dignity upon him; but when Aristobulus had put on the holy vestments, and had approached to the altar at a festival, the multitude, in great crowds, fell into tears; whereupon the child was sent by night to Jericho, and was there dipped by the Galls, at Herod's command, in a pool till he was drowned.

3. (438) For these reasons Mariamne reproached Herod, and his sister and mother, after a most contumelious manner, while he was dumb on account of his affection for her; yet had the women great indignation at her, and raised a calumny against her, that she was false to his bed; which thing they thought most likely to move Herod to anger. (439) They also contrived to have many other circumstances believed, in order to make the thing more credible, and accused her of having sent her picture into Egypt to Antony, and that her lust was so extravagant, as to have thus showed herself, though she was absent, to a man that ran mad after women, and to a man that had it in his power to use violence to her. (440) This charge fell like a thunderbolt upon Herod, and put him into disorder; and that especially, because his love to her occasioned him to be jealous, and because he considered with himself that Cleopatra was a shrewd woman, and that on her account Lysanias the king was taken off, as well as Malichus the Arabian; for his fear did not only extend to the dissolving of his marriage, but to the danger of his life.

4. (441) When therefore he was about to take a journey abroad, he committed his wife to Joseph, his sister Salome's husband, as to one who would be faithful to him, and bare him good-will on account of their kindred; he also gave him a secret injunction, that if Antony slew him, he should slay her. But Joseph, without any ill design, and only in order to demonstrate the king's love to his wife, how he could not bear to think of being separated from her, even by death itself, discovered this grand secret to her; (442) upon which, when Herod was come back, and as they talked together, and he confirmed his love to her by many oaths, and assured her that he had never such an affection for any other woman as he had for her,—" Yes," says she, "thou didst, to be sure, demonstrate thy love to me by the injunctions thou gavest Joseph, when thou commandedst him to kill me."

5. (443) When he heard that this grand secret was discovered, he was like a distracted man, and said that Joseph would never have disclosed that injunction of his, unless he had debauched her. His passion also made him stark mad, and leaping out of his bed, he ran about the palace after a wild manner; at which time his sister Salome took the opportunity also to blast her reputation, and confirmed his suspicion about Joseph; whereupon, out of his ungovernable jealousy and rage, he commanded both of them to be slain immediately; (444) but as soon as ever his passion was over, he repented of what he had done, and as soon as his anger was worn off, his affections were kindled again. And indeed the flame of his desires for her was so ardent, that he could not think she was dead, but would appear, under his disorders, to speak to her as if she were still alive, till he were better instructed by time, when his grief and trouble, now she was dead, appeared as great as his affection had been for her while she was living.

John William Waterhouse's Mariamne Leaving the Judgement Seat of Herod, *1887.*
(Forbes Magazine Collection, via Wikimedia Commons)

CHAPTER 23.

CALUMNIES AGAINST THE SONS OF MARIAMNE. ANTIPATER IS PREFERRED BEFORE THEM. THEY ARE ACCUSED BEFORE CAESAR, AND HEROD IS RECONCILED TO THEM.

1. (445) NOW Mariamne's sons were heirs to that hatred which had been borne their mother; and when they considered the greatness of Herod's crime towards her, they were suspicious of him as of an enemy of theirs; and this first while they were educated at Rome, but still more when they were returned to Judea. This temper of theirs increased upon them as they grew up to be men; (446) and when they were come to an age fit for marriage, the one of them married their aunt Salome's daughter, which Salome had been the accuser of their mother; the other married the daughter of Archelaus, king of Cappadocia. And now they used boldness in speaking, as well as bore hatred in their minds. (447) Now those that calumniated them took a handle from such their boldness, and certain of them spake now more plainly to the king that there were treacherous designs laid against him by both his sons; and he that was son-in-law to Archelaus, relying upon his father-in-law, was preparing to fly away, in order to accuse Herod before Caesar; (448) and when Herod's head had been long enough filled with these calumnies, he brought Antipater, whom he had by Doris, into favor again, as a defense to him against his other sons, and began all the ways he possibly could to prefer him before them.

2. (449) But these sons were not able to bear this change in their affairs; but when they saw him that was born of a mother of no family, the nobility of their birth made them unable to contain their indignation; but whensoever they were uneasy, they showed the anger they had at it. And as these sons did day after day improve in that their anger, (450) Antipater already exercised all his own abilities, which were very great, in flattering his father, and in contriving many sorts of calumnies against his brethren, while he told some stories of them himself, and put it upon other proper persons to raise other stories against them, till at length he entirely cut his brethren off from all hopes of succeeding to the kingdom; (451) for he was already publicly put into his father's will as his successor. Accordingly, he was sent with royal ornaments, and other marks of royalty, to Caesar, excepting the diadem. He was

also able in time to introduce his mother again into Mariamne's bed. The two sorts of weapons he made use of against his brethren were flattery and calumny, whereby he brought matters privately to such a pass, that the king had thoughts of putting his sons to death.

3. (452) So the father drew Alexander as far as Rome, and charged him with an attempt of poisoning him before Caesar. Alexander could hardly speak for lamentation; but having a judge that was more skillful than Antipater, and more wise than Herod, he modestly avoided laying any imputation upon his father, but with great strength of reason confuted the calumnies laid against him; (453) and when he had demonstrated the innocency of his brother, who was in the like danger with himself, he at last bewailed the craftiness of Antipater, and the disgrace they were under. He was enabled also to justify himself, not only by a clear conscience, which he carried within him, but by his eloquence; for he was a shrewd man in making speeches. (454) And upon his saying at last, that if his father objected this crime to them, it was in his power to put them to death, he made all the audience weep; and he brought Caesar to that pass, as to reject the accusations, and to reconcile their father to them immediately. But the conditions of this reconciliation were these, that they should in all things be obedient to their father, and that he should have power to leave the kingdom to which of them he pleased.

4. (455) After this the king came back from Rome, and seemed to have forgiven his sons upon these accusations; but still so that he was not without his suspicions of them. They were followed by Antipater, who was the fountain-head of those accusations; yet did not he openly discover his hatred to them, as revering him that had reconciled them. (456) But as Herod sailed by Cilicia, he touched at Eleusa, where Archelaus treated them in the most obliging manner, and gave him thanks for the deliverance of his son-in-law, and was much pleased at their reconciliation; and this the more, because he had formerly written to his friends at Rome that they should be assisting to Alexander at his trial. So he conducted Herod as far as Zephyrium, and made him presents to the value of thirty talents.

5. (457) Now when Herod was come to Jerusalem, he gathered the people together, and presented to them his three sons, and gave them an apologetic account of his absence, and thanked God greatly, and thanked Caesar greatly also, for settling his house when it was under disturbances, and had procured concord among his sons, which was of greater consequence than the kingdom itself, (458)—"and which I will render still more firm; for Caesar hath put into my power to dispose of the government, and to appoint my successor. Accordingly, in way of requital for his kindness, and in order to provide for mine own advantage, I do declare that these three sons of mine shall be kings. And, in the first place, I pray for the approbation of God to what I am about; and, in the next place, I desire your approbation also. The age of one of them, and the nobility of the other two, shall procure them the succession. Nay, indeed, my kingdom is so large that it may be sufficient for more kings. (459) Now do you keep those in their places whom Caesar hath joined, and their father hath appointed; and do not you pay undue or unequal respects to them, but to every one according to the prerogative of their births; for he that pays such respects unduly, will thereby not make him that is honored beyond what his age requires so joyful, as he will make him that is dishonored sorrowful. (460) As for the kindred and friends that are to converse with them, I will appoint them to each of them, and will so constitute them, that they may be securities for their concord; as well knowing that the ill tempers of those with whom they converse will produce quarrels and contentions among them; but that if these with whom they converse be of good tempers, they will preserve their natural affections for one another. (461) But still I desire that not these only, but all the captains of my army, have for the present their hopes placed on me alone; for I do not give away my kingdom to these my sons, but give them royal honors only; whereby it will come to pass that they will enjoy the sweet parts of government as rulers themselves, but that the burden of administration will rest upon myself whether I will or not. (462) And let everyone consider what age I am of, how I have conducted my life, and what piety I have exercised; for my age is not so great that men may soon expect the end of my life; nor have I indulged such a luxurious way of living as cuts men off when they are young; and we have been so religious towards God, that we [have reason to hope we] may arrive at a very great age. (463) But for such as cultivate a friendship with my sons, so as to aim at my destruction, they shall be punished by me on their account. I am not one who envy my own children, and therefore forbid men to pay them great respect; but I know that such [extravagant] respects are the way to make them insolent. (464) And if everyone that comes near them does but revolve this in his mind, that if he prove a good man, he shall receive a reward from me, but that if he prove seditious, his ill-intended complaisance shall get him nothing from him to whom it is shown, I suppose they will all be of my side, that is, of my sons' side; for it will be for their advantage that I reign, and that I be at concord with them. (465) But do you, O my good children, reflect upon the holiness of nature itself, by whose means natural affection is preserved, even among wild beasts; in the next place, reflect upon Caesar, who hath made this reconciliation among us; and in the third place, reflect upon me, who entreat you to do what I have power to command you,—continue brethren. I give you royal garments, and royal honors; and I pray to God to preserve what I have determined, in case you be at concord one with another." (466) When the king had thus spoken, and had saluted every one of his sons after an obliging manner, he dismissed the multitude; some of which gave their assent to what he had said, and wished it might take effect accordingly; but for those who wished for a change of affairs, they pretended they did not so much as hear what he said.

CHAPTER 24.

THE MALICE OF ANTIPATER AND DORIS. ALEXANDER IS VERY UNEASY ON GLAPHYRA'S ACCOUNT. HEROD PARDONS PHERORAS, WHOM HE SUSPECTED, AND SALOME WHOM HE KNEW TO MAKE MISCHIEF AMONG THEM. HEROD'S EUNUCHS ARE TORTURED AND ALEXANDER IS BOUND.

1. (467) BUT now the quarrel that was between them still accompanied these brethren when they parted, and the suspicions they had one of the other grew worse. Alexander and Aristobulus were much grieved that the privilege of the first-born was confirmed to Antipater; as was Antipater very angry at his brethren that they were to succeed him. (468) But then this last being of a disposition that was mutable and politic, he knew how to hold his tongue, and used a great deal of cunning, and thereby concealed the hatred he bore to them; while the former, depending on the nobility of their births, had every thing upon their tongues which was in their minds. Many also there were who provoked them further, and many of their [seeming] friends insinuated themselves into their acquaintance, to spy out what they did. (469) Now everything that was said by Alexander was presently brought to Antipater,

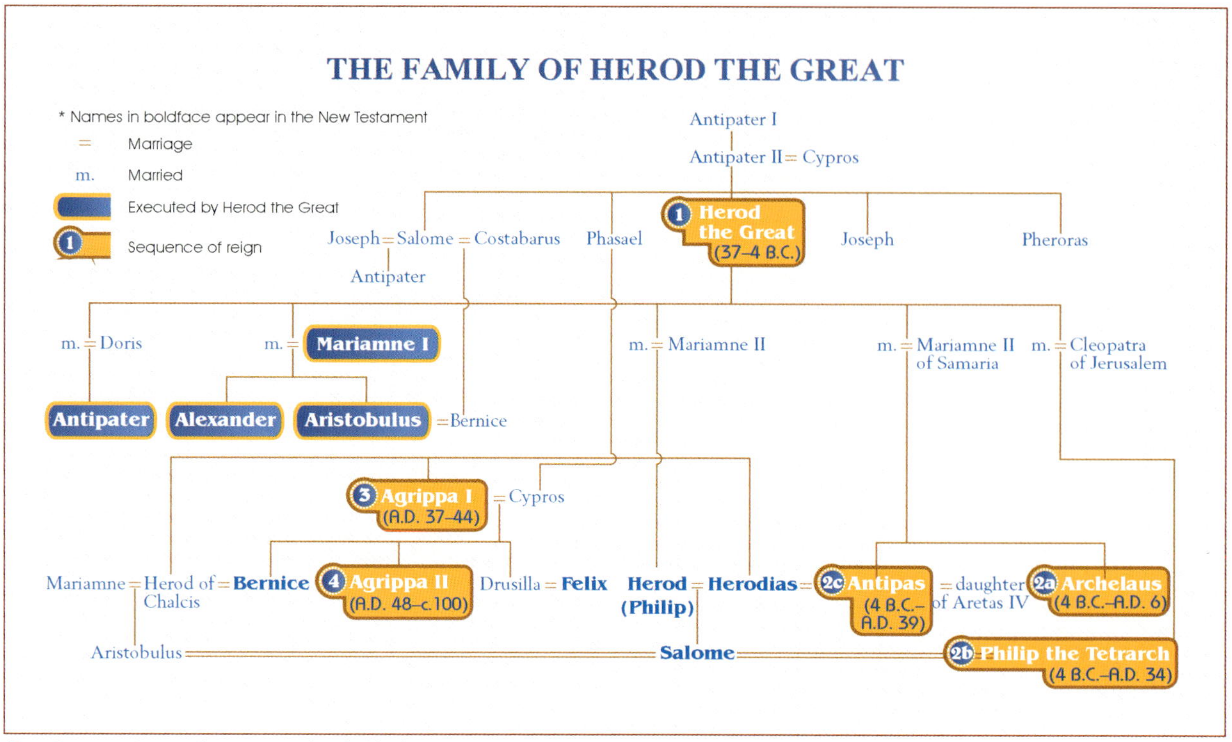

(from *Greatness Grace & Glory: Carta's Atlas of Biblical Biography* / Paul H. Wright; © Carta Jerusalem)

and from Antipater it was brought to Herod with additions. Nor could the young man say any thing in the simplicity of his heart, without giving offense, but what he said was still turned to calumny against him. And if he had been at any time a little free in his conversation, great imputations were forged from the smallest occasions. (470) Antipater also was perpetually setting some to provoke him to speak, that the lies he raised of him might seem to have some foundation of truth; and if, among the many stories that were given out, but one of them could be proved true, that was supposed to imply the rest to be true also. And as to Antipater's friends, they were all either naturally so cautious in speaking, or had been so far bribed to conceal their thoughts, that nothing of these grand secrets got abroad by their means. Nor should one be mistaken if he called the life of Antipater a mystery of wickedness; for he either corrupted Alexander's acquaintance with money, or got into their favor by flatteries; by which two means he gained all his designs, and brought them to betray their master, and to steal away, and reveal what he either did or said. (471) Thus did he act a part very cunningly in all points, and wrought himself a passage by his calumnies with the greatest shrewdness; while he put on a face as if he were a kind brother to Alexander and Aristobulus, but suborned other men to inform of what they did to Herod. And when any thing was told against Alexander, he would come in, and pretend [to be of his side], and would begin to contradict what was said; but would afterward contrive matters so privately, that the king should have an indignation at him. (472) His general aim was this,—to lay a plot, and to make it believed that Alexander lay in wait to kill his father; for nothing afforded so great a confirmation to these calumnies as did Antipater's apologies for him.

2. (473) By these methods Herod was inflamed, and as much as his natural affection to the young men did every day diminish, so much did it increase towards Antipater. The courtiers also inclined to the same conduct, some of their own accord, and others by the king's injunction, as particularly did Ptolemy, the king's dearest friend, as also the king's brethren, and all his children; for Antipater was all in all; and what was the bitterest part of all to Alexander, Antipater's mother was also all in all; she was one that gave counsel against them, and was more harsh than a step-mother, and one that hated the queen's sons more than is usual to hate sons-in-law. (474) All men did therefore already pay their respects to Antipater, in hopes of advantage; and it was the king's command which alienated every body [from the brethren], he having given this charge to his most intimate friends, that they should not come near, nor pay any regard, to Alexander, or to his friends. Herod was also become terrible, not only to his domestics about the court, but to his friends abroad; for Caesar had given such a privilege to no other king as he had given to him, which was this,—that he might fetch back any one that fled from him, even out of a city that was not under his own jurisdiction. (475) Now the young men were not acquainted with the calumnies raised against them; for which reason they could not guard themselves against them, but fell under them; for their father did not make any public complaints against either of them; though in a little time they perceived how things were by his coldness to them, and by the great uneasiness he showed upon any thing that troubled him. Antipater had also made their uncle Pheroras to be their enemy, as well as their aunt Salome, while he was always talking with her, as with a wife, and irritating her against them. (476) Moreover, Alexander's wife, Glaphyra, augmented this hatred against them, by deriving her nobility and genealogy [from great persons], and pretending that she was a lady superior to all others in that kingdom, as being derived by her father's side from Temenus, and by her mother's side from Darius [I], the son of Hystaspes. (477) She also frequently reproached Herod's sister and wives with the ignobility of their descent; and that they were every one chosen by him for their beauty, but not for their family. Now those wives of his were not a few; it being of old permitted to the Jews to marry many wives (cf. Matthew 19:8; Mark 10:5), and this king delighting in many; all which hated Alexander, on account of Glaphyra's boasting and reproaches.

3. (478) Nay, Aristobulus had raised a quarrel between himself and Salome, who was his mother-in-law, besides the anger he had conceived at Glaphyra's reproaches; for he perpetually upbraided his wife with the meanness of her family, and complained, that as

he had married a woman of a low family, so had his brother Alexander married one of royal blood. (479) At this Salome's daughter wept, and told it her with this addition, that Alexander threatened the mothers of his other brethren, that when he should come to the crown, he would make them weave with their maidens, and would make those brothers of his country schoolmasters; and brake this jest upon them, that they had been very carefully instructed, to fit them for such an employment. Hereupon Salome could not contain her anger, but told all to Herod; nor could her testimony be suspected, since it was against her own son-in-law. (480) There was also another calumny that ran abroad and inflamed the king's mind; for he heard that these sons of his were perpetually speaking of their mother, and, among their lamentations for her, did not abstain from cursing him; and that when he made presents of any of Mariamne's garments to his later wives, these threatened that in a little time, instead of royal garments, they would clothe theft in no better than hair-cloth.

4. (481) Now upon these accounts, though Herod was somewhat afraid of the young men's high spirit, yet did he not despair of reducing them to a better mind; but before he went to Rome, whither he was now going by sea, he called them to him, and partly threatened them a little, as a king; but for the main, he admonished them as a father, and exhorted them to love their brethren, and told them that he would pardon their former offenses, if they would amend for the time to come. (482) But they refuted the calumnies that had been raised of them, and said they were false, and alleged that their actions were sufficient for their vindication; and said withal, that he himself ought to shut his ears against such tales, and not be too easy in believing them, for that there would never be wanting those that would tell lies to their disadvantage, as long as any would give ear to them.

5. (483) When they had thus soon pacified him, as being their father, they got clear of the present fear they were in. Yet did they see occasion for sorrow in some time afterward; for they knew that Salome, as well as their uncle Pheroras, were their enemies; who were both of them heavy and severe persons, and especially Pheroras, who was a partner with Herod in all the affairs of the kingdom, excepting his diadem. He had also a hundred talents of his own revenue, and enjoyed the advantage of all the land beyond Jordan, which he had received as a gift from his brother, who had asked of Caesar to make him a tetrarch, as he was made accordingly. Herod had also given him a wife out of the royal family, who was no other than his own wife's sister, and after her death had solemnly espoused to him his own eldest daughter, with a dowry of three hundred talents; (484) but Pheroras refused to consummate this royal marriage, out of his affection to a maid-servant of his. Upon which account Herod was very angry, and gave that daughter in marriage to a brother's son of his, [Joseph,] who was slain afterward by the Parthians; but in some time he laid aside his anger against Pheroras, and pardoned him, as one not able to overcome his foolish passion for the maid-servant.

6. (485) Nay, Pheroras had been accused long before, while the queen [Mariamne] was alive, as if he were in a plot to poison Herod; and there came then so great a number of informers, that Herod himself, though he was an exceeding lover of his brethren, was brought to believe what was said, and to be afraid of it also. And when he had brought many of those that were under suspicion to the torture, he came at last to Pheroras's own friends; (486) none of which did openly confess the crime, but they owned that he had made preparation to take her whom he loved, and run away to the Parthians. Costobarus also, the husband of Salome, to whom the king had given her in marriage, after her former husband had been put to death for adultery, was instrumental in bringing about this contrivance and flight of his. (487) Nor did Salome escape all calumny upon herself; for her brother Pheroras accused her that she had made an agreement to marry Silleus, the procurator of Obodas [III], king of Arabia, who was at bitter enmity with Herod; but when she was convicted of this, and of all that Pheroras had accused her of, she obtained her pardon. The king also pardoned Pheroras himself the crimes he had been accused of.

7. (488) But the storm of the whole family was removed to Alexander, and all of it rested upon his head. There were three eunuchs who were in the highest esteem with the king, as was plain by the offices they were in about him; for one of them was appointed to be his butler, another of them got his supper ready for him, and the third put him into bed, and lay down by him. (489) Now Alexander had prevailed with these men, by large gifts, to let him use them after an obscene manner; which, when it was told to the king, they were tortured, and found guilty, and presently confessed the criminal conversation he had with them. They also discovered the promises by which they were induced so to do, and how they were deluded by Alexander, (490) who had told them that they ought not to fix their hopes upon Herod, an old man, and one so shameless as to color his hair, unless they thought that would make him young again; but that they ought to fix their attention to him who was to be his successor in the kingdom, whether he would or not; and who in no long time would avenge himself on his enemies, and make his friends happy and blessed, and themselves in the first place; (491) that the men of power did already pay respects to Alexander privately, and that the captains of the soldiery, and the officers, did secretly come to him.

8. (492) These confessions did so terrify Herod, that he durst not immediately publish them; but he sent spies abroad privately, by night and by day, who should make a close inquiry after all that was done and said; and when any were but suspected [of treason], he put them to death, (493) insomuch that the palace was full of horribly unjust proceedings; for every body forged calumnies, as they were themselves in a state of enmity or hatred against others; and many there were who abused the king's bloody passion to the disadvantage of those with whom they had quarrels, and lies were easily believed, and punishments were inflicted sooner than the calumnies were forged. He who had just then been accusing another was accused himself, and was led away to execution together with him whom he had convicted; for the danger the king was in of his life made examinations be very short. (494) He also proceeded to such a degree of bitterness, that he could not look on any of those that were not accused with a pleasant countenance, but was in the most barbarous disposition towards his own friends. Accordingly, he forbade a great many of them to come to court, and to those whom he had not power to punish actually he spake harshly. (495) But for Antipater, he insulted Alexander, now he was under his misfortunes, and got a stout company of his kindred together, and raised all sorts of calumny against him; and for the king, he was brought to such a degree of terror by those prodigious slanders and contrivances, that he fancied he saw Alexander coming to him with a drawn sword in his hand. (496) So he caused him to be seized upon immediately, and bound, and fell to examining his friends by torture, many of whom died [under the torture], but would discover nothing, nor say any thing against their consciences; but some of them, being forced to speak falsely by the pains they endured, said that Alexander, and his brother

Aristobulus, plotted against him, and waited for an opportunity to kill him as he was hunting, and then fly away to Rome. (497) These accusations though they were of an incredible nature, and only framed upon the great distress they were in, were readily believed by the king, who thought it some comfort to him, after he had bound his son, that it might appear he had not done it unjustly.

CHAPTER 25.

ARCHELAUS PROCURES A RECONCILIATION BETWEEN ALEXANDER, PHERORAS, AND HEROD.

1. (498) NOW as to Alexander, since he perceived it impossible to persuade his father [that he was innocent], he resolved to meet his calamities, how severe soever they were; so he composed four books against his enemies, and confessed that he had been in a plot; but declared withal that the greatest part [of the courtiers] were in a plot with him, and chiefly Pheroras and Salome; nay, that Salome once came and forced him to lie with her in the night time, whether he would or no. (499) These books were put into Herod's hands, and made a great clamor against the men in power. And now it was that Archelaus came hastily into Judea, as being affrighted for his son-in-law and his daughter; and he came as a proper assistant, and in a very prudent manner, and by a stratagem he obliged the king not to execute what he had threatened; (500) for when he was come to him, he cried out, "Where in the world is this wretched son-in-law of mine? Where shall I see the head of him which contrived to murder his father, which I will tear to pieces with my own hands? I will do the same also to my daughter, who hath such a fine husband; for although she be not a partner in the plot, yet, by being the wife of such a creature, she is polluted. (501) And I cannot but admire at thy patience, against whom this plot is laid, if Alexander be still alive; for as I came with what haste I could from Cappadocia, I expected to find him put to death for his crimes long ago; but still, in order to make an examination with thee about my daughter, whom, out of regard to thee and by dignity, I had espoused to him in marriage; but now we must take counsel about them both; and if thy paternal affection be so great, that thou canst not punish thy son, who hath plotted against thee, let us change our right hands, and let us succeed one to the other in expressing our rage upon this occasion."

Landscape view of Cappadocia in central Anatolia. (photo Carlesmari, via Wikimedia Commons)

2. (502) When he had made this pompous declaration, he got Herod to remit of his anger, though he were in disorder, who thereupon gave him the books which Alexander had composed to be read by him; and as he came to every head, he considered of it, together with Herod. So Archelaus took hence the occasion for that stratagem which he made use of, and by degrees he laid the blame on those men whose names were in these books, and especially upon Pheroras; (503) and when he saw that the king believed him [to he in earnest], he said, "We must consider whether the young man be not himself plotted against by such a number of wicked wretches, and not thou plotted against by the young man; for I cannot see any occasion for his falling into so horrid a crime, since he enjoys the advantages of royalty already, and has the expectation of being one of thy successors; I mean this, unless there were some persons that persuade him to it, and such persons as make an ill use of the facility they know there is to persuade young men; for by such persons, not only young men are sometimes imposed upon, but old men also, and by them sometimes are the most illustrious families and kingdoms overturned."

3. (504) Herod assented to what he had said, and, by degrees, abated of his anger against Alexander, but was more angry at Pheroras; for the principal subject of the four books was Pheroras; who perceiving that the king's inclinations changed on a sudden, and that Archelaus's friendship could do every thing with him, and that he had no honorable method of preserving himself, he procured his safety by his impudence. So he left Alexander, and had recourse to Archelaus, (505) who told him that he did not see how he could get him excused, now he was directly caught in so many crimes, whereby it was evidently demonstrated that he had plotted against the king, and had been the cause of those misfortunes which the young man was now under, unless he would moreover leave off his cunning knavery, and his denials of what he was charged withal, and confess the charge, and implore pardon of his brother, who still had a kindness for him; but that if he would do so, he would afford him all the assistance he was able.

4. (506) With this advice Pheroras complied, and putting himself into such a habit as might most move compassion, he came with black cloth upon his body, and tears in his eyes, and threw himself down at Herod's feet, and begged his pardon for what he had done, and confessed that he had acted very wickedly, and was guilty of every thing that he had been accused of, and lamented that disorder of his mind, and distraction which his love to a woman, he said, had brought him to. (507) So when Archelaus had brought Pheroras to accuse and bear witness against himself, he then made an excuse for him, and mitigated Herod's anger towards him, and this by using certain domestical examples; for that when he had suffered much greater mischiefs from a brother of his own, he preferred the obligations of nature before the passion of revenge; because it is in kingdoms as it is in gross bodies, where some member or other is ever swelled by the body's weight, in which case it is not proper to cut off such member, but to heal it by a gentle method of cure.

5. (508) Upon Archelaus's saying this, and much more to the same purpose, Herod's displeasure against Pheroras was mollified; yet did he persevere in his own indignation against Alexander, and said he would have his daughter divorced, and taken away from him, and this till he had brought Herod to that pass, that, contrary to his former behavior to him, he petitioned Archelaus for the young man, and that he would let his daughter continue espoused to him: but Archelaus made him strongly believe that he

would permit her to be married to any one else, but not to Alexander, because he looked upon it as a very valuable advantage, that the relation they had contracted by that affinity, and the privileges that went along with it, might be preserved. (509) And when the king said that his son would take it for a great favor to him, if he would not dissolve that marriage, especially since they had already children between the young man and her, and since that wife of his was so well beloved by him, and that as while she remains his wife she would be a great preservative to him, and keep him from offending, as he had formerly done; so if she should be once torn away from him, she would be the cause of his falling into despair, because such young men's attempts are best mollified when they are diverted from them by settling their affections at home. (510) So Archelaus complied with what Herod desired, but not without difficulty, and was both himself reconciled to the young man, and reconciled his father to him also. However, he said he must, by all means, be sent to Rome to discourse with Caesar, because he had already written a full account to him of this whole matter.

6. (511) Thus a period was put to Archelaus's stratagem, whereby he delivered his son-in-law out of the dangers he was in; but when these reconciliations were over, they spent their time in feastings and agreeable entertainments. And when Archelaus was going away, Herod made him a present of seventy talents, with a golden throne set with precious stones, and some eunuchs, and a concubine who was called Pannychis. He also paid due honors to every one of his friends according to their dignity. (512) In like manner did all the king's kindred, by his command, make glorious presents to Archelaus; and so he was conducted on his way by Herod and his nobility as far as Antioch.

Tetradrachma of Caesar Augustus (27 B.C.–A.D. 14) minted in Antioch. (photo Classical Numismatic Group, Inc. http://www.cngcoins.com)

CHAPTER 26.

HOW EURYCLES CALUMNIATED THE SONS OF MARIAMNE; AND HOW EUARATUS OF COS'S APOLOGY FOR THEM HAD NO EFFECT.

1. (513) NOW a little afterward there came into Judea a man that was much superior to Archelaus's stratagems, who did not only overturn that reconciliation that had been so wisely made with Alexander, but proved the occasion of his ruin. He was a Lacedemonian, and his name was Eurycles. He was so corrupt a man, that out of the desire of getting money, he chose to live under a king, for Greece could not suffice his luxury. (514) He presented Herod with splendid gifts, as a bait which he laid in order to compass his ends, and quickly received them back again manifold; yet did he esteem bare gifts as nothing, unless he imbrued the kingdom in blood by his purchases. (515) Accordingly, he imposed upon the king by flattering him, and by talking subtlely to him, as also by the lying encomiums which he made upon him; for as he soon perceived Herod's blind side, so he said and did every thing that might please him, and thereby became one of his most intimate friends; for both the king and all that were about him had a great regard for this Spartan, on account of his country.

2. (516) Now as soon as this fellow perceived the rotten parts of the family, and what quarrels the brothers had one with another, and in what disposition the father was towards each of them, he chose to take his lodging at the first in the house of Antipater, but deluded Alexander with a pretense of friendship to him, and falsely claimed to be an old acquaintance of Archelaus; for which reason he was presently admitted into Alexander's familiarity as a faithful friend. He also soon recommended himself to his brother Aristobulus. (517) And when he had thus made trial of these several persons, he imposed upon one of them by one method, and upon another by another. But he was principally hired by Antipater, and so betrayed Alexander, and this by reproaching Antipater, because, while he was the eldest son he overlooked the intrigues of those who stood in the way of his expectations; and by reproaching Alexander, because he who was born of a queen, and was married to a king's daughter, permitted one that was born of a mean woman to lay claim to the succession, and this when he had Archelaus to support him in the most complete manner. (518) Nor was his advice thought to be other than faithful by the young man, because of his pretended friendship with Archelaus; on which account it was that Alexander lamented to him Antipater's behavior with regard to himself, and this without concealing any thing from him; and how it was no wonder if Herod, after he had killed their mother, should deprive them of her kingdom. Upon this Eurycles pretended to commiserate his condition, and to grieve with him. (519) He also, by a bait that he laid for him, procured Aristobulus to say the same things. Thus did he inveigle both the brothers to make complaints of their father, and then went to Antipater, and carried these grand secrets to him. He also added a fiction of his own, as if his brothers had laid a plot against him, and were almost ready to come upon him with their drawn swords. For this intelligence he received a great sum of money, and on that account he commended Antipater before his father, (520) and at length undertook the work of bringing Alexander and Aristobulus to their graves, and accused them before their father. So he came to Herod, and told him that he would save his life, as a requital for the favors he had received from him, and would preserve his light [of life] by way of retribution for his kind entertainment; for that a sword had been long whetted, and Alexander's right hand had been long stretched out against him; but that he had laid impediments in his way, prevented his speed, and that by pretending to assist him in his design: (521) how Alexander said that Herod was not contented to reign in a kingdom that belonged to others, and to make dilapidations in their mother's government after he had killed her; but besides all this, that he introduced a spurious successor, and proposed to give the kingdom of their ancestors to that pestilent fellow Antipater:—that he would now appease the ghosts of Hyrcanus and Mariamne, by taking vengeance on him; for that it was not fit for him to take the succession to the government from such a father without bloodshed: (522) that many things happen every day to provoke him so to do, insomuch that he can say nothing at all, but it affords occasion for calumny against him; for that if any mention be made of nobility of birth, even in other cases, he is abused unjustly, while his father would say that nobody, to be sure, is of noble birth but Alexander, and that his father was inglorious for want of such nobility. If they be at any time hunting, and he says nothing, he gives offense; and if he commends any body, they take it in way of jest. (523) That they always find their father unmercifully severe, and have no natural affection for any of them but for Antipater; on which accounts, if this plot does not take, he is very willing to die; but that in case he kill his father, he hath sufficient opportunities for saving himself. In the first place, he hath Archelaus his father-in-law to whom he can easily fly; and

in the next place, he hath Caesar, who had never known Herod's character to this day; (524) for that he shall not appear then before him with that dread he used to do when his father was there to terrify him; and that he will not then produce the accusations that concerned himself alone, but would, in the first place, openly insist on the calamities of their nation, and how they are taxed to death, and in what ways of luxury and wicked practices that wealth is spent which was gotten by bloodshed; what sort of persons they are that get our riches, and to whom those cities belong upon whom he bestows his favors; (525) that he would have inquiry made what became of his grandfather [Hyrcanus], and his mother [Mariamne], and would openly proclaim the gross wickedness that was in the kingdom; on which accounts he should not be deemed a parricide.

3. (526) When Eurycles had made this portentous speech, he greatly commended Antipater, as the only child that had an affection for his father, and on that account was an impediment to the other's plot against him. Hereupon the king, who had hardly repressed his anger upon the former accusations, was exasperated to an incurable degree. (527) At which time Antipater took another occasion to send in other persons to his father to accuse his brethren, and to tell him that they had privately discoursed with Jucundus and Tyrannus, who had once been masters of the horse to the king, but for some offenses had been put out of that honorable employment. Herod was in a very great rage at these informations, and presently ordered those men to be tortured; (528) yet did not they confess anything of what the king had been informed; but a certain letter was produced, as written by Alexander to the governor of a castle, to desire him to receive him and Aristobulus into the castle when he had killed his father, and to give them weapons, and what other assistance he could, upon that occasion. (529) Alexander said that this letter was a forgery of Diophantus. This Diophantus was the king's secretary, a bold man, and cunning in counterfeiting any one's hand; and after he had counterfeited a great number, he was at last put to death for it. Herod did also order the governor of the castle to be tortured, but got nothing out of him of what the accusations suggested.

4. (530) However, although Herod found the proofs too weak, he gave order to have his sons kept in custody; for till now they had been at liberty. He also called that pest of his family, and forger of all this vile accusation, Eurycles, his savior and benefactor, and gave him a reward of fifty talents. Upon which he prevented any accurate accounts that could come of what he had done, by going immediately into Cappadocia, and there he got money of Archelaus, having the impudence to pretend that he had reconciled Herod to Alexander. (531) He thence passed over into Greece, and used what he had thus wickedly gotten to the like wicked purposes. Accordingly, he was twice accused before Caesar, that he had filled Achaia with sedition, and had plundered its cities; and so he was sent into banishment. And thus was he punished for what wicked actions he had been guilty of about Aristobulus and Alexander.

5. (532) But it will now be worth while to put Euaratus of Cos in opposition to this Spartan; for as he was one of Alexander's most intimate friends, and came to him in his travels at the same time that Eurycles came; so the king put the question to him, whether those things of which Alexander was accused were true? (533) He assured him upon oath that he had never heard any such things from the young men; yet did this testimony avail nothing for the clearing those miserable creatures; for Herod was only disposed and most ready to hearken to what made against them, and every one was most agreeable to him that would believe they were guilty, and showed their indignation at them.

CHAPTER 27.

HEROD BY CAESAR'S DIRECTION ACCUSES HIS SONS AT EURYTUS. THEY ARE NOT PRODUCED BEFORE THE COURTS BUT YET ARE CONDEMNED; AND IN A LITTLE TIME THEY ARE SENT TO SEBASTE, AND STRANGLED THERE.

1. (534) MOREOVER, Salome exasperated Herod's cruelty against his sons; for Aristobulus was desirous to bring her, who was his mother-in-law and his aunt, into the like dangers with themselves; so he sent to her to take care of her own safety, and told her that the king was preparing to put her to death, on account of the accusation that was laid against her, as if when she formerly endeavored to marry herself to Sylleus the Arabian, she had discovered the king's grand secrets to him, who was the king's enemy; (535) and this it was that came as the last storm, and entirely sunk the young men when they were in great danger before. For Salome came running to the king, and informed him of what admonition had been given her; whereupon he could bear no longer, but commanded both the young men to be bound, and kept the one asunder from the other. He also sent Volumnius, the general of his army, to Caesar immediately, as also his friend Olympus with him, who carried the informations in writing along with them. (536) Now as soon as they had sailed to Rome, and delivered the king's letters to Caesar, Caesar was mightily troubled at the case of the young men; yet did not he think he ought to take the power from the fa-

Main colonnaded street of ancient Tyre (al-Mina) in Lebanon. (photo Heretiq, via Wikimedia Commons)

ther of condemning his sons; (537) so he wrote back to him, and appointed him to have the power over his sons; but said withal, that he would do well to make an examination into this matter of the plot against him in a public court, and to take for his assessors his own kindred, and the governors of the province. And if those sons be found guilty, to put them to death; but if they appear to have thought of no more than flying away from him, that he should moderate their punishment.

2. (538) With these directions Herod complied, and came to Berytus, where Caesar had ordered the court to be assembled, and got the judicature together. The presidents sat first, as Caesar's letters had appointed, who were Saturninus and Pedanius, and their lieutenants that were with them, with whom was the procurator Volumnius also; next to them sat the king's kinsmen and friends, with Salome also, and Pheroras; after whom sat the principal men of all Syria, excepting Archelaus; for Herod had a suspicion of him, because he was Alexander's father-in-law. (539) Yet did not he produce his sons in open court; and this was done very cunningly, for he knew well enough that had they but appeared only, they would certainly have been pitied; and if withal they had been suffered to speak, Alexander would easily have answered what they were accused of; but they were in custody at Platane, a village of the Sidonians.

3. (540) So the king got up, and inveighed against his sons, as if they were present; and as for that part of the accusation that they had plotted against him, he urged it but faintly, because he was destitute of proofs; but he insisted before the assessors on the reproaches, and jests, and injurious carriage, and ten thousand the like offenses against him, which were heavier than death itself; and when nobody contradicted him, he moved them to pity his case, as though he had been condemned himself, now he had gained a bitter victory against his sons. So he asked every one's sentence, (541) which sentence was first of all given by Saturninus, and was this: That he condemned the young men, but not to death; for that it was not fit for him, who had three sons of his own now present, to give his vote for the destruction of the sons of another. The two lieutenants also gave the like vote; some others there were also who followed their example; (542) but Volumnius began to vote on the more melancholy side, and all those that came after him condemned the young men to die, some out of flattery, and some out of hatred to Herod; but none out of indignation at their crimes. (543) And now all Syria and Judea was in great expectation, and waited for the last act of this tragedy; yet did nobody, suppose that Herod would be so barbarous as to murder his children: however, he carried them away to Tyre, and thence sailed to Cesarea, and deliberated with himself what sort of death the young men should suffer.

4. (544) Now there was a certain old soldier of the king's, whose name was Tero, who had a son that was very familiar with and a friend to Alexander, and who himself particularly loved the young men. This soldier was in a manner distracted, out of the excess of the indignation he had at what was doing; and at first he cried out aloud, as he went about, that justice was trampled under foot; that truth was perished, and nature confounded; and that the life of man was full of iniquity, and every thing else that passion could suggest to a man who spared not his own life; (545) and at last he ventured to go to the king, and said, "Truly I think thou art a most miserable man, when thou hearkenest to most wicked wretches, against those that ought to be dearest to thee; since thou hast frequently resolved that Pheroras and Salome should be put to death, and yet believest them against thy sons; while these, by cutting off the succession of thine own sons, leave all wholly to Antipater, and thereby choose to have thee such a king as may be thoroughly in their own power. (546) However, consider whether this death of Antipater's brethren will not make him hated by the soldiers; for there is nobody but commiserates the young men; and of the captains, a great many show their indignation at it openly." Upon his saying this, he named those that had such indignation; but the king ordered those men, with Tero himself and his son, to be seized upon immediately.

5. (547) At which time there was a certain barber, whose name was Trypho. This man leaped out from among the people in a kind of madness, and accused himself, and said, "This Tero endeavored to persuade me also to cut thy throat with my razor, when I trimmed thee, and promised that Alexander should give me large presents for so doing." (548) When Herod heard this, he examined Tero, with his son and the barber, by the torture; but as the others denied the accusation, and he said nothing further, Herod gave order that Tero should be racked more severely; (549) but his son, out of pity to his father, promised to discover the whole to the king, if he would grant [that his father should be no longer tortured]. When he had agreed to this, he said that his father, at the persuasion of Alexander, had an intention to kill him. Now some said this was forged, in order to free his father from his torments; and some said it was true.

6. (550) And now Herod accused the captains and Tero in an assembly of the people, and brought the people together in a body against them; and accordingly there were they put to death, together with [Trypho] the barber; they were killed by the pieces of wood and the stones that were thrown at them. (551) He also sent his sons to Sebaste, a city not far from Cesarea, and ordered them to be there strangled; and as what he had ordered was executed immediately, so he commanded that their dead bodies should be brought to the fortress Alexandrium, to be buried with Alexander, their grandfather by the mother's side. And this was the end of Alexander and Aristobulus.

CHAPTER 28.

HOW ANTIPATER IS HATED OF ALL MEN; AND HOW THE KING ESPOUSES THE SONS OF THOSE THAT HAD BEEN SLAIN TO HIS KINDRED; BUT THAT ANTIPATER MADE HIM CHANGE THEM FOR OTHER WOMEN, OF HEROD'S MARRIAGES, AND CHILDREN.

1. (552) BUT an intolerable hatred fell upon Antipater from the nation, though he had now an indisputable title to the succession, because they all knew that he was the person who contrived all the calumnies against his brethren. However, he began to be in a terrible fear, as he saw the posterity of those that had been slain growing up; for Alexander had two sons by Glaphyra, Tigranes and Alexander; and Aristobulus had Herod, and Agrippa [I], and Aristobulus, his sons, with Herodias and Mariamne [III], his daughters, (553) and all by Bernice, Salome's daughter. As for Glaphyra, Herod, as soon as he had killed Alexander, sent her back, together with her portion, to Cappadocia. He married Bernice, Aristobulus's daughter, to Antipater's uncle by his mother, and it was Antipater who, in order to reconcile her to him, when she had been at variance with him, contrived this match; (554) he also got into Pheroras's favor, and into the favor of Caesar's friends, by presents, and other ways of obsequiousness, and sent no small sums of money to Rome; Saturninus also, and his friends in Syria, were all well replenished with the presents he made them; yet the more he gave,

the more he was hated, as not making these presents out of generosity, but spending his money out of fear. (555) Accordingly, it so fell out that the receivers bore him no more good-will than before, but that those to whom he gave nothing were his more bitter enemies. However, he bestowed his money every day more and more profusely, on observing that, contrary to his expectations, the king was taking care about the orphans, and discovering at the same time his repentance for killing their fathers, by his commiseration of those that sprang from them.

2. (556) Accordingly, Herod got together his kindred and friends, and set before them the children, and, with his eyes full of tears, said thus to them: "It was an unlucky fate that took away from me these children's fathers, which children are recommended to me by that natural commiseration which their orphan condition requires; however, I will endeavor, though I have been a most unfortunate father, to appear a better grandfather, and to leave these children such curators after myself as are dearest to me. (557) I therefore betroth thy daughter, Pheroras, to the elder of these brethren, the children of Alexander, that thou mayst be obliged to take care of them. I also betroth to thy son, Antipater, the daughter of Aristobulus; be thou therefore a father to that orphan; and my son Herod [Philip] shall have her sister, whose grandfather, by the mother's side, was high priest. (558) And let everyone that loves me be of my sentiments in these dispositions, which none that hath an affection for me will abrogate. And I pray God that he will join these children together in marriage, to the advantage of my kingdom, and of my posterity; and may he look down with eyes more serene upon them than he looked upon their fathers."

3. (559) While he spake these words he wept, and joined the children's fight hands together; after which he embraced them every one after an affectionate manner, and dismissed the assembly. Upon this, Antipater was in great disorder immediately, and lamented publicly at what was done; for he supposed that this dignity which was conferred on these orphans was for his own destruction, even in his father's lifetime, and that he should run another risk of losing the government, if Alexander's sons should have both Archelaus [a king], and Pheroras a tetrarch, to support them. (560) He also considered how he was himself hated by the nation, and how they pitied these orphans; how great affection the Jews bare to those brethren of his when they were alive, and how gladly they remembered them now they had perished by his means. So he resolved by all the ways possible to get these espousals dissolved.

4. (561) Now he was afraid of going subtlely about this matter with his father, who was hard to be pleased, and was presently moved upon the least suspicion: so he ventured to go to him directly, and to beg of him before his face not to deprive him of that dignity which he had been pleased to bestow upon him; and that he might not have the bare name of a king, while the power was in other persons; for that he should never be able to keep the government, if Alexander's son was to have both his grandfather Archelaus and Pheroras for his curators; (562) and he besought him earnestly, since there were so many of the royal family alive, that he would change those [intended] marriages. Now the king had nine wives, and children by seven of them; Antipater was himself born of Doris, and Herod Philip of Mariamne, the high priest's daughter; Antipas also and [Herod] Archelaus were by Malthace, the Samaritan, as was his daughter Olympias, which his brother Joseph's son had married. By Cleopatra of Jerusalem he had Herod and Philip; and by Pallas, Phasaelus; (563) he had also two daughters, Roxana and Salome, the one by Phedra, and the other by Elpis; he had also two wives that had no children, the one his first cousin, and the other his niece; and besides these he had two daughters, the sisters of Alexander and Aristobulus, by Mariamne. Since, therefore, the royal family was so numerous, Antipater prayed him to change these intended marriages.

5. (564) When the king perceived what disposition he was in towards these orphans, he was angry at it, and a suspicion came into his mind as to those sons whom he had put to death, whether that had not been brought about by the false tales of Antipater; (565) so that at that time he made Antipater a long and a peevish answer, and bid him begone. Yet was he afterwards prevailed upon cunningly by his flatteries, and changed the marriages; he married Aristobulus's daughter to him, and his son to Pheroras's daughter.

6. (566) Now one may learn, in this instance, how very much this flattering Antipater could do,—even what Salome in the like circumstances could not do; for when she, who was his sister, and who, by the means of Julia, Caesar's wife, earnestly desired leave to be married to Sylleus the Arabian, Herod swore he would esteem her his bitter enemy, unless she would leave off that project: he also caused her, against her own consent, to be married to Alexas, a friend of his, and that one of her daughters should be married to Alexas's son, and the other to Antipater's uncle by the mother's side. And for the daughters the king had by Mariamne, the one was married to Antipater, his sister's son, and the other to his brother's son, Phasaelus.

CHAPTER 29.

ANTIPATER BECOMES INTOLERABLE. HE IS SENT TO ROME, AND CARRIES HEROD'S TESTAMENT WITH HIM; PHERORAS LEAVES HIS BROTHER, THAT HE MAY KEEP HIS WIFE. HE DIES AT HOME.

1. (567) NOW when Antipater had cut off the hopes of the orphans, and had contracted such affinities as would be most for his own advantage, he proceeded briskly, as having a certain expectation of the kingdom; and as he had now assurance added to his wickedness, he became intolerable; for not being able to avoid the hatred of all people, he built his security upon the terror he struck into them. Pheroras also assisted him in his designs, looking upon him as already fixed in the kingdom. (568) There was also a company of women in the court, which excited new disturbances; for Pheroras's wife, together with her mother and sister, as also Antipater's mother, grew very impudent in the palace. She also was so insolent as to affront the king's two daughters, on which account the king hated her to a great degree; yet although these women were hated by him, they domineered over others: (569) there was only Salome who opposed their good agreement, and informed the king of their meetings, as not being for the advantage of his affairs. And when those women knew what calumnies she had raised against them, and how much Herod was displeased, they left off their public meetings, and friendly entertainments of one another; nay, on the contrary, they pretended to quarrel one with another when the king was within hearing. The like dissimulation did Antipater make use of; and when matters were public, he opposed Pheroras; (570) but still they had private cabals and merry meetings in the night time; nor did the observation of others do any more than confirm their mutual agreement. However, Salome knew every thing they did, and told every thing to Herod.

2. (571) But he was inflamed with anger at them, and chiefly at Pheroras's wife; for Salome had principally accused her. So he got

an assembly of his friends and kindred together, and there accused this woman of many things, and particularly of the affronts she had offered his daughters; and that she had supplied the Pharisees with money, by way of rewards for what they had done against him, and had procured his brother to become his enemy, by giving him love potions. (572) At length he turned his speech to Pheroras, and told him that he would give him his choice of these two things: Whether he would keep in with his brother, or with his wife? And when Pheroras said that he would die rather than forsake his wife? Herod, not knowing what to do further in that matter, turned his speech to Antipater, and charged him to have no intercourse either with Pheroras's wife, or with Pheroras himself, or with any one belonging to her. Now though Antipater did not transgress that his injunction publicly, yet did he in secret come to their night meetings; (573) and because he was afraid that Salome observed what he did, he procured, by the means of his Italian friends, that he might go and live at Rome; for when they wrote that it was proper for Antipater to be sent to Caesar for some time, Herod made no delay, but sent him, and that with a splendid attendance, and a great deal of money, and gave him his testament to carry with him,—wherein Antipater had the kingdom bequeathed to him, and wherein Herod was named for Antipater's successor; that Herod, I mean, who was the son of Mariamne [II], the high priest's daughter.

3. (574) Sylleus also, the Arabian, sailed to Rome, without any regard to Caesar's injunctions, and this in order to oppose Antipater with all his might, as to that law-suit which Nicolaus had with him before. This Sylleus had also a great contest with Aretas his own king; for he had slain many others of Aretas's friends, and particularly Sohemus, the most potent man in the city Petra. (575) Moreover, he had prevailed with Phabatus, who was Herod's steward, by giving him a great sum of money, to assist him against Herod; but when Herod gave him more, he induced him to leave Sylleus, and by this means he demanded of him all that Caesar had required of him to pay. But when Sylleus paid nothing of what he was to pay, and did also accuse Phabatus to Caesar, and said that he was not a steward for Caesar's advantage, but for Herod's, (576) Phabatus was angry at him on that account, but was still in very great esteem with Herod, and discovered Sylleus's grand secrets, and told the king that Sylleus had corrupted Corinthus, one of the guards of his body, by bribing him, and of whom he must therefore have a care. Accordingly, the king complied; for this Corinthus, though he was brought up in Herod's kingdom, yet was he by birth an Arabian; (577) so the king ordered him to be taken up immediately, and not only him, but two other Arabians, who were caught with him; the one of them was Sylleus's friend, the other the head of a tribe. These last, being put to the torture, confessed that they had prevailed with Corinthus, for a large sum of money, to kill Herod; and when they had been further examined before Saturninus, the president of Syria, they were sent to Rome.

4. (578) However, Herod did not leave off importuning Pheroras, but proceeded to force him to put away his wife; yet could he not devise any way by which he could bring the woman herself to punishment, although he had many causes of hatred to her; till at length he was in such great uneasiness at her, that he cast both her and his brother out of his kingdom. (579) Pheroras took this injury very patiently, and went away into his own tetrarchy, [Perea beyond Jordan,] and sware that there should be but one end put to his flight, and that should be Herod's death; and that he would never return while he was alive. Nor indeed would he return when his brother was sick, although he earnestly sent for him to come to him, because he had a mind to leave some injunctions with him before he died; (580) but Herod unexpectedly recovered. A little afterward Pheroras himself fell sick, when Herod showed great moderation; for he came to him, and pitied his case, and took care of him; but his affection for him did him no good, for Pheroras died a little afterward. (581) Now though Herod had so great an affection for him to the last day of his life, yet was a report spread abroad that he had killed him by poison. However, he took care to have his dead body carried to Jerusalem, and appointed a very great mourning to the whole nation for him, and bestowed a most pompous funeral upon him. And this was the end that one of Alexander's and Aristobulus's murderers came to.

CHAPTER 30.

WHEN HEROD MADE INQUIRY ABOUT PHERORAS'S DEATH A DISCOVERY WAS MADE THAT ANTIPATER HAD PREPARED A POISONOUS DRAUGHT FOR HIM. HEROD CASTS DORIS AND HER ACCOMPLICES, AS ALSO MARIAMNE, OUT OF THE PALACE AND BLOTS HER SON HEROD OUT OF HIS TESTAMENT.

1. (582) BUT now the punishment was transferred unto the original author, Antipater, and took its rise from the death of Pheroras; for certain of his freed-men came with a sad countenance to the king, and told him that his brother had been destroyed by poison, and that his wife had brought him somewhat that was prepared after an unusual manner, and that, upon his eating it, he presently fell into his distemper; (583) that Antipater's mother and sister, two days before, brought a woman out of Arabia that was skillful in mixing such drugs, that she might prepare a love potion for Pheroras; and that instead of a love potion, she had given him deadly poison; and that this was done by the management of Sylleus, who was acquainted with that woman.

2. (584) The king was deeply affected with so many suspicions, and had the maid-servants and some of the free women also tortured; one of which cried out in her agonies, "May that God that governs the earth and the heaven punish this author of all these our miseries, Antipater's mother!" The king took a handle from this confession, and proceeded to inquire further into the truth of the matter. (585) So this woman discovered the friendship of Antipater's mother to Pheroras, and Antipater's women, as also their secret meetings, and that Pheroras and Antipater had drunk with them for a whole night together as they returned from the king, and would not suffer any body, either man-servant or maidservant, to be there; while one of the free women discovered the matter.

3. (586) Upon this Herod tortured the maid-servants every one by themselves separately, who all unanimously agreed in the foregoing discoveries, and that accordingly by agreement they went away, Antipater to Rome, and Pheroras to Perea; for that they oftentimes talked to one another thus: That after Herod had slain Alexander and Aristobulus, he would fall upon them, and upon their wives, because, after he Mariamne and her children he would spare nobody; and that for this reason it was best to get as far off the wild beast as they were able:—(587) and that Antipater oftentimes lamented his own case before his mother, and said to her, that he had already gray hairs upon his head, and that his father grew younger again every day, and that perhaps death would overtake him before he should begin to be a king in earnest; and that in case Herod should die, which yet nobody knew when it would be, the enjoyment of the succession could certainly be but for a little time; (588) for that these heads of Hydra, the sons of Alexander and Aristobulus, were growing up: that he was deprived by his father

of the hopes of being succeeded by his children, for that his successor after his death was not to be any one of his own sons, but Herod the son of Mariamne [II]: that in this point Herod was plainly distracted, to think that his testament should therein take place; for he would take care that not one of his posterity should remain, (589) because he was of all fathers the greatest hater of his children. Yet does he hate his brother still worse; whence it was that he a while ago gave himself a hundred talents, that he should not have any intercourse with Pheroras. And when Pheroras said, Wherein have we done him any harm? Antipater replied, "I wish he would but deprive us of all we have, and leave us naked and alive only; but it is indeed impossible to escape this wild beast, who is thus given to murder, who will not permit us to love any person openly, although we be together privately; yet may we be so openly too, if we have but the courage and the hands of men."

4. (590) These things were said by the women upon the torture; as also that Pheroras resolved to fly with them to Perea. Now Herod gave credit to all they said, on account of the affair of the hundred talents; for he had no discourse with any body about them, but only with Antipater. So he vented his anger first of all against Antipater's mother, and took away from her all the ornaments which he had given her, which cost a great many talents, and cast her out of the palace a second time. (591) He also took care of Pheroras's women after their tortures, as being now reconciled to them; but he was in great consternation himself, and inflamed upon every suspicion, and had many innocent persons led to the torture, out of his fear lest he should leave any guilty person untortured.

5. (592) And now it was that he betook himself to examine Antipater of Samaria, who was the steward of [his son] Antipater; and upon torturing him, he learned that Antipater had sent for a potion of deadly poison for him out of Egypt, by Antiphilus, a companion of his; that Theudio, the uncle of Antipater, had it from him, and delivered it to Pheroras; for that Antipater had charged him to take his father off while he was at Rome, and so free him from the suspicion of doing it himself: that Pheroras also committed this potion to his wife. (593) Then did the king send for her, and bid her bring to him what she had received immediately. So she came out of her house as if she would bring it with her, but threw herself down from the top of the house, in order to prevent any examination and torture from the king. However, it came to pass, as it seems by the providence of God, when he intended to bring Antipater to punishment, that she fell not upon her head, but upon other parts of her body, and escaped. (594) The king, when she was brought to him, took care of her, (for she was at first quite senseless upon her fall,) and asked her why she had thrown herself down; and gave her his oath, that if she would speak the real truth, he would excuse her from punishment; but that if she concealed any thing, he would have her body torn to pieces by torments, and leave no part. of it to be buried.

6. (595) Upon this the woman paused a little, and then said, "Why do I spare to speak of these grand secrets, now Pheroras is dead? that would only tend to save Antipater, who is all our destruction. Hear then, O king, and be thou, and God himself, who cannot be deceived, witnesses to the truth of what I am going to say. (596) When thou didst sit weeping by Pheroras as he was dying, then it was that he called me to him, and said, My dear wife, I have been greatly mistaken as to the disposition of my brother towards me, and have hated him that is so affectionate to me, and have contrived to kill him who is in such disorder for me before I am dead. As for myself, I receive the recompence of my impiety; but do thou bring what poison was left with us by Antipater, and which thou keepest in order to destroy him, and consume it immediately in the fire in my sight, that I may not be liable to the avenger in the invisible world. (597) This I brought as he bid me, and emptied the greatest part of it into the fire, but reserved a little of it for my own use against uncertain futurity, and out of my fear of thee."

7. (598) When she had said this, she brought the box, which had a small quantity of this potion in it: but the king let her alone, and transferred the tortures to Antiphilus's mother and brother; who both confessed that Antiphilus brought the box out of Egypt, and that they had received the potion from a brother of his, who was a physician at Alexandria. (599) Then did the ghosts of Alexander and Aristobulus go round all the palace, and became the inquisitors and discoverers of what could not otherwise have been found out and brought such as were the freest from suspicion to be examined; whereby it was discovered that Mariamne, the high priest's daughter, was conscious of this plot; and her very brothers, when they were tortured, declared it so to be. (600) Whereupon the king avenged this insolent attempt of the mother upon her son, and blotted Herod, whom he had by her, out of his treament, who had been before named therein as successor to Antipater.

CHAPTER 31.

ANTIPATER IS CONVICTED BY BATHYLLUS; BUT HE STILL RETURNS FROM ROME WITHOUT KNOWING IT. HEROD BRINGS HIM TO HIS TRIAL.

1. (601) AFTER these things were over, Bathyllus came under examination, in order to convict Antipater, who proved the concluding attestation to Antipater's designs; for indeed he was no other than his freed-man. This man came, and brought another deadly potion, the poison of asps, and the juices of other serpents, that if the first potion did not do the business, Pheroras and his wife might be armed with this also to destroy the king. (602) He brought also an addition to Antipater's insolent attempt against his father, which was the letters which he wrote against his brethren, Archelaus and Philip, which were the king's sons, and educated at Rome, being yet youths, but of generous dispositions. (603) Antipater set himself to get rid of these as soon as he could, that they might not be prejudicial to his hopes; and to that end he forged letters against them in the name of his friends at Rome. Some of these he corrupted by bribes to write how they grossly reproached their father, and did openly bewail Alexander and Aristobulus, and were uneasy at their being recalled; for their father had already sent for them, which was the very thing that troubled Antipater.

2. (604) Nay, indeed, while Antipater was in Judea, and before he was upon his journey to Rome, he gave money to have the like letters against them sent from Rome, and then came to his father, who as yet had no suspicion of him, and apologized for his brethren, and alleged on their behalf that some of the things contained in those letters were false, and others of them were only youthful errors. (605) Yet at the same time that he expended a great deal of his money, by making presents to such as wrote against his brethren, did he aim to bring his accounts into confusion, by buying costly garments, and carpets of various contextures, with silver and gold cups, and a great many more curious things, that so, among the view great expenses laid out upon such furniture, he might conceal the money he had used in hiring men [to write the letters]; for he brought in an account of his expenses, amounting to two hundred talents, his main pretense for which was file law-suit he had been in with Sylleus. (606) So while all his rogueries, even those of a lesser sort also, were covered by his greater

villainy, while all the examinations by torture proclaimed his attempt to murder his father, and the letters proclaimed his second attempt to murder his brethren; yet did no one of those that came to Rome inform him of his misfortunes in Judea, although seven months had intervened between his conviction and his return, so great was the hatred which they all bore to him. (607) And perhaps they were the ghosts of those brethren of his that had been murdered that stopped the mouths of those that intended to have told him. He then wrote from Rome, and informed his [friends] that he would soon come to them, and how he was dismissed with honor by Caesar.

3. (608) Now the king, being desirous to get this plotter against him into his hands, and being also afraid lest he should some way come to the knowledge how his affairs stood, and be upon his guard, he dissembled his anger in his epistle to him, as in other points he wrote kindly to him, and desired him to make haste, because if he came quickly, he would then lay aside the complaints he had against his mother; for Antipater was not ignorant that his mother had been expelled out of the palace. (609) However, he had before received a letter, which contained an account of the death of Pheroras, at Tarentum, and made great lamentations at it; for which some commended him, as being for his own uncle; though probably this confusion arose on account of his having thereby failed in his plot [on his father's life]; and his tears were more for the loss of him that was to have been subservient therein, than for [an uncle] Pheroras: moreover, a sort of fear came upon him as to his designs, lest the poison should have been discovered. (610) However, when he was in Cilicia, he received the forementioned epistle from his father, and made great haste accordingly. But when he had sailed to Celenderis, a suspicion came into his mind relating to his mother's misfortunes; as if his soul foreboded some mischief to itself. (611) Those therefore of his friends which were the most considerate advised him not rashly to go to his father, till he had learned what were the occasions why his mother had been ejected, because they were afraid that he might be involved in the calumnies that had been cast upon his mother: (612) but those that were less considerate, and had more regard to their own desires of seeing their native country, than to Antipater's safety, persuaded him to make haste home, and not, by delaying his journey, afford his father ground for an ill suspicion, and give a handle to those that raised stories against him; for that in case any thing had been moved to his disadvantage, it was owing to his absence, which durst not have been done had he been present. And they said it was absurd to deprive himself of certain happiness, for the sake of an uncertain suspicion, and not rather to return to his father, and take the royal authority upon him, which was in a state of fluctuation on his account only. (613) Antipater complied with this last advice, for Providence hurried him on [to his destruction]. So he passed over the sea, and landed at Sebastus, the haven of Cesarea.

4. (614) And here he found a perfect and unexpected solitude, while every body avoided him, and nobody durst come at him; for he was equally hated by all men; and now that hatred had liberty to show itself, and the dread men were in at the king's anger made men keep from him; for the whole city [of Jerusalem] was filled with the rumors about Antipater, and Antipater himself was the only person who was ignorant of them; for as no man was dismissed more magnificently when he began his voyage to Rome so was no man now received back with greater ignominy. (615) And indeed he began already to suspect what misfortunes there were in Herod's family; yet did he cunningly conceal his suspicion; and while he was inwardly ready to die for fear, he put on a forced

As Lugdunum I (RIC 230), head of Augustus r., countermarked "VAR" (Varus). (By Fotografie für das Bildarchiv der Abteilung, via Wikimedia Commons)

boldness of countenance. (616) Nor could he now fly any whither, nor had he any way of emerging out of the difficulties which encompassed him; nor indeed had he even there any certain intelligence of the affairs of the royal family, by reason of the threats the king had given out: yet had he some small hopes of better tidings; for perhaps nothing had been discovered; or if any discovery had been made, perhaps he should be able to clear himself by impudence and artful tricks, which were the only things he relied upon for his deliverance.

5. (617) And with these hopes did he screen himself, till he came to the palace, without any friends with him; for these were affronted, and shut out at the first gate. Now Varus, the president of Syria, happened to be in the palace [at this juncture]; so Antipater went in to his father, and, putting on a bold face, he came near to salute him. (618) But Herod stretched out his hands, and turned his head away from him, and cried out, "Even this is an indication of a parricide, to be desirous to get me into his arms, when he is under such heinous accusations. God confound thee, thou vile wretch; do not thou touch me, till thou hast cleared thyself of these crimes that are charged upon thee. I appoint thee a court where thou art to be judged, and this Varus, who is very seasonably here, to be thy judge; and get thou thy defense ready against tomorrow, for I give thee so much time to prepare suitable excuses for thyself." (619) And as Antipater was so confounded, that he was able to make no answer to this charge, he went away; but his mother and wife came to him, and told him of all the evidence they had gotten against him. Hereupon he recollected himself, and considered what defense he should make against the accusations.

CHAPTER 32.

ANTIPATER IS ACCUSED BEFORE VARUS, AND IS CONVICTED OF LAYING A PLOT [AGAINST HIS FATHER] BY THE STRONGEST EVIDENCE. HEROD PUTS OFF HIS PUNISHMENT TILL HE SHOULD BE RECOVERED, AND IN THE MEAN TIME ALTERS HIS TESTAMENT.

1. (620) NOW the day following the king assembled a court of his kinsmen and friends, and called in Antipater's friends also. Herod himself, with Varus, were the presidents; and Herod called for all the witnesses, and ordered them to be brought in; among whom some of the domestic servants of Antipater's mother were brought in also, who had but a little while before been caught, as they were carrying the following letter from her to her son: "Since all those things have been already discovered to thy father, do not thou come to him, unless thou canst procure some assistance from Caesar." (621) When this and the other witnesses were introduced, Antipater came in, and falling on his face before his father's feet, he said, "Father, I beseech thee, do not condemn me beforehand, but let thy ears be unbiassed, and attend to my defense; for if thou wilt give me leave, I will demonstrate that I am innocent."

2. (622) Hereupon Herod cried out to him to hold his peace, and spake thus to Varus: "I cannot but think that thou, Varus, and every other upright judge, will determine that Antipater is a vile wretch. I am also afraid that thou wilt abhor my ill fortune, and judge me

also myself worthy of all sorts of calamity for begetting such children; while yet I ought rather to be pitied, who have been so affectionate a father to such wretched sons; (623) for when I had settled the kingdom on my former sons, even when they were young, and when, besides the charges of their education at Rome, I had made them the friends of Caesar, and made them envied by other kings, I found them plotting against me. These have been put to death, and that, in great measure, for the sake of Antipater; for as he was then young, and appointed to be my successor, I took care chiefly to secure him from danger: (624) but this profligate wild beast, when he had been over and above satiated with that patience which I showed him, he made use of that abundance I had given him against myself; for I seemed to him to live too long, and he was very uneasy at the old age I was arrived at; nor could he stay any longer, but would be a king by parricide. And justly I am served by him for bringing him back out of the country to court, when he was of no esteem before, and for thrusting out those sons of mine that were born of the queen, and for making him a successor to my dominions. (625) I confess to thee, O Varus, the great folly I was guilty for I provoked those sons of mine to act against me, and cut off their just expectations for the sake of Antipater; and indeed what kindness did I do them; that could equal what I have done to Antipater? to I have, in a manner, yielded up my royal while I am alive, and whom I have openly named for the successor to my dominions in my testament, and given him a yearly revenue of his own of fifty talents, and supplied him with money to an extravagant degree out of my own revenue; and when he was about to sail to Rome, I gave him three talents, and recommended him, and him alone of all my children, to Caesar, as his father's deliverer. (626) Now what crimes were those other sons of mine guilty of like these of Antipater? and what evidence was there brought against them so strong as there is to demonstrate this son to have plotted against me? (627) Yet does this parricide presume to speak for himself, and hopes to obscure the truth by his cunning tricks. Thou, O Varus, must guard thyself against him; for I know the wild beast, and I foresee how plausibly he will talk, and his counterfeit lamentation. This was he who exhorted me to have a care of Alexander when he was alive, and not to intrust my body with all men! This was he who came to my very bed, and looked about lest any one should lay snares for me! This was he who took care of my sleep, and secured me from fear of danger, who comforted me under the trouble I was in upon the slaughter of my sons, and looked to see what affection my surviving brethren bore me! This was my protector, and the guardian of my body! (628) And when I call to mind, O Varus, his craftiness upon every occasion, and his art of dissembling, I can hardly believe that I am still alive, and I wonder how I have escaped such a deep plotter of mischief. However, since some fate or other makes my house desolate, and perpetually raises up those that are dearest to me against me, I will, with tears, lament my hard fortune, and privately groan under my lonesome condition; yet am I resolved that no one who thirsts after my blood shall escape punishment, although the evidence should extend itself to all my sons."

3. (629) Upon Herod's saying this, he was interrupted by the confusion he was in; but ordered Nicolaus, one of his friends, to produce the evidence against Antipater. But in the mean time Antipater lifted up his head, (for he lay on the ground before his father's feet,) and cried out aloud, (630) "Thou, O father, hast made my apology for me; for how can I be a parricide, whom thou thyself confessest to have always had for thy guardian? Thou callest my filial affection prodigious lies and hypocrisy! how then could it be that I, who was so subtle in other matters, should here be so mad as not to understand that it was not easy that he who committed so horrid a crime should be concealed from men, but impossible that he should be concealed from the Judge of heaven, who sees all things, and is present everywhere? (631) or did not I know what end my brethren came to, on whom God inflicted so great a punishment for their evil designs against thee? And indeed what was there that could possibly provoke me against thee? Could the hope of being king do it? I was a king already. Could I suspect hatred from thee? No. Was not I beloved by thee? And what other fear could I have? Nay, by preserving thee safe, I was a terror to others. (632) Did I want money? No; for who was able to expend so much as myself? Indeed, father, had I been the most execrable of all mankind, and had I had the soul of the most cruel wild beast, must I not have been overcome with the benefits thou hadst bestowed upon me? whom, as thou thyself sayest, thou broughtest [into the palace]; whom thou didst prefer before so many of thy sons; whom thou madest a king in thine own lifetime, and, by the vast magnitude of the other advantages thou bestowedst on me, thou madest me an object of envy. (633) O miserable man! that thou shouldst undergo this bitter absence, and thereby afford a great opportunity for envy to arise against thee, and a long space for such as were laying designs against thee! Yet was I absent, father, on thy affairs, that Sylleus might not treat thee with contempt in thine old age. Rome is a witness to my filial affection, and so is Caesar, the ruler of the habitable earth, who oftentimes called me Philopater. Take here the letters he hath sent thee, they are more to be believed than the calumnies raised here; these letters are my only apology; these I use as the demonstration of that natural affection I have to thee. (634) Remember that it was against my own choice that I sailed [to Rome], as knowing the latent hatred that was in the kingdom against me. It was thou, O father, however unwillingly, who hast been my ruin, by forcing me to allow time for calumnies against me, and envy at me. However, I am come hither, and am ready to hear the evidence there is against me. If I be a parricide, I have passed by land and by sea, without suffering any misfortune on either of them: (635) but this method of trial is no advantage to me; for it seems, O father, that I am already condemned, both before God and before thee; and as I am already condemned, I beg that thou wilt not believe the others that have been tortured, but let fire be brought to torment me; let the racks march through my bowels; have no regard to any lamentations that this polluted body can make; for if I be a parricide, I ought not to die without torture." (636) Thus did Antipater cry out with lamentation and weeping, and moved all the rest, and Varus in particular, to commiserate his case. Herod was the only person whose passion was too strong to permit him to weep, as knowing that the testimonies against him were true.

4. (637) And now it was that, at the king's command, Nicolaus, when he had premised a great deal about the craftiness of Antipater, and had prevented the effects of their commiseration to him, afterwards brought in a bitter and large accusation against him, ascribing all the wickedness that had been in the kingdom to him, and especially the murder of his brethren; and demonstrated that they had perished by the calumnies he had raised against them. He also said that he had laid designs against them that were still alive, as if they were laying plots for the succession; and (said he) how can it be supposed that he who prepared poison for his father should abstain from mischief as to his brethren? (638) He then proceeded to convict him of the attempt to poison Herod, and gave an account in order of the several discoveries that had been made; and had great indignation as to the affair of Pheroras, because Antipater had been for making him murder his brother, and

had corrupted those that were dearest to the king, and filled the whole palace with wickedness; and when he had insisted on many other accusations, and the proofs for them, he left off.

5. (639) Then Varus bid Antipater make his defense; but he lay along in silence, and said no more but this, "God is my witness that I am entirely innocent." So Varus asked for the potion, and gave it to be drunk by a condemned malefactor, who was then in prison, who died upon the spot. (640) So Varus, when he had had a very private discourse with Herod, and had written an account of this assembly to Caesar, went away, after a day's stay. The king also bound Antipater, and sent away to inform Caesar of his misfortunes.

6. (641) Now after this it was discovered that Antipater had laid a plot against Salome also; for one of Antiphilus's domestic servants came, and brought letters from Rome, from a maid-servant of Julia, [Caesar's wife,] whose name was Acme. By her a message was sent to the king, that she had found a letter written by Salome, among Julia's papers, and had sent it to him privately, out of her good-will to him. (642) This letter of Salome contained the most bitter reproaches of the king, and the highest accusations against him. Antipater had forged this letter, and had corrupted Acme, and persuaded her to send it to Herod. (643) This was proved by her letter to Antipater, for thus did this woman write to him: "As thou desirest, I have written a letter to thy father, and have sent that letter, and am persuaded that the king will not spare his sister when he reads it. Thou wilt do well to remember what thou hast promised when all is accomplished."

7. (644) When this epistle was discovered, and what the epistle forged against Salome contained, a suspicion came into the king's mind, that perhaps the letters against Alexander were also forged: he was moreover greatly disturbed, and in a passion, because he had almost slain his sister on Antipater's account. He did no longer delay therefore to bring him to punishment for all his crimes; (645) yet when he was eagerly pursuing Antipater, he was restrained by a severe distemper he fell into. However, he sent all account to Caesar about Acme, and the contrivances against Salome; (646) he sent also for his testament, and altered it, and therein made Antipas king, as taking no care of Archelaus and Philip, because Antipater had blasted their reputations with him; but he bequeathed to Caesar, besides other presents that he gave him, a thousand talents; as also to his wife, and children, and friends, and freed-men about five hundred: he also bequeathed to all others a great quantity of land, and of money, and showed his respects to Salome his sister, by giving her most splendid gifts. And this was what was contained in his testament, as it was now altered.

CHAPTER 33.

THE GOLDEN EAGLE IS CUT TO PIECES. HEROD'S BARBARITY WHEN HE WAS READY TO DIE. HE ATTEMPTS TO KILL HIMSELF. HE COMMANDS ANTIPATER TO BE SLAIN. HE SURVIVES HIM FIVE DAYS AND THEN DIES.

1. (647) NOW Herod's distemper became more and more severe to him, and this because these his disorders fell upon him in his old age, and when he was in a melancholy condition; for he was already seventy years of age, and had been brought by the calamities that happened to him about his children, whereby he had no pleasure in life, even when he was in health; the grief also that Antipater was still alive aggravated his disease, whom he resolved to put to death now not at random, but as soon as he should be well again, and resolved to have him slain [in a public manner].

2. (648) There also now happened to him, among his other calamities, a certain popular sedition. There were two men of learning in the city [Jerusalem,] who were thought the most skillful in the laws of their country, and were on that account had in very great esteem all over the nation; they were, the one Judas, the son of Sepphoris, and the other Mattbias, the son of Margalus. (649) There was a great concourse of the young men to these men when they expounded the laws, and there got together every day a kind of an army of such as were growing up to be men. Now when these men were informed that the king was wearing away with melancholy, and with a distemper, they dropped words to their acquaintance, how it was now a very proper time to defend the cause of God, and to pull down what had been erected contrary to the laws of their country; (650) for it was unlawful there should be any such thing in the temple as images, or faces, or the like representation of any animal whatsoever. Now the king had put up a golden eagle over the great gate of the temple, which these learned men exhorted them to cut down; and told them, that if there should any danger arise, it was a glorious thing to die for the laws of their country; because that the soul was immortal, and that an eternal enjoyment of happiness did await such as died on that account; while the mean-spirited, and those that were not wise enough to show a right love of their souls, preferred a death by a disease, before that which is the result of a virtuous behavior.

3. (651) At the same time that these men made this speech to their disciples, a rumor was spread abroad that the king was dying, which made the young men set about the work with greater boldness; they therefore let themselves down from the top of the temple with thick cords, and this at midday, and while a great number of people were in the temple, and cut down that golden eagle with axes. (652) This was presently told to the king's captain of the temple, who came running with a great body of soldiers, and caught about forty of the young men, and brought them to the king. (653) And when he asked them, first of all, whether they had been so hardy as to cut down the golden eagle, they confessed they had done so; and when he asked them by whose command they had done it, they replied, at the command of the law of their country; and when he further asked them how they could be so joyful when they were to be put to death, they replied, because they should enjoy greater happiness after they were dead. **(cf. John 11:24)**

4. (654) At this the king was in such an extravagant passion, that he overcame his disease [for the time,] and went out, and spake to the people; wherein he made a terrible accusation against those men, as being guilty of sacrilege, and as making greater attempts under pretense of their law, and he thought they deserved to be punished as impious persons. (655) Whereupon the people were afraid lest a great number should be found guilty and desired that when he had first punished those that put them upon this work, and then those that were caught in it, he would leave off his anger as to the rest. With this the king complied, though not without difficulty, and ordered those that had let themselves down, together with their Rabbins, to be burnt alive, but delivered the rest that were caught to the proper officers, to be put to death by them.

5. (656) After this, the distemper seized upon his whole body, and greatly disordered all its parts with various symptoms; for there was a gentle fever upon him, and an intolerable itching over all the surface of his body, and continual pains in his colon, and dropsical turnouts about his feet, and an inflammation of the abdomen, and a putrefaction of his privy member, that produced worms. Besides which he had a difficulty of breathing upon him, and could not breathe but when he sat upright, and had a convulsion of all

The remains of Herodium. (photo Samuel Magal)

his members, insomuch that the diviners said those diseases were a punishment upon him for what he had done to the Rabbins. (657) Yet did he struggle with his numerous disorders, and still had a desire to live, and hoped for recovery, and considered of several methods of cure. Accordingly, he went over Jordan, and made use of those hot baths at Callirrhoe, which ran into the lake Asphaltitis, but are themselves sweet enough to be drunk. And here the physicians thought proper to bathe his whole body in warm oil, by letting it down into a large vessel full of oil; whereupon his eyes failed him, and he came and went as if he was dying; (658) and as a tumult was then made by his servants, at their voice he revived again. Yet did he after this despair of recovery, and gave orders that each soldier should have fifty drachmae a-piece, and that his commanders and friends should have great sums of money given them.

6. (659) He then returned back and came to Jericho, in such a melancholy state of body as almost threatened him with present death, when he proceeded to attempt a horrid wickedness; for he got together the most illustrious men of the whole Jewish nation, out of every village, into a place called the Hippodrome, and there shut them in. (660) He then called for his sister Salome, and her husband Alexas, and made this speech to them: "I know well enough that the Jews will keep a festival upon my death however, it is in my power to be mourned for on other accounts, and to have a splendid funeral, if you will but be subservient to my commands. Do you but take care to send soldiers to encompass these men that are now in custody, and slay them immediately upon my death, and then all Judea, and every family of them, will weep at it, whether they will or no."

7. (661) These were the commands he gave them; when there came letters from his ambassadors at Rome, whereby information was given that Acme was put to death at Caesar's command, and that Antipater was condemned to die; however, they wrote withal, that if Herod had a mind rather to banish him, Caesar permitted him so to do. (662) So he for a little while revived, and had a desire to live; but presently after he was overborne by his pains, and was disordered by want of food, and by a convulsive cough, and endeavored to prevent a natural, death; so he took an apple, and asked for a knife for he used to pare apples and eat them; he then looked round about to see that there was nobody to hinder him, and lift up his right hand as if he would stab himself; but Achiabus, his first cousin, came running to him, and held his hand, and hindered him from so doing; (663) on which occasion a very great lamentation was made in the palace, as if the king were expiring. As soon as ever Antipater heard that, he took courage, and with joy in his looks, besought his keepers, for a sum of money, to loose him and let him go; but the principal keeper of the prison did not only obstruct him in that his intention, but ran and told the king what his design was; (664) hereupon the king cried out louder than his distemper would well bear, and immediately sent some of his guards and slew Antipater; he also gave order to have him buried at Hyrcanium, and altered his testament again, and therein made Archelaus, his eldest son, and the brother of Antipas, his successor, and made Antipas tetrarch.

8. (665) So Herod, having survived the slaughter of his son five days, died, having reigned thirty-four years since he had caused Antigonus to be slain, and obtained his kingdom; but thirty-seven years since he had been made king by the Romans. (666) Now as for his fortune, it was prosperous in all other respects, if ever any other man could be so, since, from a private man, he obtained the kingdom, and kept it so long, and left it to his own sons; but still in his domestic affairs he was a most unfortunate man. Now, before the soldiers knew of his death, Salome and her husband came out and dismissed those that were in bonds, whom the king had commanded to be slain, and told them that he had altered his mind, and would have every one of them sent to their own homes. When these men were gone, Salome, told the soldiers [the king was dead], and got them and the rest of the multitude together to an assembly, in the amphitheater at Jericho, (667) where Ptolemy, who was intrusted by the king with his signet ring, came before them, and spake of the happiness the king had attained, and comforted the multitude, and read the epistle which had been left for the soldiers, wherein he earnestly exhorted them to bear good-will to his successor; (668) and after he had read the epistle, he opened and read his testament, wherein Philip was to inherit Trachonitis, and the neighboring countries, and Antipas was to be tetrarch, as we said before, and Archelaus was made king. (669) He had also been commanded to carry Herod's ring to Caesar, and the settlements he had made, sealed up, because Caesar was to be lord of all the settlements he had made, and was to confirm his testament; and he ordered that the dispositions he had made were to be kept as they were in his former testament.

9. (670) So there was an acclamation made to Archelaus, to congratulate him upon his advancement; and the soldiers, with the multitude, went round about in troops, and promised him their good-will, and besides, prayed God to bless his government. After this, they betook themselves to prepare for the king's funeral; (671) and Archelaus omitted nothing of magnificence therein, but brought out all the royal ornaments to augment the pomp of the deceased. There was a bier all of gold, embroidered with precious stones, and a purple bed of various contexture, with the dead body upon it, covered with purple; and a diadem was put upon his head, and a crown of gold above it, and a sceptre in his right hand; (672) and near to the bier were Herod's sons, and a multitude of his kindred; next to which came his guards, and the regiment of Thracians, the Germans, also and Gauls, all accounted as if they were going to war; (673) but the rest of the army went foremost, armed, and following their captains and officers in a regular manner; after whom five hundred of his domestic servants and freedmen followed, with sweet spices in their hands: and the body was carried two hundred furlongs, to Herodium, where he had given order to be buried. And this shall suffice for the conclusion of the life of Herod.

BOOK II

FROM THE DEATH OF HEROD TILL VESPASIAN WAS SENT TO SUBDUE THE JEWS BY NERO

CHAPTER 1.

ARCHELAUS MAKES A FUNERAL FEAST FOR THE PEOPLE, ON THE ACCOUNT OF HEROD. AFTER WHICH A GREAT TUMULT IS RAISED BY THE MULTITUDE AND HE SENDS THE SOLDIERS OUT UPON THEM, WHO DESTROY ABOUT THREE THOUSAND OF THEM.

1. (1) NOW the necessity which Archelaus was under of taking a journey to Rome was the occasion of new disturbances; for when he had mourned for his father seven days, (cf. Deuteronomy 26:14; Ezekiel 24:17; Jeremiah 16:7) and had given a very expensive funeral feast to the multitude, (which custom is the occasion of poverty to many of the Jews, because they are forced to feast the multitude; for if any one omits it, he is not esteemed a holy person,) he put on a white garment, and went up to the temple, (2) where the people accosted him with various acclamations. He also spake kindly to the multitude from an elevated seat and a throne of gold, and returned them thanks for the zeal they had shown about his father's funeral, and the submission they had made to him, as if he were already settled in the kingdom; but he told them withal, that he would not at present take upon him either the authority of a king, or the names thereto belonging, until Caesar, who is made lord of this whole affair by the testament, confirm the succession; (3) for that when the soldiers would have set the diadem on his head at Jericho, he would not accept of it; but that he would make abundant requitals, not to the soldiers only, but to the people, for their alacrity and good-will to him, when the superior lords [the Romans] should have given him a complete title to the kingdom; for that it should be his study to appear in all things better than his father.

2. (4) Upon this the multitude were pleased, and presently made a trial of what he intended, by asking great things of him; for some made a clamor that he would ease them in their taxes; others, that he would take off the duties upon commodities; and some, that he would loose those that were in prison; in all which cases he answered readily to their satisfaction, in order to get the good-will of the multitude; after which he offered [the proper] sacrifices, and feasted with his friends. (5) And here it was that a great many of those that desired innovations came in crowds towards the evening, and began then to mourn on their own account, when the public mourning for the king was over. These lamented those that were put to death by Herod, because they had cut down the golden eagle that had been over the gate of the temple. (6) Nor was this mourning of a private nature, but the lamentations were very great, the mourning solemn, and the weeping such as was loudly heard all over the city, as being for those men who had perished for the laws of their country, and for the temple. (7) They cried out that a punishment ought to be inflicted for these men upon those that were honored by Herod; and that, in the first place, the man whom he had made high priest should be deprived; and that it was fit to choose a person of greater piety and purity than he was.

3. (8) At these clamors Archelaus was provoked, but restrained himself from taking vengeance on the authors, on account of the haste he was in of going to Rome, as fearing lest, upon his making war on the multitude, such an action might detain him at home. Accordingly, he made trial to quiet the innovators by persuasion, rather than by force, and sent his general in a private way to them, and by him exhorted them to be quiet. (9) But the seditious threw stones at him, and drove him away, as he came into the temple, and before he could say any thing to them. The like treatment they showed to others, who came to them after him, many of which were sent by Archelaus, in order to reduce them to sobriety, and these answered still on all occasions after a passionate manner; and it openly appeared that they would not be quiet, if their numbers were but considerable. (10) And indeed, at the feast of unleavened bread, which was now at hand, and is by the Jews called the Passover, and used to be celebrated with a great number of sacrifices, an innumerable multitude of the people came out of the country to worship; some of these stood in the temple bewailing the Rabbins [that had been put to death], and procured their sustenance by begging, in order to support their sedition. (11) At this Archelaus was aftrighted, and privately sent a tribune, with his cohort of soldiers, upon them, before the disease should spread over the whole multitude, and gave orders that they should constrain those that began the tumult, by force, to be quiet. At these the whole multitude were irritated, and threw stones at many of the soldiers, and killed them; but the tribune fled away wounded, and had much ado to escape so. (12) After which they betook themselves to their sacrifices, as if they had done no mischief; nor did it appear to Archelaus that the multitude could be restrained without bloodshed; so he sent his whole army upon them, the footmen in great multitudes, by the way of the city, and the horsemen by the way of the plain, (13) who, falling upon them on the sudden, as they were

The temple facade, from M. Avi-Yonah's Second Temple model of Jerusalem, now on display at The Israel Museum. (photo Samuel Magal)

offering their sacrifices, destroyed about three thousand of them; but the rest of the multitude were dispersed upon the adjoining mountains: these were followed by Archelaus's heralds, who commanded every one to retire to their own homes, whither they all went, and left the festival.

CHAPTER 2.

ARCHELAUS GOES TO ROME WITH A GREAT NUMBER OF HIS KINDRED. HE IS THERE ACCUSED BEFORE CAESAR BY ANTIPATER; BUT IS SUPERIOR TO HIS ACCUSERS IN JUDGMENT BY THE MEANS OF THAT DEFENSE WHICH NICOLAUS MADE FOR HIM.

1. (14) ARCHELAUS went down now to the sea-side, with his mother and his friends, Poplas, and Ptolemy, and Nicolaus, and left behind him Philip, to be his steward in the palace, and to take care of his domestic affairs. (15) Salome went also along with him with her sons, as did also the king's brethren and sons-in-law. These, in appearance, went to give him all the assistance they were able, in order to secure his succession, but in reality to accuse him for his breach of the laws by what he had done at the temple.

2. (16) But as they were come to Cesarea, Sabinus, the procurator of Syria, met them; he was going up to Judea, to secure Herod's effects; but Varus, [president of Syria,] who was come thither, restrained him from going any farther. This Varus Archelaus had sent for, by the earnest entreaty of Ptolemy. (17) At this time, indeed, Sabinus, to gratify Varus, neither went to the citadels, nor did he shut up the treasuries where his father's money was laid up, but promised that he would lie still, until Caesar should have taken cognizance of the affair. So he abode at Cesarea; (18) but as soon as those that were his hinderance were gone, when Varus was gone to Antioch, and Archelaus was sailed to Rome, he immediately went on to Jerusalem, and seized upon the palace. And when he had called for the governors of the citadels, and the stewards [of the king's private affairs], he tried to sift out the accounts of the money, and to take possession of the citadels. (19) But the governors of those citadels were not unmindful of the commands laid upon them by Archelaus, and continued to guard them, and said the custody of them rather belonged to Caesar than to Archelaus.

3. (20) In the meantime, Antipas went also to Rome, to strive for the kingdom, and to insist that the former testament, wherein he was named to be king, was valid before the latter testament. Salome had also promised to assist him, as had many of Archelaus's kindred, who sailed along with Archelaus himself also. (21) He also carried along with him his mother, and Ptolemy, the brother of Nicolaus, who seemed one of great weight, on account of the great trust Herod put in him, he having been one of his most honored friends. However, Antipas depended chiefly upon Ireneus, the orator; upon whose authority he had rejected such as advised him to yield to Archelaus, because he was his elder brother, and because the second testament gave the kingdom to him. (22) The inclinations also of all Archelaus's kindred, who hated him, were removed to Antipas, when they came to Rome; although in the first place every one rather desired to live under their own laws [without a king], and to be under a Roman governor; but if they should fail in that point, these desired that Antipas might be their king.

4. (23) Sabinus did also afford these his assistance to the same purpose by letters he sent, wherein he accused Archelaus before Caesar, and highly commended Antipas. (24) Salome also, and those with her, put the crimes which they accused Archelaus of in order, and put them into Caesar's hands; and after they had done that,

Coins of Archelaus (left) and Antipas. (Carta archives)

Archelaus wrote down the reasons of his claim, and, by Ptolemy, sent in his father's ring, and his father's accounts. (25) And when Caesar had maturely weighed by himself what both had to allege for themselves, as also had considered of the great burden of the kingdom, and largeness of the revenues, and withal the number of the children Herod had left behind him, and had moreover read the letters he had received from Varus and Sabinus on this occasion, he assembled the principal persons among the Romans together, (in which assembly Caius, the son of Agrippa, and his daughter Julias, but by himself adopted for his own son, sat in the first seat,) and gave the pleaders leave to speak.

5. (26) Then stood up Salome's son, Antipater, (who of all Archelaus's antagonists was the shrewdest pleader,) and accused him in the following speech: That Archelaus did in words contend for the kingdom, but that in deeds he had long exercised royal authority, and so did but insult Caesar in desiring to be now heard on that account, since he had not staid for his determination about the succession, (27) and since he had suborned certain persons, after Herod's death, to move for putting the diadem upon his head; since he had set himself down in the throne, and given answers as a king, and altered the disposition of the army, and granted to some higher dignities; (28) that he had also complied in all things with the people in the requests they had made to him as to their king, and had also dismissed those that had been put into bonds by his father for most important reasons. Now, after all this, he desires the shadow of that royal authority, whose substance he had already seized to himself, and so hath made Caesar lord, not of things, but of words. (29) He also reproached him further, that his mourning for his father was only pretended, while he put on a sad countenance in the day time, but drank to great excess in the night; from which behavior, he said, the late disturbance among the multitude came, while they had an indignation thereat. (30) And indeed the purport of his whole discourse was to aggravate Archelaus's crime in slaying such a multitude about the temple, which multitude came to the festival, but were barbarously slain in the midst of their own sacrifices; and he said there was such a vast number of dead bodies heaped together in the temple, as even a foreign war, that should come upon them [suddenly], before it was denounced, could not have heaped together. (31) And he added, that it was the foresight his father had of that his barbarity which made him never give him any hopes of the kingdom, but when his mind was more infirm than his body, and he was not able to reason soundly, and did not well know what was the character of that son, whom in his second testament he made his successor; and this was done by him at a time when he had no complaints to make of him whom he had named before, when he was sound in body, and when his mind was free from all passion. (32) That, however, if any one should suppose Herod's judgment, when he was sick, was superior to that at another time, yet

had Archelaus forfeited his kingdom by his own behavior, and those his actions, which were contrary to the law, and to its disadvantage. Or what sort of a king will this man be, when he hath obtained the government from Caesar, who hath slain so many before he hath obtained it!

6. (33) When Antipater had spoken largely to this purpose, and had produced a great number of Archelaus's kindred as witnesses, to prove every part of the accusation, he ended his discourse. (34) Then stood up Nicolaus to plead for Archelaus. He alleged that the slaughter in the temple could not be avoided; that those that were slain were become enemies not to Archelaus's kingdom, only, but to Caesar, who was to determine about him. (35) He also demonstrated that Archelaus's accusers had advised him to perpetrate other things of which he might have been accused. But he insisted that the latter testament should, for this reason, above all others, be esteemed valid, because Herod had therein appointed Caesar to be the person who should confirm the succession; (36) for he who showed such prudence as to recede from his own power, and yield it up to the lord of the world, cannot be supposed mistaken in his judgment about him that was to be his heir; and he that so well knew whom to choose for arbitrator of the succession could not be unacquainted with him whom he chose for his successor.

7. (37) When Nicolaus had gone through all he had to say, Archelaus came, and fell down before Caesar's knees, without any noise;—upon which he raised him up, after a very obliging manner, and declared that truly he was worthy to succeed his father. However, he still made no firm determination in his case; (38) but when he had dismissed those assessors that had been with him that day, he deliberated by himself about the allegations which he had heard, whether it were fit to constitute any of those named in the testaments for Herod's successor, or whether the government should be parted among all his posterity, and this because of the number of those that seemed to stand in need of support therefrom.

CHAPTER 3.

THE JEWS FIGHT A GREAT BATTLE WITH SABINUS'S SOLDIERS, AND A GREAT DESTRUCTION IS MADE AT JERUSALEM.

1. (39) NOW before Caesar had determined any thing about these affairs, Malthace, Archelaus's mother, fell sick and died. Letters also were brought out of Syria from Varus, about a revolt of the Jews. (40) This was foreseen by Varus, who accordingly, after Archelaus was sailed, went up to Jerusalem to restrain the promoters of the sedition, since it was manifest that the nation would not be at rest; so he left one of those legions which he brought with him out of Syria in the city, (41) and went himself to Antioch. But Sabinus came, after he was gone, and gave them an occasion of making innovations; for he compelled the keepers of the citadels to deliver them up to him, and made a bitter search after the king's money, as depending not only on the soldiers which were left by Varus, but on the multitude of his own servants, all which he armed and used as the instruments of his covetousness. (42) Now when that feast, which was observed after seven weeks, and which the Jews called Pentecost, (i.e. the 50th day,) was at hand, its name being taken from the number of the days [after the passover], the people got together, but not on account of the accustomed Divine worship, but of the indignation they had ['at the present state of affairs']. (43) Wherefore an immense multitude ran together, out of Galilee, and Idumea, and Jericho, and Perea, that was beyond Jordan; but the people that naturally belonged to Judea itself were above the rest, both in number, and in the alacrity of the men. (44) So they distributed themselves into three parts, and pitched their camps in three places; one at the north side of the temple, another at the south side, by the Hippodrome, and the third part were at the palace on the west. So they lay round about the Romans on every side, and besieged them.

2. (45) Now Sabinus was aftrighted, both at their multitude, and at their courage, and sent messengers to Varus continually, and besought him to come to his succor quickly; for that if he delayed, his legion would be cut to pieces. (46) As for Sabinus himself, he got up to the highest tower of the fortress, which was called Phasaelus; it is of the same name with Herod's brother, who was destroyed by the Parthians; and then he made signs to the soldiers of that legion to attack the enemy; for his astonishment was so great, that he durst not go down to his own men. (47) Hereupon the soldiers were prevailed upon, and leaped out into the temple, and fought a terrible battle with the Jews; in which, while there were none over their heads to distress them, they were too hard for them, by their skill, and the others' want of skill, in war; (48) but when once many of the Jews had gotten up to the top of the cloisters, and threw their darts downwards, upon the heads of the Romans, there were a great many of them destroyed. Nor was it easy to avenge themselves upon those that threw their weapons from on high, nor was it more easy for them to sustain those who came to fight them hand to hand.

3. (49) Since therefore the Romans were sorely afflicted by both these circumstances, they set fire to the cloisters, which were works to be admired, both on account of their magnitude and costliness. Whereupon those that were above them were presently encompassed with the flame, and many of them perished therein; as many of them also were destroyed by the enemy, who came suddenly upon them; some of them also threw themselves down from the walls backward, and some there were who, from the desperate condition they were in, prevented the fire, by killing themselves with their own swords; (50) but so many of them as crept out from the walls, and came upon the Romans, were easily mastered by them, by reason of the astonishment they were under; until at last some of the Jews being destroyed, and others dispersed by the terror they were in, the soldiers fell upon the

Scale model of the three Herodian towers: Phasaelus, Hippicus, and Mariamne, from left to right. (photo Berthold Werner, via Wikimedia Commons)

treasure of God, which w now deserted, and plundered about four hundred talents, of which sum Sabinus got together all that was not carried away by the soldiers.

4. (51) However, this destruction of the works [about the temple], and of the men, occasioned a much greater number, and those of a more warlike sort, to get together, to oppose the Romans. These encompassed the palace round, and threatened to deploy all that were in it, unless they went their ways quickly; for they promised that Sabinus should come to no harm, if he would go out with his legion. (52) There were also a great many of the king's party who deserted the Romans, and assisted the Jews; yet did the most warlike body of them all, who were three thousand of the men of Sebaste, go over to the Romans. Rufus also, and Gratus, their captains, did the same, (Gratus having the foot of the king's party under him, and Rufus the horse,) each of whom, even without the forces under them, were of great weight, on account of their strength and wisdom, which turn the scales in war. (53) Now the Jews in the siege, tried to break down walls of the fortress, and cried out to Sabinus and his party, that they should go their ways, and not prove a hinderance to them, now they hoped, after a long time, to recover that ancient liberty which their forefathers had enjoyed. (54) Sabinus indeed was well contented to get out of the danger he was in, but he distrusted the assurances the Jews gave him, and suspected such gentle treatment was but a bait laid as a snare for them: this consideration, together with the hopes he had of succor from Varus, made him bear the siege still longer.

CHAPTER 4.

HEROD'S VETERAN SOLDIERS BECOME TUMULTUOUS. THE ROBBERIES OF JUDAS. SIMON AND ATHRONOEUS TAKE THE NAME OF KING UPON THEM.

1. (55) AT this time there were great disturbances in the country, and that in many places; and the opportunity that now offered itself induced a great many to set up for kings. And indeed in Idumea two thousand of Herod's veteran soldiers got together, and armed and fought against those of the king's party; against whom Achiabus, the king's first cousin, fought, and that out of some of the places that were the most strongly fortified; but so as to avoid a direct conflict with them in the plains. (56) In Sepphoris also, a city of Galilee, there was one Judas (the son of that arch-robber Hezekias, who formerly overran the country, and had been subdued by king Herod); this man got no small multitude together, and brake open the place where the royal armor was laid up, and armed those about him, and attacked those that were so earnest to gain the dominion.

2. (57) In Perea also, Simon, one of the servants to the king, relying upon the handsome appearance and tallness of his body, put a diadem upon his own head also; he also went about with a company of robbers that he had gotten together, and burnt down the royal palace that was at Jericho, and many other costly edifices besides, and procured himself very easily spoils by rapine, as snatching them out of the fire. (58) And he had soon burnt down all the fine edifices, if Gratus, the captain of the foot of the king's party, had not taken the Trachonite archers, and the most warlike of Sebaste, and met the man. (59) His footmen were slain in the battle in abundance; Gratus also cut to pieces Simon himself, as he was flying along a strait valley, when he gave him an oblique stroke upon his neck, as he ran away, and brake it. The royal palaces that were near Jordan at Betharamptha were also burnt down by some other of the seditious that came out of Perea.

ROMAN JERICHO—PLAN

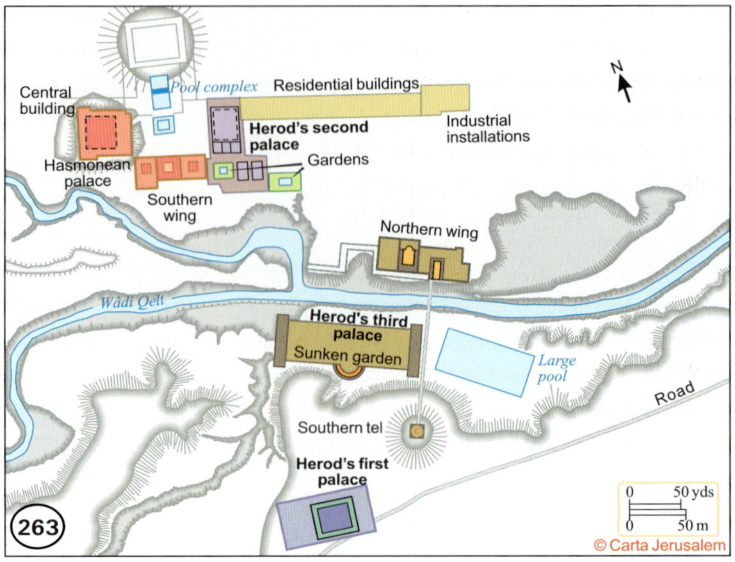

3. (60) At this time it was that a certain shepherd ventured to set himself up for a king; he was called Athrongeus. It was his strength of body that made him expect such a dignity, as well as his soul, which despised death; and besides these qualifications, he had four brethren like himself. (61) He put a troop of armed men under each of these his brethren, and made use of them as his generals and commanders, when he made his incursions, while he did himself act like a king, and meddled only with the more important affairs; (62) and at this time he put a diadem about his head, and continued after that to overrun the country for no little time with his brethren, and became their leader in killing both the Romans and those of the king's party; nor did any Jew escape him, if any gain could accrue to him thereby. (63) He once ventured to encompass a whole troop of Romans at Emmaus, who were carrying corn and weapons to their legion; his men therefore shot their arrows and darts, and thereby slew their centurion Arius, and forty of the stoutest of his men, while the rest of them, who were in danger of the same fate, upon the coming of Gratus, with those of Sebaste, to their assistance, escaped. (64) And when these men had thus served both their own countrymen and foreigners, and that through this whole war, three of them were, after some time, subdued; the eldest by Archelaus, the two next by falling into the hands of Gratus and Ptolemeus; but the fourth delivered himself up to Archelaus, upon his giving him his right hand for his security. (65) However, this their end was not till afterward, while at present they filled all Judea with a piratic war.

CHAPTER 5.

VARUS COMPOSES THE TUMULTS IN JUDEA AND CRUCIFIES ABOUT TWO THOUSAND OF THE SEDITIOUS.

1. (66) UPON Varus's reception of the letters that were written by Sabinus and the captains, he could not avoid being afraid for the whole legion [he had left there]. So he made haste to their relief, (67) and took with him the other two legions, with the four troops of horsemen to them belonging, and marched to Ptolemais; having given orders for the auxiliaries that were sent by the kings and governors of cities to meet him there. Moreover, he received from the people of Berytus, as he passed through their city, fifteen hundred armed men. (68) Now as soon as the other body of auxiliaries were come to Ptolemais, as well as Aretas the Arabian, (who, out of the hatred he bore to Herod, brought a great army of horse and foot,) Varus sent a part of his army presently to Galilee, which lay

near to Ptolemais, and Caius, one of his friends, for their captain. This Caius put those that met him to flight, and took the city Sepphoris, and burnt it, and made slaves of its inhabitants; (69) but as for Varus himself, he marched to Samaria with his whole army, where he did not meddle with the city itself, because he found that it had made no commotion during these troubles, but pitched his camp about a certain village which was called Aras. It belonged to Ptolemy, and on that account was plundered by the Arabians, who were very angry even at Herod's friends also. (70) He thence marched on to the village Sampho, another fortified place, which they plundered, as they had done the other. As they carried off all the money they lighted upon belonging to the public revenues, all was now full of fire and bloodshed, and nothing could resist the plunders of the Arabians. (71) Emmaus was also burnt, upon the flight of its inhabitants, and this at the command of Varus, out of his rage at the slaughter of those that were about Arias.

2. (72) Thence he marched on to Jerusalem, and as soon as he was but seen by the Jews, he made their camps disperse themselves; (73) they also went away, and fled up and down the country. But the citizens received him, and cleared themselves of having any hand in this revolt, and said that they had raised no commotions, but had only been forced to admit the multitude, because of the festival, and that they were rather besieged together with the Romans, than assisted those that had revolted. (74) There had before this met him Joseph, the first cousin of Archelaus, and Gratus, together with Rufus, who led those of Sebaste, as well as the king's army: there also met him those of the Roman legion, armed after their accustomed manner; for as to Sabinus, he durst not come into Varus's sight, but was gone out of the city before this, to the sea-side. (75) But Varus sent a part of his army into the country, against those that had been the authors of this commotion, and as they caught great numbers of them, those that appeared to have been the least concerned in these tumults he put into custody, but such as were the most guilty he crucified; these were in number about two thousand.

3. (76) He was also informed that there continued in Idumea ten thousand men still in arms; but when he found that the Arabians did not act like auxiliaries, but managed the war according to their own passions, and did mischief to the country otherwise than he intended, and this out of their hatred to Herod, he sent them away, but made haste, with his own legions, to march against those that had revolted; (77) but these, by the advice of Achiabus, delivered themselves up to him before it came to a battle. Then did Varus forgive the multitude their offenses, but sent their captains to Caesar to be examined by him. (78) Now Caesar forgave the rest, but gave orders that certain of the king's relations (for some of those that were among them were Herod's kinsmen) should be put to death, because they had engaged in a war against a king of their own family. (79) When therefore Varus had settled matters at Jerusalem after this manner, and had left the former legion there as a garrison, he returned to Antioch.

CHAPTER 6.

THE JEWS GREATLY COMPLAIN OF ARCHELAUS AND DESIRE THAT THEY MAY BE MADE SUBJECT TO ROMAN GOVERNORS. BUT WHEN CAESAR HAD HEARD WHAT THEY HAD TO SAY, HE DISTRIBUTED HEROD'S DOMINIONS AMONG HIS SONS ACCORDING TO HIS OWN PLEASURE.

1. (80) BUT now came another accusation from the Jews against Archelaus at Rome, which he was to answer to. It was made by those ambassadors who, before the revolt, had come, by Varus's permission, to plead for the liberty of their country; those that came were fifty in number, but there were more than eight thousand of the Jews at Rome who supported them. (81) And when Caesar had assembled a council of the principal Romans in Apollo's temple, that was in the palace, (this was what he had himself built and adorned, at a vast expense,) the multitude of the Jews stood with the ambassadors, and on the other side stood Archelaus, with his friends; (82) but as for the kindred of Archelaus, they stood on neither side; for to stand on Archelaus's side, their hatred to him, and envy at him, would not give them leave, while yet they were afraid to be seen by Caesar with his accusers. (83) Besides these, there were present Archelaus's brother Philip, being sent thither beforehand, out of kindness by Varus, for two reasons: the one was this, that he might be assisting to Archelaus; and the other was this, that in case Caesar should make a distribution of what Herod possessed among his posterity, he might obtain some share of it.

2. (84) And now, upon the permission that was given the accusers to speak, they, in the first place, went over Herod's breaches of their law, and said that he was not a king, but the most barbarous of all tyrants, and that they had found him to be such by the sufferings they underwent from him; that when a very great number had been slain by him, those that were left had endured such miseries, that they called those that were dead happy men; (85) that he had not only tortured the bodies of his subjects, but entire cities, and had done much harm to the cities of his own country, while

Remains of the Temple of Apollo, Rome. (photo Jensens, via Wikimedia Commons)

THE DIVISION OF HEROD'S KINGDOM 4 B.C.–A.D. 6

he adorned those that belonged to foreigners; and he shed the blood of Jews, in order to do kindnesses to those people that were out of their bounds; (86) that he had filled the nation full of poverty, and of the greatest iniquity, instead of that happiness and those laws which they had anciently enjoyed; that, in short, the Jews had borne more calamities from Herod, in a few years, than had their forefathers during all that interval of time that had passed since they had come out of Babylon, and returned home, in the reign of Xerxes: (87) that, however, the nation was come to so low a condition, by being inured to hardships, that they submitted to his successor of their own accord, though he brought them into bitter slavery; (88) that accordingly they readily called Archelaus, though he was the son of so great a tyrant, king, after the decease of his father, and joined with him in mourning for the death of Herod, and in wishing him good success in that his succession; (89) while yet this Archelaus, lest he should be in danger of not being thought the genuine son of Herod, began his reign with the murder of three thousand citizens; as if he had a mind to offer so many bloody sacrifices to God for his government, and to fill the temple with the like number of dead bodies at that festival: (90) that, however, those that were left after so many miseries, had just reason to consider now at last the calamities they had undergone, and to oppose themselves, like soldiers in war, to receive those stripes upon their faces [but not upon their backs, as hitherto]. Whereupon they prayed that the Romans would have compassion upon the [poor] remains of Judea, and not expose what was left of them to such as barbarously tore them to pieces, (91) and that they would join their country to Syria, and administer the government by their own commanders, whereby it would [soon] be demonstrated that those who are now under the calumny of seditious persons, and lovers of war, know how to bear governors that are set over them, if they be but tolerable ones. (92) So the Jews concluded their accusation with this request. Then rose up Nicolaus, and confuted the accusations which were brought against the kings, and himself accused the Jewish nation, as hard to be ruled, and as naturally disobedient to kings. He also reproached all those kinsmen of Archelaus who had left him, and were gone over to his accusers.

3. (93) So Caesar, after he had heard both sides, dissolved the assembly for that time; but a few days afterward, he gave the one half of Herod's kingdom to Archelaus, by the name of Ethnarch, and promised to make him king also afterward, if he rendered himself worthy of that dignity. (94) But as to the other half, he divided it into two tetrarchies, and gave them to two other sons of Herod, the one of them to Philip, and the other to that Antipas who contested the kingdom with Archelaus. (95) Under this last was Perea and Galilee, with a revenue of two hundred talents; but Batanea, and Trachonitis, and Auranitis, and certain parts of Zeno's house about Jamnia, with a revenue of a hundred talents, were made subject to Philip; (96) while Idumea, and all Judea, and Samaria were parts of the ethnarchy of Archelaus, although Samaria was eased of one quarter of its taxes, out of regard to their not having revolted with the rest of the nation. (97) He also made subject to him the following cities, viz. Strato's Tower, and Sebaste, and Joppa, and Jerusalem; but as to the Grecian cities, Gaza, and Gadara, and Hippos, he cut them off from the kingdom, and added them to Syria. Now the revenue of the country that was given to Archelaus was four hundred talents. (98) Salome also, besides what the king had left her in his testaments, was now made mistress of Jamnia, and Ashdod, and Phasaelis. Caesar did moreover bestow upon her the royal palace of Ascalon; by all which she got together a revenue of sixty talents; but he put her house under the ethnarchy of Archelaus. (99) And for the rest of Herod's offspring, they received what was bequeathed to them in his testaments; but, besides that, Caesar granted to Herod's two virgin daughters five hundred thousand [drachmae] of silver, and gave them in marriage to the sons of Pheroras: (100) but after this family distribution, he gave between them what had been bequeathed to him by Herod, which was a thousand talents, reserving to himself only some inconsiderable presents, in honor of the deceased.

CHAPTER 7.

THE HISTORY OF THE SPURIOUS ALEXANDER. ARCHELAUS IS BANISHED AND GLAPHYRA DIES, AFTER WHAT WAS TO HAPPEN TO BOTH OF THEM HAD BEEN SHOWED THEM IN DREAMS.

1. (101) In the meantime, there was a man, who was by birth a Jew, but brought up at Sidon with one of the Roman freed-men, who falsely pretended, on account of the resemblance of their countenances, that he was that Alexander who was slain by Herod. This

man came to Rome, in hopes of not being detected. (102) He had one who was his assistant, of his own nation, and who knew all the affairs of the kingdom, and instructed him to say how those that were sent to kill him and Aristobulus had pity upon them, and stole them away, by putting bodies that were like theirs in their places. (103) This man deceived the Jews that were at Crete, and got a great deal of money of them for traveling in splendor; and thence sailed to Melos, where he was thought so certainly genuine, that he got a great deal more money, and prevailed with those that had treated him to sail along with him to Rome. (104) So he landed at Dicearchia, [Puteoli,] and got very large presents from the Jews who dwelt there, and was conducted by his father's friends as if he were a king; nay, the resemblance in his countenance procured him so much credit, that those who had seen Alexander, and had known him very well, would take their oaths that he was the very same person. (105) Accordingly, the whole body of the Jews that were at Rome ran out in crowds to see him, and an innumerable multitude there was which stood in the narrow places through which he was carried; for those of Melos were so far distracted, that they carried him in a sedan, and maintained a royal attendance for him at their own proper charges.

2. (106) But Caesar, who knew perfectly well the lineaments of Alexander's face, because he had been accused by Herod before him, discerned the fallacy in his countenance, even before he saw the man. However, he suffered the agreeable fame that went of him to have some weight with him, and sent Celadus, one who well knew Alexander, and ordered him to bring the young man to him. (107) But when Caesar saw him, he immediately discerned a difference in his countenance; and when he had discovered that his whole body was of a more robust texture, and like that of a slave, he understood the whole was a contrivance. (108) But the impudence of what he said greatly provoked him to be angry at him; for when he was asked about Aristobulus, he said that he was also preserved alive, and was left on purpose in Cyprus, for fear of treachery, because it would be harder for plotters to get them both into their power while they were separate. (109) Then did Caesar take him by himself privately, and said to him, "I will give thee thy life, if thou wilt discover who it was that persuaded thee to forge such stories." So he said that he would discover him, and followed Caesar, and pointed to that Jew who abused the resemblance of his face to get money; for that he had received more presents in every city than ever Alexander did when he was alive. (110) Caesar laughed at the contrivance, and put this spurious Alexander among his rowers, on account of the strength of his body, but ordered him that persuaded him to be put to death. But for the people of Melos, they had been sufficiently punished for their folly, by the expenses they had been at on his account.

3. (111) And now Archelaus took possession of his ethnarchy, and used not the Jews only, but the Samaritans also, barbarously; and this out of his resentment of their old quarrels with him. Whereupon they both of them sent ambassadors against him to Caesar; and in the ninth year of his government he was banished to Vienna, a city of Gaul, and his effects were put into Caesar's treasury. (112) But the report goes, that before he was sent for by Caesar, he seemed to see nine ears of corn, full and large, but devoured by oxen. When, therefore, he had sent for the diviners, and some of the Chaldeans, and inquired of them what they thought it portended; (113) and when one of them had one interpretation, and another had another, Simon, one of the sect of Essens, said that he thought the ears of corn denoted years, and the oxen denoted a mutation of things, because by their ploughing they made an alteration of the country. That therefore he should reign as many years as there were ears of corn; and after he had passed through various alterations of fortune, should die. Now five days after Archelaus had heard this interpretation he was called to his trial.

4. (114) I cannot also but think it worthy to be recorded what dream Glaphyra, the daughter of Archelaus, king of Cappadocia, had, who had at first been wife to Alexander, who was the brother of Archelaus, concerning whom we have been discoursing. This Alexander was the son of Herod the king, by whom he was put to death, as we have already related. (115) This Glaphyra was married, after his death, to Juba, king of Libya; and, after his death, was returned home, and lived a widow with her father. Then it was that Archelaus, the ethnarch, saw her, and fell so deeply in love with her, that he divorced Mariamne, who was then his wife, and married her. (116) When, therefore, she was come into Judea, and had been there for a little while, she thought she saw Alexander stand by her, and that he said to her; "Thy marriage with the king of Libya might have been sufficient for thee; but thou wast not contented with him, but art returned again to my family, to a third husband; and him, thou impudent woman, hast thou chosen for thine husband, who is my brother. However, I shall not overlook the injury thou hast offered me; I shall [soon] have thee again, whether thou wilt or no." Now Glaphyra hardly survived the narration of this dream of hers two days.

CHAPTER 8.

ARCHELAUS'S ETHNARCHY IS REDUCED INTO A [ROMAN] PROVINCE. THE SEDITION OF JUDAS OF GALILEE. THE THREE SECTS.

1. (117) AND now Archelaus's part of Judea was reduced into a province, and Coponius, one of the equestrian order among the Romans, was sent as a procurator, having the power of [life and] death put into his hands by Caesar. (118) Under his administration it was that a certain Galilean, whose name was Judas, prevailed with his countrymen to revolt, and said they were cowards if they would endure to pay a tax to the Romans and would after God submit to mortal men as their lords. This man was a teacher of a peculiar sect of his own, and was not at all like the rest of those their leaders.

2. (119) For there are three philosophical sects among the Jews. The followers of the first of which are the Pharisees; of the second, the Sadducees; and the third sect, which pretends to a severer discipline, are called Essens. These last are Jews by birth, and seem to have a greater affection for one another than the other sects have. (120) These Essens reject pleasures as an evil, but esteem continence, and the conquest over our passions, to be virtue. They neglect wedlock, but choose out other persons children, while they are pliable, and fit for learning, and esteem them to be of their kindred, and form them according to their own manners. (121) They do not absolutely deny the fitness of marriage, and the succession of mankind thereby continued; but they guard against the lascivious behavior of women, and are persuaded that none of them preserve their fidelity to one man.

3. (122) These men are despisers of riches, and so very communicative as raises our admiration. Nor is there any one to be found among them who hath more than another; for it is a law among them, that those who come to them must let what they have be common to the whole order,—insomuch that among them all there is no appearance of poverty, or excess of riches, but every one's possessions are intermingled with every other's possessions; and so there is, as it were, one patrimony among all the brethren.

Remains of the so-called Essene community at Khirbet Qumran. (photo Samuel Magal)

(123) They think that oil is a defilement; and if any one of them be anointed without his own approbation, it is wiped off his body; for they think to be sweaty is a good thing, as they do also to be clothed in white garments. They also have stewards appointed to take care of their common affairs, who every one of them have no separate business for any, but what is for the uses of them all.

4. (124) They have no one certain city, but many of them dwell in every city; and if any of their sect come from other places, what they have lies open for them, just as if it were their own; and they go in to such as they never knew before, as if they had been ever so long acquainted with them. (125) For which reason they carry nothing at all with them when they travel into remote parts, though still they take their weapons with them, for fear of thieves. Accordingly, there is, in every city where they live, one appointed particularly to take care of strangers, and to provide garments and other necessaries for them. (126) But the habit and management of their bodies is such as children use who are in fear of their masters. Nor do they allow of the change of or of shoes till be first torn to pieces, or worn out by time. (127) Nor do they either buy or sell any thing to one another; but every one of them gives what he hath to him that wanteth it, and receives from him again in lieu of it what may be convenient for himself; and although there be no requital made, they are fully allowed to take what they want of whomsoever they please.

5. (128) And as for their piety towards God, it is very extraordinary; for before sun-rising they speak not a word about profane matters, but put up certain prayers which they have received from their forefathers, as if they made a supplication for its rising. (129) After this every one of them are sent away by their curators, to exercise some of those arts wherein they are skilled, in which they labor with great diligence till the fifth hour. After which they assemble themselves together again into one place; and when they have clothed themselves in white veils, they then bathe their bodies in cold water. And after this purification is over, they every one meet together in an apartment of their own, into which it is not permitted to any of another sect to enter; while they go, after a pure manner, into the dining-room, as into a certain holy temple, (130) and quietly set themselves down; upon which the baker lays them loaves in order; the cook also brings a single plate of one sort of food, and sets it before every one of them; (131) but a priest says grace before meat; and it is unlawful for any one to taste of the food before grace be said. The same priest, when he hath dined, says grace again after meat; and when they begin, and when they end, they praise God, as he that bestows their food upon them; after which they lay aside their [white] garments, and betake themselves to their labors again till the evening; (132) then they return home to supper, after the same manner; and if there be any strangers there, they sit down with them. Nor is there ever any clamor or disturbance to pollute their house, but they give every one leave to speak in their turn; (133) which silence thus kept in their house appears to foreigners like some tremendous mystery; the cause of which is that perpetual sobriety they exercise, and the same settled measure of meat and drink that is allotted them, and that such as is abundantly sufficient for them.

6. (134) And truly, as for other things, they do nothing but according to the injunctions of their curators; only these two things are done among them at everyone's own free-will, which are to assist those that want it, and to show mercy; for they are permitted of their own accord to afford succor to such as deserve it, when they stand in need of it, and to bestow food on those that are in distress; but they cannot give any thing to their kindred without the curators. (135) They dispense their anger after a just manner, and restrain their passion. They are eminent for fidelity, and are the ministers of peace; whatsoever they say also is firmer than an oath; but swearing is avoided by them, and they esteem it worse than perjury (cf. Matthew 6:34; 23:16; James 5:12) for they say that he who cannot be believed without [swearing by] God is already condemned. (136) They also take great pains in studying the writings of the ancients, and choose out of them what is most for the advantage of their soul and body; and they inquire after such roots and medicinal stones as may cure their distempers.

7. (137) But now if any one hath a mind to come over to their sect, he is not immediately admitted, but he is prescribed the same method of living which they use for a year, while he continues excluded'; and they give him also a small hatchet, and the fore-mentioned girdle, and the white garment. (138) And when he hath given evidence, during that time, that he can observe their continence, he approaches nearer to their way of living, and is made a partaker of the waters of purification; yet is he not even now admitted to live with them; for after this demonstration of his fortitude, his temper is tried two more years; and if he appear to be worthy, they then admit him into their society. (139) And before he is allowed to touch their common food, he is obliged to take tremendous oaths, that, in the first place, he will exercise piety towards God, and then that he will observe justice towards men, and that he will do no harm to any one, either of his own accord, or by the command of others; that he will always hate the wicked, and be assistant to the righteous; (140) that he will ever show fidelity to all men, and especially to those in authority, because no one obtains the government without God's assistance; and that if he be in authority, he will at no time whatever abuse his authority, nor endeavor to outshine his subjects either in his garments, or any other finery; (141) that he will be perpetually a lover of truth, and propose to himself to reprove those that tell lies; that he will keep his hands clear from theft, and his soul from unlawful gains; and that he will neither conceal any thing from those of his own sect, nor discover any of their doctrines to others, no, not though anyone should compel him so to do at the hazard of his life. (142)

Moreover, he swears to communicate their doctrines to no one any otherwise than as he received them himself; that he will abstain from robbery, and will equally preserve the books belonging to their sect, and the names of the angels [or messengers]. These are the oaths by which they secure their proselytes to themselves.

8. (143) But for those that are caught in any heinous sins, they cast them out of their society; and he who is thus separated from them does often die after a miserable manner; for as he is bound by the oath he hath taken, and by the customs he hath been engaged in, he is not at liberty to partake of that food that he meets with elsewhere, but is forced to eat grass, and to famish his body with hunger, till he perish; (144) for which reason they receive many of them again when they are at their last gasp, out of compassion to them, as thinking the miseries they have endured till they came to the very brink of death to be a sufficient punishment for the sins they had been guilty of.

9. (145) But in the judgments they exercise they are most accurate and just, nor do they pass sentence by the votes of a court that is fewer than a hundred. And as to what is once determined by that number, it is unalterable. What they most of all honor, after God himself, is the name of their legislator [Moses], whom if any one blaspheme he is punished capitally. (146) They also think it a good thing to obey their elders, and the major part. Accordingly, if ten of them be sitting together, no one of them will speak while the other nine are against it. (147) They also avoid spitting in the midst of them, or on the right side. Moreover, they are stricter than any other of the Jews in resting from their labors on the seventh day; for they not only get their food ready the day before, that they may not be obliged to kindle a fire on that day, but they will not remove any vessel out of its place, nor go to stool thereon. (148) Nay, on other days they dig a small pit, a foot deep, with a paddle (which kind of hatchet is given them when they are first admitted among them); and covering themselves round with their garment, that they may not affront the Divine rays of light, they ease themselves into that pit, (149) after which they put the earth that was dug out again into the pit; and even this they do only in the more lonely places, which they choose out for this purpose; and although this easement of the body be natural, yet it is a rule with them to wash themselves after it, as if it were a defilement to them.

PLAN OF KHIRBET QUMRAN

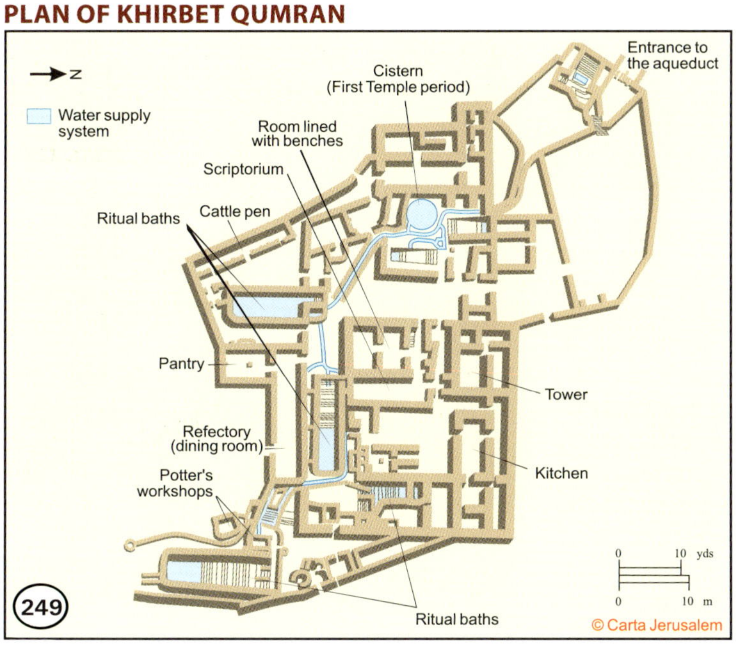

10. (150) Now after the time of their preparatory trial is over, they are parted into four classes; and so far are the juniors inferior to the seniors, that if the seniors should be touched by the juniors, they must wash themselves, as if they had intermixed themselves with the company of a foreigner. (151) They are long-lived also, insomuch that many of them live above a hundred years, by means of the simplicity of their diet; nay, as I think, by means of the regular course of life they observe also. They condemn the miseries of life, and are above pain, by the generosity of their mind. And as for death, if it will be for their glory, they esteem it better than living always; (152) and indeed our war with the Romans gave abundant evidence what great souls they had in their trials, wherein, although they were tortured and distorted, burnt and torn to pieces, and went through all kinds of instruments of torment, that they might be forced either to blaspheme their legislator, or to eat what was forbidden them, yet could they not be made to do either of them, no, nor once to flatter their tormentors, or to shed a tear; (153) but they smiled in their very pains, and laughed those to scorn who inflicted the torments upon them, and resigned up their souls with great alacrity, as expecting to receive them again.

11. (154) For their doctrine is this: That bodies are corruptible, and that the matter they are made of is not permanent; but that the souls are immortal, and continue for ever; and that they come out of the most subtile air, and are united to their bodies as to prisons, into which they are drawn by a certain natural enticement; (155) but that when they are set free from the bonds of the flesh, they then, as released from a long bondage, rejoice and mount upward. And this is like the opinions of the Greeks, that good souls have their habitations beyond the ocean, in a region that is neither oppressed with storms of rain or snow, or with intense heat, but that this place is such as is refreshed by the gentle breathing of a west wind, that is perpetually blowing from the ocean; while they allot to bad souls a dark and tempestuous den, full of never-ceasing punishments. (156) And indeed the Greeks seem to me to have followed the same notion, when they allot the islands of the blessed to their brave men, whom they call heroes and demi-gods; and to the souls of the wicked, the region of the ungodly, in Hades, where their fables relate that certain persons, such as Sisyphus, and Tantalus, and Ixion, and Tityus, are punished; which is built on this first supposition, that souls are immortal; and thence are those exhortations to virtue and dehortations from wickedness collected; (157) whereby good men are bettered in the conduct of their life by the hope they have of reward after their death; and whereby the vehement inclinations of bad men to vice are restrained, by the fear and expectation they are in, that although they should lie concealed in this life, they should suffer immortal punishment after their death. (158) These are the Divine doctrines of the Essens about the soul, which lay an unavoidable bait for such as have once had a taste of their philosophy.

12. (159) There are also those among them who undertake to foretell things to come, by reading the holy books, and using several sorts of purifications, and being perpetually conversant in the discourses of the prophets; and it is but seldom that they miss in their predictions.

13. (160) Moreover, there is another order of Essens, who agree with the rest as to their way of living, and customs, and laws, but differ from them in the point of marriage, as thinking that by not marrying they cut off the principal part of human life, which is the prospect of succession; nay, rather, that if all men should be of the same opinion, the whole race of mankind would fail. (161) Howev-

Site of Caesarea Philippi (modern Banias), with a view of the cave and niches overlooking the spring. (photo eigenes Foto, via Wikimedia Commons)

er, they try their spouses for three years; and if they find that they have their natural purgations thrice, as trials that they are likely to be fruitful, they then actually marry them. But they do not use to accompany with their wives when they are with child, as a demonstration that they do not many out of regard to pleasure, but for the sake of posterity. Now the women go into the baths with some of their garments on, as the men do with somewhat girded about them. And these are the customs of this order of Essens.

14. (162) But then as to the two other orders at first mentioned, the Pharisees are those who are esteemed most skillful in the exact explication of their laws, and introduce the first sect. These ascribe all to fate [or providence], and to God, (163) and yet allow, that to act what is right, or the contrary, is principally in the power of men, although fate does co-operate in every action. They say that all souls are incorruptible, but that the souls of good men only are removed into other bodies,—but that the souls of bad men are subject to eternal punishment. (164) But the Sadducees are those that compose the second order, and take away fate entirely, and suppose that God is not concerned in our doing or not doing what is evil; (165) and they say, that to act what is good, or what is evil, is at men's own choice, and that the one or the other belongs so to every one, that they may act as they please. They also take away the belief of the immortal duration of the soul, and the punishments and rewards in Hades. (166) Moreover, the Pharisees are friendly to one another, and are for the exercise of concord, and regard for the public; but the behavior of the Sadducees one towards another is in some degree wild, and their conversation with those that are of their own party is as barbarous as if they were strangers to them. And this is what I had to say concerning the philosophic sects among the Jews.

CHAPTER 9.

THE DEATH OF SALOME. THE CITIES WHICH HEROD AND PHILIP BUILT. PILATE OCCASIONS DISTURBANCES. TIBERIUS PUTS AGRIPPA INTO BONDS BUT CAIUS FREES HIM FROM THEM, AND MAKES HIM KING. HEROD ANTIPAS IS BANISHED.

1. (167) AND now as the ethnarchy of Archelaus was fallen into a Roman province, the other sons of Herod, Philip, and that Herod who was called Antipas, each of them took upon them the administration of their own tetrarchies; for when Salome died, she bequeathed to Julia, the wife of Augustus, both her toparchy, and Jamriga, as also her plantation of palm trees that were in Phasaelis. (168) But when the Roman empire was translated to Tiberius, the son of Julia, upon the death of Augustus, who had reigned fifty-seven years, six months, and two days, both Herod and Philip continued in their tetrarchies; and the latter of them built the city Cesarea [Philippi], at the fountains of Jordan, and in the region of Paneas; as also the city [Bethsaida-]Julias, in the lower Gaulonitis. Herod also built the city Tiberias in Galilee, and in Perea [beyond Jordan] another that was also called [Livias-]Julias.

2. (169) Now Pilate, who was sent as procurator into Judea by Tiberius, sent by night those images of Caesar that are called ensigns into Jerusalem. (170) This excited a very among great tumult among the Jews when it was day; for those that were near them were astonished at the sight of them, as indications that their laws were trodden under foot; for those laws do not permit any sort of image to be brought into the city. Nay, besides the indignation which the citizens had themselves at this procedure, a vast number of people came running out of the country. (171) These came zealously to Pilate to Cesarea, and besought him to carry those ensigns out of Jerusalem, and to preserve them their ancient laws inviolable; but upon Pilate's denial of their request, they fell down prostrate upon the ground, and continued immovable in that posture for five days and as many nights.

3. (172) On the next day Pilate sat upon his tribunal, in the open market-place, and called to him the multitude, as desirous to give them an answer; and then gave a signal to the soldiers, that they should all by agreement at once encompass the Jews with their weapons; (173) so the band of soldiers stood round about the Jews in three ranks. The Jews were under the utmost consternation at that unexpected sight. Pilate also said to them that they should be cut in pieces, unless they would admit of Caesar's images, and gave intimation to the soldiers to draw their naked swords. (174) Hereupon the Jews, as it were at one signal, fell down in vast numbers together, and exposed their necks bare, and cried out that they were sooner ready to be slain, than that their law should be transgressed. Hereupon Pilate was greatly surprised at their prodigious superstition, and gave order that the ensigns should be presently carried out of Jerusalem.

Tiberius Caesar. (photo R. Steven Notley)

4. (175) After this he raised another disturbance, by expending that sacred treasure which is called Corban (cf. Mark 7:11, 12) upon aqueducts, whereby he brought water from the distance of four hundred furlongs. At this the multitude had indignation; and when Pilate was come to Jerusalem, they came about his tribunal, and made a clamor at it. (176) Now when he was apprized aforehand of this disturbance, he mixed his own soldiers in their armor with the multitude, and ordered them to conceal themselves under the habits of private men, and not indeed to use their swords, but with their staves to beat those that made the clamor. He then gave the signal from his tribunal [to do as he had bidden them]. (177) Now the Jews were so sadly beaten, that many of them perished by the stripes they received, and many of them perished as trodden to death by themselves; by which means the multitude was astonished at the calamity of those that were slain, and held their peace.

5. (178) In the mean time Agrippa [I], the son of that Aristobulus [IV] who had been slain by his father Herod, came to Tiberius, to accuse Herod the tetrarch; who not admitting of his accusation, he staid at Rome, and cultivated a friendship with others of the men of note, but principally with Caius the son of Germanicus, who was then but a private person. (179) Now this Agrippa, at a certain time, feasted Caius; and as he was very complaisant to him on several other accounts, he at length stretched out his hands, and openly wished that Tiberius might die, and that he might quickly see him emperor of the world. (180) This was told to Tiberius by one of Agrippa's domestics, who thereupon was very angry, and ordered Agrippa to be bound, and had him very ill-treated in the prison for six months, until Tiberius died, after he had reigned twenty-two years, six months, and three days.

6. (181) But when Caius was made Caesar, he released Agrippa from his bonds, and made him king of Philip's tetrarchy, who was now dead; but when Agrippa had arrived at that degree of dignity, he inflamed the ambitious desires of Herod the tetrarch, (182) who was chiefly induced to hope for the royal authority by his wife Herodias, who reproached him for his sloth, and told him that it was only because he would not sail to Caesar that he was destitute of that great dignity; for since Caesar had made Agrippa a king, from a private person, much mole would he advance him from a tetrarch to that dignity. (183) These arguments prevailed with Herod, so that he came to Caius, by whom he was punished for his ambition, by being banished into Spain; for Agrippa followed him, in order to accuse him; to whom also Caius gave his tetrarchy, by way of addition. So Herod died in Spain, whither his wife had followed him.

CHAPTER 10.

CAIUS COMMANDS THAT HIS STATUE SHOULD BE SET UP IN THE TEMPLE ITSELF; AND WHAT PETRONIUS DID THEREUPON.

1. (184) NOW Caius Caesar did so grossly abuse the fortune he had arrived at, as to take himself to be a god, and to desire to be so called also, and to cut off those of the greatest nobility out of his country. He also extended his impiety as far as the Jews. (185) Accordingly, he sent Petronius with an army to Jerusalem, to place his statues in the temple, and commanded him that, in case the Jews would not admit of them, he should slay those that opposed it, and carry all the rest of the nation into captivity: (186) but God concerned himself with these his commands. However, Petronius marched out of Antioch into Judea, with three legions, and many Syrian auxiliaries. (187) Now as to the Jews, some of them could not

Caius, successor of Tiberius Caesar. (photo Siren-Com, via Wikimedia Commons)

believe the stories that spake of a war; but those that did believe them were in the utmost distress how to defend themselves, and the terror diffused itself presently through them all; for the army was already come to Ptolemais.

2. (188) This Ptolemais is a maritime city of Galilee, built in the great plain. It is encompassed with mountains: that on the east side, sixty furlongs off, belongs to Galilee; but that on the south belongs to Carmel, which is distant from it a hundred and twenty furlongs; and that on the north is the highest of them all, and is called by the people of the country, The Ladder of the Tyrians, which is at the distance of a hundred furlongs. (189) The very small river Belus runs by it, at the distance of two furlongs; near which there is Menmon's monument, and hath near it a place no larger than a hundred cubits, which deserves admiration; (190) for the place is round and hollow, and affords such sand as glass is made of; which place, when it hath been emptied by the many ships there loaded, it is filled again by the winds, which bring into it, as it were on purpose, that sand which lay remote, and was no more than bare common sand, while this mine presently turns it into glassy sand. (191) And what is to me still more wonderful, that glassy sand which is superfluous, and is once removed out of the place, becomes bare common sand again. And this is the nature of the place we are speaking of.

3. (192) But now the Jews got together in great numbers with their wives and children into that plain that was by Ptolemais, and made supplication to Petronius, first for their laws, and, in the next place, for themselves. So he was prevailed upon by the multitude of the supplicants, and by their supplications, and left his army and the statues at Ptolemais, (193) and then went forward into Galilee, and called together the multitude and all the men of note to Tiberias, and showed them the power of the Romans, and the threatenings of Caesar; and, besides this, proved that their petition was unreasonable, because (194) while all the nations in subjection to them had placed the images of Caesar in their several cities, among the rest of their gods, for them alone to oppose it, was almost like the behavior of revolters, and was injurious to Caesar.

4. (195) And when they insisted on their law, and the custom of their country, and how it was not only not permitted them to make either an image of God, or indeed of a man, and to put it in any despicable part of their country, much less in the temple itself, Petronius replied, "And am not I also," said he, "bound to keep the law of my own lord? For if I transgress it, and spare you, it is but

just that I perish; while he that sent me, and not I, will commence a war against you; for I am under command as well as you." (196) Hereupon the whole multitude cried out that they were ready to suffer for their law. Petronius then quieted them, and said to them, "Will you then make war against Caesar?" (197) The Jews said, "We offer sacrifices twice every day for Caesar, and for the Roman people;" but that if he would place the images among them, he must first sacrifice the whole Jewish nation; and that they were ready to expose themselves, together with their children and wives, to be slain. (198) At this Petronius was astonished, and pitied them, on account of the inexpressible sense of religion the men were under, and that courage of theirs which made them ready to die for it; so they were dismissed without success.

5. (199) But on the following days he got together the men of power privately, and the multitude publicly, and sometimes he used persuasions to them, and sometimes he gave them his advice; but he chiefly made use of threatenings to them, and insisted upon the power of the Romans, and the anger of Caius; and besides, upon the necessity he was himself under [to do as he was enjoined]. (200) But as they could be no way prevailed upon, and he saw that the country was in danger of lying without tillage; (for it was about seed time that the multitude continued for fifty days together idle;) so he at last got them together, (201) and told them that it was best for him to run some hazard himself; "for either, by the Divine assistance, I shall prevail with Caesar, and shall myself escape the danger as well as you, which will he matter of joy to us both; or, in case Caesar continue in his rage, I will be ready to expose my own life for such a great number as you are." Whereupon he dismissed the multitude, who prayed greatly for his prosperity; and he took the army out of Ptolemais, and returned to Antioch; (202) from whence he presently sent an epistle to Caesar, and informed him of the irruption he had made into Judea, and of the supplications of the nation; and that unless he had a mind to lose both the country and the men in it, he must permit them to keep their law, and must countermand his former injunction. (203) Caius answered that epistle in a violent-way, and threatened to have Petronius put to death for his being so tardy in the execution of what he had commanded. But it happened that those who brought Caius's epistle were tossed by a storm, and were detained on the sea for three months, while others that brought the news of Caius's death had a good voyage. Accordingly, Petronius received the epistle concerning Caius seven and twenty days before he received that which was against himself.

Bust of Emperor Claudius. (photo Marie-Lan Nguyen; Farnese Collection, Naples National Archaeological Museum)

Coin of Agrippa I. (Carta archives)

CHAPTER 11.

CONCERNING THE GOVERNMENT OF CLAUDIUS, AND THE REIGN OF AGRIPPA. CONCERNING THE DEATHS OF AGRIPPA AND OF HEROD AND WHAT CHILDREN THEY BOTH LEFT BEHIND THEM.

1. (204) NOW when Caius had reigned three years and eight months, and had been slain by treachery, Claudius was hurried away by the armies that were at Rome to take the government upon him; (205) but the senate, upon the reference of the consuls, Sentis Saturninus, and Pomponins Secundus, gave orders to the three regiments of soldiers that staid with them to keep the city quiet, and went up into the capitol in great numbers, and resolved to oppose Claudius by force, on account of the barbarous treatment they had met with from Caius; and they determined either to settle the nation under an aristocracy, as they had of old been governed, or at least to choose by vote such a one for emperor as might be worthy of it.

2. (206) Now it happened that at this time Agrippa sojourned at Rome, and that both the senate called him to consult with them, and at the same time Claudius sent for him out of the camp, that he might be serviceable to him, as he should have occasion for his service. So he, perceiving that Claudius was in effect made Caesar already, went to him, (207) who sent him as an ambassador to the senate, to let them know what his intentions were: that, in the first place, it was without his seeking that he was hurried away by the soldiers; moreover, that he thought it was not just to desert those soldiers in such their zeal for him, and that if he should do so, his own fortune would be in uncertainty; for that it was a dangerous case to have been once called to the empire. (208) He added further, that he would administer the government as a good prince, and not like a tyrant; for that he would be satisfied with the honor of being called emperor, but would, in every one of his actions, permit them all to give him their advice; for that although he had not been by nature for moderation, yet would the death of Caius afford him a sufficient demonstration how soberly he ought to act in that station.

3. (209) This message was delivered by Agrippa; to which the senate replied, that since they had an army, and the wisest counsels on their side, they would not endure a voluntary slavery. And when Claudius heard what answer the senate had made, he sent Agrippa to them again, with the following message: That he could not bear the thoughts of betraying them that had given their oaths to be true to him; and that he saw he must fight, though unwillingly, against such as he had no mind to fight; (210) that, however, [if it must come to that,] it was proper to choose a place without the city for the war, because it was not agreeable to piety to pollute the temples of their own city with the blood of their own countrymen, and this only on occasion of their imprudent conduct. And when Agrippa had heard this message, he delivered it to the senators.

4. (211) In the mean time, one of the soldiers belonging to the senate drew his sword, and cried out, "O my fellow soldiers, what is the meaning of this choice of ours, to kill our brethren, and to use violence to our kindred that are with Claudius? while we may have him for our emperor whom no one can blame, and who hath so many just reasons [to lay claim to the government]; and this with regard to those against whom we are going to fight." (212) When he had said this, he marched through the whole senate, and carried all the soldiers along with him. Upon which all the patricians were immediately in a great fright at their being thus deserted. But still, because there appeared no other way whither they could turn themselves for deliverance, they made haste the same way with the soldiers, and went to Claudius. (213) But those that had the greatest luck in flattering the good fortune of Claudius betimes met them before the walls with their naked swords, and there was reason to fear that those that came first might have been in danger, before Claudius could know what violence the soldiers were going to offer them, had not Agrippa ran before, and told him what a dangerous thing they were going about, and that unless he restrained the violence of these men, who were in a fit of madness against the patricians, he would lose those on whose account it was most desirable to rule, and would be emperor over a desert.

5. (214) When Claudius heard this, he restrained the violence of the soldiery, and received the senate into the camp, and treated them after an obliging manner, and went out with them presently to offer their thank-offerings to God, which were proper upon, his first coming to the empire. (215) Moreover, he bestowed on Agrippa his whole paternal kingdom immediately, and added to it, besides those countries that had been given by Augustus to Herod, Trachonitis and Auranitis, and still besides these, that kingdom which was called the kingdom of Lysanius. (216) This gift he declared to the people by a decree, but ordered the magistrates to have the donation engraved on tables of brass, and to be set up in the capitol. (217) He bestowed on his brother Herod, who was also his son-in-law, by marrying [his daughter] Bernice, the kingdom of Chalcis.

6. (218) So now riches flowed in to Agrippa by his enjoyment of so large a dominion; nor did he abuse the money he had on small matters, but he began to encompass Jerusalem with such a wall, which, had it been brought to perfection, had made it impracticable for the Romans to take it by siege; (219) but his death, which happened at Cesarea, before he had raised the walls to their due height, prevented him. He had then reigned three years, as he had governed his tetrarchies three other years. (220) He left behind him three daughters, born to him by Cypros, Bernice, Mariamne, and Drusilla, and a son born of the same mother, whose name was Agrippa [II]: he was left a very young child, so that Claudius made the country a Roman province, and sent Cuspius Fadus to be its procurator, and after him Tiberius Alexander, who, making no alterations of the ancient laws, kept the nation in tranquillity. (221) Now after this, Herod the king of Chalcis died, and left behind him two sons, born to him of his brother's daughter Bernice; their names were Bernie Janus and Hyrcanus. [He also left behind him] Aristobulus, whom he had by his former wife Mariamne. There was besides another brother of his that died a private person, his name was also Aristobulus, who left behind him a daughter, whose name was Jotape: (222) and these, as I have formerly said, were the children of Aristobulus [IV] the son of Herod, which Aristobulus and Alexander were born to Herod by Mariamne [I], and were slain by him. But as for Alexander's posterity, they reigned in Armenia.

THE KINGDOM OF AGRIPPA I A.D. 37–44

CHAPTER 12.

MANY TUMULTS UNDER CUMANUS, WHICH WERE COMPOSED BY QUADRATUS. FELIX IS PROCURATOR OF JUDEA. AGRIPPA IS ADVANCED FROM CHALCIS TO A GREATER KINGDOM.

1. (223) NOW after the death of Herod, king of Chalcis, Claudius set Agrippa, the son of Agrippa, over his uncle's kingdom, while Cumanus took upon him the office of procurator of the rest, which was a Roman province, and therein he succeeded [Tiberius] Alexander; under which Cureanus began the troubles, and the Jews' ruin came on; (224) for when the multitude were come together to Jerusalem, to the feast of unleavened bread, and a Roman cohort stood over the cloisters of the temple, (for they always were armed, and kept guard at the festivals, to prevent any innovation which the multitude thus gathered together might make,) one of the soldiers pulled back his garment, and cowering down after an indecent manner, turned his breech to the Jews, and spake such words as you might expect upon such a posture. (225) At

Coin of Agrippa II.
(Carta archives)

this the whole multitude had indignation, and made a clamor to Cumanus, that he would punish the soldier; while the rasher part of the youth, and such as were naturally the most tumultuous, fell to fighting, and caught up stones, and threw them at the soldiers. (226) Upon which Cumanus was afraid lest all the people should make an assault upon him, and sent to call for more armed men, who, when they came in great numbers into the cloisters, the Jews were in a very great consternation; and being beaten out of the temple, they ran into the city; (227) and the violence with which they crowded to get out was so great, that they trod upon each other, and squeezed one another, till ten thousand of them were killed, insomuch that this feast became the cause of mourning to the whole nation, and every family lamented their own relations.

2. (228) Now there followed after this another calamity, which arose from a tumult made by robbers; for at the public road at Bethhoron, one Stephen, a servant of Caesar, carried some furniture, which the robbers fell upon and seized. (229) Upon this Cureanus sent men to go round about to the neighboring villages, and to bring their inhabitants to him bound, as laying it to their charge that they had not pursued after the thieves, and caught them. Now here it was that a certain soldier, finding the sacred book of the law, tore it to pieces, and threw it into the fire. (230) Hereupon the Jews were in great disorder, as if their whole country were in a flame, and assembled themselves so many of them by their zeal for their religion, as by an engine, and ran together with united clamor to Cesarea, to Cumanus, and made supplication to him that he would not overlook this man, who had offered such an affront to God, and to his law; but punish him for what he had done. (231) Accordingly, he, perceiving that the multitude would not be quiet unless they had a comfortable answer from him, gave order that the soldier should be brought, and drawn through those that required to have him punished, to execution, which being done, the Jews went their ways.

3. (232) After this there happened a fight between the Galileans and the Samaritans; it happened at a village called Geman, which is situated in the great plain of Samaria; where, as a great number of Jews were going up to Jerusalem to the feast [of tabernacles,] a certain Galilean was slain; (233) and besides, a vast number of people ran together out of Galilee, in order to fight with the Samaritans. But the principal men among them came to Cumanus, and besought him that, before the evil became incurable, he would come into Galilee, and bring the authors of this murder to punishment; for that there was no other way to make the multitude separate without coming to blows. However, Cumanus postponed their supplications to the other affairs he was then about, and sent the petitioners away without success.

4. (234) But when the affair of this murder came to be told at Jerusalem, it put the multitude into disorder, and they left the feast; and without any generals to conduct them, they marched with great violence to Samaria; nor would they be ruled by any of the magistrates that were set over them, (235) but they were managed by one Eleazar, the son of Dineus, and by Alexander, in these their thievish and seditious attempts. These men fell upon those that were ill the neighborhood of the Acrabatene toparchy, and slew them, without sparing any age, and set the villages on fire.

5. (236) But Cumanus took one troop of horsemen, called the troop of Sebaste, out of Cesarea, and came to the assistance of those that were spoiled; he also seized upon a great number of those that followed Eleazar, and slew more of them. (237) And as for the rest of the multitude of those that went so zealously to fight with the Samaritans, the rulers of Jerusalem ran out clothed with sackcloth, and having ashes on their head, and begged of them to go their ways, lest by their attempt to revenge themselves upon the Samaritans they should provoke the Romans to come against Jerusalem; to have compassion upon their country and temple, their children and their wives, and not bring the utmost dangers of destruction upon them, in order to avenge themselves upon one Galilean only. (238) The Jews complied with these persuasions of theirs, and dispersed themselves; but still there were a great number who betook themselves to robbing, in hopes of impunity; and rapines and insurrections of the bolder sort happened over the

THE KINGDOM OF AGRIPPA II A.D. 44–46

whole country. (239) And the men of power among the Samaritans came to Tyre, to Ummidius Quadratus, the president of Syria, and desired that they that had laid waste the country might be punished: (240) the great men also of the Jews, and Jonathan the son of Ananus the high priest, came thither, and said that the Samaritans were the beginners of the disturbance, on account of that murder they had committed; and that Cumanus had given occasion to what had happened, by his unwillingness to punish the original authors of that murder.

6. (241) But Quadratus put both parties off for that time, and told them, that when he should come to those places, he would make a diligent inquiry after every circumstance. After which he went to Cesarea, and crucified all those whom Cumanus had taken alive; (242) and when from thence he was come to the city Lydda, he heard the affair of the Samaritans, and sent for eighteen of the Jews, whom he had learned to have been concerned in that fight, and beheaded them; (243) but he sent two others of those that were of the greatest power among them, and both Jonathan and Ananias, the high priests, as also Artanus the son of this Ananias, and certain others that were eminent among the Jews, to Caesar; as he did in like manner by the most illustrious of the Samaritans. (244) He also ordered that Cureanus [the procurator] and Celer the tribune should sail to Rome, in order to give an account of what had been done to Caesar. When he had finished these matters, he went up from Lydda to Jerusalem, and finding the multitude celebrating their feast of unleavened bread without any tumult, he returned to Antioch.

7. (245) Now when Caesar at Rome had heard what Cumanus and the Samaritans had to say, (where it was done in the hearing of Agrippa, who zealously espoused the cause of the Jews, as in like manner many of the great men stood by Cumanus,) he condemned the Samaritans, and commanded that three of the most powerful men among them should be put to death; he banished Cumanus, (246) and sent Celer bound to Jerusalem, to be delivered over to the Jews to be tormented; that he should be drawn round the city, and then beheaded.

8. (247) After this Caesar sent Felix, (cf. Acts 24:5) the brother of Pallas, to be procurator of Galilee, and Samaria, and Perea, and removed Agrippa from Chalcis unto a greater kingdom; for he gave him the tetrarchy which had belonged to Philip, which contained Batanea, Trachonitis, and Gaulonitis: he added to it the kingdom of Lysanius, and that province [Abilene] which Varus had governed. (248) But Claudius himself, when he had administered the government thirteen years, eight months, and twenty days, died, and left Nero to be his successor in the empire, whom he had adopted by his wife Agrippina's delusions, in order to be his successor, although he had a son of his own, whose name was Britannicus, by Messalina his former wife, and a daughter whose name was Octavia, (249) whom he had married to Nero; he had also another daughter by Petina, whose name was Antonia.

CHAPTER 13.

NERO ADDS FOUR CITIES TO AGRIPPA'S KINGDOM; BUT THE OTHER PARTS OF JUDEA WERE UNDER FELIX. THE DISTURBANCES WHICH WERE RAISED BY THE SICARII THE MAGICIANS AND AN EGYPTIAN FALSE PROPHET. THE JEWS AND SYRIANS HAVE A CONTEST AT CESAREA.

1. (250) NOW as to the many things in which Nero acted like a madman, out of the extravagant degree of the felicity and riches

Nero, from the Augustan area on the Palatine Hill. (photo Jastrow, via Wikimedia Commons)

which he enjoyed, and by that means used his good fortune to the injury of others; and after what manner he slew his brother, and wife, and mother, from whom his barbarity spread itself to others that were most nearly related to him; (251) and how, at last, he was so distracted that he became an actor in the scenes, and upon the theater,—I omit to say any more about them, because there are writers enough upon those subjects every where; but I shall turn myself to those actions of his time in which the Jews were concerned.

2. (252) Nero therefore bestowed the kingdom of the Lesser Armenia upon Aristobulus, Herod's son, and he added to Agrippa's kingdom four cities, with the toparchies to them belonging; I mean Abila, and that Julias which is in Perea, Tarichea[e] also, and Tiberias of Galilee; but over the rest of Judea he made Felix procurator. (253) This Felix took Eleazar the arch-robber, and many that were with him, alive, when they had ravaged the country for twenty years together, and sent them to Rome; but as to the number of the robbers whom he caused to be crucified, and of those who were caught among them, and whom he brought to punishment, they were a multitude not to be enumerated.

3. (254) When the country was purged of these, there sprang up another sort of robbers in Jerusalem, which were called Sicarii, who slew men in the day time, and in the midst of the city; (255) this they did chiefly at the festivals, when they mingled themselves among the multitude, and concealed daggers under their garments, with which they stabbed those that were their enemies; and when any fell down dead, the murderers became a part of those that had indignation against them; by which means they appeared persons of such reputation, that they could by no means be discovered. (256) The first man who was slain by them was Jonathan the high priest, after whose death many were slain every day, while the fear men were in of being so served was more afflicting than the calamity itself; (257) and while everybody expected death every hour, as men do in war, so men were obliged to look before them, and to take notice of their enemies at a great distance; nor, if their friends were coming to them, durst they trust them any longer; but, in the midst of their suspicions and guarding of themselves, they were slain. Such was the celerity of the plotters against them, and so cunning was their contrivance.

4. (258) There was also another body of wicked men gotten together, not so impure in their actions, but more wicked in their intentions, which laid waste the happy state of the city no less than did these murderers. (259) These were such men as deceived and de-

The Mount of Olives. (photo Ana Paula Hirama, via Wikimedia Commons)

luded the people under pretense of Divine inspiration, but were for procuring innovations and changes of the government; and these prevailed with the multitude to act like madmen, and went before them into the wilderness, as pretending that God would there show them the signals of liberty. (260) But Felix thought this procedure was to be the beginning of a revolt; so he sent some horsemen and footmen both armed, who destroyed a great number of them.

5. (261) But there was an Egyptian false prophet that did the Jews more mischief than the former; for he was a cheat, and pretended to be a prophet also, and got together thirty thousand men that were deluded by him; (262) these he led round about from the wilderness to the mount which was called the Mount of Olives, and was ready to break into Jerusalem by force from that place; and if he could but once conquer the Roman garrison and the people, he intended to domineer over them by the assistance of those guards of his that were to break into the city with him. (263) But Felix prevented his attempt, and met him with his Roman soldiers, while all the people assisted him in his attack upon them, insomuch that when it came to a battle, the Egyptian ran away, with a few others, while the greatest part of those that were with him were either destroyed or taken alive; but the rest of the multitude were dispersed every one to their own homes, and there concealed themselves.

6. (264) Now when these were quieted, it happened, as it does in a diseased body, that another part was subject to an inflammation; for a company of deceivers and robbers got together, and persuaded the Jews to revolt, and exhorted them to assert their liberty, inflicting death on those that continued in obedience to the Roman government, and saying, that such as willingly chose slavery ought to be forced from such their desired inclinations; (265) for they parted themselves into different bodies, and lay in wait up and down the country, and plundered the houses of the great men, and slew the men themselves, and set the villages on fire; and this till all Judea was filled with the effects of their madness. And thus the flame was every day more and more blown up, till it came to a direct war.

7. (266) There was also another disturbance at Cesarea,—those Jews who were mixed with the Syrians that lived there rising a tumult against them. The Jews pretended that the city was theirs, and said that he who built it was a Jew, meaning king Herod. The Syrians confessed also that its builder was a Jew; but they still said, however, that the city was a Grecian city; for that he who set up statues and temples in it could not design it for Jews. (267) On which account both parties had a contest with one another; and this contest increased so much, that it came at last to arms, and the bolder sort of them marched out to fight; for the elders of the Jews were not able to put a stop to their own people that were disposed to be tumultuous, and the Greeks thought it a shame for them to be overcome by the Jews. (268) Now these Jews exceeded the others in riches and strength of body; but the Grecian part had the advantage of assistance from the soldiery; for the greatest part of the Roman garrison was raised out of Syria; and being thus related to the Syrian part, they were ready to assist it. (269) However, the governors of the city were concerned to keep all quiet, and whenever they caught those that were most for fighting on either side, they punished them with stripes and bands. Yet did not the sufferings of those that were caught affright the remainder, or make them desist; but they were still more and more exasperated, and deeper engaged in the sedition. (270) And as Felix came once into the market-place, and commanded the Jews, when they had beaten the Syrians, to go their ways, and threatened them if they would not, and they would not obey him, he sent his soldiers out upon them, and slew a great many of them, upon which it fell out that what they had was plundered. And as the sedition still continued, he chose out the most eminent men on both sides as ambassadors to Nero, to argue about their several privileges.

CHAPTER 14.

FESTUS SUCCEEDS FELIX WHO IS SUCCEEDED BY ALBINUS AS HE IS BY FLORUS; WHO BY THE BARBARITY OF HIS GOVERNMENT FORCES THE JEWS INTO THE WAR.

1. (271) NOW it was that Festus succeeded Felix as procurator, and made it his business to correct those that made disturbances in the country. So he caught the greatest part of the robbers, and destroyed a great many of them. (272) But then Albinus, who succeeded Festus, did not execute his office as the other had done; nor was there any sort of wickedness that could be named but he had a hand in it. (273) Accordingly, he did not only, in his political capacity, steal and plunder every one's substance, nor did he only burden the whole nation with taxes, but he permitted the relations of such as were in prison for robbery, and had been laid there, either by the senate of every city, or by the former procurators, to redeem them for money; and no body remained in the prisons as a malefactor but he who gave him nothing. (274) At this time it was that the enterprises of the seditious at Jerusalem were very formidable; the principal men among them purchasing leave of Albinus to go on with their seditious practices; while that part of the people who delighted in disturbances joined themselves to such as had fellowship with Albinus; (275) and every one of these wicked wretches were encompassed with his own band of robbers, while he himself, like an arch-robber, or a tyrant, made a figure among his company, and abused his authority over those about him, in order to plunder those that lived quietly. (276) The effect of which was this, that those who lost their goods were forced to hold their peace, when they had reason to show great indignation at what they had suffered; but those who had escaped were forced to flatter him that deserved to be punished, out of the fear

they were in of suffering equally with the others. Upon the Whole, nobody durst speak their minds, but tyranny was generally tolerated; and at this time were those seeds sown which brought the city to destruction.

2. (277) And although such was the character of Albinus, yet did Gessius Florus who succeeded him, demonstrate him to have been a most excellent person, upon the comparison; for the former did the greatest part of his rogueries in private, and with a sort of dissimulation; but Gessius did his unjust actions to the harm of the nation after a pompous manner; and as though he had been sent as an executioner to punish condemned malefactors, he omitted no sort of rapine, or of vexation; (278) where the case was really pitiable, he was most barbarous, and in things of the greatest turpitude he was most impudent. Nor could any one outdo him in disguising the truth; nor could any one contrive more subtle ways of deceit than he did. He indeed thought it but a petty offense to get money out of single persons; so he spoiled whole cities, and ruined entire bodies of men at once, and did almost publicly proclaim it all the country over, that they had liberty given them to turn robbers, upon this condition, that he might go shares with them in the spoils they got. (279) Accordingly, this his greediness of gain was the occasion that entire toparchies were brought to desolation, and a great many of the people left their own country, and fled into foreign provinces.

3. (280) And truly, while Cestius Gallus was president of the province of Syria, nobody durst do so much as send an embassage to him against Florus; but when he was come to Jerusalem, upon the approach of the feast of unleavened bread, the people came about him not fewer in number than three millions these besought him to commiserate the calamities of their nation, and cried out upon Florus as the bane of their country. (281) But as he was present, and stood by Cestius, he laughed at their words. However, Cestius, when he had quieted the multitude, and had assured them that he would take care that Florus should hereafter treat them in a more gentle manner, returned to Antioch. (282) Florus also conducted him as far as Cesarea, and deluded him, though he had at that very time the purpose of showing his anger at the nation, and procuring a war upon them, by which means alone it was that he supposed he might conceal his enormities; (283) for he expected that if the peace continued, he should have the Jews for his accusers before Caesar; but that if he could procure them to make

Stained glass window in St Paul's Cathedral, Melbourne, depicting a scene from the Book of Acts with St. Paul, Porcius Festus, Agrippa and Berenice. (St. Anselm, via Wikimedia Commons)

a revolt, he should divert their laying lesser crimes to his charge, by a misery that was so much greater; he therefore did every day augment their calamities, in order to induce them to a rebellion.

4. (284) Now at this time it happened that the Grecians at Cesarea had been too hard for the Jews, and had obtained of Nero the government of the city, and had brought the judicial determination: at the same time began the war, in the twelfth year of the reign of Nero, and the seventeenth of the reign of Agrippa, in the month of Artemisins [Jyar.] (285) Now the occasion of this war was by no means proportionable to those heavy calamities which it brought upon us. For the Jews that dwelt at Cesarea had a synagogue near the place, whose owner was a certain Cesarean Greek: the Jews had endeavored frequently to have purchased the possession of the place, and had offered many times its value for its price; (286) but as the owner overlooked their offers, so did he raise other buildings upon the place, in way of affront to them, and made working-shops of them, and left them but a narrow passage, and such as was very troublesome for them to go along to their synagogue. Whereupon the warmer part of the Jewish youth went hastily to the workmen, and forbade them to build there; (287) but as Florus would not permit them to use force, the great men of the Jews, with John the publican, being in the utmost distress what to do, persuaded Florus, with the offer of eight talents, to hinder the work. (288) He then, being intent upon nothing but getting money, promised he would do for them all they desired of him, and then went away from Cesarea to Sebaste, and left the sedition to take its full course, as if he had sold a license to the Jews to fight it out.

5. (289) Now on the next day, which was the seventh day of the week, when the Jews were crowding apace to their synagogue, a certain man of Cesarea, of a seditious temper, got an earthen vessel, and set it with the bottom upward, at the entrance of that synagogue, and sacrificed birds. This thing provoked the Jews to an incurable degree, because their laws were affronted, and the place was polluted. (290) Whereupon the sober and moderate part of the Jews thought it proper to have recourse to their governors again, while the seditious part, and such as were in the fervor of their youth, were vehemently inflamed to fight. The seditions also among the Gentiles of Cesarea stood ready for the same purpose; for they had, by agreement, sent the man to sacrifice beforehand [as ready to support him;] so that it soon came to blows. (291) Hereupon Jucundus, the master of the horse, who was ordered to prevent the fight, came thither, and took away the earthen vessel, and endeavored to put a stop to the sedition; but when he was overcome by the violence of the people of Cesarea, the Jews caught up their books of the law, and retired to Narbata, which was a place to them belonging, distant from Cesarea sixty furlongs. (292) But John, and twelve of the principal men with him, went to Florus, to Sebaste, and made a lamentable complaint of their case, and besought him to help them; and with all possible decency, put him in mind of the eight talents they had given him; but he had the men seized upon, and put in prison, and accused them for carrying the books of the law out of Cesarea.

6. (293) Moreover, as to the citizens of Jerusalem, although they took this matter very ill, yet did they restrain their passion; but Florus acted herein as if he had been hired, and blew up the war into a flame, and sent some to take seventeen talents out of the sacred treasure, and pretended that Caesar wanted them. (294) At this the people were in confusion immediately, and ran together to the temple, with prodigious clamors, and called upon Caesar by

NEW TESTAMENT JERUSALEM

name, and besought him to free them from the tyranny of Florus. (295) Some also of the seditious cried out upon Florus, and cast the greatest reproaches upon him, and carried a basket about, and begged some spills of money for him, as for one that was destitute of possessions, and in a miserable condition. Yet was not he made ashamed hereby of his love of money, but was more enraged, and provoked to get still more; (296) and instead of coming to Cesarea, as he ought to have done, and quenching the flame of war, which was beginning thence, and so taking away the occasion of any disturbances, on which account it was that he had received a reward [of eight talents], he marched hastily with an army of horsemen and footmen against Jerusalem, that he might gain his will by the arms of the Romans, and might, by his terror, and by his threatenings, bring the city into subjection.

7. (297) But the people were desirous of making Florus ashamed of his attempt, and met his soldiers with acclamations, and put themselves in order to receive him very submissively. (298) But he sent Capito, a centurion, beforehand, with fifty soldiers, to bid them go back, and not now make a show of receiving him in an obliging manner, whom they had so foully reproached before; (299) and said that it was incumbent on them, in case they had generous souls, and were free speakers, to jest upon him to his face, and appear to be lovers of liberty, not only in words, but with their weapons also. (300) With this message was the multitude amazed; and upon the coming of Capito's horsemen into the midst of them, they were dispersed before they could salute Florus, or manifest their submissive behavior to him. Accordingly, they retired to their own houses, and spent that night in fear and confusion of face.

8. (301) Now at this time Florus took up his quarters at the palace; and on the next day he had his tribunal set before it, and sat upon it, when the high priests, and the men of power, and those of the greatest eminence in the city, came all before that tribunal; (302) upon which Florus commanded them to deliver up to him those that had reproached him, and told them that they should themselves partake of the vengeance to them belonging, if they did not produce the criminals; but these demonstrated that the people were peaceably disposed, and they begged forgiveness for those that had spoken amiss; (303) for that it was no wonder at all that in so great a multitude there should be some more daring than they ought to be, and, by reason of their younger age, foolish also; and that it was impossible to distinguish those that offended from the rest, while every one was sorry for what he had done, and denied it out of fear of what would follow: (304) that he ought, however, to provide for the peace of the nation, and to take such counsels as might preserve the city for the Romans, and rather for the sake of a great number of innocent people to forgive a few that were guilty, than for the sake of a few of the wicked to put so large and good a body of men into disorder.

9. (305) Florus was more provoked at this, and called out aloud to the soldiers to plunder that which was called the Upper Market-place, and to slay such as they met with. So the soldiers, taking this exhortation of their commander in a sense agreeable to their desire of gain, did not only plunder the place they were sent to, but forcing themselves into every house, they slew its inhabitants; (306) so the citizens fled along the narrow lanes, and the soldiers slew those that they caught, and no method of plunder was omitted; they also caught many of the quiet people, and brought them before Florus, whom he first chastised with stripes, and then crucified. (307) Accordingly, the whole number of those that were destroyed that day, with their wives and children, (for they did not spare even the infants themselves,) was about three thousand and six hundred. (308) And what made this calamity the heavier was this new method of Roman barbarity; for Florus ventured then to do what no one had done before, that is, to have men of the equestrian order whipped (cf. Acts 22:25–29) and nailed to the cross before his tribunal; who, although they were by birth Jews, yet were they of Roman dignity notwithstanding.

CHAPTER 15.

CONCERNING BERNICE'S PETITION TO FLORUS, TO SPARE THE JEWS, BUT IN VAIN; AS ALSO HOW, AFTER THE SEDITIOUS FLAME WAS QUENCHED, IT WAS KINDLED AGAIN BY FLORUS.

1. (309) ABOUT this very time king Agrippa was going to Alexandria, to congratulate Alexander upon his having obtained the government of Egypt from Nero; (310) but as his sister Bernice was come to Jerusalem, and saw the wicked practices of the soldiers, she was sorely affected at it, and frequently sent the masters of her horse and her guards to Florus, and begged of him to leave off

these slaughters; (311) but he would not comply with her request, nor have any regard either to the multitude of those already slain, or to the nobility of her that interceded, but only to the advantage he should make by this plundering; (312) nay, this violence of the soldiers brake out to such a degree of madness, that it spent itself on the queen herself; for they did not only torment and destroy those whom they had caught under her very eyes, but indeed had killed herself also, unless she had prevented them by flying to the palace, and had staid there all night with her guards, which she had about her for fear of an insult from the soldiers. (313) Now she dwelt then at Jerusalem, in order to perform a vow which she had made to God; for it is usual with those that had been either afflicted with a distemper, or with any other distresses, to make vows; and for thirty days before they are to offer their sacrifices, to abstain from wine, and to shave the hair of their head. (314) Which things Bernice was now performing, and stood barefoot before Florus's tribunal, and besought him [to spare the Jews]. Yet could she neither have any reverence paid to her, nor could she escape without some danger of being slain herself.

2. (315) This happened upon the sixteenth day of the month Artemisius [Jyar]. Now, on the next day, the multitude, who were in a great agony, ran together to the Upper Market-place, and made the loudest lamentations for those that had perished; and the greatest part of the cries were such as reflected on Florus; (316) at which the men of power were aftrighted, together with the high priests, and rent their garments, and fell down before each of them, and besought them to leave off, and not to provoke Florus to some incurable procedure, besides what they had already suffered. (317) Accordingly, the multitude complied immediately, out of reverence to those that had desired it of them, and out of the hope they had that Florus would do them no more injuries.

3. (318) So Florus was troubled that the disturbances were over, and endeavored to kindle that flame again, and sent for the high priests, with the other eminent persons, and said the only demonstration that the people would not make any other innovations should be this, that they must go out and meet the soldiers that were ascending from Cesarea, whence two cohorts were coming; (319) and while these men were exhorting the multitude so to do, he sent beforehand, and gave directions to the centurions of the cohorts, that they should give notice to those that were under them not to return the Jews' salutations; and that if they made any reply to his disadvantage, they should make use of their weapons. (320) Now the high priests assembled the multitude in the temple, and desired them to go and meet the Romans, and to salute the cohorts very civilly, before their miserable case should become incurable. Now the seditious part would not comply with these persuasions; but the consideration of those that had been destroyed made them incline to those that were the boldest for action.

4. (321) At this time it was that every priest, and every servant of God, brought out the holy vessels, and the ornamental garments wherein they used to minister in sacred things. The harpers also, and the singers of hymns, came out with their instruments of music, and fell down before the multitude, and begged of them that they would preserve those holy ornaments to them, and not provoke the Romans to carry off those sacred treasures. (322) You might also see then the high priests themselves, with dust sprinkled in great plenty upon their heads, with bosoms deprived of any covering but what was rent; these besought every one of the eminent men by name, and the multitude in common, that they would not for a small offense betray their country to those that were desirous to have it laid waste; (323) saying, "What benefit will it bring to the soldiers to have a salutation from the Jews? or what amendment of your affairs will it bring you, if you do not now go out to meet them? (324) and that if they saluted them civilly, all handle would be cut off from Florus to begin a war; that they should thereby gain their country, and freedom from all further sufferings; and that, besides, it would be a sign of great want of command of themselves, if they should yield to a few seditious persons, while it was fitter for them who were so great a people to force the others to act soberly."

5. (325) By these persuasions, which they used to the multitude and to the seditious, they restrained some by threatenings, and others by the reverence that was paid them. After this they led them out, and they met the soldiers quietly, and after a composed manner, and when they were come up with them, they saluted them; but when they made no answer, the seditious exclaimed against Florus, which was the signal given for falling upon them. (326) The soldiers therefore encompassed them presently, and struck them with their clubs; and as they fled away, the horsemen trampled them down, so that a great many fell down dead by the strokes of the Romans, and more by their own violence in crushing one another. (327) Now there was a terrible crowding about the gates, and while every body was making haste to get before another, the flight of them all was retarded, and a terrible destruction there was among those that fell down, for they were suffocated, and broken to pieces by the multitude of those that were uppermost; nor could any of them be distinguished by his relations in order to the care of his funeral; (328) the soldiers also who beat them, fell upon those whom they overtook, without showing them any mercy, and thrust the multitude through the place called Bezetha, as they forced their way, in order to get in and seize upon the temple, and the tower Antonia. Florus also being desirous to get those places into his possession, brought such as were with him out of the king's palace, and would have compelled them to get as far as the citadel [Antonia;] (329) but his attempt failed, for the people immediately turned back upon him, and stopped the violence of his attempt; and as they stood upon the tops of their houses, they threw their darts at the Romans, who, as they were sorely galled thereby, because those weapons came from above, and they were not able to make a passage through the multitude, which stopped up the narrow passages, they retired to the camp which was at the palace.

Remains of the pool of Bethesda (Bezetha), north of the temple in Jerusalem. (photo Samuel Magal)

6. (330) But for the seditious, they were afraid lest Florus should come again, and get possession of the temple, through Antonia; so they got immediately upon those cloisters of the temple that joined to Antonia, and cut them down. (331) This cooled the avarice of Florus; for whereas he was eager to obtain the treasures of God [in the temple], and on that account was desirous of getting into Antonia, as soon as the cloisters were broken down, he left off his attempt; he then sent for the high priests and the sanhedrim, and told them that he was indeed himself going out of the city, but that he would leave them as large a garrison as they should desire. (332) Hereupon they promised that they would make no innovations, in case he would leave them one band; but not that which had fought with the Jews, because the multitude bore ill-will against that band on account of what they had suffered from it; so he changed the band as they desired, and, with the rest of his forces, returned to Cesarea.

CHAPTER 16.

CESTIUS SENDS NEOPOLITANUS THE TRIBUNE TO SEE IN WHAT CONDITION THE AFFAIRS OF THE JEWS WERE. AGRIPPA MAKES A SPEECH TO THE PEOPLE OF THE JEWS THAT HE MAY DIVERT THEM FROM THEIR INTENTIONS OF MAKING WAR WITH THE ROMANS.

1. (333) HOWEVER, Florus contrived another way to oblige the Jews to begin the war, and sent to Cestius, and accused the Jews falsely of revolting [from the Roman government], and imputed the beginning of the former fight to them, and pretended they had been the authors of that disturbance, wherein they were only the sufferers. Yet were not the governors of Jerusalem silent upon this occasion, but did themselves write to Cestius, as did Bernice also, about the illegal practices of which Florus had been guilty against the city; (334) who, upon reading both accounts, consulted with his captains [what he should do]. Now some of them thought it best for Cestius to go up with his army, either to punish the revolt, if it was real, or to settle the Roman affairs on a surer foundation, if the Jews continued quiet under them; but he thought it best himself to send one of his intimate friends beforehand, to see the state of affairs, and to give him a faithful account of the intentions of the Jews. (335) Accordingly, he sent one of his tribunes, whose name was Neopolitanus, who met with king Agrippa as he was returning from Alexandria, at Jamnia, and told him who it was that sent him, and on what errands he was sent.

2. (336) And here it was that the high priests, and men of power among the Jews, as well as the sanhedrim, came to congratulate the king [upon his safe return]; and after they had paid him their respects, they lamented their own calamities, and related to him what barbarous treatment they had met with from Florus. (337) At which barbarity Agrippa had great indignation, but transferred, after a subtle manner, his anger towards those Jews whom he really pitied, that he might beat down their high thoughts of themselves, and would have them believe that they had not been so unjustly treated, in order to dissuade them from avenging themselves. (338) So these great men, as of better understanding than the rest, and desirous of peace, because of the possessions they had, understood that this rebuke which the king gave them was intended for their good; but as to the people, they came sixty furlongs out of Jerusalem, and congratulated both Agrippa and Neopolitanus; (339) but the wives of those that had been slain came running first of all and lamenting. The people also, when they heard their mourning, fell into lamentations also, and besought Agrippa to assist them: they also cried out to Neopolitanus, and complained of the many miseries they had endured under Florus; and they showed them, when they were come into the city, how the market-place was made desolate, and the houses plundered. (340) They then persuaded Neopolitanus, by the means of Agrippa, that he would walk round the city, with one only servant, as far as Siloam, that he might inform himself that the Jews submitted to all the rest of the Romans, and were only displeased at Florus, by reason of his exceeding barbarity to them. So he walked round, and had sufficient experience of the good temper the people were in, and then went up to the temple, (341) where he called the multitude together, and highly commended them for their fidelity to the Romans, and earnestly exhorted them to keep the peace; and having performed such parts of Divine worship at the temple as he was allowed to do, he returned to Cestius.

3. (342) But as for the multitude of the Jews, they addressed themselves to the king, and to the high priests, and desired they might have leave to send ambassadors to Nero against Florus, and not by their silence afford a suspicion that they had been the occasions of such great slaughters as had been made, and were disposed to revolt, alleging that they should seem to have been the first beginners of the war, if they did not prevent the report by showing who it was that began it; (343) and it appeared openly that they would not be quiet, if any body should hinder them from sending such an embassage. But Agrippa, although he thought it too dangerous a thing for them to appoint men to go as the accusers of Florus, yet did he not think it fit for him to overlook them, as they were in a disposition for war. (344) He therefore called the multitude together into a large gallery, and placed his sister Bernice in the house of the Asamoneans, that she might be seen by them, (which house was over the gallery, at the passage to the upper city, where the bridge joined the temple to the gallery,) and spake to them as follows:

4. (345) "Had I perceived that you were all zealously disposed to go to war with the Romans, and that the purer and more sincere part of the people did not propose to live in peace, I had not come out to you, nor been so bold as to give you counsel; for all discourses that tend to persuade men to do what they ought to do are superfluous, when the hearers are agreed to do the contrary. (346) But because some are earnest to go to war because they are young, and without experience of the miseries it brings, and because some are for it out of an unreasonable expectation of regaining their liberty, and because others hope to get by it, and are therefore earnestly bent upon it, that in the confusion of your affairs they may gain what belongs to those that are too weak to resist them, I have thought proper to get you all together, and to say to you what I think to be for your advantage; that so the former may grow wiser, and change their minds, and that the best men may come to no harm by the ill conduct of some others. (347) And let not any one be tumultuous against me, in case what they hear me say do not please them; for as to those that admit of no cure, but are resolved upon a revolt, it will still be in their power to retain the same sentiments after my exhortation is over; but still my discourse will fall to the ground, even with a relation to those that have a mind to hear me, unless you will all keep silence. (348) I am well aware that many make a tragical exclamation concerning the injuries that have been offered you by your procurators, and concerning the glorious advantages of liberty; but before I begin the inquiry, who you are that must go to war, and who they are against whom you must fight, I shall first separate those pretenses that are by some connected together; (349) for if you aim at avenging yourselves on those that have done you injury, why do you pretend this to be a war for recovering your lib-

THE ROMAN EMPIRE

Roman infantry officers

(from *The Land of Jesus Then & Now* / G. S. P. Freeman-Grenville)

erty? but if you think all servitude intolerable, to what purpose serve your complaint against your particular governors? for if they treated you with moderation, it would still be equally an unworthy thing to be in servitude. (350) Consider now the several cases that may be supposed, how little occasion there is for your going to war. Your first occasion is the accusations you have to make against your procurators; now here you ought to be submissive to those in authority, and not give them any provocation; (351) but when you reproach men greatly for small offenses, you excite those whom you reproach to be your adversaries; for this will only make them leave off hurting you privately, and with some degree of modesty, and to lay what you have waste openly. (352) Now nothing so much damps the force of strokes as bearing them with patience; and the quietness of those who are injured diverts the injurious persons from afflicting. But let us take it for granted that the Roman ministers are injurious to you, and are incurably severe; yet are they not all the Romans who thus injure you; nor hath Caesar, against whom you are going to make war, injured you: it is not by their command that any wicked governor is sent to you; for they who are in the west cannot see those that are in the east; nor indeed is it easy for them there even to hear what is done in these parts. (353) Now it is absurd to make war with a great many for the sake of one, to do so with such mighty people for a small cause; and this when these people are not able to know of what you complain: (354) nay, such crimes as we complain of may soon be corrected, for the same procurator will not continue for ever; and probable it is that the successors will come with more moderate inclinations. But as for war, if it be once begun, it is not easily laid down again, nor borne without calamities coming therewith. (355) However, as to the desire of recovering your liberty, it is unseasonable to indulge it so late; whereas you ought to have labored earnestly in old time that you might never have lost it; for the first experience of slavery was hard to be endured, and the struggle that you might never have been subject to it would have been just; (356) but that slave who hath been once brought into subjection, and then runs away, is rather a refractory slave than a lover of liberty; for it was then the proper time for doing all that was possible, that you might never have admitted the Romans [into your city], when Pompey came first into the country. (357) But so it was, that our ancestors and their kings, who were in much better circumstances than we are, both as to money, and strong bodies, and [valiant] souls, did not bear the onset of a small body of the Roman army. And yet you, who have now accustomed yourselves to obedience from one generation to another, and who are so much inferior to those who first submitted, in your circumstances will venture to oppose the entire empire of the Romans. (358) While those Athenians, who, in order to preserve the liberty of Greece, did once set fire to their own city; who pursued Xerxes, that proud prince, when he sailed upon the land, and walked upon the sea, and could not be contained by the seas, but conducted such an army as was too broad for Europe; and made him run away like a fugitive in a single ship, and brake so great a part of Asia at the Lesser Salamis; are yet at this time servants to the Romans; and those injunctions which are sent from Italy become laws to the principal governing city of Greece. (359) Those Lacedemonians also who got the great victories at Thermopylae and Platea, and had Agesilaus [for their king], and searched every corner of Asia, are contented to admit the same lords. (360) Those Macedonians also, who still fancy what great men their Philip and Alexander were, and see that the latter had promised them the empire over the world, these bear so great a change, and pay their obedience to those whom fortune hath advanced in their stead. (361) Moreover, ten thousand other nations there are who had greater reason than we to claim their entire liberty, and yet do submit. You are the only people who think it a disgrace to be servants to those to whom all the world hath submitted. What sort of an army do you rely on? What are the arms you depend on? Where is your fleet, that may seize upon the Roman seas? and where are those treasures which may be sufficient for your undertakings? (362) Do you suppose, I pray you, that you are to make war with the Egyptians, and with the Arabians? Will you not carefully reflect upon the Roman empire? Will you not estimate your own weakness? Hath not your army been often beaten even by your neighboring nations, while the power of the Romans is invincible in all parts of the habitable earth? (363) nay, rather they seek for somewhat still beyond that; for all Euphrates is not a sufficient boundary for them on the east side, nor the Danube on the north; and for their southern limit, Libya hath been searched over by them, as far as countries uninhabited, as is Cadiz their limit on the west; nay, indeed, they have sought for another habitable earth beyond the ocean, and have carried their arms as far as such British islands as were never known before. (364) What therefore do you pretend to? Are you richer than the Gauls, stronger than the Germans, wiser than the Greeks, more numerous than all men upon the habitable earth? What confidence is it that elevates you to oppose the Romans? (365) Perhaps it will be said, It is hard to endure slavery. Yes; but how much harder is this to the Greeks, who were esteemed the noblest of all people under the sun! These, though they inhabit in a large country, are in subjection to six bundles of Roman rods. It is the same case with the Macedonians, who have juster reason to claim their liberty than you have. (366) What is the case of five hundred cities of Asia? Do they not submit to a single governor, and to the consular bundle of rods? What need I speak of the Henlochi, and Colchi and the nation of Tauri, those that inhabit the Bosphorus, and the nations about Pontus, and Meotis, (367) who formerly knew not so much as a lord of their own, but are now subject to three thousand armed men, and where forty long ships keep the sea in peace, which before was not navigable, and very tempestuous? (368) How strong a plea may Bithynia, and Cappadocia, and the people of Pamphylia, the Lycians, and Cilicians, put in for liberty! But they are made tributary without an army. What are the circumstances of the Thracians, whose country extends in breadth five days' journey, and in length seven, and is of a much more harsh constitution, and much more defensible, than yours, and by the rigor of its cold sufficient to keep off armies from attacking them? do not they submit to two thousand men of the Roman garrisons? (369) Are not the Illyrians, who inhabit the country adjoining, as far as Dalmatia and the Danube, governed by barely two legions? by which also they put a stop to the incursions of the Daeians. And for the (370) Dalmatians, who have made such frequent insurrections in order to regain their liberty, and who could never before be so thoroughly subdued, but that they always gathered their forces together again, revolted, yet are they now very quiet under one Roman legion. (371) Moreover, if eat advantages might provoke any people to revolt, the Gauls might do it best of all, as being so thoroughly walled round by nature; on the east side by the Alps, on the north by the river Rhine, on the south by the Pyrenean mountains, and on the west by the ocean. (372) Now although these Gauls have such obstacles before them to prevent any attack upon them, and have no fewer than three hundred and five nations among them, nay have, as one may say, the fountains of domestic happiness within themselves, and send out plentiful streams of happiness over almost the whole world, these bear to be tributary to the Romans, and derive their prosperous condition from them; (373) and they undergo this, not because they are of effeminate minds, or because they are of an ignoble stock, as having borne a war of eighty years in order to preserve their liberty; but by reason of the great regard they have to the power of the Romans, and their good fortune, which is of greater efficacy than their arms. These Gauls, therefore, are kept in servitude by twelve hundred soldiers, which are hardly so many as are their cities; (374) nor hath the gold dug out of the mines of Spain been sufficient for the support of a war to preserve their liberty, nor could their vast distance from the Romans by land and by sea do it; nor could the martial tribes of the Lusitanians and Spaniards escape; no more could the ocean, with its tide, which yet was terrible to the ancient inhabitants. (375) Nay, the Romans have extended their arms beyond the pillars of Hercules, and have walked among the clouds, upon the Pyrenean mountains, and have subdued these nations. And one legion is a sufficient guard for these people, although they were so hard to be conquered, and at a distance so remote from Rome. (376) Who is there among you that hath not heard of the great number of the Germans? You have, to be sure, yourselves seen them to be strong and tall, and that frequently, since the Romans have them among their captives everywhere; (377) yet these Germans, who dwell in an immense country, who have minds greater than their bodies, and a soul that despises death, and who are in rage more fierce than wild beasts, have the Rhine for the boundary of their enterprises, and are tamed by eight Roman legions. Such of them as were taken captive became their servants; and the rest of the entire nation were obliged to save themselves by flight. (378) Do you also, who depend on the walls of Jerusalem, consider what a wall the Britons had; for the Romans sailed away to them, an subdued them while they were encompassed by the ocean, and inhabited an island that is not less than the [continent of this] habitable earth; and four legions are a sufficient guard to so large an island. (379) And why should I speak much more about this matter, while the Parthians, that most warlike body of men, and lords of so many nations, and encompassed with such mighty forces, send hostages to the Romans? whereby you may see, if you please, even in Italy, the noblest nation of the East, under the notion of peace, submitting to serve them. (380) Now when almost all people under the sun submit to the Roman arms, will you be the only people that make war against them? and this without regarding the fate of the Carthaginians, who, in the midst of their brags of the great Hannibal, and the nobility of their Phoenician original, fell by the hand of Scipio. (381) Nor indeed have the Cyrenians, derived from the Lacedemonians, nor the Marmaridites, a nation extended as far as the regions uninhabitable for want of water, nor have the Syrtes, a place terrible to such as barely hear it described, the Nasamons and Moors, and the immense multitude of the Numidians, been able to put a stop to the Roman valor. (382) And as for the third part of the habitable earth, [Akica,] whose nations are so many that it is not easy to number them, and which is bounded by the Atlantic Sea and the pillars of Hercules, and feeds an innumerable multitude of Ethiopians, as far as the Red Sea, these have the Romans subdued entirely. (383) And besides the annual fruits of the earth, which maintain the multi-

The French Pyrenées viewed from the Ossau Valley. (photo Myrabella, via Wikimedia Commons)

tude of the Romans for eight months in the year, this, over and above, pays all sorts of tribute, and affords revenues suitable to the necessities of the government. Nor do they, like you, esteem such injunctions a disgrace to them, although they have but one Roman legion that abides among them. (384) And indeed what occasion is there for showing you the power of the Romans over remote countries, when it is so easy to learn it from Egypt, in your neighborhood? (385) This country is extended as far as the Ethiopians, and Arabia the Happy, and borders upon India; it hath seven millions five hundred thousand men, besides the inhabitants of Alexandria, as may be learned from the revenue of the poll tax; yet it is not ashamed to submit to the Roman government, although it hath Alexandria as a grand temptation to a revolt, by reason it is so full of people and of riches, and is besides exceeding large, (386) its length being thirty furlongs, and its breadth no less than ten; and it pays more tribute to the Romans in one month than you do in a year; nay, besides what it pays in money, it sends corn to Rome that supports it for four months [in the year]: it is also walled round on all sides, either by almost impassable deserts, or seas that have no havens, or by rivers, or by lakes; (387) yet have none of these things been found too strong for the Roman good fortune; however, two legions that lie in that city are a bridle both for the remoter parts of Egypt, and for the parts inhabited by the more noble Macedonians. (388) Where then are those people whom you are to have for your auxiliaries? Must they come from the parts of the world that are uninhabited? for all that are in the habitable earth are [under the] Romans. Unless any of you extend his hopes as far as beyond the Euphrates, and suppose that those of your own nation that dwell in Adiabene will come to your assistance; (389) but certainly these will not embarrass themselves with an unjustifiable war, nor, if they should follow such ill advice, will the Parthians permit them so to do; for it is their concern to maintain the truce that is between them and the Romans, and they will be supposed to break the covenants between them, if any under their government march against the Romans. (390) What remains, therefore, is this, that you have recourse to Divine assistance; but this is already on the side of the Romans; for it is impossible that so vast an empire should be settled without God's providence. (391) Reflect upon it, how impossible it is for your zealous observations of your religious customs to be here preserved, which are hard to be observed even when you fight with those whom you are able to conquer; and how can you then most of all hope for God's assistance, when, by being forced to transgress his law, you will make him turn his face from you? (392) and if you do observe the custom of the sabbath days, and will not be revealed on to do any thing thereon, you will easily be taken, as were your forefathers by Pompey, who was the busiest in his siege on those days on which the besieged rested. (393) But if in time of war you transgress the law of your country, I cannot tell on whose account you will afterward go to war; for your concern is but one, that you do nothing against any of your forefathers; (394) and how will you call upon God to assist you, when you are voluntarily transgressing against his religion? Now all men that go to war do it either as depending on Divine or on human assistance; but since your going to war will cut off both those assistances, those that are for going to war choose evident destruction. (395) What hinders you from slaying your children and wives with your own hands, and burning this most excellent native city of yours? for by this mad prank you will, however, escape the reproach of being beaten. (396) But it were best, O my friends, it were best, while the vessel is still in the haven, to foresee the impending storm, and not to set sail out of the port into the middle of the hurricanes; for we justly pity those who fall into great misfortunes without fore-seeing them; but for him who rushes into manifest ruin, he gains reproaches [instead of commiseration]. (397) But certainly no one can imagine that you can enter into a war as by agreement, or that when the Romans have got you under their power, they will use you with moderation, or will not rather, for an example to other nations, burn your holy city, and utterly destroy your whole nation; for those of you who shall survive the war will not be able to find a place whither to flee, since all men have the Romans for their lords already, or are afraid they shall have hereafter. (398) Nay, indeed, the danger concerns not those Jews that dwell here only, but those of them which dwell in other cities also; for there is no people upon the habitable earth which have not some portion of you among them, (399) whom your enemies will slay, in case you go to war, and on that account also; and so every city which hath Jews in it will be filled with slaughter for the sake of a few men, and they who slay them will be pardoned; but if that slaughter be not made by them, consider how wicked a thing it is to take arms against those that are so kind to you. (400) Have pity, therefore, if not on your children and wives, yet upon this your metropolis, and its sacred walls; spare the temple, and preserve the holy house, with its holy furniture, for yourselves; for if the Romans get you under their power, they will no longer abstain from them, when their former abstinence shall have been so ungratefully requited. (401) I call to witness your sanctuary, and the holy angels of God, and this country common to us all, that I have not kept back any thing that is for your preservation; and if you will follow that advice which you ought to do, you will have that peace which will be common to you and to me; but if you indulge four passions, you will run those hazards which I shall be free from."

5. (402) When Agrippa had spoken thus, both he and his sister wept, and by their tears repressed a great deal of the violence of the people; but still they cried out, that they would not fight against the Romans, but against Florus, on account of what they had suffered by his means. To which Agrippa replied, that what they had already done was like such as make war against the Romans; "for you have not paid the tribute which is due to Caesar and you have cut off the cloisters [of the temple] from joining to the tower Antonia. You will therefore prevent any occasion of revolt if you will but join these together again, and if you will but pay your tribute; for the citadel does not now belong to Florus, nor are you to pay the tribute money to Florus."

Half-shekel coin minted in year 3 of the First Jewish Revolt (A.D. 66–70). (Classical Numismatic Group, Inc. http://www.cngcoins.com)

CHAPTER 17.

HOW THE WAR OF THE JEWS WITH THE ROMANS BEGAN, AND CONCERNING MANAHEM.

1. (405) THIS advice the people hearkened to, and went up into the temple with the king and Bernice, and began to rebuild the cloisters; the rulers also and senators divided themselves into the villages, and collected the tributes, and soon got together forty talents, which was the sum that was deficient. (406) And thus did Agrippa then put a stop to that war which was threatened. Moreover, he attempted to persuade the multitude to obey Florus, until Caesar should send one to succeed him; but they were hereby more provoked, and cast reproaches upon the king, and got him excluded out of the city; nay, some of the seditious had the impudence to throw stones at him. (407) So when the king saw that the violence of those that were for innovations was not to be restrained, and being very angry at the contumelies he had received, he sent their rulers, together with their men of power, to Florus, to Cesarea, that he might appoint whom he thought fit to collect the tribute in the country, while he retired into his own kingdom.

2. (408) And at this time it was that some of those that principally excited the people to go to war made an assault upon a certain fortress called Masada. They took it by treachery, and slew the Romans that were there, and put others of their own party to keep it. (409) At the same time Eleazar, the son of Ananias the high priest, a very bold youth, who was at that time governor of the temple, persuaded those that officiated in the Divine service to receive no gift or sacrifice for any foreigner. And this was the true beginning of our war with the Romans; for they rejected the sacrifice of Caesar on this account; (410) and when many of the high priests and principal men besought them not to omit the sacrifice, which it was customary for them to offer for their princes, they would not be prevailed upon. These relied much upon their multitude, for the most flourishing part of the innovators assisted them; but they had the chief regard to Eleazar, the governor of the temple.

3. (411) Hereupon the men of power got together, and conferred with the high priests, as did also the principal of the Pharisees; and thinking all was at stake, and that their calamities were becoming incurable, took counsel what was to be done. Accordingly, they determined to try what they could do with the seditious by words, and assembled the people before the brazen gate, which was that gate of the inner temple [court of the priests] which looked toward the sun-rising. (412) And, in the first place, they showed the great indignation they had at this attempt for a revolt, and for their bringing so great a war upon their country; after which they confuted their pretense as unjustifiable, and told them that their forefathers had adorned their temple in great part with donations bestowed on them by foreigners, and had always received what had been presented to them from foreign nations; (413) and that they had been so far from rejecting any person's sacrifice (which would be the highest instance of impiety,) that they had themselves placed those donation about the temple which were still visible, and had remained there so long a time; (414) that they did now irritate the Romans to take arms against them, and invited them to make war upon them, and brought up novel rules of a strange Divine worship, and determined to run the hazard of having their city condemned for impiety, while they would not allow any foreigner, but Jews only, either to sacrifice or to worship therein. (415) And if such a law should be introduced in the case of a single private person only, he would have indignation at it, as an instance of inhumanity determined against him; while they have no regard to the Romans or to Caesar, and forbid even their oblations to be received also; (416) that however they cannot but fear, lest, by thus rejecting their sacrifices, they shall not be allowed to offer their own; and that this city will lose its principality, unless they grow wiser quickly, and restore the sacrifices as formerly, and indeed amend the injury [they have offered foreigners] before the report of it comes to the ears of those that have been injured.

4. (417) And as they said these things, they produced those priests that were skillful in the customs of their country, who made the report that all their forefathers had received the sacrifices from foreign nations. But still not one of the innovators would hearken to what was said; nay, those that ministered about the temple would not attend their Divine service, but were preparing matters for beginning the war. (418) So the men of power perceiving that the sedition was too hard for them to subdue, and that the danger which would arise from the Romans would come upon them first of all, endeavored to save themselves, and sent ambassadors, some to Florus, the chief of which was Simon the son of Ananias; and others to Agrippa, among whom the most eminent were Saul, and Antipas, and Costobarus, who were of the king's kindred; (419) and they desired of them both that they would come with an army to the city, and cut off the seditious before it should be too hard to be subdued. (420) Now this terrible message was good news to

THE OUTBREAK OF THE FIRST REVOLT AGAINST ROME
A.D. 66

Florus; and because his design was to have a war kindled, he gave the ambassadors no answer at all. (421) But Agrippa was equally solicitous for those that were revolting, and for those against whom the war was to be made, and was desirous to preserve the Jews for the Romans, and the temple and metropolis for the Jews; he was also sensible that it was not for his own advantage that the disturbances should proceed; so he sent three thousand horsemen to the assistance of the people out of Auranitis, and Batanea, and Trachonitis, and these under Darius, the master of his horse, and Philip the son of Jacimus, the general of his army.

5. (422) Upon this the men of power, with the high priests, as also all the part of the multitude that were desirous of peace, took courage, and seized upon the upper city [Mount Sion;] for the seditious part had the lower city and the temple in their power; (423) so they made use of stones and slings perpetually against one another, and threw darts continually on both sides; and sometimes it happened that they made incursions by troops, and fought it out hand to hand, while the seditious were superior in boldness, but the king's soldiers in skill. (424) These last strove chiefly to gain the temple, and to drive those out of it who profaned it; as did the seditious, with Eleazar, besides what they had already, labor to gain the upper city. Thus were there perpetual slaughters on both sides for seven days' time; but neither side would yield up the parts they had seized on.

6. (425) Now the next day was the festival of Xylophory; upon which the custom was for every one to bring wood for the altar (that there might never be a want of fuel for that fire which was unquenchable and always burning). Upon that day they excluded the opposite party from the observation of this part of religion. And when they had joined to themselves many of the Sicarii, who crowded in among the weaker people, (that was the name for such robbers as had under their bosoms swords called Sicae,) they grew bolder, and carried their undertaking further; (426) insomuch that the king's soldiers were overpowered by their multitude and boldness; and so they gave way, and were driven out of the upper city by force. The others then set fire to the house of Ananias the high priest, and to the palaces of Agrippa and Bernice; (427) after which they carried the fire to the place where the archives were reposited, and made haste to burn the contracts belonging to their creditors, and thereby to dissolve their obligations for paying their debts; and this was done in order to gain the multitude of those who had been debtors, and that they might persuade the poorer sort to join in their insurrection with safety against the more wealthy; so the keepers of the records fled away, and the rest set fire to them. (428) And when they had thus burnt down the nerves of the city, they fell upon their enemies; at which time some of the men of power, and of the high priests, went into the vaults under ground, and concealed themselves, (429) while others fled with the king's soldiers to the upper palace, and shut the gates immediately; among whom were Ananias the high priest, and the ambassadors that had been sent to Agrippa. And now the seditious were contented with the victory they had gotten, and the buildings they had burnt down, and proceeded no further.

7. (430) But on the next day, which was the fifteenth of the month Lous, [Ab,] they made an assault upon Antonia, and besieged the garrison which was in it two days, and then took the garrison, and slew them, and set the citadel on fire; (431) after which they marched to the palace, whither the king's soldiers were fled, and parted themselves into four bodies, and made an attack upon the walls. As for those that were within it, no one had the courage to

The Antonia fortress at the northwest corner of the Temple Mount. (from M. Avi-Yonah's Second Temple model, now on display at The Israel Museum; photo Samuel Magal)

Aerial view of Masada, looking southeast. (photo Samuel Magal)

sally out, because those that assaulted them were so numerous; but they distributed themselves into the breast-works and turrets, and shot at the besiegers, whereby many of the robbers fell under the walls; (432) nor did they cease to fight one with another either by night or by day, while the seditious supposed that those within would grow weary for want of food, and those without supposed the others would do the like by the tediousness of the siege.

8. (433) In the meantime, one Manahem, the son of Judas, that was called the Galilean, (who was a very cunning sophister, and had formerly reproached the Jews under Cyrenius, that after God they were subject to the Romans,) took some of the men of note with him, and retired to Masada, (434) where he broke open king Herod's armory, and gave arms not only to his own people, but to other robbers also. These he made use of for a guard, and returned in the state of a king to Jerusalem; he became the leader of the sedition, and gave orders for continuing the siege; (435) but they wanted proper instruments, and it was not practicable to undermine the wall, because the darts came down upon them from above. But still they dug a mine from a great distance under one of the towers, and made it totter; and having done that, they set on fire what was combustible, and left it; (436) and when the foundations were burnt below, the tower fell down suddenly. Yet did they then meet with another wall that had been built within, for the besieged were sensible beforehand of what they were doing, and probably the tower shook as it was undermining; so they provided themselves of another fortification; (437) which when the besiegers unexpectedly saw, while they thought they had already gained the place, they were under some consternation. However, those that were within sent to Manahem, and to the other leaders of the sedition, and desired they might go out upon a capitulation: this was granted to the king's soldiers and their own countrymen only, who went out accordingly; (438) but the Romans that were left alone were greatly dejected, for they were not able to force their way through such a multitude; and to desire them to give them their right hand for their security, they thought it would be a reproach to them; and besides, if they should give it them, they durst not depend upon it; (439) so they deserted their camp, as easily taken, and ran away to the royal towers,—that called Hippicus, that called Phasaelus, and that called Mariamne. (440) But Manahem and his party fell upon the place whence the soldiers were fled, and slew as many of them as they could catch, before they got up to the towers, and plundered what they left behind them, and set fire to their camp. This was executed on the sixth day of the month Gorpieus [Elul].

9. (441) But on the next day the high priest was caught where he had concealed himself in an aqueduct; he was slain, together with Hezekiah his brother, by the robbers: hereupon the seditious besieged the towers, and kept them guarded, lest any one of the soldiers should escape. (442) Now the overthrow of the places of strength, and the death of the high priest Ananias, so puffed up Manahem, that he became barbarously cruel; and as he thought he had no antagonist to dispute the management of affairs with him, he was no better than an insupportable tyrant; (443) but Eleazar and his party, when words had passed between them, how it was not proper when they revolted from the Romans, out of the desire of liberty, to betray that liberty to any of their own people, and to bear a lord, who, though he should be guilty of no violence, was yet meaner than themselves; as also, that in case they were obliged to set some one over their public affairs, it was fitter they should give that privilege to any one rather than to him; they made an assault upon him in the temple; (444) for he went up thither to worship in a pompous manner, and adorned with royal garments, and had his followers with him in their armor. (445) But Eleazar and his party fell violently upon him, as did also the rest of the people; and taking up stones to attack him withal, they threw them at the sophister, and thought, that if he were once ruined, the entire sedition would fall to the ground. (446) Now Manahem and his party made resistance for a while; but when they perceived that the whole multitude were falling upon them, they fled which way every one was able; those that were caught were slain, and those that hid themselves were searched for. (447) A few there were of them who privately escaped to Masada, among whom was Eleazar, the son of Jairus, who was of kin to Manahem, and acted the part of a tyrant at Masada afterward. (448) As for Manahem himself, he ran away to the place called Ophla, and there lay skulking in private; but they took him alive, and drew him out before them all; they then tortured him with many sorts of torments, and after all slew him, as they did by those that were captains under him also, and particularly by the principal instrument of his tyranny, whose name was Apsalom.

10. (449) And, as I said, so far truly the people assisted them, while they hoped this might afford some amendment to the seditious practices; but the others were not in haste to put an end to the

war, but hoped to prosecute it with less danger, now they had slain Manahem. (450) It is true, that when the people earnestly desired that they would leave off besieging the soldiers, they were the more earnest in pressing it forward, and this till Metilius, who was the Roman general, sent to Eleazar, and desired that they would. give them security to spare their lives only; but agreed to deliver up their arms, and what else they had with them. (451) The others readily complied with their petition, sent to them Gorion, the son of Nicodemus, and Ananias, the son of Sadduk, and Judas, the son of Jonathan, that they might give them the security of their right hands, and of their oaths; after which Metilius brought down his soldiers; (452) which soldiers, while they were in arms, were not meddled with by any of the seditious, nor was there any appearance of treachery; but as soon as, according to the articles of capitulation, they had all laid down their shields and their swords, and were under no further suspicion of any harm, but were going away, (453) Eleazar's men attacked them after a violent manner, and encompassed them round, and slew them, while they neither defended themselves, nor entreated for mercy, but only cried out upon the breach of their articles of capitulation and their oaths. (454) And thus were all these men barbarously murdered, excepting Metilius; for when he entreated for mercy, and promised that he would turn Jew, and be circumcised, they saved him alive, but none else. This loss to the Romans was but light, there being no more than a few slain out of an immense army; but still it appeared to be a prelude to the Jews' own destruction, (455) while men made public lamentation when they saw that such occasions were afforded for a war as were incurable; that the city was all over polluted with such abominations, from which it was but reasonable to expect some vengeance, even though they should escape revenge from the Romans; so that the city was filled with sadness, and every one of the moderate men in it were under great disturbance, as likely themselves to undergo punishment for the wickedness of the seditious; (456) for indeed it so happened that this murder was perpetrated on the sabbath day, on which day the Jews have a respite from their works on account of Divine worship.

CHAPTER 18.

THE CALAMITIES AND SLAUGHTERS THAT CAME UPON THE JEWS.

1. (457) NOW the people of Cesarea had slain the Jews that were among them on the very same day and hour [when the soldiers were slain], which one would think must have come to pass by the direction of Providence; insomuch that in one hour's time above twenty thousand Jews were killed, and all Cesarea was emptied of its Jewish inhabitants; for Florus caught such as ran away, and sent them in bonds to the galleys. (458) Upon which stroke that the Jews received at Cesarea, the whole nation was greatly enraged; so they divided themselves into several parties, and laid waste the villages of the Syrians, and their neighboring cities, Philadelphia, and Sebonitis, and Gerasa, and Pella, and Scythopolis, (459) and after them Gadara, and Hippos; and falling upon Gaulonitis, some cities they destroyed there, and some they set on fire, and then went to Kedasa, belonging to the Tyrians, and to Ptolemais, and to Gaba, and to Cesarea; (460) nor was either Sebaste [Samaria] or Askelon able to oppose the violence with which they were attacked; and when they had burnt these to the ground; they entirely demolished Anthedon and Gaza; many also of the villages that were about every one of those cities were plundered, and an immense slaughter was made of the men who were caught in them.

2. (461) However, the Syrians were even with the Jews in the multitude of the men whom they slew; for they killed those whom they caught in their cities, and that not only out of the hatred they bare them, as formerly, but to prevent the danger under which they were from them; (462) so that the disorders in all Syria were terrible, and every city was divided into two armies, encamped one against another, and the preservation of the one party was in the destruction of the other; (463) so the day time was spent in shedding of blood, and the night in fear, which was of the two the more terrible; for when the Syrians thought they had ruined the Jews, they had the Judaizers in suspicion also; and as each side did not care to slay those whom they only suspected on the other, so did they greatly fear them when they were mingled with the other, as if they were certainly foreigners. (464) Moreover, greediness of gain was a provocation to kill the opposite party, even to such as had of old appeared very mild and gentle towards them; for they without fear plundered the effects of the slain, and carried off the spoils of those whom they slew to their own houses, as if they had been gained in a set battle; and he was esteemed a man of honor who got the greatest share, as having prevailed over the greatest number of his enemies. (465) It was then common to see cities filled with dead bodies, still lying unburied, and those of old men, mixed with infants, all dead, and scattered about together; women also lay amongst them, without any covering for their nakedness: you might then see the whole province full of inexpressible calamities, while the dread of still more barbarous practices which were threatened was every where greater than what had been already perpetrated.

3. (466) And thus far the conflict had been between Jews and foreigners; but when they made excursions to Scythopolis, they found Jew that acted as enemies; for as they stood in battle-array with those of Scythopolis, and preferred their own safety before their relation to us, they fought against their own countrymen; (467) nay, their alacrity was so very great, that those of Scythopolis suspected them. These were afraid, therefore, lest they should make an assault upon the city in the night time, and, to their great misfortune, should thereby make an apology for themselves to their own people for their revolt from them. So they commanded them, that in case they would confirm their agreement and demonstrate their fidelity to them, who were of a different nation, they should go out of the city, with their families to a neighboring grove; (468) and when they had done as they were commanded, without suspecting any thing, the people of Scythopolis lay still

Part of the high-level aqueduct at Caesarea, Roman period. (photo Christianpentzold, via Wikimedia Commons)

The Roman theater at Scythopolis. (photo Samuel Magal)

for the interval of two days, to tempt them to be secure; but on the third night they watched their opportunity, and cut all their throats, some as they lay unguarded, and some as they lay asleep. The number that was slain was above thirteen thousand, and then they plundered them of all that they had.

4. (469) It will deserve our relation what befell Simon; he was the son of one Saul, a man of reputation among the Jews. This man was distinguished from the rest by the strength of his body, and the boldness of his conduct, although he abused them both to the mischieving of his countrymen; (470) for he came every day and slew a great many of the Jews of Scythopolis, and he frequently put them to flight, and became himself alone the cause of his army's conquering. (471) But a just punishment overtook him for the murders he had committed upon those of the same nation with him; for when the people of Scythopolis threw their darts at them in the grove, he drew his sword, but did not attack any of the enemy; for he saw that he could do nothing against such a multitude; but he cried out after a very moving manner, and said, (472) "O you people of Scythopolis, I deservedly suffer for what I have done with relation to you, when I gave you such security of my fidelity to you, by slaying so many of those that were related to me. Wherefore we very justly experience the perfidiousness of foreigners, while we acted after a most wicked manner against our own nation. I will therefore die, polluted wretch as I am, by nine own hands; for it is not fit I should die by the hand of our enemies; (473) and let the same action be to me both a punishment for my great crimes, and a testimony of my courage to my commendation, that so no one of our enemies may have it to brag of, that he it was that slew me, and no one may insult upon me as I fall." (474) Now when he had said this, he looked round about him upon his family with eyes of commiseration and of rage (that family consisted of a wife and children, and his aged parents); (475) so, in the first place, he caught his father by his grey hairs, and ran his sword through him, and after him he did the same to his mother, who willingly received it; and after them he did the like to his wife and children, every one almost offering themselves to his sword, as desirous to prevent being slain by their enemies; (476) so when he had gone over all his family, he stood upon their bodies to be seen by all, and stretching out his right hand, that his action might be observed by all, he sheathed his entire sword into his own bowels. This young man was to be pitied, on account of the strength of his body and the courage of his soul; but since he had assured foreigners of his fidelity [against his own countrymen], he suffered deservedly.

5. (477) Besides this murder at Scythopolis, the other cities rose up against the Jews that were among them; those of Askelon slew two thousand five hundred, and those of Ptolemais two thousand, and put not a few into bonds; (478) those of Tyre also put a great number to death, but kept a greater number in prison; moreover, those of Hippos, and those of Gadara, did the like while they put to death the boldest of the Jews, but kept those of whom they were afraid in custody; as did the rest of the cities of Syria, according as they every one either hated them or were afraid of them; (479) only the Antiochians the Sidonians, and Apamians spared those that dwelt with them, and would not endure either to kill any of the Jews, or to put them in bonds. And perhaps they spared them, because their own number was so great that they despised their attempts. But I think the greatest part of this favor was owing to their commiseration of those whom they saw to make no innovations. (480) As for the Gerasans, they did no harm to those that abode with them; and for those who had a mind to go away, they conducted them as far as their borders reached.

6. (481) There was also a plot laid against the Jews in Agrippa's kingdom; for he was himself gone to Cestius Gallus, to Antioch, but had left one of his companions, whose name was Noarus, to take care of the public affairs; which Noarus was of kin to king Sohemus. (482) Now there came certain men seventy in number, out of Batanea, who were the most considerable for their families and prudence of the rest of the people; these desired to have an army put into their hands, that if any tumult should happen, they might have about them a guard sufficient to restrain such as might rise up against them. (483) This Noarus sent out some of the king's armed men by night, and slew all those [seventy] men; which bold action he ventured upon without the consent of Agrippa, and was such a lover of money, that he chose to be so wicked to his own countrymen, though he brought ruin on the kingdom thereby; and thus cruelly did he treat that nation, and this contrary to the laws also, until Agrippa was informed of it, who did not indeed dare to put him to death, out of regard to Sohemus; but still he put an end to his procuratorship immediately. (484) But as to the seditious, they took the citadel which was called Cypros, and was above Jericho, and cut the throats of the garrison, and utterly demolished the fortifications. (485) This was about the same time that the multitude of the Jews that were at Macherus persuaded the Romans who were in garrison to leave the place, and deliver it up to them. (486) These Romans being in great fear, lest the place should be taken by force, made an agreement with them to depart upon certain conditions; and when they had obtained the security they desired, they delivered up the citadel, into which the people of Macherus put a garrison for their own security, and held it in their own power.

7. (487) But for Alexandria, the sedition of the people of the place against the Jews was perpetual, and this from that very time when Alexander [the Great], upon finding the readiness of the Jews in assisting him against the Egyptians, and as a reward for

such their assistance, gave them equal privileges in this city with the Grecians themselves; (488) which honorary reward continued among them under his successors, who also set apart for them a particular place, that they might live without being polluted [by the Gentiles], and were thereby not so much intermixed with foreigners as before; they also gave them this further privilege, that they should be called Macedonians. Nay, when the Romans got possession of Egypt, neither the first Caesar, nor any one that came after him, thought of diminishing the honors which Alexander had bestowed on the Jews. (489) But still conflicts perpetually arose with the Grecians; and although the governors did every day punish many of them, yet did the sedition grow worse; (490) but at this time especially, when there were tumults in other places also, the disorders among them were put into a greater flame; for when the Alexandrians had once a public assembly, to deliberate about an embassage they were sending to Nero, a great number of Jews came flocking to the theater; (491)but when their adversaries saw them, they immediately cried out, and called them their enemies, and said they came as spies upon them; upon which they rushed out, and laid violent hands upon them; and as for the rest, they were slain as they ran away; but there were three men whom they caught, and hauled them along, in order to have them burnt alive; (492) but all the Jews came in a body to defend them, who at first threw stones at the Grecians, but after that they took lamps, and rushed with violence into the theater, and threatened that they would burn the people to a man; and this they had soon done, unless Tiberius Alexander, the governor of the city, had restrained their passions. (493) However, this man did not begin to teach them wisdom by arms, but sent among them privately some of the principal men, and thereby entreated them to be quiet, and not provoke the Roman army against them; but the seditious made a jest of the entreaties of Tiberius, and reproached him for so doing.

Alexander the Great.

8. (494) Now when he perceived that those who were for innovations would not be pacified till some great calamity should overtake them, he sent out upon them those two Roman legions that were in the city, and together with them five thousand other soldiers, who, by chance, were come together out of Libya, to the ruin of the Jews. They were also permitted not only to kill them, but to plunder them of what they had, and to set fire to their houses. (495) These soldiers rushed violently into that part of the city that was called Delta, where the Jewish people lived together, and did as they were bidden, though not without bloodshed on their own side also; for the Jews got together, and set those that were the best armed among them in the forefront, and made a resistance for a great while; but when once they gave back, they were destroyed unmercifully; (496) and this their destruction was complete, some being caught in the open field, and others forced into their houses, which houses were first plundered of what was in them, and then set on fire by the Romans; wherein no mercy was shown to the infants, and no regard had to the aged; but they went on in the slaughter of persons of every age, (497) till all the place was overflowed with blood, and fifty thousand of them lay dead upon heaps; nor had the remainder been preserved, had they not betaken themselves to supplication. So Alexander commiserated their condition, and gave orders to the Romans to retire; (498) accordingly, these being accustomed to obey orders, left off killing at the first intimation; but the populace of Alexandria bare so very great hatred to the Jews, that it was difficult to recall them, and it was a hard thing to make them leave their dead bodies.

9. (499) And this was the miserable calamity which at this time befell the Jews at Alexandria. Hereupon Cestius thought fit no longer to lie still, while the Jews were everywhere up in arms; (500) so he took out of Antioch the twelfth legion entire, and out of each of the rest he selected two thousand, with six cohorts of footmen, and four troops of horsemen, besides those auxiliaries which were sent by the kings; of which Antiochus sent two thousand horsemen, and three thousand footmen, with as many archers; and Agrippa sent the same number of footmen, and one thousand horsemen; (501) Sohemus also followed with four thousand, a third part whereof were horsemen, but most part were archers, and thus did he march to Ptolemais. (502) There were also great numbers of auxiliaries gathered together from the [free] cities, who indeed had not the same skill in martial affairs, but made up in their alacrity and in their hatred to the Jews what they wanted in skill. There came also along with Cestius Agrippa himself, both as a guide in his march over the country, and a director what was fit to be done; (503) so Cestius took part of his forces, and marched hastily to Zabulon, a strong city of Galilee, which was called the City of Men, and divides the country of Ptolemais from our nation; (504) this he found deserted by its men, the multitude having fled to the mountains, but full of all sorts of good things; those he gave leave to the soldiers to plunder, and set fire to the city, although it was of admirable beauty, and had its houses built like those in Tyre, and Sidon, and Berytus. (505) After this he overran all the country, and seized upon whatsoever came in his way, and set fire to the villages that were round about them, and then returned to Ptolemais. (506) But when the Syrians, and especially those of Berytus, were busy in plundering, the Jews pulled up their courage again, for they knew that Cestius was retired, and fell upon those that were left behind unexpectedly, and destroyed about two thousand of them.

Altar of Julius Magnus, centurion of the Legio XII Fulminata, discovered in the sand dunes of Caesarea. (photo אור פ, via Wikimedia Commons)

10. (507) And now Cestius himself marched from Ptolemais, and came to Cesarea; but he sent part of his army before him to Joppa, and gave order, that if they could take that city [by surprise] they should keep it; but that in case the citizens should perceive they were coming to attack them, that they then should stay for him, and for the rest of the army. (508) So some of them made a brisk march by the sea-side, and some by land, and so coming upon them on both sides, they took the city with ease; and as the inhabitants had made no provision beforehand for a flight, nor had gotten any thing ready for fighting, the soldiers fell upon them, and slew them all, with their families, and then plundered and burnt the city. (509) The number of the slain was eight thousand four hundred. In like manner, Cestius sent also a considerable body of horsemen to the toparchy of Narbatene, that adjoined to Cesarea, who destroyed the country, and slew a great multitude of its people; they also plundered what they had, and burnt their villages.

11. (510) But Cestius sent Gallus, the commander of the twelfth legion, into Galilee, and delivered to him as many of his forces as he supposed sufficient to subdue that nation. (511) He was received by the strongest city of Galilee, which was Sepphoris, with acclamations of joy; which wise conduct of that city occasioned the rest of the cities to be in quiet; while the seditious part and the robbers ran away to that mountain which lies in the very middle of Galilee, and is situated over against Sepphoris; it is called Asamon. So Gallus brought his forces against them; (512) but while those men were in the superior parts above the Romans, they easily threw their darts upon the Romans, as they made their approaches, and slew about two hundred of them. But when the Romans had gone round the mountains, and were gotten into the parts above their enemies, the others were soon beaten; nor could they who had only light armor on sustain the force of them that fought them armed all over; nor when they were beaten could they escape the enemies' horsemen; insomuch that only some few concealed themselves in certain places hard to be come at, among the mountains, while the rest, above two thousand in number, were slain.

THE CAMPAIGN OF CESTIUS GALLUS A.D. 66

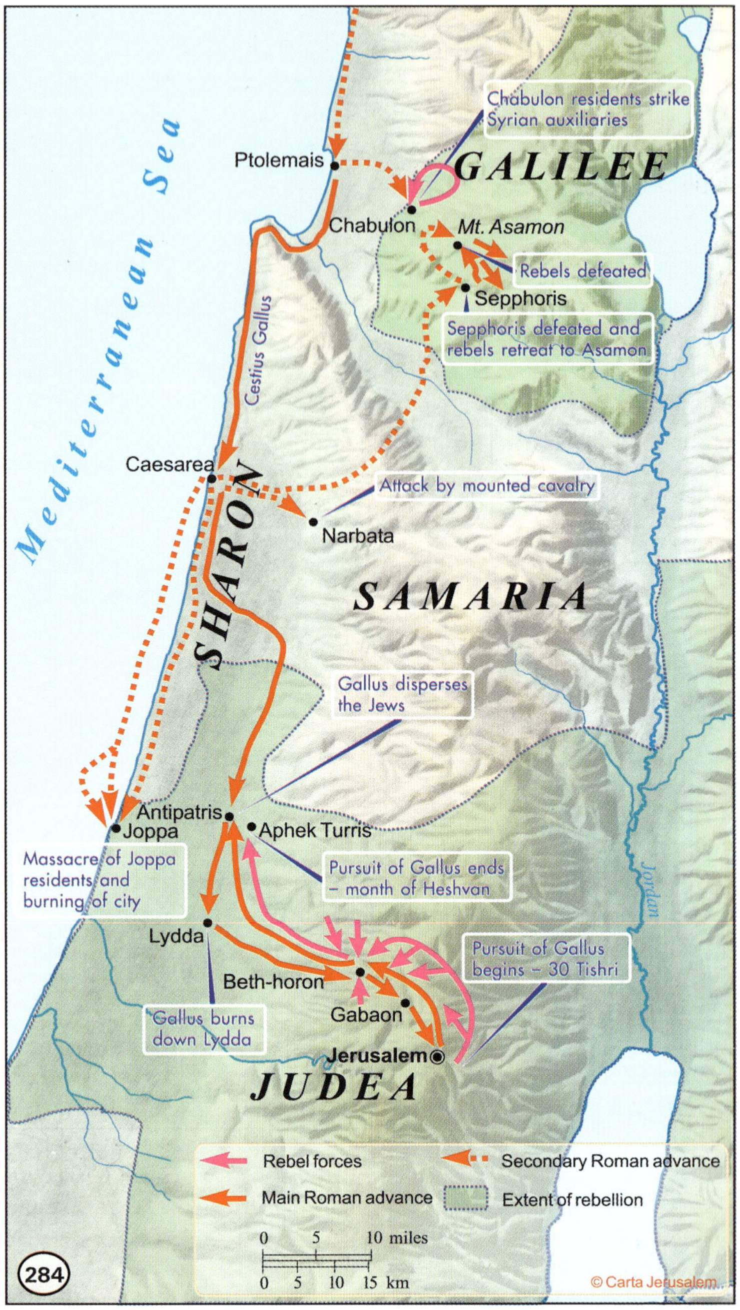

CHAPTER 19.

WHAT CESTIUS DID AGAINST THE JEWS; AND HOW, UPON HIS BESIEGING JERUSALEM, HE RETREATED FROM THE CITY WITHOUT ANY JUST OCCASION IN THE WORLD. AS ALSO WHAT SEVERE CALAMITIES HE UNDER WENT FROM THE JEWS IN HIS RETREAT.

1. (513) AND now Gallus, seeing nothing more that looked towards an innovation in Galilee, returned with his army to Cesarea: but Cestius removed with his whole army, and marched to Antipatris; and when he was informed that there was a great body of Jewish forces gotten together in a certain tower called Aphek [Turris], he sent a party before to fight them; (514) but this party dispersed the Jews by affrighting them before it came to a battle: so they came, and finding their camp deserted, they burnt it, as well as the villages that lay about it. (515) But when Cestius had marched from Antipatris to Lydda, he found the city empty of its men, for the whole multitude were gone up to Jerusalem to the feast of tabernacles; (516) yet did he destroy fifty of those that showed themselves, and burnt the city, and so marched forwards; and ascending by Bethoron, he pitched his camp at a certain place called Gabao, fifty furlongs distant from Jerusalem.

2. (517) But as for the Jews, when they saw the war approaching to their metropolis, they left the feast, and betook themselves to their arms; and taking courage greatly from their multitude, went in a sudden and disorderly manner to the fight, with a great noise, and without any consideration had of the rest of the seventh day, although the Sabbath was the day to which they had the greatest regard; (518) but that rage which made them forget the religious observation [of the sabbath] made them too hard for their enemies in the fight: with such violence therefore did they fall upon the Romans, as to break into their ranks, and to march through the midst of them, making a great slaughter as they went, (519) insomuch that unless the horsemen, and such part of the footmen as were not yet tired in the action, had wheeled round, and succored that part of the army which was not yet broken, Cestius, with his whole army, had been in danger: however, five hundred and fifteen of the Romans were slain, of which number four hundred were footmen, and the rest horsemen, while the Jews lost only twenty-two, (520) of whom the most valiant were the kinsmen of Monobazus, king of Adiabene, and their names were Monobazus and Kenedeus; and next to them were Niger of Perea, and Silas of Babylon, who had deserted from king Agrippa to the Jews; for he had formerly served in his army. (521) When the front of the Jewish army had been cut off, the Jews retired into the city; but still Simon, the son of Giora, fell upon the backs of the Romans, as

they were ascending up Bethoron, and put the hindmost of the army into disorder, and carried off many of the beasts that carded the weapons of war, and led them into the city. (522) But as Cestius tarried there three days, the Jews seized upon the elevated parts of the city, and set watches at the entrances into the city, and appeared openly resolved not to rest when once the Romans should begin to march.

3. (523) And now when Agrippa observed that even the affairs of the Romans were likely to be in danger, while such an immense multitude of their enemies had seized upon the mountains round about, he determined to try what the Jews would agree to by words, as thinking that he should either persuade them all to desist from fighting, or, however, that he should cause the sober part of them to separate themselves from the opposite party. (524) So he sent Borceus and Phebus, the persons of his party that were the best known to them, and promised them that Cestius should give them his right hand, to secure them of the Romans' entire forgiveness of what they had done amiss, if they would throw away their arms, and come over to them; (525) but the seditious, fearing lest the whole multitude, in hopes of security to themselves, should go over to Agrippa, resolved immediately to fall upon and kill the ambassadors; (526) accordingly they slew Phebus before he said a word, but Borceus was only wounded, and so prevented his fate by flying away. And when the people were very angry at this, they had the seditious beaten with stones and clubs, and drove them before them into the city.

4. (527) But now Cestius, observing that the disturbances that were begun among the Jews afforded him a proper opportunity to attack them, took his whole army along with him, and put the Jews to flight, and pursued them to Jerusalem. (528) He then pitched his camp upon the elevation called Scopus, [or watch-tower,] which was distant seven furlongs from the city; yet did not he assault them in three days' time, out of expectation that those within might perhaps yield a little; and in the mean time he sent out a great many of his soldiers into neighboring villages, to seize upon their corn. And on the fourth day, which was the thirtieth of the month Hyperbereteus, [Tisri,] when he had put his army in array, he brought it into the city. (529) Now for the people, they were kept under by the seditious; but the seditious themselves were greatly affrighted at the good order of the Romans, and retired from the suburbs, and retreated into the inner part of the city, and into the temple. (530) But when Cestius was come into the city, he set the part called Bezetha, which is called Cenopolis, [or the new city,] on fire; as he did also to the timber market; after which he came into the upper city, and pitched his camp over against the royal palace; (531) and had he but at this very time attempted to get within the walls by force, he had won the city presently, and the war had been put an end to at once; but Tyrannius Priseus, the muster-master of the army, and a great number of the officers of the horse, had been corrupted by Florus, and diverted him from that his attempt; (532) and that was the occasion that this war lasted so very long, and thereby the Jews were involved in such incurable calamities.

5. (533) In the mean time, many of the principal men of the city were persuaded by Ananus, the son of Jonathan, and invited Cestius into the city, and were about to open the gates for him; (534) but he overlooked this offer, partly out of his anger at the Jews, and partly because he did not thoroughly believe they were in earnest; whence it was that he delayed the matter so long, that the seditious perceived the treachery, and threw Ananus and those of his party down from the wall, and, pelting them with stones, drove them into their houses; but they stood themselves at proper distances in the towers, and threw their darts at those that were getting over the wall. (535) Thus did the Romans make their attack against the wall for five days, but to no purpose. But on the next day Cestius took a great many of his choicest men, and with them the archers, and attempted to break into the temple at the northern quarter of it; (536) but the Jews beat them off from the cloisters, and repulsed them several times when they were gotten near to the wall, till at length the multitude of the darts cut them off, and made them retire; (537) but the first rank of the Romans rested their shields upon the wall, and so did those that were behind them, and the like did those that were still more backward, and guarded themselves with what they call Testudo, [the back of] a tortoise, upon which the darts that were thrown fell, and slided off without doing them any harm; so the soldiers undermined the wall, without being themselves hurt, and got all things ready for setting fire to the gate of the temple.

6. (538) And now it was that a horrible fear seized upon the seditious, insomuch that many of them ran out of the city, as though it were to be taken immediately; but the people upon this took courage, and where the wicked part of the city gave ground, thither did they come, in order to set open the gates, and to admit Cestius as their benefactor, (539) who, had he but continued the siege a little longer, had certainly taken the city; but it was, I suppose, owing to the aversion God had already at the city and the sanctuary, that he was hindered from putting an end to the war that very day.

7. (540) It then happened that Cestius was not conscious either how the besieged despaired of success, nor how courageous the people were for him; and so he recalled his soldiers from the place, and by despairing of any expectation of taking it, without having received any disgrace, he retired from the city, without any reason in the world. (541) But when the robbers perceived this unexpected retreat of his, they resumed their courage, and ran after the hinder parts of his army, and destroyed a considerable number of both their horsemen and footmen; (542) and now Cestius lay all night at the camp which was at Scopus; and as he went off farther next day, he thereby invited the enemy to follow him, who still fell upon the hindmost, and destroyed them; they also fell upon the flank on each side of the army, and threw darts upon them obliquely, (543) nor durst those that were hindmost turn back upon those who wounded them behind, as imagining that the multitude of those that pursued them was immense; nor did they venture to drive away those that pressed upon them on each side, because they were heavy with their arms, and were afraid of breaking their ranks to pieces, and because they saw the Jews were light, and ready for making incursions upon them. And this was the reason why the Romans suffered greatly, without being able to revenge themselves upon their enemies; (544) so they were galled all the way, and their ranks were put into disorder, and those that were thus put out of their ranks were slain; among whom were Priscus, the commander of the sixth legion, and Longinus, the tribune, and Emilius Secundus, the commander of a troop of horsemen. So it was not without difficulty that they got to Gabao, their former camp, and that not without the loss of a great part of their baggage. (545) There it was that Cestius staid two days, and was in great distress to know what he should do in these circumstances; but when on the third day he saw a still much greater number of enemies, and all the parts round about him full of Jews, he understood that his delay was to his own detriment, and that if he staid any longer there, he should have still more enemies upon him.

8. (546) That therefore he might fly the faster, he gave orders to cast

View of Mount Scopus today, looking northeast. (photo Deror avi, via Wikimedia Common)

away what might hinder his army's march; so they killed the mules and other creatures, excepting those that carried their darts and machines, which they retained for their own use, and this principally because they were afraid lest the Jews should seize upon them. He then made his army march on as far as Bethoron. (547) Now the Jews did not so much press upon them when they were in large open places; but when they were penned up in their descent through narrow passages, then did some of them get before, and hindered them from getting out of them; and others of them thrust the hinder-most down into the lower places; and the whole multitude extended themselves over against the neck of the passage, and covered the Roman army with their darts. (548) In which circumstances, as the footmen knew not how to defend themselves, so the danger pressed the horsemen still more, for they were so pelted, that they could not march along the road in their ranks, and the ascents were so high, that the cavalry were not able to march against the enemy; (549) the precipices also and valleys into which they frequently fell, and tumbled down, were such on each side of them, that there was neither place for their flight, nor any contrivance could be thought of for their defense; till the distress they were at last in was so great, that they betook themselves to lamentations, and to such mournful cries as men use in the utmost despair: the joyful acclamations of the Jews also, as they encouraged one another, echoed the sounds back again, these last composing a noise of those that at once rejoiced and were in a rage. (550) Indeed, things were come to such a pass, that the Jews had almost taken Cestius's entire army prisoners, had not the night come on, when the Romans fled to Bethoron, and the Jews seized upon all the places round about them, and watched for their coming out [in the morning].

9. (551) And then it was that Cestius, despairing of obtaining room for a public march, contrived how he might best run away; and when he had selected four hundred of the most courageous of his soldiers, he placed them at the strongest of their fortifications, and gave order, that when they went up to the morning guard, they should erect their ensigns, that the Jews might be made to believe that the entire army was there still, while he himself took the rest of his forces with him, and marched, without any noise, thirty furlongs. (552) But when the Jews perceived, in the morning, that the camp was empty, they ran upon those four hundred who had deluded them, and immediately threw their darts at them, and slew them; and then pursued after Cestius. (553) But he had already made use of a great part of the night in his flight, and still marched quicker when it was day; insomuch that the soldiers, through the astonishment and fear they were in, left behind them their engines for sieges, and for throwing of stones, and a great part of the instruments of war. (554) So the Jews went on pursuing the Romans as far as Antipatris; after which, seeing they could not overtake them, they came back, and took the engines, and spoiled the dead bodies, and gathered the prey together which the Romans had left behind them, and came back running and singing to their metropolis; (555) while they had themselves lost a few only, but had slain of the Romans five thousand and three hundred footmen, and three hundred and eighty horsemen. This defeat happened on the eighth day of the month Dius, [Marchesvan,] in the twelfth year of the reign of Nero.

CHAPTER 20.

CESTIUS SENDS AMBASSADORS TO NERO. THE PEOPLE OF DAMASCUS SLAY THOSE JEWS THAT LIVED WITH THEM. THE PEOPLE OF JERUSALEM AFTER THEY HAD [LEFT OFF] PURSUING CESTIUS, RETURN TO THE CITY AND GET THINGS READY FOR ITS DEFENSE AND MAKE A GREAT MANY GENERALS FOR, THEIR ARMIES AND PARTICULARLY JOSEPHUS THE WRITER OF THESE BOOKS. SOME ACCOUNT OF HIS ADMINISTRATION.

1. (556) AFTER this calamity had befallen Cestius, many of the most eminent of the Jews swam away from the city, as from a ship when it was going to sink; Costobarus, therefore, and Saul, who were brethren, together with Philip, the son of Jacimus, who was the commander of king Agrippa's forces, ran away from the city, and went to Cestius. (557) But then how Antipas, who had been besieged with them in the king's palace, but would not fly away with them, was afterward slain by the seditious, we shall relate hereafter. (558) However, Cestius sent Saul and his friends, at their own desire, to Achaia, to Nero, to inform him of the great distress they were in, and to lay the blame of their kindling the war upon Florus, as hoping to alleviate his own danger, by provoking his indignation against Florus.

2. (559) In the mean time, the people of Damascus, when they were informed of the destruction of the Romans, set about the slaughter of those Jews that were among them; (560) and as they had them already cooped up together in the place of public exercises, which they had done out of the suspicion they had of them, they thought they should meet with no difficulty in the attempt; yet did they distrust their own wives, which were almost all of them addicted to the Jewish religion; (561) on which account it was that their greatest concern was, how they might conceal these things

from them; so they came upon the Jews, and cut their throats, as being in a narrow place, in number ten thousand, and all of them unarmed, and this in one hour's time, without any body to disturb them.

3. (562) But as to those who had pursued after Cestius, when they were returned back to Jerusalem, they overbore some of those that favored the Romans by violence, and some them persuaded [by entreaties] to join with them, and got together in great numbers in the temple, and appointed a great many generals for the war. (563) Joseph also, the son of Gorion, and Ananus the high priest, were chosen as governors of all affairs within the city, and with a particular charge to repair the walls of the city; (564) for they did not ordain Eleazar the son of Simon to that office, although he had gotten into his possession the prey they had taken from the Romans, and the money they had taken from Cestius, together with a great part of the public treasures, because they saw he was of a tyrannical temper, and that his followers were, in their behavior, like guards about him. (565) However, the want they were in of Eleazar's money, and the subtle tricks used by him, brought all so about, that the people were circumvented, and submitted themselves to his authority in all public affairs.

4. (566) They also chose other generals for Idumea; Jesus, the son of Sapphias, one of the high priests; and Eleazar, the son of Ananias, the high priest; they also enjoined Niger, the then governor of Idumea, who was of a family that belonged to Perea, beyond Jordan, and was thence called the Peraite, that he should be obedient to those fore-named commanders. (567) Nor did they neglect the care of other parts of the country; but Joseph the son of Simon was sent as general to Jericho, as was Manasseh to Perea, and John, the Esscue, to the toparchy of Thamna; Lydda was also added to his portion, and Joppa, and Emmaus. (568) But John, the son of Matthias, was made governor of the toparchies of Gophnitica and Acrabattene; as was Josephus, the son of Matthias, of both the Galilees. Gamala also, which was the strongest city in those parts, was put under his command.

5. (569) So every one of the other commanders administered the affairs of his portion with that alacrity and prudence they were masters of; but as to Josephus, when he came into Galilee, his first care was to gain the good-will of the people of that country, as sensible that he should thereby have in general good success, although he should fail in other points. (570) And being conscious to himself that if he communicated part of his power to the great men, he should make them his fast friends; and that he should gain the same favor from the multitude, if he executed his commands by persons of their own country, and with whom they were well acquainted; he chose out seventy of the most prudent men, and those elders in age, and appointed them to be rulers of all Galilee, (571) as he chose seven judges in every city to hear the lesser quarrels; for as to the greater causes, and those wherein life and death were concerned, he enjoined they should be brought to him and the seventy elders.

6. (572) Josephus also, when he had settled these rules for determining causes by the law, with regard to the people's dealings one with another, betook himself to make provisions for their safety against external violence; (573) and as he knew the Romans would fall upon Galilee, he built walls in proper places about Jotapata, and Bersabe, and Selamis; and besides these, about Caphareccho, and Japha, and Sigo, and what they call Mount Tabor, and Taricheae, and Tiberias. Moreover, he built walls about the caves near the lake of Gennesar, which places lay in the Lower Galilee; the same he did to the places of Upper Galilee, as well as to the rock called the Rock of the Achabari, and to Seph, and Jamnith, and Meroth; (574) and in Gaulonitis he fortified Seleucia, and Sogane, and Gamala; but as to those of Sepphoris, they were the only people to whom he gave leave to build their own walls, and this because he perceived they were rich and wealthy, and ready to go to war, without standing in need of any injunctions for that purpose. (575) The case was the same with Gischala, which had a wall built about it by John the son of Levi himself, but with the consent of Josephus; but for the building of the rest of the fortresses, he labored together with all the other builders, and was present to give all the necessary orders for that purpose. (576) He also got together an army out of Galilee, of more than a hundred thousand young men, all of which he armed with the old weapons which he had collected together and prepared for them.

7. (577) And when he had considered that the Roman power became invincible, chiefly by their readiness in obeying orders, and the constant exercise of their arms, he despaired of teaching these his men the use of their arms, which was to be obtained by experience; but observing that their readiness in obeying orders was

The fortified hill of Gamala in the Golan. (photo Samuel Magal)

Gush Halav (Jish), home of John of Gischala. Shown here are remains of the synagogue, facing northwest. (photo Sean Leatherbury/Manar al-Athar)

owing to the multitude of their officers, he made his partitions in his army more after the Roman manner, and appointed a great many subalterns. (578) He also distributed the soldiers into various classes, whom he put under captains of tens, and captains of hundreds, and then under captains of thousands; and besides these, he had commanders of larger bodies of men. (579) He also taught them to give the signals one to another, and to call and recall the soldiers by the trumpets, how to expand the wings of an army, and make them wheel about; and when one wing hath had success, to turn again and assist those that were hard set, and to join in the defense of what had most suffered. (580) He also continually instructed them ill what concerned the courage of the soul, and the hardiness of the body; and, above all, he exercised them for war, by declaring to them distinctly the good order of the Romans, and that they were to fight with men who, both by the strength of their bodies and courage of their souls, had conquered in a manner the whole habitable earth. (581) He told them that he should make trial of the good order they would observe in war, even before it came to any battle, in case they would abstain from the crimes they used to indulge themselves in, such as theft, and robbery, and rapine, and from defrauding their own countrymen, and never to esteem the harm done to those that were so near of kin to them to be any advantage to themselves; (582) for that wars are then managed the best when the warriors preserve a good conscience; but that such as are ill men in private life will not only have those for enemies which attack them, but God himself also for their antagonist.

8. (583) And thus did he continue to admonish them. Now he chose for the war such an army as was sufficient, i.e. sixty thousand footmen, and two hundred and fifty horsemen; and besides these, on which he put the greatest trust, there were about four thousand five hundred mercenaries; he had also six hundred men as guards of his body. (584) Now the cities easily maintained the rest of his army, excepting the mercenaries, for every one of the cities enumerated above sent out half their men to the army, and retained the other half at home, in order to get provisions for them; insomuch that the one part went to the war, and the other part to their work, and so those that sent out their corn were paid for it by those that were in arms, by that security which they enjoyed from them.

CHAPTER 21.

CONCERNING JOHN OF GISCHALA. JOSEPHUS USES STRATAGEMS AGAINST THE PLOTS JOHN LAID AGAINST HIM AND RECOVERS CERTAIN CITIES WHICH HAD REVOLTED FROM HIM.

1. (585) NOW as Josephus was thus engaged in the administration of the affairs of Galilee, there arose a treacherous person, a man of Gischala, the son of Levi, "whose name was John. His character was that of a very cunning and very knavish person, beyond the ordinary rate of the other men of eminence there, and for wicked practices he had not his fellow any where. Poor he was at first, and for a long time his wants were a hinderance to him in his wicked designs. (586) He was a ready liar, and yet very sharp in gaining credit to his fictions: he thought it a point of virtue to delude people, and would delude even such as were the dearest to him. (587) He was a hypocritical pretender to humanity, but where he had hopes of gain, he spared not the shedding of blood: his desires were ever carried to great things, and he encouraged his hopes from those mean wicked tricks which he was the author of. He had a peculiar knack at thieving; but in some time he got certain companions in his impudent practices; at first they were but few, but as he proceeded on in his evil course, they became still more and more numerous. (588) He took care that none of his partners should be easily caught in their rogueries, but chose such out of the rest as had the strongest constitutions of body, and the greatest courage of soul, together with great skill in martial affairs; as he got together a band of four hundred men, who came principally out of the country of Tyre, and were vagabonds that had run away from its villages; (589) and by the means of these he laid waste all Galilee, and irritated a considerable number, who were in great expectation of a war then suddenly to arise among them.

2. (590) However, John's want of money had hitherto restrained him in his ambition after command, and in his attempts to advance himself. But when he saw that Josephus was highly pleased with the activity of his temper, he persuaded him, in the first place, to intrust him with the repairing of the walls of his native city, [Gischala,] in which work he got a great deal of money from the rich citizens. (591) He after that contrived a very shrewd trick, and pretending that the Jews who dwelt in Syria were obliged to make use of oil that was made by others than those of their own nation, he desired leave of Josephus to send oil to their borders; (592) so he bought four amphorae with such Tyrian money as was of the value of four Attic drachmae, and sold every half-amphora at the same price. And as Galilee was very fruitful in oil, and was peculiarly so at that time, by sending away great quantities, and having the sole privilege so to do, he gathered an immense sum of money together, which money he immediately used to the disadvantage of him who gave him that privilege; (593) and, as he supposed, that if he could once overthrow Josephus, he should himself obtain the government of Galilee; so he gave orders to the robbers that

were under his command to be more zealous in their thievish expeditions, that by the rise of many that desired innovations in the country, he might either catch their general in his snares, as he came to the country's assistance, and then kill him; or if he should overlook the robbers, he might accuse him for his negligence to the people of the country. (594) He also spread abroad a report far and near that Josephus was delivering up the administration of affairs to the Romans; and many such plots did he lay, in order to ruin him.

3. (595) Now at the same time that certain young men of the village Dabaritta, who kept guard in the Great Plain laid snares for Ptolemy, who was Agrippa's and Bernice's steward, and took from him all that he had with him; among which things there were a great many costly garments, and no small number of silver cups, and six hundred pieces of gold; (596) yet were they not able to conceal what they had stolen, but brought it all to Josephus, to Taricheae. (597) Hereupon he blamed them for the violence they had offered to the king and queen, and deposited what they brought to him with Eneas, the most potent man of Taricheae, with an intention of sending the things back to the owners at a proper time; which act of Josephus brought him into the greatest danger; (598) for those that had stolen the things had an indignation at him, both because they gained no share of it for themselves, and because they perceived beforehand what was Josephus's intention, and that he would freely deliver up what had cost them so much pains to the king and queen. These ran away by night to their several villages, and declared to all men that Josephus was going to betray them: they also raised great disorders in all the neighboring cities, insomuch that in the morning a hundred thousand armed men came running together; (599) which multitude was crowded together in the hippodrome at Taricheae, and made a very peevish clamor against him; while some cried out, that they should depose the traitor; and others, that they should burn him. Now John irritated a great many, as did also one Jesus, the son of Sapphias, who was then governor of Tiberias. (600) Then it was that Josephus's friends, and the guards of his body, were so affrighted at this violent assault of the multitude, that they all fled away but four; and as he was asleep, they awaked him, as the people were going to set fire to the house. (601) And although those four that remained with him persuaded him to run away, he was neither surprised at his being himself deserted, nor at the great multitude that came against him, but leaped out to them with his clothes rent, and ashes sprinkled on his head, with his hands behind him, and his sword hanging at his neck. (602) At this sight his friends, especially those of Taricheae, commiserated his condition; but those that came out of the country, and those in their neighborhood, to whom his government seemed burdensome, reproached him, and bid him produce the money which belonged to them all immediately, and to confess the agreement he had made to betray them; (603) for they imagined, from the habit in which he appeared, that he would deny nothing of what they suspected concerning him, and that it was in order to obtain pardon that he had put himself entirely into so pitiable a posture. (604) But this humble appearance was only designed as preparatory to a stratagem of his, who thereby contrived to set those that were so angry at him at variance one with another about the things they were angry at. However, he promised he would confess all: (605) hereupon he was permitted to speak, when he said, "I did neither intend to send this money back to Agrippa, nor to gain it myself; for I did never esteem one that was your enemy to be my friend, nor did I look upon what would tend to your disadvantage to be my advantage. But, (606) O you people of Taricheae, I saw that your city stood in more need than others of fortifications for your security, and that it wanted money in order for the building it a wall. I was also afraid lest the people of Tiberias and other cities should lay a plot to seize upon these spoils, and therefore it was that I intended to retain this money privately, that I might encompass you with a wall. (607) But if this does not please you, I will produce what was brought me, and leave it to you to plunder it; but if I have conducted myself so well as to please you, you may if you please punish your benefactor."

4. (608) Hereupon the people of Taricheae loudly commended him; but those of Tiberias, with the rest of the company, gave him hard names, and threatened what they would do to him; so both sides left off quarrelling with Josephus, and fell on quarrelling with one another. So he grew bold upon the dependence he had on his friends, which were the people of Taricheae, and about forty thousand in number, and spake more freely to the whole multitude, and reproached them greatly for their rashness; (609) and told them, that with this money he would build walls about Taricheae, and would put the other cities in a state of security also; for that they should not want money, if they would but agree for whose benefit it was to be procured, and would not suffer themselves to be irritated against him who procured it for them.

5. (610) Hereupon the rest of the multitude that had been deluded retired; but yet so that they went away angry, and two thousand of them made an assault upon him in their armor; and as he was al-

TIBERIAS—PLAN OF THE ROMAN-BYZANTINE CITY

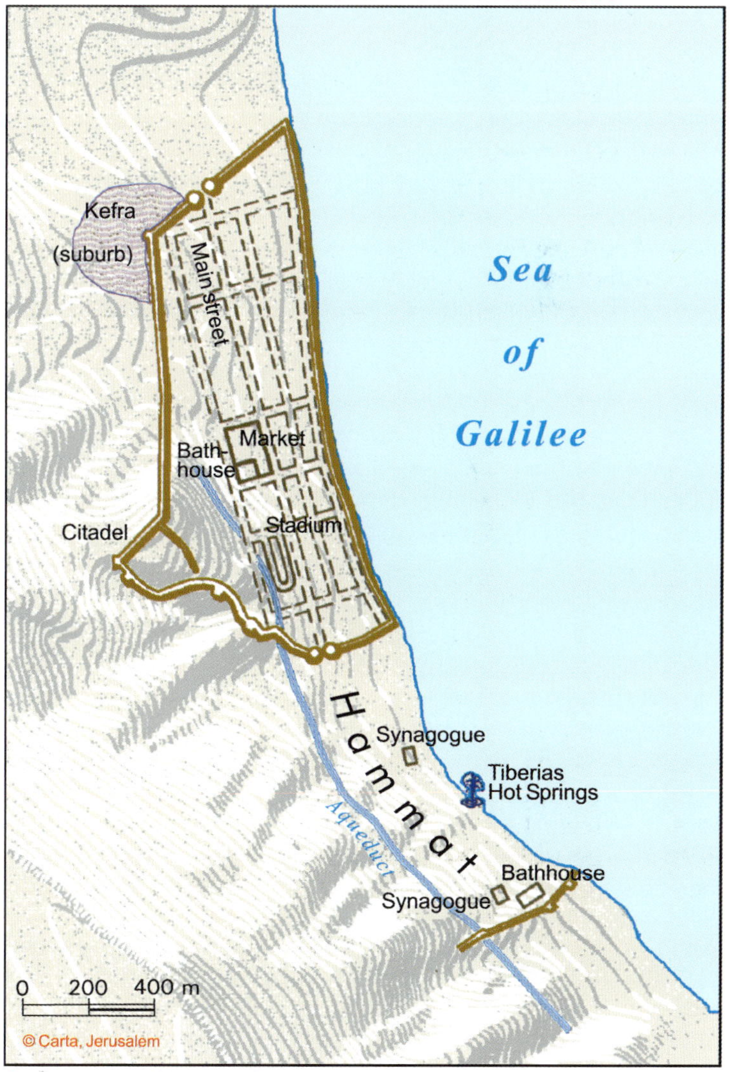

(from *Carta's Atlas of the Period of the Second Temple: Mishnah and the Talmud* / M. Avi-Yonah)

Tiberias today, looking northeast. (photo Samuel Magal)

ready gone to his own house, they stood without and threatened him. (611) On which occasion Josephus again used a second stratagem to escape them; for he got upon the top of his house, and with his right hand desired them to be silent, and said to them, "I cannot tell what you would have, nor can hear what you say, for the confused noise you make;" but he said that he would comply with all their demands, in case they would but send some of their number in to him that might talk with him about it. (612) And when the principal of them, with their leaders, heard this, they came into the house. He then drew them to the most retired part of the house, and shut the door of that hall where he put them, and then had them whipped till every one of their inward parts appeared naked. In the mean time the multitude stood round the house, and supposed that he had a long discourse with those that were gone in about what they claimed of him. (613) He had then the doors set open immediately, and sent the men out all bloody, which so terribly aftrighted those that had before threatened him, that they threw away their arms and ran away.

6. (614) But as for John, his envy grew greater [upon this escape of Josephus], and he framed a new plot against him; he pretended to be sick, and by a letter desired that Josephus would give him leave to use the hot baths that were at Tiberias, for the recovery of his health. (615) Hereupon Josephus, who hitherto suspected nothing of John's plots against him, wrote to the governors of the city, that they would provide a lodging and necessaries for John; which favors, when he had made use of, in two days' time he did what he came about; some he corrupted with delusive frauds, and others with money, and so persuaded them to revolt from Josephus. (616) This Silas, who was appointed guardian of the city by Josephus, wrote to him immediately, and informed him of the plot against him; which epistle when Josephus had received, he marched with great diligence all night, and came early in the morning to Tiberias; (617) at which time the rest of the multitude met him. But John, who suspected that his coming was not for his advantage, sent however one of his friends, and pretended that he was sick, and that being confined to his bed, he could not come to pay him his respects. (618) But as soon as Josephus had got the people of Tiberias together in the stadium, and tried to discourse with them about the letters that he had received, John privately sent some armed men, and gave them orders to slay him. (619) But when the people saw that the armed men were about to draw their swords, they cried out; at which cry Josephus turned himself about, and when he saw that the swords were just at his throat, he marched away in great haste to the sea-shore, and left off that speech which he was going to make to the people, upon an elevation of six cubits high. He then seized on a ship which lay in the haven, and leaped into it, with two of his guards, and fled away into the midst of the lake.

7. (620) But now the soldiers he had with him took up their arms immediately, and marched against the plotters; but Josephus was afraid lest a civil war should be raised by the envy of a few men, and bring the city to ruin; so he sent some of his party to tell them, that they should do no more than provide for their own safety; that they should not kill any body, nor accuse any for the occasion they had afforded [of disorder]. (621) Accordingly, these men obeyed his orders, and were quiet; but the people of the neighboring country, when they were informed of this plot, and of the plotter, they got together in great multitudes to oppose John. But he prevented their attempt, and fled away to Gischala, his native city, (622) while the Galileans came running out of their several cit-

ies to Josephus; and as they were now become many ten thousands of armed men, they cried out, that they were come against John the common plotter against their interest, and would at the same time burn him, and that city which had received him. (623) Hereupon Josephus told them that he took their good-will to him kindly, but still he restrained their fury, and intended to subdue his enemies by prudent conduct, rather than by slaying them; (624) so he excepted those of every city which had joined in this revolt with John, by name, who had readily been shown him by these that came from every city, and caused public proclamation to be made, that he would seize upon the effects of those that did not forsake John within five days' time, and would burn both their houses and their families with fire. (625) Whereupon three thousand of John's party left him immediately, who came to Josephus, and threw their arms down at his feet. John then betook himself, together with his two thousand Syrian runagates, from open attempts, to more secret ways of treachery. (626) Accordingly, he privately sent messengers to Jerusalem, to accuse Josephus, as having to great power, and to let them know that he would soon come as a tyrant to their metropolis, unless they prevented him. (627) This accusation the people were aware of beforehand, but had no regard to it. However, some of the grandees, out of envy, and some of the rulers also, sent money to John privately, that he might be able to get together mercenary soldiers, in order to fight Josephus; they also made a decree of themselves, and this for recalling him from his government, yet did they not think that decree sufficient; (628) so they sent withal two thousand five hundred armed men, and four persons of the highest rank amongst them; Joazar the son of Nomicus, and Ananias the son of Sadduk, as also Simon and Judas the sons of Jonathan, all very able men in speaking, that these persons might withdraw the good-will of the people from Josephus. These had it in charge, that if he would voluntarily come away, they should permit him to [come and] give an account of his conduct; but if he obstinately insisted upon continuing in his government, they should treat him as an enemy. (629) Now Josephus's friends had sent him word that an army was coming against him, but they gave him no notice beforehand what the reason of their coming was, that being only known among some secret councils of his enemies; and by this means it was that four cities revolted from him immediately, Sepphoris, and Gamala, and Gischala, and Tiberias. (630) Yet did he recover these cities without war; and when he had routed those four commanders by stratagems, and had taken the most potent of their warriors, he sent them to Jerusalem; (631) and the people [of Galilee] had great indignation at them, and were in a zealous disposition to slay, not only these forces, but those that sent them also, had not these forces prevented it by running away.

8. (632) Now John was detained afterward within the walls of Gischala, by the fear he was in of Josephus; but within a few days Tiberias revolted again, the people within it inviting king Agrippa [to return to the exercise of his authority there]. (633) And when he did not come at the time appointed, and when a few Roman horsemen appeared that day, they expelled Josephus out of the city. (634) Now this revolt of theirs was presently known at Taricheae; and as Josephus had sent out all the soldiers that were with him to gather corn, he knew not how either to march out alone against the revolters, or to stay where he was, because he was afraid the king's soldiers might prevent him if he tarried, and might get into the city; for he did not intend to do any thing on the next day, because it was the sabbath day, and would hinder his proceeding. (635) So he contrived to circumvent the revolters by a stratagem; and in the first place he ordered the gates of Taricheae to be shut, that nobody might go out and inform [those of Tiberias], for whom it was intended, what stratagem he was about; he then got together all the ships that were upon the lake, which were found to be two hundred and thirty, and in each of them he put no more than four mariners. So he sailed to Tiberias with haste, (636) and kept at such a distance from the city, that it was not easy for the people to see the vessels, and ordered that the empty vessels should float up and down there, while himself, who had but seven of his guards with him, and those unarmed also, went so near as to be seen; (637) but when his adversaries, who were still reproaching him, saw him from the walls, they were so astonished that they supposed all the ships were full of armed men, and threw down their arms, and by signals of intercession they besought him to spare the city.

Roman bust thought to be that of Josephus. (original in Ny Carlsberg Glyptotek)

9. (637) Upon this Josephus threatened them terribly, and reproached them, that when they were the first that took up arms against the Romans, they should spend their force beforehand in civil dissensions, and do what their enemies desired above all things; and that besides they should endeavor so hastily to seize upon him, who took care of their safety, and had not been ashamed to shut the gates of their city against him that built their walls; that, however, he would admit of any intercessors from them that might make some excuse for them, and with whom he would make such agreements as might be for the city's security. (639) Hereupon ten of the most potent men of Tiberias came down to him presently; and when he had taken them into one of his vessels, he ordered them to be carried a great way off from the city. He then commanded that fifty others of their senate, such as were men of the greatest eminence, should come to him, that they also might give him some security on their behalf. (640) After which, under one new pretense or another, he called forth others, one after another, to make the leagues between them. (641) He then gave order to the masters of those vessels which he had thus filled to sail away immediately for Taricheae, and to confine those men in the prison there; till at length he took all their senate, consisting of six hundred persons, and about two thousand of the populace, and carried them away to Taricheae.

10. (642) And when the rest of the people cried out, that it was one Clitus that was the chief author of this revolt, they desired him to spend his anger upon him [only]; but Josephus, whose intention it was to slay nobody, commanded one Levius, belonging to his guards, to go out of the vessel, in order to cut off both Clitus's hands; (643) yet was Levius afraid to go out by himself alone to such a large body of enemies, and refused to go. Now Clitus saw that Josephus was in a great passion in the ship, and ready to leap out of it, in order to execute the punishment himself; he begged there-

Remains of the synagogue at Gischala. (photo Samuel Magal)

fore from the shore, that he would leave him one of his hands; (644) which Josephus agreed to, upon condition that he would himself cutoff the other hand; accordingly he drew his sword, and with his right hand cut off his left, so great was the fear he was in of Josephus himself. (645) And thus he took the people of Tiberias prisoners, and recovered the city again with empty ships and seven of his guard. Moreover, a few days afterward he retook Gischala, which had revolted with the people of Sepphoris, and gave his soldiers leave to plunder it; (646) yet did he get all the plunder together, and restored it to the inhabitants; and the like he did to the inhabitants of Sepphoris and Tiberias. For when he had subdued those cities, he had a mind, by letting them be plundered, to give them some good instruction, while at the same time he regained their good-will by restoring them their money again.

CHAPTER 22.

THE JEWS MAKE ALL READY FOR THE WAR; AND SIMON, THE SON OF GIORAS, FALLS TO PLUNDERING.

1. (647) AND thus were the disturbances of Galilee quieted, when, upon their ceasing to prosecute their civil dissensions, they betook themselves to make preparations for the war with the Romans. (648) Now in Jerusalem the high priest Artanus, and do as many of the men of power as were not in the interest of the Romans, both repaired the walls, and made a great many warlike instruments, insomuch that (649) in all parts of the city darts and all sorts of armor were upon the anvil. Although the multitude of the young men were engaged in exercises, without any regularity, and all places were full of tumultuous doings; yet the moderate sort were exceedingly sad; and a great many there were who, out of the prospect they had of the calamities that were coming upon them, made great lamentations. (650) There were also such omens observed as were understood to be forerunners of evils by such as loved peace, but were by those that kindled the war interpreted so as to suit their own inclinations; and the very state of the city, even before the Romans came against it, was that of a place doomed to destruction. (651) However, Ananus's concern was this, to lay aside, for a while, the preparations for the war, and to persuade the seditious to consult their own interest, and to restrain the madness of those that had the name of zealots; but their violence was too hard for him; and what end he came to we shall relate hereafter.

2. (652) But as for the Acrabbene toparchy, Simon, the son of Gioras, got a great number of those that were fond of innovations together, and betook himself to ravage the country; nor did he only harass the rich men's houses, but tormented their bodies, and appeared openly and beforehand to affect tyranny in his government. (653) And when an army was sent against him by Artanus, and the other rulers, he and his band retired to the robbers that were at Masada, and staid there, and plundered the country of Idumea with them, till both Ananus and his other adversaries were slain; (654) and until the rulers of that country were so afflicted with the multitude of those that were slain, and with the continual ravage of what they had, that they raised an army, and put garrisons into the villages, to secure them from those insults. And in this state were the affairs of Judea at that time.

BOOK III

FROM VESPASIAN'S COMING TO SUBDUE THE JEWS TO THE TAKING OF GAMALA

CHAPTER 1.

VESPASIAN IS SENT INTO SYRIA BY NERO IN ORDER TO MAKE WAR WITH THE JEWS.

1. (1) WHEN Nero was informed of the Romans' ill success in Judea, a concealed consternation and terror, as is usual in such cases, fell upon him; although he openly looked very big, and was very angry, (2) and said that what had happened was rather owing to the negligence of the commander, than to any valor of the enemy: and as he thought it fit for him, who bare the burden of the whole empire, to despise such misfortunes, he now pretended so to do, and to have a soul superior to all such sad accidents whatsoever. Yet did the disturbance that was in his soul plainly appear by the solicitude he was in [how to recover his affairs again].

Vespasian. (Capitoline Museum, Rome; photo Samuel Magal)

2. (3) And as he was deliberating to whom he should commit the care of the East, now it was in so great a commotion, and who might be best able to punish the Jews for their rebellion, and might prevent the same distemper from seizing upon the neighboring nations also,—(4) he found no one but Vespasian equal to the task, and able to undergo the great burden of so mighty a war, seeing he was growing an old man already in the camp, and from his youth had been exercised in warlike exploits: he was also a man that had long ago pacified the west, and made it subject to the Romans, when it had been put into disorder by the Germans; he had also recovered to them Britain by his arms, (5) which had been little known before whereby he procured to his father Claudius to have a triumph bestowed on him without any sweat or labor of his own.

3. (6) So Nero esteemed these circumstances as favorable omens, and saw that Vespasian's age gave him sure experience, and great skill, and that he had his sons as hostages for his fidelity to himself, and that the flourishing age they were in would make them fit instruments under their father's prudence. Perhaps also there was some interposition of Providence, which was paving the way for Vespasian's being himself emperor afterwards. (7) Upon the whole, he sent this man to take upon him the command of the armies that were in Syria; but this not without great encomiums and flattering compellations, such as necessity required, and such as might mollify him into complaisance. (8) So Vespasian sent his son Titus from Achaia, where he had been with Nero, to Alexandria, to bring back with him from thence the fifth and the tenth legions, while he himself, when he had passed over the Hellespont, came by land into Syria, where he gathered together the Roman forces, with a considerable number of auxiliaries from the kings in that neighborhood.

CHAPTER 2.

A GREAT SLAUGHTER ABOUT ASCALON. VESPASIAN COMES TO PTOLEMAIS.

1. (9) Now the Jews, after they had beaten Cestius, were so much elevated with their unexpected success, that they could not govern their zeal, but, like people blown up into a flame by their good fortune, carried the war to remoter places. Accordingly, they presently got together a great multitude of all their most hardy soldiers, and marched away for Ascalon. (10) This is an ancient city that is distant from Jerusalem five hundred and twenty furlongs, and was always an enemy to the Jews; on which account they determined to make their first effort against it, and to make their approaches to it as near as possible. (11) This excursion was led on by three men, who were the chief of them all, both for strength and sagacity; Niger, called the Persite, Silas of Babylon, and besides them John the Essene. (12) Now Ascalon was strongly walled about, but had almost no assistance to be relied on [near them], for the garrison consisted of one cohort of footmen, and one troop of horsemen, whose captain was Antonius.

2. (13) These Jews, therefore, out of their anger, marched faster than ordinary, and, as if they had come but a little way, approached very near the city, and were come even to it; (14) but Antonius, who was not unapprized of the attack they were going to make upon the

Ancient ramparts of Ascalon. (photo Azaria Alon)

city, drew out his horsemen beforehand, and being neither daunted at the multitude, nor at the courage of the enemy, received their first attacks with great bravery; and when they crowded to the very walls, he beat them off. (15) Now the Jews were unskillful in war, but were to fight with those who were skillful therein; they were footmen to fight with horsemen; they were in disorder, to fight those that were united together; they were poorly armed, to fight those that were completely so; they were to fight more by their rage than by sober counsel, and were exposed to soldiers that were exactly obedient; and did every thing they were bidden upon the least intimation. (16) So they were easily beaten; for as soon as ever their first ranks were once in disorder, they were put to flight by the enemy's cavalry, and those of them that came behind such as crowded to the wall fell upon their own party's weapons, and became one another's enemies; and this so long till they were all forced to give way to the attacks of the horsemen, and were dispersed all the plain over, which plain was wide, and all fit for the horsemen; (17) which circumstance was very commodious for the Romans, and occasioned the slaughter of the greatest number of the Jews; for such as ran away, they could overrun them, and make them turn back; and when they had brought them back after their flight, and driven them together, they ran them through, and slew a vast number of them, insomuch that others encompassed others of them, and drove them before them whithersoever they turned themselves, and slew them easily with their arrows; (18) and the great number there were of the Jews seemed a solitude to themselves, by reason of the distress they were in, while the Romans had such good success with their small number, that they seemed to themselves to be the greater multitude. (19) And as the former strove zealously under their misfortunes, out of the shame of a sudden flight, and hopes of the change in their success, so did the latter feel no weariness by reason of their good fortune; insomuch that the fight lasted till the evening, till ten thousand men of the Jews' side lay dead, with two of their generals, John and Silas, (20) and the greater part of the remainder were wounded, with Niger, their remaining general, who fled away together to a small city of Idumea, called Sallis. (21) Some few also of the Romans were wounded in this battle.

3. (22) Yet were not the spirits of the Jews broken by so great a calamity, but the losses they had sustained rather quickened their resolution for other attempts; for, overlooking the dead bodies which lay under their feet, they were enticed by their former glorious actions to venture on a second destruction; (23) so when they had lain still so little a while that their wounds were not yet thoroughly cured, they got together all their forces, and came with greater fury, and in much greater numbers, to Ascalon. (24) But their former ill fortune followed them, as the consequence of their unskilfulness, and other deficiencies in war; (25) for Antonius laid ambushes for them in the passages they were to go through, where they fell into snares unexpectedly, and where they were encompassed about with horsemen, before they could form themselves into a regular body for fighting, and were above eight thousand of them slain; so all the rest of them ran away, and with them Niger, who still did a great many bold exploits in his flight. However, they were driven along together by the enemy, who pressed hard upon them, into a certain strong tower belonging to a village called Bezedeh. (26) However, Antonius and his party, that they might neither spend any considerable time about this tower, which was hard to be taken, nor suffer their commander, and the most courageous man of them all, to escape from them, they set the wall on fire; (27) and as the tower was burning, the Romans went away rejoicing, as taking it for granted that Niger was destroyed; but he leaped out of the tower into a subterraneous cave, in the innermost part of it, and was preserved; and on the third day afterward he spake out of the ground to those that with great lamentation were searching for him, in order to give him a decent funeral; (28) and when he was come out, he filled all the Jews with an unexpected joy, as though he were preserved by God's providence to be their commander for the time to come.

4. (29) And now Vespasian took along with him his army from Antioch, (which is the metropolis of Syria, and without dispute deserves the place of the third city in the habitable earth that was under the Roman empire, both in magnitude, and other marks of prosperity,) where he found king Agrippa, with all his forces, waiting for his coming, and marched to Ptolemais. (30) At this city also the inhabitants of Sepphoris of Galilee met him, who were for peace with the Romans. (31) These citizens had beforehand taken care of their own safety, and being sensible of the power of the Romans, they had been with Cestius Gallus before Vespasian came, and had given their faith to him, and received the security of his right hand, (32) and had received a Roman garrison; and at this time withal they received Vespasian, the Roman general, very kindly, and readily promised that they would assist him against their own countrymen. (33) Now the general delivered them, at their desire, as many horsemen and footmen as he thought sufficient to oppose the incursions of the Jews, if they should come

Part of Upper Galilee, with Mount Hermon in background. (photo Itamar Grinberg, Israel_photo_gallery, via Wikimedia Commons)

Aerial view of Acre (ancient Ptolemais) on the Mediterranean coast. (photo Samuel Magal)

against them. (34) And indeed the danger of losing Sepphoris would be no small one, in this war that was now beginning, seeing it was the largest city of Galilee, and built in a place by nature very strong, and might be a security of the whole nation's [fidelity to the Romans].

CHAPTER 3.

A DESCRIPTION OF GALILEE, SAMARIA, AND JUDEA.

1. (35) NOW Phoenicia and Syria encompass about the Galilees, which are two, and called the Upper Galilee and the Lower. They are bounded toward the sun-setting, with the borders of the territory belonging to Ptolemais, and by Carmel; which mountain had formerly belonged to the Galileans, but now belonged to the Tyrians; (36) to which mountain adjoins Gaba, which is called the City of Horsemen, because those horsemen that were dismissed by Herod the king dwelt therein; (37) they are bounded on the south with Samaria and Scythopolis, as far as the river Jordan; on the east with Hippeae and Gadaris, and also with Gaulonitis, and the borders of the kingdom of Agrippa; (38) its northern parts are hounded by Tyre, and the country of the Tyrians. As for that Galilee which is called the Lower, it, extends in length from Tiberias to Zabulon, and of the maritime places Ptolemais is its neighbor; (39) its breadth is from the village called Xaloth, which lies in the great plain, as far as Bersabe, from which beginning also is taken the breadth of the Upper Galilee, as far as the village Baca, which divides the land of the Tyrians from it; (40) its length is also from Meloth to Thella, a village near to Jordan.

2. (41) These two Galilees, of so great largeness, and encompassed with so many nations of foreigners, have been always able to make a strong resistance on all occasions of war; (42) for the Galileans are inured to war from their infancy, and have been always very numerous; nor hath the country been ever destitute of men of courage, or wanted a numerous set of them; for their soil is universally rich and fruitful, and full of the plantations of trees of all sorts, insomuch that it invites the most slothful to take pains in its cultivation, by its fruitfulness; (43) accordingly, it is all cultivated by its inhabitants, and no part of it lies idle. Moreover, the cities lie here very thick, and the very many villages there are here are every where so full of people, by the richness of their soil, that the very least of them contain above fifteen thousand inhabitants.

3. (44) In short, if any one will suppose that Galilee is inferior to Perea in magnitude, he will be obliged to prefer it before it in its strength; for this is all capable of cultivation, and is every where fruitful; but for Perea, which is indeed much larger in extent, the greater part of it is desert and rough, and much less disposed for the production of the milder kinds of fruits; (45) yet hath it a moist soil [in other parts], and produces all kinds of fruits, and its plains are planted with trees of all sorts, while yet the olive tree, the vine, and the palm tree are chiefly cultivated there. It is also sufficiently watered with torrents, which issue out of the mountains, and with springs that never fail to run, even when the torrents fail them, as they do in the dog-days. (46) Now the length of Perea is from Macherus to Pella, and its breadth from Philadelphia to Jordan; (47) its northern parts are bounded by Pella, as we have already said, as well as its Western with Jordan; the land of Moab is its southern border, and its eastern limits reach to Arabia, and Silbonitis, and besides to Philadelphene and Gerasa.

4. (48) Now as to the country of Samaria, it lies between Judea and Galilee; it begins at a village that is in the great plain called Ginea, and ends at the Acrabbene toparchy, and is entirely of the same nature with Judea; (49) for both countries are made up of hills and valleys, and are moist enough for agriculture, and are very fruitful. They have abundance of trees, and are full of autumnal fruit, both that which grows wild, and that which is the effect of cultivation. They are not naturally watered by many rivers, but derive their chief moisture from rain-water, of which they have no want; (50) and for those rivers which they have, all their waters are exceeding sweet: by reason also of the excellent grass they have, their cattle yield more milk than do those in other places; and, what is the greatest sign of excellency and of abundance, they each of them

Aerial view of the Temple Mount today in Jerusalem, the heart of Judea. (photo Samuel Magal)

are very full of people.

5. (51) In the limits of Samaria and Judea lies the village Anuath, which is also named Borceos. This is the northern boundary of Judea. The southern parts of Judea, if they be measured lengthways, are bounded by a village adjoining to the confines of Arabia; the Jews that dwell there call it Jordan. However, its breadth is extended from the river Jordan to Joppa. (52) The city Jerusalem is situated in the very middle; on which account some have, with sagacity enough, called that city the Navel of the country. (53) Nor indeed is Judea destitute of such delights as come from the sea, since its maritime places extend as far as Ptolemais: (54) it was parted into eleven portions, of which the royal city Jerusalem was the supreme, and presided over all the neighboring country, as the head does over the body. As to the other cities that were inferior to it, they presided over their several toparchies; (55) Gophna was the second of those cities, and next to that Acrabatta, after them Thamna, and Lydda, and Emmaus, and Pella, and Idumea, and Engaddi, and Herodium, and Jericho; (56) and after them came Jamnia and Joppa, as presiding over the neighboring people; and besides these there was the region of Gamala, and Gaulonitis, and Batanea, and Trachonitis, which are also parts of the kingdom of Agrippa. (57) This [last] country begins at Mount Libanus, and the fountains of Jordan, and reaches breadthways to the lake of Tiberias; and in length is extended from a village called Arpha, as far as Julias. Its inhabitants are a mixture of Jews and Syrians. (58) And thus have I, with all possible brevity, described the country of Judea, and those that lie round about it.

CHAPTER 4.

JOSEPHUS MAKES AN ATTEMPT UPON SEPPHORIS BUT IS REPELLED. TITUS COMES WITH A GREAT ARMY TO PTOLEMAIS.

1. (59) NOW the auxiliaries which were sent to assist the people of Sepphoris, being a thousand horsemen, and six thousand footmen, under Placidus the tribune, pitched their camp in two bodies in the great plain. The foot were put into the city to be a guard to it, but the horse lodged abroad in the camp. (60) These last, by marching continually one way or other, and overrunning the parts of the adjoining country, were very troublesome to Josephus and his men; they also plundered all the places that were out of the city's liberty, and intercepted such as durst go abroad. (61) On this account it was that Josephus marched against the city, as hoping to take what he had lately encompassed with so strong a wall, before they revolted from the rest of the Galileans, that the Romans would have much ado to take it; by which means he proved too weak, and failed of his hopes, both as to the forcing the place, and as to his prevailing with the people of Sepphoris to deliver it up to him. (62) By this means he provoked the Romans to treat the country according to the law of war; nor did the Romans, out of the anger they bore at this attempt, leave off, either by night or by day, burning the places in the plain, and stealing away the cattle that were in the country, and killing whatsoever appeared capable of fighting perpetually, and leading the weaker people as slaves into captivity; (63) so that Galilee was all over filled with fire and blood; nor was it exempted from any kind of misery or calamity, for the only refuge they had was this, that when they were pursued, they could retire to the cities which had walls built them by Josephus.

2. (64) But as to Titus, he sailed over from Achaia to Alexandria, and that sooner than the winter season did usually permit; so he took with him those forces he was sent for, and marching with great expedition, he came suddenly to Ptolemais, (65) and there finding his father, together with the two legions, the fifth and the tenth, which were the most eminent legions of all, he joined them to that fifteenth legion which was with his father; (66) eighteen cohorts

Coin of the Legio X Fretensis. (original in The British Museum, London)

followed these legions; there came also five cohorts from Cesarea, with one troop of horsemen, and five other troops of horsemen from Syria. (67) Now these ten cohorts had severally a thousand footmen, but the other thirteen cohorts had no more than six hundred footmen apiece, with a hundred and twenty horsemen. (68) There were also a considerable number of auxiliaries got together, that came from the kings Antiochus, and Agrippa, and Sohemus, each of them contributing one thousand footmen that were archers, and a thousand horsemen. Malchus also, the king of Arabia, sent a thousand horsemen, besides five thousand footmen, the greatest part of which were archers; (69) so that the whole army, including the auxiliaries sent by the kings, as well horsemen as footmen, when all were united together, amounted to sixty thousand, besides the servants, who, as they followed in vast numbers, so because they had been trained up in war with the rest, ought not to be distinguished from the fighting men; for as they were in their masters' service in times of peace, so did they undergo the like dangers with them in times of war, insomuch that they were inferior to none, either in skill or in strength, only they were subject to their masters.

CHAPTER 5.

A DESCRIPTION OF THE ROMAN ARMIES AND ROMAN CAMPS AND OF OTHER PARTICULARS FOR WHICH THE ROMANS ARE COMMENDED.

1. (70) NOW here one cannot but admire at the precaution of the Romans, in providing themselves of such household servants, as might not only serve at other times for the common offices of life, but might also be of advantage to them in their wars. (71) And, indeed, if any one does but attend to the other parts of their military discipline, he will be forced to confess that their obtaining so large a dominion hath been the acquisition of their valor, and not the bare gift of fortune; (72) for they do not begin to use their weapons first in time of war, nor do they then put their hands first into motion, while they avoided so to do in times of peace; but, as if their weapons did always cling to them, they have never any truce from warlike exercises; nor do they stay till times of war admonish them to use them; (73) for their military exercises differ not at all from the real use of their arms, but every soldier is every day exercised, and that with great diligence, as if it were in time of war, which is the reason why they bear the fatigue of battles so easily; (74) for neither can any disorder remove them from their usual regularity, nor can fear affright them out of it, nor can labor tire them; which firmness of conduct makes them always to overcome those that have not the same firmness; (75) nor would he be mistaken that should call those their exercises unbloody battles, and their battles bloody exercises. (76) Nor can their enemies easily surprise them with the suddenness of their incursions; for as soon as they have marched into an enemy's land, they do not begin to fight till they have walled their camp about; (77) nor is the fence they raise rashly made, or uneven; nor do they all abide ill it, nor do those that are in it take their places at random; but if it happens that the ground is uneven, it is first leveled: their camp is also four-square by measure, (78) and carpenters are ready, in great numbers, with their tools, to erect their buildings for them.

2. (79) As for what is within the camp, it is set apart for tents, but the outward circumference hath the resemblance to a wall, and is adorned with towers at equal distances, (80) where between the towers stand the engines for throwing arrows and darts, and for slinging stones, and where they lay all other engines that can annoy the enemy, all ready for their several operations. (81) They also erect four gates, one at every side of the circumference, and those large enough for the entrance of the beasts, and wide enough for making excursions, if occasion should require. (82) They divide the camp within into streets, very conveniently, and place the tents of the commanders in the middle; but in the very midst of all is the general's own tent, in the nature of a temple, (83) insomuch, that it appears to be a city built on the sudden, with its market-place, and place for handicraft trades, and with seats for the officers superior and inferior, where, if any differences arise, their causes are heard and determined. (84) The camp, and all that is in it, is encompassed with a wall round about, and that sooner than one would imagine, and this by the multitude and the skill of the laborers; and, if occasion require, a trench is drawn round the whole, whose depth is four cubits, and its breadth equal.

3. (85) When they have thus secured themselves, they live together by companies, with quietness and decency, as are all their other affairs managed with good order and security. Each company hath also their wood, and their corn, and their water brought them, when they stand in need of them; (86) for they neither sup nor dine as they please themselves singly, but all together. Their times also for sleeping, and watching, and rising are notified beforehand by the sound of trumpets, nor is any thing done without such a signal; (87) and in the morning the soldiery go every one to their centurions, and these centurions to their tribunes, to salute them; with whom all the superior officers go to the general of the whole army, (88) who then gives them of course the watchword and other orders, to be by them cared to all that are under their command; which is also observed when they go to fight, and thereby they turn themselves about on the sudden, when there is occasion for making sallies, as they come back when they are recalled in crowds also.

4. (89) Now when they are to go out of their camp, the trumpet gives a sound, at which time nobody lies still, but at the first intimation they take down their tents, and all is made ready for their going out; (90) then do the trumpets sound again, to order them to get ready for the march; then do they lay their baggage suddenly upon their mules, and other beasts of burden, and stand, as at the place of starting, ready to march; when also they set fire to their camp, and this they do because it will be easy for them to erect another camp, and that it may not ever be of use to their enemies. (91) Then do the trumpets give a sound the third time, that they are to go out, in order to excite those that on any account are a little tardy, that so no one may be out of his rank when the army marches. (92) Then does the crier stand at the general's right hand, and asks them thrice, in their own tongue, whether they be now ready to go out to war or not? To which they reply as often, with a loud and cheerful voice, saying, "We are ready." And this they do almost before the question is asked them: they do this as filled with a kind of martial fury, and at the same time that they so cry out, they lift up their right hands also.

5. (93) When, after this, they are gone out of their camp, they all march without noise, and in a decent manner, and every one keeps his own rank, as if they were going to war. The footmen are armed with breastplates and head-pieces, and have swords on each side; (94) but the sword which is upon their left side is much longer than the other, for that on the right side is not longer than a span. (95) Those footmen also that are chosen out from the rest to be about the general himself have a lance and a buckler, but the rest of the foot soldiers have a spear and a long buckler, besides a saw and a basket, a pick-axe and an axe, a thong of leather and a hook, with provisions for three days, so that a footman hath no

Remains of a Roman camp near Masada. (photo Samuel Magal)

great need of a mule to carry his burdens. (96) The horsemen have a long sword on their right sides, axed a long pole in their hand; a shield also lies by them obliquely on one side of their horses, with three or more darts that are borne in their quiver, having broad points, and not smaller than spears. They have also head-pieces and breastplates, in like manner as have all the footmen. (97) And for those that are chosen to be about the general, their armor no way differs from that of the horsemen belonging to other troops; and he always leads the legions forth to whom the lot assigns that employment.

6. (98) This is the manner of the marching and resting of the Romans, as also these are the several sorts of weapons they use. But when they are to fight, they leave nothing without forecast, nor to be done off-hand, but counsel is ever first taken before any work is begun, and what hath been there resolved upon is put in execution presently; (99) for which reason they seldom commit any errors; and if they have been mistaken at any time, they easily correct those mistakes. (100) They also esteem any errors they commit upon taking counsel beforehand to be better than such rash success as is owing to fortune only; because such a fortuitous advantage tempts them to be inconsiderate, while consultation, though it may sometimes fail of success, hath this good in it, that it makes men more careful hereafter; (101) but for the advantages that arise from chance, they are not owing to him that gains them; and as to what melancholy accidents happen unexpectedly, there is this comfort in them, that they had however taken the best consultations they could to prevent them.

7. (102) Now they so manage their preparatory exercises of their weapons, that not the bodies of the soldiers only, but their souls may also become stronger: they are moreover hardened for war by fear; (103) for their laws inflict capital punishments, not only for soldiers running away from the ranks, but for slothfulness and inactivity, though it be but in a lesser degree; as are their generals more severe than their laws, for they prevent any imputation of cruelty toward those under condemnation, by the great rewards they bestow on the valiant soldiers; (104) and the readiness of obeying their commanders is so great, that it is very ornamental in peace; but when they come to a battle, the whole army is but one body, (105) so well coupled together are their ranks, so sudden are their turnings about, so sharp their hearing as to what orders are given them, so quick their sight of the ensigns, and so nimble are their hands when they set to work; (106) whereby it comes to pass that what they do is done quickly, and what they suffer they bear with the greatest patience. Nor can we find any examples where they have been conquered in battle, when they came to a close fight, either by the multitude of the enemies, or by their stratagems, or by the difficulties in the places they were in; no, nor by fortune neither, for their victories have been surer to them than fortune could have granted them. (107) In a case, therefore, where counsel still goes before action, and where, after taking the best advice, that advice is followed by so active an army, what wonder is it that Euphrates on the east, the ocean on the west, the most fertile regions of Libya on the south, and the Danube and the Rhine on the north, are the limits of this empire? One might well say that the Roman possessions are not inferior to the Romans themselves.

8. (108) This account I have given the reader, not so much with the intention of commending the Romans, as of comforting those that have been conquered by them, and for the deterring others from attempting innovations under their government. (109) This

discourse of the Roman military conduct may also perhaps be of use to such of the curious as are ignorant of it, and yet have a mind to know it. I return now from this digression.

CHAPTER 6.

PLACIDUS ATTEMPTS TO TAKE JOTAPATA AND IS BEATEN OFF. VESPASIAN MARCHES INTO GALILEE.

1. (110) AND now Vespasian, with his son Titus, had tarried some time at Ptolemais, and had put his army in order. But when Placidus, who had overrun Galilee, and had besides slain a number of those whom he had caught, (which were only the weaker part of the Galileans, and such as were of timorous souls,) (111) saw that the warriors ran always to those cities whose walls had been built by Josephus, he marched furiously against Jotapata, which was of them all the strongest, as supposing he should easily take it by a sudden surprise, and that he should thereby obtain great honor to himself among the commanders, and bring a great advantage to them in their future campaign; because if this strongest place of them all were once taken, the rest would be so affrighted as to surrender themselves. (112) But he was mightily mistaken in his undertaking; for the men of Jotapata were apprized of his coming to attack them, and came out of the city, and expected him there. So they fought the Romans briskly when they least expected it, being both many in number, and prepared for fighting, and of great alacrity, as esteeming their country, their wives, and their children to be in danger, (113) and easily put the Romans to flight, and wounded many of them, and slew seven of them; because their retreat was not made in a disorderly manner, because the strokes only touched the surface of their bodies, which were covered with their armor in all parts, and because the Jews did rather throw their weapons upon them from a great distance, than venture to come hand to hand with them, and had only light armor on, while the others were completely armed. (114) However, three men of the Jews' side were slain, and a few wounded; so Placidus, finding himself unable to assault the city, ran away.

2. (115) But as Vespasian had a great mind to fall upon Galilee, he marched out of Ptolemais, having put his army into that order wherein the Romans used to march. (116) He ordered those auxiliaries which were lightly armed, and the archers, to march first, that they might prevent any sudden insults from the enemy, and might search out the woods that looked suspiciously, and were capable of ambuscades. (117) Next to these followed that part of the Romans which was completely armed, both footmen and horsemen. Next to these followed ten out of every hundred, carrying along with them their arms, and what was necessary to measure out a camp withal; (118) and after them, such as were to make the road even and straight, and if it were any where rough and hard to be passed over, to plane it, and to cut down the woods that hindered their march, that the army might not be in distress, or tired with their march. (119) Behind these he set such carriages of the army as belonged both to himself and to the other commanders, with a considerable number of their horsemen for their security. (120) After these he marched himself, having with him a select body of footmen, and horsemen, and pikemen. After these came the peculiar cavalry of his own legion, for there were a hundred and twenty horsemen that peculiarly belonged to every legion. (121) Next to these came the mules that carried the engines for sieges, and the other warlike machines of that nature. (122) After these came the commanders of the cohorts and tribunes, having about them soldiers chosen out of the rest. (123) Then came the ensigns encompassing the eagle, which is at the head of every Roman legion, the king, and the strongest of all birds, which seems to them a signal of dominion, and an omen that they shall conquer all against whom they march; (124) these sacred ensigns are followed by the trumpeters. Then came the main army in their squadrons and battalions, with six men in depth, which were followed at last by a centurion, who, according to custom, observed the rest. (125) As for the servants of every legion, they all followed the footmen, and led the baggage of the soldiers, which was borne by the mules and other beasts of burden. (126) But behind all the legions carne the whole multitude of the mercenaries; and those that brought up the rear came last of all for the security of the whole army, being both footmen, and those in their armor also, with a great number of horsemen.

Roman legionary eagle.

3. (127) And thus did Vespasian march with his army, and came to the bounds of Galilee, where he pitched his camp and restrained his soldiers, who were eager for war; he also showed his army to the enemy, in order to affright them, and to afford them a season for repentance, to see whether they would change their minds before it came to a battle, and at the same time he got things ready for besieging their strong minds. (128) And indeed this sight of the

VESPASIAN'S CAMPAIGN IN GALILEE A.D. 67

general brought many to repent of their revolt, and put them all into a consternation; (129) for those that were in Josephus's camp, which was at the city called Garis, not far from Sepphoris, when they heard that the war was come near them, and that the Romans would suddenly fight them hand to hand, dispersed themselves and fled, not only before they came to a battle, but before the enemy ever came in sight, (130) while Josephus and a few others were left behind; and as he saw that he had not an army sufficient to engage the enemy, that the spirits of the Jews were sunk, and that the greater part would willingly come to terms, if they might be credited, (131) he already despaired of the success of the whole war, and determined to get as far as he possibly could out of danger; so he took those that staid along with him, and fled to Tiberias.

CHAPTER 7.

VESPASIAN, WHEN HE HAD TAKEN THE CITY GADARA MARCHES TO JOTAPATA. AFTER A LONG SIEGE THE CITY IS BETRAYED BY A DESERTER, AND TAKEN BY VESPASIAN.

1. (132) SO Vespasian marched to the city Gadara, and took it upon the first onset, because he found it destitute of any considerable number of men grown up and fit for war. (133) He came then into it, and slew all the youth, the Romans having no mercy on any age whatsoever; and this was done out of the hatred they bore the nation, and because of the iniquity they had been guilty of in the affair of Cestius. (134) He also set fire not only to the city itself, but to all the villas and small cities that were round about it; some of them were quite destitute of inhabitants, and out of some of them he carried the inhabitants as slaves into captivity.

2. (135) As to Josephus, his retiring to that city which he chose as the most fit for his security, put it into great fear; for the people of Tiberias did not imagine that he would have run away, unless he had entirely despaired of the success of the war. (136) And indeed, as to that point, they were not mistaken about his opinion; for he saw whither the affairs of the Jews would tend at last, and was sensible that they had but one way of escaping, and that was by repentance. (137) However, although he expected that the Romans would forgive him, yet did he chose to die many times over, rather than to betray his country, and to dishonor that supreme command of the army which had been intrusted with him, or to live happily under those against whom he was sent to fight. (138) He determined, therefore, to give an exact account of affairs to the principal men at Jerusalem by a letter, that he might not, by too much aggrandizing the power of the enemy, make them too timorous; nor, by relating that their power beneath the truth, might encourage them to stand out when they were perhaps disposed to repentance. (139) He also sent them word, that if they thought of coming to terms, they must suddenly write him an answer; or if they resolved upon war, they must send him an army sufficient to fight the Romans. (140) Accordingly, he wrote these things, and sent messengers immediately to carry his letter to Jerusalem.

3. (141) Now Vespasian was very desirous of demolishing Jotapata, for he had gotten intelligence that the greatest part of the enemy had retired thither, and that it was, on other accounts, a place of great security to them. Accordingly, he sent both footmen and horsemen to level the road, which was mountainous and rocky, not without difficulty to be traveled over by footmen, but absolutely impracticable for horsemen. (142) Now these workmen accomplished what they were about in four days' time, and opened a broad way for the army. On the fifth day, which was the twenty-first of the month Artemisius, (Jyar,) Josephus prevented him, and came from Tiberias, and went into Jotapata, and raised the drooping spirits of the Jews. (143) And a certain deserter told this good news to Vespasian, that Josephus had removed himself thither, which made him make haste to the city, as supposing that with taking that he should take all Judea, in case he could but withal get Josephus under his power. (144) So he took this news to be of the vastest advantage to him, and believed it to be brought about by the providence of God, that he who appeared to be the most prudent man of all their enemies, had, of his own accord, shut

Tel Yodfat (Jotapata) in Galilee. (photo Samuel Magal)

himself up in a place of sure custody. Accordingly, he sent Placidus with a thousand horsemen, and Ebutius a decurion, a person that was of eminency both in council and in action, to encompass the city round, that Josephus might not escape away privately.

4. (145) Vespasian also, the very next day, took his whole army and followed them, and by marching till late in the evening, arrived then at Jotapata; (146) and bringing his army to the northern side of the city, he pitched his camp on a certain small hill which was seven furlongs from the city, and still greatly endeavored to be well seen by the enemy, to put them into a consternation; (147) which was indeed so terrible to the Jews immediately, that no one of them durst go out beyond the wall. (148) Yet did the Romans put off the attack at that time, because they had marched all the day, although they placed a double row of battalions round the city, with a third row beyond them round the whole, which consisted of cavalry, in order to stop up every way for an exit; (149) which thing making the Jews despair of escaping, excited them to act more boldly; for nothing makes men fight so desperately in war as necessity.

5. (150) Now when the next day an assault was made by the Romans, the Jews at first staid out of the walls and opposed them, and met them, as having formed themselves a camp before the city walls. (151) But when Vespasian had set against them the archers and slingers, and the whole multitude that could throw to a great distance, he permitted them to go to work, while he himself, with the footmen, got upon an acclivity, whence the city might easily be taken. Josephus was then in fear for the city, and leaped out, and all the Jewish multitude with him; (152) these fell together upon the Romans in great numbers, and drove them away from the wall, and performed a great many glorious and bold actions. Yet did they suffer as much as they made the enemy suffer; (153) for as despair of deliverance encouraged the Jews, so did a sense of shame equally encourage the Romans. These last had skill as well as strength; the other had only courage, which armed them, and made them fight furiously. (154) And when the fight had lasted all day, it was put an end to by the coming on of the night. They had wounded a great many of the Romans, and killed of them thirteen men; of the Jews' side seventeen were slain, and six hundred wounded.

6. (155) On the next day the Jews made another attack upon the Romans, and went out of the walls and fought a much more desperate battle with them titan before. For they were now become more courageous than formerly, and that on account of the unexpected good opposition they had made the day before, as they found the Romans also to fight more desperately; (156) for a sense of shame inflamed these into a passion, as esteeming their failure of a sudden victory to be a kind of defeat. (157) Thus did the Romans try to make an impression upon the Jews till the fifth day continually, while the people of Jotapata made sallies out, and fought at the walls most desperately; nor were the Jews affrighted at the strength of the enemy, nor were the Romans discouraged at the difficulties they met with in taking the city.

7. (158) Now Jotapata is almost all of it built on a precipice, having on all the other sides of it every way valleys immensely deep and steep, insomuch that those who would look down would have their sight fail them before it reaches to the bottom. It is only to be come at on the north side, where the utmost part of the city is built on the mountain, as it ends obliquely at a plain. (159) This mountain Josephus had encompassed with a wall when he fortified the city, that its top might not be capable of being seized upon by the enemies. (160) The city is covered all round with other mountains, and can no way be seen till a man comes just upon it. And this was the strong situation of Jotapata.

Reconstruction of Roman javelins and shields at Jotapata. (artist Shuki Zerach, Israel National Parks Authority; photo Samuel Magal)

8. (161) Vespasian, therefore, in order to try how he might overcome the natural strength of the place, as well as the bold defense of the Jews, made a resolution to prosecute the siege with vigor. To that end he called the commanders that were under him to a council of war, and consulted with them which way the assault might be managed to the best advantage. (162) And when the resolution was there taken to raise a bank against that part of the wall which was practicable, he sent his whole army abroad to get the materials together. So when they had cut down all the trees on the mountains that adjoined to the city, and had gotten together a vast heap of stones, (163) besides the wood they had cut down, some of them brought hurdles, in order to avoid the effects of the darts that were shot from above them. These hurdles they spread over their banks, under cover whereof they formed their bank, and so were little or nothing hurt by the darts that were thrown upon them from the wall, (164) while others pulled the neighboring hillocks to pieces, and perpetually brought earth to them; so that while they were busy three sorts of ways, nobody was idle. (165) However, the Jews cast great stones from the walls upon the hurdles which protected the men, with all sorts of darts also; and the noise of what could not reach them was yet so terrible, that it was some impediment to the workmen.

Jotapata viewed from one of the caves in the area. (photo Samuel Magal)

9. (166) Vespasian then set the engines for throwing stones and darts round about the city. The number of the engines was in all a hundred and sixty, and bid them fall to work, and dislodge those that were upon the wall. (167) At the same time such engines as were intended for that purpose threw at once lances upon them with a great noise, and stones of the weight of a talent were thrown by the engines that were prepared for that purpose, together with fire, and a vast multitude of arrows, which made the wall so dangerous, that the Jews durst not only not come upon it, but durst not come to those parts within the walls which were reached by the engines; (168) for the multitude of the Arabian archers, as well also as all those that threw darts and slung stones, fell to work at the same time with the engines. (169) Yet did not the others lie still, when they could not throw at the Romans from a higher place; for they then made sallies out of the city, like private robbers, by parties, and pulled away the hurdles that covered the workmen, and killed them when they were thus naked; and when those workmen gave way, these cast away the earth that composed the bank, and burnt the wooden parts of it, together with the hurdles, (170) till at length Vespasian perceived that the intervals there were between the works were of disadvantage to him; for those spaces of ground afforded the Jews a place for assaulting the Romans. So he united the hurdles, and at the same time joined one part of the army to the other, which prevented the private excursions of the Jews.

10. (171) And when the bank was now raised, and brought nearer than ever to the battlements that belonged to the walls, Josephus thought it would be entirely wrong in him if he could make no contrivances in opposition to theirs, and that might be for the city's preservation; so he got together his workmen, and ordered them to build the wall higher; (172) and while they said that this was impossible to be done while so many darts were thrown at them, he invented this sort of cover for them: (173) He bid them fix piles, and expand before them the raw hides of oxen newly killed, that these hides by yielding and hollowing themselves when the stones were thrown at them might receive them, for that the other darts would slide off them, and the fire that was thrown would be quenched by the moisture that was in them. And these he set before the workmen, (174) and under them these workmen went on with their works in safety, and raised the wall higher, and that both by day and by night, fill it was twenty cubits high. He also built a good number of towers upon the wall, and fitted it to strong battlements. (175) This greatly discouraged the Romans, who in their own opinions were already gotten within the walls, while they were now at once astonished at Josephus's contrivance, and at the fortitude of the citizens that were in the city.

11. (176) And now Vespasian was plainly irritated at the great subtlety of this stratagem, and at the boldness of the citizens of Jotapata; (177) for taking heart again upon the building of this wall, they made fresh sallies upon the Romans, and had every day conflicts with them by parties, together with all such contrivances, as robbers make use of, and with the plundering of all that came to hand, as also with the setting fire to all the other works; (178) and this till Vespasian made his army leave off fighting them, and resolved to lie round the city, and to starve them into a surrender, (179) as supposing that either they would be forced to petition him for mercy by want of provisions, or if they should have the courage to hold out till the last, they should perish by famine: (180) and he concluded he should conquer them the more easily in fighting, if he gave them an interval, and then fell upon them when they were weakened by famine; but still he gave orders that they should guard against their coming out of the city.

12. (181) Now the besieged had plenty of corn within the city, and indeed of all necessaries, but they wanted water, because there was no fountain in the city, the people being there usually satisfied with rain water; yet is it a rare thing in that country to have rain in summer, (182) and at this season, during the siege, they were in great distress for some contrivance to satisfy their thirst; and they were very sad at this time particularly, as if they were already in want of water entirely, (183) for Josephus seeing that the city abounded with other necessaries, and that the men were of good courage, and being desirous to protract the siege to the Romans longer than they expected, ordered their drink to be given them by measure; (184) but this scanty distribution of water by measure was deemed by them as a thing more hard upon them than the want of it; and their not being able to drink as much as they would made them more desirous of drinking than they otherwise had been; nay, they were as much disheartened hereby as if they were come to the last degree of thirst. Nor were the Romans unacquainted with the state they were in, (185) for when they stood over against them, beyond the wall, they could see them running together, and taking their water by measure, which made them throw their javelins thither the place being within their reach, and kill a great many of them.

13. (186) Hereupon Vespasian hoped that their receptacles of water would in no long time be emptied, and that they would be forced

to deliver up the city to him; (187) but Josephus being minded to break such his hope, gave command that they should wet a great many of their clothes, and hang them out about the battlements, till the entire wall was of a sudden all wet with the running down of the water. (188) At this sight the Romans were discouraged, and under consternation, when they saw them able to throw away in sport so much water, when they supposed them not to have enough to drink themselves. This made the Roman general despair of taking the city by their want of necessaries, and to betake himself again to arms, and to try to force them to surrender, (189) which was what the Jews greatly desired; for as they despaired of either themselves or their city being able to escape, they preferred a death in battle before one by hunger and thirst.

14. (190) However, Josephus contrived another stratagem besides the foregoing, to get plenty of what they wanted. (191) There was a certain rough and uneven place that could hardly be ascended, and on that account was not guarded by the soldiers; so Josephus sent out certain persons along the western parts of the valley, and by them sent letters to whom he pleased of the Jews that were out of the city, and procured from them what necessaries soever they wanted in the city in abundance; (192) he enjoined them also to creep generally along by the watch as they came into the city, and to cover their backs with such sheep-skins as had their wool upon them, that if any one should spy them out in the night time, they might be believed to be dogs. This was done till the watch perceived their contrivance, and encompassed that rough place about themselves.

15. (193) And now it was that Josephus perceived that the city could not hold out long, and that his own life would be in doubt if he continued in it; so he consulted how he and the most potent men of the city might fly out of it. When the multitude understood this, they came all round about him, and begged of him not to overlook them while they entirely depended on him, and him alone; (194) for that there was still hope of the city's deliverance, if he would stay with them, because every body would undertake any pains with great cheerfulness on his account, and in that case there would be some comfort for them also, though they should be taken: (195) that it became him neither to fly from his enemies, nor to desert his friends, nor to leap out of that city, as out of a ship that was sinking in a storm, into which he came when it was quiet and in a calm; (196) for that by going away he would be the cause of drowning the city, because nobody would then venture to oppose the enemy when he was once gone, upon whom they wholly confided.

16. (197) Hereupon Josephus avoided letting them know that he was to go away to provide for his own safety, but told them that he would go out of the city for their sakes; (198) for that if he staid with them, he should be able to do them little good while they were in a safe condition; and that if they were once taken, he should only perish with them to no purpose; but that if he were once gotten free from this siege, he should be able to bring them very great relief; (199) for that he would then immediately get the Galileans together, out of the country, in great multitudes, and draw the Romans off their city by another war. (200) That he did not see what advantge he could bring to them now, by staying among them, but only provoke the Romans to besiege them more closely, as esteeming it a most valuable thing to take him; but that if they were once informed that he was fled out of the city, they would greatly remit of their eagerness against it. (201) Yet did not this plea move the people, but inflamed them the more to hang about him. Accordingly, both the children and the old men, and the women with their infants, came mourning to him, and fell down before him, and all of them caught hold of his feet, and held him fast, (202) and besought him, with great lamentations, that he would take his share with them in their fortune; and I think they did this, not that they envied his deliverance, but that they hoped for their own; for they could not think they should suffer any great misfortune, provided Josephus would but stay with them.

17. (203) Now Josephus thought, that if he resolved to stay, it would be ascribed to their entreaties; and if he resolved to go away by force, he should be put into custody. His commiseration also of the people under their lamentations had much broken that his eagerness to leave them; so he resolved to stay, (204) and arming himself with the common despair of the citizens, he said to them, "Now is the time to begin to fight in earnest, when there is no hope of deliverance left. It is a brave thing to prefer glory before life, and to set about some such noble undertaking as may be remembered by late posterity." (205) Having said this, he fell to work immediately, and made a sally, and dispersed the enemies' out-guards, and ran as far as the Roman camp itself, and pulled the coverings of their tents to pieces, that were upon their banks, and set fire to their works. (206) And this was the manner in which he never left off fighting, neither the next day, nor the day after it, but went on with it for a considerable number of both days and nights.

Jotapata with the reconstructed javelins and shields in the distance. (artist Shuki Zerach, Israel National Parks Authority; photo Samuel Magal)

(left and below) Front and side views of a Roman battering ram, reconstructed, from Jotapata. (artist Shuki Zerach, Israel National Parks Authority; photo Samuel Magal)

18. (207) Upon this, Vespasian, when he saw the Romans distressed by these sallies, (though they were ashamed to be made to run away by the Jews; and when at any time they made the Jews run away, their heavy armor would not let them pursue them far; while the Jews, when they had performed any action, and before they could be hurt themselves, still retired into the city,) (208) ordered his armed men to avoid their onset, and not fight it out with men under desperation, (209) while nothing is more courageous than despair; but that their violence would be quenched when they saw they failed of their purposes, as fire is quenched when it wants fuel; (210) and that it was proper for the Romans to gain their victories as cheap as they could, since they are not forced to fight, but only to enlarge their own dominions. (211) So he repelled the Jews in great measure by the Arabian archers, and the Syrian slingers, and by those that threw stones at them, nor was there any intermission of the great number of their offensive engines. (212) Now the Jews suffered greatly by these engines, without being able to escape from them; and when these engines threw their stones or javelins a great way, and the Jews were within their reach, they pressed hard upon the Romans, and fought desperately, without sparing either soul or body, one part succoring another by turns, when it was tired down.

19. (213) When, therefore, Vespasian looked upon himself as in a manner besieged by these sallies of the Jews, and when his banks were now not far from the walls, he determined to make use of his battering ram. (214) This battering ram is a vast beam of wood like the mast of a ship, its forepart is armed with a thick piece of iron at the head of it, which is so carved as to be like the head of a ram, whence its name is taken. (215) This ram is slung in the air by ropes passing over its middle, and is hung like the balance in a pair of scales from another beam, and braced by strong beams that pass on both sides of it, in the nature of a cross. (216) When this ram is pulled backward by a great number of men with united force, and then thrust forward by the same men, with a mighty noise, it batters the walls with that iron part which is prominent. (217) Nor is there any tower so strong, or walls so broad, that can resist any more than its first batteries, but all are forced to yield to it at last. (218) This was the experiment which the Roman general betook himself to, when he was eagerly bent upon taking the city; but found lying in the field so long to be to his disadvantage, because the Jews would never let him be quiet. (219) So these Romans brought the several engines for galling an enemy nearer to the walls, that they might reach such as were upon the wall, and endeavored to frustrate their attempts; these threw stones and javelins at them; in the like manner did the archers and slingers come both together closer to the wall. (220) This brought matters to such a pass that none of the Jews durst mount the walls, and then it was that the other Romans brought the battering ram that was cased with hurdles all over, and in the tipper part was secured by skins that covered it, and this both for the security of themselves and of the engine. (221) Now, at the very first stroke of this engine, the wall was shaken, and a terrible clamor was raised by the people within the city, as if they were already taken.

20. (222) And now, when Josephus saw this ram still battering the same place, and that the wall would quickly be thrown down by it, he resolved to elude for a while the force of the engine. (223) With this design he gave orders to fill sacks with chaff, and to hang them down before that place where they saw the ram always battering, that the stroke might be turned aside, or that the place might feel less of the strokes by the yielding nature of the chaff. (224) This contrivance very much delayed the attempts of the Romans, because, let them remove their engine to what part they pleased, those that were above it removed their sacks, and placed them over against the strokes it made, insomuch that the wall was no way hurt, and this by diversion of the strokes, (225) till the Romans made an opposite contrivance of long poles, and by tying hooks at their ends, cut off the sacks. (226) Now when the battering ram thus recovered its force, and the wall having been but newly built, was giving way, Josephus and those about him had afterward immediate recourse to fire, to defend themselves withal; (227) whereupon they took what materials soever they had that were but dry, and made a sally three ways, and set fire to the machines,

and the hurdles, and the banks of the Romans themselves; (228) nor did the Romans well know how to come to their assistance, being at once under a consternation at the Jews' boldness, and being prevented by the flames from coming to their assistance; for the materials being dry with the bitumen and pitch that were among them, as was brimstone also, the fire caught hold of every thing immediately, and what cost the Romans a great deal of pains was in one hour consumed.

21. (229) And here a certain Jew appeared worthy of our relation and commendation; he was the son of Sameas, and was called Eleazar, and was born at Saab, in Galilee. (230) This man took up a stone of a vast bigness, and threw it down from the wall upon the ram, and this with so great a force, that it broke off the head of the engine. He also leaped down, and took up the head of the ram from the midst of them, and without any concern carried it to the top of the wall, (231) and this while he stood as a fit mark to he pelted by all his enemies. Accordingly, he received the strokes upon his naked body, and was wounded with five darts; (232) nor did he mind any of them while he went up to the top of the wall, where he stood in the sight of them all, as an instance of the greatest boldness; after which he drew himself on a heap with his wounds upon him, and fell down together with the head of the ram. (233) Next to him, two brothers showed their courage; their names were Netir and Philip, both of them of the village Ruma, and both of them Galileans also; these men leaped upon the soldiers of the tenth legion, and fell upon the Romans with such a noise and force as to disorder their ranks, and to put to flight all upon whomsoever they made their assaults.

22. (234) After these men's performances, Josephus, and the rest of the multitude with him, took a great deal of fire, and burnt both the machines and their coverings, with the works belonging to the fifth and to the tenth legion, which they put to flight; when others followed them immediately, and buried those instruments and all their materials under ground. (235) However, about the evening, the Romans erected the battering ram again, against that part of the wall which had suffered before; (236) where a certain Jew that defended the city from the Romans hit Vespasian with a dart in his foot, and wounded him a little, the distance being so great, that no mighty impression could be made by the dart thrown so far off. However, this caused the greatest disorder among the Romans; (237) for when those who stood near him saw his blood, they were disturbed at it, and a report went abroad, through the whole army, that the general was wounded, while the greatest part left the siege, and came running together with surprise and fear to the general; (238) and before them all came Titus, out of the concern he had for his father, insomuch that the multitude were in great confusion, and this out of the regard they had for their general, and by reason of the agony that the son was in. Yet did the father soon put an end to the son's fear, and to the disorder the army was under, (239) for being superior to his pains, and endeavoring soon to be seen by all that had been in a fright about him, he excited them to fight the Jews more briskly; for now every body was willing to expose himself to danger immediately, in order to avenge their general; and then they encouraged one another with loud voices, and ran hastily to the walls.

23. (240) But still Josephus and those with him, although they fell down dead one upon another by the darts and stones which the engines threw upon them, yet did not they desert the wall, but fell upon those who managed the ram, under the protection of the hurdles, with fire, and iron weapons, and stones; (241) and these could do little or nothing, but fell themselves perpetually, while they were seen by those whom they could not see, (242) for the light of their own flame shone about them, and made them a most visible mark to the enemy, as they were in the day time, while the engines could not be seen at a great distance, and so what was thrown at them was hard to be avoided; (243) for the force with which these engines threw stones and darts made them hurt several at a time, and the violent noise of the stones that were cast by the engines was so great, that they carried away the pinnacles of the wall, and broke off the corners of the towers; (244) for no body of men could be so strong as not to be overthrown to the last rank by the largeness of the stones. (245) And any one may learn the force of the engines by what happened this very night; for as one of those that stood round about Josephus was near the wall, his head was carried away by such a stone, and his skull was flung as far as three furlongs. (246) In the day time also, a woman with child had her belly so violently struck, as she was just come out of her house, that the infant was carried to the distance of half a furlong, so great was the force of that engine. (247) The noise of the instruments themselves was very terrible, the sound of the darts and stones that were thrown by them was so also; (248) of the same sort was that noise the dead bodies made, when they were dashed against the wall; and indeed dreadful was the clamor which these things raised in the women within the city, which was echoed back at the same time by the cries of such as were slain; (249) while the whole space of ground whereon they fought ran with blood, and the wall might have been ascended over by the bodies of the dead carcasses; (250) the mountains also contributed to increase the noise by their echoes; nor was there on that night any thing of terror wanting that could either affect the hearing or the sight: (251) yet did a great part of those that fought so hard for Jotapata fall manfully, as were a great part of them wounded. (252) However, the morning watch was come ere the wall yielded to the machines employed against it, though it had been battered without intermission. However, those within covered their bodies with their armor, and raised works over against that part which was thrown down, before those machines were laid by which the Romans were to ascend into the city.

24. (253) In the morning Vespasian got his army together, in order to take the city [by storm], after a little recreation upon the hard

Stone bullets of an ancient Roman ballista. (Archaeological museum Gunzenhausen [Bavaria]; photo Wolfgang Sauber, via Wikimedia Commons)

pains they had been at the night before; (254) and as he was desirous to draw off those that opposed him from the places where the wall had been thrown down, he made the most courageous of the horsemen get off their horses, and placed them in three ranks over against those ruins of the wall, but covered with their armor on every side, and with poles in their hands, that so these might begin their ascent as soon as the instruments for such ascent were laid; (255) behind them he placed the flower of the footmen; but for the rest of the horse, he ordered them to extend themselves over against the wall, upon the whole hilly country, in order to prevent any from escaping out of the city when it should be taken; (256) and behind these he placed the archers round about, and commanded them to have their darts ready to shoot. The same command he gave to the slingers, and to those that managed the engines, (257) and bid them to take up other ladders, and have them ready to lay upon those parts of the wall which were yet untouched, that the besieged might be engaged in trying to hinder their ascent by them, and leave the guard of the parts that were thrown down, while the rest of them should be overborne by the darts cast at them, and might afford his men an entrance into the city.

25. (258) But Josephus, understanding the meaning of Vespasian's contrivance, set the old men, together with those that were tired out, at the sound parts of the wall, as expecting no harm from those quarters, but set the strongest of his men at the place where the wall was broken down, and before them all six men by themselves, among whom he took his share of the first and greatest danger. (259) He also gave orders, that when the legions made a shout, they should stop their ears, that they might not be affrighted at it, and that, to avoid the multitude of the enemy's darts, they should bend down on their knees, and cover themselves with their shields, and that they should retreat a little backward for a while, till the archers should have emptied their quivers; (260) but that when the Romans should lay their instruments for ascending the walls, they should leap out on the sudden, and with their own instruments should meet the enemy, and that every one should strive to do his best, in order not to defend his own city, as if it were possible to be preserved, but in order to revenge it, when it was already destroyed; (261) and that they should set before their eyes how their old men were to be slain, and their children and wives were to be killed immediately by the enemy; and that they would beforehand spend all their fury, on account of the calamities just coming upon them, and pour it out on the actors.

Iron arrowheads from the Roman period. (Gäubodenmuseum; photo Wolfgang Sauber, via Wikimedia Commons)

26. (262) And thus did Josephus dispose of both his bodies of men; but then for the useless part of the citizens, the women and children, when they saw their city encompassed by a threefold army, (for none of the usual guards that had been fighting before were removed,) when they also saw, not only the walls thrown down, but their enemies with swords in their hands, as also the hilly country above them shining with their weapons, and the darts in the hands of the Arabian archers, they made a final and lamentable outcry of the destruction, as if the misery were not only threatened, but actually come upon them already. (263) But Josephus ordered the women to be shut up in their houses, lest they should render the warlike actions of the men too effeminate, by making them commiserate their condition, and commanded them to hold their peace, and threatened them if they did not, while he came himself before the breach, where his allotment was; (264) for all those who brought ladders to the other places, he took no notice of them, but earnestly waited for the shower of arrows that was coming.

27. (265) And now the trumpeters of the several Roman legions sounded together, and the army made a terrible shout; and the darts, as by order, flew so last, that they intercepted the light. (266) However, Josephus's men remembered the charges he had given them, they stopped their ears at the sounds, and covered their bodies against the darts; (267) and as to the engines that were set ready to go to work, the Jews ran out upon them, before those that should have used them were gotten upon them. (268) And now, on the ascending of the soldiers, there was a great conflict, and many actions of the hands and of the soul were exhibited; while the Jews did earnestly endeavor, in the extreme danger they were in, not to show less courage than those who, without being in danger, fought so stoutly against them; (269) nor did they leave struggling with the Romans till they either fell down dead themselves, or killed their antagonists. (270) But the Jews grew weary with defending themselves continually, and had not enough to come in their places, and succor them; while, on the side of the Romans, fresh men still succeeded those that were tired; and still new men soon got upon the machines for ascent, in the room of those that were thrust down; those encouraging one another, and joining side to side with their shields, which were a protection to them, they became a body of men not to be broken; and as this band thrust away the Jews, as though they were themselves but one body, they began already to get upon the wall.

28. (271) Then did Josephus take necessity for his counselor in this utmost distress, (which necessity is very sagacious in invention when it is irritated by despair,) and gave orders to pour scalding oil upon those whose shields protected them. (272) Whereupon they soon got it ready, being many that brought it, and what they brought being a great quantity also, and poured it on all sides upon the Romans, and threw down upon them their vessels as they were still hissing from the heat of the fire: (273) this so burnt the Romans, that it dispersed that united band, who now tumbled clown from the wall with horrid pains, (274) for the oil did easily run down the whole body from head to foot, under their entire armor, and fed upon their flesh like flame itself, its fat and unctuous nature rendering it soon heated and slowly cooled; (275) and as the men were cooped up in their head-pieces and breastplates, they could no way get free from this burning oil; they could only leap and roll about in their pains, as they fell down from the bridges they had laid. And as they thus were beaten back, and retired to their own party, who still pressed them forward, they were easily wounded by those that were behind them.

29. (276) However, in this ill success of the Romans, their courage did not fail them, nor did the Jews want prudence to oppose them; for the Romans, although they saw their own men thrown down, and in a miserable condition, yet were they vehemently bent against those that poured the oil upon them; while every one reproached the man before him as a coward, and one that hindered him from exerting himself; (277) and while the Jews made use of another stratagem to prevent their ascent, and poured boiling fenugreek upon the boards, in order to make them slip and fall down; (278) by which means neither could those that were coming up, nor those that were going down, stand on their feet; but some of them fell backward upon the machines on which they ascended, and were trodden upon; many of them fell down upon the bank they had raised, (279) and when they were fallen upon it were slain by the Jews; for when the Romans could not keep their feet, the Jews being freed from fighting hand to hand, had leisure to throw their darts at them. (280) So the general called off those soldiers in the evening that had suffered so sorely, (281) of whom the number of the slain was not a few, while that of the wounded was still greater; but of the people of Jotapata no more than six men were killed, although more than three hundred were carried off wounded. (282) This fight happened on the twentieth day of the month Desius [Sivan].

30. (283) Hereupon Vespasian comforted his army on occasion of what happened, and as he found them angry indeed, but rather wanting somewhat to do than any further exhortations, (284) he gave orders to raise the banks still higher, and to erect three towers, each fifty feet high, and that they should cover them with plates of iron on every side, that they might be both firm by their weight, and not easily liable to be set on fire. (285) These towers he set upon the banks, and placed upon them such as could shoot darts and arrows, with the lighter engines for throwing stones and darts also; and besides these, he set upon them the stoutest men among the slingers, (286) who not being to be seen by reason of the height they stood upon, and the battlements that protected them, might throw their weapons at those that were upon the wall, and were easily seen by them. (287) Hereupon the Jews, not being easily able to escape those darts that were thrown down upon their heads, nor to avenge themselves on those whom they could not see, and perceiving that the height of the towers was so great, that a dart which they threw with their hand could hardly reach it, and that the iron plates about them made it very hard to come at them by fire, they ran away from the walls, and fled hastily out of the city, and fell upon those that shot at them. (288) And thus did the people of Jotapata resist the Romans, while a great number of them were every day killed, without their being able to retort the evil upon their enemies; nor could they keep them out of the city without danger to themselves.

31. (289) About this time it was that Vespasian sent out Trajan against a city called Japha, that lay near to Jotapata, and that desired innovations, and was puffed up with the unexpected length of the opposition of Jotapata. This Trajan was the commander of the tenth legion, and to him Vespasian committed one thousand horsemen, and two thousand footmen. (290) When Trajan came to the city, he found it hard to be taken, for besides the natural strength of its situation, it was also secured by a double wall; but when he saw the people of this city coming out of it, and ready to fight him, he joined battle with them, and after a short resistance which they made, he pursued after them; (291) and as they fled to their first wall, the Romans followed them so closely, that they fell in together with them: (292) but when the Jews were endeavoring to get again within their second wall, their fellow citizens shut them out, as being afraid that the Romans would force themselves in with them. (293) It was certainly God therefore who brought the Romans to punish the Galileans, and did then expose the people of the city every one of them manifestly to be destroyed by their bloody enemies; (294) for they fell upon the gates in great crowds, and earnestly calling to those that kept them, and that by their names also, yet had they their throats cut in the very midst of their supplications; (295) for the enemy shut the gates of the first wall, and their own citizens shut the gates of the second, (296) so they were enclosed between two walls, and were slain in great numbers together; many of them were run through by swords of their own men, and many by their own swords, besides an immense number that were slain by the Romans. Nor had they any courage to revenge themselves; for there was added to the consternation they were in from the enemy, their being betrayed by their own friends, which quite broke their spirits; (297) and at last they died, cursing not the Romans, but their own citizens, till they were all destroyed, being in number twelve thousand. (298) So Trajan gathered that the city was empty of people that could fight, and although there should a few of them be therein, he supposed that they would be too timorous to venture upon any opposition; so he reserved the taking of the city to the general. Accordingly, he sent messengers to Vespasian, and desired him to send his son Titus to finish the victory he had gained. (299) Vespasian hereupon imagining there might be some pains still necessary, sent his son with an army of five hundred horsemen, and one thousand footmen. (300) So he came quickly to the city, and put his army in order, and set Trajan over the left wing, while he had the right himself, and led them to the siege: (301) and when the soldiers brought ladders to be laid against the wall on every side, the Galileans opposed them from above for a while; but soon afterward they left the walls. (302) Then did Titus's men leap into the city, and seized upon it presently; but when those that were in it were gotten together, there was a fierce battle between them; (303) for the men of power fell upon the Romans in the narrow streets, and the women threw whatsoever came next to hand at them, (304) and sustained a fight with them for six hours' time; but when the fighting men were spent, the rest of the multitude had their throats cut, partly in the open air, and partly in their own houses, both young and old together. So there were no males now remaining, besides infants, which, with the women, were carried as slaves into captivity; (305) so that the number of the slain, both now in the city and at the former fight, was fifteen thousand, and the captives were two thousand one hundred and thirty. (306) This calamity befell the Galileans on the twenty-fifth day of the month Desius [Sivan.]

Bust of Trajan. (Louvre Museum; photo Clio20, via Wikimedia Commons))

32. (307) Nor did the Samaritans escape their share of misfortunes at this time; for they assembled themselves together upon file mountain called Gerizzim, which is with them a holy mountain, and there they remained; which collection of theirs, as well as the courageous minds they showed, could not but threaten somewhat of war; (308) nor were they rendered wiser by the miseries

Ancient ruins on the top of Mount Geriz[z]im. (photo Ovedc, via Wikimedia Commons)

that had come upon their neighboring cities. They also, notwithstanding the great success the Romans had, marched on in an unreasonable manner, depending on their own weakness, and were disposed for any tumult upon its first appearance. (309) Vespasian therefore thought it best to prevent their motions, and to cut off the foundation of their attempts. For although all Samaria had ever garrisons settled among them, yet did the number of those that were come to Mount Gerizzim, and their conspiracy together, give ground for fear what they would be at; (310) he therefore sent I thither Cerealis, the commander of the fifth legion, with six hundred horsemen, and three thousand footmen, (311) who did not think it safe to go up to the mountain, and give them battle, because many of the enemy were on the higher part of the ground; so he encompassed all the lower part of the mountain with his army, and watched them all that day. (312) Now it happened that the Samaritans, who were now destitute of water, were inflamed with a violent heat, (for it was summer time, and the multitude had not provided themselves with necessaries,) (313) insomuch that some of them died that very day with heat, while others of them preferred slavery before such a death as that was, and fled to the Romans; (314) by whom Cerealis understood that those which still staid there were very much broken by their misfortunes. So he went up to the mountain, and having placed his forces round about the enemy, he, in the first place, exhorted them to take the security of his right hand, and come to terms with him, and thereby save themselves; and assured them, that if they would lay down their arms, he would secure them from any harm; (315) but when he could not prevail with them, he fell upon them and slew them all, being in number eleven thousand and six hundred. This was done on the twenty-seventh day of the month Desius [Sivan]. And these were the calamities that befell the Samaritans at this time.

33. (316) But as the people of Jotapata still held out manfully, and bore up tinder their miseries beyond all that could be hoped for, on the forty-seventh day [of the siege] the banks cast up by the Romans were become higher than the wall; (317) on which day a certain deserter went to Vespasian, and told him how few were left in the city, and how weak they were, (318) and that they had been so worn out with perpetual watching, and as perpetual fighting, that they could not now oppose any force that came against them, and that they might he taken by stratagem, if any one would attack them; (319) for that about the last watch of the night, when they thought they might have some rest from the hardships they were under, and when a morning sleep used to come upon them, as they were thoroughly weary, he said the watch used to fall asleep; accordingly his advice was, that they should make their attack at that hour. (320) But Vespasian had a suspicion about this deserter, as knowing how faithful the Jews were to one another, (321) and how much they despised any punishments that could be inflicted on them; this last because one of the people of Jotapata had undergone all sorts of torments, and though they made him pass through a fiery trial of his enemies in his examination, yet would he inform them nothing of the affairs within the city, and as he was crucified, smiled at them. (322) However, the probability there was in the relation itself did partly confirm the truth of what the deserter told them, and they thought he might probably speak truth. However, Vespasian thought they should be no great sufferers if the report was a sham; so he commanded them to keep the man in custody, and prepared the army for taking the city.

34. (323) According to which resolution they marched without noise, at the hour that had been told them, to the wall; (324) and it was Titus himself that first got upon it, with one of his tribunes, Domitius Sabinus, and had a few of the fifteenth legion along with him. (325) So they cut the throats of the watch, and entered the city very quietly. After these came Cerealis the tribune, and Placidus, and led on those that were tinder them. (326) Now when the citadel was taken, and the enemy were in the very midst of the city, and when it was already day, yet was not the taking of the city known by those that held it; (327) for a great many of them were fast asleep, and a great mist, which then by chance fell upon the city, hindered those that got up from distinctly seeing the case they were in, (328) till the whole Roman army was gotten in, and they were raised up only to find the miseries they were under; and as they were slaying, they perceived the city was taken. (329) And for the Romans, they so well remembered what they had suffered during the siege, that they spared none, nor pitied any, but drove the people down the precipice from the citadel, and slew them as they drove them down; (330) at which time the difficulties of the place hindered those that were still able to fight from defending themselves; for as they were distressed in the narrow streets, and could not keep their feet sure along the precipice, they were overpowered with the crowd of those that came fighting them down from the citadel. (331) This provoked a great many, even of those chosen men that were about Josephus, to kill themselves with their own hands; for when they saw that they could kill none of the Romans, they resolved to prevent being killed by the Romans, and got together in great numbers in the utmost parts of the city, and killed themselves.

35. (332) However, such of the watch as at the first perceived they were taken, and ran away as fast as they could, went up into one of the towers on the north side of the city, and for a while defended themselves there; but as they were encompassed with a multi-

tude of enemies, they tried to use their right hands when it was too late, and at length they cheerfully offered their necks to be cut off by those that stood over them. (333) And the Romans might have boasted that the conclusion of that siege was without blood [on their side] if there had not been a centurion, Antonius, who was slain at the taking of the city. His death was occasioned by the following treachery; (334) for there was one of those that were fled into the caverns, which were a great number, who desired that this Antonius would reach him his right hand for his security, and would assure him that he would preserve him, and give him his assistance in getting up out of the cavern; (335) accordingly, he incautiously reached him his right hand, when the other man prevented him, and stabbed him under his loins with a spear, and killed him immediately.

36. (336) And on this day it was that the Romans slew all the multitude that appeared openly; but on the following days they searched the hiding-places, and fell upon those that were under ground, and in the caverns, and went thus through every age, excepting the infants and the women, (337) and of these there were gathered together as captives twelve hundred; and as for those that were slain at the taking of the city, and in the former fights, they were numbered to be forty thousand. (338) So Vespasian gave order that the city should be entirely demolished, and all the fortifications burnt down. (339) And thus was Jotapata taken, in the thirteenth year of the reign of Nero, on the first day of the month Panemus [Tamuz].

Modern memorial to the defenders of Jotapata (Yodfat). (photo Hedva Sanderovitz, Pikiwiki Israel, via Wikimedia Commons)

CHAPTER 8.

HOW JOSEPHUS WAS DISCOVERED BY A WOMAN, AND WAS WILLING TO DELIVER HIMSELF UP TO THE ROMANS; AND WHAT DISCOURSE HE HAD WITH HIS OWN MEN, WHEN THEY ENDEAVORED TO HINDER HIM; AND WHAT HE SAID TO VESPASIAN, WHEN HE WAS BROUGHT TO HIM; AND AFTER WHAT MANNER VESPASIAN USED HIM AFTERWARD.

1. (340) AND now the Romans searched for Josephus, both out of the hatred they bore him, and because their general was very desirous to have him taken; for he reckoned that if he were once taken, the greatest part of the war would be over. They then searched among the dead, and looked into the most concealed recesses of the city; (341) but as the city was first taken, he was assisted by a certain supernatural providence; for he withdrew himself from the enemy when he was in the midst of them, and leaped into a certain deep pit, whereto there adjoined a large den at one side of it, which den could not be seen by those that were above ground; (342) and there he met with forty persons of eminency that had concealed themselves, and with provisions enough to satisfy them for not a few days. (343) So in the daytime he hid himself from the enemy, who had seized upon all places, and in the night time he got up out of the den and looked about for some way of escaping, and took exact notice of the watch; but as all places were guarded every where on his account, that there was no way of getting off unseen, he went down again into the den. (344) Thus he concealed himself two days; but on the third day, when they had taken a woman who had been with them, he was discovered. Whereupon Vespasian sent immediately and zealously two tribunes, Paulinus and Gallicanus, and ordered them to give Josephus their right hands as a security for his life, and to exhort him to come up.

2. (345) So they came and invited the man to come up, and gave him assurances that his life should be preserved: but they did not prevail with him; (346) for he gathered suspicions from the probability there was that one who had done so many things against the Romans must suffer for it, though not from the mild temper of those that invited him. However, he was afraid that he was invited to come up in order to be punished, until Vespasian sent besides these a third tribune, Nicanor, to him; he was one that was well known to Josephus, and had been his familiar acquaintance in old time. (347) When he was come, he enlarged upon the natural mildness of the Romans towards those they have once conquered; and told him that he had behaved himself so valiantly, that the commanders rather admired than hated him; (348) that the general was very desirous to have him brought to him, not in order to punish him, for that he could do though he should not come voluntarily, but that he was determined to preserve a man of his courage. (349) He moreover added this, that Vespasian, had he been resolved to impose upon him, would not have sent to him a friend of his own, nor put the fairest color upon the vilest action, by pretending friendship and meaning perfidiousness; nor would he have himself acquiesced, or come to him, had it been to deceive him.

3. (350) Now as Josephus began to hesitate with himself about Nicanor's proposal, the soldiery were so angry, that they ran hastily to set fire to the den; but the tribune would not permit them so to do, as being very desirous to take the man alive. (351) And now, as Nicanor lay hard at Josephus to comply, and he understood how the multitude of the enemies threatened him, he called to mind the dreams which he had dreamed in the night time, whereby God had signified to him beforehand both the future calamities of the Jews, and the events that concerned the Roman emperors. (352) Now Josephus was able to give shrewd conjectures about the interpretation of such dreams as have been ambiguously delivered by God. Moreover, he was not unacquainted with the prophecies contained in the sacred books, as being a priest himself, and of the posterity of priests: (353) and just then was he in an ecstasy; and setting before him the tremendous images of the dreams he had lately had, he put up a secret prayer to God, (354) and said, "Since it pleaseth thee, who hast created the Jewish nation, to depress the same, and since all their good fortune is gone over to the Romans, and since thou hast made choice of this soul of mine to foretell what is to come to pass hereafter, I willingly give them my hands, and am content to live. And I protest openly that I do not go over to the Romans as a deserter of the Jews, but as a minister from thee."

4. (355) When he had said this, he complied with Nicanor's invitation. But when those Jews who had fled with him understood that

he yielded to those that invited him to come up, they came about him in a body, and cried out, (356) "Nay, indeed, now may the laws of our forefathers, which God ordained himself, well groan to purpose; that God we mean who hath created the souls of the Jews of such a temper, that they despise death. (357) O Josephus! art thou still fond of life? and canst thou bear to see the light in a state of slavery? How soon hast thou forgotten thyself! How many hast thou persuaded to lose their lives for liberty! (358) Thou hast therefore had a false reputation for manhood, and a like false reputation for wisdom, if thou canst hope for preservation from those against whom thou hast fought so zealously, and art however willing to be preserved by them, if they be in earnest. (359) But although the good fortune of the Romans hath made thee forget thyself, we ought to take care that the glory of our forefathers may not be tarnished. We will lend thee our right hand and a sword; and if thou wilt die willingly, thou wilt die as general of the Jews; (360) but if unwillingly, thou wilt die as a traitor to them." As soon as they said this, they began to thrust their swords at him, and threatened they would kill him, if he thought of yielding himself to the Romans.

5. (361) Upon this Josephus was afraid of their attacking him, and yet thought he should be a betrayer of the commands of God, if he died before they were delivered. So he began to talk like a philosopher to them in the distress he was then in, (362) when he said thus to them: "O my friends, why are we so earnest to kill ourselves? and why do we set our soul and body, which are such dear companions, at such variance? (363) Can anyone pretend that I am not the man I was formerly? Nay, the Romans are sensible how that matter stands well enough. It is a brave thin to die in war; but so that it be according to the law of war, by the hand of conquerors. (364) If, therefore, I avoid death from the sword of the Romans, I am truly worthy to be killed by my own sword, and my own hand; but if they admit of mercy, and would spare their enemy, how much more ought we to have mercy upon ourselves, and to spare ourselves? For it is certainly a foolish thing to do that to ourselves which we quarrel with them for doing to us. (365) I confess freely that it is a brave thing to die for liberty; but still so that it be in war, and done by those who take that liberty from us; but in the present case our enemies do neither meet us in battle, nor do they kill us. Now he is equally a coward who will not die when he is obliged to die, and he who will die when he is not obliged so to do. (366) What are we afraid of, when we will not go up to the Romans? Is it death? (367) If so, what we are afraid of, when we but suspect our enemies will inflict it on us, shall we inflict it on ourselves for certain? But it may be said we must be slaves. (368) And are we then in a clear state of liberty at present? It may also be said that it is a manly act for one to kill himself. No, certainly, but a most unmanly one; as I should esteem that pilot to be an arrant coward, who, out of fear of a storm, should sink his ship of his own accord. (369) Now self-murder is a crime most remote from the common nature of all animals, and an instance of impiety against God our Creator; (370) nor indeed is there any animal that dies by its own contrivance, or by its own means, for the desire of life is a law engraven in them all; on which account we deem those that openly take it away from us to be our enemies, and those that do it by treachery are punished for so doing. (371) And do not you think that God is very angry when a man does injury to what he hath bestowed on him? For from him it is that we have received our being, and we ought to leave it to his disposal to take that being away from us. (372) The bodies of all men are indeed mortal, and are created out of corruptible matter; but the soul is ever immortal, and is a portion of the divinity that inhabits our bodies. Besides, if anyone destroys or abuses a depositum he hath received from a mere man, he is esteemed a wicked and perfidious person; but then if any one cast out of his body this Divine depositum, can we imagine that he who is thereby affronted does not know of it? (373) Moreover, our law justly ordains that slaves which run away from their master shall be punished, though the masters they run away from may have been wicked masters to them. And shall we endeavor to run away from God, who is the best of all masters, and not guilty of impiety? (374) Do not you know that those who depart out of this life according to the law of nature, and pay that debt which was received from God, when he that lent it us is pleased to require it back again, enjoy eternal fame; that their houses and their posterity are sure, that their souls are pure and obedient, and obtain a most holy place in heaven, from whence, in the revolutions of ages, they are again sent into pure bodies; (375) while the souls of those whose hands have acted madly against themselves are received by the darkest place in Hades, and while God, who is their Father, punishes those that offend against either of them in their posterity? (376) for which reason God hates such doings, and the crime is punished by our most wise legislator. (377) Accordingly, our laws determine that the bodies of such as kill themselves should be exposed till the sun be set, without burial, although at the same time it be allowed by them to be lawful to bury our enemies [sooner]. (378) The laws of other nations also enjoin such men's hands to be cut off when they are dead, which had been made use of in destroying themselves when alive, while they reckoned that as the body is alien from the soul, so is the hand alien from the body. (379) It is therefore, my friends, a right thing to reason justly, and not add to the calamities which men bring upon us impiety towards our Creator. (380) If we have a mind to preserve ourselves, let us do it; for to be preserved by those our enemies, to whom we have given so many demonstrations of our courage, is no way inglorious; but if we have a mind to die, it is good to die by the hand of those that have conquered us. (381) For nay part, I will not run over to our enemies' quarters, in order to be a traitor to myself; for certainly I should then be much more foolish than those that deserted to the enemy, since they did it in order to save themselves, and I should do it for destruction, for my own destruction. (382) However, I heartily wish the Romans may prove treacherous in this matter; for if, after their offer of their right hand for security, I be slain by them, I shall die cheerfully, and carry away with me the sense of their perfidiousness, as a consolation greater than victory itself."

6. (383) Now these and many the like motives did Josephus use to these men to prevent their murdering themselves; (384) but desperation had shut their ears, as having long ago devoted themselves to die, and they were irritated at Josephus. They then ran upon him with their swords in their hands, one from one quarter, and another from another, and called him a coward, and everyone of them appeared openly as if he were ready to smite him; (385) but he calling to one of them by name, and looking like a general to another, and taking a third by the hand, and making a fourth ashamed of himself, by praying him to forbear, and being in this condition distracted with various passions, (as he well might in the great distress he was then in,) he kept off every one of their swords from killing him, and was forced to do like such wild beasts as are encompassed about on every side, who always turn themselves against those that last touched them. (386) Nay, some of their right hands were debilitated by the reverence they bare to their general in these his fatal calamities, and their swords dropped out of their hands; and not a few of them there were, who, when they aimed to smite him with their swords, they were not thoroughly either willing or able to do it.

7. (387) However, in this extreme distress, he was not destitute of his usual sagacity; but trusting himself to the providence of God, he put his life into hazard [in the manner following]: (388) "And now,"

said he, "since it is resolved among you that you will die, come on, let us commit our mutual deaths to determination by lot. He whom the lot falls to first, let him be killed by him that hath the second lot, (389) and thus fortune shall make its progress through us all; nor shall any of us perish by his own right hand, for it would be unfair if, when the rest are gone, somebody should repent and save himself." This proposal appeared to them to be very just; (390) and when he had prevailed with them to determine this matter by lots, he drew one of the lots for himself also. He who had the first lot laid his neck bare to him that had the next, as supposing that the general would die among them immediately; for they thought death, if Josephus might but die with them, was sweeter than life; (391) yet was he with another left to the last, whether we must say it happened so by chance, or whether by the providence of God. And as he was very desirous neither to be condemned by the lot, nor, if he had been left to the last, to imbrue his right hand in the blood of his countrymen, he persuaded him to trust his fidelity to him, and to live as well as himself.

8. (392) Thus Josephus escaped in the war with the Romans, and in this his own war with his friends, and was led by Nicanor to Vespasian. (393) But now all the Romans ran together to see him; and as the multitude pressed one upon another about their general, there was a tumult of a various kind; while some rejoiced that Josephus was taken, and some threatened him, and some crowded to see him very near; (394) but those that were more remote cried out to have this their enemy put to death, while those that were near called to mind the actions he had done, and a deep concern appeared at the change of his fortune. (395) Nor were there any of the Roman commanders, how much soever they had been enraged at him before, but relented when they came to the sight of him. (396) Above all the rest, Titus's own valor, and Josephus's own patience under his afflictions, made him pity him, as did also the commiseration of his age, when he recalled to mind that but a little while ago he was fighting, but lay now in the hands of his enemies, which made him consider the power of fortune, and how quick is the turn of affairs in war, and how no state of men is sure; (397) for which reason he then made a great many more to be of the same pitiful temper with himself, and induced them to commiserate Josephus. He was also of great weight in persuading his father to preserve him. (398) However, Vespasian gave strict orders that he should be kept with great caution, as though he would in a very little time send him to Nero.

9. (399) When Josephus heard him give those orders, he said that he had somewhat in his mind that he would willingly say to himself alone. When therefore they were all ordered to withdraw, excepting Titus and two of their friends, he said, (400) "Thou, O Vespasian, thinkest no more than that thou hast taken Josephus himself captive; but I come to thee as a messenger of greater tidings; for had not I been sent by God to thee, I knew what was the law of the Jews in this case? and how it becomes generals to die. (401) Dost thou send me to Nero? For why? Are Nero's successors till they come to thee still alive? Thou, O Vespasian, art Caesar and emperor, thou, and this thy son. (402) Bind me now still faster, and keep me for thyself, for thou, O Caesar, are not only lord over me, but over the land and the sea, and all mankind; and certainly I deserve to be kept in closer custody than I now am in, in order to be punished, if I rashly affirm anything of God." (403) When he had said this, Vespasian at present did not believe him, but supposed that Josephus said this as a cunning trick, in order to his own preservation; (404) but in a little time he was convinced, and believed what he said to be true, God himself erecting his expectations, so as to think of obtaining the empire, and by other signs fore-showing his advancement. (405) He also found Josephus to have spoken truth on other occasions; for one of those friends that were present at that secret conference said to Josephus, "I cannot but wonder how thou couldst not foretell to the people of Jotapata that they should be taken, nor couldst foretell this captivity which hath happened to thyself, unless what thou now sayest be a vain thing, in order to avoid the rage that is risen against thyself." (406) To which Josephus replied, "I did foretell to the people of Jotapata that they would be taken on the forty-seventh day, and that I should be caught alive by the Romans." (407) Now when Vespasian had inquired of the captives privately about these predictions, he found them to be true, and then he began to believe those that concerned himself. (408) Yet did he not set Josephus at liberty from his hands, but bestowed on him suits of clothes, and other precious gifts; he treated him also in a very obliging manner, and continued so to do, Titus still joining his interest ill the honors that were done him.

CHAPTER 9.

HOW JOPPA WAS TAKEN, AND TIBERIAS DELIVERED UP.

1. (409) NOW Vespasian returned to Ptolemais on the fourth day of the month Panemus, [Tamus] and from thence he came to Cesarea, which lay by the sea-side. This was a very great city of Judea, and for the greatest part inhabited by Greeks: (410) the citizens here received both the Roman army and its general, with all sorts of acclamations and rejoicings, and this partly out of the good-will they bore to the Romans, but principally out of the hatred they bore to those that were conquered by them; on which account they came clamoring against Josephus in crowds, and desired he might be put to death. (411) But Vespasian passed over this petition concerning him, as offered by the injudicious multitude, with a

Roman remains at Cesarea. (photo Samuel Magal)

Old Jaffa (Joppa) today. (photo yeowatzup from Katlenburg-Lindau, Germany, via Wikimedia Commons)

bare silence. (412) Two of the legions also he placed at Cesarea, that they might there take their winter-quarters, as perceiving the city very fit for such a purpose; but he placed the tenth and the fifth at Scythopolis, that he might not distress Cesarea with the entire army. (413) This place was warm even in winter, as it was suffocating hot in the summer time, by reason of its situation in a plain, and near to the sea [of Galilee].

2. (414) In the mean time, there were gathered together as well such as had seditiously got out from among their enemies, as those that had escaped out of the demolished cities, which were in all a great number, and repaired Joppa, which had been left desolate by Cestius, that it might serve them for a place of refuge; (415) and because the adjoining region had been laid waste in the war, and was not capable of supporting them, they determined to go off to sea. (416) They also built themselves a great many piratical ships, and turned pirates upon the seas near to Syria, and Phoenicia, and Egypt, and made those seas unnavigable to all men. (417) Now as soon as Vespasian knew of their conspiracy, he sent both footmen and horsemen to Joppa, which was unguarded in the night time; (418) however, those that were in it perceived that they should be attacked, and were afraid of it; yet did they not endeavor to keep the Romans out, but fled to their ships, and lay at sea all night, out of the reach of their darts.

3. (419) Now Joppa is not naturally a haven, for it ends in a rough shore, where all the rest of it is straight, but the two ends bend towards each other, (420) where there are deep precipices, and great stones that jut out into the sea, and where the chains wherewith Andromeda was bound have left their footsteps, which attest to the antiquity of that fable. (421) But the north wind opposes and beats upon the shore, and dashes mighty waves against the rocks which receive them, and renders the haven more dangerous than the country they had deserted. (422) Now as those people of Joppa were floating about in this sea, in the morning there fell a violent wind upon them; it is called by those that sail there "the black north wind," (423) and there dashed their ships one against another, and dashed some of them against the rocks, and carried many of them by force, while they strove against the opposite waves, into the main sea; for the shore was so rocky, and had so many of the enemy upon it, that they were afraid to come to land; nay, the waves rose so very high, that they drowned them; (424) nor was there any place whither they could fly, nor any way to save themselves; while they were thrust out of the sea, by the violence of the wind, if they staid where they were, and out of the city by the violence of the Romans. And much lamentation there was when the ships were dashed against one another, and a terrible noise when they were broken to pieces; (425) and some of the multitude that were in them were covered with waves, and so perished, and a great many were embarrassed with shipwrecks. But some of them thought that to die by their own swords was lighter than by the sea, and so they killed themselves before they were drowned; (426) although the greatest part of them were carried by the waves, and dashed to pieces against the abrupt parts of the rocks, insomuch that the sea was bloody a long way, and the maritime parts were full of dead bodies; for the Romans came upon those that were carried to the shore, and destroyed them; (427) and the number of the bodies that were thus thrown out of the sea was four thousand and two hundred. The Romans also took the city without opposition, and utterly demolished it.

4. (428) And thus was Joppa taken twice by the Romans in a little time; (429) but Vespasian, in order to prevent these pirates from coming thither any more, erected a camp there, where the citadel of Joppa had been, and left a body of horse in it, with a few footmen, (430) that these last might stay there and guard the camp, and the horsemen might spoil the country that lay round it, and might destroy the neighboring villages and smaller cities. (431) So these troops overran the country, as they were ordered to do, and every day cut to pieces and laid desolate the whole region.

5. (432) But now, when the fate of Jotapata was related at Jerusalem, a great many at the first disbelieved it, on account of the vastness of the calamity, and because they had no eye-witness to attest the truth of what was related about it; for not one person was saved to be a messenger of that news, (433) but a fame was spread abroad at random that the city was taken, as such fame usually spreads bad news about. (434) However, the truth was known by degrees, from the places near Jotapata, and appeared to all to be too true. Yet were there fictitious stories added to what was really done; for it was reported that Josephus was slain at the taking of the city, (435) which piece of news filled Jerusalem full of sorrow. In every house also, and among all to whom any of the slain were allied, there was a lamentation for them; but the mourning for the commander was a public one; (436) and some mourned for those that had lived with them, others for their kindred, others for their friends, and others for their brethren, but all mourned for Josephus; (437) insomuch that the lamentation did not cease in the city before the thirtieth day; and a great many hired mourners, **(cf. Matthew 11:17)** with their pipes, who should begin the melancholy ditties for them.

6. (438) But as the truth came out in time, it appeared how the affairs of Jotapata really stood; yet was it found that the death of Josephus was a fiction; and when they understood that he was alive, and was among the Romans, and that the commanders treated him at another rate than they treated captives, they were as vehemently angry at him now as they had showed their good-

will before, when he appeared to have been dead. (439) He was also abused by some as having been a coward, and by others as a deserter; and the city was full of indignation at him, and of reproaches cast upon him; their rage was also aggravated by their afflictions, and more inflamed by their ill success; (440) and what usually becomes an occasion of caution to wise men, I mean affliction, became a spur to them to venture on further calamities, and the end of one misery became still the beginning of another; (441) they therefore resolved to fall on the Romans the more vehemently, as resolving to be revenged on him in revenging themselves on the Romans. (442) And this was the state of Jerusalem as to the troubles which now came upon it.

7. (443) But Vespasian, in order to see the kingdom of Agrippa, while the king persuaded himself so to do, (partly in order to his treating the general and his army in the best and most splendid manner his private affairs would enable him to do, and partly that he might, by their means, correct such things as were amiss in his government,) he removed from that Cesarea which was by the sea-side, and went to that which is called Cesarea Philippi (cf. Matthew 16:13; Mark 8:27) (444) and there he refreshed his army for twenty days, and was himself feasted by king Agrippa, where he also returned public thanks to God for the good success he had had in his undertakings. (445) But as soon as he was informed that Tiberias was fond of innovations, and that Taricheae had revolted, both which cities were parts of the kingdom of Agrippa, and was satisfied within himself that the Jews were every where perverted [from their obedience to their governors], he thought it seasonable to make an expedition against these cities, and that for the sake of Agrippa, and in order to bring his cities to reason. (446) So he sent away his son Titus to [the other] Cesarea, that he might bring the army that lay there to Scythopolis, which is the largest city of Decapolis, and in the neighborhood of Tiberias, (447) whither he came, and where he waited for his son. He then came with three legions, and pitched his camp thirty furlongs off Tiberias, at a certain station easily seen by the innovators; it is named Sennabris. (448) He also sent Valerian, a decurion, with fifty horsemen, to speak peaceably to those that were in the city, and to exhort them to give him assurances of their fidelity; for he had heard that the people were desirous of peace, but were obliged by some of the seditious part to join with them, and so were forced to fight for them. (449) When Valerian had marched up to the place, and was near the wall, he alighted off his horse, and made those that were with him to do the same, that they might not be thought to come to skirmish with them; but before they could come to a discourse one with another, the most potent men among the seditious made a sally upon them armed; (450) their leader was one whose name was Jesus, the son of Shaphat, the principal head of a band of robbers. (451) Now Valerian, neither thinking it safe to fight contrary to the commands of the general, though he were secure of a victory, and knowing that it was a very hazardous undertaking for a few to fight with many, for those that were unprovided to fight those that were ready, (452) and being on other accounts surprised at this unexpected onset of the Jews, he ran away on foot, as did five of the rest in like manner, and left their horses behind them; which horses Jesus led away into the city, and rejoiced as if they had taken them in battle, and not by treachery.

Remains of the Roman gate at Tiberias. (photo Hanay, via Wikimedia Commons)

8. (453) Now the seniors of the people, and such as were of principal authority among them, fearing what would be the issue of this matter, fled to the camp of the Romans; (454) they then took their king along with them, and fell down before Vespasian, to supplicate his favor, and besought him not to overlook them, nor to impute the madness of a few to the whole city, (455) to spare a people that have been ever civil and obliging to the Romans; but to bring the authors of this revolt to due punishment, who had hitherto so watched them, that though they were zealous to give them the security of their right hands of a long time, yet could they not accomplish the same. (456) With these supplications the general complied, although he were very angry at the whole city about the carrying off his horses, (457) and this because he saw that Agrippa was under a great concern for them. So when Vespasian and Agrippa had accepted of their right hands by way of security, Jesus and his party thought it not safe for them to continue at Tiberias, so they ran away to Taricheae. (458) The next day Vespasian sent Trajan before with some horsemen to the citadel, to make trial of the multitude, whether they were all disposed for peace; (459) and as soon as he knew that the people were of the same mind with the petitioner, he took his army, and went to the city; upon which the citizens opened to him their gates, and met him with acclamations of joy, and called him their savior and benefactor. (460) But as the army was a great while in getting in at the gates, they were so narrow, Vespasian commanded the south wall to be broken down, and so made a broad passage for their entrance. (461) However, he charged them to abstain from rapine and injustice, in order to gratify the king; and on his account spared the rest of the wall, while the king undertook for them that they should continue [faithful to the Romans] for the time to come. And thus did he restore this city to a quiet state, after it had been grievously afflicted by the sedition.

CHAPTER 10.

HOW TARICHEAE WAS TAKEN. A DESCRIPTION OF THE RIVER JORDAN, AND OF THE COUNTRY OF GENNESARETH.

1. (462) AND now Vespasian pitched his camp between this city and Taricheae, but fortified his camp more strongly, as suspecting that he should be forced to stay there, and have a long war; (463) for all the innovators had gotten together at Taricheae, as relying upon the strength of the city, and on the lake that lay by it. This lake is called by the people of the country the Lake of Gennesareth. (464) The city itself is situated like Tiberias, at the bottom of a mountain, and on those sides which are not washed by the sea, had been strongly fortified by Josephus, though not so strongly as Tiberias; (465) for the wall of Tiberias had been built at the beginning of the Jews' revolt, when he had great plenty of money, and great

Aerial view of Magdala-Taricheae on the shore of the Sea of Galilee (Lake Gennesareth). (photo AVRAMGR, via Wikimedia Commons)

power, but Taricheae partook only the remains of that liberality. (466) Yet had they a great number of ships gotten ready upon the lake, that, in case they were beaten at land, they might retire to them; and they were so fitted up, that they might undertake a sea-fight also. (467) But as the Romans were building a wall about their camp, Jesu[s] and his party were neither affrighted at their number, nor at the good order they were in, but made a sally upon them; (468) and at the very first onset the builders of the wall were dispersed; and these pulled what little they had before built to pieces; but as soon as they saw the armed men getting together, and before they had suffered any thing themselves, they retired to their own men. But then the Romans pursued them, and drove them into their ships, (469) where they launched out as far as might give them the opportunity of reaching the Romans with what they threw at them, and then cast anchor, and brought their ships close, as in a line of battle, and thence fought the enemy from the sea, who were themselves at land. (470) But Vespasian hearing that a great multitude of them were gotten together in the plain that was before the city, he thereupon sent his son, with six hundred chosen horsemen, to disperse them.

2. (471) But when Titus perceived that the enemy was very numerous, he sent to his father, and informed him that he should want more forces. But as he saw a great many of the horsemen eager to fight, and that before any succors could come to them, and that yet some of them were privately under a sort of consternation at the multitude of the Jews, he stood in a place whence he might be heard, and said to them, (472) "My brave Romans! for it is right for me to put you in mind of what nation you are, in the beginning of my speech, that so you may not be ignorant who you are, and who they are against whom we are going to fight. (473) For as to us, Romans, no part of the habitable earth hath been able to escape our hands hitherto; but as for the Jews, that I may speak of them too, though they have been already beaten, yet do they not give up the cause; and a sad thing it would be for us to grow wealthy under good success, when they bear up under their misfortunes. (474) As to the alacrity which you show publicly, I see it, and rejoice at it; yet am I afraid lest the multitude of the enemy should bring a concealed fright upon some of you: (475) let such a one consider again, who we are that are to fight, and who those are against whom we are to fight. Now these Jews, though they be very bold and great despisers of death, are but a disorderly body, and unskillful in war, and may rather be called a rout than an army; while I need say nothing of our skill and our good order; for this is the reason why we Romans alone are exercised for war in time of peace, that we may not think of number for number when we come to fight with our enemies: (476) for what advantage should we reap by our continual sort of warfare, if we must still be equal in number to such as have not been used to war. (477) Consider further, that you are to have a conflict with men in effect unarmed, while you are well armed; with footmen, while you are horsemen; with those that have no good general, while you have one; and as these advantages make you in effect manifold more than you are, so do their disadvantages mightily diminish their number. (478) Now it is not the multitude of men, though they be soldiers, that manages wars with success, but it is their bravery that does it, though they be but a few; for a few are easily set in battle-array, and can easily assist one another, while over-numerous armies are more hurt by themselves than by their enemies. (479) It is boldness and rashness, the effects of madness, that conduct the Jews. Those passions indeed make a great figure when they succeed, but are quite extinguished upon the least ill success; but we are led on by courage, and obedience, and fortitude, which shows itself indeed in our good fortune, but still does not for ever desert us in our ill fortune. (480) Nay, indeed, your fighting is to be on greater motives than those of the Jews; for although they run the hazard of war for liberty, and for their country, yet what can be a greater motive to us than glory? and that. it may never be said, that after we have got dominion of the habitable earth, the Jews are able to confront us. (481) We must also reflect upon this, that there is no fear of our suffering any incurable disaster in the present case; for those that are ready to assist us are many, and at hand also; yet it is in our power to seize upon this victory ourselves; and I think we ought to prevent the coming of those my father is sending to us for our assistance, that our success may be peculiar to ourselves, and of greater reputation to us. (482) And I cannot but think this an opportunity wherein my father, and I, and you shall be all put to the trial, whether he be worthy of his former glorious performances, whether I be his son in reality, and whether you be really my soldiers; for it is usual for my father to conquer; and for myself, I should not bear the thoughts of returning to him if I were once taken by the enemy. (483) And how will you be able to avoid being ashamed, if you do not show equal courage with your commander, when he goes before you into danger? For you know very well that I shall go into the danger first, and make the first

attack upon the enemy. (484) Do not you therefore desert me, but persuade yourselves that God will be assisting to my onset. Know this also before we begin, that we shall now have better success than we should have, if we were to fight at a distance."

3. (485) As Titus was saying this, an extraordinary fury fell upon the men; and as Trajan was already come before the fight began, with four hundred horsemen, they were uneasy at it, because the reputation of the victory would be diminished by being common to so many. (486) Vespasian had also sent both Antonius and Silo, with two thousand archers, and had given it them in charge to seize upon the mountain that was over against the city, and repel those that were upon the wall; (487) which archers did as they were commanded, and prevented those that attempted to assist them that way; And now Titus made his own horse march first against the enemy, as did the others with a great noise after him, and extended themselves upon the plain as wide as the enemy which confronted them; by which means they appeared much more numerous than they really were. (488) Now the Jews, although they were surprised at their onset, and at their good order, made resistance against their attacks for a little while; but when they were pricked with their long poles, and overborne by the violent noise of the horsemen, they came to be trampled under their feet; (489) many also of them were slain on every side, which made them disperse themselves, and run to the city, as fast as every one of them were able. (490) So Titus pressed upon the hindmost, and slew them; and of the rest, some he fell upon as they stood on heaps, and some he prevented, and met them in the mouth, and run them through; many also he leaped upon as they fell one upon another, and trod them down, (491) and cut off all the retreat they had to the wall, and turned them back into the plain, till at last they forced a passage by their multitude, and got away, and ran into the city.

4. (492) But now there fell out a terrible sedition among them within the city; for the inhabitants themselves, who had possessions there, and to whom the city belonged, were not disposed to fight from the very beginning; and now the less so, because they had been beaten; (493) but the foreigners, which were very numerous, would force them to fight so much the more, insomuch that there was a clamor and a tumult among them, as all mutually angry one at another. (494) And when Titus heard this tumult, for he was not far from the wall, he cried out," Fellow soldiers, now is the time;

Ornately decorated limestone artifact from the remains of a first-century synagogue at Magdala-Taricheae. (photo R. Steven Notley)

Secondary use of stones and column drums to block up the streets at Magdala-Taricheae, perhaps to fortify the site. (photo R. Steven Notley)

and why do we make any delay, when God is giving up the Jews to us? Take the victory which is given you: do not you hear what a noise they make? (495) Those that have escaped our hands are ill an uproar against one another. We have the city if we make haste; but besides haste, we must undergo some labor, and use some courage; for no great thing uses to be accomplished without danger: (496) accordingly, we must not only prevent their uniting again, which necessity will soon compel them to do, but we must also prevent the coming of our own men to our assistance, that, as few as we are, we may conquer so great a multitude, and may ourselves alone take the city:"

5. (497) As soon as ever Titus had said this, he leaped upon his horse, and rode apace down to the lake; by which lake he marched, and entered into the city the first of them all, as did the others soon after him. (498) Hereupon those that were upon the walls were seized with a terror at the boldness of the attempt, nor durst any one venture to fight with him, or to hinder him; so they left guarding the city, and some of those that were about Jesus fled over the country, (499) while others of them ran down to the lake, and met the enemy in the teeth, and some were slain as they were getting up into the ships, but others of them as they attempted to overtake those that were already gone aboard. (500) There was also a great slaughter made in the city, while those foreigners that had not fled away already made opposition; but the natural inhabitants were killed without fighting: for in hopes of Titus's giving them his right hand for their security, and out of a consciousness that they had not given any consent to the war, they avoided fighting, (501) till Titus had slain the authors of this revolt, and then put a stop to any further slaughters, out of commiseration of these inhabitants of the place. (502) But for those that had fled to the lake, upon seeing the city taken, they sailed as far as they possibly could from the enemy.

6. (503) Hereupon Titus sent one of his horsemen to his father, and let him know the good news of what he had done; (504) at which, as was natural, he was very joyful, both on account of the courage and glorious actions of his son; for he thought that now the greatest part of the war was over. He then came thither himself, and set men to guard the city, and gave them command to take care that nobody got privately out of it, but to kill such as attempted so to do. (505) And on the next day he went down to the lake, and commanded that vessels should be fitted up, in order to pursue those

The southern end of the lake of Gennesareth (Sea of Galilee), looking east. (photo Samuel Magal)

that had escaped in the ships. These vessels were quickly gotten ready accordingly, because there was great plenty of materials, and a great number of artificers also.

7. (506) Now this lake of Gennesareth is so called from the country adjoining to it. Its breadth is forty furlongs, and its length one hundred and forty; its waters are sweet, and very agreeable for drinking, (507) for they are finer than the thick waters of other fens; the lake is also pure, and on every side ends directly at the shores, and at the sand; it is also of a temperate nature when you draw it up, and of a more gentle nature than river or fountain water, and yet always cooler than one could expect in so diffuse a place as this is. (508) Now when this water is kept in the open air, it is as cold as that snow which the country people are accustomed to make by night in summer. There are several kinds of fish in it, different both to the taste and the sight from those elsewhere. (509) It is divided into two parts by the river Jordan. Now Panium is thought to be the fountain of Jordan, but in reality it is carried thither after an occult manner from the place called Phiala: (510) this place lies as you go up to Trachonitis, and is a hundred and twenty furlongs from Cesarea, and is not far out of the road on the right hand; (511) and indeed it hath its name of Phiala [vial or bowl] very justly, from the roundness of its circumference, as being round like a wheel; its water continues always up to its edges, without either sinking or running over. (512) And as this origin of Jordan was formerly not known, it was discovered so to be when Philip was tetrarch of Trachonitis; (513) for he had chaff thrown into Phiala, and it was found at Paninto, where the ancients thought the fountain-head of the river was, whither it had been therefore carried [by the waters]. (514) As for Panium itself, its natural beauty had been improved by the royal liberality of Agrippa, and adorned at his expenses. (515) Now Jordan's visible stream arises from this cavern, and divides the marshes and fens of the lake Semechonitis; when it hath run another hundred and twenty furlongs, it first passes by the city Julias, and then passes through the middle of the lake Gennesareth; after which it runs a long way over a desert, and then makes its exit into the lake Asphaltitis.

8. (516) The country also that lies over against this lake hath the same name of Gennesareth; its nature is wonderful as well as its beauty; its soil is so fruitful that all sorts of trees can grow upon it, and the inhabitants accordingly plant all sorts of trees there; for the temper of the air is so well mixed, that it agrees very well with those several sorts, (517) particularly walnuts, which require the coldest air, flourish there in vast plenty; there are palm trees also, which grow best in hot air; fig trees also and olives grow near them, which yet require an air that is more temperate. (518) One may call this place the ambition of nature, where it forces those plants that are naturally enemies to one another to agree together; it is a happy contention of the seasons, as if every one of them laid claim to this country; (519) for it not only nourishes different sorts of autumnal fruit beyond men's expectation, but preserves them a great while; it supplies men with the principal fruits, with grapes and figs continually, during ten months of the year and the rest of the fruits as they become ripe together through the whole year; for besides the good temperature of the air, it is also watered from a most fertile fountain. The people of the country call it Capharnaum. (520) Some have thought it to be a vein of the Nile, because it produces the Coracin fish as well as that lake does which is near to Alexandria. (521) The length of this country extends itself along the banks of this lake that bears the same name for thirty furlongs, and is in breadth twenty, And this is the nature of that place.

9. (522) But now, when the vessels were gotten ready, Vespasian put upon ship-board as many of his forces as he thought sufficient to be too hard for those that were upon the lake, and set sail after them. Now these which were driven into the lake could neither fly to the land, where all was in their enemies' hand, and in war against them; nor could they fight upon the level by sea, (523) for their ships were small and fitted only for piracy; they were too weak to fight with Vespasian's vessels, and the mariners that were in them were so few, that they were afraid to come near the Romans, who attacked them in great numbers. (524) However, as they sailed round about the vessels, and sometimes as they came near them, they threw stones at the Romans when they were a good way off, or came closer and fought them; (525) yet did they receive the greatest harm themselves in both cases. As for the stones they threw at the Romans, they only made a sound one after another, for they threw them against such as were in their armor, while the Roman darts could reach the Jews themselves; and when they ventured to come near the Romans, they became sufferers themselves before they could do any harm to the ether, and were drowned, they and their ships together. (526) As for those that endeavored to come to an actual fight, the Romans ran many of them through with their long poles. Sometimes the Romans leaped into their ships, with swords in their hands, and slew them; but when some of them met the vessels, the Romans caught them by the middle, and destroyed at once their ships and themselves who were taken in them. (527) And for such as were drowning in the sea, if they lifted their heads up above the water, they were either killed by darts, or caught by the vessels; but if, in the desperate case they were in, they attempted to swim to their enemies, the Romans cut off either their heads or their hands; (528) and indeed they were destroyed after various manners every where, till the rest being put to flight, were forced to get upon the land, while the vessels encompassed them about [on the sea]: (529) but as many of these were repulsed when they were getting ashore, they were killed by the darts upon the lake; and the Romans leaped out of their vessels, and destroyed a great many more upon the land: one might then see the lake all bloody, and full of dead bodies, for not one of them escaped. (530) And a terrible stink, and a very sad sight there was on the following days over that country; for as for the shores, they were full of shipwrecks, and of dead bodies all swelled; and as the dead bodies were inflamed by the sun, and putrefied, they corrupted the air, insomuch that the misery was not only the object of commiseration to the Jews, but to those that hated them, and had been the authors of that misery. (531) This was the upshot of the sea-fight. The number of the slain, including those that were killed in the city before, was six thousand and five hundred.

10. (532) After this fight was over, Vespasian sat upon his tribunal at Taricheae, in order to distinguish the foreigners from the old inhabitants; for those foreigners appear to have begun the war. So he deliberated with the other commanders, whether he ought to save those old inhabitants or not. (532) And when those commanders alleged that the dismission of them would be to his own disadvantage, because, when they were once set at liberty, they would not be at rest, since they would be people destitute of proper habitations, and would he able to compel such as they fled to fight against us, (534) Vespasian acknowledged that they did not deserve to be saved, and that if they had leave given them to fly away, they would make use of it against those that gave them that leave. But still he considered with himself after what manner they should be slain (535) for if he had them slain there, he suspected the people of the country would thereby become his enemies; for that to be sure they would never bear it, that so many that had been supplicants to him should be killed; and to offer violence to them, after he had given them assurances of their lives, he could not himself bear to do it. (536) However, his friends were too hard for him, and pretended that nothing against Jews could be any impiety, and that he ought to prefer what was profitable before what was fit to be done, where both could not be made consistent. (537) So he gave them an ambiguous liberty to do as they advised, and permitted the prisoners to go along no other road than that which led to Tiberias only. (538) So they readily believed what they desired to be true, and went along securely, with their effects, the way which was allowed them, while the Romans seized upon all the road that led to Tiberias, that none of them might go out of it, and shut them up in the city. (539) Then came Vespasian, and ordered them all to stand in the stadium, and commanded them to kill the old men, together with the others that were useless, which were in number a thousand and two hundred. (540) Out of the young men he chose six thousand of the strongest, and sent them to Nero, to dig through the Isthmus, and sold the remainder for slaves, being thirty thousand and four hundred, besides such as he made a present of to Agrippa; (541) for as to those that belonged to his kingdom, he gave him leave to do what he pleased with them; however, the king sold these also for slaves; (542) but for the rest of the multitude, who were Trachonites, and Gaulanites, and of Hippos, and some of Gadara, the greatest part of them were seditious persons and fugitives, who were of such shameful characters, that they preferred war before peace. These prisoners were taken on the eighth day of the month Gorpiaeus [Elul].

The plain of Gennesareth with the lake in background, looking northeast. (photo Samuel Magal)

BOOK IV

FROM THE SIEGE OF GAMALA TO THE COMING OF TITUS TO BESIEGE JERUSALEM

CHAPTER 1.

THE SIEGE AND TAKING OF GAMALA.

1. (1) NOW all those Galileans who, after the taking of Jotapata, had revolted from the Romans, did, upon the conquest of Taricheae, deliver themselves up to them again. And the Romans received all the fortresses and the cities, excepting Gischala and those that had seized upon Mount Tabor; (2) Gamala also, which is a city ever against Tarichem, but on the other side of the lake, conspired with them. This city lay upon the borders of Agrippa's kingdom, as also did Sogana and Seleucia. And these were both parts of Gaulanitis; for Sogana was a part of that called the Upper Gaulanitis, as was Gamala of the Lower; (3) while Seleucia was situated at the lake Semechouitis, which lake is thirty furlongs in breadth, and sixty in length; its marshes reach as far as the place Daphne, which in other respects is a delicious place, and hath such fountains as supply water to what is called Little Jordan, under the temple of the golden calf, where it is sent into Great Jordan. (4) Now Agrippa had united Sogana and Seleucia by leagues to himself, at the very beginning of the revolt from the Romans; yet did not Gamala accede to them, but relied upon the difficulty of the place, which was greater than that of Jotapata, (5) for it was situated upon a rough ridge of a high mountain, with a kind of neck in the middle: where it begins to ascend, it lengthens itself, and declines as much downward before as behind, insomuch that it is like a camel in figure, from whence it is so named, although the people of the country do not pronounce it accurately. (6) Both on the side and the face there are abrupt parts divided from the rest, and ending in vast deep valleys; yet are the parts behind, where they are joined to the mountain, somewhat easier of ascent than the other; but then the people belonging to the place have cut an oblique ditch there, and made that hard to be ascended also. (7) On its acclivity, which is straight, houses are built, and those very thick and close to one another. The city also hangs so strangely, that it looks as if it would fall down upon itself, so sharp is it at the top. (8) It is exposed to the south, and its southern mount, which reaches to an immense height, was in the nature of a citadel to the city; and above that was a precipice, not walled about, but extending itself to an immense depth. There was also a spring of water within the wall, at the utmost limits of the city.

General view of Gamala in the Golan Heights. (photo Samuel Magal)

Roman ballista stones at Gamala. (photo Staselnik, via Wikimedia Commons)

2. (9) As this city was naturally hard to be taken, so had Josephus, by building a wall about it, made it still stronger, as also by ditches and mines under ground. (10) The people that were in it were made more bold by the nature of the place than the people of Jotapata had been, but it had much fewer fighting men in it; and they had such a confidence in the situation of the place, that they thought the enemy could not be too many for them; for the city had been filled with those that had fled to it for safety, on account of its strength; on which account they had been able to resist those whom Agrippa sent to besiege it for seven months together.

3. (11) But Vespasian removed from Emmaus, where he had last pitched his camp before the city Tiberias, (now Emmaus, if it be interpreted, may be rendered "a warm bath," for therein is a spring of warm water, useful for healing,) and came to Gamala; (12) yet was its situation such that he was not able to encompass it all round with soldiers to watch it; but where the places were practicable, he set men to watch it, and seized upon the mountain which was over it. (13) And as the legions, according to their usual custom, were fortifying their camp upon that mountain, he began to cast up banks at the bottom, at the part towards the east, where the highest tower of the whole city was, and where the fifteenth legion pitched their camp; while the fifth legion did duty over against the midst of the city, and whilst the tenth legion filled up the ditches and the valleys. (14) Now at this time it was that as king Agrippa was come nigh the walls, and was endeavoring to speak to those that were on the walls about a surrender, he was hit with a stone on his right elbow by one of the slingers; (15) he was then immediately surrounded with his own men. But the Romans were excited to set about the siege, by their indignation on the king's account, and by their fear on their own account, (16) as concluding that those men would omit no kinds of barbarity against foreigners and enemies, who where so enraged against one of their own nation, and one that advised them to nothing but what was for their own advantage.

4. (17) Now when the banks were finished, which was done on the sudden, both by the multitude of hands, and by their being accustomed to such work, they brought the machines; (18) but Chares and Joseph, who were the most potent men in the city, set their armed men in order, though already in a fright, because they did not suppose that the city could hold out long, since they had not a sufficient quantity either of water, or of other necessaries. (19) However, these their leaders encouraged them, and brought them out upon the wall, and for a while indeed they drove away those that were bringing the machines; but when those machines threw darts and stones at them, they retired into the city; (20) then did the Romans bring battering rams to three several places, and made the wall shake [and fall]. They then poured in over the parts of the wall that were thrown down, with a mighty sound of trumpets and noise of armor, and with a shout of the soldiers, and brake in by force upon those that were in the city; (22) but these men fell upon the Romans for some time, at their first entrance, and prevented their going any further, and with great courage beat them back; and the Romans were so overpowered by the greater multitude of the people, who beat them on every side, that they were obliged to run into the upper parts of the city. Whereupon the people turned about, and fell upon their enemies, who had attacked them, and thrust them down to the lower parts, and as they were distressed by the narrowness and difficulty of the place, slew them; (23) and as these Romans could neither beat those back that were above them, nor escape the force of their own men that were forcing their way forward, they were compelled to fly into their enemies' houses, which were low; (24) but these houses being thus full, of soldiers, whose weight they could not bear, fell down suddenly; and when one house fell, it shook down a great many of those that were under it, as did those do to such as were under them. (25) By this means a vast number of the Romans perished; for they were so terribly distressed, that although they saw the houses subsiding, they were compelled to leap upon the tops of them; so that a great many were ground to powder by these ruins, and a great many of those that got from under them lost some of their limbs, but still a greater number were suffocated by the dust that arose from those ruins. (26) The people of Gamala supposed this to be an assistance afforded them by God, and without regarding what damage they suffered themselves, they pressed forward, and thrust the enemy upon the tops of their houses; and when they stumbled in the sharp and narrow streets, and were perpetually falling down, they threw their stones or darts at them, and slew them. (27) Now the very ruins afforded them stones enow; and for iron weapons, the dead men of the enemies' side afforded them what they wanted; for drawing the swords of those that were dead, they made use of them to despatch such as were only half dead; (28) nay, there were a great number who, upon their falling down from the tops of the houses, stabbed themselves, and died after that manner; (29) nor indeed was it easy for those that were beaten back to fly away; for they were so unacquainted with the

Reconstruction of a Roman catapult at Gamala. (photo Staselnik, via Wikimedia Commons)

Remains at Gamala, showing breach in the city wall. (photo Samuel Magal)

(below) Remains of the synagogue at Gamala. (photo Samuel Magal)

ways, and the dust was so thick, that they wandered about without knowing one another, and fell down dead among the crowd.

5. (30) Those therefore that were able to find the ways out of the city retired. (31) But now Vespasian always staid among those that were hard set; for he was deeply affected with seeing the ruins of the city falling upon his army, and forgot to take care of his own preservation. He went up gradually towards the highest parts of the city before he was aware, and was left in the midst of dangers, having only a very few with him; (32) for even his son Titus was not with him at that time, having been then sent into Syria to Mucianus. (33) However, he thought it not safe to fly, nor did he esteem it a fit thing for him to do; but calling to mind the actions he had done from his youth, and recollecting his courage, as if he had been excited by a divine fury, he covered himself and those that were with him with their shields, and formed a testudo over

both their bodies and their armor, (34) and bore up against the enemy's attacks, who came running down from the top of the city; and without showing any dread at the multitude of the men or of their darts, he endured all, until the enemy took notice of that divine courage that was within him, and remitted of their attacks; (35) and when they pressed less zealously upon him, he retired, though without showing his back to them till he was gotten out of the walls of the city. (36) Now a great number of the Romans fell in this battle, among whom was Ebutius, the decurion, a man who appeared not only in this engagement, wherein he fell, but every where, and in former engagements, to be of the truest courage, and one that had done very great mischief to the Jews. (37) But there was a centurion whose name was Gallus, who, during this disorder, being encompassed about, he and ten other soldiers privately crept into the house of a certain person, (38) where he heard them talking at supper, what the people intended to do against the Romans, or about themselves (for both the man himself and those with him were Syrians). So he got up in the night time, and cut all their throats, and escaped, together with his soldiers, to the Romans.

6. (39) And now Vespasian comforted his army, which was much dejected by reflecting on their ill success, and because they had never before fallen into such a calamity, and besides this, because they were greatly ashamed that they had left their general alone in great dangers. (40) As to what concerned himself, he avoided to say any thing, that he might by no means seem to complain of it; but he said that "we ought to bear manfully what usually falls out in war, and this, by considering what the nature of war is, and how it can never be that we must conquer without bloodshed on our own side; for there stands about us that fortune which is of its own nature mutable; (41) that while they had killed so many ten thousands of the Jews, they had now paid their small share of the reckoning to fate; (42) and as it is the part of weak people to be too much puffed up with good success, so is it the part of cowards to be too much aftrighted at that which is ill; for the change from the one to the other is sudden on both sides; and he is the best warrior who is of a sober mind under misfortunes, that he may continue in that temper, and cheerfully recover what had been lost formerly; (43) and as for what had now happened, it was neither owing to their own effeminacy, nor to the valor of the Jews, but the difficulty of the place was the occasion of their advantage, and of our disappointment. (44) Upon reflecting on which matter one might blame your zeal as perfectly ungovernable; for when the enemy had retired to their highest fastnesses, you ought to have restrained yourselves, and not, by presenting yourselves at the top of the city, to be exposed to dangers; but upon your having obtained the lower parts of the city, you ought to have provoked those that had retired thither to a safe and settled battle; whereas, in rushing so hastily upon victory, you took no care of your safety. (45) But this incautiousness in war, and this madness of zeal, is not a Roman maxim. While we perform all that we attempt by skill and good order, that procedure is the part of barbarians, and is what the Jews chiefly support themselves by. (46) We ought therefore to return to our own virtue, and to be rather angry than any longer dejected at this unlucky misfortune, (47) and let everyone seek for his own consolation from his own hand; for by this means he will avenge those that have been destroyed, and punish those that have killed them. (48) For myself, I will endeavor, as I have now done, to go first before you against your enemies in every engagement, and to be the last that retires from it."

7. (49) So Vespasian encouraged his army by this speech; but for the people of Gamala, it happened that they took courage for a little while, upon such great and unaccountable success as they had had. (50) But when they considered with themselves that they had now no hopes of any terms of accommodation, and reflecting upon it that they could not get away, and that their provisions began already to be short, they were exceedingly cast down, and their courage failed them; (51) yet did they not neglect what might be for their preservation, so far as they were able, but the most courageous among them guarded those parts of the wall that were beaten down, while the more infirm did the same to the rest of the wall that still remained round the city. (52) And as the Romans raised their banks, and attempted to get into the city a second time, a great many of them fled out of the city through impracticable valleys, where no guards were placed, as also through subterraneous caverns; (53) while those that were afraid of being caught, and for that reason staid in the city, perished for want of food; for what food they had was brought together from all quarters, and reserved for the fighting men.

Plaque commemorating the Jewish defenders of Gamala. (photo Samuel Magal)

8. (54) And these were the hard circumstances that the people of Gamala were in. But now Vespasian went about other work by the by, during this siege, and that was to subdue those that had seized upon Mount Tabor, a place that lies in the middle between the great plain and Scythopolis, (55) whose top is elevated as high as thirty furlongs and is hardly to be ascended on its north side; its top is a plain of twenty-six furlongs, and all encompassed with a wall. (56) Now Josephus erected this so long a wall in forty days'

General view of Mount Tabor. (photo Samuel Magal)

time, and furnished it with other materials, and with water from below, for the inhabitants only made use of rain water. (57) As therefore there was a great multitude of people gotten together upon this mountain, Vespasian sent Placidus with six hundred horsemen thither. (58) Now, as it was impossible for him to ascend the mountain, he invited many of them to peace, by the offer of his right hand for their security, and of his intercession for them. (59) Accordingly they came down, but with a treacherous design, as well as he had the like treacherous design upon them on the other side; for Placidus spoke mildly to them, as aiming to take them, when he got them into the plain; they also came down, as complying with his proposals, but it was in order to fall upon him when he was not aware of it: (60) however, Placidus's stratagem was too hard for theirs; for when the Jews began to fight, he pretended to run away, and when they were in pursuit of the Romans, he enticed them a great way along the plain, and then made his horsemen turn back; whereupon he beat them, and slew a great number of them, and cut off the retreat of the rest of the multitude, and hindered their return. (61) So they left Tabor, and fled to Jerusalem, while the people of the country came to terms with him, for their water failed them, and so they delivered up the mountain and themselves to Placidus.

9. (62) But of the people of Gamala, those that were of the bolder sort fled away and hid themselves, while the more infirm perished by famine; (63) but the men of war sustained the siege till the two and twentieth day of the month Hyperberetmus, [Tisri,] when three soldiers of the fifteenth legion, about the morning watch, got under a high tower that was near them, and undermined it, without making any noise; (64) nor when they either came to it, which was in the night time, nor when they were under it, did those that guarded it perceive them. These soldiers then upon their coming avoided making a noise, and when they had rolled away five of its strongest stones, they went away hastily; (65) whereupon the tower fell down on a sudden, with a very great noise, and its guard fell headlong with it; so that those that kept guard at other places were under such disturbance, that they ran away; (66) the Romans also slew many of those that ventured to oppose them, among whom was Joseph, who was slain by a dart, as he was running away over that part of the wall that was broken down: (67) but as those that were in the city were greatly aftrighted at the noise, they ran hither and thither, and a great consternation fell upon them, as though all the enemy had fallen in at once upon them. (68) Then it was that Chares, who was ill, and under the physician's hands, gave up the ghost, the fear he was in greatly contributing to make his distemper fatal to him. (69) But the Romans so well remembered their former ill success, that they did not enter the city till the three and twentieth day of the forementioned month.

10. (70) At which time Titus, who was now returned, out of the indignation he had at the destruction the Romans had undergone while he was absent, took two hundred chosen horsemen and some footmen with him, and entered without noise into the city. (71) Now as the watch perceived that he was coming, they made a noise, and betook themselves to their arms; and as that his entrance was presently known to those that were in the city, some of them caught hold of their children and their wives, and drew them after them, and fled away to the citadel, with lamentations and cries, while others of them went to meet Titus, and were killed perpetually; (72) but so many of them as were hindered from running up to the citadel, not knowing what in the world to do, fell among the Roman guards, while the groans of those that were killed were prodigiously great every where, and blood ran down over all the lower parts of the city, from the upper. (73) But then Vespasian himself came to his assistance against those that had fled to the citadel, and brought his whole army with him; now this upper part of the city was every way rocky, and difficult of ascent, and elevated to a vast altitude, and very full of people on all sides,

and encompassed with precipices, (75) whereby the Jews cut off those that came up to them, and did much mischief to others by their darts, and the large stones which they rolled down upon them, while they were themselves so high that the enemy's darts could hardly reach them. (76) However, there arose such a Divine storm against them as was instrumental to their destruction; this carried the Roman darts upon them, and made those which they threw return back, and drove them obliquely away from them; (77) nor could the Jews indeed stand upon their precipices, by reason of the violence of the wind, having nothing that was stable to stand upon, nor could they see those that were ascending up to them; (78) so the Romans got up and surrounded them, and some they slew before they could defend themselves, and others as they were delivering up themselves; and the remembrance of those that were slain at their former entrance into the city increased their rage against them now; (79) a great number also of those that were surrounded on every side, and despaired of escaping, threw their children and their wives, and themselves also, down the precipices, into the valley beneath, which, near the citadel, had been dug hollow to a vast depth; (80) but so it happened, that the anger of the Romans appeared not to be so extravagant as was the madness of those that were now taken, while the Romans slew but four thousand, whereas the number of those that had thrown themselves down was found to be five thousand: (81) nor did anyone escape except two women, who were the daughters of Philip, and Philip himself was the son of a certain eminent man called Jacimus, who had been general of king Agrippa's army; (82) and these did therefore escape, because they lay concealed from the rage of the Romans when the city was taken; for otherwise they spared not so much as the infants, of which many were flung down by them from the citadel. (83) And thus was Gamala taken on the three and twentieth day of the month Hyperberetens, [Tisri,] whereas the city had first revolted on the four and twentieth day of the month Gorpieus [Elul].

CHAPTER 2.

THE SURRENDER OF GISCHALA; WHILE JOHN FLIES AWAY FROM IT TO JERUSALEM.

1. (84) NOW no place of Galilee remained to be taken but the small city of Gischala, whose multitude yet were desirous of peace; for they were generally husbandmen, and always applied themselves to cultivate the fruits of the earth. However, there were a great number that belonged to a band of robbers, that were already corrupted, and had crept in among them, and some of the governing part of the citizens were sick of the same distemper. (85) It was John, the son of a certain man whose name was Levi, that drew them into this rebellion, and encouraged them in it. He was a cunning knave, and of a temper that could put on various shapes; very rash in expecting great things, and very sagacious in bringing about what he hoped for. It was known to every body that he was fond of war, in order to thrust himself into authority; (86) and the seditious part of the people of Gischala were under his management, by whose means the populace, who seemed ready to send ambassadors in order to a surrender, waited for the coming of the Romans in battle-array. (87) Vespasian sent against them Titus, with a thousand horsemen, but withdrew the tenth legion to Scythopolis, (88) while he returned to Cesarea with the two other legions, that he might allow them to refresh themselves after their long and hard campaign, thinking withal that the plenty which was in those cities would improve their bodies and their spirits, against the difficulties they were to go through afterwards; (89) for he saw there would be occasion for great pains about Jerusalem, which was not yet taken, because it was the royal city, and the principal city of the whole nation, and because those that had run away from the war in other places got all together thither. (90) It was also naturally strong, and the walls that were built round it made him not a little concerned about it. Moreover, he esteemed the men that were in it to be so courageous and bold, that even without the consideration of the walls, it would be hard to subdue them; (91) for which reason he took care of and exercised his soldiers beforehand for the work, as they do wrestlers before they begin their undertaking.

2. (92) Now Titus, as he rode out to Gischala, found it would be easy for him to take the city upon the first onset; but knew withal, that if he took it by force, the multitude would be destroyed by the soldiers without mercy. (Now he was already satiated with the shedding of blood, and pitied the major part, who would then perish, without distinction, together with the guilty.) So he was rather desirous the city might be surrendered up to him on terms. (93) Accordingly, when he saw the wall full of those men that were of the corrupted party, he said to them,—That he could not but wonder what it was they depended on, when they alone staid to fight the Romans, after every other city was taken by them, (94) especially when they have seen cities much better fortified than theirs is overthrown by a single attack upon them; while as many as have intrusted themselves to the security of the Romans' right hands, which he now offers to them, without regarding their former insolence, do enjoy their own possessions in safety; (95) for that while they had hopes of recovering their liberty, they might be pardoned; but that their continuance still in their opposition, when they saw that to be impossible, was inexcusable; (96) for that if they will not comply with such humane offers, and right hands for security, they should have experience of such a war as would spare nobody, and should soon be made sensible that their wall would be but a trifle, when battered by the Roman machines; in depending on which they demonstrate themselves to be the only Galileans that were no better than arrogant slaves and captives.

Remains of the ancient synagogue at Gush Halav (Gischala). (photo Samuel Magal)

3. (97) Now none of the populace durst not only make a reply, but durst not so much as get upon the wall, for it was all taken up by the robbers, who were also the guard at the gates, in order to prevent any of the rest from going out, in order to propose terms of submission, and from receiving any of the horsemen into the city. (98) But John returned Titus this answer: That for himself he was content to hearken to his proposals, and that he would either persuade or force those that refused them. (99) Yet he said that Titus ought to have such regard to the Jewish law, as to grant them leave to celebrate that day, which was the seventh day of the week, on which it was unlawful not only to remove their arms, but even to treat of peace also; (100) and that even the Romans were not ignorant how the period of the seventh day was among them a cessation from all labors; and that he who should compel them to transgress the law about that day would be equally guilty with those that were compelled to transgress it: (101) and that this delay could be of no disadvantage to him; for why should anybody think of doing any thing in the night, unless it was to fly away? which he might prevent by placing his camp round about them; (102) and that they should think it a great point gained, if they might not be obliged to transgress the laws of their country; and that it would be a right thing for him, who designed to grant them peace, without their expectation of such a favor, to preserve the laws of those they saved inviolable. (103) Thus did this man put a trick upon Titus, not so much out of regard to the seventh day as to his own preservation, for he was afraid lest he should be quite deserted if the city should be taken, and had his hopes of life in that night, and in his flight therein. (104) Now this was the work of God, who therefore preserved this John, that he might bring on the destruction of Jerusalem; as also it was his work that Titus was prevailed with by this pretense for a delay, and that he pitched his camp further off the city at Cydessa. (105) This Cydessa was a strong Mediterranean village of the Tyrians, which always hated and made war against the Jews; it had also a great number of inhabitants, and was well fortified, which made it a proper place for such as were enemies to the Jewish nation.

4. (106) Now, in the night time, when John saw that there was no Roman guard about the city, he seized the opportunity directly, and, taking with him not only the armed men that where about him, but a considerable number of those that had little to do, together with their families, he fled to Jerusalem. (107) And indeed, though the man was making haste to get away, and was tormented with fears of being a captive, or of losing his life, yet did he prevail with himself to take out of the city along with him a multitude of women and children, as far as twenty furlongs; but there he left them as he proceeded further on his journey, where those that were left behind made sad lamentations; (108) for the farther every one of them was come from his own people, the nearer they thought themselves to be to their enemies. They also affrighted themselves with this thought, that those who would carry them into captivity were just at hand, and still turned themselves back at the mere noise they made themselves in this their hasty flight, as if those from whom they fled were just upon them. (109) Many also of them missed their ways, and the earnestness of such as aimed to outgo the rest threw down many of them. (110) And indeed there was a miserable destruction made of the women and children; while some of them took courage to call their husbands and kinsmen back, and to beseech them, with the bitterest lamentations, to stay for them; (111) but John's exhortation, who cried out to them to save themselves, and fly away, prevailed. He said also, that if the Romans should seize upon those whom they left behind, they would be revenged on them for it. So this multitude that run thus away was dispersed abroad, according as each of them was able to run, one faster or slower than another.

5. (112) Now on the next day Titus came to the wall, to make the agreement; (113) whereupon the people opened their gates to him, and came out to him, with their children and wives, and made acclamations of joy to him, as to one that had been their benefactor, and had delivered the city out of custody; (114) they also informed him of John's flight, and besought him to spare them, and to come in, and bring the rest of those that were for innovations to punishment. (115) But Titus, not so much regarding the supplications of the people, sent part of his horsemen to pursue after John, but they could not overtake him, for he was gotten to Jerusalem before; they also slew six thousand of the women and children who went out with him, but returned back, and brought with them almost three thousand. (116) However, Titus was greatly displeased that he had not been able to bring this John, who had deluded him, to punishment; yet he had captives enough, as well as the corrupted part of the city, to satisfy his anger, when it missed of John. (117) So he entered the city in the midst of acclamations of joy; and when he had given orders to the soldiers to pull down a small part of the wall, as of a city taken in war, he repressed those that had disturbed the city rather by threatenings than by executions; (118) for he thought that many would accuse innocent persons, out of their own private animosities and quarrels, if he should at-

Eastern facade of the Roman temple at Tel Kedesh (Cydessa). (photo Natalinasser, via Wikimedia Commons)

tempt to distinguish those that were worthy of punishment from the rest; and that it was better to let a guilty person alone in his fears, that to destroy with him any one that did not deserve it; (119) for that probably such a one might be taught prudence, by the fear of the punishment he had deserved, and have a shame upon him for his former offenses, when he had been forgiven; but that the punishment of such as have been once put to death could never be retrieved. (120) However, he placed a garrison in the city for its security, by which means he should restrain those that were for innovations, and should leave those that were peaceably disposed in greater security. And thus was all Galilee taken, but this not till after it had cost the Romans much pains before it could be taken by them.

CHAPTER 3.

CONCERNING JOHN OF GISCHALA. CONCERNING THE ZEALOTS AND THE HIGH PRIEST ANANUS; AS ALSO HOW THE JEWS RAISE SEDITIONS ONE AGAINST ANOTHER [IN JERUSALEM].

1. (121) NOW upon John's entry into Jerusalem, the whole body of the people were in an uproar, and ten thousand of them crowded about every one of the fugitives that were come to them, and inquired of them what miseries had happened abroad, (122) when their breath was so short, and hot, and quick, that of itself it declared the great distress they were in; yet did they talk big under their misfortunes, and pretended to say that they had not fled away from the Romans, but came thither in order to fight them with less hazard; (123) for that it would be an unreasonable and a fruitless thing for them to expose themselves to desperate hazards about Gischala, and such weak cities, whereas they ought to lay up their weapons and their zeal, and reserve it for their metropolis. (124) But when they related to them the taking of Gischala, and their decent departure, as they pretended, from that place, many of the people understood it to be no better than a flight; (125) and especially when the people were told of those that were made captives, they were in great confusion, and guessed those things to be plain indications that they should be taken also. (126) But for John, he was very little concerned for those whom he had left behind him, but went about among all the people, and persuaded them to go to war, by the hopes he gave them. He affirmed that the affairs of the Romans were in a weak condition, and extolled his own power. (127) He also jested upon the ignorance of the unskillful, as if those Romans, although they should take to themselves wings, could never fly over the wall of Jerusalem, who found such great difficulties in taking the villages of Galilee, and had broken their engines of war against their walls.

2. (128) These harangues of John's corrupted a great part of the young men, and puffed them up for the war; but as to the more prudent part, and those in years, there was not a man of them but foresaw what was coming, and made lamentation on that account, as if the city was already undone; (129) and in this confusion were the people. But then it must be observed, that the multitude that came out of the country were at discord before the Jerusalem sedition began; (130) for Titus went from Gischala to Cesates, and Vespasian from Cesarea to Jamnia and Azotus, and took them both; and when he had put garrisons into them, he came back with a great number of the people, who were come over to him, upon his giving them his right hand for their preservation. (131) There were besides disorders and civil wars in every city; and all those that were at quiet from the Romans turned their hands one against another. There was also a bitter contest between those that were fond of war, and those that were desirous for peace. (132) At the first this quarrelsome temper caught hold of private families, who could not agree among themselves; after which those people that were the dearest to one another brake through all restraints with regard to each other, and every one associated with those of his own opinion, and began already to stand in opposition one to another; (133) so that seditions arose every where, while those that were for innovations, and were desirous of war, by their youth and boldness, were too hard for the aged and prudent men. (134) And, in the first place, all the people of every place betook themselves to rapine; after which they got together in bodies, in order to rob the people of the country, insomuch that for barbarity and iniquity those of the same nation did no way differ from the Romans; nay, it seemed to be a much lighter thing to be ruined by the Romans than by themselves.

3. (135) Now the Roman garrisons, which guarded the cities, partly out of their uneasiness to take such trouble upon them, and partly out of the hatred they bare to the Jewish nation, did little or nothing towards relieving the miserable, till the captains of these troops of robbers, being satiated with rapines in the country, got all together from all parts, and became a band of wickedness, and all together crept into Jerusalem, (136) which was now become a city without a governor, and, as the ancient custom was, received without distinction all that belonged to their nation; and these they then received, because all men supposed that those who came so fast into the city came out of kindness, and for their assistance, (137) although these very men, besides the seditions they raised, were otherwise the direct cause of the city's destruction also; for as they were an unprofitable and a useless multitude, they spent those provisions beforehand which might otherwise have been sufficient for the fighting men. Moreover, besides the bringing on of the war, they were the occasions of sedition and famine therein.

4. (138) There were besides these other robbers that came out of the country, and came into the city, and joining to them those that were worse than themselves, omitted no kind of barbarity; (139) for they did not measure their courage by their rapines and plunderings only, but preceded as far as murdering men; and this not in the night time or privately, or with regard to ordinary men, but did it openly in the day time, and began with the most eminent persons in the city; (140) for the first man they meddled with was Antipas, one of the royal lineage, and the most potent man in the whole city, insomuch that the public treasures were committed to his care; (141) him they took and confined; as they did in the next place to Levias, a person of great note, with Sophas, the son of Raguel, both which were of royal lineage also. And besides these, they did the same to the principal men of the country. (142) This caused a terrible consternation among the people, and everyone contented himself with taking care of his own safety, as they would do if the city had been taken in war.

5. (143) But these were not satisfied with the bonds into which they had put the men forementioned; nor did they think it safe for them to keep them thus in custody long, (144) since they were men very powerful, and had numerous families of their own that were able to avenge them. Nay, they thought the very people would perhaps be so moved at these unjust proceedings, as to rise in a body against them; it was therefore resolved to have them slain; (145) accordingly, they sent one John, who was the most bloody-minded of them all, to do that execution: this man was also called "the son of Dorcas," (cf. Acts 9:36) in the language of our country. Ten more men went along with him into the prison, with their swords drawn, and so they cut the throats of those that were in custody there. (146) The grand lying pretence these men made for so flagrant an enormity was this, that these men had had conferences

List of High Priests in the Herodian-Roman Period	
Ananelus	37–36 B.C.
Aristobulus III, paternal grandson of Aristobulus. He was the last of the Hasmoneans; II and brother of Herod's wife Mariamne (second wife of Herod).	36 B.C.
Ananelus (restored)	36–30 B.C.
Joshua ben Fabus	30–23 B.C.
Simon ben Boethus (his daughter Mariamne was third wife of Herod the Great)	23–5 B.C.
Matthias ben Theophilus	5–4 B.C.
Joazar ben Boethus	4 B.C.
Eleazar ben Boethus	4–3 B.C.
Joshua ben Sie	3 B.C. – ?
Joazar ben Boethus (restored)	? – A.D. 6
Ananus ben Seth	6–15
Ishmael ben Fabus	15–16
Eleazar ben Ananus	16–17
Simon ben Camithus	17–18
Joseph Caiaphas (son-in-law of the high priest Ananus ben Seth)	18–36
Jonathan ben Ananus	36–37
Theophilus ben Ananus	37–41
Simon Cantatheras ben Boethus	41–43
Matthias ben Ananus	43
Elioneus ben Simon Cantatheras	43–44
Jonathan ben Ananus	44 (restored)
Josephus ben Camydus	44–46
Ananias ben Nebedeus	46–58
Jonathan	58
Ishmael ben Fabus	58–62 (restored?)
Joseph Cabi ben Simon	62–63
Ananus ben Ananus	63
Joshua ben Damneus	63
Joshua ('Jesus') ben Gamaliel (his wife Martha belonged to family of Boethus)	63–64
Mattathias ben Theophilus	65–66
Phannias ben Samuel	67–70

with the Romans for a surrender of Jerusalem to them; and so they said they had slain only such as were traitors to their common liberty. Upon the whole, they grew the more insolent upon this bold prank of theirs, as though they had been the benefactors and saviors of the city.

6. (147) Now the people were come to that degree of meanness and fear, and these robbers to that degree of madness, that these last took upon them to appoint high priests. (148) So when they had disannulled the succession, according to those families out of which the high priests used to be made, they ordained certain unknown and ignoble persons for that office, that they might have their assistance in their wicked undertakings; (149) for such as obtained this highest of all honors, without any desert, were forced to comply with those that bestowed it on them. (150) They also set the principal men at variance one with another, by several sorts of contrivances and tricks, and gained the opportunity of doing what they pleased, by the mutual quarrels of those who might have obstructed their measures; till at length, when they were satiated with the unjust actions they had done towards men, they transferred their contumelious behavior to God himself, and came into the sanctuary with polluted feet.

7. (151) And now the multitude were going to rise against them already; for Ananus, the ancientest of the high priests, persuaded them to it. He was a very prudent man, and had perhaps saved the city if he could but have escaped the hands of those that plotted against him. These men made the temple of God a strong hold for them, and a place whither they might resort, in order to avoid the troubles they feared from the people; the sanctuary was now become a refuge, and a shop of tyranny. (152) They also mixed jesting among the miseries they introduced, which was more intolerable than what they did; (153) for in order to try what surprise the people would be under, and how far their own power extended, they undertook to dispose of the high priesthood by casting lots for it, whereas, as we have said already, it was to descend by succession in a family. (154) The pretense they made for this strange attempt was an ancient practice, while they said that of old it was determined by lot; but in truth, it was no better than a dissolution of an undeniable law, and a cunning contrivance to seize upon the government, derived from those that presumed to appoint governors as they themselves pleased.

8. (155) Hereupon they sent for one of the pontifical tribes, which is called Eniachim, and cast lots which of it should be the high priest. By fortune the lot so fell as to demonstrate their iniquity after the plainest manner, for it fell upon one whose name was Phannias, the son of Samuel, of the village Aphtha. He was a man not only unworthy of the high priesthood, but that did not well know what the high priesthood was, such a mere rustic was he! (156) yet did they hail this man, without his own consent, out of the country, as if they were acting a play upon the stage, and adorned him with a counterfeit thee; they also put upon him the sacred garments, and upon every occasion instructed him what he was to do. (157) This horrid piece of wickedness was sport and pastime with them, but occasioned the other priests, who at a distance saw their law made a jest of, to shed tears, and sorely lament the dissolution of such a sacred dignity.

9. (158) And now the people could no longer bear the insolence of this procedure, but did all together run zealously, in order to overthrow that tyranny; (159) and indeed they were Gorion the son of Josephus, and Symeon the son of Gamaliel, who encouraged them, by going up and down when they were assembled together in crowds, and as they saw them alone, to bear no longer, but to inflict punishment upon these pests and plagues of their freedom, and to purge the temple of these bloody polluters of it. (160) The best esteemed also of the high priests, Jesus the son of Gamalas, and Ananus the son of Ananus when they were at their assemblies, bitterly reproached the people for their sloth, and excited them against the zealots; (161) for that was the name they went by, as if they were zealous in good undertakings, and were not rather zealous in the worst actions, and extravagant in them beyond the example of others.

10. (162) And now, when the multitude were gotten together to an assembly, and every one was in indignation at these men's seizing upon the sanctuary, at their rapine and murders, but had not yet begun their attacks upon them, (the reason of which was this,

VESPASIAN'S CAMPAIGN IN JUDEA; INTERNAL CONFLICT AMONG THE JEWS A.D. 67

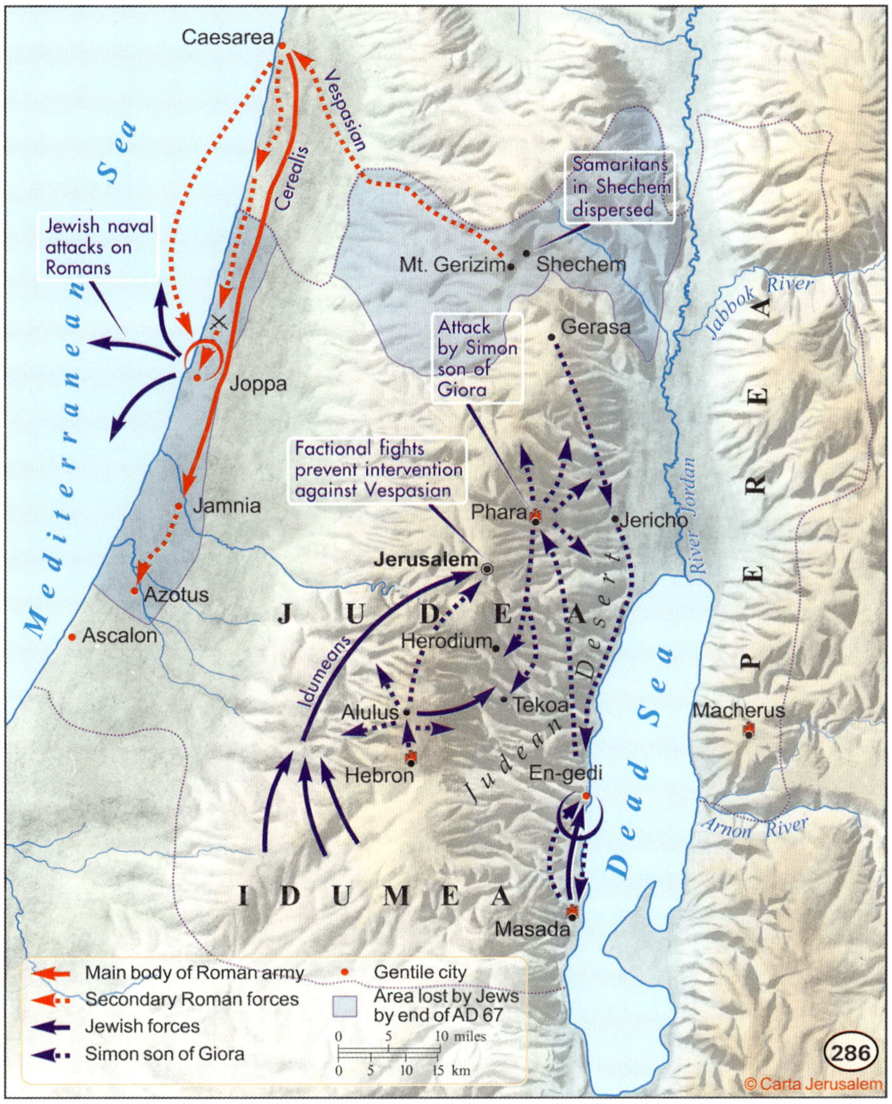

that they imagined it to be a difficult thing to suppress these zealots, as indeed the case was,) Ananus stood in the midst of them, and casting his eyes frequently at the temple, and having a flood of tears in his eyes, (163) he said, "Certainly it had been good for me to die before I had seen the house of God full of so many abominations, or these sacred places, that ought not to be trodden upon at random, filled with the feet of these blood-shedding villains; (164) yet do I, who am clothed with the vestments of the high priesthood, and am called by that most venerable name [of high priest], still live, and am but too fond of living, and cannot endure to undergo a death which would be the glory of my old age; and if I were the only person concerned, and as it were in a desert, I would give up my life, and that alone for God's sake; (165) for to what purpose is it to live among a people insensible of their calamities, and where there is no notion remaining of any remedy for the miseries that are upon them? for when you are seized upon, you bear it! and when you are beaten, you are silent! and when the people are murdered, nobody dare so much as send out a groan openly! (166) O bitter tyranny that we are under! But why do I complain of the tyrants? Was it not you, and your sufferance of them, that have nourished them? (167) Was it not you that overlooked those that first of all got together, for they were then but a few, and by your silence made them grow to be many; and by conniving at them when they took arms, in effect armed them against yourselves? (168) You ought to have then prevented their first attempts, when they fell a reproaching your relations; but by neglecting that care in time, you have encouraged these wretches to plunder men. When houses were pillaged, nobody said a word, which was the occasion why they carried off the owners of those houses; and when they were drawn through the midst of the city, nobody came to their assistance. (169) They then proceeded to put those whom you have betrayed into their hands into bonds. I do not say how many and of what characters those men were whom they thus served; but certainly they were such as were accused by none, and condemned by none; and since nobody succored them when they were put into bonds, (170) the consequence was, that you saw the same persons slain. We have seen this also; so that still the best of the herd of brute animals, as it were, have been still led to be sacrificed, when yet nobody said one word, or moved his right hand for their preservation. (171) Will you bear, therefore, will you bear to see your sanctuary trampled on? and will you lay steps for these profane wretches, upon which they may mount to higher degrees of insolence? Will not you pluck them down from their exaltation? for even by this time they had proceeded to higher enormities, if they had been able to overthrow any thing greater than the sanctuary. (172) They have seized upon the strongest place of the whole city; you may call it the temple, if you please, though it be like a citadel or fortress. Now, while you have tyranny in so great a degree walled in, and see your enemies over your heads, to what purpose is it to take counsel? and what have you to support your minds withal? (173) Perhaps you wait for the Romans, that they may protect our holy places: are our matters then brought to that pass? and are we come to that degree of misery, that our enemies themselves are expected to pity us? (174) O wretched creatures! will not you rise up and turn upon those that strike you? which you may observe in wild beasts themselves, that they will avenge themselves on those that strike them. Will you not call to mind, every one of you, the calamities you yourselves have suffered? nor lay before your eyes what afflictions you yourselves have undergone? and will not such things sharpen your souls to revenge? (175) Is therefore that most honorable and most natural of our passions utterly lost, I mean the desire of liberty? Truly we are in love with slavery, and in love with those that lord it over us, as if we had received that principle of subjection from our ancestors; (176) yet did they undergo many and great wars for the sake of liberty, nor were they so far overcome by the power of the Egyptians, or the Medes, but that still they did what they thought fit, notwithstanding their commands to the contrary. (177) And what occasion is there now for a war with the Romans? (I meddle not with determining whether it be an advantageous and profitable war or not.) What pretense is there for it? (178) Is it not that we may enjoy our liberty? Besides, shall we not bear the lords of the habitable earth to be lords over us, and yet bear tyrants of our own country? (179) Although I must say that submission to foreigners may be borne, because fortune hath already doomed us to it, while submission to wicked people of our own nation is too unmanly, and brought upon us by our own consent. (180) However, since I have had occasion to mention the Romans, I will not conceal a thing that, as I am speaking, comes into my mind, and affects me considerably;

Model of the Second Temple in Jerusalem and the outer court (Court of the Gentiles) of the sanctuary. (by M. Avi-Yonah, now on display at The Israel Museum; photo Samuel Magal)

it is this, that though we should be taken by them, (God forbid the event should be so!) yet can we undergo nothing that will be harder to be borne than what these men have already brought upon us. (181) How then can we avoid shedding of tears, when we see the Roman donations in our temple, while we withal see those of our own nation taking our spoils, and plundering our glorious metropolis, and slaughtering our men, from which enormities those Romans themselves would have abstained? (182) to see those Romans never going beyond the bounds allotted to profane persons, nor venturing to break in upon any of our sacred customs; nay, having a horror on their minds when they view at a distance those sacred walls; (183) while some that have been born in this very country, and brought up in our customs, and called Jews, do walk about in the midst of the holy places, at the very time when their hands are still warm with the slaughter of their own countrymen. (184) Besides, can any one be afraid of a war abroad, and that with such as will have comparatively much greater moderation than our own people have? For truly, if we may suit our words to the things they represent, it is probable one may hereafter find the Romans to be the supporters of our laws, and those within ourselves the subverters of them. (185) And now I am persuaded that every one of you here comes satisfied before I speak that these overthrowers of our liberties deserve to be destroyed, and that nobody can so much as devise a punishment that they have not deserved by what they have done, and that you are all provoked against them by those their wicked actions, whence you have suffered so greatly. (186) But perhaps many of you are aftrighted at the multitude of those zealots, and at their audaciousness, as well as at the advantage they have over us in their being higher in place than we are; (187) for these circumstances, as they have been occasioned by your negligence, so will they become still greater by being still longer neglected; for their multitude is every day augmented, by every ill man's running away to those that are like to themselves, (188) and their audaciousness is therefore inflamed, because they meet with no obstruction to their designs. And for their higher place, they will make use of it for engines also, if we give them time to do so; (189) but be assured of this, that if we go up to fight them, they will be made tamer by their own consciences, and what advantages they have in the height of their situation they will lose by the opposition of their reason; (190) perhaps also God himself, who hath been affronted by them, will make what they throw at us return against themselves, and these impious wretches will be killed by their own darts: let us but make our appearance before them, and they will come to nothing. (191) However, it is a right thing, if there should be any danger in the attempt, to die before these holy gates, and to spend our very lives, if not for the sake of our children and wives, yet for God's sake, and for the sake of his sanctuary. (192) I will assist you both with my counsel and with my hand; nor shall any sagacity of ours be wanting for your support; nor shall you see that I will be sparing of my body neither."

11. (193) By these motives Ananus encouraged the multitude to go against the zealots, although he knew how difficult it would be to disperse them, because of their multitude, and their youth, and the courage of their souls; but chiefly because of their consciousness of what they had done, since they would not yield, as not so much as hoping for pardon at the last for those their enormities. (194) However, Ananus resolved to undergo whatever sufferings might come upon him, rather than overlook things, now they were in such great confusion. (195) So the multitude cried out to him, to lead them on against those whom he had described in his exhortation to them, and every one of them was most readily disposed to run any hazard whatsoever on that account.

12. (196) Now while Ananus was choosing out his men, and putting those that were proper for his purpose in array for fighting, the zealots got information of his undertaking, (for there were some who went to them, and told them all that the people were doing,) and were irritated at it, and leaping out of the temple in crowds, and by parties, spared none whom they met with. (197) Upon this Ananus got the populace together on the sudden, who were more numerous indeed than the zealots, but inferior to them in arms, because they had not been regularly put into array for fighting; (198) but the alacrity that every body showed supplied all their defects on both sides, the citizens taking up so great a passion as was stronger than arms, and deriving a degree of courage from the temple more forcible than any multitude whatsoever; (199) and indeed these citizens thought it was not possible for them to dwell in the city, unless they could cut off the robbers that were in it. The zealots also thought that unless they prevailed, there would be no punishment so bad but it would be inflicted on them. So their conflicts were conducted by their passions; (200)

and at the first they only cast stones at each other in the city, and before the temple, and threw their javelins at a distance; but when either of them were too hard for the other, they made use of their swords; and great slaughter was made on both sides, and a great number were wounded. (201) As for the dead bodies of the people, their relations carried them out to their own houses; but when any of the zealots were wounded, he went up into the temple, and defiled that sacred floor with his blood, insomuch that one may say it was their blood alone that polluted our sanctuary. (202) Now in these conflicts the robbers always sallied out of the temple, and were too hard for their enemies; but the populace grew very angry, and became more and more numerous, and reproached those that gave back, and those behind would not afford room to those that were going off, but forced them on again, till at length they made their whole body to turn against their adversaries, (203) and the robbers could no longer oppose them, but were forced gradually to retire into the temple; when Ananus and his party fell into it at the same time together with them. **(cf. Matthew 21:12, 13; Mark 11:15–17)** (204) This horribly affrighted the robbers, because it deprived them of the first court; so they fled into the inner court immediately, and shut the gates. (205) Now Ananus did not think fit to make any attack against the holy gates, although the other threw their stones and darts at them from above. He also deemed it unlawful to introduce the multitude into that court before they were purified; (206) he therefore chose out of them all by lot six thousand armed men, and placed them as guards in the cloisters; (207) so there was a succession of such guards one after another, and every one was forced to attend in his course; although many of the chief of the city were dismissed by those that then took on them the government, upon their hiring some of the poorer sort, and sending them to keep the guard in their stead.

13. (208) Now it was John who, as we told you, ran away from Gischala, and was the occasion of all these being destroyed. He was a man of great craft, and bore about him in his soul a strong passion after tyranny, and at a distance was the adviser in these actions; (209) and indeed at this time he pretended to be of the people's opinion, and went all about with Ananus when he consulted the great men every day, and in the night time also when he went round the watch; but he divulged their secrets to the zealots, and every thing that the people deliberated about was by his means known to their enemies, even before it had been well agreed upon by themselves. (210) And by way of contrivance how he might not be brought into suspicion, he cultivated the greatest friendship possible with Ananus, and with the chief of the people; (211) yet did this overdoing of his turn against him, for he flattered them so extravagantly, that he was but the more suspected; and his constant attendance everywhere, even when he was not invited to be present, made him strongly suspected of betraying their secrets to the enemy; (212) for they plainly perceived that they understood all the resolutions taken against them at their consultations. Nor was there any one whom they had so much reason to suspect of that discovery as this John; (213) yet was it not easy to get quit of him, so potent was he grown by his wicked practices. He was also supported by many of those eminent men, who were to be consulted upon all considerable affairs; it was therefore thought reasonable to oblige him to give them assurance of his good-will upon oath; (214) accordingly John took such an oath readily, that he would be on the people's side, and would not betray any of their counsels or practices to their enemies, and would assist them in overthrowing those that attacked them, and that both by his hand and his advice. (215) So Ananus and his party believed his oath, and did now receive him to their consultations without further suspicion; nay, so far did they believe him, that they sent him as their ambassador into the temple to the zealots, with proposals of accommodation; for they were very desirous to avoid the pollution of the temple as much as they possibly could, and that no one of their nation should be slain therein.

14. (216) But now this John, as if his oath had been made to the zealots, and for confirmation of his good-will to them, and not against them, went into the temple, and stood in the midst of them, and spake as follows: That he had run many hazards o, their accounts, and in order to let them know of every thing that was secretly contrived against them by Ananus and his party; (217) but that both he and they should be cast into the most imminent danger, unless some providential assistance were afforded them; (218) for that Ananus made no longer delay, but had prevailed with the people to send ambassadors to Vespasian, to invite him to come presently and take the city; and that he had appointed a fast for the next day against them, that they might obtain admission into the temple on a religious account, or gain it by force, and fight with them there; (219) that he did not see how long they could either endure a siege, or how they could fight against so many enemies. He added further, that it was by the providence of God he was himself sent as an ambassador to them for an accommodation; for that Artanus did therefore offer them such proposals, that he might come upon them when they were unarmed; (220) that they ought to choose one of these two methods, either to intercede with those that guarded them, to save their lives, or to provide some foreign assistance for themselves; (221) that if they fostered themselves with the hopes of pardon, in case they were subdued, they had forgotten what desperate things they had done, or could suppose, that as soon as the actors repented, those that had suffered by them must be presently reconciled to them; (222) while those that have done injuries, though they pretend to repent of them, are frequently hated by the others for that sort of repentance; and that the sufferers, when they get the power into their hands, are usually still more severe upon the actors; (223) that the friends and kindred of those that had been destroyed would always be laying plots against them; and that a large body of people were very angry on account of their gross breaches of their laws, and [illegal] judicatures, insomuch that although some part might commiserate them, those would be quite overborne by the majority.

CHAPTER 4.

THE IDUMEANS BEING SENT FOR BY THE ZEALOTS, CAME IMMEDIATELY TO JERUSALEM; AND WHEN THEY WERE EXCLUDED OUT OF THE CITY, THEY LAY ALL NIGHT THERE. JESUS ONE OF THE HIGH PRIESTS MAKES A SPEECH TO THEM; AND SIMON THE IDUMEAN MAKES A REPLY TO IT.

1. (224) NOW, by this crafty speech, John made the zealots afraid; yet durst he not directly name what foreign assistance he meant, but in a covert way only intimated at the Idumeans. But now, that he might particularly irritate the leaders of the zealots, he calumniated Ananus, that he was about a piece of barbarity, and did in a special manner threaten them. (225) These leaders were Eleazar, the son of Simon, who seemed the most plausible man of them all, both in considering what was fit to be done, and in the execution of what he had determined upon, and Zacharias, the son of Phalek; both of whom derived their families from the priests. (226) Now when these two men had heard, not only the common threatenings which belonged to them all, but those peculiarly leveled against themselves; and besides, how Artanus and his party, in order to secure their own dominion, had invited the Romans to come to them, for that also was part of John's lie; they hesitated

Aerial view of ancient Idumea (today's northern Negev), with the Dead Sea salt ponds in the distance. (photo Godot13, via Wikimedia Commons)

a great while what they should do, considering the shortness of the time by which they were straitened; (227) because the people were prepared to attack them very soon, and because the suddenness of the plot laid against them had almost cut off all their hopes of getting any foreign assistance; for they might be under the height of their afflictions before any of their confederates could be informed of it. (228) However, it was resolved to call in the Idumeans; so they wrote a short letter to this effect: That Ananus had imposed on the people, and was betraying their metropolis to the Romans; that they themselves had revolted from the rest, and were in custody in the temple, on account of the preservation of their liberty; (229) that there was but a small time left wherein they might hope for their deliverance; and that unless they would come immediately to their assistance, they should themselves be soon in the power of Artanus, and the city would be in the power of the Romans. They also charged the messengers to tell many more circumstances to the rulers of the Idumeans. (230) Now there were two active men proposed for the carrying this message, and such as were able to speak, and to persuade them that things were in this posture, and, what was a qualification still more necessary than the former, they were very swift of foot; (231) for they knew well enough that these would immediately comply with their desires, as being ever a tumultuous and disorderly nation, always on the watch upon every motion, delighting in mutations; and upon your flattering them ever so little, and petitioning them, they soon take their arms, and put themselves into motion, and make haste to a battle, as if it were to a feast. (232) There was indeed occasion for quick despatch in the carrying of this message, in which point the messengers were no way defective. Both their names were Ananias; and they soon came to the rulers of the Idumeans.

2. (233) Now these rulers were greatly surprised at the contents of the letter, and at what those that came with it further told them; whereupon they ran about the nation like madmen, and made proclamation that the people should come to war; (234) so a multitude was suddenly got together, sooner indeed than the time appointed in the proclamation, and every body caught up their arms, in order to maintain the liberty of their metropolis; (235) and twenty thousand of them were put into battle-array, and came to Jerusalem, under four commanders, John, and Jacob the son of Sosas; and besides these were Simon, the son of Cathlas, and Phineas, the son of Clusothus.

3. (236) Now this exit of the messengers was not known either to Ananus or to the guards, but the approach of the Idumeans was known to him; for as he knew of it before they came, he ordered the gates to be shut against them, and that the walls should be guarded. (237) Yet did not he by any means think of fighting against them, but, before they came to blows, to try what persuasions would do. (238) Accordingly, Jesus, the eldest of the high priests next to Artanus, stood upon the tower that was over against them, and said thus: "Many troubles indeed, and those of various kinds, have fallen upon this city, yet in none of them have I so much wondered at her fortune as now, when you are come to assist wicked men, and this after a manner very extraordinary; (239) for I see that you are come to support the vilest of men against us, and this with so great alacrity, as you could hardly put on the like, in case our metropolis had called you to her assistance against barbarians. (240) And if I had perceived that your army was composed of men like unto those who invited them, I had not deemed your attempt so absurd; for nothing does so much cement the minds of men together as the alliance there is between their manners. But now for these men who have invited you, if you were to examine them one by one, every one of them would be found to have deserved ten thousand deaths; (241) for the very rascality and offscouring of the whole country, who have spent in debauchery their own substance, and, by way of trial beforehand, have madly plundered the neighboring villages and cities, in the upshot of all, have privately run together into this holy city. (242) They are robbers, who by their prodigious wickedness have profaned this most sacred floor, and who are to be now seen drinking themselves drunk in the sanctuary, and expending the spoils of those whom they have slaughtered upon their unsatiable bellies. (243) As for the multitude that is with you, one may see them so decently adorned in their armor, as it would become them to be had their metropolis called them to her assistance against foreigners. What can a man call this procedure of yours but the sport of fortune, when he sees a whole nation coming to protect a sink of wicked wretches? (244) I have for a good while been in doubt what it could possibly be that should move you to do this so suddenly; because certainly you would not take on your armor on the behalf of robbers, and against a people of kin to you, without some very great cause for your so doing. (245) But we have an item that the Romans are pretended, and that we are supposed to be going to betray this city to them; for some of your men have lately made a clamor about those matters, and have said they are come to set their metropolis free. Now we cannot but admire at these wretches in their devising such a lie as this against us; (246) for they knew there was no other way to irritate against us men that were naturally desirous of liberty, and on that account the best disposed to fight against foreign enemies, but by framing a tale as if we were going to betray that most desirable thing, liberty. (247) But you ought to consider what sort of people they are that raise this calumny, and against what sort of people that calumny is raised, and to gather the truth of things, not by fictitious speeches, but out of the actions of both parties;

(248) for what occasion is there for us to sell ourselves to the Romans, while it was in our power not to have revolted from them at the first, or when we had once revolted, to have returned under their dominion again, and this while the neighboring countries were not yet laid waste? (249) whereas it is not an easy thing to be reconciled to the Romans, if we were desirous of it, now they have subdued Galilee, and are thereby become proud and insolent; and to endeavor to please them at the time when they are so near us, would bring such a reproach upon us as were worse than death. (250) As for myself, indeed, I should have preferred peace with them before death; but now we have once made war upon them, and fought with them, I prefer death, with reputation, before living in captivity under them. (251) But further, whether do they pretend that we, who are the rulers of the people, have sent thus privately to the Romans, or hath it been done by the common suffrages of the people? (252) If it be ourselves only that have done it, let them name those friends of ours that have been sent, as our servants, to manage this treachery. Hath any one been caught as he went out on this errand, or seized upon as he came back? Are they in possession of our letters? (253) How could we be concealed from such a vast number of our fellow citizens, among whom we are conversant every hour, while what is done privately in the country is, it seems, known by the zealots, who are but few in number, and under confinement also, and are not able to come out of the temple into the city. (254) Is this the first time that they are become sensible how they ought to be punished for their insolent actions? For while these men were free from the fear they are now under, there was no suspicion raised that any of us were traitors. (255) But if they lay this charge against the people, this must have been done at a public consultation, and not one of the people must have dissented from the rest of the assembly; in which case the public fame of this matter would have come to you sooner than any particular indication. (256) But how could that be? Must there not then have been ambassadors sent to confirm the agreements? And let them tell us who this ambassador was that was ordained for that purpose. (257) But this is no other than a pretense of such men as are loath to die, and are laboring to escape those punishments that hang over them; for if fate had determined that this city was to be betrayed into its enemies' hands, no other than these men that accuse us falsely could have the impudence to do it, there being no wickedness wanting to complete their impudent practices but this only, that they become traitors. (258) And now you Idumeans are come hither already with your arms, it is your duty, in the first place, to be assisting to your metropolis, and to join with us in cutting off those tyrants that have infringed the rules of our regular tribunals, that have trampled upon our laws, and made their swords the arbitrators of right and wrong; (259) for they have seized upon men of great eminence, and under no accusation, as they stood in the midst of the market-place, and tortured them with putting them into bonds, and, without bearing to hear what they had to say, or what supplications they made, they destroyed them. (260) You may, if you please, come into the city, though not in the way of war, and take a view of the marks still remaining of what I now say, and may see the houses that have been depopulated by their rapacious hands, with those wives and families that are in black, mourning for their slaughtered relations; as also you may hear their groans and lamentations all the city over; for there is nobody but hath tasted of the incursions of these profane wretches, (261) who have proceeded to that degree of madness, as not only to have transferred their impudent robberies out of the country, and the remote cities, into this city, the very face and head of the whole nation, but out of the city into the temple also; (262) for that is now made their receptacle and refuge, and the fountain-head whence their preparations are made against us. And this place, which is adored by the habitable world, and honored by such as only know it by report, as far as the ends of the earth, is trampled upon by these wild beasts born among ourselves. (263) They now triumph in the desperate condition they are already in, when they hear that one people is going to fight against another people, and one city against another city, and that your nation hath gotten an army together against its own bowels. (264) Instead of which procedure, it were highly fit and reasonable, as I said before, for you to join with us in cutting off these wretches, and in particular to be revenged on them for putting this very cheat upon you; I mean, for having the impudence to invite you to assist them, of whom they ought to have stood in fear, as ready to punish them. (265) But if you have some regard to these men's invitation of you, yet may you lay aside your arms, and come into the city under the notion of our kindred, and take upon you a middle name between that of auxiliaries and of enemies, and so become judges in this case. (266) However, consider what these men will gain by being called into judgment before you, for such undeniable and such flagrant crimes, who would not vouchsafe to hear such as had no accusations laid against them to speak a word for themselves. However, let them gain this advantage by your coming. (267) But still, if you will neither take our part in that indignation we have at these men, nor judge between us, the third thing I have to propose is this, that you let us both alone, and neither insult upon our calamities, nor abide with these plotters against their metropolis; (268) for though you should have ever so great a suspicion that some of us have discoursed with the Romans, it is in your power to watch the passages into the city; and in case any thing that we have been accused of is brought to light, then to come and defend your metropolis, and to inflict punishment on those that are found guilty; for the enemy cannot prevent you who are so near to the city. (269) But if, after all, none of these proposals seem acceptable and moderate, do not you wonder that the gates are shut against you, while you bear your arms about you."

4. (270) Thus spake Jesus; yet did not the multitude of the Idumeans give any attention to what he said, but were in a rage, because they did not meet with a ready entrance into the city. The generals also had indignation at the offer of laying down their arms, and looked upon it as equal to a captivity, to throw them away at any man's injunction whomsoever. (271) But Simon, the son of Cathlas, one of their commanders, with much ado quieted the tumult of his own men, and stood so that the high priests might hear him, and said as follows: (272) "I can no longer wonder that the patrons of liberty are under custody in the temple, since there are those that shut the gates of our common city to their own nation, (273) and at the same time are prepared to admit the Romans into it; nay, perhaps are disposed to crown the gates with garlands at their coming, while they speak to the Idumeans from their own towers, and enjoin them to throw down their arms which they have taken up for the preservation of its liberty. (274) And while they will not intrust the guard of our metropolis to their kindred, profess to make them judges of the differences that are among them; nay, while they accuse some men of having slain others without a legal trial, they do themselves condemn a whole nation after an ignominious manner, (275) and have now walled up that city from their own nation, which used to be open to even all foreigners that came to worship there. (276) We have indeed come in great haste to you, and to a war against our own countrymen; and the reason why we have made such haste is this, that we may preserve that freedom

which you are so unhappy as to betray. (277) You have probably been guilty of the like crimes against those whom you keep in custody, and have, I suppose, collected together the like plausible pretenses against them also that you make use of against us; (278) after which you have gotten the mastery of those within the temple, and keep them in custody, while they are only taking care of the public affairs. You have also shut the gates of the city in general against nations that are the most nearly related to you; and while you give such injurious commands to others, you complain that you have been tyrannized over by them, and fix the name of unjust governors upon such as are tyrannized over by yourselves. (279) Who can bear this your abuse of words, while they have a regard to the contrariety of your actions, unless you mean this, that those Idumeans do now exclude you out of your metropolis, whom you exclude from the sacred offices of your own country? (280) One may indeed justly complain of those that are besieged in the temple, that when they had courage enough to punish those tyrants whom you call eminent men, and free from any accusations, because of their being your companions in wickedness, they did not begin with you, and thereby cut off beforehand the most dangerous parts of this treason. (281) But if these men have been more merciful than the public necessity required, we that are Idumeans will preserve this house of God, and will fight for our common country, and will oppose by war as well those that attack them from abroad, as those that betray them from within. (282) Here will we abide before the walls in our armor, until either the Romans grow weary in waiting for you, or you become friends to liberty, and repent of what you have done against it."

5. (283) And now did the Idumeans make an acclamation to what Simon had said; but Jesus went away sorrowful, as seeing that the Idumeans were against all moderate counsels, and that the city was besieged on both sides. (284) Nor indeed were the minds of the Idumeans at rest; for they were in a rage at the injury that had been offered them by their exclusion out of the city; and when they thought the zealots had been strong, but saw nothing of theirs to support them, they were in doubt about the matter, and many of them repented that they had come thither. (285) But the shame that would attend them in case they returned without doing any thing at all, so far overcame that their repentance, that they lay all night before the wall, though in a very bad encampment; (286) for there broke out a prodigious storm in the night, with the utmost violence, and very strong winds, with the largest showers of rain, with continued lightnings, terrible thunderings, and amazing concussions and bellowings of the earth, that was in an earthquake. (287) These things were a manifest indication that some destruction was coming upon men, when the system of the world was put into this disorder; and any one would guess that these wonders foreshowed some grand calamities that were coming.

6. (288) Now the opinion of the Idumeans and of the citizens was one and the same. The Idumeans thought that God was angry at their taking arms, and that they would not escape punishment for their making war upon their metropolis. Ananus and his party thought that they had conquered without fighting, and that God acted as a general for them; (289) but truly they proved both ill conjectures at what was to come, and made those events to be ominous to their enemies, while they were themselves to undergo the ill effects of them; (290) for the Idumeans fenced one another by uniting their bodies into one band, and thereby kept themselves warm, and connecting their shields over their heads, were not so much hurt by the rain. (291) But the zealots were more deeply concerned for the danger these men were in than they were for themselves, and got together, and looked about them to see whether they could devise any means of assisting them. (292) The hotter sort of them thought it best to force their guards with their arms, and after that to fall into the midst of the city, and publicly open the gates to those that came to their assistance; (293) as supposing the guards would be in disorder, and give way at such an unexpected attempt of theirs, especially as the greater part of them were unarmed and unskilled in the affairs of war; (294) and that besides the multitude of the citizens would not be easily gathered together, but confined to their houses by the storm: and that if there were any hazard in their undertaking, it became them to suffer any thing whatsoever themselves, rather than to overlook so great a multitude as were miserably perishing on their account. (295) But the more prudent part of them disapproved of this forcible method, because they saw not only the guards about them very numerous, but the walls of the city itself carefully watched, by reason of the Idumeans. (296) They also supposed that Ananus would be every where, and visit the guards every hour; (297) which indeed was done upon other nights, but was omitted that night, not by reason of any slothfulness of Ananus, but by the overbearing appointment of fate, that so both he might himself perish, and the multitude of the guards might perish with him; (298) for truly, as the night was far gone, and the storm very terrible, Ananus gave the guards in the cloisters leave to go to sleep; while it came into the heads of the zealots to make use of the saws belonging to the temple, and to cut the bars of the gates to pieces. (299) The noise of the wind, and that not inferior sound of the thunder, did here also conspire with their designs, that the noise of the saws was not heard by the others.

7. (300) So they secretly went out of the temple to the wall of the city, and made use of their saws, and opened that gate which was over against the Idumeans. (301) Now at first there came a fear upon the Idumeans themselves, which disturbed them, as imagining that Ananus and his party were coming to attack them, so that every one of them had his right hand upon his sword, in order to defend himself; but they soon came to know who they were that came to them, and were entered the city. (302) And had the Idumeans then fallen upon the city, nothing could have hindered them from destroying the people every man of them, such was the rage they were in at that time; but as they first of all made haste to get the zealots out of custody, which those that brought them in earnestly desired them to do, and not to overlook those for whose sakes they were come, in the midst of their distresses, nor to bring them into a still greater danger; (303) for that when they had once seized upon the guards, it would be easy for them to fall upon the city; but that if the city were once alarmed, they would not then be able to overcome those guards, (304) because as soon as they should perceive they were there, they would put themselves in order to fight them, and would hinder their coming into the temple.

CHAPTER 5.

THE CRUELTY OF THE IDUMEANS WHEN THEY WERE GOTTEN INTO THE TEMPLE DURING THE STORM; AND OF THE ZEALOTS. CONCERNING THE SLAUGHTER OF ANANUS, AND JESUS, AND ZACHARIAS; AND HOW THE IDUMEANS RETIRED HOME.

1. (305) THIS advice pleased the Idumeans, and they ascended through the city to the temple. The zealots were also in great expectation of their coming, and earnestly waited for them. When therefore these were entering, they also came boldly out of the inner temple, (306) and mixing themselves among the Idumeans, they attacked the guards; and some of those that were upon the watch, but were fallen asleep, they killed as they were asleep; but as those that were now awakened made a cry, the whole multi-

The Valley of Hinnom, Jerusalem, the traditional burial place of the high priest Annas (Ananias), looking east. (photo Ron Almog from Israel, via Wikimedia Commons)

tude arose, and in the amazement they were in caught hold of their arms immediately, and betook themselves to their own defense; (307) and so long as they thought they were only the zealots who attacked them, they went on boldly, as hoping to overpower them by their numbers; but when they saw others pressing in upon them also, they perceived the Idumeans were got in; (308) and the greatest part of them laid aside their arms, together with their courage, and betook themselves to lamentations. But some few of the younger sort covered themselves with their armor, and valiantly received the Idumeans, and for a while protected the multitude of old men. (309) Others, indeed, gave a signal to those that were in the city of the calamities they were in; but when these were also made sensible that the Idumeans were come in, none of them durst come to their assistance, only they returned the terrible echo of wailing, and lamented their misfortunes. A great howling of the women was excited also, and every one of the guards were in danger of being killed. (310) The zealots also joined in the shouts raised by the Idumeans; and the storm itself rendered the cry more terrible; nor did the Idumeans spare any body; for as they are naturally a most barbarous and bloody nation, and had been distressed by the tempest, they made use of their weapons against those that had shut the gates against them, (311) and acted in the same manner as to those that supplicated for their lives, and to those that fought them, insomuch that they ran through those with their swords who desired them to remember the relation there was between them, and begged of them to have regard to their common temple. (312) Now there was at present neither any place for flight, nor any hope of preservation; but as they were driven one upon another in heaps, so were they slain. Thus the greater part were driven together by force, as there was now no place of retirement, and the murderers were upon them; and, having no other way, threw themselves down headlong into the city; whereby, in my opinion, they underwent a more miserable destruction than that which they avoided, because that was a voluntary one. (313) And now the outer temple was all of it overflowed with blood; and that day, as it came on, they saw eight thousand five hundred dead bodies there.

2. (314) But the rage of the Idumeans was not satiated by these slaughters; but they now betook themselves to the city, and plundered every house, and slew every one they met; (315) and for the other multitude, they esteemed it needless to go on with killing them, but they sought for the high priests, and the generality went with the greatest zeal against them; (316) and as soon as they caught them they slew them, and then standing upon their dead bodies, in way of jest, upbraided Ananus with his kindness to the people, and Jesus with his speech made to them from the wall. (317) Nay, they proceeded to that degree of impiety, as to cast away their dead bodies without burial, although the Jews used to take so much care of the burial of men, that they took down those that were condemned and crucified, and buried them before the going down of the sun. (318) I should not mistake if I said that the death of Ananus was the beginning of the destruction of the city, and that from this very day may be dated the overthrow of her wall, and the ruin of her affairs, whereon they saw their high priest, and the procurer of their preservation, slain in the midst of their city. (319) He was on other accounts also a venerable, and a very just man; and besides the grandeur of that nobility, and dignity, and honor of which he was possessed, he had been a lover of a kind of parity, even with regard to the meanest of the people; (320) he was a prodigious lover of liberty, and an admirer of a democracy in government; and did ever prefer the public welfare before his own advantage, and preferred peace above all things; for he was thoroughly sensible that the Romans were not to be conquered. He also foresaw that of necessity a war would follow, and that unless the Jews made up matters with them very dexterously, they would be destroyed; (321) to say all in a word, if Ananus had survived, they had certainly compounded matters; for he was a shrewd man in speaking and persuading the people, and had already gotten the mastery of those that opposed his designs, or were for the war. And the Jews had then put abundance of delays in the way of the Romans, if they had had such a general as he was. (322) Jesus was also joined with him; and although he was inferior to him upon the comparison, he was superior to the rest; (323) and I cannot but think that it was because God had doomed this city to destruction, as a polluted city, and was resolved to purge his sanctuary by fire, that he cut off these their great defenders and well-wishers, (324) while those that a little before had worn the sacred garments, and had presided over the public worship; and had been esteemed venerable by those that dwelt on the whole habitable earth when they came into our city, were cast out naked, and seen to be the food of dogs and wild beasts. (325) And I cannot but imagine that virtue itself groaned at these men's case, and lamented that she was here so terribly conquered by wickedness. And this at last was the end of Ananus and Jesus.

3. (326) Now after these were slain, the zealots and the multitude of the Idumeans fell upon the people as upon a flock of profane animals, and cut their throats; (327) and for the ordinary sort, they were destroyed in what place soever they caught them. But for the noblemen and the youth, they first caught them and bound them, and shut them up in prison, and put off their slaughter, in hopes that some of them would turn over to their party; (328) but not one of them would comply with their desires, but all of them preferred death before being enrolled among such wicked wretches as acted against their own country. (329) But this refusal of theirs brought upon them terrible torments; for they were so scourged and tortured, that their bodies were not able to sustain their torments, till at length, and with difficulty, they had the favor to be slain. (330) Those whom they caught in the day time were slain in the night, and then their bodies were carried out and thrown away,

that there might be room for other prisoners; (331) and the terror that was upon the people was so great, that no one had courage enough either to weep openly for the dead man that was related to him, or to bury him; but those that were shut up in their own houses could only shed tears in secret, and durst not even groan without great caution, lest any of their enemies should hear them; (332) for if they did, those that mourned for others soon underwent the same death with those whom they mourned for. Only in the night time they would take up a little dust, and throw it upon their bodies; and even some that were the most ready to expose themselves to danger would do it in the day time: (333) and there were twelve thousand of the better sort who perished in this manner.

4. (334) And now these zealots and Idumeans were quite weary of barely killing men, so they had the impudence of setting up fictitious tribunals and judicatures for that purpose; (335) and as they intended to have Zacharias the son of Baruch, one of the most eminent of the citizens, slain,—so what provoked them against him was, that hatred of wickedness and love of liberty which were so eminent in him: he was also a rich man, so that by taking him off, they did not only hope to seize his effects, but also to get rid of a mall that had great power to destroy them. (336) So they called together, by a public proclamation, seventy of the principal men of the populace, for a show, as if they were real judges, while they had no proper authority. Before these was Zacharias accused of a design to betray their polity to the Romans, and having traitorously sent to Vespasian for that purpose. (337) Now there appeared no proof or sign of what he was accused; but they affirmed themselves that they were well persuaded that so it was, and desired that such their affirmation might he taken for sufficient evidence. (338) Now when Zacharias clearly saw that there was no way remaining for his escape from them, as having been treacherously called before them, and then put in prison, but not with any intention of a legal trial, he took great liberty of speech in that despair of his life he was under. Accordingly he stood up, and laughed at their pretended accusation, and in a few words confuted the crimes laid to his charge; (339) after which he turned his speech to his accusers, and went over distinctly all their transgressions of the law, and made heavy lamentation upon the confusion they had brought public affairs to: (340) in the meantime, the zealots grew tumultuous, and had much ado to abstain from drawing their swords, although they designed to preserve the appearance and show of judicature to the end. They were also desirous, on other accounts, to try the judges, whether they would be mindful of what was just at their own peril. (341) Now the seventy judges brought in their verdict that the person accused was not guilty, as choosing rather to die themselves with him, than to have his death laid at their doors; (342) hereupon there arose a great clamor of the zealots upon his acquittal, and they all had indignation at the judges for not understanding that the authority that was given them was but in jest. (343) So two of the boldest of them fell upon Zacharias in the middle of the temple, and slew him; and as he fell down dead, they bantered him, and said, "Thou hast also our verdict, and this will prove a more sure acquittal to thee than the other." They also threw him down from the temple immediately into the valley beneath it. (344) Moreover, they struck the judges with the backs of their swords, by way of abuse, and thrust them out of the court of the temple, and spared their lives with no other design than that, when they were dispersed among the people in the city, they might become their messengers, to let them know they were no better than slaves.

5. (345) But by this time the Idumeans repented of their coming, and were displeased at what had been done; (346) and when they were assembled together by one of the zealots, who had come privately to them, he declared to them what a number of wicked pranks they had themselves done in conjunction with those that invited them, and gave a particular account of what mischiefs had been done against their metropolis.—(347) He said that they had taken arms, as though the high priests were betraying their metropolis to the Romans, but had found no indication of any such treachery; but that they had succored those that had pretended to believe such a thing, while they did themselves the works of war and tyranny, after an insolent manner. (348) It had been indeed their business to have hindered them from such their proceedings at the first, but seeing they had once been partners with them in shedding the blood of their own countrymen, it was high time to put a stop to such crimes, and not continue to afford any more assistance to such as are subverting the laws of their forefathers; (349) for that if any had taken it ill that the gates had been shut against them, and they had not been permitted to come into the city, yet that those who had excluded them have been punished, and Ananus is dead, and that almost all those people had been destroyed in one night's time. (350) That one may perceive many

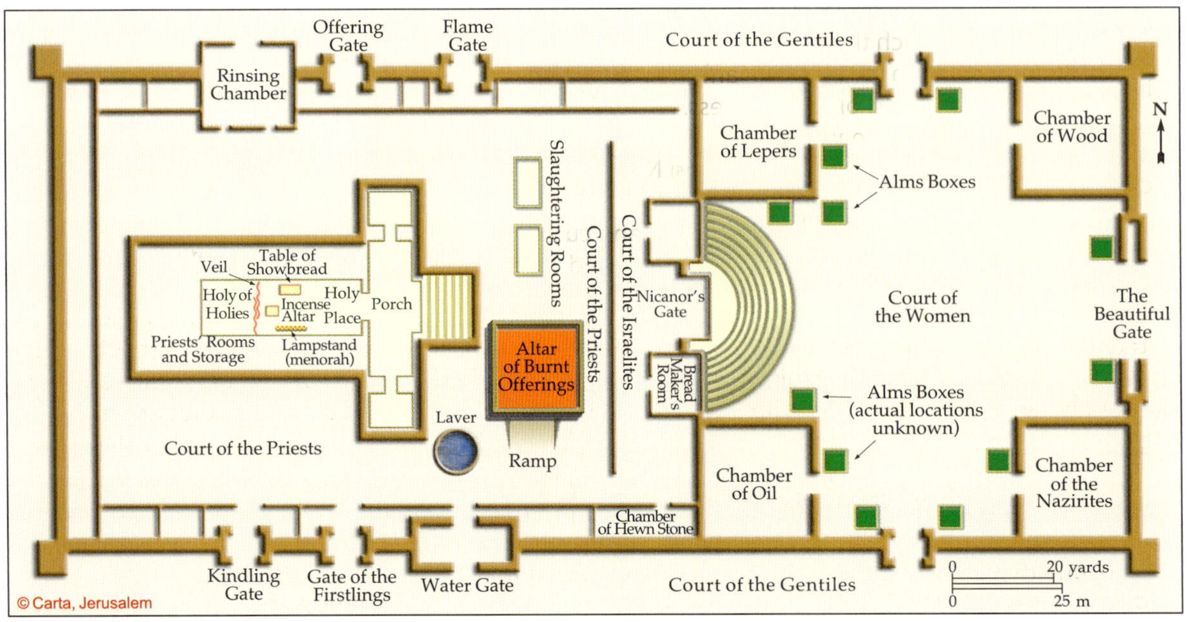

PLAN OF THE HERODIAN TEMPLE COMPOUND

(from *Greatness Grace & Glory: Carta's Atlas of Biblical Biography* / Paul H. Wright)

of themselves now repenting for what they had done, and might see the horrid barbarity of those that had invited them, and that they had no regard to such as had saved them; (351) that they were so impudent as to perpetrate the vilest things, under the eyes of those that had supported them, and that their wicked actions would be laid to the charge of the Idumeans, and would be so laid to their charge till somebody obstructs their proceedings, or separates himself from the same wicked action; (352) that they therefore ought to retire home, since the imputation of treason appears to be a calumny, and that there was no expectation of the coming of the Romans at this time, and that the government of the city was secured by such walls as cannot easily be thrown down; and, by avoiding any further fellowship with these bad men, to make some excuse for themselves, as to what they had been so far deluded, as to have been partners with them hitherto.

CHAPTER 6.

HOW THE ZEALOTS WHEN THEY WERE FREED FROM THE IDUMEANS, SLEW A GREAT MANY MORE OF THE CITIZENS; AND HOW VESPASIAN DISSUADED THE ROMANS WHEN THEY WERE VERY EARNEST TO MARCH AGAINST THE JEWS FROM PROCEEDING IN THE WAR AT THAT TIME.

1. (353) THE Idumeans complied with these persuasions; and, in the first place, they set those that were in the prisons at liberty, being about two thousand of the populace, who thereupon fled away immediately to Simon, one whom we shall speak of presently. After which these Idumeans retired from Jerusalem, and went home; (354) which departure of theirs was a great surprise to both parties; for the people, not knowing of their repentance, pulled up their courage for a while, as eased of so many of their enemies, (355) while the zealots grew more insolent not as deserted by their confederates, but as freed from such men as might hinder their designs, and plat some stop to their wickedness. (356) Accordingly, they made no longer any delay, nor took any deliberation in their enormous practices, but made use of the shortest methods for all their executions and what they had once resolved upon, they put in practice sooner than any one could imagine. (357) But their thirst was chiefly after the blood of valiant men, and men of good families; the one sort of which they destroyed out of envy, the other out of fear; for they thought their whole security lay in leaving no potent men alive; (358) on which account they slew Gorion, a person eminent in dignity, and on account of his family also; he was also for democracy, and of as great boldness and freedom of spirit as were any of the Jews whosoever; the principal thing that ruined him, added to his other advantages, was his free-speaking. (359) Nor did Niger of Perea escape their hands; he had been a man of great valor in their war with the Romans, but was now drawn through the middle of the city, (360) and, as he went, he frequently cried out, and showed the scars of his wounds; and when he was drawn out of the gates, and despaired of his preservation, he besought them to grant him a burial; but as they had threatened him beforehand not to grant him any spot of earth for a grave, which he chiefly desired of them, so did they slay him [without permitting him to be buried]. (361) Now when they were slaying him, he made this imprecation upon them, that they might undergo both famine and pestilence in this war, and besides all that, they might come to the mutual slaughter of one another; (362) all which imprecations God confirmed against these impious men, and was what came most justly upon them, when not long afterward. they tasted of their own madness in their mutual seditions one against another. (363) So when this Niger was killed, their fears of being overturned were diminished; and indeed there was no part of the people but they found out some pretense to destroy them; (364)

Judaea Capta coin minted in Rome in honor of the Roman victory over Judea. Obverse: bust of the emperor Vespasian; reverse: a Jewess seated, mourning beside a plundered statue, with "Judaea" inscribed below. (Courtesy Reuben and Edith Hecht Museum, University of Haifa)

for some were therefore slain, because they had had differences with some of them; and as to those that had not opposed them in times of peace, they watched seasonable opportunities to gain some accusation against them; and if any one did not come near them at all, he was under their suspicion as a proud man; if any one came with boldness, he was esteemed a contemner of them; (365) and if any one came as aiming to oblige them, he was supposed to have some treacherous plot against them; while the only punishment of crimes, whether they were of the greatest or smallest sort, was death. Nor could any one escape, unless he were very inconsiderable, either on account of the meanness of his birth, or on account of his fortune.

2. (366) And now all the rest of the commanders of the Romans deemed this sedition among their enemies to be of great advantage to them, and were very earnest to march to the city, and they urged Vespasian, as their lord and general in all cases, to make haste, and said to him, that "the providence of God is on our side, by setting our enemies at variance against one another; (367) that still the change in such cases may be sudden, and the Jews may quickly be at one again, either because they may be tired out with their civil miseries, or repent them of such doings." (368) But Vespasian replied, that they were greatly mistaken in what they thought fit to be done, as those that, upon the theater, love to make a show of their hands, and of their weapons, but do it at their own hazard, without considering, what was for their advantage, and for their security; (369) for that if they now go and attack the city immediately, they shall but occasion their enemies to unite together, and shall convert their force, now it is in its height, against themselves. But if they stay a while, they shall have fewer enemies, because they will be consumed in this sedition: (370) that God acts as a general of the Romans better than he can do, and is giving the Jews up to them without any pains of their own, and granting their army a victory without any danger; (371) that therefore it is their best way, while their enemies are destroying each other with their own hands, and falling into the greatest of misfortunes, which is that of sedition, to sit still as spectators of the dangers they run into, rather than to fight hand to hand with men that love murdering, and are mad one against another. (372) But if anyone imagines that the glory of victory, when it is gotten without fighting, will be more insipid, let him know this much, that a glorious success, quietly obtained, is more profitable than the dangers of a battle; (373) for we ought to esteem these that do what is agreeable to temperance and prudence no less glorious than those that have gained great reputation by their actions in war: that he shall lead on his army with greater force when their enemies are diminished, and his own army refreshed after the continual labors they had undergone. (374) However, that this is not a proper time to propose to ourselves the glory of victory; (375) for that the Jews are not now employed in making of armor or building of walls, nor indeed in getting together auxiliaries, while the advantage will be on their side who give them such opportunity of delay; but that the Jews are vexed to pieces every day by their civil wars and dissensions, and are under greater miseries, than, if they were once

taken, could be inflicted on them by us. (376) Whether therefore any one hath regard to what is for our safety, he ought to suffer these Jews to destroy one another; or whether he hath regard to the greater glory of the action, we ought by no means to meddle with those men, now they are afflicted with a distemper at home; for should we now conquer them, it would be said the conquest was not owing to our bravery, but to their sedition."

3. (377) And now the commanders joined in their approbation of what Vespasian had said, and it was soon discovered how wise an opinion he had given. And indeed many there were of the Jews that deserted every day, and fled away from the zealots, (378) although their flight was very difficult, since they had guarded every passage out of the city, and slew every one that was caught at them, as taking it for granted they were going over to the Romans; (379) yet did he who gave them money get clear off, while he only that gave them none was voted a traitor. So the upshot was this, that the rich purchased their flight by money, while none but the poor were slain. (380) Along all the roads also vast numbers of dead bodies lay in heaps, and even many of those that were so zealous in deserting at length chose rather to perish within the city; for the hopes of burial made death in their own city appear of the two less terrible to them. (381) But these zealots came at last to that degree of barbarity, as not to bestow a burial either on those slain in the city, or on those that lay along the roads; (382) but as if they had made an agreement to cancel both the laws of their country and the laws of nature, and, at the same time that they defiled men with their wicked actions, they would pollute the Divinity itself also, (383) they left the dead bodies to putrefy under the sun; and the same punishment was allotted to such as buried any as to those that deserted, which was no other than death; while he that granted the favor of a grave to another would presently stand in need of a grave himself. (384) To say all in a word, no other gentle passion was so entirely lost among them as mercy; for what were the greatest objects of pity did most of all irritate these wretches, and they transferred their rage from the living to those that had been slain, and from the dead to the living. (385) Nay, the terror was so very great, that he who survived called them that were first dead happy, as being at rest already; as did those that were under torture in the prisons, declare, that, upon this comparison, those that lay unburied were the happiest. (386) These men, therefore, trampled upon all the laws of men, and laughed at the laws of God; and for the oracles of the prophets, they ridiculed them as the tricks of jugglers; (387) yet did these prophets foretell many things concerning [the rewards of] virtue, and [punishments of] vice, which when these zealots violated, they occasioned the fulfilling of those very prophecies belonging to their own country; (388) for there was a certain ancient oracle of those men, that the city should then be taken and the sanctuary burnt, by right of war, when a sedition should invade the Jews, and their own hand should pollute the temple of God. Now while these zealots did not [quite] disbelieve these predictions, they made themselves the instruments of their accomplishment.

CHAPTER 7.

HOW JOHN TYRANNIZED OVER THE REST; AND WHAT MISCHIEFS THE ZEALOTS DID AT MASADA. HOW ALSO VESPASIAN TOOK GADARA; AND WHAT ACTIONS WERE PERFORMED BY PLACIDUS.

1. (389) BY this time John was beginning to tyrannize, and thought it beneath him to accept of barely the same honors that others had; and joining to himself by degrees a party of the wickedest of them all, he broke off from the rest of the faction. (390) This was brought about by his still disagreeing with the opinions of others, and giving out injunctions of his own, in a very imperious manner; so that it was evident he was setting up a monarchical power. (391) Now some submitted to him out of their fear of him, and others out of their good-will to him; for he was a shrewd man to entice men to him, both by deluding them and putting cheats upon them. Nay, many there were that thought they should be safer themselves, if the causes of their past insolent actions should now be reduced to one head, and not to a great many. (392) His activity was so great, and that both in action and in counsel, that he had not a few guards about him; (393) yet was there a great party of his antagonists that left him; among whom envy at him weighed a great deal, while they thought it a very heavy thing to be in subjection to one that was formerly their equal. But the main reason that moved men against him was the dread of monarchy, (394) for they could not hope easily to put an end to his power, if he had once obtained it; and yet they knew that he would have this pretense always against them, that they had opposed him when he was first advanced; while every one chose rather to suffer any thing whatsoever in war, than that, when they had been in a voluntary slavery for some time, they should afterward perish. (395) So the sedition was divided into two parts, and John reigned in opposition to his adversaries over one of them: (396) but for their leaders, they watched one another, nor did they at all, or at least very little, meddle with arms in their quarrels; but they fought earnestly against the people, and contended one with another which of them should bring home the greatest prey. (397) But because the city had to struggle with three of the greatest misfortunes, war, and tyranny, and sedition, it appeared, upon the comparison, that the war was the least troublesome to the populace of them all. Accordingly, they ran away from their own houses to foreigners, and obtained that preservation from the Romans which they despaired to obtain among their own people.

2. (398) And now a fourth misfortune arose, in order to bring our nation to destruction. (399) There was a fortress of very great strength not far from Jerusalem, which had been built by our ancient kings, both as a repository for their effects in the hazards of war, and for the preservation of their bodies at the same time. It was called Masada. (400) Those that were called Sicarii had taken possession of it formerly, but at this time they overran the neighboring countries, aiming only to procure to themselves necessaries; for the fear they were then in prevented their further ravages. (401) But when once they were informed that the Roman army lay still, and that the Jews were divided between sedition and tyranny, they boldly undertook greater matters; (402) and at the feast of unleavened bread, which the Jews celebrate in memory of their deliverance from the Egyptian bondage, when they were sent back into the country of their forefathers, they came down by night, without being discovered by those that could have prevented them, and overran a certain small city called Engaddi:—(403) in which expedition they prevented those citizens that could have stopped them, before they could arm themselves, and fight them. They also dispersed them, and cast them out of the city. As for such as could not run away, being women and children, they slew of them above seven hundred. (404) Afterward, when they had carried every thing out of their houses, and had seized upon all the fruits that were in a flourishing condition, they brought them into Masada. (405) And indeed these men laid all the villages that were about the fortress waste, and made the whole country desolate; while there came to them every day, from all parts, not a few men as corrupt as themselves. (406) At that time all the other regions of Judea that had hitherto been at rest were in motion, by means of the robbers.

View of Masada, looking southwest. (photo Samuel Magal)

Now as it is in a human body, if the principal part be inflamed, all the members are subject to the same distemper; (407) so, by means of the sedition and disorder that was in the metropolis, had the wicked men that were in the country opportunity to ravage the same. Accordingly, when every one of them had plundered their own villages, they then retired into the desert; (408) yet were these men that now got together, and joined in the conspiracy by parties, too small for an army, and too many for a gang of thieves: and thus did they fall upon the holy places (**see Luke 6:12; Acts 16:13, 16**) and the cities; (409) yet did it now so happen that they were sometimes very ill treated by those upon whom they fell with such violence, and were taken by them as men are taken in war: but still they prevented any further punishment as do robbers, who, as soon as their ravages [are discovered], run their way. Nor was there now any part of Judea that was not in a miserable condition, as well as its most eminent city also.

3. (410) These things were told Vespasian by deserters; for although the seditious watched all the passages out of the city, and destroyed all, whosoever they were, that came thither, yet were there some that had concealed themselves, and when they had fled to the Romans, persuaded their general to come to their city's assistance, and save the remainder of the people; (411) informing him withal, that it was upon account of the people's good-will to the Romans that many of them were already slain, and the survivors in danger of the same treatment. (412) Vespasian did indeed already pity the calamities these men were in, and arose, in appearance, as though he was going to besiege Jerusalem, but in reality to deliver them from a [worse] siege they were already under. (413) However, he was obliged first to overthrow what remained elsewhere, and to leave nothing out of Jerusalem behind him that might interrupt him in that siege. Accordingly, he marched against Gadara, the metropolis of Perea, which was a place of strength, and entered that city on the fourth day of the month Dystrus [Adar]; (414) for the men of power had sent an embassage to him, without the knowledge of the seditious, to treat about a surrender; which they did out of the desire they had of peace, and for saving their effects, because many of the citizens of Gadara were rich men. (415) This embassy the opposite party knew nothing of, but discovered it as Vespasian was approaching near the city. However, they despaired of keeping possession of the city, as being inferior in number to their enemies who were within the city, and seeing the Romans very near to the city; so they resolved to fly, but thought it dishonorable to do it without shedding some blood, and revenging themselves on the authors of this surrender; (416) so they seized upon Dolesus, (a person not only the first in rank and family in that city, but one that seemed the occasion of sending such an embassy,) and slew him, and treated his dead body after a barbarous manner, so very violent was their anger at him, and then ran out of the city. (417) And as now the Roman army was just upon them, the people of Gadara admitted Vespasian with joyful acclamations, and received from him the security of his right hand, as also a garrison of horsemen and footmen, to guard them against the excursions of the runagates; (418) for as to their wall, they had pulled it down before the Romans desired them so to do, that they might thereby give them assurance that they were lovers of peace, and that, if they had a mind, they could not now make war against them.

4. (419) And now Vespasian sent Placidus against those that had fled from Gadara, with five hundred horsemen, and three thousand footmen, while he returned himself to Cesarea, with the rest of the army. (420) But as soon as these fugitives saw the horsemen that pursued them just upon their backs, and before they came to a close fight, they ran together to a certain village, which was called Bethennabris, (421) where finding a great multitude of

THE ROMAN CAMPAIGN OF A.D. 68

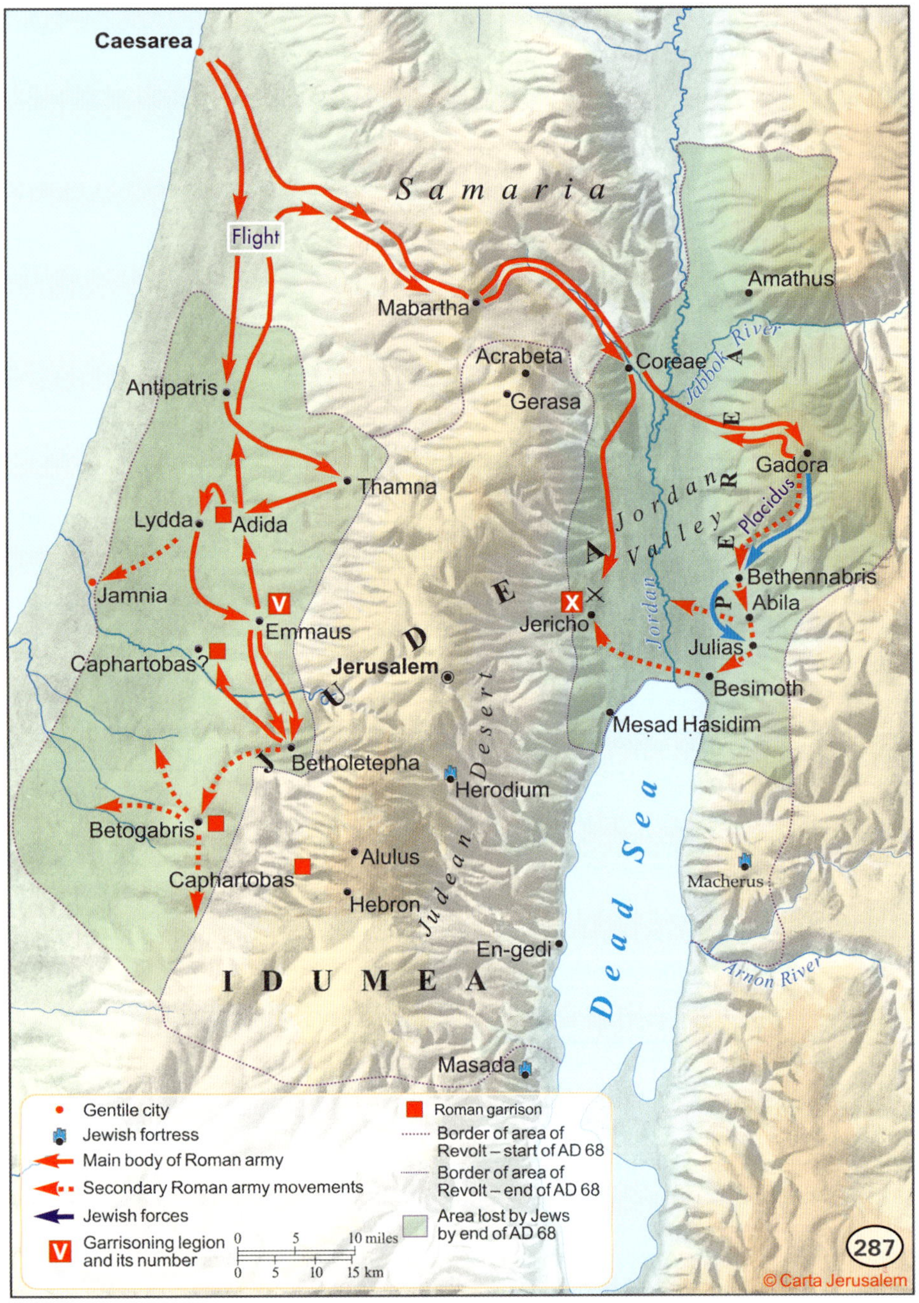

young men, and arming them, partly by their own consent, partly by force, they rashly and suddenly assaulted Placidus and the troops that were with him. (422) These horsemen at the first onset gave way a little, as contriving to entice them further off the wall; and when they had drawn them into a place fit for their purpose, they made their horse encompass them round, and threw their darts at them. (423) So the horsemen cut off the flight of the fugitives, while the foot terribly destroyed those that fought against them; (424) for those Jews did no more than show their courage, and then were destroyed; for as they fell upon the Romans when they were joined close together, and, as it were, walled about with their entire armor, they were not able to find any place where the darts could enter, nor were they any way able to break their ranks, (425) while they were themselves run through by the Roman darts, and, like the wildest of wild beasts, rushed upon the point of others' swords; so some of them were destroyed, as cut with their enemies' swords upon their faces, and others were dispersed by the horsemen.

5. (426) Now Placidus's concern was to exclude them in their flight from getting into the village; (427) and causing his horse to march continually on that side of them, he then turned short upon them, and at the same time his men made use of their darts, and easily took their aim at those that were the nearest to them, as they made those that were further off turn back by the terror they were in, till at last the most courageous of them brake through those horsemen and fled to the wall of the village. (428) And now those that guarded the wall were in great doubt what to do; for they could not bear the thoughts of excluding those that came from Gadara, because of their own people that were among them; and yet, if they should admit them, they expected to perish with them, which came to pass accordingly; (429) for as they were crowding together at the wall, the Roman horsemen were just ready to fall in with them. However, the guards prevented them, and shut the gates, when Placidus made an assault upon them, and fighting courageously till it was dark, he got possession of the wall, and of the people that were in the city, (430) when the useless multitude were destroyed; but those that were more potent ran away, and the soldiers plundered the houses, and set the village on fire. (431) As for those that ran out of the village, they stirred up such as were in the country, and exaggerating their own calamities, and telling them that the whole army of the Romans were upon them, they put them into great fear on every side; so they got in great numbers together, and fled to Jericho, (432) for they knew no other place that could afford them any hope of escaping, it being a city that had a strong wall, and a great multitude of inhabitants. (433) But Placidus, relying much upon his horsemen, and his former good success, followed them, and slew all that he overtook, as far as Jordan; and when he had driven the whole multitude to the river-side, where they were stopped by the current, (for it had been augmented lately by rains, and was not fordable,) he put his soldiers in array over against them; (434) so the necessity the others were in provoked them to hazard a battle, because there was no place whither they could flee. They then extended themselves a very great way along the banks of the river, and sustained the darts that were thrown at them, as well as the attacks of the horsemen, who beat many of them, and pushed them into the current. (435) At which fight, hand to hand, fifteen thousand of them were slain, while the number of those that were unwillingly forced to leap into Jordan was prodigious. (436) There were besides two thousand and two hundred taken prisoners. A mighty prey was taken also, consisting of asses, and sheep, and camels, and oxen.

6. (437) Now this destruction that fell upon the Jews, as it was not inferior to any of the rest in itself, so did it still appear greater than it really was; and this, because not only the whole country through which they fled was filled with slaughter, and Jordan could not be passed over, by reason of the dead bodies that were in it, but because the lake Asphaltitis was also full of dead bodies, that were carried down into it by the river. (438) And now Placidus, after this good success that he had, fell violently upon the neighboring smaller cities and villages; when he took Abila, and Julias,

The Dead Sea, known in antiquity as lake Asphaltitis, viewed from a grove of palm trees, looking east. (photo Samuel Magal)

and Bezemoth, and all those that lay as far as the lake Asphaltitis, and put such of the deserters into each of them as he thought proper. (439) He then put his soldiers on board the ships, and slew such as had fled to the lake, insomuch that all Perea had either surrendered themselves, or were taken by the Romans, as far as Macherus.

CHAPTER 8.

HOW VESPASIAN, UPON HEARING OF SOME COMMOTIONS IN GALL, MADE HASTE TO FINISH THE JEWISH WAR. A DESCRIPTION OF JERICHO, AND OF THE GREAT PLAIN; WITH AN ACCOUNT BESIDES OF THE LAKE ASPHALTITIS.

1. (440) IN the mean time, an account came that there were commotions in Gall, and that Vindex, together with the men of power in that country, had revolted from Nero; which affair is more accurately described elsewhere. (441) This report, thus related to Vespasian, excited him to go on briskly with the war; for he foresaw already the civil wars which were coming upon them, nay, that the very government was in danger; and he thought, if he could first reduce the eastern parts of the empire to peace, he should make the fears for Italy the lighter; (442) while therefore the winter was his hinderance [from going into the field], he put garrisons into the villages and smaller cities for their security; he put decurions also into the villages, and centurions into the cities: he besides this rebuilt many of the cities that had been laid waste; (443) but at the beginning of the spring he took the greatest part of his army, and led it from Cesarea to Antipatris, where he spent two days in settling the affairs of that city, and then, on the third day, he marched on, laying waste and burning all the neighboring villages. (444) And when he had laid waste all the places about the toparchy of Thamnas, he passed on to Lydda and Jamnia; and when both these cities had come over to him, he placed a great many of those that had come over to him [from other places] as inhabitants therein, and then came to Emmaus, (445) where he seized upon the passage which led thence to their metropolis, and fortified his camp, and leaving the fifth legion therein, he came to the toparchy of Bethletephon. (446) He then destroyed that place, and the neighboring places, by fire, and fortified, at proper places, the strong holds all about Idumea; (447) and when he had seized upon two villages, which were in the very midst of Idumea, Betaris and Caphartobas, he slew above ten thousand of the people, (448) and carried into captivity above a thousand, and drove away the rest of the multitude, and placed no small part of his own forces in them, who overran and laid waste the whole mountainous country; (449) while he, with the rest of his forces, returned to Emmaus, whence he came down through the country of Samaria, and hard by the city, by others called Neapolis, (or Sichem,) but by the people of that country Mabortha, to Corea, where he pitched his camp, on the second day of the month Desius [Sivan]; (450) and on the day following he came to Jericho; on which day Trajan, one of his commanders, joined him with the forces he brought out of Perea, all the places beyond Jordan being subdued already.

2. (451) Hereupon a great multitude prevented their approach, and came out of Jericho, and fled to those mountainous parts that lay over against Jerusalem, while that part which was left behind was in a great measure destroyed; (452) they also found the city desolate. It is situated in a plain; but a naked and barren mountain, of a very great length, hangs over it, (453) which extends itself to the land about Scythopolis northward, but as far as the country of Sodom, and the utmost limits of the lake Asphaltitis, southward. This mountain is all of it very uneven and uninhabited, by reason of its barrenness: (454) there is an opposite mountain that is situated over against it, on the other side of Jordan; this last begins at Julias, and the northern quarters, and extends itself southward as far as Somorrhon, which is the bounds of Petra, in Arabia. In this ridge of mountains there is one called the Iron Mountain, that runs in length as far as Moab. (455) Now the region that lies in the middle between these ridges of mountains is called the Great Plain; it reaches from the village Ginnabris, as far as the lake Asphaltitis; (456) its length is two hundred and thirty furlongs, and its breadth a hundred and twenty, and it is divided in the midst by Jordan. It hath two lakes in it, that of Asphaltitis, and that of Tiberias, whose natures are opposite to each other; for the former is salt and unfruitful, but that of Tiberias is sweet and fruitful. (457) This plain is much burnt up in summer time, and, by reason of the extraordinary heat, contains a very unwholesome air; (458) it is all destitute of water excepting the river Jordan, which water of Jordan is the occasion why those plantations of palm trees that are near its banks are more flourishing, and much more fruitful, as are those that are remote from it not so flourishing, or fruitful.

3. (459) Notwithstanding which, there is a fountain by Jericho, that

The so-called Spring of Elisha, at the foot of Jericho, as depicted here in a 19th-century engraving. (Carta collection)

runs plentifully, and is very fit for watering the ground; it arises near the old city, which Joshua, the son of Naue [Nun], the general of the Hebrews, took the first of all the cities of the land of Canaan, by right of war. (460) The report is, that this fountain, at the beginning, caused not only the blasting of the earth and the trees, but of the children born of women, and that it was entirely of a sickly and corruptive nature to all things whatsoever; but that it was made gentle, and very wholesome and fruitful, by the prophet Elisha. This prophet was familiar with Elijah, and was his successor, (461) who, when he once was the guest of the people at Jericho, and the men of the place had treated him very kindly, he both made them amends as well as the country, by a lasting favor; (462) for he went out of the city to this fountain, and threw into the current an earthen vessel full of salt; after which he stretched out his righteous hand unto heaven, and, pouring out a mild drink-offering, he made this supplication,—That the current might be mollified, and that the veins of fresh water might be opened; (463) that God also would bring into the place a more temperate and fertile air for the current, and would bestow upon the people of that country plenty of the fruits of the earth, and a succession of children; and that this prolific water might never fail them, while they continued to he righteous. (464) To these prayers Elisha **(see 2 Kings 2:21, 22)** joined proper operations of his hands, after a skillful manner, and changed the fountain; and that water, which had been the occasion of barrenness and famine before, from that time did supply a numerous posterity, and afforded great abundance to the country. (465) Accordingly, the power of it is so great in watering the ground, that if it do but once touch a country, it affords a sweeter nourishment than other waters do, when they lie so long upon them, till they are satiated with them. (466) For which reason, the advantage gained from other waters, when they flow in great plenty, is but small, while that of this water is great when it flows even in little quantities. (467) Accordingly, it waters a larger space of ground than any other waters do, and passes along a plain of seventy furlongs long, and twenty broad; wherein it affords nourishment to those most excellent gardens that are thick set with trees. (468) There are in it many sorts of palm trees that are watered by it, different from each other in taste and name; the better sort of them, when they are pressed, yield an excellent kind of honey, not much inferior in sweetness to other honey. (469) This country withal produces honey from bees; it also bears that balsam which is the most precious of all the fruits in that place, cypress trees also, and those that bear myrobalanum; so that he who should pronounce this place to be divine would not be mistaken, wherein is such plenty of trees produced as are very rare, and of the must excellent sort. (470) And indeed, if we speak of those other fruits, it will not be easy to light on any climate in the habitable earth that can well be compared to it,—what is here sown comes up in such clusters; (471) the cause of which seems to me to be the warmth of the air, and the fertility of the waters; the warmth calling forth the sprouts, and making them spread, and the moisture making every one of them take root firmly, and supplying that virtue which it

Mud plains along the Dead Sea, which used to be underwater before the lake's evaporation. (photo Samuel Magal)

stands in need of in summer time. Now this country is then so sadly burnt up, that nobody cares to come at it; (472) and if the water be drawn up before sun-rising, and after that exposed to the air, it becomes exceeding cold, and becomes of a nature quite contrary to the ambient air; (473) as in winter again it becomes warm; and if you go into it, it appears very gentle. The ambient air is here also of so good a temperature, that the people of the country are clothed in linen-only, even when snow covers the rest of Judea. (474) This place is one hundred and fifty furlongs from Jerusalem, and sixty from Jordan. The country, as far as Jerusalem, is desert and stony; but that as far as Jordan and the lake Asphaltitis lies lower indeed, though it be equally desert and barren. (475) But so much shall suffice to have said about Jericho, and of the great happiness of its situation.

4. (476) The nature of the lake Asphaltitis is also worth describing. It is, as I have said already, bitter and unfruitful. It is so light [or thick] that it bears up the heaviest things that are thrown into it; nor is it easy for any one to make things sink therein to the bottom, if he had a mind so to do. (477) Accordingly, when Vespasian went to see it, he commanded that some who could not swim should have their hands tied behind them, and be thrown into the deep, when it so happened that they all swam as if a wind had forced them upwards. (478) Moreover, the change of the color of this lake is wonderful, for it changes its appearance thrice every day; and as the rays of the sun fall differently upon it, the light is variously reflected. (479) However, it casts up black clods of bitumen in many parts of it; these swim at the top of the water, and resemble both in shape and bigness headless bulls; (480) and when the laborers that belong to the lake come to it, and catch hold of it as it hangs together, they draw it into their ships; but when the ship is full, it is not easy to cut off the rest, for it is so tenacious as to make the ship hang upon its clods till they set it loose with the menstrual blood of women, and with urine, to which alone it yields. (481) This bitumen is not only useful for the caulking of ships, but for the cure of men's bodies; accordingly, it is mixed in a great many medicines. (482) The length of this lake is five hundred and eighty furlongs, where it is extended as far as Zoar in Arabia; and its breadth is a hundred and fifty. (483) The country of Sodom borders upon it. It was of old a most happy land, both for the fruits it bore and the riches of its cities, although it be now all burnt up. (484) It is related how, for the impiety of its inhabitants, it was burnt by lightning; in consequence of which there are still the remainders of that Divine fire, and the traces [or shadows] of the five cities are still to be seen, as well as the ashes growing in their fruits; which fruits have a color as if they were fit to be eaten, but if you pluck them with your hands, they dissolve into smoke and ashes. (485) And thus what is related of this land of Sodom hath these marks of credibility which our very sight affords us.

CHAPTER 9.

THAT VESPASIAN, AFTER HE HAD TAKEN GADARA MADE PREPARATION FOR THE SIEGE OF JERUSALEM; BUT THAT, UPON HIS HEARING OF THE DEATH OF NERO, HE CHANGED HIS INTENTIONS. AS ALSO CONCERNING SIMON OF GERASA.

1. (486) AND now Vespasian had fortified all the places round about Jerusalem, and erected citadels at Jericho and Adida, and placed garrisons in them both, partly out of his own Romans, and partly out of the body of his auxiliaries. (487) He also sent Lucius Annius to Gerasa, and delivered to him a body of horsemen, and a considerable number of footmen. (488) So when he had taken the city, which he did at the first onset, he slew a thousand of those young men who had not prevented him by flying away; but he took their

Denarius coin of Galba (A.D. 68–69), minted in Rome. (Classical Numismatic Group, Inc. http://www.cngcoins.com)

families captive, and permitted his soldiers to plunder them of their effects; after which he set fire to their houses, and went away to the adjoining villages, (489) while the men of power fled away, and the weaker part were destroyed, and what was remaining was all burnt down. (490) And now the war having gone through all the mountainous country, and all the plain country also, those that were at Jerusalem were deprived of the liberty of going out of the city; for as to such as had a mind to desert, they were watched by the zealots; and as to such as were not yet on the side of the Romans, their army kept them in, by encompassing the city round about on all sides.

2. (491) Now as Vespasian was returned to Cesarea, and was getting ready with all his army to march directly to Jerusalem, he was informed that Nero was dead, after he had reigned thirteen years and eight days. (492) But as to any narration after what manner he abused his power in the government, and committed the management of affairs to those vile wretches, Nymphidius and Tigellinus, (493) his unworthy freed-men; and how he had a plot laid against him by them, and was deserted by all his guards, and ran away with four of his most trusty freed-men, and slew himself in the suburbs of Rome; and how those that occasioned his death were in no long time brought themselves to punishment; (494) how also the war in Gall ended; and how Galba was made emperor and returned out of Spain to Rome; and how he was accused by the soldiers as a pusillanimous person, and slain by treachery in the middle of the market-place at Rome, and Otho was made emperor; (495) with his expedition against the commanders of Vitellius, and his destruction thereupon; and besides what troubles there were under Vitellius, and the fight that was about the capitol; as also how Antonius Primus and Mucianus slew Vitellius, and his German legions, and thereby put an end to that civil war;—(496) I have omitted to give an exact account of them, because they are well known by all, and they are described by a great number of Greek and Roman authors; yet for the sake of the connexion of matters, and that my history may not be incoherent, I have just touched upon every thing briefly. (497) Wherefore Vespasian put off at first his expedition against Jerusalem, and stood waiting whither the empire would be transferred after the death of Nero. (498) Moreover, when he heard that Galba was made emperor, he attempted nothing till he also should send him some directions about the war: however, he sent his son Titus to him, to salute him, and to receive his commands about the Jews. Upon the very same errand did king Agrippa sail along with Titus to Galba; (499) but as they were sailing in their long ships by the coasts of Achaia, for it was winter time, they heard that Galba was slain, before they could get to him, after he had reigned seven months and as many days. After whom Otho took the government, and undertook the management of public affairs. (500) So Agrippa resolved to go on to Rome without any terror; on account of the change in the government; (501) but Titus, by a Divine impulse, sailed back from Greece to Syria, and came in great haste to Cesarea, to his father. (502) And now they were both in suspense about the public affairs, the Roman empire being then in a fluctuating condition, and did not go on with their expedition against the Jews, but thought that

The forum at Gerasa. (photo Zairon, via Wikimedia Commons)

to make any attack upon foreigners was now unseasonable, on account of the solicitude they were in for their own country.

3. (503) And now there arose another war at Jerusalem. There was a son of Giora, one Simon, by birth of Gerasa, a young man, not so cunning indeed as John [of Gischala], who had already seized upon the city, (504) but superior in strength of body and courage; on which account, when he had been driven away from that Acrabattene toparchy, which he once had, by Ananus the high priest, he came to those robbers who had seized upon Masada. (505) At the first they suspected him, and only permitted him to come with the women he brought with him into the lower part of the fortress, while they dwelt in the upper part of it themselves. (506) However, his manner so well agreed with theirs, and he seemed so trusty a man, that he went out with them, and ravaged and destroyed the country with them about Masada; (507) yet when he persuaded them to undertake greater things, he could not prevail with them so to do; for as they were accustomed to dwell in that citadel, they were afraid of going far from that which was their hiding-place; (508) but he affecting to tyrannize, and being fond of greatness, when he had heard of the death of Ananus, he left them, and went into the mountainous part of the country. So he proclaimed liberty to those in slavery, and a reward to those already free, and got together a set of wicked men from all quarters.

4. (509) And as he had now a strong body of men about him, he overran the villages that lay in the mountainous country, and when there were still more and more that came to him, he ventured to go down into the lower parts of the country, (510) and since he was now become formidable to the cities, many of the men of power were corrupted by him; so that his army was no longer composed of slaves and robbers, but a great many of the populace were obedient to him as to their king. (511) He then overran the Acrabattene toparchy, and the places that reached as far as the Great Idumea; for he built a wall at a certain village called Nain, and made use of that as a fortress for his own party's security; (512) and at the valley called Paran, he enlarged many of the caves, and many others he found ready for his purpose; these he made use of as repositories for his treasures, and receptacles for his prey, (513) and therein he laid up the fruits that he had got by rapine; and many of his partizans had their dwelling in them; and he made no secret of it that he was exercising his men beforehand, and making preparations for the assault of Jerusalem.

5. (514) Whereupon the zealots, out of the dread they were in of his attacking them, and being willing to prevent one that was growing up to oppose them, went out against him with their weapons. Simon met them, and joining battle with them, slew a considerable number of them, and drove the rest before him into the city, (515) but durst not trust so much upon his forces as to make an assault upon the walls; but he resolved first to subdue Idumea, and as he had now twenty thousand armed men, he marched to the borders of their country. (516) Hereupon the rulers of the Idumeans got together on the sudden the most warlike part of their people, about twenty-five thousand in number, and permitted the rest to be a guard to their own country, by reason of the incursions that were made by the Sicarii that were at Masada. Thus they received Simon at their borders, (517) where they fought him, and continued the battle all that day; and the dispute lay whether they had conquered him, or been conquered by him. So he went back to Nain, as did the Idumeans return home. (518) Nor was it long ere Simon came violently again upon their country; when he pitched his camp at a certain village called Thecoe, and sent Eleazar, one of his companions, to those that kept garrison at Herodium, and in order to persuade them to surrender that fortress to him. (519) The garrison received this man readily, while they knew nothing of what he came about; but as soon as he talked of the surrender of the place, they fell upon him with their drawn swords, till he found that he had no place for flight, when he threw himself down from the wall into the valley beneath; (520) so he died immediately: but the Idumeans, who were already much afraid of Simon's power, thought fit to take a view of the enemy's army before they hazarded a battle with them.

6. (521) Now there was one of their commanders named Jacob, who offered to serve them readily upon that occasion, but had it in his mind to betray them. (522) He went therefore from the village Alurus, wherein the army of the Idumeans were gotten together, and came to Simon, (523) and at the very first he agreed to betray his country to him, and took assurances upon oath from him that he should always have him in esteem, and then promised him that he would assist him in subduing all Idumea under him; (524) upon which account he was feasted after an obliging manner by Simon, and elevated by his mighty promises; and when he was returned to his own men, he at first belied the army of Simon, (525) and said it was manifold more in number than what it was; after which, he dexterously persuaded the commanders, and by degrees the whole multitude, to receive Simon, and to surrender the whole government up to him without fighting. (526) And as he was doing this, he invited Simon by his messengers, and promised him to disperse the Idumeans, which he performed also; (527) for as soon as their army was nigh them, he first of all got upon his horse, and fled, together with those whom he had corrupted; (528) hereupon a terror fell upon the whole multitude; and before it came to a close fight, they broke their ranks, and every one retired to his own home.

7. (529) Thus did Simon unexpectedly march into Idumea, without bloodshed, and made a sudden attack upon the city Hebron, and

took it; wherein he got possession of a great deal of prey, and plundered it of a vast quantity of fruit. (530) Now the people of the country say that it is an ancienter city, not only than any in that country, but than Memphis in Egypt, and accordingly its age is reckoned at two thousand and three hundred years. (531) They also relate that it had been the habitation of Abram, the progenitor of the Jews, after he had removed out of Mesopotamia; and they say that his posterity descended from thence into Egypt, (532) whose monuments are to this very time showed in that small city; the fabric of which monuments are of the most excellent marble, and wrought after the most elegant manner. (533) There is also there showed, at the distance of six furlongs from the city, a very large turpentine tree and the report goes, that this tree has continued ever since the creation of the world. (534) Thence did Simon make his progress over all Idumea, and did not only ravage the cities and villages, but lay waste the whole country; for, besides those that were completely armed, he had forty thousand men that followed him, insomuch that he had not provisions enough to suffice such a multitude. (535) Now, besides this want of provisions that he was in, he was of a barbarous disposition, and bore great anger at this nation, by which means it came to pass that Idumea was greatly depopulated; (536) and as one may see all the woods behind despoiled of their leaves by locusts, after they have been there, so was there nothing left behind Simon's army but a desert. (537) Some places they burnt down, some they utterly demolished, and whatsoever grew in the country, they either trod it down or fed upon it, and by their marches they made the ground that was cultivated harder and more untractable than that which was barren. In short, there was no sign remaining of those places that had been laid waste, that ever they had had a being.

8. (538) This success of Simon excited the zealots afresh; and though they were afraid to fight him openly in a fair battle, yet did they lay ambushes in the passes, and seized upon his wife, with a considerable number of her attendants; (539) whereupon they came back to the city rejoicing, as if they had taken Simon himself captive, and were in present expectation that he would lay down his arms, and make supplication to them for his wife; (540) but instead of indulging any merciful affection, he grew very angry at them for seizing his beloved wife; so he came to the wall of Jerusalem, and, like wild beasts when they are wounded, and cannot overtake those that wounded them, he vented his spleen upon all persons that he met with. (541) Accordingly, he caught all those that were come out of the city gates, either to gather herbs or sticks, who were unarmed and in years; he then tormented them and destroyed them, out of the immense rage he was in, and was almost ready to taste the very flesh of their dead bodies. (542) He also cut off the hands of a great many, and sent them into the city to astonish his enemies, and in order to make the people fall into a sedition, and desert those that had been the authors of his wife's seizure. (543) He also enjoined them to tell the people that Simon swore by the God of the universe, who sees all things, that unless they will re-

The palace-fortress of Herodium. (photo Samuel Magal)

THE CAMPAIGNS OF A.D. 69–70

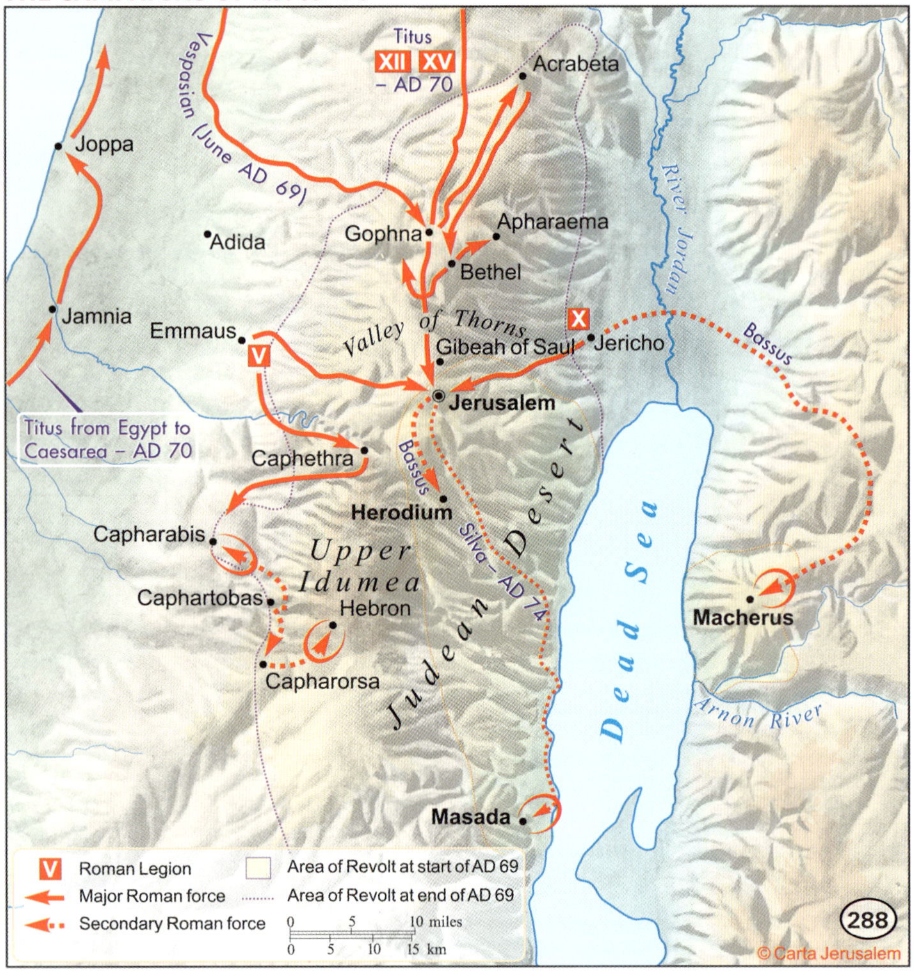

store him his wife, he will break down their wall, and inflict the like punishment upon all the citizens, without sparing any age, and without making any distinction between the guilty and the innocent. (544) These threatenings so greatly affrighted, not the people only, but the zealots themselves also, that they sent his wife back to him; when he became a little milder, and left off his perpetual blood-shedding.

9. (545) But now sedition and civil war prevailed, not only over Judea, but in Italy also; (546) for now Galba was slain in the midst of the Roman market-place; then was Otho made emperor, and fought against Vitellius, who set up for emperor also; for the legions in Germany had chosen him. (547) But when he gave battle to Valens and Cecinna, who were Vitellius's generals, at Betriacum, in Gaul, Otho gained the advantage on the first day, but on the second day Vitellius's soldiers had the victory; (548) and after much slaughter Otho slew himself, when he had heard of this defeat at Brixia, and after he had managed the public affairs three months and two days. (549) Otho's army also came over to Vitellius's generals, and he came himself down to Rome with his army. (550) But in the meantime Vespasian removed from Cesarea, on the fifth day of the month Deasius, [Sivan,] and marched against those places of Judea which were not yet overthrown. (551) So he went up to the mountainous country, and took those two toparchies that were called the Gophnitica and Acrabattene toparchies. After which he took Bethel and Ephraim, two small cities; and when he had put garrisons into them, he rode as far as Jerusalem, in which march he took many prisoners, and many captives; (552) but Cerealis, one of his commanders, took a body of horsemen and footmen, and laid waste that part of Idumea which was called the Upper Idumea, and attacked Caphethra, which pretended to be a small city, and took it at the first onset, and burnt it down. He also attacked Caphatabira, and laid siege to it, (553) for it had a very strong wall; and when he expected to spend a long time in that siege, those that were within opened their gates on the sudden, and came to beg pardon, and surrendered themselves up to him. (554) When Cerealis had conquered them, he went to Hebron, another very ancient city. I have told you already that this city is situated in a mountainous country not far off Jerusalem; and when he had broken into the city by force, what multitude and young men were left therein he slew, and burnt down the city; (555) so that as now all the places were taken, excepting Herodium, and Masada, and Macherus, which were in the possession of the robbers, so Jerusalem was what the Romans at present aimed at.

10. (556) And now, as soon as Simon had set his wife free, and recovered her from the zealots, he returned back to the remainders of Idumea, and driving the nation all before him from all quarters, he compelled a great number of them to retire to Jerusalem; (557) he followed them himself also to the city, and encompassed the wall all round again; and when he lighted upon any laborers that were coming thither out of the country, he slew them. (558) Now this Simon, who was without the wall, was a greater terror to the people than the Romans themselves, as were the zealots who were within it more heavy upon them than both of the other; and during this time did the mischievous contrivances and courage [of John] corrupt the body of the Galileans; (559) for these Galileans had advanced this John, and made him very potent, who made them suitable requital from the authority he had obtained by their means; for he permitted them to do all things that any of them desired to do, (560) while their inclination to plunder was insatiable, as was their zeal in searching the houses of the rich; and for the murdering of the men, and abusing of the women, it was sport to them. (561) They also devoured what spoils they had taken, together with their blood, and indulged themselves in feminine wantonness, without any disturbance, till they were satiated therewith; while they decked their hair, and put on women's garments, and were besmeared over with ointments; and that they might appear very comely, they had paints under their eyes, (562) and imitated not only the ornaments, but also the lusts of women, and were guilty of such intolerable uncleanness, that they invented unlawful pleasures of that sort. And thus did they roll themselves up and down the city, as in a brothel-house, and defiled it entirely with their impure actions; (563) nay, while their faces looked like the faces of women, they killed with their right hands; and when their gait was effeminate, they presently attacked men, and became warriors, and drew their swords from under their finely dyed cloaks, and ran every body through whom they alighted upon. (564) However, Simon waited for such as ran away from John, and was the more bloody of the two; and he who had escaped the tyrant within the wall was destroyed by the other that lay before the gates, (565) so that all attempts of flying and deserting to the Romans were cut off, as to those that had a mind so to do.

11. (566) Yet did the army that was under John raise a sedition against him, and all the Idumeans separated themselves from the

tyrant, and attempted to destroy him, and this out of their envy at his power, and hatred of his cruelty; (567) so they got together, and slew many of the zealots, and drove the rest before them into that royal palace that was built by Grapte, who was a relation of Izates, the king of Adiabene; (568) the Idumeans fell in with them, and drove the zealots out thence into the temple, and betook themselves to plunder John's effects; (569) for both he himself was in that palace, and therein had he laid up the spoils he had acquired by his tyranny. (570) In the meantime, the multitude of those zealots that were dispersed over the city ran together to the temple unto those that fled thither, and John prepared to bring them down against the people and the Idumeans, (571) who were not so much afraid of being attacked by them (because they were themselves better soldiers than they) as at their madness, lest they should privately sally out of the temple and get among them, and not only destroy them, but set the city on fire also. (572) So they assembled themselves together, and the high priests with them, and took counsel after what manner they should avoid their assault. (573) Now it was God who turned their opinions to the worst advice, and thence they devised such a remedy to get themselves free as was worse than the disease itself. Accordingly, in order to overthrow John, they determined to admit Simon, and earnestly to desire the introduction of a second tyrant into the city; (574) which resolution they brought to perfection, and sent Matthias, the high priest, to beseech this Simon to come ill to them, of whom they had so often been afraid. Those also that had fled from the zealots in Jerusalem joined in this request to him, out of the desire they had of preserving their houses and their effects. (575) Accordingly he, in an arrogant manner, granted them his lordly protection, and came into the city, in order to deliver it from the zealots. The people also made joyful acclamations to him, as their savior and their preserver; (576) but when he was come in, with his army, he took care to secure his own authority, and looked upon those that had invited him in to be no less his enemies than those against whom the invitation was intended.

12. (577) And thus did Simon get possession of Jerusalem, in the third year of the war, in the month Xanthicus [Nisan]; whereupon John, with his multitude of zealots, as being both prohibited from coming out of the temple, and having lost their power in the city, (for Simon and his party had plundered them of what they had,) were in despair of deliverance. (578) Simon also made an assault upon the temple, with the assistance of the people, while the others stood upon the cloisters and the battlements, and defended themselves from their assaults. (579) However, a considerable number of Simon's party fell, and many were carried off wounded; for the zealots threw their darts easily from a superior place, and seldom failed of hitting their enemies; (580) but having the advantage of situation, and having withal erected four very large towers aforehand, that their darts might come from higher places, (581) one at the north-east corner of the court, one above the Xystus, the third at another corner over against the lower city, (582) and the last was erected above the top of the Pastophoria, where one of the priests stood of course, and gave a signal beforehand, with a trumpet at the beginning of every seventh day, in the evening twilight, as also at the evening when that day was finished, as giving notice to the people when they were to leave off work, and when they were to go to work again. (583) These men also set their engines to cast darts and stones withal, upon those towers, with their archers and slingers. (584) And now Simon made his assault upon the temple more faintly, by reason that the greatest part of his men grew weary of that work; yet did he not leave off his opposition, because his army was superior to the others, although the darts which were thrown by the engines were carried a great way, and slew many of those that fought for him.

CHAPTER 10.

HOW THE SOLDIERS, BOTH IN JUDEA AND EGYPT, PROCLAIMED VESPASIAN EMPEROR; AND HOW VESPASIAN RELEASED JOSEPHUS FROM HIS BONDS.

1. (585) NOW about this very time it was that heavy calamities came about Rome on all sides; (586) for Vitellius was come from Germany with his soldiery, and drew along with him a great multitude of other men besides. And when the spaces allotted for soldiers could not contain them, he made all Rome itself his camp, and filled all the houses with his armed men; (587) which men, when they saw the riches of Rome with those eyes which had never seen such riches before, and found themselves shone round about on all sides with silver and gold, they had much ado to contain their covetous desires, and were ready to betake themselves to plunder, and to the slaughter of such as should stand in their way. And this was the state of affairs in Italy at that time.

2. (588) But when Vespasian had overthrown all the places that were near to Jerusalem, he returned to Cesarea, and heard of the troubles that were at Rome, and that Vitellius was emperor. (589) This produced indignation in him, although he well knew how to be governed as well as to govern, and could not, with any satisfaction, own him for his lord who acted so madly, and seized upon the government as if it were absolutely destitute of a governor. (590) And as this sorrow of his was violent, he was not able to support the torments he was under, nor to apply himself further in other wars, when his native country was laid waste; (591) but then, as much as his passion excited him to avenge his country, so much was he restrained by the consideration of his distance therefrom; because fortune might prevent him, and do a world of mischief before he could himself sail over the sea to Italy, especially as it was still the winter season; so he restrained his anger, how vehement soever it was at this time.

Bust of the emperor Vitellius (A.D. 69). (Ny Carlsberg Glyptothek, Copenhagen; photo Wolfgang Sauber, via Wikimedia Commons)

3. (592) But now his commanders and soldiers met in several companies, and consulted openly about changing the public affairs;—and, out of their indignation, cried out, how "at Rome there are soldiers that live delicately, and when they have not ventured so much as to hear the fame of war, they ordain whom they please for our governors, and in hopes of gain make them emperors; (593) while you, who have gone through so many labors, and are grown into years under your helmets, give leave to others to use such a power, when yet you have among yourselves one more worthy to rule than any whom they have set up. (594) Now what juster opportunity shall they ever have of requiting their generals, if they do not make use of this that is now before them? while there is so much juster reasons for Vespasian's being emperor than for Vitellius; (595) as they are themselves more deserving than those that made the other emperors; for that they have undergone as great wars as have the troops that come from Germany; (596) nor are they inferior in war to those that have brought that tyrant to Rome, nor have they undergone smaller labors than they; for that neither

THE NILE DELTA

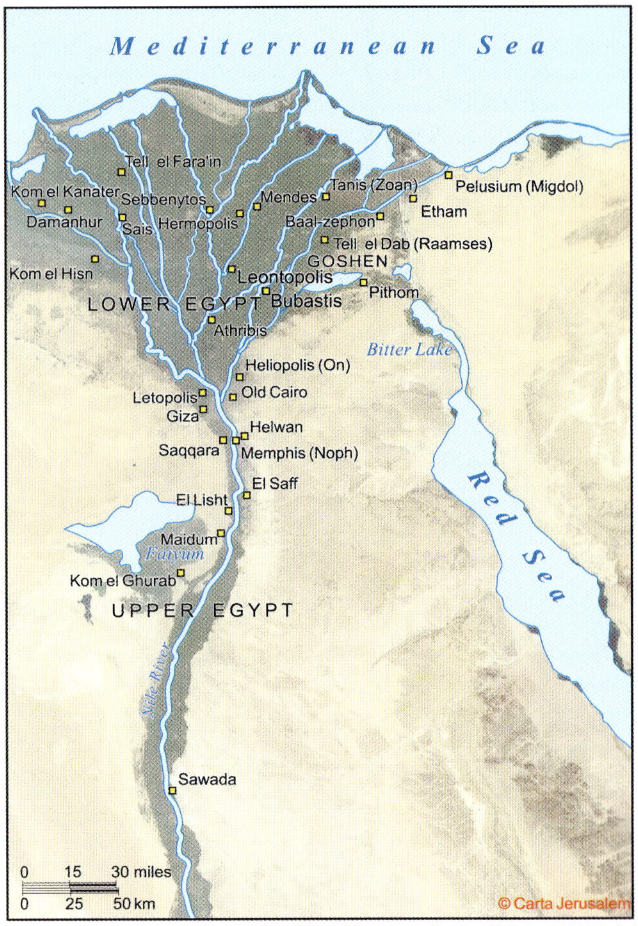

(from *Understanding the Geography of the Bible* / Menashe Har-El & Paul H. Wright)

will the Roman senate, nor people, bear such a lascivious emperor as Vitellius, if he be compared with their chaste Vespasian; nor will they endure a most barbarous tyrant, instead of a good governor, nor choose one that hath no child to preside over them, instead of him that is a father; because the advancement of men's own children to dignities is certainly the greatest security kings can have for themselves. (597) Whether, therefore, we estimate the capacity of governing from the skill of a person in years, we ought to have Vespasian,—or whether from the strength of a young man, we ought to have Titus; for by this means we shall have the advantage of both their ages, (598) for that they will afford strength to those that shall be made emperors, they having already three legions, besides other auxiliaries from the neighboring kings, and will have further all the armies in the east to support them, as also those in Europe, so they as they are out of the distance and dread of Vitellius, besides such auxiliaries as they may have in Italy itself; that is, Vespasian's brother, and his other son [Domitian]; (599) the one of whom will bring in a great many of those young men that are of dignity, while the other is intrusted with the government of the city, which office of his will be no small means of Vespasian's obtaining the government. (600) Upon the whole, the case may be such, that if we ourselves make further delays, the senate may choose an emperor, whom the soldiers, who are the saviors of the empire, will have in contempt."

4. (601) These were the discourses the soldiers had in their several companies; after which they got together in a great body, and, encouraging one another, they declared Vespasian emperor, and exhorted him to save the government, which was now in danger. (602) Now Vespasian's concern had been for a considerable time about the public, yet did he not intend to set up for governor himself, though his actions showed him to deserve it, while he preferred that safety which is in a private life before the dangers in a state of such dignity; (603) but when he refused the empire, the commanders insisted the more earnestly upon his acceptance; and the soldiers came about him, with their drawn swords in their hands, and threatened to kill him, unless he would now live according to his dignity. (604) And when he had shown his reluctance a great while, and had endeavored to thrust away this dominion from him, he at length, being not able to persuade them, yielded to their solicitations that would salute him emperor.

5. (605) So upon the exhortations of Mucianus, and the other commanders, that he would accept of the empire, and upon that of the rest of the army, who cried out that they were willing to be led against all his opposers, he was in the first place intent upon gaining the dominion over Alexandria, as knowing that Egypt was of the greatest consequence, in order to obtain the entire government, because of its supplying of corn [to Rome]; (606) which corn, if he could be master of, he hoped to dethrone Vitellius, supposing he should aim to keep the empire by force (for he would not be able to support himself, if the multitude at Rome should once be in want of food); and because he was desirous to join the two legions that were at Alexandria to the other legions that were with him. (607) He also considered with himself, that he should then have that country for a defense to himself against the uncertainty of fortune; for Egypt is hard to be entered by land, and hath no good havens by sea. (608) It hath on the west the dry deserts of Libya; and on the south Siene, that divides it from Ethiopia, as well as the cataracts of the Nile, that cannot be sailed over; and on the east the Red Sea extended as far as Coptus; (609) and it is fortified on the north by the land that reaches to Syria, together with that called the Egyptian Sea, having no havens in it for ships. (610) And thus is Egypt walled about on every side. Its length between Pelusium and Siene is two thousand furlongs, and the passage by sea from Plinthine to Pelusium is three thousand six hundred furlongs. (611) Its river Nile is navigable as far as the city called Elephantine, the forenamed cataracts hindering ships from going any farther. (612) The haven also of Alexandria is not entered by the mariners without difficulty, even in times of peace; for the passage inward is narrow, and full of rocks that lie under the water, which oblige the mariners to turn from a straight direction: (613) its left side is blocked up by works made by men's hands on both sides; on its right side lies the island called Pharus, which is situated just before the entrance, and supports a very great tower, that affords the sight of a fire to such as sail within three hundred furlongs of it, that ships may cast anchor a great way off in the night time, by reason of the difficulty of sailing nearer. (614) About this island are built very great piers, the handiwork of men, against which, when the sea dashes itself, and its waves are broken against those boundaries, the navigation becomes very troublesome, and the entrance through so narrow a passage is rendered dangerous; (615) yet is the haven itself, when you are got into it, a very safe one, and of thirty furlongs in largeness; into which is brought what the country wants in order to its happiness, as also what abundance the country affords more than it wants itself is hence distributed into all the habitable earth.

6. (616) Justly, therefore, did Vespasian desire to obtain that government, in order to corroborate his attempts upon the whole empire; so he immediately sent to Tiberius Alexander, who was then governor of Egypt and of Alexandria, and informed him what the army had put upon him, and how he, being forced to accept of the burden of the government, was desirous to have him for his confederate and supporter. (617) Now as soon as ever Alexander

had read this letter, he readily obliged the legions and the multitude to take the oath of fidelity to Vespasian, both which willingly complied with him, as already acquainted with the courage of the man, from that his conduct in their neighborhood. (618) Accordingly Vespasian, looking upon himself as already intrusted with the government, got all things ready for his journey [to Rome]. Now fame carried this news abroad more suddenly than one could have thought, that he was emperor over the east, upon which every city kept festivals, and celebrated sacrifices and oblations for such good news; (619) the legions also that were in Mysia and Pannonia, who had been in commotion a little before, on account of this insolent attempt of Vitellius, were very glad to take the oath of fidelity to Vespasian, upon his coming to the empire. (620) Vespasian then removed from Cesarea to Berytus, where many embassages came to him from Syria, and many from other provinces, bringing with them from every city crowns, and the congratulations of the people. (621) Mucianus came also, who was the president of the province, and told him with what alacrity the people [received the news of his advancement], and how the people of every city had taken the oath of fidelity to him.

7. (622) So Vespasian's good fortune succeeded to his wishes every where, and the public affairs were, for the greatest part, already in his hands; upon which he considered that he had not arrived at the government without Divine Providence, but that a righteous kind of fate had brought the empire under his power; (623) for as he called to mind the other signals, which had been a great many every where, that foretold he should obtain the government, so did he remember what Josephus had said to him when he ventured to foretell his coming to the empire while Nero was alive; (624) so he was much concerned that this man was still in bonds with him. He then called for Mucianus, together with his other commanders and friends, and, in the first place, he informed them what a valiant man Josephus had been, and what great hardships he had made him undergo in the siege of Jotapata. (625) After that he related those predictions of his which he had then suspected as fictions, suggested out of the fear he was in, but which had by time been demonstrated to be Divine. (626) "It is a shameful thing (said he) that this man, who hath foretold my coming to the empire beforehand, and been the minister of a Divine message to me, should still be retained in the condition of a captive or prisoner." So he called for Josephus, and commanded that he should be set at liberty; (627) whereupon the commanders promised themselves glorious things, froth this requital Vespasian made to a stranger. Titus was then present with his father, (628) and said, "O father, it is but just that the scandal [of a prisoner] should be taken off Josephus, together with his iron chain. For if we do not barely loose his bonds, but cut them to pieces, he will be like a man that had never been bound at all." For that is the usual method as to such as have been bound without a cause. (629) This advice was agreed to by Vespasian also; so there came a man in, and cut the chain to pieces; while Josephus received this testimony of his integrity for a reward, and was moreover esteemed a person of credit as to futurities also.

CHAPTER 11.

THAT UPON THE CONQUEST AND SLAUGHTER OF VITELLIUS VESPASIAN HASTENED HIS JOURNEY TO ROME; BUT TITUS HIS SON RETURNED TO JERUSALEM.

1. (630) AND now, when Vespasian had given answers to the embassages, and had disposed of the places of power justly, and according to every one's deserts, he came to Antioch, (631) and consulting which way he had best take, he preferred to go for Rome, rather than to march to Alexandria, because he saw that Alexandria was sure to him already, but that the affairs at Rome were put into disorder by Vitellius; (632) so he sent Mucianus to Italy, and committed a considerable army both of horsemen and footmen to him; yet was Mucianus afraid of going by sea, because it was the middle of winter, and so he led his army on foot through Cappadocia and Phrygia.

2. (633) In the meantime, Antonius Primus took the third of the legions that were in Mysia, for he was president of that province, and made haste, in order to fight Vitellius; (634) whereupon Vitellius sent away Cecinna, with a great army, having a mighty confidence in him, because of his having beaten Otho. This Cecinna marched out of Rome in great haste, and found Antonius about Cremona in Gall, which city is in the borders of Italy; (635) but when he saw there that the enemy were numerous and in good order, he durst not fight them; and as he thought a retreat dangerous, so he began to think of betraying his army to Antonius. (636) Accordingly, he assembled the centurions and tribunes that were under his command, and persuaded them to go over to Antonius, and this by diminishing the reputation of Vitellius, and by exaggerating the power of Vespasian. (637) He also told them that with the one there was no more than the bare name of dominion, but with the other was the power of it; and that it was better for them to prevent necessity, and gain favor, and, while they were likely to be overcome in battle, to avoid the danger beforehand, and go over to Antonius willingly; (638) that Vespasian was able of himself to subdue what had not yet submitted without their assistance, while Vitellius could not preserve what he had already with it.

3. (639) Cecinna said this, and much more to the same purpose, and persuaded them to comply with him; and both he and his army deserted; (640) but still the very same night the soldiers repented of what they had done, and a fear seized on them, lest perhaps Vitellius who sent them should get the better; and drawing their swords, they assaulted Cecinna, in order to kill him; and the thing had been done by them, if the tribunes had not fallen upon their knees, and besought them not to do it; (641) so the soldiers did not kill him, but put him in bonds, as a traitor, and were about to send him to Vitellius. When [Antonius] Primus heard of this, he raised up his men immediately, and made them put on their armor, and led them against those that had revolted; (642) hereupon they put themselves in order of battle, and made a resistance for a while, but were soon beaten, and fled to Cremona; then did Primus take his horsemen, and cut off their entrance into the city, and encompassed and destroyed a great multitude of them before the city, and fell into the city together with the rest, and gave leave to his soldiers to plunder it. (643) And here it was that many strangers, who were merchants, as well as many of the people of that country, perished, and among them Vitellius's whole army, being thirty thousand and two hundred, while Antonius lost no more of those that came with him from Mysia than four thousand and five hundred: (644) he then loosed Cecinna, and sent him to Vespasian to tell him the good news. So he came, and was received by him, and covered the scandal of his treachery by the unexpected honors he received from Vespasian.

4. (645) And now, upon the news that Antonius was approaching, Sabinus took courage at Rome, and assembled those cohorts of soldiers that kept watch by night, and in the night time seized upon the capitol; (646) and, as the day came on, many men of character came over to him, with Domitian, his brother's son, whose

Coin of the emperor Vespasian (A.D. 69–79). (Skokloster Castle; photo Miguel Herranz)

encouragement was of very great weight for the compassing the government. (647) Now Vitellius was not much concerned at this Primus, but was very angry with those that had revolted with Sabinus; and thirsting, out of his own natural barbarity, after noble blood, he sent out that part of the army which came along with him to fight against the capitol; (648) and many bold actions were done on this side, and on the side of those that held the temple. But at last, the soldiers that came from Germany, being too numerous for the others, got the hill into their possession, (649) where Domitian, with many other of the principal Romans, providentially escaped, while the rest of the multitude were entirely cut to pieces, and Sabinus himself was brought to Vitellius, and then slain; the soldiers also plundered the temple of its ornaments, and set it on fire. (650) But now within a day's time came Antonius, with his army, and were met by Vitellius and his army; and having had a battle in three several places, the last were all destroyed. (651) Then did Vitellius come out of the palace, in his cups, and satiated with an extravagant and luxurious meal, as in the last extremity, (652) and being drawn along through the multitude, and abused with all sorts of torments, had his head cut off in the midst of Rome, having retained the government eight months and five days and had he lived much longer, I cannot but think the empire would not have been sufficient for his lust. (653) Of the others that were slain, were numbered above fifty thousand. (654) This battle was fought on the third day of the month Apelleus [Casleu]; on the next day Mucianus came into the city with his army, and ordered Antonius and his men to leave off killing; for they were still searching the houses, and killed many of Vitellius's soldiers, and many of the populace, as supposing them to be of his party, preventing by their rage any accurate distinction between them and others. He then produced Domitian, and recommended him to the multitude, until his father should come himself; (655) so the people being now freed from their fears, made acclamations of joy for Vespasian, as for their emperor, and kept festival days for his confirmation, and for the destruction of Vitellius.

5. (656) And now, as Vespasian was come to Alexandria, this good news came from Rome, and at the same time came embassies from all his own habitable earth, to congratulate him upon his advancement; and though this Alexandria was the greatest of all cities next to Rome, it proved too narrow to contain the multitude that then came to it. (657) So upon this confirmation of Vespasian's entire government, which was now settled, and upon the unexpected deliverance of the public affairs of the Romans from ruin, Vespasian turned his thoughts to what remained unsubdued in Judea. (658) However, he himself made haste to go to Rome, as the winter was now almost over, and soon set the affairs of Alexandria in order, but sent his son Titus, with a select part of his army, to destroy Jerusalem. (659) So Titus marched on foot as far as Nicopolis, which is distant twenty furlongs from Alexandria; there he put his army on board some long ships, and sailed upon the river along the Mendesian Nomus, as far as the city Tumuis; (660) there he got out of the ships, and walked on foot, and lodged all night at a small city called Tanis. His second station was Heracleopolis, and his third Pelusium; (661) he then refreshed his army at that place for two days, and on the third passed over the mouths of the Nile at Pelusium; he then proceeded one station over the desert, and pitched his camp at the temple of the Casian Jupiter, and on the next day at Ostracine. This station had no water, but the people of the country make use of water brought from other places. (662) After this he rested at Rhinocolura, and from thence he went to Raphia, which was his fourth station. This city is the beginning of Syria. For his fifth station he pitched his camp at Gaza; (663) after which he came to Ascalon, and thence to Jamnia, and after that to Joppa, and from Joppa to Cesarea, having taken a resolution to gather all his other forces together at that place.

Fortifications of Alexandria. (by Luigi Mayer, 1803, via Wikimedia Commons)

BOOK V

FROM THE COMING OF TITUS TO BESIEGE JERUSALEM TO THE GREAT EXTREMITY TO WHICH THE JEWS WERE REDUCED

CHAPTER 1.

CONCERNING THE SEDITIONS AT JERUSALEM AND WHAT TERRIBLE MISERIES AFFLICTED THE CITY BY THEIR MEANS.

1. (1) WHEN therefore Titus had marched over that desert which lies between Egypt and Syria, in the manner forementioned, he came to Cesarea, having resolved to set his forces in order at that place, before he began the war. (2) Nay, indeed, while he was assisting his father at Alexandria, in settling that government which had been newly conferred upon them by God, it so happened that the sedition at Jerusalem was revived, and parted into three factions, and that one faction fought against the other; which partition in such evil cases may be said to be a good thing, and the effect of Divine justice. (3) Now as to the attack the zealots made upon the people, and which I esteem the beginning of the city's destruction, it hath been already explained after an accurate manner; as also whence it arose, and to how great a mischief it was increased. (4) But for the present sedition, one should not mistake if he called it a sedition begotten by another sedition, and to be like a wild beast grown mad, which, for want of food from abroad, fell now upon eating its own flesh.

2. (5) For Eleazar, the son of Simon, who made the first separation of the zealots from the people, and made them retire into the temple, appeared very angry at John's insolent attempts, which he made everyday upon the people; for this man never left off murdering; but the truth was, that he could not bear to submit to a tyrant who set up after him. (6) So he being desirous of gaining the entire power and dominion to himself, revolted from John, and took to his assistance Judas the son of Chelcias, and Simon the son of Ezron, who were among the men of greatest power. There was also with him Hezekiah, the son of Chobar, a person of eminence. (7) Each of these were followed by a great many of the zealots; these seized upon the inner court of the temple and laid their arms upon the holy gates, and over the holy fronts of that court. (8) And because they had plenty of provisions, they were of good courage, for there was a great abundance of what was consecrated to sacred uses, and they scrupled not the making use of them; yet were they afraid, on account of their small number; and when they had laid up their arms there, they did not stir from the place they were in. (9) Now as to John, what advantage he had above Eleazar in the multitude of his followers, the like disadvantage he had in the situation he was in, since he had his enemies over his head; and as he could not make any assault upon them without some terror, so was his anger too great to let them be at rest; (10) nay, although he suffered more mischief from Eleazar and his party than he could inflict upon them, yet would he not leave off assaulting them, insomuch that there were continual sallies made one against another, as well as darts thrown at one another, and the temple was defiled every where with murders.

3. (11) But now the tyrant Simon, the son of Gioras, whom the people had invited in, out of the hopes they had of his assistance in the great distresses they were in, having in his power the upper city, and a great part of the lower, did now make more vehement assaults upon John and his party, because they were fought against from above also; yet was he beneath their situation when he attacked them, as they were beneath the attacks of the others above them. (12) Whereby it came to pass that John did both receive and inflict great damage, and that easily, as he was fought against on both sides; and the same advantage that Eleazar and his party had over him, since he was beneath them, the same advantage had he, by his higher situation, over Simon. (13) On which account he easily repelled the attacks that were made from beneath, by the weapons thrown from their hands only; but was obliged to repel those that threw their darts from the temple above him, by his engines of war; (14) for he had such engines as threw darts, and javelins, and stones, and that in no small number, by which he did not only defend himself from such as fought against him, but slew moreover many of the priests, as they were about their sacred ministrations. (15) For notwithstanding these men were mad with all sorts of impiety, yet did they still admit those that desired to offer their sacrifices, although they took care to search the people of their own country beforehand, and both suspected and watched them; while they were not so much afraid of strangers, who, although they had gotten leave of them, how cruel soever they were, to come into that court, were yet often destroyed by this sedition; (16) for those darts that were thrown by the engines came with that force, that they went over all the buildings, and reached as far as the altar, and the temple itself, and fell upon the priests, and those that were about the sacred offices; (17) insomuch that many persons who came thither with great zeal from the ends of the earth, to offer sacrifices at this celebrated place, which was esteemed holy by all mankind, fell down before their own sacrifices themselves, and sprinkled that altar which was venerable among all men, both Greeks and Barbarians, with their own blood; (18) till the dead bodies of strangers were mingled together with those of their own country, and those of profane persons with those of the priests, and the blood of all sorts of dead carcasses stood in lakes in the holy courts themselves. (19) And now, "O must wretched city, what misery so great

Roman arrowheads. (Museo Della Civita Romano; photo Samuel Magal)

as this didst thou suffer from the Romans, when they came to purify thee from thy intestine hatred! 'For thou couldst be no longer a place fit for God, nor couldst thou long continue in being, after thou hadst been a sepulcher for the bodies of thy own people, and hadst made the holy house itself a burying-place in this civil war of thine. Yet mayst thou again grow better, if perchance thou wilt hereafter appease the anger of that God who is the author of thy destruction." (20) But I must restrain myself from these passions by the rules of history, since this is not a proper time for domestical lamentations, but for historical narrations; I therefore return to the operations that follow in this sedition.

4. (21) And now there were three treacherous factions in the city, the one parted from the other. Eleazar and his party, that kept the sacred first-fruits, came against John in their cups. Those that were with John plundered the populace, and went out with zeal against Simon. This Simon had his supply of provisions from the city, in opposition to the seditious. (22) When, therefore, John was assaulted on both sides, he made his men turn about, throwing his darts upon those citizens that came up against him, from the cloisters he had in his possession, while he opposed those that attacked him from the temple by his engines of war. (23) And if at any time he was freed from those that were above him, which happened frequently, from their being drunk and tired, he sallied out with a great number upon Simon and his party; (24) and this he did always in such parts of the city as he could come at, till he set on fire those houses that were full of corn, and of all other provisions. The same thing was done by Simon, when, upon the other's retreat, he attacked the city also; as if they had, on purpose, done it to serve the Romans, by destroying what the city had laid up against the siege, and by thus cutting off the nerves of their own power. (25) Accordingly, it so came to pass, that all the places that were about the temple were burnt down, and were become an intermediate desert space, ready for fighting on both sides of it; and that almost all that corn was burnt, which would have been sufficient for a siege of many years. (26) So they were taken by the means of the famine, which it was impossible they should have been, unless they had thus prepared the way for it by this procedure.

Gravestone in Mamertine Prison, with the names of illustrious prisoners who were locked up, awaiting execution. Among them, Simon bar [son of] Giora. (photo Lalupa, via Wikimedia Commons)

5. (27) And now, as the city was engaged in a war on all sides, from these treacherous crowds of wicked men, the people of the city, between them, were like a great body torn in pieces. (28) The aged men and the women were in such distress by their internal calamities, that they wished for the Romans, and earnestly hoped for an external war, in order to their delivery from their domestical miseries. (29) The citizens themselves were under a terrible consternation and fear; nor had they any opportunity of taking counsel, and of changing their conduct; nor were there any hopes of coming to an agreement with their enemies; nor could such as had a mind flee away; (30) for guards were set at all places, and the heads of the robbers, although they were seditious one against another in other respects, yet did they agree in killing those that were for peace with the Romans, or were suspected of an inclination to desert them, as their common enemies. (31) They agreed in nothing but this, to kill those that were innocent. The noise also of those that were fighting was incessant, both by day and by night; but the lamentations of those that mourned exceeded the other; (32) nor was there ever any occasion for them to leave off their lamentations, because their calamities came perpetually one upon another, although the deep consternation they were in prevented their outward wailing; but being constrained by their fear to conceal their inward passions, they were inwardly tormented, without daring to open their lips in groans. (33) Nor was any regard paid to those that were still alive, by their relations; nor was there any care taken of burial for those that were dead; the occasion of both which was this, that every one despaired of himself; for those that were not among the seditious had no great desires of any thing, as expecting for certain that they should very soon be destroyed; (34) but for the seditious themselves, they fought against each other, while they trod upon the dead bodies as they lay heaped one upon another, and taking up a mad rage from those dead bodies that were under their feet, became the fiercer thereupon. (35) They, moreover, were still inventing somewhat or other that was pernicious against themselves; and when they had resolved upon any thing, they executed it without mercy, and omitted no method of torment or of barbarity. (36) Nay, John abused the sacred materials, and employed them in the construction of his engines of war; for the people and the priests had formerly determined to support the temple, and raise the holy house twenty cubits higher; for king Agrippa had at a very great expense, and with very great pains, brought thither such materials as were proper for that purpose, being pieces of timber very well worth seeing, both for their straightness and their largeness; (37) but the war coming on, and interrupting the work, John had them cut, and prepared for the building him towers, he finding them long enough to oppose from them those his adversaries that thought him from the temple that was above him. (38) He also had them brought and erected behind the inner court over against the west end of the cloisters, where alone he could erect them ; whereas the other sides of that court had so many steps as would not let them come nigh enough the cloisters.

6. (39) Thus did John hope to be too hard for his enemies by these

engines constructed by his impiety; but God himself demonstrated that his pains would prove of no use to him, by bringing the Romans upon him, before he had reared any of his towers; (40) for Titus, when he had gotten together part of his forces about him, and had ordered the rest to meet him at Jerusalem, marched out of Cesarea. (41) He had with him those three legions that had accompanied his father when he laid Judea waste, together with that twelfth legion which had been formerly beaten with Cestius; which legion, as it was otherwise remarkable for its valor, so did it march on now with greater alacrity to avenge themselves on the Jews, as remembering what they had formerly suffered from them. (42) Of these legions he ordered the fifth to meet him, by going through Emmaus, and the tenth to go up by Jericho; he also moved himself, together with the rest; besides whom, marched those auxiliaries that came from the kings, being now more in number than before, together with a considerable number that came to his assistance from Syria. (43) Those also that had been selected out of these four legions, and sent with Mucianus to Italy, had their places filled up out of these soldiers that came out of Egypt with Titus; (44) who were two thousand men, chosen out of the armies at Alexandria. There followed him also three thousand drawn from those that guarded the river Euphrates; (45) as also there came Tiberius Alexander, who was a friend of his, most valuable, both for his good-will to him, and for his prudence. He had formerly been governor of Alexandria, (46) but was now thought worthy to be general of the army [under Titus]. The reason of this was, that he had been the first who encouraged Vespasian very lately to accept this his new dominion, and joined himself to him with great fidelity, when things were uncertain, and fortune had not yet declared for him. He also followed Titus as a counselor, very useful to him in this war, both by his age and skill in such affairs.

Bust of Titus. (Capitoline Museum, Rome; photo Samuel Magal)

CHAPTER 2.

HOW TITUS MARCHED TO JERUSALEM, AND HOW HE WAS IN DANGER AS HE WAS TAKING A VIEW OF THE CITY OF THE PLACE ALSO WHERE HE PITCHED HIS CAMP

1. (47) NOW, as Titus was upon his march into the enemy's country, the auxiliaries that were sent by the kings marched first, having all the other auxiliaries with them; after whom followed those that were to prepare the roads and measure out the camp; then came the commander's baggage, and after that the other soldiers, who were completely armed to support them; then came Titus himself, having with him another select body; and then came the pikemen; after whom came the horse belonging to that legion. (48) All these came before the engines; and after these engines came the tribunes and the leaders of the cohorts, with their select bodies; after these came the ensigns, with the eagle; and before those ensigns came the trumpeters belonging to them; next these came the main body of the army in their ranks, every rank being six deep; (49) the servants belonging to every legion came after these; and before these last their baggage; the mercenaries came last, and those that guarded them brought up the rear. (50) Now Titus, according to the Roman usage, went in the front of the army after a decent manner, and marched through Samaria to Gophna, a city that had been formerly taken by his father, and was then garrisoned by Roman soldiers; (51) and when he had lodged there one night, he marched on in the morning; and when he had gone as far as a day's march, he pitched his camp at that valley which the Jews, in their own tongue, call "the Valley of Thorns," near a certain village called Gabaothsath, which signifies "the Hill of Saul," being distant from Jerusalem about thirty furlongs. (52) There it was that he chose out six hundred select horsemen, and went to take a view of the city, to observe what strength it was of, and how courageous the Jews were; whether, when they saw him, and before they came to a direct battle, they would be affrighted and submit; (53) for he had been informed what was really true, that the people who were fallen under the power of the seditious and the robbers were greatly desirous of peace; but being too weak to rise up against the rest, they lay still.

2. (54) Now, so long as he rode along the straight road which led to the wall of the city, nobody appeared out of the gates; (55) but when he went out of that road, and declined towards the tower Psephinus, and led the band of horsemen obliquely, an immense number of the Jews leaped out suddenly at the towers called the "Women's Towers," through that gate which was over against the monuments of queen Helena, and intercepted his horse; (56) and standing directly opposite to those that still ran along the road, hindered them from joining those that had declined out of it. They intercepted Titus also, with a few other. (57) Now it was here impossible for him to go forward, because all the places had trenches dug in them from the wall, to preserve the gardens round about, and were full of gardens obliquely situated, and of many hedges; (58) and to return back to his own men, he saw it was also impossible, by reason of the multitude of the enemies that lay between them; many of whom did not so much as know that the king was in any danger, but supposed him still among them. (59) So he perceived that his preservation must be wholly owing to his own courage, and turned his horse about, and cried out aloud to those that were about him to follow him, and ran with violence into the midst of his enemies, in order to force his way through them to his own men. (60) And hence we may principally learn, that both the success of wars, and the dangers that kings (**cf. Matthew 2:22; 10:18; 17:25; John 19:15; 1 Timothy 2:2; 1 Peter 2:13, 17**) are in, are under the providence of God; (61) for while such a number of darts were thrown at Titus, when he had neither his head-piece on, nor his breastplate, (for, as I told you, he went out not to fight, but

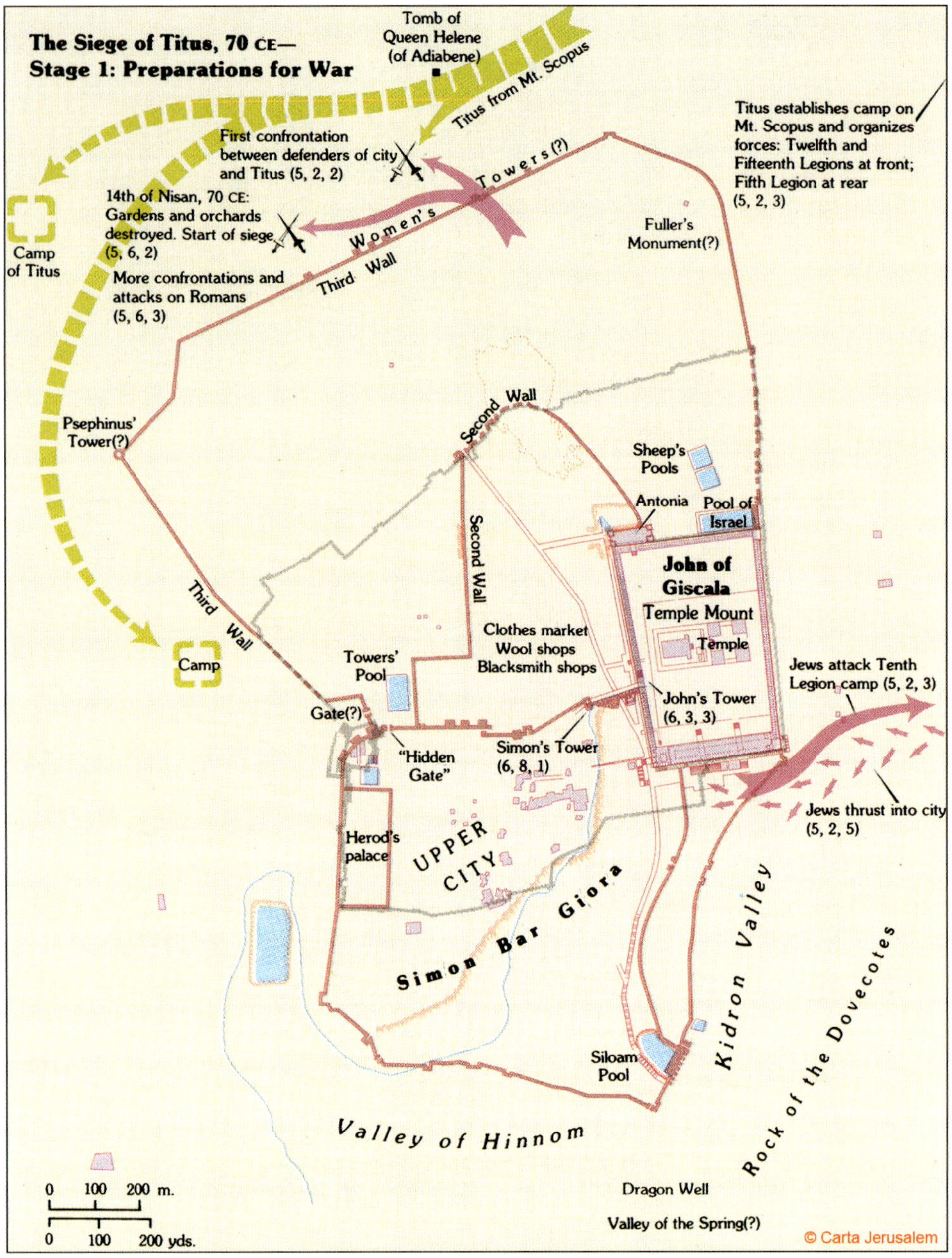

(from *The Carta Jerusalem Atlas* / Dan Bahat)

to view the city,) none of them touched his body, but went aside without hurting him; as if all of them missed him on purpose, and only made a noise as they passed by him. (62) So he diverted those perpetually with his sword that came on his side, and overturned many of those that directly met him, and made his horse ride over those that were overthrown. (63) The enemy indeed made a shout at the boldness of Caesar, and exhorted one another to rush upon him. Yet did these against whom he marched fly away, and go off from him in great numbers; (64) while those that were in the same danger with him kept up close to him, though they were wounded both on their backs and on their sides; for they had each of them but this one hope of escaping, if they could assist Titus in opening himself a way, that he might not be encompassed round by his enemies before he got away from them. (65) Now there were two of those that were with him, but at some distance; the one of which the enemy compassed round, and slew him with their darts, and his horse also; but the other they slew as he leaped down from his horse, and carried off his horse with them. But Titus escaped with the rest, and came safe to the camp. (66) So this success of the Jews' first attack raised their minds, and gave them an ill-grounded hope; and this short inclination of fortune, on their side, made them very courageous for the future.

3. (67) But now, as soon as that legion that had been at Emmaus was joined to Caesar at night, he removed thence, when it was day, and came to a place called Scopus; from whence the city began already to be seen, and a plain view might be taken of the great temple. Accordingly, this place, on the north quarter of the city, and joining thereto, was a plain, and very properly named Scopus, [the prospect,] (68) and was no more than seven furlongs distant from it. And here it was that Titus ordered a camp to be fortified for two legions that were to be together; but ordered another camp to be fortified, at three furlongs farther distance behind them, for the fifth legion; for he thought that, by marching in the night, they might be tired, and might deserve to be covered from the enemy, and with less fear might fortify themselves; (69) and as these were now beginning to build, the tenth legion, who came through Jericho, was already come to the place, where a certain party of armed men had formerly lain, to guard that pass into the city, and had been taken before by Vespasian. (70) These legions had orders to encamp at the distance of six furlongs from Jerusalem, at the mount called the Mount of Olives which lies over against the city on the east side, and is parted from it by a deep valley, interposed between them, which is named Cedron.

4. (71) Now when hitherto the several parties in the city had been dashing one against another perpetually, this foreign war, now suddenly come upon them after a violent manner, put the first stop to their contentions one against another; (72) and as the seditious now saw with astonishment the Romans pitching three several camps, they began to think of an awkward sort of concord, and said one to another, (73) "What do we here, and what do we mean, when we suffer three fortified walls to be built to coop us in, that we shall not be able to breathe freely? while the enemy is securely building a kind of city in opposition to us, and while we sit still within our own walls, and become spectators only of what they are doing, with our hands idle, and our armor laid by, as if they were about somewhat that was for our good and advantage. (74) We are, it seems, (so did they cry out,) only courageous against ourselves, while the Romans are likely to gain the city without bloodshed by our sedition." (75) Thus did they encourage one another when they were gotten together, and took their armor immediately, and ran out upon the tenth legion, and fell upon the Romans with great eagerness, and with a prodigious shout, as they were fortifying their camp. (76) These Romans were caught in different parties, and this in order to perform their several works, and on that account had in great measure laid aside their arms; for they thought the Jews would not have ventured to make a sally upon them; and had they been disposed so to do, they supposed their sedition would have distracted them. So they were put into disorder unexpectedly; (77) when some of hem left their works they were about, and immediately marched off, while many ran to their arms, but were smitten and slain before they could turn back upon the enemy. (78) The Jews became still more and more in number, as encouraged by

the good success of those that first made the attack; and while they had such good fortune, they seemed both to themselves and to the enemy to be many more than they really were. (79) The disorderly way of their fighting at first put the Romans also to a stand, who had been constantly used to fight skillfully in good order, and with keeping their ranks, and obeying the orders that were given them; for which reason the Romans were caught unexpectedly, and were obliged to give way to the assaults that were made upon them. (80) Now when these Romans were overtaken, and turned back upon the Jews, they put a stop to their career; yet when they did not take care enough of themselves through the vehemency of their pursuit, they were wounded by them; but as still more and more Jews sallied out of the city, the Romans were at length brought into confusion, and put to fight, and ran away from their camp. (81) Nay, things looked as though the entire legion would have been in danger, unless Titus had been informed of the case they were in, and had sent them succors immediately. So he reproached them for their cowardice, and brought those back that were running away, (82) and fell himself upon the Jews on their flank, with those select troops that were with him, and slew a considerable number, and wounded more of them, and put them all to flight, and made them run away hastily down the valley. (83) Now as these Jews suffered greatly in the declivity of the valley, so when they were gotten over it, they turned about, and stood over against the Romans, having the valley between them, and there fought with them. (84) Thus did they continue the fight till noon; but when it was already a little after noon, Titus set those that came to the assistance of the Romans with him, and those that belonged to the cohorts, to prevent the Jews from making any more sallies, and then sent the rest of the legion to the upper part of the mountain, to fortify their camp.

5. (85) This march of the Romans seemed to the Jews to be a flight; and as the watchman who was placed upon the wall gave a signal by shaking his garment, there came out a fresh multitude of Jews, and that with such mighty violence, that one might compare it to the running of the most terrible wild beasts. (86) To say the truth, none of those that opposed them could sustain the fury with which they made their attacks; but, as if they had been cast out of an engine, they brake the enemies' ranks to pieces, who were put to flight, and ran away to the mountain; (87) none but Titus himself, and a few others with him, being left in the midst of the acclivity. Now these others, who were his friends, despised the danger they were in, and were ashamed to leave their general, (88) earnestly exhorting him to give way to these Jews that are fond of dying, and not to run into such dangers before those that ought to stay before him; to consider what his fortune was, and not, by supplying the place of a common soldier, to venture to turn back upon the enemy so suddenly; and this because he was general in the war, and lord of the habitable earth, on whose preservation the public affairs do all depend. (89) These persuasions Titus seemed not so much as to hear, but opposed those that ran upon him, and smote them on the face; and when he had forced them to go back, he slew them: he also fell upon great numbers as they marched down the hill, and thrust them forward; (90) while those men were so amazed at his courage and his strength, that they could not fly directly to the city, but declined from him on both sides, and pressed after those that fled up the hill; yet did he still fall upon their flank, and put a stop to their fury. (91) In the meantime, a disorder and a terror fell again upon those that were fortifying their camp at the top of the hill, upon their seeing those beneath them running away; insomuch that the whole legion was dispersed, (92) while they thought that the sallies of the Jews

View of the Temple Mount from the Mount of Olives cemetery, with the valley of Cedron in between. (photo Samuel Magal)

Roman soldier armed with shield and lance. (Museo Della Civita Romano; photo Samuel Magal)

upon them were plainly insupportable, and that Titus was himself put to flight; because they took it for granted, that, if he had staid, the rest would never have fled for it. (93) Thus were they encompassed on every side by a kind of panic fear, and some dispersed themselves one way, and some another, till certain of them saw their general in the very midst of an action, and being under great concern for him, they loudly proclaimed the danger he was in to the entire legion; (94) and now shame made them turn back, and they reproached one another that they did worse than run away, by deserting Caesar. So they used their utmost force against the Jews, and declining from the straight declivity, they drove them on heaps into the bottom of the valley. Then did the Jews turn about and fight them; (95) but as they were themselves retiring, and now, because the Romans had the advantage of the ground, and were above the Jews, they drove them all into the valley. (96) Titus also pressed upon those that were near him, and sent the legion again to fortify their camp; while he, and those that were with him before, opposed the enemy, and kept them from doing further mischief; (97) insomuch that, if I may be allowed neither to add any thing out of flattery, nor to diminish any thing out of envy, but to speak the plain truth, Caesar did twice deliver that entire legion when it was in jeopardy, and gave them a quiet opportunity of fortifying their camp.

CHAPTER 3.

HOW THE SEDITION WAS AGAIN REVIVED WITHIN JERUSALEM AND YET THE JEWS CONTRIVED SNARES FOR THE ROMANS. HOW TITUS ALSO THREATENED HIS SOLDIERS FOR THEIR UNGOVERNABLE RASHNESS.

1. (98) AS now the war abroad ceased for a while, the sedition within was revived; (99) and on the feast of unleavened bread, which was now come, it being the fourteenth day of the month Xanthicus, [Nisan,] when it is believed the Jews were first freed from the Egyptians, Eleazar and his party opened the gates of this [inmost court of the] temple, and admitted such of the people as were desirous to worship God into it. (100) But John made use of this festival as a cloak for his treacherous designs, and armed the most inconsiderable of his own party, the greater part of whom were not purified, with weapons concealed under their garments, and sent them with great zeal into the temple, in order to seize upon it; which armed men, when they were gotten in, threw their garments away, and presently appeared in their armor. (101) Upon which there was a very great disorder and disturbance about the holy house; while the people, who had no concern in the sedition, supposed that this assault was made against all without distinction, as the zealots thought it was made against themselves only. (102) So these left off guarding the gates any longer, and leaped down from their battlements before they came to an engagement, and fled away into the subterranean caverns of the temple; while the people that stood trembling at the altar, and about the holy house, were rolled on heaps together, and trampled upon, and were beaten both with wooden and with iron weapons without mercy. (103) Such also as had differences with others slew many persons that were quiet, out of their own private enmity and hatred, as if they were opposite to the seditious; and all those that had formerly offended any of these plotters were now known, and were now led away to the slaughter; (104) and when they had done abundance of horrid mischief to the guiltless, they granted a truce to the guilty, and let those go off that came cut of the caverns. These followers of John also did now seize upon this inner temple, and upon all the warlike engines therein, and then ventured to oppose Simon. (105) And thus that sedition, which had been divided into three factions, was now reduced to two.

2. (106) But Titus, intending to pitch his camp nearer to the city than Scopus, placed as many of his choice horsemen and footmen as he thought sufficient opposite to the Jews, to prevent their sallying out upon them, while he gave orders for the whole army to level the distance, as far as the wall of the city. (107) So they threw down all the hedges and walls which the inhabitants had made about their gardens and groves of trees, and cut down all the fruit trees that lay between them and the wall of the city, and filled up all the hollow places and the chasms, (108) and demolished the rocky precipices with iron instruments; and thereby made all the place level from Scopus to Herod's monuments, which adjoined to the pool called the Serpent's Pool.

3. (109) Now at this very time the Jews contrived the following stratagem against the Romans. (110) The bolder sort of the seditious went out at the towers, called the Women's Towers, as if they had been ejected out of the city by those who were for peace, and rambled about as if they were afraid of being assaulted by the Romans, and were in fear of one another; (111) while those that stood upon the wall, and seemed to be of the people's side, cried out aloud for peace, and entreated they might have security for their lives given them, and called for the Romans, promising to open the gates to them; and as they cried out after that manner, they threw stones at their own people, as though they would drive them away from the gates. (112) These also pretended that they were excluded by force, and that they petitioned those that were within to let them in; and rushing upon the Romans perpetually, with violence, they then came back, and seemed to be in great disorder. (113) Now the Roman soldiers thought this cunning stratagem of theirs was to be believed real, and thinking they had the one party under their power, and could punish them as they pleased, and hoping that the other party would open their gates to them, set to the execution of their designs accordingly. (114) But for Titus himself, he had this surprising conduct of the Jews in suspicion; for whereas he had invited them to come to terms of accommodation, by Josephus, but one day before, he could then receive no civil answer

from them; so he ordered the soldiers to stay where they were. (115) However, some of them that were set in the front of the works prevented him, and catching up their arms ran to the gates; (116) whereupon those that seemed to have been ejected at the first retired; but as soon as the soldiers were gotten between the towers on each side of the gate, the Jews ran out and encompassed them round, and fell upon them behind, (117) while that multitude which stood upon the wall threw a heap of stones and darts of all kinds at them, insomuch that they slew a considerable number, and wounded many more; (118) for it was not easy for the Romans to escape, by reason those behind them pressed them forward; besides which, the shame they were under for being mistaken, and the fear they were in of their commanders, engaged them to persevere in their mistake; (119) wherefore they fought with their spears a great while, and received many blows from the Jews, though indeed they gave them as many blows again, and at last repelled those that had encompassed them about, while the Jews pursued them as they retired, and followed them, and threw darts at them as far as the monuments of queen Helena.

4. (120) After this these Jews, without keeping any decorum, grew insolent upon their good fortune, and jested upon the Romans for being deluded by the trick they bad put upon them, and making a noise with beating their shields, leaped for gladness, and made joyful exclamations; (121) while these soldiers were received with threatenings by their officers, and with indignation by Caesar himself, [who spake to them thus]: These Jews, who are only conducted by their madness, do every thing with care and circumspection; they contrive stratagems, and lay ambushes, and fortune gives success to their stratagems, because they are obedient, and preserve their goodwill and fidelity to one another; (122) while the Romans, to whom fortune uses to be ever subservient, by reason of their good order, and ready submission to their commanders, have now had ill success by their contrary behavior, and by not being able to restrain their hands from action, they have been caught; and that which is the most to their reproach, they have gone on without their commanders, in the very presence of Caesar. (123) "Truly," says Titus, "the laws of war cannot but groan heavily, as will my father also himself, when he shall be informed of this wound that hath been given us, (124) since he who is grown old in wars did never make so great a mistake. Our laws of war do also ever inflict capital punishment on those that in the least break into good order, while at this time they have seen an entire army run into disorder. (125) However, those that have been so insolent shall be made immediately sensible, that even they who conquer among the Romans without orders for fighting are to be under disgrace." (126) When Titus had enlarged upon this matter before the commanders, it appeared evident that he would execute the law against all those that were concerned; so these soldiers' minds sunk down in despair, as expecting to be put to death, and that justly and quickly. (127) However, the other legions came round about Titus, and entreated his favor to these their fellow soldiers, and made supplication to him, that he would pardon the rashness of a few, on account of the better obedience of all the rest; and promised for them that they should make amends for their present fault, by their more virtuous behavior for the time to come.

5. (128) So Caesar complied with their desires, and with what prudence dictated to him also; for he esteemed it fit to punish single persons by real executions, but that the punishment of great multitudes should proceed no further than reproofs; (129) so he was reconciled to the soldiers, but gave them a special charge to act more wisely for the future; and he considered with himself how he might be even with the Jews for their stratagem. (130) And now when the space between the Romans and the wall had been leveled, which was done in four days, and as he was desirous to bring the baggage of the army, with the rest of the multitude that followed him, safely to the camp, he set the strongest part of his army over against that wall which lay on the north quarter of the city, and over against the western part of it, and made his army seven deep, (131) with the foot-men placed before them, and the horsemen behind them, each of the last in three ranks, whilst the archers stood in the midst in seven ranks. (132) And now as the Jews were prohibited, by so great a body of men, from making sallies upon the Romans, both the beasts that bare the burdens, and belonged to the three legions, and the rest of the multitude, marched on without any fear. (133) But as for Titus himself, he was but about two furlongs distant from the wall, at that part of it where was the corner (cf. 2 Chronicles 26:9) and over against that tower which was called Psephinus, at which tower the compass of the wall belonging to the north bended, and extended itself over against the west; (134) but the other part of the army fortified itself at the tower called Hippicus, and was distant, in like manner, by two furlongs from the city. (135) However, the tenth legion continued in its own place, upon the Mount of Olives.

Serpent's Pool, known today as the Sultan's Pool, now dry, is situated at the foot of Yemin Moshe (in background) and opposite the Old City of Jerusalem. (photo Ron Almog, via Wikimedia Commons)

CHAPTER 4.

THE DESCRIPTION OF JERUSALEM.

1. (136) THE city of Jerusalem was fortified with three walls, on such parts as were not encompassed with unpassable valleys; for in such places it had but one wall. The city was built upon two hills, which are opposite to one another, and have a valley to divide them asunder; at which valley the corresponding rows of houses on both hills end. (137) Of these hills, that which contains the upper city is much higher, and in length more

The Western Wall plaza, site of the Xystus and council-house. (photo Samuel Magal)

direct. Accordingly, it was called the "Citadel," by king David; he was the father of that Solomon who built this temple at the first; but it is by us called the "Upper Market-place." But the other hill, which was called "Acra," and sustains the lower city, is of the shape of a moon when she is horned; (138) over against this there was a third hill, but naturally lower than Acra, and parted formerly from the other by a broad valley. (139) However, in those times when the Asamoneans reigned, they filled up that valley with earth, and had a mind to join the city to the temple. They then took off part of the height of Acra, and reduced it to be of less elevation than it was before, that the temple might be superior to it. (140) Now the Valley of the Cheesemongers, as it was called, and was that which we told you before distinguished the hill of the upper city from that of the lower, extended as far as Siloam; for that is the name of a fountain which hath sweet water in it, and this in great plenty also. (141) But on the outsides, these hills are surrounded by deep valleys, and by reason of the precipices to them belonging on both sides they are every where unpassable.

Late 19th century photograph of the Tombs of the Kings. (Library of Congress)

2. (142) Now, of these three walls, the old one was hard to be taken, both by reason of the valleys, and of that hill on which it was built, and which was above them. (143) But besides that great advantage, as to the place where they were situated, it was also built very strong; because David and Solomon, and the following kings, were very zealous about this work. (144) Now that wall began on the north, at the tower called "Hippicus," and extended as far as the "Xystus," a place so called, and then, joining to the council-house, ended at the west cloister of the temple. (145) But if we go the other way westward, it began at the same place, and extended through a place called "Bethso," to the gate of the Essens; and after that it

went southward, having its bending above the fountain Siloam, where it also bends again towards the east at Solomon's pool, and reaches as far as a certain place which they called "Ophlas," where it was joined to the eastern cloister of the temple. (146) The second wall took its beginning from that gate which they called "Gennath," which belonged to the first wall; it only encompassed the northern quarter of the city, and reached as far as the tower Antonia. (147) The beginning of the third wall was at the tower Hippicus, whence it reached as far as the north quarter of the city, and the tower Psephinus, and then was so far extended till it came over against the monuments of Helena, which Helena was queen of Adiabene, the daughter of Izates; it then extended further to a great length, and passed by the sepulchral caverns of the kings, and bent again at the tower of the corner, at the monument which is called the "Monument of the Fuller," and joined to the old wall at the valley called the "Valley of Cedron." (148) It was Agrippa who encompassed the parts added to the old city with this wall, which had been all naked before; for as the city grew more populous, it gradually crept beyond its old limits, (149) and those parts of it that stood northward of the temple, and joined that hill to the city, made it considerably larger, and occasioned that hill, which is in number the fourth, and is called "Bezetha," to be inhabited also. It lies over against the tower Antonia, but is divided from it by a deep valley, (150) which was dug on purpose, and that in order to hinder the foundations of the tower of Antonia from joining to this hill, and thereby affording an opportunity for getting to it with ease, and hindering the security that arose from its superior elevation; (151) for which reason also that depth of the ditch made the elevation of the towers more remarkable. This new-built part of the city was called "Bezetha," in our language, which, if interpreted in the Grecian language, may be called "the New City." (152) Since, therefore, its inhabitants stood in need of a covering, the father of the present king, and of the same name with him, Agrippa, began that wall we spoke of; but he left off building it when he had only laid the foundations, out of the fear he was in of Claudius Caesar, lest he should suspect that so strong a wall was built in order to make some innovation in public affairs; (153) for the city could no way have been taken if that wall had been finished in the manner it was begun; as its parts were connected together by stones twenty cubits long, and ten cubits broad, which could never have been either easily undermined by any iron tools, or shaken by any engines. (154) The wall was, however, ten cubits wide, and it would probably have had a height greater than that, had not his zeal who began it been hindered from exerting itself. (155) After this, it was erected with great diligence by the Jews, as high as twenty cubits, above which it had battlements of two cubits, and turrets of three cubits altitude, insomuch that the entire altitude extended as far as twenty-five cubits.

3. (156) Now the towers that were upon it were twenty cubits in breadth, and twenty cubits in height; they were square and solid, as was the wall itself, wherein the niceness of the joints, and the beauty of the stones, were no way inferior to those of the holy house itself. (157) Above this solid altitude of the towers, which was twenty cubits, there were rooms of great magnificence, and over them upper rooms, and cisterns to receive rain-water. They were many in number, and the steps by which you ascended up to them were every one broad: (158) of these towers then the third wall had ninety, and the spaces between them were each two hundred cubits; but in the middle wall were forty towers, and the old wall

M. Avi-Yonah's scale model of the upper city of Jerusalem during the Second Temple period, now at the Israel Museum. (photo Samuel Magal)

Scale model of the three Herodian towers, from left to right, Phasaelus, Hippicus and Mariamne. (photo Zachary Wong)

was parted into sixty, (159) while the whole compass of the city was thirty-three furlongs. Now the third wall was all of it wonderful; yet was the tower Psephinus elevated above it at the north-west corner, and there Titus pitched his own tent; (160) for being seventy cubits high it both afforded a prospect of Arabia at sun-rising, as well as it did of the utmost limits of the Hebrew possessions at the sea westward. Moreover, it was an octagon, (161) and over against it was the tower Hippicus, and hard by two others were erected by king Herod, in the old wall. These were for largeness, beauty, and strength beyond all that were in the habitable earth; (162) for besides the magnanimity of his nature, and his magnificence towards the city on other occasions, he built these after such an extraordinary manner, to gratify his own private affections, and dedicated these towers to the memory of those three persons who had been the dearest to him, and from whom he named them. They were his brother, his friend, and his wife. This wife he had slain, out of his love [and jealousy], as we have already related; the other two he lost in war, as they were courageously fighting. (163) Hippicus, so named from his friend, was square; its length and breadth were each twenty-five cubits, and its height thirty, and it had no vacuity in it. (164) Over this solid building, which was composed of great stones united together, there was a reservoir twenty cubits deep, (165) over which there was a house of two stories, whose height was twenty-five cubits, and divided into several parts; over which were battlements of two cubits, and turrets all round of three cubits high, insomuch that the entire height added together amounted to fourscore cubits. (166) The second tower, which he named from his brother Phasaelus, had its breadth and its height equal, each of them forty cubits; (167) over which was its solid height of forty cubits; over which a cloister went round about, whose height was ten cubits, and it was covered from enemies by breast-works and bulwarks. (168) There was also built over that cloister another tower, parted into magnificent rooms, and a place for bathing; so that this tower wanted nothing that might make it appear to be a royal palace. (169) It was also adorned with battlements and turrets, more than was the foregoing, and the entire altitude was about ninety cubits; the appearance of it resembled the tower of Pharus, which exhibited a fire to such as sailed to Alexandria, but was much larger than it in compass. This was now converted to a house, wherein Simon exercised his tyrannical authority. (170) The third tower was Mariamne, for that was his queen's name; it was solid as high as twenty cubits; its breadth and its length were twenty cubits, and were equal to each other; (171) its upper buildings were more magnificent, and had greater variety, than the other towers had; for the king thought it most proper for him to adorn that which was denominated from his wife, better than those denominated from men, as those were built stronger than this that bore his wife's name. The entire height of this tower was fifty cubits.

4. (172) Now as these towers were so very tall, they appeared much taller by the place on which they stood; (173) for that very old wall wherein they were was built on a high hill, and was itself a kind of elevation that was still thirty cubits taller; over which were the towers situated, and thereby were made much higher to appearance. (174) The largeness also of the stones was wonderful; for they were not made of common small stones, nor of such large ones only as men could carry, but they were of white marble, cut out of the rock; (175) each stone was twenty cubits in length, and ten in breadth, and five in depth. They were so exactly united to one another, that each tower looked like one entire rock of stone, so growing naturally, and afterward cut by the hand of the artificers into their present shape and corners; so little, or not at all, did their joints or connexion appear. (176) Now as these towers were themselves on the north side of the wall, the king had a palace inwardly thereto adjoined, which exceeds all my ability to describe it; (177) for it was so very curious as to want no cost nor skill in its construction, but was entirely walled about to the height of thirty cubits, and was adorned with towers at equal distances, and with large bed-chambers, that would contain beds for a hundred guests a-piece, (178) in which the variety of the stones is not to be expressed; for a large quantity of those that were rare of that kind was collected together. Their roofs were also wonderful, both for the length of the beams, and the splendor of their ornaments. (179) The number of the rooms was also very great, and the variety of the figures that were about them was prodigious; their furniture was complete, and the greatest part of the vessels that were put in them was of silver and gold. (180) There were besides many porticoes, one beyond another, round about, and in each of those porticoes curious pillars; yet were all the courts that were exposed to the air everywhere green. (181) There were, moreover, several groves of trees, and long walks through them, with deep canals, and cisterns, that in several parts were filled with brazen statues, through which the water ran out. There were withal many dovecourts of tame pigeons about the canals. (182) But indeed it is not possible to give a complete description of these palaces; and the very remembrance of them is a torment to one, as putting one in mind what vastly rich buildings that fire which was kindled by the robbers hath consumed; (183) for these were not burnt by the Romans, but by these internal plotters, as we have already related, in the beginning of their rebellion. That fire began at the tower of Antonia, and went on to the palaces, and consumed the upper parts of the three towers themselves.

CHAPTER 5.

A DESCRIPTION OF THE TEMPLE.

1. (184) NOW this temple, as I have already said, was built upon a strong hill. At first the plain at the top was hardly sufficient for the holy house and the altar, for the ground about it was very uneven, and like a precipice; (185) but when king Solomon, who was the person that built the temple, had built a wall to it on its east side, there was then added one cloister founded on a bank cast up for it, and on the other parts the holy house stood naked. But in future ages the people added new banks, and the hill became a larger plain. (186) They then broke down the wall on the north side, and took in as much as sufficed afterward for the compass of the entire temple. (187) And when they had built walls on three sides of the temple round about, from the bottom of the hill, and had performed a work that was greater than could be hoped for, (in which work long ages were spent by them, as well as all their sacred treasures were exhausted, which were still replenished by those tributes which were sent to God from the whole habitable earth,) they then encompassed their upper courts with cloisters, as well as they [afterward] did the lowest [court of the] temple. (188) The lowest part of this was erected to the height of three hundred cubits, and in some places more; yet did not the entire depth of the foundations appear, for they brought earth, and filled up the valleys, as being desirous to make them on a level with the narrow streets of the city; (189) wherein they made use of stones of forty cubits in magnitude; for the great plenty of money they then had, and the liberality of the people, made this attempt of theirs to succeed to an incredible degree; and what could not be so much as hoped for as ever to be accomplished, was, by perseverance and length of time, brought to perfection.

2. (190) Now for the works that were above these foundations, these were not unworthy of such foundations; for all the cloisters were double, and the pillars to them belonging were twenty-five cubits in height, and supported the cloisters. These pillars were of one entire stone each of them, and that stone was white marble; (191) and the roofs were adorned with cedar, curiously graven. The natural magnificence, and excellent polish, and the harmony of the joints in these cloisters, afforded a prospect that was very remarkable; nor was it on the outside adorned with any work of the painter or engraver. (192) The cloisters [of the outmost court] were in breadth thirty cubits, while the entire compass of it was by measure six furlongs, including the tower of Antonia; those entire courts that were exposed to the air were laid with stones of all sorts. (193) When you go through these [first] cloisters, unto the second [court of the] temple, there was a partition made of stone all round, whose height was three cubits: its construction was very elegant; (194) upon it stood pillars, at equal distances from one another, declaring the law of purity, some in Greek, and some in Roman letters, that "no foreigner should go within that sanctuary" for that second [court of the] temple was called "the Sanctuary," (195) and was ascended to by fourteen steps from the first court. This court was four-square, and had a wall about it peculiar to itself; (196) the height of its buildings, although it were on the outside forty cubits, was hidden by the steps, and on the inside that height was but twenty-five cubits; for it being built over against a higher part of the hill with steps, it was no further to be entirely discerned within, being covered by the hill itself. (197) Beyond these thirteen steps there was the distance of ten cubits; this was all plain; (198) whence there were other steps, each of five cubits a-piece, that led to the gates, which gates on the north and south sides were eight, on each of those sides four, and of necessity two

M. Avi-Yonah's scale model of the Herodian temple, now on display at The Israel Museum in Jerusalem. (photo Samuel Magal)

Greek inscription banning Gentiles from entering the sanctified area of the Temple Mount. (photo R. Steven Notley)

on the east. For since there was a partition built for the women on that side, as the proper place wherein they were to worship, there was a necessity for a second gate for them: this gate was cut out of its wall, over against the first gate. (199) There was also on the other sides one southern and one northern gate, through which was a passage into the court of the women; for as to the other gates, the women were not allowed to pass through them; nor when they went through their own gate could they go beyond their own wall. This place was allotted to the women of our own country, and of other countries, provided they were of the same nation, and that equally. (200) The western part of this court had no gate at all, but the wall was built entire on that side. But then the cloisters which were betwixt the gates extended from the wall inward, before the chambers; for they were supported by very fine and large pillars. These cloisters were single, and, excepting their magnitude, were no way inferior to those of the lower court.

3. (201) Now nine of these gates were on every side covered over with gold and silver, as were the jambs of their doors and their lintels; but there was one gate that was without the [inward court of the] holy house, which was of Corinthian brass, and greatly excelled those that were only covered over with silver and gold. (202) Each gate had two doors, whose height was severally thirty cubits, and their breadth fifteen. (203) However, they had large spaces within of thirty cubits, and had on each side rooms, and those, both in breadth and in length, built like towers, and their height was above forty cubits. Two pillars did also support these rooms, and were in circumference twelve cubits. (204) Now the magnitudes of the other gates were equal one to another; but that over the Corinthian gate, which opened on the east over against the gate of the holy house itself, was much larger; (205) for its height was fifty cubits; and its doors were forty cubits; and it was adorned after a most costly manner, as having much richer and thicker plates of silver and gold upon them than the other. These nine gates had that silver and gold poured upon them by Alexander, the father of Tiberius [Alexander]. (206) Now there were fifteen steps, which led away from the wall of the court of the women to this greater gate; whereas those that led thither from the other gates were five steps shorter.

4. (207) As to the holy house itself, which was placed in the midst [of the inmost court], that most sacred part of the temple, it was ascended to by twelve steps; and in front its height and its breadth were equal, and each a hundred cubits, though it was behind forty cubits narrower; for on its front it had what may be styled shoulders on each side, that passed twenty cubits further. (208) Its first gate was seventy cubits high, and twenty-five cubits broad; but this gate had no doors; for it represented the universal visibility of heaven, and that it cannot be excluded from any place. Its front was covered with gold all over, and through it the first part of the house, that was more inward, did all of it appear; which, as it was very large, so did all the parts about the more inward gate appear to shine to those that saw them; (209) but then, as the entire house was divided into two parts within, it was only the first part of it that was open to our view. Its height extended all along to ninety cubits in height, and its length was fifty cubits, and its breadth twenty. (210) But that gate which was at this end of the first part of the house was, as we have already observed, all over covered with gold, as was its whole wall about it; it had also golden vines above it, from which clusters of grapes hung as tall as a man's height. (211) But then this house, as it was divided into two parts, the inner part was lower than the appearance of the outer, and had golden doors of fifty-five cubits altitude, and sixteen in breadth; (212) but before these doors there was a veil of equal largeness with the doors. It was a Babylonian curtain, embroidered with blue, and fine linen, and scarlet, and purple, and of a contexture that was truly wonderful. Nor was this mixture of colors without its mystical interpretation, but was a kind of image of the universe; (213) for by the scarlet there seemed to be enigmatically signified fire, by the fine flax the earth, by the blue the air, and by the purple the sea; two of them having their colors the foundation of this resemblance; but the fine flax and the purple have their own origin for that foundation, the earth producing the one, and the sea the other. (214) This curtain had also embroidered upon it all that was mystical in the heavens, excepting that of the [twelve] signs, representing living creatures.

5. (215) When any persons entered into the temple, its floor received them. This part of the temple therefore was in height sixty cubits, and its length the same; whereas its breadth was but twenty cubits: (216) but still that sixty cubits in length was divided again, and the first part of it was cut off at forty cubits, and had in it three things that were very wonderful and famous among all mankind, the candlestick, the table [of shew-bread], and the altar of incense. (217) Now the seven lamps signified the seven planets; for so many there were springing out of the candlestick. Now the twelve loaves that were upon the table signified the circle of the zodiac and the year; (218) but the altar of incense, by its thirteen kinds of sweet-smelling spices with which the sea replenished it, signified that God is the possessor of all things that are both in the uninhabitable and habitable parts of the earth, and that they are all to be dedicated to his use. (219) But the inmost part of the temple of all was of twenty cubits. This was also separated from the outer part by a veil. In this there was nothing at all. It was inaccessible and inviolable, and not to be seen by any; and was called the Holy of Holies. (220) Now, about the sides of the lower part of the temple, there were little houses, with passages out of one into another; there were a great many of them, and they were of three stories high; there were also entrances on each side into them from the gate of the temple. (221) But the superior part of the temple had no such little houses any further, because the temple was there narrower, and forty cubits higher, and of a smaller body than the lower parts of it. Thus we collect that the whole height, including the sixty cubits from the floor, amounted to a hundred cubits.

6. (222) Now the outward face of the temple in its front wanted nothing that was likely to surprise either men's minds or their eyes; for it was covered all over with plates of gold of great weight, and, at the first rising of the sun, reflected back a very fiery splendor, and

(left) The priestly garments and (right) detail of the breastplate. (Carta collection)

made those who forced themselves to look upon it to turn their eyes away, just as they would have done at the sun's own rays. (223) But this temple appeared to strangers, when they were coming to it at a distance, like a mountain covered with snow; for as to those parts of it that were not gilt, they were exceeding white. (224) On its top it had spikes with sharp points, to prevent any pollution of it by birds sitting upon it. Of its stones, some of them were forty-five cubits in length, five in height, and six in breadth. (225) Before this temple stood the altar, fifteen cubits high, and equal both in length and breadth; each of which dimensions was fifty cubits. The figure it was built in was a square, and it had corners like horns; and the passage up to it was by an insensible acclivity. It was formed without any iron tool, nor did any such iron tool so much as touch it at any time. (226) There was also a wall of partition, about a cubit in height, made of fine stones, and so as to be grateful to the sight; this encompassed the holy house and the altar, and kept the people that were on the outside off from the priests. (227) Moreover, those that had the gonorrhea and the leprosy were excluded out of the city entirely; women also, when their courses were upon them, were shut out of the temple; nor when they were free from that impurity, were they allowed to go beyond the limit before-mentioned; men also, that were not thoroughly pure, were prohibited to come into the inner [court of the] temple; nay, the priests themselves that were not pure were prohibited to come into it also.

7. (228) Now all those of the stock of the priests that could not minister by reason of some defect in their bodies, came within the partition, together with those that had no such imperfection, and had their share with them by reason of their stock, but still made use of none except their own private garments; for nobody but he that officiated had on his sacred garments; (229) but then those priests that were without any blemish upon them went up to the altar clothed in fine linen. They abstained chiefly from wine, out of this fear, lest otherwise they should transgress some rules of their ministration. (230) The high priest did also go up with them; not always indeed, but on the seventh days and new moons, and if any festivals belonging to our nation, which we celebrate every year, happened. (231) When he officiated, he had on a pair of breeches that reached beneath his privy parts to his thighs, and had on an inner garment of linen, together with a blue garment, round, without seam, with fringe work, and reaching to the feet. There were also golden bells that hung upon the fringes, and pomegranates intermixed among them. The bells signified thunder, and the pomegranates lightning. (232) But that girdle that tied the garment to the breast was embroidered with five rows of various colors, of gold, and purple, and scarlet, as also of fine linen and blue, with which colors we told you before the veils of the temple were embroidered also. (233) The like embroidery was upon the ephod; but the quantity of gold therein was greater. Its figure was that of a stomacher for the breast. There were upon it two golden buttons like small shields, which buttoned the ephod to the garment; in these buttons were enclosed two very large and very excellent sardonyxes, having the names of the tribes of that nation engraved upon them: (234) on the other part there hung twelve stones, three in a row one way, and four in the other; a sardius, a topaz, and an emerald; a carbuncle, a jasper, and a sapphire; an agate, an amethyst, and a ligure; an onyx, a beryl, and a chrysolite; upon every one of which was again engraved one of the forementioned names of the tribes. (235) A mitre also of fine linen encompassed his head, which was tied by a blue ribbon, about which there was another golden crown, in which was engraven the sacred name [of God]: it consists of four vowels. (236) However, the high priest did not wear these garments at other times, but a more plain habit; he only did it when he went into the most sacred part of the temple, which he did but once in a year, on that day when our custom is for all of us to keep a fast to God. (237) And thus much concerning the city and the temple; but for the customs and laws hereto relating, we shall speak more accurately another time; for there remain a great many things thereto relating which have not been here touched upon.

SUPPLIES TO THE TEMPLE AND THE BRINGING OF THE *OMER*

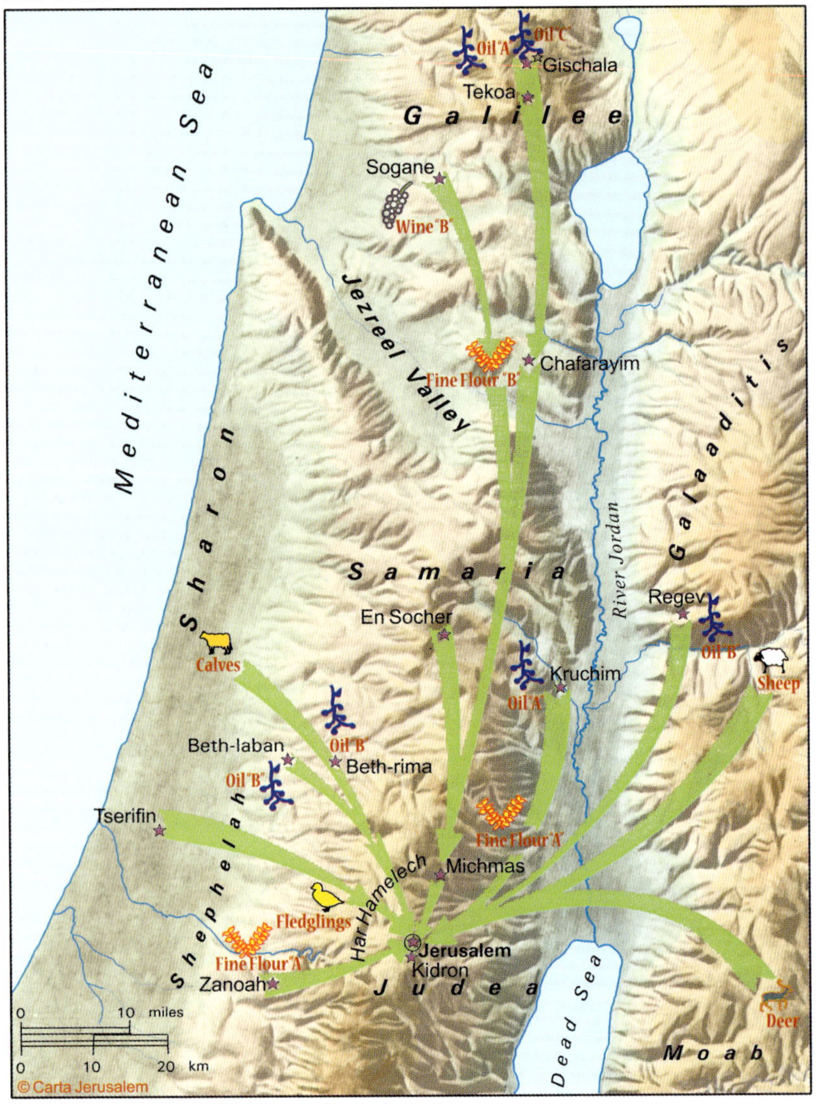

(from *Jerusalem City of the Great King* / R. Steven Notley)

8. (238) Now as to the tower of Antonia, it was situated at the corner of two cloisters of the court of the temple; of that on the west, and that on the north; it was erected upon a rock of fifty cubits in height, and was on a great precipice; it was the work of king Herod, wherein he demonstrated his natural magnanimity. (239) In the first place, the rock itself was covered over with smooth pieces of stone, from its foundation, both for ornament, and that any one who would either try to get up or to go down it might not be able to hold his feet upon it. (240) Next to this, and before you come to the edifice of the tower itself, there was a wall three cubits high; but within that wall all the space of the tower of Antonia itself was built upon, to the height of forty cubits. (241) The inward parts had the largeness and form of a palace, it being parted into all kinds of rooms and other conveniences, such as courts, and places for bathing, and broad spaces for camps; insomuch that, by having all conveniences that cities wanted, it might seem to be composed of several cities, but by its magnificence it seemed a palace. (242) And as the entire structure resembled that of a tower, it contained also four other distinct towers at its four corners; whereof the others were but fifty cubits high; whereas that which lay upon the southeast corner was seventy cubits high, that from thence the whole temple might be viewed; (243) but on the corner where it joined to the two cloisters of the temple, it had passages down to them both, through which the guard (244) (for there always lay in this tower a Roman legion) went several ways among the cloisters, with their arms, on the Jewish festivals, in order to watch the people, that they might not there attempt to make any innovations; (245) for the temple was a fortress that guarded the city, as was the tower of Antonia a guard to the temple; and in that tower were the guards of those three. There was also a peculiar fortress belonging to the upper city, which was Herod's palace; (246) but for the hill Bezetha, it was divided from the tower Antonia, as we have already told you; and as that hill on which the tower of Antonia stood was the highest of these three, so did it adjoin to the new city, and was the only place that hindered the sight of the temple on the north. (247) And this shall suffice at present to have spoken about the city and the walls about it, because I have proposed to myself to make a more accurate description of it elsewhere.

CHAPTER 6.

CONCERNING THE TYRANTS SIMON AND JOHN. HOW ALSO AS TITUS WAS GOING ROUND THE WALL OF THIS CITY NICANOR WAS WOUNDED BY A DART; WHICH ACCIDENT PROVOKED TITUS TO PRESS ON THE SIEGE.

1. (248) NOW the warlike men that were in the city, and the multitude of the seditious that were with Simon, were ten thousand, besides the Idumeans. Those ten thousand had fifty commanders, over whom this Simon was supreme. (249) The Idumeans that paid him homage were five thousand, and had eight commanders, among whom those of greatest fame were Jacob the son of Sosas, and Simon the son of Cathlas. (250) Jotre, who had seized upon the temple, had six thousand armed men under twenty commanders; the zealots also that had come over to him, and left off their opposition, were two thousand four hundred, and had the same commander that they had formerly, Eleazar, together with Simon the son of Arinus. (251) Now, while these factions fought one against another, the people were their prey on both sides, as we have said already; and that part of the people who would not join with them in their wicked practices were plundered by both factions. (252) Simon held the upper city, and the great wall as far as Cedron, and as much of the old wall as bent from Siloam to the east, and which went down to the palace of Monobazus, who was king of the Adiabeni, beyond Euphrates; (253) he also held that fountain, and the Acra, which was no other than the lower city; he also held all that reached to the palace of queen Helena, the mother of Monobazus. (254) But John held the temple, and the parts thereto adjoining, for a great way, as also Ophla, and the valley called "the Valley of Cedron;" and when the parts that were interposed between their possessions were burnt by them, they left a space wherein they might fight with each other; (255) for this internal sedition did not cease even when the Romans were encamped near their very wall. But although they had grown wiser at the first onset the Romans made upon them, this lasted but a while; for they returned to their former madness, and separated one from another, and fought it out, and did everything that the besiegers could desire them to do; (256) for they never suffered any thing that was worse from the Romans than they made each other suffer; nor was there any misery endured by the city after these men's actions that could be esteemed new. But it was most of all unhappy before it was overthrown, while those that took it did it a greater kindness (257) for I venture to affirm that the sedition destroyed the city, and the Romans destroyed the sedition, which it was a much harder thing to do than to destroy the walls; so that we may justly ascribe our misfortunes to our own people, and the just vengeance taken on them to the Romans; as to which matter let every one determine

by the actions on both sides.

2. (258) Now when affairs within the city were in this posture, Titus went round the city on the outside with some chosen horsemen, and looked about for a proper place where he might make an impression upon the walls; (259) but as he was in doubt where he could possibly make an attack on any side, (for the place was no way accessible where the valleys were, and on the other side the first wall appeared too strong to be shaken by the engines,) he thereupon thought it best to make his assault upon the monument of John the high priest; (260) for there it was that the first fortification was lower, and the second was not joined to it, the builders neglecting to build strong where the new city was not much inhabited; here also was an easy passage to the third wall, through which he thought to take the upper city, and, through the tower of Antonia, the temple itself. (261) But at this time, as he was going round about the city, one of his friends, whose name was Nicanor, was wounded with a dart on his left shoulder, as he approached, together with Josephus, too near the wall, and attempted to discourse to those that were upon the wall, about terms of peace; for he was a person known by them. (262) On this account it was that Caesar, as soon as he knew their vehemence, that they would not hear even such as approached them to persuade them to what tended to their own preservation, was provoked to press on the siege. He also at the same time gave his soldiers leave to set the suburbs on fire, and ordered that they should bring timber together, and raise banks against the city; (263) and when he had parted his army into three parts, in order to set about those works, he placed those that shot darts and the archers in the midst of the banks that were then raising; before whom he placed those engines that threw javelins, and darts, and stones, that he might prevent the enemy from sallying out upon their works, and might hinder those that were upon the wall from being able to obstruct them. (264) So the trees were now cut down immediately, and the suburbs left naked. But now while the timber was carrying to raise the banks, and the whole army was earnestly engaged in their works, the Jews were not, however, quiet; (265) and it happened that the people of Jerusalem, who had been hitherto plundered and murdered, were now of good courage, and supposed they should have a breathing time, while the others were very busy in opposing their enemies without the city, and that they should now be avenged on those that had been the authors of their miseries, in case the Romans did but get the victory.

3. (266) However, John staid behind, out of his fear of Simon, even while his own men were earnest in making a sally upon their enemies without. (267) Yet did not Simon lie still, for he lay near the place of the siege; he brought his engines of war, and disposed of them at due distances upon the wall, both those which they took from Cestius formerly, and those which they got when they seized the garrison that lay in the tower Antonia. (268) But though they had these engines in their possession, they had so little skill in using them, that they were in great measure useless to them; but a few there were who had been taught by deserters how to use them, which they did use, though after an awkward manner. So they cast stones and arrows at those that were making the banks; they also ran out upon them by companies, and fought with them. (269) Now those that were at work covered themselves with hurdles spread over their banks, and their engines were opposed to them when they made their excursions. The engines, that all the legions had ready prepared for them, were admirably contrived; but still more extraordinary ones belonged to the tenth legion: those that threw darts and those that threw stones were more forcible and larger than the rest, by which they not only repelled the excursions of

M. Avi-Yonah's scale model of the palaces of the kings of Adiabene, south of the Temple Mount. (now at the Israel Museum; photo Samuel Magal)

the Jews, but drove those away that were upon the walls also. (270) Now the stones that were cast were of the weight of a talent, and were carried two furlongs and further. The blow they gave was no way to be sustained, not only by those that stood first in the way, but by those that were beyond them for a great space. (271) As for the Jews, they at first watched the coming of the stone, for it was of a white color, and could therefore not only be perceived by the great noise it made, but could be seen also before it came by its brightness; (272) accordingly the watchmen that sat upon the towers gave them notice when the engine was let go, and the stone came from it, and cried out aloud, in their own country language, THE STONE COMETH so those that were in its way stood off, and threw themselves down upon the ground; by which means, and by their thus guarding themselves, the stone fell down and did them no harm. (273) But the Romans contrived how to prevent that by blacking the stone, who then could aim at them with success, when the stone was not discerned beforehand, as it had been till then; and so they destroyed many of them at one blow. (274) Yet did not the Jews, under all this distress, permit the Romans to raise their banks in quiet; but they shrewdly and boldly exerted themselves, and repelled them both by night and by day.

4. (275) And now, upon the finishing the Roman works, the workmen measured the distance there was from the wall, and this by lead and a line, which they threw to it from their banks; for they could not measure it any otherwise, because the Jews would shoot at them, if they came to measure it themselves; and when they found that the engines could reach the wall, they brought

Reconstruction of a Roman siege tower and a battering ram protruding from it.
(Museo Della Civita Romano; photo Samuel Magal)

them thither. (276) Then did Titus set his engines at proper distances, so much nearer to the wall, that the Jews might not be able to repel them, and gave orders they should go to work; (277) and when thereupon a prodigious noise echoed round about from three places, and that on the sudden there was a great noise made by the citizens that were within the city, and no less a terror fell upon the seditious themselves; whereupon both sorts, seeing the common danger they were in, contrived to make a like defense. (278) So those of different factions cried out one to another, that they acted entirely as in concert with their enemies; whereas they ought however, notwithstanding God did not grant them a lasting concord, in their present circumstances, to lay aside their enmities one against another, and to unite together against the Romans. Accordingly, Simon gave those that came from the temple leave, by proclamation, to go upon the wall; John also himself, though he could not believe Simon was in earnest, gave them the same leave. (279) So on both sides they laid aside their hatred and their peculiar quarrels, and formed themselves into one body; they then ran round the walls, and having a vast number of torches with them, they threw them at the machines, and shot darts perpetually upon those that impelled those engines which battered the wall; (280) nay, the bolder sort leaped out by troops upon the hurdles that covered the machines, and pulled them to pieces, and fell upon those that belonged to them, and beat them, not so much by any skill they had, as principally by the boldness of their attacks. (281) However, Titus himself still sent assistance to those that were the hardest set, and placed both horsemen and archers on the several sides of the engines, and thereby beat off those that brought the fire to them; he also thereby repelled those that shot stones or darts from the towers, and then set the engines to work in good earnest; (282) yet did not the wall yield to these blows, excepting where the battering ram of the fifteenth legion moved the corner of a tower, while the wall itself continued unhurt; (283) for the wall was not presently in the same danger with the tower, which was extant far above it; nor could the fall of that part of the tower easily break down any part of the wall itself together with it.

5. (284) And now the Jews intermitted their sallies for a while; but when they observed the Romans dispersed all abroad at their works, and in their several camps, (for they thought the Jews had retired out of weariness and fear,) they all at once made a sally at the tower Hippicus, through an obscure gate, and at the same time brought fire to burn the works, and went boldly up to the Romans, and to their very fortifications themselves, (285) where, at the cry they made, those that were near them came presently to their assistance, and those farther off came running after them; and here the boldness of the Jews was too hard for the good order of the Romans; and as they beat those whom they first fell upon, so they pressed upon those that were now gotten together. (286) So this fight about the machines was very hot, while the one side tried hard to set them on fire, and the other side to prevent it; on both sides there was a confused cry made, and many of those in the forefront of the battle were slain. (287) However, the Jews were now too hard for the Romans, by the furious assaults they made like madmen; and the fire caught hold of the works, and both all those works, and the engines themselves, had been in danger of being burnt, had not many of these select soldiers that came from Alexandria opposed themselves to prevent it, and had they not behaved themselves with greater courage than they themselves supposed they could have done; for they outdid those in this fight that had greater reputation than themselves before. This was the state of things till Caesar took the stoutest of his horsemen, and attacked the enemy, (288) while he himself slew twelve of those that were in the forefront of the Jews; which death of these men, when the rest of the multitude saw, they gave way, and he pursued them, and drove them all into the city, and saved the works from the fire. (289) Now it happened at this fight that a certain Jew was taken alive, who, by Titus's order, was crucified before the wall, to see whether the rest of them would be aftrighted, and abate of their obstinacy. (290) But after the Jews were retired, John, who was commander of the Idumeans, and was talking to a certain soldier of his acquaintance before the wall, was wounded by a dart shot at him by an Arabian, and died immediately, leaving the greatest lamentation to the Jews, and sorrow to the seditious. For he was a man of great eminence, both for his actions and his conduct also.

CHAPTER 7.

HOW ONE OF THE TOWERS ERECTED BY THE ROMANS FELL DOWN OF ITS OWN ACCORD; AND HOW THE ROMANS AFTER GREAT SLAUGHTER HAD BEEN MADE GOT POSSESSION OF THE FIRST WALL. HOW ALSO TITUS MADE HIS ASSAULTS UPON THE SECOND WALL; AS ALSO CONCERNING LONGINUS THE ROMAN, AND CASTOR THE JEW.

1. (291) NOW, on the next night, a surprising disturbance fell upon the Romans; (292) for whereas Titus had given orders for the erection of three towers of fifty cubits high, that by setting men upon them at every bank, he might from thence drive those away who

were upon the wall, it so happened that one of these towers fell down about midnight; (293) and as its fall made a very great noise, fear fell upon the army, and they, supposing that the enemy was coming to attack them, ran all to their arms. (294) Whereupon a disturbance and a tumult arose among the legions, and as nobody could tell what had happened, they went on after a disconsolate manner; and seeing no enemy appear, they were afraid one of another, (295) and everyone demanded of his neighbor the watchword with great earnestness, as though the Jews had invaded their camp. And now were they like people under a panic fear, till Titus was informed of what had happened, and gave orders that all should be acquainted with it; and then, though with some difficulty, they got clear of the disturbance they had been under.

2. (296) Now these towers were very troublesome to the Jews, who otherwise opposed the Romans very courageously; for they shot at them out of their lighter engines from those towers, as they did also by those that threw darts, and the archers, and those that flung stones. (297) For neither could the Jews reach those that were over them, by reason of their height; and it was not practicable to take them, nor to overturn them, they were so heavy, nor to set them on fire, because they were covered with plates of iron. (298) So they retired out of the reach of the darts, and did no longer endeavor to hinder the impression of their rams, which, by continually beating upon the wall, did gradually prevail against it; (299) so that the wall already gave way to the Nico, for by that name did the Jews themselves call the greatest of their engines, because it conquered all things. And now they were for a long while grown weary of fighting, and of keeping guards, and were retired to lodge in the night time at a distance from the wall. (300) It was on other accounts also thought by them to be superfluous to guard the wall, there being besides that two other fortifications still remaining, and they being slothful, and their counsels having been ill concerted on all occasions; so a great many grew lazy and retired. (301) Then the Romans mounted the breach, where Nico had made one, and all the Jews left the guarding that wall, and retreated to the second wall; so those that had gotten over that wall opened the gates, and received all the army within it. (302) And thus did the Romans get possession of this first wall, on the fifteenth day of the siege, which was the seventh day of the month Artemisius, [Jyar,] when they demolished a great part of it, as well as they did of the northern parts of the city, which had been demolished also by Cestius formerly.

3. (303) And now Titus pitched his camp within the city, at that place which was called "the Camp of the Assyrians," having seized upon all that lay as far as Cedron, but took care to be out of the reach of the Jews' darts. He then presently began his attacks, (304) upon which the Jews divided themselves into several bodies, and courageously defended that wall; while John and his faction did it from the tower of Antonia, and from the northern cloister of the temple, and fought the Romans before the monuments of king Alexander; and Sireoh's army also took for their share the spot of ground that was near John's monument, and fortified it as far as to that gate where water was brought in to the tower Hippicus. (305) However, the Jews made violent sallies, and that frequently also, and in bodies together out of the gates, and there fought the Romans; and when they were pursued all together to the wall, they were beaten in those fights, as wanting the skill of the Romans. But when they fought them from the walls, they were too hard for them; (306) the Romans being encouraged by their power, joined to their skill, as were the Jews by their boldness, which was nourished by the fear they were in, and that hardiness which is natural to our nation under calamities; they were also encouraged still by

The line of the first wall can be traced here underneath the Ottoman wall south of the Citadel. (photo Samuel Magal)

the hope of deliverance, as were the Romans by their hopes of subduing them in a little time. (307) Nor did either side grow weary; but attacks and rightings upon the wall, and perpetual sallies out in bodies, were there all the day long; nor were there any sort of warlike engagements that were not then put in use. (308) And the night itself had much ado to part them, when they began to fight in the morning; nay, the night itself was passed without sleep on both sides, and was more uneasy than the day to them, while the one was afraid lest the wall should be taken, and the other lest the Jews should make sallies upon their camps; both sides also lay in their armor during the night time, and thereby were ready at the first appearance of light to go to the battle. (309) Now among the Jews the ambition was who should undergo the first dangers, and thereby gratify their commanders. Above all, they had a great veneration and dread of Simon; and to that degree was he regarded by every one of those that were under him, that at his command they were very ready to kill themselves with their own hands. (310) What made the Romans so courageous was their usual custom of conquering and disuse of being defeated, their constant wars, and perpetual warlike exercises, and the grandeur of their dominion; and what was now their chief encouragement—Titus who was present every where with them all; (311) for it appeared a terrible thing to grow weary while Caesar was there, and fought bravely as well as they did, and was himself at once an eye-witness of such as behaved themselves valiantly, and he who was to reward them also. It was, besides, esteemed an advantage at present to have any one's valor known by Caesar; on which account many of them appeared to have more alacrity than strength to answer it. (312) And now, as the Jews were about this time standing in array before the wall, and that in a strong body, and while both parties were throwing their darts at each other, Longinus, one of the equestrian order, leaped out of the army of the Romans, and leaped into the very midst of the army of the Jews; (313) and as they dispersed themselves upon the attack, he slew two of their men of the greatest courage; one of them he struck in his mouth as he was coming to meet him, the other was slain by him by that very dart which he drew out of the body of the other, with which he ran this man through his side as he was running away from him; and when he had done this, he first of all ran out of the midst of his enemies to his own side. (314) So this man signalized himself for his valor, and many there were who were ambitious of gaining the like reputation. (315) And now the Jews were unconcerned at what they suffered themselves from the Romans, and were only solicitous about what mischief they could do them; and death itself seemed a small matter to them, if at the same time they could but kill any one of their enemies. (316) But Titus took care to secure his own soldiers from harm, as well as to have them overcome their enemies. He also said that inconsiderate violence was madness, and that this alone was the true courage that was joined with good conduct. He therefore commanded his men to take care, when they fought their enemies, that they received no harm from them at the same time, and thereby show themselves to be truly valiant men.

4. (317) And now Titus brought one of his engines to the middle tower of the north part of the wall, in which a certain crafty Jew, whose name was Castor, lay in ambush, with ten others like himself, the rest being fled away by reason of the archers. (318) These men lay still for a while, as in great fear, under their breastplates; but when the tower was shaken, they arose, and Castor did then stretch out his hand, as a petitioner, and called for Caesar, and by his voice moved his compassion, and begged of him to have mercy upon them; (319) and Titus, in the innocency of his heart, believing him to be in earnest, and hoping that the Jews did now repent, stopped the working of the battering ram, and forbade them to shoot at the petitioners, and bid Castor say what he had a mind to say to him. (320) He said that he would come down, if he would give him his right hand for his security. To which Titus replied, that he was well pleased with such his agreeable conduct, and would be well pleased if all the Jews would be of his mind, and that he was ready to give the like security to the city. (321) Now five of the ten dissembled with him, and pretended to beg for mercy, while the rest cried out aloud that they would never be slaves to the Romans, while it was in their power to die in a state of freedom. (322) Now while these men were quarrelling for a long while, the attack was delayed; Castor also sent to Simon, and told him that they might take some time for consultation about what was to be done, because he would elude the power of the Romans for a considerable time. And at the same time that he sent thus to him, he appeared openly to exhort those that were obstinate to accept of Titus's hand for their security; (323) but they seemed very angry at it, and brandished their naked swords upon the breastworks, and struck themselves upon their breast, and fell down as if they had been slain. (324) Hereupon Titus, and those with him, were amazed at the courage of the men; and as they were not able to see exactly what was done, they admired at their great fortitude, and pitied their calamity. (325) During this interval, a certain person shot a dart at Castor, and wounded him in his nose; whereupon he presently pulled out the dart, and showed it to Titus, and complained that this was unfair treatment; so Caesar reproved him that shot the dart, and sent Josephus, who then stood by him, to give his right hand to Castor. (326) But Josephus said that he would not go to him, because these pretended petitioners meant nothing that was good; he also restrained those friends of his who were zealous to go to him. But still there was one Eneas, a deserter, who said he would go to him. (327) Castor also called to them, that somebody should come and receive the money which he had with him; this made Eneas the more earnestly to run to him with his bosom open. (328) Then did Castor take up a great stone, and threw it at him, which missed him, because he guarded himself against it; but still it wounded another soldier that was coining to him. (329) When Caesar understood that this was a delusion, he perceived that mercy in war is a pernicious thing, because such cunning tricks have less place under the exercise of greater severity. So he caused the engine to work more strongly than before, on account of his anger at the deceit put upon him. (330) But Castor and his companions set the tower on fire when it began to give way, and leaped through the flame into a hidden vault that was under it, which made the Romans further suppose that they were men of great courage, as having cast themselves into the fire.

CHAPTER 8.

HOW THE ROMANS TOOK THE SECOND WALL TWICE, AND GOT ALL READY FOR TAKING THE THIRD WALL.

1. (331) NOW Caesar took this wall there on the fifth day after he had taken the first; and when the Jews had fled from him, he entered into it with a thousand armed men, and those of his choice troops, and this at a place where were the merchants of wool, the braziers, and the market for cloth, and where the narrow streets led obliquely to the wall. (332) Wherefore, if Titus had either demolished a larger part of the wall immediately, or had come in, and, according to the law of war, had laid waste what was left, his victory would not, I suppose, have been mixed with any loss to himself. (333) But now, out of the hope he had that he should make the Jews ashamed of their obstinacy, by not being willing, when he was able, to afflict them more than he needed to do, he did

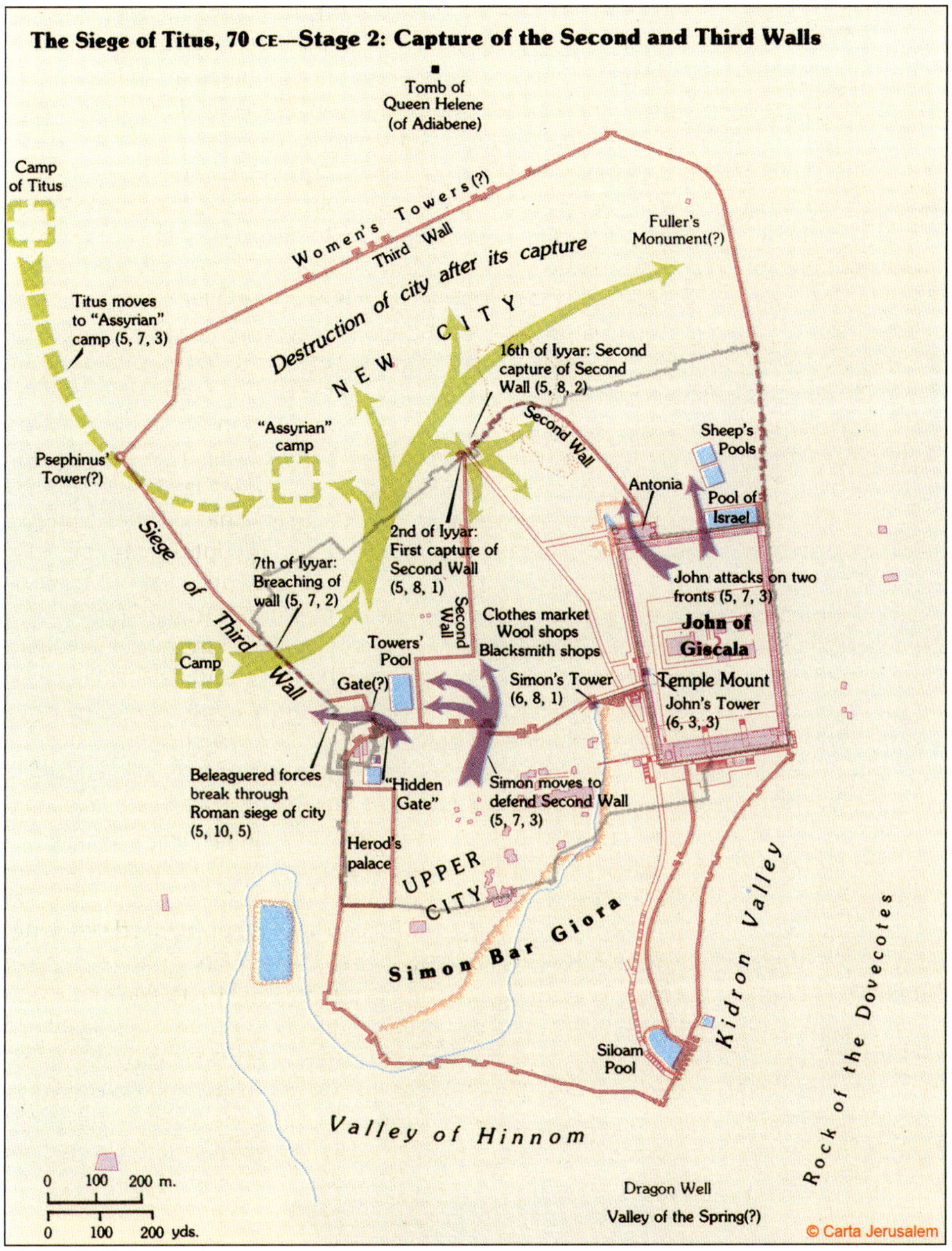

(from *The Carta Jerusalem Atlas* / Dan Bahat)

not widen the breach of the wall, in order to make a safer retreat upon occasion; for he did not think they would lay snares for him that did them such a kindness. (334) When therefore he came in, he did not permit his soldiers to kill any of those they caught, nor to set fire to their houses neither; nay, he gave leave to the seditious, if they had a mind, to fight without any harm to the people, and promised to restore the people's effects to them; for he was very desirous to preserve the city for his own sake, and the temple for the sake of the city. (335) As to the people, he had them of a long time ready to comply with his proposals; but as to the fighting men, this humanity of his seemed a mark of his weakness, and they imagined that he made these proposals because he was not able to take the rest of the city. (336) They also threatened death to the people, if they should any one of them say a word about a surrender. They moreover cut the throats of such as talked of a peace, and then attacked those Romans that were come within the wall. Some of them they met in the narrow streets, and some they fought against from their houses, while they made a sudden sally out at the upper gates, (337) and assaulted such Romans as were beyond the wall, till those that guarded the wall were so affrighted, that they leaped down from their towers, and retired to their several camps: (338) upon which a great noise was made by the Romans that were within, because they were encompassed round on every side by their enemies; as also by them that were without, because they were in fear for those that were left in the city. Thus did the Jews grow more numerous perpetually, and had great advantages over the Romans, by their full knowledge of those narrow lanes; and they wounded a great many of them, and fell upon them, and drove them out of the city. (339) Now these Romans were at present forced to make the best resistance they could; for they were not able, in great numbers, to get out at the breach in the wall, it was so narrow. It is also probable that all those that were gotten within had been cut to pieces, if Titus had not sent them succors; (340) for he ordered the archers to stand at the upper ends of these narrow lakes, and he stood himself where was the greatest multitude of his enemies, and with his darts he put a stop to them; as with him did Domitius Sabinus also, a valiant man, and one that in this battle appeared so to be. (341) Thus did Caesar continue to shoot darts at the Jews continually, and to hinder them from coming upon his men, and this until all his soldiers had retreated out of the city.

2. (342) And thus were the Romans driven out, after they had possessed themselves of the second wall. Whereupon the fighting men that were in the city were lifted up in their minds, and were elevated upon this their good success, and began to think that the Romans would never venture to come into the city any more; and that if they kept within it themselves, they should not be any more conquered. (343) For God had blinded their minds for the transgressions they had been guilty of, nor could they see how much greater forces the Romans had than those that were now expelled, no more than they could discern how a famine was creeping upon them; (344) for hitherto they had fed themselves out of the public miseries, and drank the blood of the city. But now poverty had for a long time seized upon the better part, and a great many had died already for want of necessaries; (345) although the seditious indeed supposed the destruction of the people to be an easement to themselves; for they desired that none others might be preserved but such as were against a peace with the Romans, and were resolved to live in opposition to them, and they were pleased when the multitude of those of a contrary opinion were consumed, as being then freed from a heavy burden. (346) And this was their disposition of mind with regard to those that were within the city, while they covered themselves with their armor, and prevented the Romans, when they were trying to get into the city again, and made a wall of their own bodies over against that part of the wall that was cast down. Thus did they valiantly defend themselves for three days; but on the fourth day they could not support themselves against the vehement assaults of Titus but were compelled by force to fly whither they had fled before; (347) so he quietly possessed himself again of that wall, and demolished it entirely. And when he had put a garrison into the towers that were on the south parts of the city, he contrived how he might assault the third wall.

CHAPTER 9.

TITUS WHEN THE JEWS WERE NOT AT ALL MOLLIFIED BY HIS LEAVING OFF THE SIEGE FOR A WHILE, SET HIMSELF AGAIN TO PROSECUTE THE SAME; BUT SOON SENT JOSEPHUS TO DISCOURSE WITH HIS OWN COUNTRYMEN ABOUT PEACE.

1. (348) A RESOLUTION was now taken by Titus to relax the siege for a little while, and to afford the seditious an interval for consideration, and to see whether the demolishing of their second wall would not make them a little more compliant, or whether they were not somewhat afraid of a famine, because the spoils they had gotten by rapine would not be sufficient for them long; so he made use of this relaxation in order to compass his own designs. (349) Accordingly, as the usual appointed time when he must distribute subsistence money to the soldiers was now come, he gave orders that the commanders should put the army into battle-array, in the face of the enemy, and then give every one of the soldiers their pay. (350) So the soldiers, according to custom, opened the cases wherein their arms before lay covered, and marched with their breastplates on, as did the horsemen lead their horses in their fine trappings. (351) Then did the places that were before the city shine very splendidly for a great way; nor was there any thing so grateful to Titus's own men, or so terrible to the enemy, as that sight. (352) For the whole old wall, and the north side of the temple, were full of spectators, and one might see the houses full of such as looked at them; nor was there any part of the city which was not covered over with their multitudes; (353) nay, a very great consternation seized upon the hardiest of the Jews themselves, when they saw all the army in the same place, together with the fineness of their arms, and the good order of their men. (354) And I cannot but think that the seditious would have changed their minds at that sight, unless the crimes they had committed against the people had been so horrid, that they despaired of forgiveness from the Romans; (355) but as they believed death with torments must be their punishment, if they did not go on in the defense of the city, they thought it much better to die in war. Fate also prevailed so far over them, that the innocent were to perish with the guilty, and the city was to be destroyed with the seditious that were in it.

2. (356) Thus did the Romans spend four days in bringing this subsistence-money to the several legions. But on the fifth day, when no signs of peace appeared to come from the Jews, Titus divided his legions, and began to raise banks, both at the tower of Antonia and at John's monument. Now his designs were to take the upper city at that monument, and the temple at the tower of Antonia; for if the temple were not taken, it would be dangerous to keep the city itself; (357) so at each of these parts he raised him banks, each legion raising one. (358) As for those that wrought at John's monument, the Idumeans, and those that were in arms with Simon, made sallies upon them, and put some stop to them; while John's party, and the multitude of zealots with them, did the like to those that were before the tower of Antonia. (359) These Jews were now too hard for the Romans, not only in direct fighting, because they stood upon the higher ground, but because they had now learned to use their own engines; for their continual use of them one day after another did by degrees improve their skill about them; for of one sort of engines for darts they had three hundred, and forty for stones; by the means of which they made it more tedious for the Romans to raise their banks. (360) But then Titus, knowing that the city would be either saved or destroyed for himself, did not only proceed earnestly in the siege, but did not omit to have the Jews exhorted to repentance; (361) so he mixed good counsel with his works for the siege. And being sensible that exhortations are frequently more effectual than arms, he persuaded them to surrender the city, now in a manner already taken, and thereby to save themselves, and sent Josephus to speak to them in their own language; for he imagined they might yield to the persuasion of a countryman of their own.

3. (362) So Josephus went round about the wall, and tried to find a place that was out of the reach of their darts, and yet within their hearing, and besought them, in many words, to spare themselves, to spare their country and their temple, and not to be more obdurate in these cases than foreigners themselves; (363) for that the Romans, who had no relation to those things, had a reverence for their sacred rites and places, although they belonged to their enemies, and had till now kept their hands off from meddling with them; while such as were brought up under them, and, if they be preserved, will be the only people that will reap the benefit of them, hurry on to have them destroyed. (364) That certainly they have seen their strongest walls demolished, and that the wall still remaining was weaker than those that were already taken. That they must know the Roman power was invincible, and that they had been used to serve them; (365) for, that in case it be allowed a right thing to fight for liberty, that ought to have been done at first; but for them that have once fallen under the power of the Romans, and have now submitted to them for so many long years, to pretend to shake off that yoke afterward, was the work of such as had a mind to die miserably, not of such as were lovers of liberty. (366) Besides, men may well enough grudge at the dishonor of owning ignoble masters over them, but ought not to do so to those who have all things under their command; for what part of the world is there that hath escaped the Romans, unless it be such as are of no use for violent heat, or for violent cold? (367) And evident it is that fortune is on all hands gone over to them; and that God, when he had gone round the nations with this dominion, is now settled in Italy. That, moreover, it is a strong and fixed law, even among brute beasts, as well as among men, to yield to those that are too strong for them; and to stiffer those to have the dominion who are too hard (368) for the rest in war; for which reason it was that their forefathers, who were far superior to them, both in their souls and bodies, and other advantages, did yet submit to the Romans, which they would not have suffered, had they not known that God was with them. (369) As for themselves, what can they depend on in this their opposition, when the greatest part of their city is already taken? and when those that are within it are under greater miseries than if they were taken, although their walls be still standing? (370) For that the Romans are not unacquainted with that famine which is in the city, whereby the people are already consumed, and the fighting men will in a little time be so too; (371) for although the Romans should leave off the siege, and not fall upon the city with their swords in their hands, yet was there an insuperable war that beset them within, and was augmented every hour, unless they were able to wage war with famine, and fight against it, or could alone conquer their natural appetites. (372) He added this further, how right a thing it was to change their conduct before their calamities were become incurable, and to have recourse to such advice as might preserve them, while opportunity was offered them for so doing; for that the Romans would not be mindful of their past actions to their disadvantage, unless they persevered in their insolent behavior to the end; because they were naturally mild in their conquests, and preferred what was profitable, before what their passions dictated to them; (373) which profit of theirs lay not in leaving the city empty of inhabitants, nor the country a desert; on which account Caesar did now

offer them his right hand for their security. Whereas, if he took the city by force, he would not save any of them, and this especially, if they rejected his offers in these their utmost distresses; (374) for the walls that were already taken could not but assure them that the third wall would quickly be taken also. And though their fortifications should prove too strong for the Romans to break through them, yet would the famine fight for the Romans against them.

4. (375) While Josephus was making this exhortation to the Jews, many of them jested upon him from the wall, and many reproached him; nay, some threw their darts at him: but when he could not himself persuade them by such open good advice, he betook himself to the histories belonging to their own nation, (376) and cried out aloud, "O miserable creatures! are you so unmindful of those that used to assist you, that you will fight by your weapons and by your hands against the Romans? When did we ever conquer any other nation by such means? (377) and when was it that God, who is the Creator of the Jewish people, did not avenge them when they had been injured? Will not you turn again, and look back, and consider whence it is that you fight with such violence, and how great a Supporter you have profanely abused? Will not you recall to mind the prodigious things done for your forefathers and this holy place, and how great enemies of yours were by him subdued under you? (378) I even tremble myself in declaring the works of God before your ears, that are unworthy to hear them; however, hearken to me, that you may be informed how you fight not only against the Romans, but against God himself. (379) In old times there was one Necao, king of Egypt, who was also called Pharaoh; he came with a prodigious army of soldiers, and seized queen Sarah, the mother of our nation. (380) What did Abraham our progenitor then do? Did he defend himself from this injurious person by war, although he had three hundred and eighteen captains under him, and an immense army under each of them? Indeed he deemed them to be no number at all without God's assistance, and only spread out his hands towards this holy place, which you have now polluted, and reckoned upon him as upon his invincible supporter, instead of his own army. (381) Was not our queen sent back, without any defilement, to her husband, the very next evening?—while the king of Egypt fled away, adoring this place which you have defiled by shedding thereon the blood of your own countrymen; and he also trembled at those visions which he saw in the night season, and bestowed both silver and gold on the Hebrews, as on a people beloved by God. (382) Shall I say nothing, or shall I mention the removal of our fathers into Egypt, who, when they were used tyrannically, and were fallen under the power of foreign kings for four hundred ears together, and might have defended themselves by war and by fighting, did yet do nothing but commit themselves to God! (383) Who is there that does not know that Egypt was overrun with all sorts of wild beasts, and consumed by all sorts of distempers? how their land did not bring forth its fruit? how the Nile failed of water? how the ten plagues of Egypt followed one upon another? and how by those means our fathers were sent away under a guard, without any bloodshed, and without running any dangers, because God conducted them as his peculiar servants? (384) Moreover, did not Palestine groan under the ravage the Assyrians made, when they carried away our sacred ark? as did their idol Dagon, and as also did that entire nation of those that carried it away, (385) how they were smitten with a loathsome distemper in the secret parts of their bodies, when their very bowels came down together with what they had eaten, till those hands that stole it away were obliged to bring it back again, and that with the sound of cymbals and timbrels, and oth-

Sennacherib, king of Assyria. (photo Timo Roller, via Wikimedia Commons)

er oblations, in order to appease the anger of God for their violation of his holy ark. (386) It was God who then became our General, and accomplished these great things for our fathers, and this because they did not meddle with war and fighting, but committed it to him to judge about their affairs. (387) When Sennacherib, king of Assyria, brought along with him all Asia, and encompassed this city round with his army, did he fall by the hands of men? (388) were not those hands lifted up to God in prayers, without meddling with their arms, when an angel of God destroyed that prodigious army in one night? when the Assyrian king, as he rose the next day, found a hundred fourscore and five thousand dead bodies, and when he, with the remainder of his army, fled away from the Hebrews, though they were unarmed, and did not pursue them. (389) You are also acquainted with the slavery we were under at Babylon, where the people were captives for seventy years; yet were they not delivered into freedom again before God made Cyrus his gracious instrument in bringing it about; accordingly they were set free by him, and did again restore the worship of their Deliverer at his temple. (390) And, to speak in general, we can produce no example wherein our fathers got any success by war, or failed of success when without war they committed themselves to God. When they staid at home, they conquered, as pleased their Judge; but when they went out to fight, they were always disappointed: (391) for example, when the king of Babylon besieged this very city, and our king Zedekiah fought against him, contrary to what predictions were made to him by Jeremiah the prophet, he was at once taken prisoner, and saw the city and the temple demolished. Yet how much greater was the moderation of that king, than is that of your present governors, and that of the people then under him, than is that of you at this time! (392) for when Jeremiah cried out aloud, how very angry God was at them, because of their transgressions, and told them they should

The Cyrus Cylinder. (original in The British Museum, London)

relling about rapines and murders, and invent strange ways of wickedness. Nay, the temple itself is become the receptacle of all, and this Divine place is polluted by the hands of those of our own country; which place hath yet been reverenced by the Romans when it was at a distance from them, when they have suffered many of their own customs to give place to our law. (403) And, after all this, do you expect Him whom you have so impiously abused to be your supporter? To be sure then you have a right to be petitioners, and to call upon Him to assist you, so pure are your hands! (404) Did your king [Hezekiah] lift up such hands in prayer to God against the king of Assyria, when he destroyed that great army in one

be taken prisoners, unless they would surrender up their city, neither did the king nor the people put him to death; (393) but for you, (to pass over what you have done within the city, which I am not able to describe as your wickedness deserves,) you abuse me, and throw darts at me, who only exhort you to save yourselves, as being provoked when you are put in mind of your sins, and cannot bear the very mention of those crimes which you every day perpetrate. (394) For another example, when Antiochus, who was called Epiphanes, lay before this city, and had been guilty of many indignities against God, and our forefathers met him in arms, they then were slain in the battle, this city was plundered by our enemies, and our sanctuary made desolate for three years and six months. And what need I bring any more examples? (395) Indeed what can it be that hath stirred up an army of the Romans against our nation? Is it not the impiety of the inhabitants? Whence did our servitude commence? (396) Was it not derived from the seditions that were among our forefathers, when the madness of Aristobulus and Hyrcanus, and our mutual quarrels, brought Pompey upon this city, and when God reduced those under subjection to the Romans who were unworthy of the liberty they had enjoyed? (397) After a siege, therefore, of three months, they were forced to surrender themselves, although they had not been guilty of such offenses, with regard to our sanctuary and our laws, as you have; and this while they had much greater advantages to go to war than you have. (398) Do not we know what end Antigonus, the son of Aristobulus, came to, under whose reign God provided that this city should be taken again upon account of the people's offenses? When Herod, the son of Antipater, brought upon us Sosius, and Sosius brought upon us the Roman army, they were then encompassed and besieged for six months, till, as a punishment for their sins, they were taken, and the city was plundered by the enemy. (399) Thus it appears that arms were never given to our nation, but that we are always given up to be fought against, and to be taken; (400) for I suppose that such as inhabit this holy place ought to commit the disposal of all things to God, and then only to disregard the assistance of men when they resign themselves up to their Arbitrator, who is above. (401) As for you, what have you done of those things that are recommended by our legislator? and what have you not done of those things that he hath condemned? How much more impious are you than those who were so quickly taken! (402) You have not avoided so much as those sins that are usually done in secret; I mean thefts, and treacherous plots against men, and adulteries. You are quar-

night? And do the Romans commit such wickedness as did the king of Assyria, that you may have reason to hope for the like vengeance upon them? (405) Did not that king accept of money from our king on this condition, that he should not destroy the city, and yet, contrary to the oath he had taken, he came down to burn the temple? while the Romans do demand no more than that accustomed tribute which our fathers paid to their fathers; (406) and if they may but once obtain that, they neither aim to destroy this city, nor to touch this sanctuary; nay, they will grant you besides, that your posterity shall be free, and your possessions secured to you, and will preserve our holy laws inviolate to you. (407) And it is plain madness to expect that God should appear as well disposed towards the wicked as towards the righteous, since he knows when it is proper to punish men for their sins immediately; accordingly he brake the power of the Assyrians the very first night that they pitched their camp. (408) Wherefore, had he judged that our nation was worthy of freedom, or the Romans of punishment, he had immediately inflicted punishment upon those Romans, as he did upon the Assyrians, when Pompey began to meddle with our nation, or when after him Sosius came up against us, or when Vespasian laid waste Galilee, or, lastly, when Titus came first of all near to this city; (409) although Magnus and Sosius did not only suffer nothing, but took the city by force; as did Vespasian go from the war he made against you to receive the empire; and as for Titus, those springs that were formerly almost dried up when they were under your power since he is come, run more plentifully than they did before; (410) accordingly, you know that Siloam, as well as all the other springs that were without the city, did so far fail, that water was sold by distinct measures; whereas they now have such a great quantity of water for your enemies, as is sufficient not only for drink both for themselves and their cattle, but for watering their gardens also. (411) The same wonderful sign you had also experience of formerly, when the forementioned king of Babylon made war against us, and when he took the city, and burnt the temple; while yet I believe the Jews of that age were not so impious as you are. (412) Wherefore I cannot but suppose that God is fled out of his sanctuary, and stands on the side of those against whom you fight. (413) Now even a man, if he be but a good man, will fly from an impure house, and will hate those that are in it; and do you persuade yourselves that God will abide with you in your iniquities, who sees all secret things, and hears what is kept most private? (414) Now what crime is there, I pray you, that is so much as kept secret among you, or is concealed by you? nay, what is there that is not open to your very enemies? for you show your transgressions after a pompous manner, and contend one with another which of you shall be more wicked than another; and you make a public demonstration of your injustice, as if it were virtue. (415) However, there is a place left for your preservation, if you be willing to accept of it; and God is easily reconciled to those that confess their faults, and repent of them. (416) O hard-hearted wretches as you are! cast away all your arms, and take pity of your country already going to ruin; return from your wicked ways, and have regard to the excellency of that city which you are going to betray, to that excellent temple with the donations of so many countries in it. (417) Who could bear to be the first that should set that temple on fire? who could be willing that these things should be no more? and what is there that can better deserve to be preserved? O insensible creatures, and more stupid than are the stones themselves! (418) And if you cannot look at these things with discerning eyes, yet, however, have pity upon your families, and set before every one of your eyes your children, and wives, and parents, who will be gradually consumed either by famine or by war. (419) I am sensible that this danger will extend to my mother, and wife, and to that family of mine who have been by no means ignoble, and indeed to one that hath been very eminent in old time; and perhaps you may imagine that it is on their account only that I give you this advice; if that be all, kill them; nay, take my own blood as a reward, if it may but procure your preservation; for I am ready to die, in case you will but return to a sound mind after my death."

Remains of the Siloam pool from the Herodian period. (photo Ian Scott, via Wikimedia Commons)

CHAPTER 10.

HOW A GREAT MANY OF THE PEOPLE EARNESTLY ENDEAVORED TO DESERT TO THE ROMANS; AS ALSO WHAT INTOLERABLE THINGS THOSE THAT STAID BEHIND SUFFERED BY FAMINE, AND THE SAD CONSEQUENCES THEREOF.

1. (420) AS Josephus was speaking thus with a loud voice, the seditious would neither yield to what he said, nor did they deem it safe for them to alter their conduct; but as for the people, they had a great inclination to desert to the Romans; (421) accordingly, some of them sold what they had, and even the most precious things that had been laid up as treasures by them, for every small matter, and swallowed down pieces of gold, that they might not be found out by the robbers; and when they had escaped to the Romans, went to stool, and had wherewithal to provide plentifully for themselves; (422) for Titus let a great number of them go away into the country, whither they pleased. And the main reasons why they were so ready to desert were these: That now they should be freed from those miseries which they had endured in that city, and yet should not be in slavery to the Romans: (423) however, John and Simon, with their factions, did more carefully watch these men's going out than they did the coming in of the Romans; and if any one did but afford the least shadow of suspicion of such an intention, his throat was cut immediately.

2. (424) But as for the richer sort, it proved all one to them whether they staid in the city, or attempted to get out of it; for they were equally destroyed in both cases; for every such person was put to death under this pretense, that they were going to desert, but in reality that the robbers might get what they had. The madness of the seditious did also increase together with their famine, and both those miseries were every day inflamed more and more; (425) for there was no corn which any where appeared publicly, but the robbers came running into, and searched men's private houses; and then, if they found any, they tormented them, because they had denied they had any; and if they found none, they tormented them worse, because they supposed they had more carefully concealed it. (426) The indication they made use of whether they had any or not was taken from the bodies of these miserable wretches; which, if they were in good case, they supposed they were in no want at all of food; but if they were wasted away, they walked off without searching any further; nor did they think it proper to kill such as these, because they saw they would very soon die of themselves for want of food. (427) Many there were indeed who sold what they had for one measure; it was of wheat, if they were of the richer sort; but of barley, if they were poorer. When these had so done, they shut themselves up in the inmost rooms of their houses, and ate the corn they had gotten; some did it without grinding it, by reason of the extremity of the want they were in, and others baked bread of it, according as necessity and fear dictated to them: (428) a table was nowhere laid for a distinct meal, but they snatched the bread out of the fire, half-baked, and ate it very hastily.

3. (429) It was now a miserable case, and a sight that would justly bring tears into our eyes, how men stood as to their food, while the more powerful had more than enough, and the weaker were lamenting [for want of it.] But the famine was too hard for all other passions, and it is destructive to nothing so much as to modesty; for what was

otherwise worthy of reverence was in this case despised; (430) insomuch that children pulled the very morsels that their fathers were eating out of their very mouths, and what was still more to be pitied, so did the mothers do as to their infants; and when those that were most dear were perishing under their hands, they were not ashamed to take from them the very last drops that might preserve their lives: (431) and while they ate after this manner, yet were they not concealed in so doing; but the seditious every where came upon them immediately, and snatched away from them what they had gotten from others; (432) for when they saw any house shut up, this was to them a signal that the people within had gotten some food; whereupon they broke open the doors, and ran in, and took pieces of what they were eating almost up out of their very throats, and this by force: (433) the old men, who held their food fast, were beaten; and if the women hid what they had within their hands, their hair was torn for so doing; nor was there any commiseration shown either to the aged or to the infants, but they lifted up children from the ground as they hung upon the morsels they had gotten, and shook them down upon the floor. (434) But still they were more barbarously cruel to those that had prevented their coming in, and had actually swallowed down what they were going to seize upon, as if they had been unjustly defrauded of their right. (435) They also invented terrible methods of torments to discover where any food was, and they were these to stop up the passages of the privy parts of the miserable wretches, and to drive sharp stakes up their fundaments; and a man was forced to bear what it is terrible even to hear, in order to make him confess that he had but one loaf of bread, or that he might discover a handful of barley-meal that was concealed; (436) and this was done when these tormentors were not themselves hungry; for the thing had been less barbarous had necessity forced them to it; but this was done to keep their madness in exercise, and as making preparation of provisions for themselves for the following days. (437) These men went also to meet those that had crept out of the city by night, as far as the Roman guards, to gather some plants and herbs that grew wild; and when those people thought they had got clear of the enemy, they snatched from them what they had brought with them, (438) even while they had frequently entreated them, and that by calling upon the tremendous name of God, to give them back some part of what they had brought; though these would not give them the least crumb, and they were to be well contented that they were only spoiled, and not slain at the same time.

Sign of famine. (photo Samuel Magal)

4. (439) These were the afflictions which the lower sort of people suffered from these tyrants' guards; but for the men that were in dignity, and withal were rich, they were carried before the tyrants themselves; some of whom were falsely accused of laying treacherous plots, and so were destroyed; others of them were charged with designs of betraying the city to the Romans; but the readiest way of all was this, to suborn somebody to affirm that they were resolved to desert to the enemy. (440) And he who was utterly despoiled of what he had by Simon was sent back again to John, as of those who had been already plundered by Jotre, Simon got what remained; insomuch that they drank the blood of the populace to one another, and divided the dead bodies of the poor creatures between them; (441) so that although, on account of their ambition after dominion, they contended with each other, yet did they very well agree in their wicked practices; for he that did not communicate what he got by the miseries of others to the other tyrant seemed to be too little guilty, and in one respect only; and he that did not partake of what was so communicated to him grieved at this, as at the loss of what was a valuable thing, that he had no share in such barbarity.

5. (442) It is therefore impossible to go distinctly over every instance of these men's iniquity. I shall therefore speak my mind here at once briefly:—That neither did any other city ever suffer such miseries, nor did any age ever breed a generation more fruitful in wickedness than this was, from the beginning of the world. (443) Finally, they brought the Hebrew nation into contempt, that they might themselves appear comparatively less impious with regard to strangers. They confessed what was true, that they were the slaves, the scum, and the spurious and abortive offspring of our nation, (444) while they overthrew the city themselves, and forced the Romans, whether they would or no, to gain a melancholy reputation, by acting gloriously against them, and did almost draw that fire upon the temple, which they seemed to think came too slowly; (445) and indeed when they saw that temple burning from the upper city, they were neither troubled at it, nor did they shed any tears on that account, while yet these passions were discovered among the Romans themselves; which circumstances we shall speak of hereafter in their proper place, when we come to treat of such matters.

CHAPTER 11.

HOW THE JEWS WERE CRUCIFIED BEFORE THE WALLS OF THE CITY CONCERNING ANTIOCHUS EPIPHANES; AND HOW THE JEWS OVERTHREW THE BANKS THAT HAD BEEN RAISED BY THE ROMANS.

1. (446) SO now Titus's banks were advanced a great way, notwithstanding his soldiers had been very much distressed from the wall. He then sent a party of horsemen, and ordered they should lay ambushes for those that went out into the valleys to gather food. (447) Some of these were indeed fighting men, who were not contented with what they got by rapine; but the greater part of them were poor people, who were deterred from deserting by the concern they were under for their own relations; (448) for they could not hope to escape away, together with their wives and children, without the knowledge of the seditious; nor could they think of leaving these relations to be slain by the robbers on their account; (449) nay, the severity of the famine made them bold in thus going out; so nothing remained but that, when they were concealed from the robbers, they should be taken by the enemy; and when they were going to be taken, they were forced to defend themselves for fear of being punished; as after they had fought, they thought it too late to make any supplications for mercy; so

Crucifixion, a Roman punishment learned from Carthage. (Carta collection)

they were first whipped, and then tormented with all sorts of tortures, before they died, and were then crucified before the wall of the city. (450) This miserable procedure made Titus greatly to pity them, while they caught every day five hundred Jews; nay, some days they caught more: yet it did not appear to be safe for him to let those that were taken by force go their way, and to set a guard over so many he saw would be to make such as great deal them useless to him. The main reason why he did not forbid that cruelty was this, that he hoped the Jews might perhaps yield at that sight, out of fear lest they might themselves afterwards be liable to the same cruel treatment. (451) So the soldiers, out of the wrath and hatred they bore the Jews, nailed those they caught, one after one way, and another after another, to the crosses, by way of jest, when their multitude was so great, that room was wanting for the crosses, and crosses wanting for the bodies.

2. (452) But so far were the seditious from repenting at this sad sight, that, on the contrary, they made the rest of the multitude believe otherwise; (453) for they brought the relations of those that had deserted upon the wall, with such of the populace as were very eager to go over upon the security offered them, and showed them what miseries those underwent who fled to the Romans; and told them that those who were caught were supplicants to them, and not such as were taken prisoners. (454) This sight kept many of those within the city who were so eager to desert, till the truth was known; yet did some of them run away immediately as unto certain punishment, esteeming death from their enemies to be a quiet departure, if compared with that by famine. (455) So Titus commanded that the hands of many of those that were caught should be cut off, that they might not be thought deserters, and might be credited on account of the calamity they were under, and sent them in to John and Simon, (456) with this exhortation, that they would now at length leave off [their madness], and not force him to destroy the city, whereby they would have those advantages of repentance, even in their utmost distress, that they would preserve their own lives, and so find a city of their own, and that temple which was their peculiar. (457) He then went round about the banks that were cast up, and hastened them, in order to show that his words should in no long time be followed by his deeds. (458) In answer to which the seditious cast reproaches upon Caesar himself, and upon his father also, and cried out, with a loud voice, that they contemned death, and did well in preferring it before slavery; that they would do all the mischief to the Romans they could while they had breath in them; and that for their own city, since they were, as he said, to be destroyed, they had no concern about it, and that the world itself was a better temple to God than this. (459) That yet this temple would be preserved by him that inhabited therein, whom they still had for their assistant in this war, and did therefore laugh at all his threatenings, which would come to nothing, because the conclusion of the whole depended upon God only. These words were mixed with reproaches, and with them they made a mighty clamor.

3. (460) In the mean time Antiochus Epiphanes came to the city, having with him a considerable number of other armed men, and a band called the Macedonian band about him, all of the same age, tall, and just past their childhood, armed, and instructed after the Macedonian manner, whence it was that they took that name. Yet were many of them unworthy of so famous a nation; (461) for it had so happened, that the king of Commagene had flourished more than any other kings that were under the power of the Romans, till a change happened in his condition; and when he was become an old man, he declared plainly that we ought not to call any man happy before he is dead. (462) But this son of his, who was then come thither before his father was decaying, said that he could not but wonder what made the Romans so tardy in making their attacks upon the wall. Now he was a warlike man, and naturally bold in exposing himself to dangers; he was also so strong a man, that his boldness seldom failed of having success. (463) Upon this Titus smiled, and said he would share the pains of an attack with him. However, Antiochus went as he then was, and with his Macedonians made a sudden assault upon the wall; (464) and, indeed, for his own part, his strength and skill were so great, that he guarded himself from the Jewish darts, and yet shot his darts at them, while yet the young men with him were almost all sorely galled; for they had so great a regard to the promises that had been made of their courage, that they would needs persevere in their fighting, (465) and at length many of them retired, but not till they were wounded; and then they perceived that true Macedonians, if they were to be conquerors, must have Alexander's good fortune also.

4. (466) Now as the Romans began to raise their banks on the twelfth day of the month Artemisius, [Jyar,] so had they much ado to finish them by the twenty-ninth day of the same month, after they had labored hard for seventeen days continually. (467) For there were now four great banks raised, one of which was at the tower Antonia; this was raised by the fifth legion, over against the middle of that pool which was called Struthius. Another was cast up by the twelfth legion, at the distance of about twenty cubits from the other. (468) But the labors of the tenth legion, which lay a great way off these, were on the north quarter, and at the pool called Amygdalon; as was that of the fifteenth legion about thirty cubits from it, and at the high priest's monument. (469) And now, when the engines were brought, John had from within undermined the space that was over against the tower of Antonia, as far as the banks themselves, and had supported the ground over the mine with beams laid across one another, whereby the Roman works stood upon an uncertain foundation. Then did he order such materials to be brought in as were daubed over with pitch and bitumen, and set them on fire; (470) and as the cross beams that supported the banks were burning, the ditch yielded on the sudden, and the banks were shaken down, and fell into the ditch with a prodigious noise. (471) Now at the first there arose a very thick smoke and dust, as the fire was choked with the fall of the bank;

The double-vaulted Struthian pool. (photo Yaacov Harlap)

but as the suffocated materials were now gradually consumed, a plain flame brake out; (472) on which sudden appearance of the flame a consternation fell upon the Romans, and the shrewdness of the contrivance discouraged them; and indeed this accident coming upon them at a time when they thought they had already gained their point, cooled their hopes for the time to come. They also thought it would be to no purpose to take the pains to extinguish the fire, since if it were extinguished, the banks were swallowed up already [and become useless to them].

5. (473) Two days after this, Simon and his party made an attempt to destroy the other banks; for the Romans had brought their engines to bear there, and began already to make the wall shake. (474) And here one Tephtheus, of Garsis, a city of Galilee, and Megassarus, one who was derived from some of queen Mariamne's servants, and with them one from Adiabene, he was the son of Nabateus, and called by the name of Chagiras, from the ill fortune he had, the word signifying "a lame man," snatched some torches, and ran suddenly upon the engines. (475) Nor were there during this war any men that ever sallied out of the city who were their superiors, either in their boldness, or in the terror they struck into their enemies. (476) For they ran out upon the Romans, not as if they were enemies, but friends, without fear or delay; nor did they leave their enemies till they had rushed violently through the midst of them, and set their machines on fire. (477) And though they had darts thrown at them on every side, and were on every side assaulted with their enemies' swords, yet did they not withdraw themselves out of the dangers they were in, till the fire had caught hold of the instruments; (478) but when the flame went up, the Romans came running from their camp to save their engines. Then did the Jews hinder their succors from the wall, and fought with those that endeavored to quench the fire, without any regard to the danger their bodies were in. (479) So the Romans pulled the engines out of the fire, while the hurdles that covered them were on fire; but the Jews caught hold of the battering rams through the flame itself, and held them fast, although the iron upon them was become red hot; and now the fire spread itself from the engines to the banks, and prevented those that came to defend them; (480) and all this while the Romans were encompassed round about with the flame; and, despairing of saying their works from it, they retired to their camp. (481) Then did the Jews become still more and more in number by the coming of those that were within the city to their assistance; and as they were very bold upon the good success they had had, their violent assaults were almost irresistible; nay, they proceeded as far as the fortifications of the enemies' camp, and fought with their guards. (482) Now there stood a body of soldiers in array before that camp, which succeeded one another by turns in their armor; and as to those, the law of the Romans was terrible, that he who left his post there, let the occasion be whatsoever it might be, he was to die for it; (483) so that body of soldiers, preferring rather to die in fighting courageously, than as a punishment for their cowardice, stood firm; and at the necessity these men were in of standing to it, many of the others that had run away, out of shame, turned back again; (484) and when they had set the engines against the wall, they put the multitude from coming more of them out of the city, [which they could the more easily do] because they had made no provision for preserving or guarding their bodies at this time; for the Jews fought now hand to hand with all that came in their way, and, without any caution, fell against the points of their enemies' spears, and attacked them bodies against bodies; for they were now too hard for the Romans, not so much by their other warlike actions, as by these courageous assaults they made upon them; (485) and the Romans gave way more to their boldness than they did to the sense of the harm they had received from them.

6. (486) And now Titus was come from the tower of Antonia, whither he was gone to look out for a place for raising other banks, and reproached the soldiers greatly for permitting their own walls to be in danger, when they had taken the wails of their enemies, and sustained the fortune of men besieged, while the Jews were allowed to sally out against them, though they were already in a sort of prison. (487) He then went round about the enemy with some chosen troops, and fell upon their flank himself; so the Jews, who had been before assaulted in their faces, wheeled about to Titus, and continued the fight. The armies also were now mixed one among another, and the dust that was raised so far hindered them from seeing one another, and the noise that was made so far hindered them from hearing one another, that neither side could discern an enemy from a friend. (488) However, the Jews did not flinch, though not so much from their real strength, as from their despair of deliverance. The Romans also would not yield, by reason of the regard they had to glory, and to their reputation in war, and because Caesar himself went into the danger before them; (489) insomuch that I cannot but think the Romans would in the conclusion have now taken even the whole multitude of the Jews, so very angry were they at them, had these not prevented the upshot of the battle, and retired into the city. (490) However, seeing the banks of the Romans were demolished, these Romans were very much east down upon the loss of what had cost them so long pains, and this in one hour's time. And many indeed despaired of taking the city with their usual engines of war only.

CHAPTER 12.

TITUS THOUGHT FIT TO ENCOMPASS THE CITY ROUND WITH A WALL; AFTER WHICH THE FAMINE CONSUMED THE PEOPLE BY WHOLE HOUSES AND FAMILIES TOGETHER.

1. (491) AND now did Titus consult with his commanders what was to be done. Those that were of the warmest tempers thought he should bring the whole army against the city and storm the wall; (492) for that hitherto no more than a part of their army had fought with the Jews; but that in case the entire army was to come at once, they would not be able to sustain their attacks, but would be overwhelmed by their darts. (493) But of those that were for a more cautious management, some were for raising their banks again; and others advised to let the banks alone, but to lie still before the city, to guard against the coming out of the Jews, and against their carrying provisions into the city, and so to leave the enemy to the famine, and this without direct fighting with them; (494) for that despair was not to be conquered, especially as to those who are desirous to die by the sword, while a more terrible misery than that is reserved for them. (495) However, Titus did not think it fit for so great an army to lie entirely idle, and that yet it was in vain to fight with those that would be destroyed one by another; (496) he also showed them how impracticable it was to cast up any more banks, for want of materials, and to guard against the Jews coming out still more impracticable; as also, that to encompass the whole city round with his army was not very easy, by reason of its magnitude, and the difficulty of the situation, (497) and on other accounts dangerous, upon the sallies the Jews might make out of the city. For although they might guard the known passages out of the place, yet would they, when they found themselves under the greatest distress, contrive secret passages out, as being well acquainted with all such places; and if any provisions were carried in by stealth, the siege would thereby be longer delayed. (498) He also owned that he was afraid that the length of time thus to be spent would diminish the glory of his success; for though it be true that length of time will perfect everything, yet that to do what we do in a little time is still necessary to the gaining reputation. (499) That therefore his opinion was, that if they aimed at quickness joined with security, they must build a wall round about the whole city; which was, he thought, the only way to prevent the Jews from coming out any way, and that then they would either entirely despair of saving the city, and so would surrender it up to him, or be still the more easily conquered when the famine had further weakened them; (500) for that besides this wall, he would not lie entirely at rest afterward, but would take care then to have banks raised again, when those that would oppose them were become weaker. (501) But that if anyone should think such a work to be too great, and not to be finished without much difficulty, he ought to consider that it is not fit for Romans to undertake any small work, and that none but God himself could with ease accomplish any great thing whatsoever.

2. (502) These arguments prevailed with the commanders. So Titus gave orders that the army should be distributed to their several shares of this work; and indeed there now came upon the soldiers a certain divine fury, so that they did not only part the whole wall that was to be built among them, nor did only one legion strive with another, but the lesser divisions of the army did the same; (503) insomuch that each soldier was ambitious to please his decurion, each decurion his centurion, each centurion his tribune, and the ambition of the tribunes was to please their superior commanders, while Caesar himself took notice of and rewarded the like contention in those commanders; for he went round about the works many times every day, and took a view of what was done. Titus began the wall from the camp of the Assyrians, where his own camp was pitched, and drew it down to the lower parts of Cenopolis; thence it went along the valley of Cedron, to the Mount of Olives; (505) it then bent towards the south, and encompassed the mountain as far as the rock called Peristereon, and that other hill which lies next it, and is over the valley which reaches to Siloam; whence it bended again to the west, and went down to the valley of the Fountain, (506) beyond which it went up again at the monument of Ananus the high priest, and encompassing that mountain where Pompey had formerly pitched his camp, (507) it returned back to the north side of the city, and was carried on as far as a certain village called "The House of the Erebinthi;" after which it encompassed Herod's monument, and there, on the east, was joined to Titus's own camp, where it began. (508) Now the length of this wall was forty furlongs, one only abated. Now at this wall without were erected thirteen places to keep garrison in, whose circumferences, put together, amounted to ten furlongs; (509) the whole was completed in three days; so that what would naturally have required some months was done in so short an interval as is incredible. (510) When Titus had therefore encompassed the city with this wall, and put garrisons into proper places, be went round the wall, at the first watch of the night, and observed how the guard was kept; the second watch he allotted to Alexander; the commanders of legions took the third watch. (511) They also cast lots among themselves who should be upon the watch in the night time, and who should go all night long round the spaces that were interposed between the garrisons.

3. (512) So all hope of escaping was now cut off from the Jews, together with their liberty of going out of the city. Then did the famine widen its progress, and devoured the people by whole houses and families; (513) the upper rooms were full of women and chil-

Reconstruction showing the use of a Roman siege tower and battering ram against a fortification. (Museo Della Civita Romano; photo Samuel Magal)

Aerial view of the Temple Mount today, looking north. (photo Samuel Magal)

dren that were dying by famine, and the lanes of the city were full of the dead bodies of the aged; the children also and the young men wandered about the market-places like shadows, all swelled with the famine, and fell down dead, wheresoever their misery seized them. (514) As for burying them, those that were sick themselves were not able to do it; and those that were hearty and well were deterred from doing it by the great multitude of those dead bodies, and by the uncertainty there was how soon they should die themselves; for many died as they were burying others, and many went to their coffins before that fatal hour was come. (515) Nor was there any lamentations made under these calamities, nor were heard any mournful complaints; but the famine confounded all natural passions; for those who were just going to die looked upon those that were gone to rest before them with dry eyes and open mouths. A deep silence also, and a kind of deadly night, had seized upon the city; while yet the robbers were still more terrible than these miseries were themselves; (516) for they brake open those houses which were no other than graves of dead bodies, and plundered them of what they had; and carrying off the coverings of their bodies, went out laughing, and tried the points of their swords in their dead bodies; and, in order to prove what metal they were made of they thrust some of those through that still lay alive upon the ground; (517) but for those that entreated them to lend them their right hand and their sword to despatch them, they were too proud to grant their requests, and left them to be consumed by the famine. Now every one of these died with their eyes fixed upon the temple, and left the seditious alive behind them. (518) Now the seditious at first gave orders that the dead should be buried out of the public treasury, as not enduring the stench of their dead bodies. But afterwards, when they could not do that, they had them cast down from the walls into the valleys beneath.

4. (519) However, when Titus, in going his rounds along those valleys, saw them full of dead bodies, and the thick putrefaction running about them, he gave a groan; and, spreading out his hands to heaven, called God to witness that this was not his doing; (520) and such was the sad case of the city itself. But the Romans were very joyful, since none of the seditious could now make sallies out of the city, because they were themselves disconsolate, and the famine already touched them also. These Romans besides had great plenty of corn and other necessaries out of Syria, and out of the neighboring provinces; (521) many of whom would stand near to the wall of the city, and show the people what great quantities of provisions they had, and so make the enemy more sensible of their famine, by the great plenty, even to satiety, which they had themselves. (522) However, when the seditious still showed no inclinations of yielding, Titus, out of his commiseration of the people that remained, and out of his earnest desire of rescuing what was still left out of these miseries, began to raise his banks again, although materials for them were hard to he come at; (523) for all the trees that were about the city had been already cut down for the making of the former banks. Yet did the soldiers bring with them other materials from the distance of ninety furlongs, and thereby raised banks in four parts, much greater than the former, though this was done only at the tower of Antonia. (524) So Caesar went his rounds through the legions, and hastened on the works, and showed the robbers that they were now in his hands. (525) But these men, and these only, were incapable of repenting of the wickednesses they had been guilty of; and separating their souls from their bodies,

they used them both as if they belonged to other folks, and not to themselves. (526) For no gentle affection could touch their souls, nor could any pain affect their bodies, since they could still tear the dead bodies of the people as dogs do, and fill the prisons with those that were sick.

CHAPTER 13.

THE GREAT SLAUGHTERS AND SACRILEGE THAT WERE IN JERUSALEM.

1. (527) ACCORDINGLY Simon would not suffer Matthias, by whose means he got possession of the city, to go off without torment. This Matthias was the son of Boethus, and was one of the high priests, one that had been very faithful to the people, and in great esteem with them; (528) he, when the multitude were distressed by the zealots, among whom John was numbered, persuaded the people to admit this Simon to come in to assist them, while he had made no terms with him, nor expected any thing that was evil from him. (529) But when Simon was come in, and had gotten the city under his power, he esteemed him that had advised them to admit him as his enemy equally with the rest, as looking upon that advice as a piece of his simplicity only; (530) so he had him then brought before him, and condemned to die for being on the side of the Romans, without giving him leave to make his defense. He condemned also his three sons to die with him; for as to the fourth, he prevented him by running away to Titus before. And when he begged for this, that he might be slain before his sons, and that as a favor, on account that he had procured the gates of the city to be opened to him, he gave order that he should be slain the last of them all; (531) so he was not slain till he had seen his sons slain before his eyes, and that by being produced over against the Romans; for such a charge had Simon given to Artanus, the son of Bamadus, who was the most barbarous of all his guards. He also jested upon him, and told him that he might now see whether those to whom he intended to go over would send him any succors or not; but still he forbade their dead bodies should be buried. (532) After the slaughter of these, a certain priest, Ananias, the son of Masambalus, a person of eminency, as also Aristens, the scribe of the sanhedrim, and born at Emmaus, and with them fifteen men of figure among the people, were slain. (533) They also kept Josephus's father in prison, and made public proclamation, that no citizen whosoever should either speak to him himself, or go into his company among others, for fear he should betray them. They also slew such as joined in lamenting these men, without any further examination.

2. (534) Now when Judas, the son of Judas, who was one of Simon's under officers, and a person intrusted by him to keep one of the towers, saw this procedure of Simon, he called together ten of those under him, that were most faithful to him, (perhaps this was done partly out of pity to those that had so barbarously been put to death, but principally in order to provide for his own safety,) and spoke thus to them: (535) "How long shall we bear these miseries? or what hopes have we of deliverance by thus continuing faithful to such wicked wretches? (536) Is not the famine already come against us? Are not the Romans in a manner gotten within the city? Is not Simon become unfaithful to his benefactors? and is there not reason to fear he will very soon bring us to the like punishment, while the security the Romans offer us is sure? Come on, let us surrender up this wall, and save ourselves and the city. (537) Nor will Simon be very much hurt, if, now he despairs of deliverance, he be brought to justice a little sooner than he thinks on." (538) Now these ten were prevailed upon by those arguments; so he sent the rest of those that were under him, some one way, and some another, that no discovery might be made of what they had resolved upon. Accordingly, he called to the Romans from the tower about the third hour; (539) but they, some of them out of pride, despised what he said, and others of them did not believe him to be in earnest, though the greatest number delayed the matter, as believing they should get possession of the city in a little time, without any hazard. (540) But when Titus was just coming thither with his armed men, Simon was acquainted with the matter before he came, and presently took the tower into his own custody, before it was surrendered, and seized upon these men, and put them to death in the sight of the Romans themselves; and when he had mangled their dead bodies, he threw them down before the wall of the city.

3. (541) In the meantime, Josephus, as he was going round the city, had his head wounded by a stone that was thrown at him; upon which he fell down as giddy. Upon which fall of his the Jews made a sally, and he had been hurried away into the city, if Caesar had not sent men to protect him immediately; (542) and as these men were fighting, Josephus was taken up, though he heard little of what was done. So the seditious supposed they had now slain that man whom they were the most desirous of killing, and made thereupon a great noise, in way of rejoicing. (543) This accident was told in the city, and the multitude that remained became very disconsolate at the news, as being persuaded that he was really dead, on whose account alone they could venture to desert to the Romans. (544) But when Josephus's mother heard in prison that her son was dead, she said to those that watched about her, That she had always been of opinion, since the siege of Jotapata, [that he would be slain,] and she should never enjoy him alive any more. (545) She also made great lamentation privately to the maidservants that were about her, and said, That this was all the advantage she had of bringing so extraordinary a person as this son into the world; that she should not be able even to bury that son of hers, by whom she expected to have been buried herself. (546) However, this false report did not put his mother to pain, nor afford merriment to the robbers, long; for Josephus soon recovered of his wound, and came out, and cried out aloud, That it would not be long ere they should be punished for this wound they had given him. He also made a fresh exhortation to the people to come out upon the security that would be given them. (547) This sight of Josephus encouraged the people greatly, and brought a great consternation upon the seditious.

4. (548) Hereupon some of the deserters, having no other way, leaped down from the wall immediately, while others of them went out of the city with stones, as if they would fight them; but thereupon they fled away to the Romans. But here a worse fate accompanied these than what they had found within the city; and they met with a quicker despatch from the too great abundance they had among the Romans, than they could have done from the famine among the Jews; (549) for when they came first to the Romans, they were puffed up by the famine, and swelled like men in a dropsy; after which they all on the sudden overfilled those bodies that were before empty, and so burst asunder, excepting such only as were skillful enough to restrain their appetites, and by degrees took in their food into bodies unaccustomed thereto. (550) Yet did another plague seize upon those that were thus preserved; for there was found among the Syrian deserters a certain person who was caught gathering pieces of gold out of the excrements of the Jews' bellies; for the deserters used to swallow such pieces of gold, as we told you before, when they came out, and for these did the seditious search them all; for there was a great quantity of gold

The golden lampstand (menorah) from the temple, as depicted on the Arch of Titus in Rome. (Carta collection)

in the city, insomuch that as much was now sold [in the Roman camp] for twelve Attic [drams], as was sold before for twenty-five. (551) But when this contrivance was discovered in one instance, the fame of it filled their several camps, that the deserters came to them full of gold. So the multitude of the Arabians, with the Syrians, cut up those that came as supplicants, and searched their bellies. (552) Nor does it seem to me that any misery befell the Jews that was more terrible than this, since in one night's time about two thousand of these deserters were thus dissected.

5. (553) When Titus came to the knowledge of this wicked practice, he had like to have surrounded those that had been guilty of it with his horse, and have shot them dead; and he had done it, had not their number been so very great, and those that were liable to this punishment would have been manifold more than those whom they had slain. (554) However, he called together the commanders of the auxiliary troops he had with him, as well as the commanders of the Roman legions, (for some of his own soldiers had been also guilty herein, as he had been informed,) (555) and had great indignation against both sorts of them, and said to them, "What! have any of my own soldiers done such things as this out of the uncertain hope of gain, without regarding their own weapons, which are made of silver and gold? (556) Moreover, do the Arabians and Syrians now first of all begin to govern themselves as they please, and to indulge their appetites in a foreign war, and then, out of their barbarity in murdering men, and out of their hatred to the Jews, get it ascribed to the Romans?" for this infamous practice was said to be spread among some of his own soldiers also. (557) Titus then threatened that he would put such men to death, if any of them were discovered to be so insolent as to do so again; moreover, he gave it in charge to the legions, that they should make a search after such as were suspected, and should bring them to him. (558) But it appeared that the love of money was too hard for all their dread of punishment, and a vehement desire of gain is natural to men, and no passion is so venturesome as covetousness; (559) otherwise such passions have certain bounds, and are subordinate to fear. But in reality it was God who condemned the whole nation, and turned every course that was taken for their preservation to their destruction. (560) This, therefore, which was forbidden by Caesar under such a threatening, was ventured upon privately against the deserters, and these barbarians would go out still, and meet those that ran away before any saw them, and looking about them to see that no Roman spied them, they dissected them, and pulled this polluted money out of their bowels; (561) which money was still found in a few of them, while yet a great many were destroyed by the bare hope there was of thus getting by them, which miserable treatment made many that were deserting to return back again into the city.

6. (562) But as for John, when he could no longer plunder the people, he betook himself to sacrilege, and melted down many of the sacred utensils, which had been given to the temple; as also many of those vessels which were necessary for such as ministered about holy things, the caldrons, the dishes, and the tables; nay, he did not abstain from those pouring vessels that were sent them by Augustus and his wife; (563) for the Roman emperors did ever both honor and adorn this temple; whereas this man, who was a Jew, seized upon what were the donations of foreigners, (564) and said to those that were with him, that it was proper for them to use Divine things, while they were fighting for the Divinity, without fear, and that such whose warfare is for the temple should live of the temple; (565) on which account he emptied the vessels of that sacred wine and oil, which the priests kept to be poured on the burnt-offerings, and which lay in the inner court of the temple, and distributed it among the multitude, who, in their anointing themselves and drinking, used [each of them] above an hin of them. (566) And here I cannot but speak my mind, and what the concern I am under dictates to me, and it is this: I suppose, that had the Romans made any longer delay in coming against these villains, that the city would either have been swallowed up by the ground opening upon them, or been overflowed by water, or else been destroyed by such thunder as the country of Sodom perished by, for it had brought forth a generation of men much more atheistical than were those that suffered such punishments; for by their madness it was that all the people came to be destroyed.

7. (567) And, indeed, why do I relate these particular calamities? while Manneus, the son of Lazarus, came running to Titus at this very time, and told him that there had been carried out through that one gate, which was intrusted to his care, no fewer than a hundred and fifteen thousand eight hundred and eighty dead bodies, in the interval between the fourteenth day of the month Xanthieus, [Nisan,] when the Romans pitched their camp by the city, and the first day of the month Panemus [Tamuz]. (568) This was itself a prodigious multitude; and though this man was not himself set as a governor at that gate, yet was he appointed to pay the public stipend for carrying these bodies out, and so was obliged of necessity to number them, while the rest were buried by their relations; though all their burial was but this, to bring them away, and cast them out of the city. (569) After this man there ran away to Titus many of the eminent citizens, and told him the entire number of the poor that were dead, and that no fewer than six hundred thousand were thrown out at the gates, though still the number of the rest could not be discovered; (570) and they told him further, that when they were no longer able to carry out the dead bodies of the poor, they laid their corpses on heaps in very large houses, and shut them up therein; (571) as also that a medimnus of wheat was sold for a talent; and that when, a while afterward, it was not possible to gather herbs, by reason the city was all walled about, some persons were driven to that terrible distress as to search the common sewers and old dunghills of cattle, and to eat the dung which they got there; and what they of old could not endure so much as to see they now used for food. (572) When the Romans barely heard all this, they commiserated their case; while the seditious, who saw it also, did not repent, but suffered the same distress to come upon themselves; for they were blinded by that fate which was already coming upon the city, and upon themselves also.

BOOK VI

FROM THE GREAT EXTREMITY TO WHICH THE JEWS WERE REDUCED TO THE TAKING OF JERUSALEM BY TITUS

CHAPTER 1.

THAT THE MISERIES STILL GREW WORSE; AND HOW THE ROMANS MADE AN ASSAULT UPON THE TOWER OF ANTONIA.

1. (1) THUS did the miseries of Jerusalem grow worse and worse every day, and the seditious were still more irritated by the calamities they were under, even while the famine preyed upon themselves, after it had preyed upon the people. (2) And indeed the multitude of carcasses that lay in heaps one upon another was a horrible sight, and produced a pestilential stench, which was a hinderance to those that would make sallies out of the city, and fight the enemy: but as those were to go in battle-array, who had been already used to ten thousand murders, and must tread upon those dead bodies as they marched along, (3) so were not they terrified, nor did they pity men as they marched over them; nor did they deem this affront offered to the deceased to be any ill omen to themselves; (4) but as they had their right hands already polluted with the murders of their own countrymen, and in that condition ran out to fight with foreigners, they seem to me to have cast a reproach upon God himself, as if he were too slow in punishing them; for the war was not now gone on with as if they had any hope of victory; for they gloried after a brutish manner in that despair of deliverance they were already in. (5) And now the Romans, although they were greatly distressed in getting together their materials, raised their banks in one and twenty days, after they had cut down all the trees that were in the country that adjoined to the city, and that for ninety furlongs round about, as I have already related. (6) And truly the very view itself of the country was a melancholy thing; for those places which were before adorned with trees and pleasant gardens were now become a desolate country every way, and its trees were all cut down: (7) nor could any foreigner that had formerly seen Judea and the most beautiful suburbs of the city, and now saw it as a desert, but lament and mourn sadly at so great a change: (8) for the war had laid all the signs of beauty quite waste: nor if any one that had known the place before, had come on a sudden to it now, would he have known it again; but though he were at the city itself, yet would he have inquired for it notwithstanding.

2. (9) And now the banks were finished, they afforded a foundation for fear both to the Romans and to the Jews; (10) for the Jews expected that the city would be taken, unless they could burn those banks, as did the Romans expect that, if these were once burnt down, they should never be able to take it; (11) for there was a mighty scarcity of materials, and the bodies of the soldiers began to fail with such hard labors, as did their souls faint with so many instances of ill success; (12) nay, the very calamities themselves that were in the city proved a greater discouragement to the Romans than those within the city; for they found the fighting men of the Jews to be not at all mollified among such their sore afflictions, (13) while they had themselves perpetually less and less hopes of success, and their banks were forced to yield to the stratagems of the enemy, their engines to the firmness of their wall, and their closest fights to the boldness of their attack; and, what was their greatest discouragement of all, they found the Jews' courageous souls to be superior to the multitude of the miseries they were under, by their sedition, their famine, and the war itself; (14) insomuch that they were ready to imagine that the violence of their attacks was invincible, and that the alacrity they showed would not be discouraged by their calamities; for what would not those be able to bear if they should be fortunate, who turned their very misfortunes to the improvement of their valor! These considerations made the Romans to keep a stronger guard about their banks than they formerly had done.

3. (15) But now John and his party took care for securing themselves afterward, even in case this wall should be thrown down, and fell to their work before the battering rams were brought against them. (16) Yet did they not compass what they endeavored to do, but as they were gone out with their torches, they came back under great discouragement before they came near to the banks; and the reasons were these: (17) that, in the first place, their conduct did not seem to be unanimous, but they went out in distinct parties, and at distinct intervals, and after a slow manner, and timorously, and, to say all in a word, without a Jewish courage; for they were now defective in what is peculiar to our nation, that is, in boldness, in violence of assault, and in running upon the enemy all together, and in persevering in what they go about, though they do not at first succeed in it; (18) but they now went out in a more languid manner than usual, and at the same time found the Romans set in array, and more courageous than ordinary, (19) and that they guarded their banks both with their bodies and their

Reconstruction of a Roman siege machine with battering ram. (Museo Della Civita Romano; photo Samuel Magal)

A Roman catapult. (Museo Della Civita Romano; photo Samuel Magal)

entire armor, and this to such a degree on all sides, that they left no room for the fire to get among them, and that every one of their souls was in such good courage, that they would sooner die than desert their ranks; (20) for besides their notion that all their hopes were cut off, in case these their works were once burnt, the soldiers were greatly ashamed that subtlety should quite be too hard for courage, madness for armor, multitude for skill, and Jews for Romans. (21) The Romans had now also another advantage, in that their engines for sieges co-operated with them in throwing darts and stones as far as the Jews, when they were coming out of the city; whereby the man that fell became an impediment to him that was next to him, as did the danger of going farther make them less zealous in their attempts; (22) and for those that had run under the darts, some of them were terrified by the good order and closeness of the enemies' ranks before they came to a close fight, and others were pricked with their spears, and turned back again; at length they reproached one another for their cowardice, and retired without doing any thing. This attack was made upon the first day of the month Panemus [Tamuz.] (23) So when the Jews were retreated, the Romans brought their engines, although they had all the while stones thrown at them from the tower of Antonia, and were assaulted by fire and sword, and by all sorts of darts, which necessity afforded the Jews to make use of; (24) for although these had great dependence on their own wall, and a contempt of the Roman engines, yet did they endeavor to hinder the Romans from bringing them. (25) Now these Romans struggled hard, on the contrary, to bring them, as deeming that this zeal of the Jews was in order to avoid any impression to be made on the tower of Antonia, because its wall was but weak, and its foundations rotten. (26) However, that tower did not yield to the blows given it from the engines; yet did the Romans bear the impressions made by the enemies' darts which were perpetually cast at them, and did not give way to any of those dangers that came upon them from above, and so they brought their engines to bear. (27) But then, as they were beneath the other, and were sadly wounded by the stones thrown down upon them, some of them threw their shields over their bodies, and partly with their hands, and partly with their bodies, and partly with crows, they undermined its foundations, and with great pains they removed four of its stones. (28) Then night came upon both sides, and put an end to this struggle for the present; however, that night the wall was so shaken by the battering rams in that place where John had used his stratagem before, and had undermined their banks, that the ground then gave way, and the wall fell down suddenly.

4. (29) When this accident had unexpectedly happened, the minds of both parties were variously affected; (30) for though one would expect that the Jews would be discouraged, because this fall of their wall was unexpected by them, and they had made no provision in that case, yet did they pull up their courage, because the tower of Antonia itself was still standing; (31) as was the unexpected joy of the Romans at this fall of the wall soon quenched by the sight they had of another wall, which John and his party had built within it. (32) However, the attack of this second wall appeared to be easier than that of the former, because it seemed a thing of greater facility to get up to it through the parts of the former wall that were now thrown down. This new wall appeared also to be much weaker than the tower of Antonia, and accordingly the Romans imagined that it had been erected so much on the sudden, that they should soon overthrow it: yet did not any body venture now to go up to this wall; for that such as first ventured so to do must certainly be killed.

5. (33) And now Titus, upon consideration that the alacrity of soldiers in war is chiefly excited by hopes and by good words, and that exhortations and promises do frequently make men to forget the hazards they run, nay, sometimes to despise death itself, got together the most courageous part of his army, and tried what he could do with his men by these methods. (34) "O fellow soldiers," said he, "to make an exhortation to men to do what hath no peril in it, is on that very account inglorious to such to whom that exhortation is made; and indeed so it is in him that makes the exhortation, an argument of his own cowardice also. (35) I therefore think that such exhortations ought then only to be made use of when affairs are in a dangerous condition, and yet are worthy of being attempted by every one themselves; (36) accordingly, I am fully of the same opinion with you, that it is a difficult task to go up this wall; but that it is proper for those that desire reputation for their valor to struggle with difficulties in such cases will then appear, when I have particularly shown that it is a brave thing to die with glory, and that the courage here necessary shall not go unrewarded in those that first begin the attempt. (37) And let my first argument to move you to it be taken from what probably some would think reasonable to dissuade you, I mean the constancy and patience of these Jews, even under their ill successes; (38) for it is unbecoming you, who are Romans and my soldiers, who have in peace been taught how to make wars, and who have also been used to conquer in those wars, to be inferior to Jews, either in action of the hand, or in courage of the soul, and this especially when you are at the conclusion of your victory, and are assisted by God himself; (39) for as to our misfortunes, they have been owing to the madness of the Jews, while their sufferings have been owing to your valor, and to the assistance God hath afforded you; (40)

for as to the seditions they have been in, and the famine they are under, and the siege they now endure, and the fall of their walls without our engines, what can they all be but demonstrations of God's anger against them, and of his assistance afforded us? (41) It will not therefore be proper for you, either to show yourselves inferior to those to whom you are really superior, or to betray that Divine assistance which is afforded you. (42) And, indeed, how can it be esteemed otherwise than a base and unworthy thing, that while the Jews, who need not be much ashamed if they be deserted, because they have long learned to be slaves to others, do yet despise death, that they may be so no longer; and do make sallies into the very midst of us frequently, no in hopes of conquering us, but merely for a demonstration of their courage; (43) we, who have gotten possession of almost all the world that belongs to either land or sea, to whom it will be a great shame if we do not conquer them, do not once undertake any attempt against our enemies wherein there is much danger, but sit still idle, with such brave arms as we have, (44) and only wait till the famine and fortune do our business themselves, and this when we have it in our power, with some small hazard, to gain all that we desire! (45) For if we go up to this tower of Antonia, we gain the city; for if there should be any more occasion for fighting against those within the city, which I do not suppose there will, since we shall then be upon the top of the hill and be upon our enemies before they can have taken breath, these advantages promise us no less than a certain and sudden victory. (46) As for myself, I shall at present wave any commendation of those who die in war, and omit to speak of the immortality of those men who are slain in the midst of their martial bravery; yet cannot I forbear to imprecate upon those who are of a contrary disposition, that they may die in time of peace, by some distemper or other, since their souls are condemned to the grave, together with their bodies. (47) For what man of virtue is there who does not know, that those souls which are severed from their fleshly bodies in battles by the sword are received by the ether, that purest of elements, and joined to that company which are placed among the stars; that they become good demons, and propitious heroes, and show themselves as such to their posterity afterwards? (48) while upon those souls that wear away in and with their distempered bodies comes a subterranean night to dissolve them to nothing, and a deep oblivion to take away all the remembrance of them, and this notwithstanding they be clean from all spots and defilements of this world; so that, in this ease, the soul at the same time comes to the utmost bounds of its life, and of its body, and of its memorial also. (49) But since he hath determined that death is to come of necessity upon all men, a sword is a better instrument for that purpose than any disease whatsoever. Why is it not then a very mean thing for us not to yield up that to the public benefit which we must yield up to fate? (50) And this discourse have I made, upon the supposition that those who at first attempt to go upon this wall must needs be killed in the attempt, though still men of true courage have a chance to escape even in the most hazardous undertakings. (51) For, in the first place, that part of the former wall that is thrown down is easily to be ascended; and for the new-built wall, it is easily destroyed. Do you, therefore, many of you, pull up your courage, and set about this work, and do you mutually encourage and assist one another; and this your bravery will soon break the hearts of your enemies; (52) and perhaps such a glorious undertaking as yours is may be accomplished without bloodshed. For although it be justly to be supposed that the Jews will try to hinder you at your first beginning to go up to them; yet when you have once concealed yourselves from them, and driven them away by force, they will not be able to sustain your efforts against them any longer, though but a few of you prevent them, and get over the wall. (53) As for that person who first mounts the wall, I should blush for shame if I did not make him to be envied of others, by those rewards I would bestow upon him. If such a one escape with his life, he shall have the command of others that are now but his equals; although it be true also that the greatest rewards will accrue to such as die in the attempt."

6. (54) Upon this speech of Titus, the rest of the multitude were affrighted at so great a danger. But there was one, whose name was Sabinus, a soldier that served among the cohorts, and a Syrian by birth, who appeared to be of very great fortitude, both in the actions he had done, and the courage of his soul he had shown; (55) although anybody would have thought, before he came to his work, that he was of such a weak constitution of body, that he was not fit to be a soldier; for his color was black, his flesh was lean and thin, and lay close together; but there was a certain heroic soul that dwelt in this small body, which body was indeed much too narrow for that peculiar courage which was in him. (56) Accordingly he was the first that rose up, when he thus spake: "I readily surrender up myself to thee, O Caesar; I first ascend the wall, (57) and I heartily wish that my fortune may follow my courage and my resolution And if some ill fortune grudge me the success of my undertaking, take notice that my ill success will not be unexpected, but that I choose death voluntarily for thy sake." (58) When he had said this, and had spread out his sheild over his head with his left hand, and hill, with his right hand, drawn his sword, he marched up to the wall, just about the sixth hour of the day. (59) There followed him eleven others, and no more, that resolved to imitate his bravery; but still this was the principal person of them all, and went first, as excited by a divine fury. (60) Now those that guarded the wall shot at them from thence, and cast innumerable darts upon them from every side; they also rolled very large stones upon them, which overthrew some of those eleven that were with him. (61) But as for Sabinus himself, he met the darts that were cast at him and though he was overwhelmed with them, yet did he not leave off the violence of his attack before he had gotten up on the top of the wall, and had put the enemy to flight. (62) For as the Jews were astonished at his great strength, and the bravery of his soul, and as, withal, they imagined more of them had got upon the wall than really had, they were put to flight. (63) And now one cannot but complain here of fortune, as still envious at virtue, and always hindering the performance of glorious achievements: (64) this was the case of the man before us, when he had just obtained his purpose; for he then stumbled at a certain large stone, and fell down upon it headlong, with a very great noise. Upon which the Jews turned back, and when they saw him to be alone, and fallen down also, they threw darts at him from every side. (65) However, he got upon his knee, and covered himself with his shield, and at the first defended himself against them, and wounded many of those that came near him; (66) but he was soon forced to relax his right hand, by the multitude of the wounds that had been given him, till at length he was quite covered over with darts before he gave up the ghost. He was one who deserved a better fate, by reason of his bravery; but, as might be expected, he fell under so vast an attempt. (67) As for the rest of his partners, the Jews dashed three of them to pieces with stones, and slew them as they were gotten up to the top of the wall; the other eight being wounded, were pulled down, and carried back to the camp. These things were done upon the third day of the month Panemus [Tamuz].

7. (68) Now two days afterward twelve of those men that were on the forefront, and kept watch upon the banks, got together, and called to them the standard-bearer of the fifth legion, and two

others of a troop of horsemen, and one trumpeter; these went without noise, about the ninth hour of the night, through the ruins, to the tower of Antonia; and when they had cut the throats of the first guards of the place, as they were asleep, they got possession of the wall, and ordered the trumpeter to sound his trumpet. (69) Upon which the rest of the guard got up on the sudden, and ran away, before any body could see how many they were that were gotten up; for, partly from the fear they were in, and partly from the sound of the trumpet which they heard, they imagined a great number of the enemy were gotten up. (70) But as soon as Caesar heard the signal, he ordered the army to put on their armor immediately, and came thither with his commanders, and first of all ascended, as did the chosen men that were with him. (71) And as the Jews were flying away to the temple, they fell into that mine which John had dug under the Roman banks. (72) Then did the seditious of both the bodies of the Jewish army, as well that belonging to John as that belonging to Simon, drive them away; and indeed were no way wanting as to the highest degree of force and alacrity; (73) for they esteemed themselves entirely ruined if once the Romans got into the temple, as did the Romans look upon the same thing as the beginning of their entire conquest. (74) So a terrible battle was fought at the entrance of the temple, while the Romans were forcing their way, in order to get possession of that temple, and the Jews were driving them back to the tower of Antonia; (75) in which battle the darts were on both sides useless, as well as the spears, and both sides drew their swords, and fought it out hand to hand. Now during this struggle the positions of the men were undistinguished on both sides, and they fought at random, the men being intermixed one with another, and confounded, by reason of the narrowness of the place; while the noise that was made fell on the ear after an indistinct manner, because it was so very loud. (76) Great slaughter was now made on both sides, and the combatants trod upon the bodies and the armor of those that were dead, and dashed them to pieces. (77) Accordingly, to which side soever the battle inclined, those that had the advantage exhorted one another to go on, as did those that were beaten make great lamentation. But still there was no room for flight, nor for pursuit, but disorderly revolutions and retreats, while the armies were intermixed one with another; (78) but those that were in the first ranks were under the necessity of killing or being killed, without any way for escaping; for those on both sides that came behind forced those before them to go on, without leaving any space between the armies. (79) At length the Jews' violent zeal was too hard for the Romans' skill, and the battle already inclined entirely that way; for the fight had lasted from the ninth hour of the night till the seventh hour of the day, (80) while the Jews came on in crowds, and had the danger the temple was in for their motive; the Romans having no more here than a part of their army; for those legions, on which the soldiers on that side depended, were not come up to them. So it was at present thought sufficient by the Romans to take possession of the tower of Antonia.

8. (81) But there was one Julian, a centurion, that came from Eithynia, a man he was of great reputation, whom I had formerly seen in that war, and one of the highest fame, both for his skill in war, his strength of body, and the courage of his soul. (82) This man, seeing the Romans giving ground, and ill a sad condition, (for he stood by Titus at the tower of Antonia,) leaped out, and of himself alone put the Jews to flight, when they were already conquerors, and made them retire as far as the corner of the inner court of the temple; from him the multitude fled away in crowds, as supposing that neither his strength nor his violent attacks could be those of a

M. Avi-Yonah's scale model of the temple mount and the four towers of the Antonia, looking east, now on display at The Israel Museum. (photo Samuel Magal)

mere man. (83) Accordingly, he rushed through the midst of the Jews, as they were dispersed all abroad, and killed those that he caught. Nor, indeed, was there any sight that appeared more wonderful in the eyes of Caesar, or more terrible to others, than this. (84) However, he was himself pursued by fate, which it all not possible that he, who was but a mortal man, should escape; (85) for as he had shoes all full of thick and sharp nails as had every one of the other soldiers, so when he ran on the pavement of the temple, he slipped, and fell down upon his back with a very great noise, which was made by his armor. This made those that were running away to turn back; (86) whereupon those Romans that were in the tower of Antonia set up a great shout, as they were in fear for the man. But the Jews got about him in crowds, and struck at him with their spears and with their swords on all sides. (87) Now he received a great many of the strokes of these iron weapons upon his shield, and often attempted to get up again, but was thrown down by those that struck at him; yet did he, as he lay along, stab many of them with his sword. (88) Nor was he soon killed, as being covered with his helmet and his breastplate in all those parts of his body where he might be mortally wounded; he also pulled his neck close to his body, till all his other limbs were shattered, and nobody durst come to defend him, and then he yielded to his fate. (89) Now Caesar was deeply affected on account of this man of so great fortitude, and especially as he was killed in the sight of so many people; he was desirous himself to come to his assistance, but the place would not give him leave, while such as could have done it were too much terrified to attempt it. (90) Thus when Julian had struggled with death a great while, and had let but few of those that had given him his mortal wound go off unhurt, he had at last his throat cut, though not without some difficulty, and left behind him a very great fame, not only among the Romans, and with Caesar himself, but among his enemies also; (91) then did the Jews catch up his dead body, and put the Romans to flight again, and shut them up in the tower of Antonia. (92) Now those that most signalized themselves, and fought most zealously in this battle of the Jewish side, were one Alexas and Gyphtheus, of John's party, and of Simon's party were Malachias, and Judas the son of Merto, and James the son of Sosas, the commander of the Idumeans; and of the zealots, two brethren, Simon and Judas, the sons of Jairus.

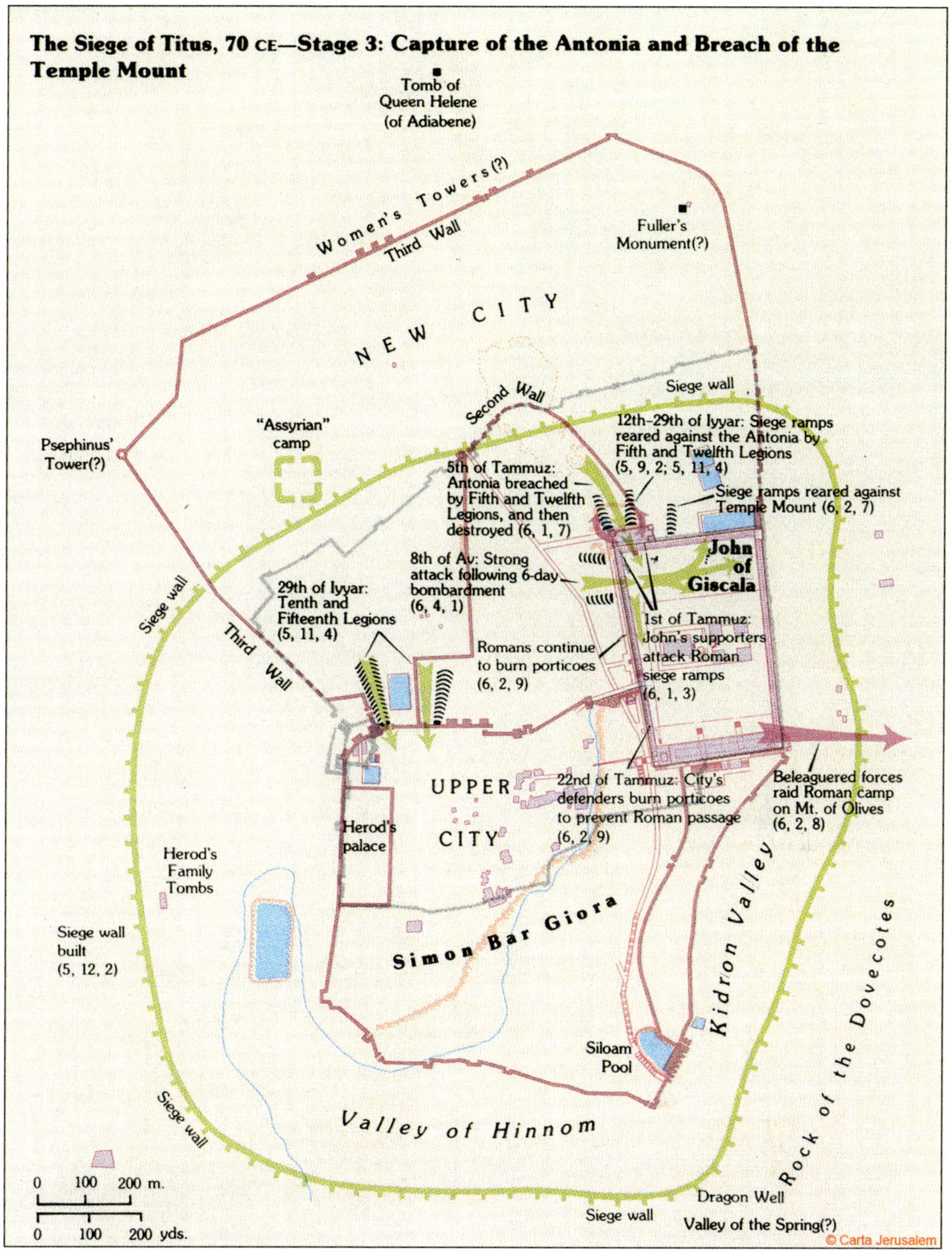

(from *The Carta Jerusalem Atlas* / Dan Bahat)

CHAPTER 2.

HOW TITUS GAVE ORDERS TO DEMOLISH THE TOWER OF ANTONIA AND THEN PERSUADED JOSEPHUS TO EXHORT THE JEWS AGAIN [TO A SURRENDER].

1. (93) AND now Titus gave orders to his soldiers that were with him to dig up the foundations of the tower of Antonia, and make him a ready passage for his army to come up; (94) while he himself had Josephus brought to him, (for he had been informed that on that very day, which was the seventeenth day **(cf. Daniel 9:27)** of Panemus, [Tamuz,] the sacrifice called "the Daily Sacrifice" had failed, and had not been offered to God, for want of men to offer it, and that the people were grievously troubled at it,) (95) and commanded him to say the same things to John that he had said before, that if he had any malicious inclination for fighting, he might come out with as many of his men as he pleased, in order to fight, without the danger of destroying either his city or temple; but that he desired he would not defile the temple, nor thereby offend against God. That he might, if he pleased, offer the sacrifices which were now discontinued by any of the Jews whom he should pitch upon. (96) Upon this Josephus stood in such a place where he might be heard, not by John only, but by many more, and then declared to them what Caesar had given him in charge, and this in the Hebrew language. (97) So he earnestly prayed them to spare their own city, and to prevent that fire which was just ready to seize upon the temple, and to offer their usual sacrifices to God therein. (98) At these words of his a great sadness and silence were observed among the people. But the tyrant himself cast many reproaches upon Josephus, with imprecations besides; and at last added this withal, that he did never fear the taking of the city, because it was God's own city. (99) In answer to which Josephus said thus with a loud voice: "To be sure thou hast kept this city won-

Stone window railing from the palace of Jehoiachim at Ramat Rachel. (Carta collection)

derfully pure for God's sake; the temple also continues entirely unpolluted! Nor hast thou been guilty of ally impiety against him for whose assistance thou hopest! He still receives his accustomed sacrifices! (100) Vile wretch that thou art! if any one should deprive thee of thy daily food, thou wouldst esteem him to be an enemy to thee; but thou hopest to have that God for thy supporter in this war whom thou hast deprived of his everlasting worship; (101) and thou imputest those sins to the Romans, who to this very time take care to have our laws observed, and almost compel these sacrifices to be still offered to God, which have by thy means been intermitted! (102) Who is there that can avoid groans and lamentations at the amazing change that is made in this city? since very foreigners and enemies do now correct that impiety which thou hast occasioned; while thou, who art a Jew, and wast educated in our laws, art become a greater enemy to them than the others. (103) But still, John, it is never dishonorable to repent, and amend what hath been done amiss, even at the last extremity. Thou hast an instance before thee in Jechoniah [Jehoiachim], the king of the Jews, if thou hast a mind to save the city, (104) who, when the king of Babylon made war against him, did of his own accord go out of this city before it was taken, and did undergo a voluntary captivity with his family, that the sanctuary might not be delivered up to the enemy, and that he might not see the house of God set on fire; (105) on which account he is celebrated among all the Jews, in their sacred memorials, and his memory is become immortal, and will be conveyed fresh down to our posterity through all ages. (106) This, John, is an excellent example in such a time of danger, and I dare venture to promise that the Romans shall still forgive thee. (107) And take notice that I, who make this exhortation to thee, am one of thine own nation; I, who am a Jew, do make this promise to thee. And it will become thee to consider who I am that give thee this counsel, and whence I am derived; for while I am alive I shall never be in such slavery, as to forego my own kindred, or forget the laws of our forefathers. (108) Thou hast indignation at me again, and makest a clamor at me, and reproachest me; indeed I cannot deny but I am worthy of worse treatment than all this amounts to, because, in opposition to fate, I make this kind invitation to thee, and endeavor to force deliverance upon those whom God hath condemned. (109) And who is there that does not know what the writings of the ancient prophets contain in them,—and particularly that oracle which is just now going to be fulfilled upon this miserable city? For they foretold that this city should be then taken when somebody shall begin the slaughter of his own countrymen. (110) And are not both the city and the entire temple now full of the dead bodies of your countrymen? It is God, therefore, it is God himself who is bringing on this fire, to purge that city and temple by means of the Romans, and is going to pluck up this city, which is full of your pollutions."

2. (111) As Josephus spoke these words, with groans and tears in his eyes, his voice was intercepted by sobs. (112) However, the Romans could not but pity the affliction he was under, and wonder at his conduct. But for John, and those that were with him, they were but the more exasperated against the Romans on this account, and were desirous to get Josephus also into their power: (113) yet did that discourse influence a great many of the better sort; and truly some of them were so afraid of the guards set by the seditious, that they tarried where they were, but still were satisfied that both they and the city were doomed to destruction. Some also there were who, watching a proper opportunity when they might quietly get away, fled to the Romans, (114) of whom were the high priests Joseph and Jesus, and of the sons of high priests three, whose father was Ishmael, who was beheaded in Cyrene, and four sons of Matthias, as also one son of the other Matthias, who ran away after his father's death, and whose father was slain by Simon the son of Gioras, with three of his sons, as I have already related; many also of the other nobility went over to the Romans, together with the high priests. (115) Now Caesar not only received these men very kindly in other respects, but, knowing they would not willingly live after the customs of other nations, he sent them to Gophna, and desired them to remain there for the present, and told them, that when he was gotten clear of this war, he would restore each of them to their possessions again; (116) so they cheerfully retired to that small city which was allotted them, without fear of any danger. But as they did not appear, the seditious gave out again that these deserters were slain by the Romans, which was done in order to deter the rest from running away, by fear of the like treatment. (117) This trick of theirs succeeded now for a while, as did the like trick before; for the rest were hereby deterred from deserting, by fear of the like treatment.

3. (118) However, when Titus had recalled those men from Gophna, he gave orders that they should go round the wall, together with Josephus, and show themselves to the people; upon which a great many fled to the Romans. (119) These men also got in a great number together, and stood before the Romans, and besought the seditious, with groans and tears in their eyes, in the first place to receive the Romans entirely into the city, and save that their own place of residence again; (120) but that, if they would not agree to such a proposal, they would at least depart out of the temple, and save the holy house for their own use; for that the Romans would not venture to set the sanctuary on fire but under the most pressing necessity. (121) Yet did the seditious still more and more contradict them; and while they cast loud and bitter reproaches upon these deserters, they also set their engines for throwing of darts, and javelins, and stones upon the sacred gates of the temple, at due distances from one another, insomuch that all the space round about within the temple might be compared to a burying-ground, so great was the number of the dead bodies therein; as might the holy house itself be compared to a citadel. (122) Accordingly, these men rushed upon these holy places in their armor, that were otherwise unapproachable, and that while their hands were yet warm with the blood of their own people which they had shed; nay, they proceeded to such great transgressions, that the very same indignation which Jews would naturally have against Romans, had they been guilty of such abuses against them, the Romans now had against Jews, for their impiety in regard to their own religious customs. (123) Nay, indeed, there were none of the Roman soldiers who did not look with a sacred horror upon the holy house, and adored it, and wished that the robbers would

repent before their miseries became incurable.

Entrance ban inscription forbidding foreigners from entering the sanctified area. The Greek inscription shown here has been reconstructed according to one found in 1871 near the "Dark Gate" on the Temple Mount. The section in the photograph is from another inscription discovered in the vicinity of the Lions' Gate in 1935. (after *QDAP* VI: 2, 1938)

4. (124) Now Titus was deeply affected with this state of things, and reproached John and his party, and said to them, "Have not you, vile wretches that you are, by our permission, put up this partition-wall before your sanctuary? (125) Have not you been allowed to put up the pillars thereto belonging, at due distances, and on it to engrave in Greek, and in your own letters, this prohibition, that no foreigner should go beyond that wall? (126) Have not we given you leave to kill such as go beyond it, though he were a Roman? And what do you do now, you pernicious villains? Why do you trample upon dead bodies in this temple? and why do you pollute this holy house with the blood of both foreigners and Jews themselves? (127) I appeal to the gods of my own country, and to every god that ever had any regard to this place; (for I do not suppose it to be now regarded by any of them;) I also appeal to my own army, and to those Jews that are now with me, and even to yourselves, that I do not force you to defile this your sanctuary; (128) and if you will but change the place whereon you will fight, no Roman shall either come near your sanctuary, or offer any affront to it; nay, I will endeavor to preserve you your holy house, whether you will or not."

5. (129) As Josephus explained these things from the mouth of Caesar, both the robbers and the tyrant thought that these exhortations proceeded from Titus's fear, and not from his good-will to them, and grew insolent upon it. (130) But when Titus saw that these men were neither to be moved by commiseration towards themselves, nor had any concern upon them to have the holy house spared, he proceeded unwillingly to go on again with the war against them. (131) He could not indeed bring all his army against them, the place was so narrow; but choosing thirty soldiers of the most valiant out of every hundred, and committing a thousand to each tribune, and making Cerealis their commander-in-chief, he gave orders that they should attack the guards of the temple about the ninth hour of that night. (132) But as he was now in his armor, and preparing to go down with them, his friends would not let him go, by reason of the greatness of the danger, and what the commanders suggested to them; (133) for they said that he would do more by sitting above in the tower of Antonia, as a dispenser of rewards to those soldiers that signalized themselves in the fight, than by coming down and hazarding his own person in the forefront of them; for that they would all fight stoutly while Caesar looked upon them. (134) With this advice Caesar complied, and said that the only reason he had for such compliance with the soldiers was this, that he might be able to judge of their courageous actions, and that no valiant soldier might lie concealed, and miss of his reward, and no cowardly soldier might go unpunished; but that he might himself be an eye-witness, and able to give evidence of all that was done, who was to be the disposer of punishments and rewards to them. (135) So he sent the soldiers about their work at the hour forementioned, while he went out himself to a higher place in the tower of Antonia, whence he might see what was done, and there waited with impatience to see the event.

6. (136) However, the soldiers that were sent did not find the guards of the temple asleep, as they hoped to have done; but were obliged to fight with them immediately hand to hand, as they rushed with violence upon them with a great shout. Now as soon as the rest within the temple heard that shout of those that were upon the watch, they ran out in troops upon them. (137) Then did the Romans receive the onset of those that came first upon them; but those that followed them fell upon their own troops, and many of them treated their own soldiers as if they had been enemies; (138) for the great confused noise that was made on both sides hindered them from distinguishing one another's voices, as did the darkness of the night hinder them from the like distinction by the sight, besides that blindness which arose otherwise also from the passion and the fear they were in at the same time; for which reason it was all one to the soldiers who it was they struck at. (139) However, this ignorance did less harm to the Romans than to the Jews, because they were joined together under their shields, and made their sallies more regularly than the others did, and each of them remembered their watch-word; (140)

M. Avi-Yonah's scale model of the Antonia, from inside the northwestern corner of the Temple Mount. (now on display at The Israel Museum; photo Samuel Magal)

while the Jews were perpetually dispersed abroad, and made their attacks and retreats at random, and so did frequently seem to one another to be enemies; for every one of them received those of their own men that came back in the dark as Romans, and made an assault upon them; (141) so that more of them were wounded by their own men than by the enemy, till, upon the coming on of the day, the nature of the right was discerned by the eye afterward. Then did they stand in battle-array in distinct bodies, and cast their darts regularly, and regularly defended themselves; (142) nor did either side yield or grow weary. The Romans contended with each other who should fight the most strenuously, both single men and entire regiments, as being under the eye of Titus; and every one concluded that this day would begin his promotion if he fought bravely. (143) What were the great encouragements of the Jews to act vigorously were, their fear for themselves and for the temple, and the presence of their tyrant, who exhorted some, and beat and threatened others, to act courageously. (144) Now, it so happened, that this fight was for the most part a stationary one, wherein the soldiers went on and came back in a short time, and suddenly; for there was no long space of ground for either of their flights or pursuits. (145) But still there was a tumultuous noise among the Romans from the tower of Antonia, who loudly cried out upon all occasions to their own men to press on courageously, when they were too hard for the Jews, and to stay when they were retiring backward; (146) so that here was a kind of theater of war; for what was done in this fight could not be concealed either from Titus, or from those that were about him. (147) At length it appeared that this fight, which began at the ninth hour of the night, was not over till past the fifth hour of the day; and that, in the same place where the battle began, neither party could say they had made the other to retire; but both the armies left the victory almost in uncertainty between them; (148) wherein those that signalized themselves on the Roman side were a great many, but on the Jewish side, and of those that were with Simon, Judas the son of Merto, and Simon the son of Josas; of the Idumeans, James and Simon, the latter of whom was the son of Cathlas, and James was the son of Sosas; of those that were with John, Gyphtheus and Alexas; and of the zealots, Simon the son of Jairus.

7. (149) In the mean time, the rest of the Roman army had, in seven days' time, overthrown [some] foundations of the tower of Antonia, and had made a ready and broad way to the temple. (150) Then did the legions come near the first court, and began to raise their banks. The one bank was over against the north-west corner of the inner temple; another was at that northern edifice which was between the two gates; (151) and of the other two, one was at the western cloister of the outer court of the temple; the other against its northern cloister. However, these works were thus far advanced by the Romans, not without great pains and difficulty, and particularly by being obliged to bring their materials from the distance of a hundred furlongs. (152) They had further difficulties also upon them; sometimes by their over-great security they were in that they should overcome the Jewish snares laid for them, and by that boldness of the Jews which their despair of escaping had inspired them withal; (153) for some of their horsemen, when they went out to gather wood or hay, let their horses feed without having their bridles on during the time of foraging; upon which horses the Jews sallied out in whole bodies, and seized them. (154) And when this was continually done, and Caesar believed what the truth was, that the horses were stolen more by the negligence of his own men than by the valor of the Jews, he determined to use greater severity to oblige the rest to take care of their horses; (155) so he commanded that one of those soldiers who had lost their horses should be capitally punished; whereby he so terrified the rest, that they preserved their horses for the time to come; for they did not any longer let them go from them to feed by themselves, but, as if they had grown to them, they went always along with them when they wanted necessaries. (156) Thus did the Romans still continue to make war against the temple, and to raise their banks against it.

8. (157) Now after one day had been interposed since the Romans ascended the breach, many of the seditious were so pressed by the famine, upon the present failure of their ravages, that they got together, and made an attack on those Roman guards that were upon the Mount of Olives, and this about the eleventh hour of the day, as supposing, first, that they would not expect such an onset, and, in the next place, that they were then taking care of their bodies, and that therefore they should easily beat them. (158) But the Romans were apprized of their coming to attack them beforehand, and, running together from the neighboring camps on the sudden, prevented them from getting over their fortification, or forcing the wall that was built about them. (159) Upon this came on a sharp fight, and here many great actions were performed on both sides; while the Romans showed both their courage and their skill in war, as did the Jews come on them with immoderate violence and intolerable passion. (160) The one part were urged on by shame, and the other by necessity; for it seemed a very shameful thing to the Romans to let the Jews go, now they were taken in a kind of net; while the Jews had but one hope of saving themselves, and that was in case they could by violence break through the Roman wall; (161) and one whose name was Pedanius, belonging to a party of horsemen, when the Jews were already beaten and forced down into the valley together, spurred his horse on their flank with great vehemence, and caught up a certain young man belonging to the enemy by his ankle, as he was running away; (162) the man was, however, of a robust body, and in his armor; so low did Pedanius bend himself downward from his horse, even as he was galloping away, and so great was the strength of his right hand, and of the rest of his body, as also such skill had he in horsemanship. (163) So this man seized upon that his prey, as upon a precious treasure, and carried him as his captive to Caesar; whereupon Titus admired the man that had seized the other for his great strength, and ordered the man that was caught to be punished [with death] for his attempt against the Roman wall, but betook himself to the siege of the temple, and to pressing on the raising of the banks.

9. (164) In the meantime, the Jews were so distressed by the fights they had been in, as the war advanced higher and higher, and creeping up to the holy house itself, that they, as it were, cut off those limbs of their body which were infected, in order to prevent the distemper's spreading further; (165) for they set the north-west cloister, which was joined to the tower of Antonia, on fire, and after that brake off about twenty cubits of that cloister, and thereby made a beginning in burning the sanctuary; (166) two days after which, or on the twenty-fourth day of the forenamed month, [Panemus or Tamuz,] the Romans set fire to the cloister that joined to the other, when the fire went fifteen cubits farther. The Jews, in like manner, cut off its roof; nor did they entirely leave off what they were about till the tower of Antonia was parted from the temple, (167) even when it was in their power to have stopped the fire; nay, they lay still while the temple was first set on fire, and deemed this spreading of the fire to be for their own advantage. (168) However, the armies were still fighting one against another about the temple, and the war was managed by continual sallies of particular parties against one another.

The Temple Mount today, looking east toward the Mount of Olives. (photo Samuel Magal)

10. (169) Now there was at this time a man among the Jews, low of stature he was, and of a despicable appearance; of no character either as to his family, or in other respects: his flame was Jonathan. He went out at the high priest John's monument, and uttered many other insolent things to the Romans, a challenged the best of them all to a single combat. (170) But many of those that stood there in the army huffed him, and many of them (as they might well be) were afraid of him. Some of them also reasoned thus, and that justly enough: that it was not fit to fight with a man that desired to die, (171) because those that utterly despaired of deliverance had, besides other passions, a violence in attacking men that could not be opposed, and had no regard to God himself; and that to hazard oneself with a person, whom, if you overcome, you do no great matter, and by whom it is hazardous that you may be taken prisoner, would be an instance, not of manly courage, but of unmanly rashness. (172) So there being nobody that came out to accept the man's challenge, and the Jew cutting them with a great number of reproaches, as cowards, (for he was a very haughty man in himself, and a great despiser of the Romans,) one whose name was Pudens, of the body of horsemen, out of his abomination of the other's words, and of his impudence withal, and perhaps out of an inconsiderate arrogance, on account of the other's lowness of stature, ran out to him, (173) and was too hard for him in other respects, but was betrayed by his ill fortune; for he fell down, and as he was down, Jonathan came running to him, and cut his throat, (174) and then, standing upon his dead body, he brandished his sword, bloody as it was, and shook his shield with his left hand, and made many acclamations to the Roman army, and exulted over the dead man, and jested upon the Romans; (175) till at length one Priscus, a centurion, shot a dart at him as he was leaping and playing the fool with himself, and thereby pierced him through; upon which a shout was set up both by the Jews and the Romans, though on different accounts. (176) So Jonathan grew giddy by the pain of his wounds, and fell down upon the body of his adversary, as a plain instance how suddenly vengeance may come upon men that have success in war, without any just deserving the same.

CHAPTER 3.

CONCERNING A STRATAGEM THAT WAS DEVISED BY THE JEWS, BY WHICH THEY BURNT MANY OF THE ROMANS; WITH ANOTHER DESCRIPTION OF THE TERRIBLE FAMINE THAT WAS IN THE CITY.

1. (177) BUT now the seditious that were in the temple did every day openly endeavor to beat off the soldiers that were upon the banks, and on the twenty-seventh day of the forenamed month [Panemus or Tamuz] contrived such a stratagem as this: (178) They filled that part of the western cloister which was between the beams, and the roof under them, with dry materials, as also with bitumen and pitch, and then retired from that place, as though they were tired with the pains they had taken; (179) at which procedure of theirs, many of the most inconsiderate among the Romans, who were carried away with violent passions, followed hard after them as they were retiring, and applied ladders to the cloister, and got up to it suddenly; but the prudent part of them, when they understood this unaccountable retreat of the Jews, stood still where they were before. (180) However, the cloister was full of those that were gone up the ladders; at which time the Jews set it all on fire; and as the flame burst out every where on the sudden, the Romans that were out of the danger were seized with a very great consternation, as were those that were in the midst of the danger in the utmost distress. (181) So when they perceived themselves surrounded with the flames, some of them threw themselves down backwards into the city, and some among their

The Masonic Hall, or Council Chamber, discovered by Charles Warren below Wilson's Arch in the Western Wall tunnels. This chamber adjoined the Xystus in Josephus's time. (photo deror_avi, via Wikimedia Commons)

enemies [in the temple]; as did many leap down to their own men, and broke their limbs to pieces; but a great number of those that were going to take these violent methods were prevented by the fire; though some prevented the fire by their own swords. (182) However, the fire was on the sudden carried so far as to surround those who would have otherwise perished. As for Caesar himself, he could not, however, but commiserate those that thus perished, although they got up thither without any order for so doing, (183) since there was no way of giving the many relief. Yet was this some comfort to those that were destroyed, that every body might see that person grieve, for whose sake they came to their end; for he cried out openly to them, and leaped up, and exhorted those that were about him to do their utmost to relieve them. (184) So every one of them died cheerfully, as carrying along with him these words and this intention of Caesar as a sepulchral monument. (185) Some there were indeed who retired into the wall of the cloister, which was broad, and were preserved out of the fire, but were then surrounded by the Jews; and although they made resistance against the Jews for a long time, yet were they wounded by them, and at length they all fell down dead.

2. (186) At the last a young man among them, whose name was Longus, became a decoration to this sad affair, and while every one of them that perished were worthy of a memorial, this man appeared to deserve it beyond all the rest. (187) Now the Jews admired this man for his courage, and were further desirous of having him slain; so they persuaded him to come down to them, upon security given him for his life. But Cornelius his brother persuaded him on the contrary, not to tarnish his own glory, nor that of the Roman army. He complied with this last advice, and lifting up his sword before both armies, he slew himself. (188) Yet there was one Artorius among those surrounded by the fire who escaped by his subtlety; for when he had with a loud voice called to him Lucius, one of his fellow soldiers that lay with him in the same tent, and said to him, "I do leave thee heir of all I have, if thou wilt come and receive me." (189) Upon this he came running to receive him readily; Artorius then threw himself down upon him, and saved his own life, while he that received him was dashed so vehemently against the stone pavement by the other's weight, that he died immediately. (190) This melancholy accident made the Romans sad for a while, but still it made them more upon their guard for the future, and was of advantage to them against the delusions of the Jews, by which they were greatly damaged through their unacquaintedness with the places, and with the nature of the inhabitants. (191) Now this cloister was burnt down as far as John's tower, which he built in the war he made against Simon over the gates that led to the Xystus. The Jews also cut off the rest of that cloister from the temple, after they had destroyed those that got up to it. (192) But the next day the Romans burnt down the northern cloister entirely, as far as the east cloister, whose common angle joined to the valley that was called Cedron, and was built over it; on which account the depth was frightful. And this was the state of the temple at that time.

3. (193) Now of those that perished by famine in the city, the number was prodigious, and the miseries they underwent were unspeakable; (194) for if so much as the shadow of any kind of food did any where appear, a war was commenced presently, and the dearest friends fell a fighting one with another about it, snatching from each other the most miserable supports of life. (195) Nor would men believe that those who were dying had no food, but the robbers would search them when they were expiring, lest any one should have concealed food in their bosoms, and counterfeited dying; (196) nay, these robbers gaped for want, and ran about stumbling and staggering along like mad dogs, and reeling against the doors of the houses like drunken men; they would also, in the great distress they were in, rush into the very same houses two or three times in one and the same day. (197) Moreover, their hunger was so intolerable, that it obliged them to chew every thing, while they gathered such things as the most sordid animals would not touch, and endured to eat them; nor did they at length abstain from girdles and shoes; and the very leather which belonged to their shields they pulled off and gnawed: (198) the very wisps of old hay became food to some; and some gathered up fibres, and sold a very small weight of them for four Attic [drachmae]. (199) But why do I describe the shameless impudence that the famine brought on men in their eating inanimate things, while I am going to relate a matter of fact, the like to which no history relates, either among the Greeks or Barbarians? It is horrible to speak of it, and incredible when heard. (200) I had indeed willingly omitted this calamity of ours, that I might not seem to deliver what is so portentous to posterity, but that I have innumerable witnesses to it in my own age; and besides, my country would have had little reason to thank me for suppressing the miseries that she underwent at this time.

4. (201) There was a certain woman that dwelt beyond Jordan, her name was Mary; her father was Eleazar, of the village Bethezob, which signifies the house of Hyssop. She was eminent for her family and her wealth, and had fled away to Jerusalem with the rest of the multitude, and was with them besieged therein at this time. (202) The other effects of this woman had been already seized upon, such I mean as she had brought with her out of Perea, and

removed to the city. What she had treasured up besides, as also what food she had contrived to save, had been also carried off by the rapacious guards, who came every day running into her house for that purpose. (203) This put the poor woman into a very great passion, and by the frequent reproaches and imprecations she cast at these rapacious villains, she had provoked them to anger against her; (204) but none of them, either out of the indignation she had raised against herself, or out of commiseration of her case, would take away her life; and if she found any food, she perceived her labors were for others, and not for herself; and it was now become impossible for her any way to find any more food, while the famine pierced through her very bowels and marrow, when also her passion was fired to a degree beyond the famine itself; nor did she consult with any thing but with her passion and the necessity she was in. She then attempted a most unnatural thing; (205) and snatching up her son, who was a child sucking at her breast, she said, "O thou miserable infant! for whom shall I preserve thee in this war, this famine, and this sedition? (206) As to the war with the Romans, if they preserve our lives, we must be slaves. This famine also will destroy us, even before that slavery comes upon us. Yet are these seditious rogues more terrible than both the other. (207) Come on; be thou my food, and be thou a fury to these seditious varlets, and a by-word to the world, which is all that is now wanting to complete the calamities of us Jews." (208) As soon as she had said this, she slew her son, and then roasted him, and eat the one half of him, and kept the other half by her concealed. (209) Upon this the seditious came in presently, and smelling the horrid scent of this food, they threatened her that they would cut her throat immediately if she did not show them what food she had gotten ready. She replied that she had saved a very fine portion of it for them, and withal uncovered what was left of her son. (210) Hereupon they were seized with a horror and amazement of mind, and stood astonished at the sight, when she said to them, "This is mine own son, and what hath been done was mine own doing! Come, eat of this food; for I have eaten of it myself! (211) Do not you pretend to be either more tender than a woman, or more compassionate than a mother; but if you be so scrupulous, and do abominate this my sacrifice, as I have eaten the one half, let the rest be reserved for me also." (212) After which those men went out trembling, being never so much affrighted at any thing as they were at this, and with some difficulty they left the rest of that meat to the mother. Upon which the whole city was full of this horrid action immediately; and while every body laid this miserable case before their own eyes, they trembled, as if this unheard of action had been done by themselves. (213) So those that were thus distressed by the famine were very desirous to die, and those already dead were esteemed happy, because they had not lived long enough either to hear or to see such miseries.

5. (214) This sad instance was quickly told to the Romans, some of whom could not believe it, and others pitied the distress which the Jews were under; but there were many of them who were hereby induced to a more bitter hatred than ordinary against our nation. (215) But for Caesar, he excused himself before God as to this matter, and said that he had proposed peace and liberty to the Jews, as well as an oblivion of all their former insolent practices; but that they, instead of concord, had chosen sedition; instead of peace, war; and before satiety and abundance, a famine. (216) That they had begun with their own hands to burn down that temple which we have preserved hitherto; and that therefore they deserved to eat such food as this was. (217) That, however, this horrid action of eating an own child ought to be covered with the overthrow of their very country itself, and men ought not to leave such a city upon the habitable earth to be seen by the sun, wherein mothers are thus fed, (218) although such food be fitter for the fathers than for the mothers to eat of, since it is they that continue still in a state of war against us, after they have undergone such miseries as these. (219) And at the same time that he said this, he reflected on the desperate condition these men must be in; nor could he expect that such men could be recovered to sobriety of mind, after they had endured those very sufferings, for the avoiding whereof it only was probable they might have repented.

CHAPTER 4.

WHEN THE BANKS WERE COMPLETED AND THE BATTERING RAMS BROUGHT, AND COULD DO NOTHING, TITUS GAVE ORDERS TO SET FIRE TO THE GATES OF THE TEMPLE; IN NO LONG TIME AFTER WHICH THE HOLY HOUSE ITSELF WAS BURNT DOWN, EVEN AGAINST HIS CONSENT.

1. (220) AND now two of the legions had completed their banks on the eighth day of the month Lous [Ab]. Whereupon Titus gave orders that the battering rams should be brought, and set over against the western edifice of the inner temple; (221) for before these were brought, the firmest of all the other engines had battered the wall for six days together without ceasing, without making any impression upon it; but the vast largeness and strong connexion of the stones were superior to that engine, and to the other battering rams also. (222) Other Romans did indeed undermine the foundations of the northern gate, and after a world of pains removed the outermost stones, yet was the gate still upheld by the inner stones, and stood still unhurt; till the workmen, despairing of all such attempts by engines and crows, brought their ladders to the cloisters. (223) Now the Jews did not interrupt them in so doing; but when they were gotten up, they fell upon them, and fought with them; some of them they thrust down, and threw them backwards headlong; others of them they met and slew; (224) they also beat many of those that went down the ladders again, and slew them with their swords before they could bring their shields to protect them; nay, some of the ladders they threw down from above when they were full of armed men; (225) a great slaughter was made of the Jews also at the same time, while those that bare the ensigns fought hard for them, as deeming it a terrible thing, and what would tend to their great shame, if they permitted them to be stolen away. (226) Yet did the Jews at length get possession of these engines, and destroyed those that had gone up the ladders, while the rest were so intimidated by what those suffered who were slain, that they retired; (227) although none of the Romans died without having done good service before his death. Of the seditious, those that had fought bravely in the former battles did the like now, as besides them did Eleazar, the brother's son of Simon the tyrant. (228) But when Titus perceived that his endeavors to spare a foreign temple turned to the damage of his soldiers, and then be killed, he gave order to set the gates on fire.

2. (229) In the meantime, there deserted to him Ananus, who came from Emmaus, the most bloody of all Simon's guards, and Archelaus, the son of Magadatus, they hoping to be still forgiven, because they left the Jews at a time when they were the conquerors. (230) Titus objected this to these men, as a cunning trick of theirs; and as he had been informed of their other barbarities towards the Jews, he was going in all haste to have them both slain. He told them that they were only driven to this desertion because of the utmost distress they were in, and did not come away of their own good disposition; and that those did not deserve to be preserved, by whom their own city was already set on fire, out of

Remains of a Roman road leading from Jerusalem to Emmaus. (photo R. Steven Notley)

which fire they now hurried themselves away. (231) However, the security he had promised deserters overcame his resentments, and he dismissed them accordingly, though he did not give them the same privileges that he had afforded to others. (232) And now the soldiers had already put fire to the gates, and the silver that was over them quickly carried the flames to the wood that was within it, whence it spread itself all on the sudden, and caught hold on the cloisters. (233) Upon the Jews seeing this fire all about them, their spirits sunk together with their bodies, and they were under such astonishment, that not one of them made any haste, either to defend himself or to quench the fire, but they stood as mute spectators of it only. (234) However, they did not so grieve at the loss of what was now burning, as to grow wiser thereby for the time to come; but as though the holy house itself had been on fire already, they whetted their passions against the Romans. (235) This fire prevailed during that day and the next also; for the soldiers were not able to burn all the cloisters that were round about together at one time, but only by pieces.

3. (236) But then, on the next day, Titus commanded part of his army to quench the fire, and to make a road for the more easy marching up of the legions, while he himself gathered the commanders together. (237) Of those there were assembled the six principal persons: Tiberius Alexander, the commander [under the general] of the whole army; with Sextus Cerealis, the commander of the fifth legion; and Larcius Lepidus, the commander of the tenth legion; and Titus Frigius, the commander of the fifteenth legion: (238) there was also with them Eternius, the leader of the two legions that came from Alexandria; and Marcus Antonius Julianus, procurator of Judea: after these came together all the rest of the procurators and tribunes. Titus proposed to these that they should give him their advice what should be done about the holy house. (239) Now some of these thought it would be the best way to act according to the rules of war, [and demolish it,] because the Jews would never leave off rebelling while that house was standing; at which house it was that they used to get all together. (240) Others of them were of opinion, that in case the Jews would leave it, and none of them would lay their arms up in it, he might save it; but that in case they got upon it, and fought any more, he might burn it; because it must then be looked upon not as a holy house, but as a citadel; and that the impiety of burning it would then belong to those that forced this to be done, and not to them. (241) But Titus said, that "although the Jews should get upon that holy house, and fight us thence, yet ought we not to revenge ourselves on things that are inanimate, instead of the men themselves;" and that he was not in any case for burning down so vast a work as that was, because this would be a mischief to the Romans themselves, as it would be an ornament to their government while it continued. (242) So Fronto, and Alexander, and Cerealis grew bold upon that declaration, and agreed to the opinion of Titus. (243) Then was this assembly dissolved, when Titus had given orders to the commanders that the rest of their forces should lie still; but that they should make use of such as were most courageous in this attack. So he commanded that the chosen men that were taken out of the cohorts should make their way through the ruins, and quench the fire.

4. (244) Now it is true that on this day the Jews were so weary, and under such consternation, that they refrained from any attacks. But on the next day they gathered their whole force together, and ran upon those that guarded the outward court of the temple very boldly, through the east gate, and this about the second hour of the day. (245) These guards received that their attack with great bravery, and by covering themselves with their shields before, as if it were with a wall, they drew their squadron close together; yet was it evident that they could not abide there very long, but would be overborne by the multitude of those that sallied out upon them, and by the heat of their passion. (246) However, Caesar seeing, from the tower of Antonia, that this squadron was likely to give way, he sent some chosen horsemen to support them. (247) Hereupon the Jews found themselves not able to sustain their onset, and upon the slaughter of those in the forefront, many of the rest were put to flight. (248) But as the Romans were going off, the Jews turned upon them, and fought them; and as those Romans came back upon them, they retreated again, until about the fifth hour of the day they were overborne, and shut themselves up in the inner [court of the] temple.

5. (249) So Titus retired into the tower of Antonia, and resolved to storm the temple the next day, early in the morning, with his whole army, and to encamp round about the holy house. (250) But as for that house, God had, for certain, long ago doomed it to the fire; and now that fatal day was come, according to the revolution of ages; it was the tenth day of the month Lous, [Ab,] upon which it was formerly burnt by the king of Babylon; (251) although these flames took their rise from the Jews themselves, and were occasioned by them; for upon Titus's retiring, the seditious lay still for a little while, and then attacked the Romans again, when those that guarded the holy house fought with those that quenched the fire that was burning the inner [court of the] temple; but these Romans put the Jews to flight, and proceeded as far as the holy house itself. (252) At which time one of the soldiers, without staying for any orders, and without any concern or dread upon him at so great an undertaking, and being hurried on by a certain divine fury, snatched somewhat out of the materials that were on fire, and being lifted up by another soldier, he set fire to a golden window, through which there was a passage to the rooms that were round about the holy house, on the north side of it. (253) As the flames went upward, the Jews made a great clamor, such as so mighty an affliction required, and ran together to prevent it; and now they spared not their lives any longer, nor suffered any thing to restrain their force, since that holy house was perishing, for whose sake it was that they kept such a guard about it.

The elders and the virgins of Jerusalem lament the desolation of the city by the king of Babylon (Lamentations 2:10); 19th century engraving. (Carta collection)

6. (254) And now a certain person came running to Titus, and told him of this fire, as he was resting himself in his tent after the last battle; whereupon he rose up in great haste, and, as he was, ran to the holy house, in order to have a stop put to the fire; (255) after him followed all his commanders, and after them followed the several legions, in great astonishment; so there was a great clamor and tumult raised, as was natural upon the disorderly motion of so great an army. (256) Then did Caesar, both by calling to the soldiers that were fighting, with a loud voice, and by giving a signal to them with his right hand, order them to quench the fire. (257) But they did not hear what he said, though he spake so loud, having their ears already dimmed by a greater noise another way; nor did they attend to the signal he made with his hand neither, as still some of them were distracted with fighting, and others with passion. But as for the legions that came running thither, neither any persuasions nor any threatenings could restrain their violence, but each one's own passion was his commander at this time; and as they were crowding into the temple together, many of them were trampled on by one another, while a great number fell among the ruins of the cloisters, which were still hot and smoking, and were destroyed in the same miserable way with those whom they had conquered; (258) and when they were come near the holy house, they made as if they did not so much as hear Caesar's orders to the contrary; but they encouraged those that were before them to set it on fire. (259) As for the seditious, they were in too great distress already to afford their assistance [towards quenching the fire]; they were every where slain, and every where beaten; and as for a great part of the people, they were weak and without arms, and had their throats cut wherever they were caught. Now round about the altar lay dead bodies heaped one upon another, as at the steps going up to it ran a great quantity of their blood, whither also the dead bodies that were slain above [on the altar] fell down.

7. (260) And now, since Caesar was no way able to restrain the enthusiastic fury of the soldiers, and the fire proceeded on more and more, he went into the holy place of the temple, with his commanders, and saw it, with what was in it, which he found to be far superior to what the relations of foreigners contained, and not inferior to what we ourselves boasted of and believed about it. (261) But as the flame had not as yet reached to its inward parts, but was still consuming the rooms that were about the holy house, and Titus supposing what the fact was, that the house itself might yet be saved, (262) he came in haste and endeavored to persuade the soldiers to quench the fire, and gave order to Liberalius the centurion, and one of those spearmen that were about him, to beat the soldiers that were refractory with their staves, and to restrain them; (263) yet were their passions too hard for the regards they had for Caesar, and the dread they had of him who forbade them, as was their hatred of the Jews, and a certain vehement inclination to fight them, too hard for them also. (264) Moreover, the hope of plunder induced many to go on, as having this opinion, that all the places within were full of money, and as seeing that all round about it was made of gold. (265) And besides, one of those that went into the place prevented Caesar, when he ran so hastily out to restrain the soldiers, and threw the fire upon the hinges of the gate, in the dark; (266) whereby the flame burst out from within the holy house itself immediately, when the commanders retired, and Caesar with them, and when nobody any longer forbade those that were without to set fire to it. And thus was the holy house burnt down, without Caesar's approbation.

8. (267) Now although any one would justly lament the destruction of such a work as this was, since it was the most admirable of all the works that we have seen or heard of, both for its curious structure and its magnitude, and also for the vast wealth bestowed upon it, as well as for the glorious reputation it had for its holiness; yet might such a one comfort himself with this thought, that it was fate that decreed it so to be, which is inevitable, both as to living creatures, and as to works and places also. (268) However, one cannot but wonder at the accuracy of this period thereto relating; for the same month and day were now observed, as I said before, wherein the holy house was burnt formerly by the Babylonians. (269) Now the number of years that passed from its first foundation, which was laid by king Solomon, till this its destruction, which happened in the second year of the reign of Vespasian, are collected to be one thousand one hundred and thirty, besides seven months and fifteen days; (270) and from the second building of it, which was done by Haggai, in the second year of Cyrus the king, till its destruction under Vespasian, there were six hundred and thirty-nine years and forty-five days.

The Siege and Destruction of Jerusalem by the Romans Under the Command of Titus, A.D. 70, *by David Roberts, 1850.*

CHAPTER 5.

THE GREAT DISTRESS THE JEWS WERE IN UPON THE CONFLAGRATION OF THE HOLY HOUSE. CONCERNING A FALSE PROPHET, AND THE SIGNS THAT PRECEDED THIS DESTRUCTION.

1. (271) WHILE the holy house was on fire, every thing was plundered that came to hand, and ten thousand of those that were caught were slain; nor was there a commiseration of any age, or any reverence of gravity, but children, and old men, and profane persons, and priests were all slain in the same manner; so that this war went round all sorts of men, and brought them to destruction, and as well those that made supplication for their lives, as those that defended themselves by fighting. (272) The flame was also carried a long way, and made an echo, together with the groans of those that were slain; and because this hill was high, and the works at the temple were very great, one would have thought the whole city had been on fire. Nor can one imagine any thing either greater or more terrible than this noise; (273) for there was at once a shout of the Roman legions, who were marching all together, and a sad clamor of the seditious, who were now surrounded with fire and sword. The people also that were left above were beaten back upon the enemy, and under a great consternation, and made sad moans at the calamity they were under; (274) the multitude also that was in the city joined in this outcry with those that were upon the hill. And besides, many of those that were worn away by the famine, and their mouths almost closed, when they saw the fire of the holy house, they exerted their utmost strength, and brake out into groans and outcries again: Pera did also return the echo, as well as the mountains round about [the city,] and augmented the force of the entire noise. (275) Yet was the misery itself more terrible than this disorder; for one would have thought that the hill itself, on which the temple stood, was seething hot, as full of fire on every part of it, that the blood was larger in quantity than the fire, and those that were slain more in number than those that slew them; (276) for the ground did no where appear visible, for the dead bodies that lay on it; but the soldiers went over heaps of those bodies, as they ran upon such as fled from them. (277) And now it was that the multitude of the robbers were thrust out [of the inner court of the temple by the Romans,] and had much ado to get into the outward court, and from thence into the city, while the remainder of the populace fled into the cloister of that outer court. (278) As for the priests, some of them plucked up from the holy house the spikes that were upon it, with their bases, which were made of lead, and shot them at the Romans instead of darts. (279) But then as they gained nothing by so doing, and as the fire burst out upon them, they retired to the wall that was eight cubits broad, and there they tarried; (280) yet did two of these of eminence among them, who might have saved themselves by going over to the Romans, or have borne up with courage, and taken their fortune with the others, throw themselves into the fire, and were burnt together with the holy house; their names were Meirus the son of Belgas, and Joseph the son of Daleus.

2. (281) And now the Romans, judging that it was in vain to spare what was round about the holy house, burnt all those places, as also the remains of the cloisters and the gates, two excepted; the one on the east side, and the other on the south; both which, however, they burnt afterward. (282) They also burnt down the treasury chambers, in which was an immense quantity of money, and an immense number of garments, and other precious goods there reposited; and, to speak all in a few words, there it was that the entire riches of the Jews were heaped up together, while the rich people had there built themselves chambers [to contain such furniture]. (283) The soldiers also came to the rest of the cloisters that were in the outer [court of the] temple, whither the women and children, and a great mixed multitude of the people, fled, in number about six thousand. (284) But before Caesar had determined any thing about these people, or given the commanders any or-

ders relating to them, the soldiers were in such a rage, that they set that cloister on fire; by which means it came to pass that some of these were destroyed by throwing themselves down headlong, and some were burnt in the cloisters themselves. Nor did any one of them escape with his life. (285) A false prophet was the occasion of these people's destruction, who had made a public proclamation in the city that very day, that God commanded them to get upon the temple, and that there they should receive miraculous signs of their deliverance. (286) Now there was then a great number of false prophets suborned by the tyrants to impose on the people, who denounced this to them, that they should wait for deliverance from God; and this was in order to keep them from deserting, and that they might be buoyed up above fear and care by such hopes. (287) Now a man that is in adversity does easily comply with such promises; for when such a seducer makes him believe that he shall be delivered from those miseries which oppress him, then it is that the patient is full of hopes of such his deliverance.

3. (288) Thus were the miserable people persuaded by these deceivers, and such as belied God himself; while they did not attend nor give credit to the signs that were so evident, and did so plainly foretell their future desolation, but, like men infatuated, without either eyes to see or minds to consider, did not regard the denunciations that God made to them. (289) Thus there was a star resembling a sword, which stood over the city, and a comet, that continued a whole year. (290) Thus also before the Jews' rebellion, and before those commotions which preceded the war, when the people were come in great crowds to the feast of unleavened bread, on the eighth day of the month Xanthicus, [Nisan,] **(cf. John 11:55; 12:1)** and at the ninth hour of the night, so great a light shone round the altar and the holy house, that it appeared to be bright day time; which lasted for half an hour. (291) This light seemed to be a good sign to the unskillful, but was so interpreted by the sacred scribes, as to portend those events that followed immediately upon it. (292) At the same festival also, a heifer, as she was led by the high priest to be sacrificed, brought forth a lamb in the midst of the temple. (293) Moreover, the eastern gate of the inner [court of the] temple, which was of brass, and vastly heavy, and had been with difficulty shut by twenty men, and rested upon a basis armed with iron, and had bolts fastened very deep into the firm floor, which was there made of one entire stone, was seen to be opened of its own accord about the sixth hour of the night. (294) Now those that kept watch in the temple came hereupon running to the captain of the temple, and told him of it; who then came up thither, and not without great difficulty was able to shut the gate again. (295) This also appeared to the vulgar to be a very happy prodigy, as if God did thereby open them the gate of happiness. But the men of learning understood it, that the security of their holy house was dissolved of its own accord, and that the gate was opened for the advantage of their enemies. (296) So these publicly declared that the signal foreshowed the desolation that was coming upon them. Besides these, a few days after that feast, on the one and twentieth day of the month Artemisius, [Jyar,] (297) a certain prodigious and incredible phenomenon appeared: I suppose the account of it would seem to be a fable, were it not related by those that saw it, (298) and were not the events that followed it of so considerable a nature as to deserve such signals; for, before sun-setting, chariots and troops of soldiers in their armor were seen (299) running about among the clouds, and surrounding of cities. Moreover, at that feast which we call Pentecost, as the priests were going by night into the inner [court of the temple,] as their custom was, to perform their sacred ministrations, they said that, in the first place, they felt a quaking, and heard a great noise, (300) and after that they heard a sound as of a great multitude, saying, "Let us remove hence." But, what is still more terrible, there was one Jesus, the son of Ananus, a plebeian and a husbandman, who, four years before the war began, and at a time when the city was in very great peace

Destruction of the Temple of Jerusalem *by Francesco Hayez (1867); detail.* (photo Samuel Magal)

and prosperity, came to that feast whereon it is our custom for every one to make tabernacles to God in the temple, (cf. Nehemiah 8:16) (301) began on a sudden to cry aloud, "A voice from the east, a voice from the west, a voice from the four winds, a voice against Jerusalem and the holy house, a voice against the bridegrooms and the brides, and a voice against this whole people!" This was his cry, as he went about by day and by night, in all the lanes of the city. (302) However, certain of the most eminent among the populace had great indignation at this dire cry of his, and took up the man, and gave him a great number of severe stripes; yet did not he either say any thing for himself, or any thing peculiar to those that chastised him, but still went on with the same words which he cried before. (303) Hereupon our rulers, supposing, as the case proved to be, that this was a sort of divine fury in the man, brought him to the Roman procurator, (304) where he was whipped till his bones were laid bare; yet he did not make any supplication for himself, nor shed any tears, but turning his voice to the most lamentable tone possible, at every stroke of the whip his answer was, "Woe, woe to Jerusalem!" (305) And when Albinus (for he was then our procurator) asked him, Who he was? and whence he came? and why he uttered such words? he made no manner of reply to what he said, but still did not leave off his melancholy ditty, till Albinus took him to be a madman, and dismissed him. (306) Now, during all the time that passed before the war began, this man did not go near any of the citizens, nor was seen by them while he said so; but he every day uttered these lamentable words, as if it were his premeditated vow, "Woe, woe to Jerusalem!" (307) Nor did he give ill words to any of those that beat him every day, nor good words to those that gave him food; but this was his reply to all men, and indeed no other than a melancholy presage of what was to come. (308) This cry of his was the loudest at the festivals; and he continued this ditty for seven years and five months, without growing hoarse, or being tired therewith, until the very time that he saw his presage in earnest fulfilled in our siege, when it ceased; (309) for as he was going round upon the wall, he cried out with his utmost force, "Woe, woe to the city again, and to the people, and to the holy house!" And just as he added at the last, "Woe, woe to myself also!" there came a stone out of one of the engines, and smote him, and killed him immediately; and as he was uttering the very same presages he gave up the ghost.

4. (310) Now if any one consider these things, he will find that God takes care of mankind, and by all ways possible foreshows to our race what is for their preservation; but that men perish by those miseries which they madly and voluntarily bring upon themselves; (311) for the Jews, by demolishing the tower of Antonia, had made their temple four-square, while at the same time they had it written in their sacred oracles, "That then should their city be taken, as well as their holy house, when once their temple should become four-square." (312) But now, what did the most elevate them in undertaking this war, was an ambiguous oracle that was also found in their sacred writings, how," about that time, one from their country should become governor of the habitable earth." (313) The Jews took this prediction to belong to themselves in particular, and many of the wise men were thereby deceived in their determination. Now this oracle certainly denoted the government of Vespasian, who was appointed emperor in Judea. (314) However, it is not possible for men to avoid fate, although they see it beforehand. (315) But these men interpreted some of these signals according to their own pleasure, and some of them they utterly despised, until their madness was demonstrated, both by the taking of their city and their own destruction.

CHAPTER 6.

HOW THE ROMANS CARRIED THEIR ENSIGNS TO THE TEMPLE, AND MADE JOYFUL ACCLAMATIONS TO TITUS. THE SPEECH THAT TITUS MADE TO THE JEWS WHEN THEY MADE SUPPLICATION FOR MERCY. WHAT REPLY THEY MADE THERETO; AND HOW THAT REPLY MOVED TITUS'S INDIGNATION AGAINST THEM.

1. (316) AND now the Romans, upon the flight of the seditious into the city, and upon the burning of the holy house itself, and of all the buildings round about it, brought their ensigns to the temple and set them over against its eastern gate; and there did they offer sacrifices to them, and there did they make Titus imperator with the greatest acclamations of joy. (317) And now all the soldiers had such vast quantities of the spoils which they had gotten by plunder, that in Syria a pound weight of gold was sold for half its former value. (318) But as for those priests that kept themselves still upon the wall of the holy house, there was a boy that, out of the thirst he was in, desired some of the Roman guards to give him their right hands as a security for his life, and confessed he was very thirsty. (319) These guards commiserated his age, and the distress he was in, and gave him their right hands accordingly. So he came down himself, and drank some water, and filled the vessel he had with him when he came to them with water, and then went off, and fled away to his own friends; (320) nor could any of those guards overtake him; but still they reproached him for his perfidiousness. To which he made this answer: "I have not broken the agreement; for the security I had given me was not in order to my staying with you, but only in order to my coming down safely, and taking up some water; both which things I have performed, and thereupon think myself to have been faithful to my engagement." (321) Hereupon those whom the child had imposed upon admired at his cunning, and that on account of his age. On the fifth day afterward, the priests that were pined with the famine came down, and when they were brought to Titus by the guards, they begged for their lives; (322) but he replied, that the time of pardon was over as to them, and that this very holy house, on whose account only they could justly hope to be preserved, was destroyed; and that it was agreeable to their office that priests should perish with the house itself to which they belonged. So he ordered them to be put to death.

2. (323) But as for the tyrants themselves, and those that were with them, when they found that they were encompassed on every side, and, as it were, walled round, without any method of escaping, they desired to treat with Titus by word of mouth. (324) Accordingly, such was the kindness of his nature, and his desire of preserving the city from destruction, joined to the advice of his friends, who now thought the robbers were come to a temper, that he placed himself on the western side of the outer [court of the] temple; (325) for there were gates on that side above the Xystus, and a bridge that connected the upper city to the temple. This bridge it was that lay between the tyrants and Caesar, and parted them; (326) while the multitude stood on each side; those of the Jewish nation about Sinran and John, with great hopes of pardon; and the Romans about Caesar, in great expectation how Titus would receive their supplication. (327) So Titus charged his soldiers to restrain their rage, and to let their darts alone, and appointed an interpreter between them, which was a sign that he was the conqueror, and first began the discourse, and said, (328) "I hope you, sirs, are now satiated with the miseries of your country, who have not bad any just notions, either of our great power, or of your own great weakness, but have, like madmen, after a violent and inconsiderate manner, made such attempts, as have brought

Aerial view of the Old City of Jerusalem, looking northwest, with the Ophel (Ophlas) seen south of the Temple Mount and the valley of Cedron to the right. (photo Samuel Magal)

your people, your city, and your holy house to destruction. (329) You have been the men that have never left off rebelling since Pompey first conquered you, and have, since that time, made open war with the Romans. (330) Have you depended on your multitude, while a very small part of the Roman soldiery have been strong enough for you? Have you relied on the fidelity of your confederates? And what nations are there, out of the limits of our dominion, that would choose to assist the Jews before the Romans? Are your bodies stronger than ours? (331) nay, you know that the [strong] Germans themselves are our servants. Have you stronger walls than we have? Pray, what greater obstacle is there than the wall of the ocean, with which the Britons are encompassed, and yet do adore the arms of the Romans. (332) Do you exceed us in courage of soul, and in the sagacity of your commanders? Nay, indeed, you cannot but know that the very Carthaginians have been conquered by us. (333) It can therefore be nothing certainly but the kindness of us Romans which hath excited you against us; who, in the first place, have given you this land to possess; and, in the next place, have set over you kings of your own nation; and, in the third place, have preserved the laws of your forefathers to you, (334) and have withal permitted you to live, either by yourselves, or among others, as it should please you: (335) and, what is our chief favor of all we have given you leave to gather up that tribute which is paid to God with such other gifts that are dedicated to him; nor have we called those that carried these donations to account, nor prohibited them; till at length you became richer than we ourselves, even when you were our enemies; and you made preparations for war against us with our own money; (336) nay, after all, when you were in the enjoyment of all these advantages, you turned your too great plenty against those that gave it you, and, like merciless serpents, have thrown out your poison against those that treated you kindly. (337) I suppose, therefore, that you might despise the slothfulness of Nero, and, like limbs of the body that are broken or dislocated, you did then lie quiet, waiting for some other time, though still with a malicious intention, and have now showed your distemper to be greater than ever, and have extended your desires as far as your impudent and immense hopes would enable you to do it. (338) At this time my father came into this country, not with a design to punish you for what you had done under Cestius, but to admonish you; (339) for had he come to overthrow your nation, he had run directly to your fountain-head, and had immediately laid this city waste; whereas he went and burnt Galilee and the neighboring parts, and thereby gave you time for repentance; (340) which instance of humanity you took for an argument of his weakness, and nourished up your impudence by our mildness. (341) When Nero was gone out of the world, you did as the wickedest wretches would have done, and encouraged yourselves to act against us by our civil dissensions, and abused that time, when both I and my father were gone away to Egypt, to make preparations for this war. Nor were you ashamed to raise disturbances against us when we were made emperors, and this while you had experienced how mild we had been, when we were no more than generals of the army. (342) But when the government was devolved upon us, and all other people did thereupon lie quiet, and even foreign nations sent embassies, and congratulated our access to the government, (343) then did you Jews show yourselves to be our enemies. You sent embassies to those of your nation that are beyond Euphrates to assist you in your raising disturbances; new walls were built by you round your city, seditions arose, and one tyrant contended against another, and a civil war broke out among you; such indeed as became none but so wicked a people as you are. (344) I then came to this city, as unwillingly sent by my father, and received melancholy injunctions from him. When I heard that the people were disposed to peace, I rejoiced at it; (345) I exhorted you to leave off these proceedings before I began this war; I spared you even when you had fought against me a great while; I gave my right hand as security to the deserters; I observed what I had promised faithfully. When they fled to me, I had compassion on many of those that I had taken captive; I tortured those that were eager for war, in order to restrain them. It was unwillingly that I brought my engines of war against your walls; I always prohibited my soldiers, when they were set upon your slaughter, from their severity against you. After every victory I persuaded you to peace, as though I had been myself conquered. (346) When I came near your temple, I again departed from the laws of war, and exhorted you to spare your own sanctuary, and to preserve your holy house to yourselves. I allowed you a quiet exit out of it, and security for your preservation; nay, if you had a mind, I gave you leave to fight in another place. Yet have you still despised every one of my proposals, and have set fire to your holy house with your own hands. (347) And now, vile wretches, do you desire to treat with me by word of mouth? To what purpose is it that you would save such a holy house as this was, which is now destroyed? What preservation can you now desire after the destruction of your temple? (348) Yet do you stand still at this very time in your armor; nor can you bring yourselves so much as to pretend to be supplicants even in this your utmost extremity. O miserable creatures! what is it you depend on? (349) Are not your people dead? is not your holy house gone? is not your city in my power? and are not your own very lives in my hands? And do you still deem it a part of valor to die? (350) However, I will not imitate your madness. If you throw down your arms, and deliver up your bodies to me, I grant you your lives; and I will act like a mild master of a family; what cannot be healed shall be punished, and the rest I will preserve for my own use."

3. (351) To that offer of Titus they made this reply: That they could not accept of it, because they had sworn never to do so; but they desired they might have leave to go through the wall that had been made about them, with their wives and children; for that they would go into the desert, and leave the city to him. (352) At this Titus had great indignation, that when they were in the case of men already taken captives, they should pretend to make their own terms with him, as if they had been conquerors. So he ordered this proclamation to be made to them, That they should no more come out to him as deserters, nor hope for any further security; (353) for that he would henceforth spare nobody, but fight them with his whole army; and that they must save themselves as well as they could; for that he would from henceforth treat them according to the laws of war. So he gave orders to the soldiers both to burn and to plunder the city; (354) who did nothing indeed that day; but on the next day they set fire to the repository of the archives, to Acra, to the council-house, and to the place called Ophlas; (355) at which time the fire proceeded as far as the palace of queen Helena, which was in the middle of Acra; the lanes also were burnt down, as were also those houses that were full of the dead bodies of such as were destroyed by famine.

4. (356) On the same day it was that the sons and brethren of Izates the king, together with many others of the eminent men of the populace, got together there, and besought Caesar to give them his right hand for their security; upon which, though he was very angry at all that were now remaining, yet did he not lay aside his old moderation, but received these men. (357) At that time, indeed, he kept them all in custody, but still bound the king's sons and kinsmen, and led them with him to Rome, in order to make them hostages for their country's fidelity to the Romans.

CHAPTER 7.

WHAT AFTERWARD BEFELL THE SEDITIOUS WHEN THEY HAD DONE A GREAT DEAL OF MISCHIEF, AND SUFFERED MANY MISFORTUNES; AS ALSO HOW CAESAR BECAME MASTER OF THE UPPER CITY.

1. (358) AND now the seditious rushed into the royal palace, into which many had put their effects, because it was so strong, and drove the Romans away from it. They also slew all the people that had crowded into it, who were in number about eight thousand four hundred, and plundered them of what they had. (359) They also took two of the Romans alive; the one was a horseman, and the other a footman. They then cut the throat of the footman, and immediately had him drawn through the whole city, as revenging themselves upon the whole body of the Romans by this one instance. (360) But the horseman said he had somewhat to suggest to them in order to their preservation; whereupon he was brought before Simon; but he having nothing to say when he was there, he was delivered to Ardalas, one of his commanders, to be punished, (361) who bound his hands behind him, and put a riband over his eyes, and then brought him out over against the Romans, as intending to cut off his head. But the man prevented that execution, and ran away to the Romans, and this while the Jewish executioner was drawing out his sword. (362) Now when he was gotten away from the enemy, Titus could not think of putting him to death; but because he deemed him unworthy of being a Roman soldier any longer, on account that he had been taken alive by the enemy, he took away his arms, and ejected him out of the legion whereto he had belonged; which, to one that had a sense of shame, was a penalty severer than death itself.

2. (363) On the next day the Romans drove the robbers out of the lower city, and set all on fire as far as Siloam. These soldiers were indeed glad to see the city destroyed. But they missed the plunder, because the seditious had carried off all their effects, and were retired into the upper city; (364) for they did not yet at all repent of the mischiefs they had done, but were insolent, as if they had done well; for, as they saw the city on fire, they appeared cheerful, and put on joyful countenances, in expectation, as they said, of death to end their miseries. Accordingly, as the people were now slain, the holy house was burnt down, and the city was on fire, there was nothing further left for the enemy to do. (365) Yet did not Josephus grow weary, even in this utmost extremity, to beg of them to spare what was left of the city; he spake largely to them about their barbarity and impiety, and gave them his advice in order to their escape; though he gained nothing thereby more than to be laughed at by them; (366) and as they could not think of surrendering themselves up, because of the oath they had taken, nor were strong enough to fight with the Romans any longer upon the square, as being surrounded on all sides, and a kind of prisoners already, yet were they so accustomed to kill people, that they could not restrain their right hands from acting accordingly. So they dispersed themselves before the city, and laid themselves in ambush among its ruins, (367) to catch those that attempted to desert to the Romans; accordingly many such deserters were caught by them, and were all slain; for these were too weak, by reason of their want of food, to fly away from them; so their dead bodies were thrown to the dogs. (368) Now every other sort of death was thought more tolerable than the famine, insomuch that, though the Jews despaired now of mercy, yet would they fly to the Romans, and would themselves, even of their own

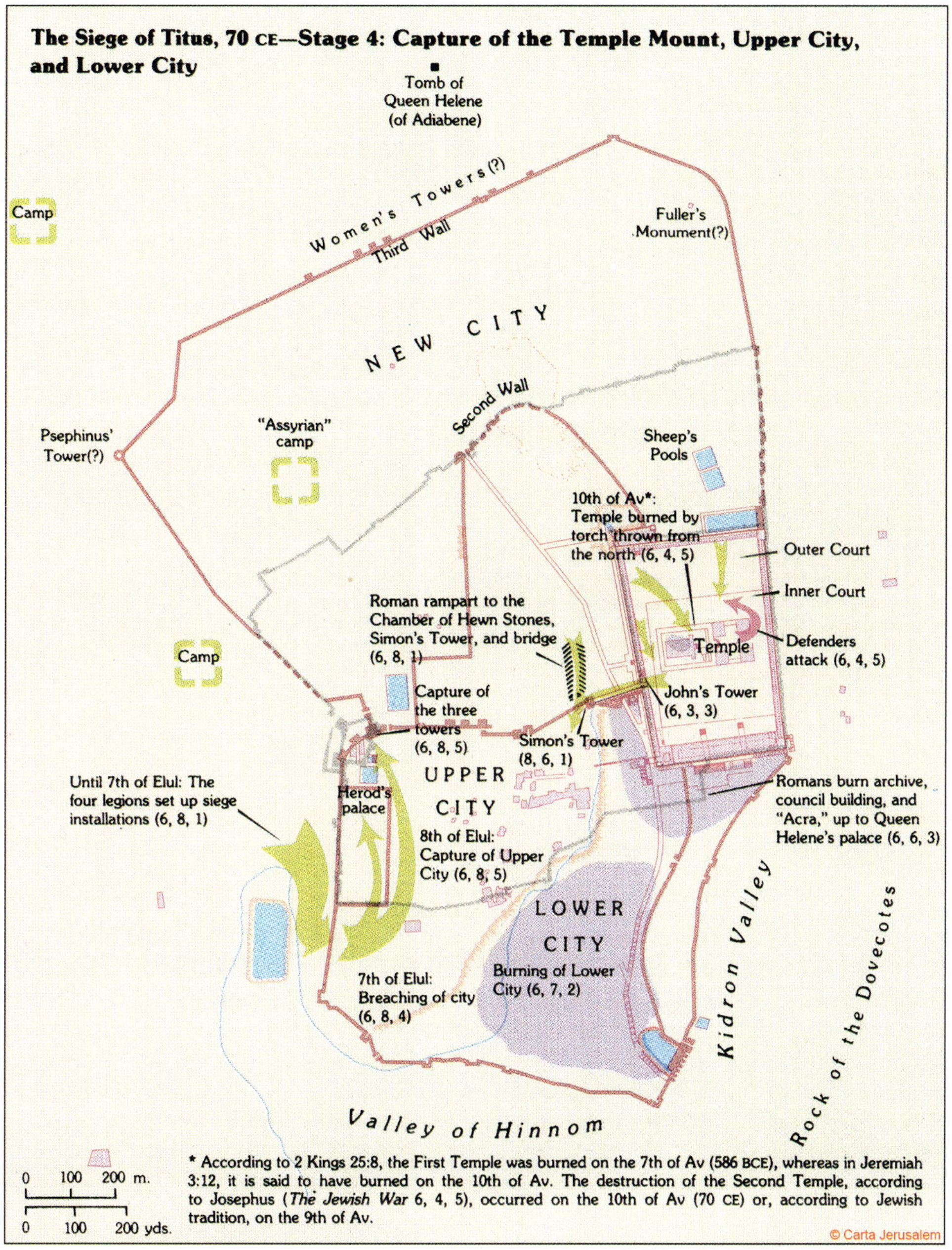

(from *The Carta Jerusalem Atlas* / Dan Bahat)

accord, fall among the murderous rebels also. (369) Nor was there any place in the city that had no dead bodies in it, but what was entirely covered with those that were killed either by the famine or the rebellion; and all was full of the dead bodies of such as had perished, either by that sedition or by that famine.

3. (370) So now the last hope which supported the tyrants, and that crew of robbers who were with them, was in the caves and caverns under ground; whither, if they could once fly, they did not expect to be searched for; but endeavored, that after the whole city should be destroyed, and the Romans gone away, they might come out again, and escape from them. (371) This was no better than a dream of theirs; for they were not able to lie hid either from God or from the Romans. (372) However, they depended on these under-ground subterfuges, and set more places on fire than did the Romans themselves; and those that fled out of their houses thus set on fire into the ditches, they killed without mercy, and pillaged them also; and if they discovered food belonging to any one, they seized upon it and swallowed it down, together with their blood also; (373) nay, they were now come to fight one with another about their plunder; and I cannot but think that, had not their destruction prevented it, their barbarity would have made them taste of even the dead bodies themselves.

CHAPTER 8.

HOW CAESAR RAISED BANKS ROUND ABOUT THE UPPER CITY [MOUNT ZION] AND WHEN THEY WERE COMPLETED, GAVE ORDERS THAT THE MACHINES SHOULD BE BROUGHT. HE THEN POSSESSED HIMSELF OF THE WHOLE CITY.

1. (374) NOW when Caesar perceived that the upper city was so steep that it could not possibly be taken without raising banks against it, he distributed the several parts of that work among his army, and this on the twentieth day of the month Lous [Ab]. (375) Now the carriage of the materials was a difficult task, since all the trees, as I have already told you, that were about the city, within the distance of a hundred furlongs, had their branches cut off already, in order to make the former banks. (376) The works that belonged to the four legions were erected on the west side of the city, over against the royal palace; (377) but the whole body of the auxiliary troops, with the rest of the multitude that were with them, [erected their banks] at the Xystus, whence they reached to the bridge, and that tower of Simon which he had built as a citadel for himself against John, when they were at war one with another.

2. (378) It was at this time that the commanders of the Idumeans got together privately, and took counsel about surrendering up themselves to the Romans. Accordingly, they sent five men to Titus, and entreated him to give them his right hand for their security. (379) So Titus thinking that the tyrants would yield, if the Idumeans, upon whom a great part of the war depended, were once withdrawn from them, after some reluctancy and delay, complied with them, and gave them security for their lives, and sent the five men back. (380) But as these Idumeans were preparing to march out, Simon perceived it, and immediately slew the five men that had gone to Titus, and took their commanders, and put them in prison, of whom the most eminent was Jacob, the son of Sosas; (381) but as for the multitude of the Idumeans, who did not at all know what to do, now their commanders were taken from them, he had them watched, and secured the walls by a more numerous garrison. (382) Yet could not that garrison resist those that were deserting; for although a great number of them were slain, yet were the deserters many more in number. (383) They were all received by the Romans, because Titus himself grew negligent as to his former orders for killing them, and because the very soldiers grew weary of killing them, and because they hoped to get some money by sparing them; (384) for they left only the populace, and sold the rest of the multitude, **(cf. Deuteronomy 28:68)** with their wives and children, and every one of them at a very low price, and that because such as were sold were very many, and the buyers were few: (385) and although Titus had made proclamation beforehand, that no deserter should come alone by himself, that so they might bring out their families with them, yet did he receive such as these also. However, he set over them such as were to distinguish some from others, in order to see if any of them de-

Mount Zion today, with the Dormition Abbey in background. (photo Dror Feitelson Pikiwiki Israel, via Wikimedia Commons)

served to be punished. (386) And indeed the number of those that were sold was immense; but of the populace above forty thousand were saved, whom Caesar let go whither every one of them pleased.

3. (387) But now at this time it was that one of the priests, the son of Thebuthus, whose name was Jesus, upon his having security given him, by the oath of Caesar, that he should be preserved, upon condition that he should deliver to him certain of the precious things that had been reposited in the temple (388) came out of it, and delivered him from the wall of the holy house two candlesticks, like to those that lay in the holy house, with tables, and cisterns, and vials, all made of solid gold, and very heavy. (389) He also delivered to him the veils and the garments, with the precious stones, and a great number of other precious vessels that belonged to their sacred worship. (390) The treasurer of the temple also, whose name was Phineas, was seized on, and showed Titus the coats and girdles of the priests, with a great quantity of purple and scarlet, which were there reposited for the uses of the veil, as also a great deal of cinnamon and cassia, with a large quantity of other sweet spices, **(cf. Exodus 31:34)** which used to be mixed together, and offered as incense to God every day. (391) A great many other treasures were also delivered to him, with sacred ornaments of the temple not a few; which things thus delivered to Titus obtained of him for this man the same pardon that he had allowed to such as deserted of their own accord.

4. (392) And now were the banks finished on the seventh day of the month Gorpieus, [Elul,] in eighteen days' time, when the Romans brought their machines against the wall. But for the seditious, some of them, as despairing of saving the city, retired from the wall to the citadel; others of them went down into the subterranean vaults, (393) though still a great many of them defended themselves against those that brought the engines for the battery; yet did the Romans overcome them by their number and by their strength; and, what was the principal thing of all, by going cheerfully about their work, while the Jews were quite dejected, and become weak. (394) Now as soon as a part of the wall was battered down, and certain of the towers yielded to the impression of the battering rams, those that opposed themselves fled away, and such a terror fell upon the tyrants, as was much greater than the occasion required; (395) for before the enemy got over the breach they were quite stunned, and were immediately for flying away. And now one might see these men, who had hitherto been so insolent and arrogant in their wicked practices, to be cast down and to tremble, insomuch that it would pity one's heart to observe the change that was made in those vile persons. (396) Accordingly, they ran with great violence upon the Roman wall that encompassed them, in order to force away those that guarded it, and to break through it, and get away. (397) But when they saw that those who had formerly been faithful to them had gone away, (as indeed they were fled whithersoever the great distress they were in persuaded them to flee,) as also when those that came running before the rest told them that the western wall was entirely overthrown, while others said the Romans were gotten in, and others that they were near, and looking out for them, (398) which were only the dictates of their fear, which imposed upon their sight, they fell upon their face, and greatly lamented their own mad conduct; and their nerves were so terribly loosed, that they could not flee away. (399) And here one may chiefly reflect on the power of God exercised upon these wicked wretches, and on the good fortune of the Romans; for these tyrants did now wholly deprive themselves of the security they had in their own power, and came down from those very towers of their own accord, wherein they could have never been taken by force, nor indeed by any other way than by famine. (400) And thus did the Romans, when they had taken such great pains about weaker walls, get by good fortune what they could never have gotten by their engines; for three of these towers were too strong for all mechanical engines whatsoever, concerning which we have treated above.

5. (401) So they now left these towers of themselves, or rather they were ejected out of them by God himself, and fled immediately to that valley which was under Siloam, where they again recovered themselves out of the dread they were in for a while, and ran violently against that part of the Roman wall which lay on that side; (402) but as their courage was too much depressed to make their attacks with sufficient force, and their power was now broken with fear and affliction, they were repulsed by the guards, and dispersing themselves at distances from each other, went down into the subterranean caverns. (403) So the Romans being now become masters of the walls, they both placed their ensigns upon the towers, and made joyful acclamations for the victory they had gained, as having found the end of this war much lighter than its beginning; for when they had gotten upon the last wall, without any bloodshed, they could hardly believe what they found to be true; but seeing nobody to oppose them, they stood in doubt what such an unusual solitude could mean. (404) But when they went in numbers into the lanes of the city with their swords drawn, they slew those whom they overtook without and set fire to the

Sewage channel, lined with large Herodian stones, found under a street that ran northward from Siloam up along the Western Wall. Many of the city's inhabitants found refuge in these channels during the Roman siege. (photo Dan Bahat)

houses whither the Jews were fled, and burnt every soul in them, and laid waste a great many of the rest; (405) and when they were come to the houses to plunder them, they found in them entire families of dead men, and the upper rooms full of dead corpses, that is, of such as died by the famine; they then stood in a horror at this sight, and went out without touching any thing. (406) But although they had this commiseration for such as were destroyed in that manner, yet had they not the same for those that were still alive, but they ran every one through whom they met with, and obstructed the very lanes with their dead bodies, and made the whole city run down with blood, to such a degree indeed that the fire of many of the houses was quenched with these men's blood. (407) And truly so it happened, that though the slayers left off at the evening, yet did the fire greatly prevail in the night; and as all was burning, came that eighth day of the month Gorpieus [Elul] upon Jerusalem, (408) a city that had been liable to so many miseries during this siege, that, had it always enjoyed as much happiness from its first foundation, it would certainly have been the envy of the world. Nor did it on any other account so much deserve these sore misfortunes, as by producing such a generation of men as were the occasions of this its overthrow.

CHAPTER 9.

WHAT INJUNCTIONS CAESAR GAVE WHEN HE WAS COME WITHIN THE CITY. THE NUMBER OF THE CAPTIVES AND OF THOSE THAT PERISHED IN THE SIEGE; AS ALSO CONCERNING THOSE THAT HAD ESCAPED INTO THE SUBTERRANEAN CAVERNS, AMONG WHOM WERE THE TYRANTS SIMON AND JOHN THEMSELVES.

1. (409) Now when Titus was come into this [upper] city, he admired not only some other places of strength in it, but particularly those strong towers which the tyrants in their mad conduct had relinquished; (410) for when he saw their solid altitude, and the largeness of their several stones, and the exactness of their joints, as also how great was their breadth, and how extensive their length, he expressed himself after the manner following: (411) "We have certainly had God for our assistant in this war, and it was no other than God who ejected the Jews out of these fortifications; for what could the hands of men or any machines do towards overthrowing these towers?" (412) At which time he had many such discourses to his friends; he also let such go free as had been bound by the tyrants, and were left in the prisons. (413) To conclude, when he entirely demolished the rest of the city, and overthrew its walls, he left these towers as a monument of his good fortune, which had proved his auxiliaries, and enabled him to take what could not otherwise have been taken by him.

2. (414) And now, since his soldiers were already quite tired with killing men, and yet there appeared to be a vast multitude still remaining alive, Caesar gave orders that they should kill none but those that were in arms, and opposed them, but should take the rest alive. (415) But, together with those whom they had orders to slay, they slew the aged and the infirm; but for those that were in their flourishing age, and who might be useful to them, they drove them together into the temple, and shut them up within the walls of the court of the women; (416) over which Caesar set one of his freed-men, as also Fronto, one of his own friends; which last was to determine every one's fate, according to his merits. (417) So this Fronto slew all those that had been seditious and robbers, who were impeached one by another; but of the young men he chose out the tallest and most beautiful, and reserved them for the triumph; (418) and as for the rest of the multitude that were above seventeen years old, he put them into bonds, and sent them to the Egyptian mines (**cf. Deuteronomy 28:68; Jeremiah 44:7; Hosea 8:13; 9:3; 9:4, 5; 2 Samuel 15:10–13**). Titus also sent a great number into the provinces, as a present to them, that they might be destroyed upon their theatres, by the sword and by the wild beasts; but those that were under seventeen years of age were sold for slaves. (419) Now during the days wherein Fronto was distinguishing these men, there perished, for want of food, eleven thousand; some of whom did not taste any food, through the hatred their guards bore to them; and others would not take in any when it was given them. The multitude also was so very great, that they were in want even of corn for their sustenance.

3. (420) Now the number of those that were carried captive during this whole war was collected to be ninety-seven thousand; as was the number of those that perished during the whole siege eleven hundred thousand, (421) the greater part of whom were indeed of the same nation [with the citizens of Jerusalem], but not belonging to the city itself; for they were come up from all the country to the feast of unleavened bread, and were on a sudden shut up by an army, which, at the very first, occasioned so great a straitness among them, that there came a pestilential destruction upon them, and soon afterward such a famine, as destroyed them more suddenly. (422) And that this city could contain so many people in it, is manifest by that number of them which was taken under Cestius, who being desirous of informing Nero of the power of the city, who otherwise was disposed to contemn that nation, entreated the high priests, if the thing were possible, to take the number of their whole multitude. (423) So these high priests, upon the coming of that feast which is called the Passover, when they slay their sacrifices, from the ninth hour till the eleventh, but so that a company not less than ten belong to every sacrifice, (for it is not lawful for them to feast singly by themselves,) and many of us are twenty in a company, (424) found the number of sacrifices was two hundred and fifty-six thousand five hundred; (425) which, upon the allowance of no more than ten that feast together, amounts to two millions seven hundred thousand and two hundred persons

Triumphal parade of Roman soldiers carry the temple vessels, relief on the Arch of Titus, Rome. (photo Samuel Magal)

that were pure and holy; (426) for as to those that have the leprosy, or the gonorrhea, or women that have their monthly courses, or such as are otherwise polluted, it is not lawful for them to be partakers of this sacrifice; (427) nor indeed for any foreigners neither, who come hither to worship.

4. (428) Now this vast multitude is indeed collected out of remote places, but the entire nation was now shut up by fate as in prison, and the Roman army encompassed the city when it was crowded with inhabitants. (429) Accordingly, the multitude of those that therein perished exceeded all the destructions that either men or God ever brought upon the world; for, to speak only of what was publicly known, the Romans slew some of them, some they carried captives, and others they made a search for under ground, and when they found where they were, they broke up the ground and slew all they met with. (430) There were also found slain there above two thousand persons, partly by their own hands, and partly by one another, but chiefly destroyed by the famine; (431) but then the ill savor of the dead bodies was most offensive to those that lighted upon them, insomuch that some were obliged to get away immediately, while others were so greedy of gain, that they would go in among the dead bodies that lay on heaps, and tread upon them; (432) for a great deal of treasure was found in these caverns, and the hope of gain made every way of getting it to be esteemed lawful. Many also of those that had been put in prison by the tyrants were now brought out; for they did not leave off their barbarous cruelty at the very last: (433) yet did God avenge himself upon them both, in a manner agreeable to justice. As for John, he wanted food, together with his brethren, in these caverns, and begged that the Romans would now give him their right hand for his security, which he had often proudly rejected before; but for Simon, he struggled hard with the distress he was in, fill he was forced to surrender himself, as we shall relate hereafter; (434) so he was reserved for the triumph, and to be then slain; as was John condemned to perpetual imprisonment. And now the Romans set fire to the extreme parts of the city, and burnt them down, and entirely demolished its walls.

CHAPTER 10.

THAT WHEREAS THE CITY OF JERUSALEM HAD BEEN FIVE TIMES TAKEN FORMERLY, THIS WAS THE SECOND TIME OF ITS DESOLATION. A BRIEF ACCOUNT OF ITS HISTORY.

1. (435) AND thus was Jerusalem taken, in the second year of the reign of Vespasian, on the eighth day of the month Gorpeius [Elul]. It had been taken five times before, though this was the second time of its desolation; (436) for Shishak, the king of Egypt, and after him Antiochus, and after him Pompey, and after them Sosius and Herod, took the city, but still preserved it; (437) but before all these, the king of Babylon conquered it, and made it desolate, one thousand four hundred and sixty-eight years and six months after it was built. (438) But he who first built it was a potent man among the Canaanites, and is in our own tongue called [Melchisedek], the Righteous King, for such he really was; on which account he was [there] the first priest of God, and first built a temple [there], and called the city Jerusalem, which was formerly called Salem. (439) However, David, the king of the Jews, ejected the Canaanites, and settled his own people therein. It was demolished entirely by the Babylonians, four hundred and seventy-seven years and six months after him. (440) And from king David, who was the first of the Jews who reigned therein, to this destruction under Titus, were one thousand one hundred and seventy-nine years; (441) but from its first building, till this last destruction, were two thousand one hundred and seventy-seven years; (442) yet hath not its great antiquity, nor its vast riches, nor the diffusion of its nation over all the habitable earth, nor the greatness of the veneration paid to it on a religious account, been sufficient to preserve it from being destroyed. And thus ended the siege of Jerusalem.

BOOK VII

FROM THE TAKING OF JERUSALEM BY TITUS TO THE SEDITION OF THE JEWS AT CYRENE

CHAPTER 1.

HOW THE ENTIRE CITY OF JERUSALEM WAS DEMOLISHED, EXCEPTING THREE TOWERS; AND HOW TITUS COMMENDED HIS SOLDIERS IN A SPEECH MADE TO THEM, AND DISTRIBUTED REWARDS TO THEM AND THEN DISMISSED MANY OF THEM.

1. (1) NOW as soon as the army had no more people to slay or to plunder, because there remained none to be the objects of their fury, (for they would not have spared any, had there remained any other work to be done,) Caesar gave orders that they should now demolish the entire city and temple, but should leave as many of the towers standing as were of the greatest eminency; that is, Phasaelus, and Hippicus, and Mariamne; and so much of the wall as enclosed the city on the west side. (2) This wall was spared, in order to afford a camp for such as were to lie in garrison, as were the towers also spared, in order to demonstrate to posterity what kind of city it was, and how well fortified, which the Roman valor had subdued; (3) but for all the rest of the wall, it was so thoroughly laid even with the ground by those that dug it up to the foundation, that there was left nothing to make those that came thither believe it had ever been inhabited. (4) This was the end which Jerusalem came to by the madness of those that were for innovations; a city otherwise of great magnificence, and of mighty fame among all mankind.

2. (5) But Caesar resolved to leave there, as a guard, the tenth legion, with certain troops of horsemen, and companies of footmen. So, having entirely completed this war, he was desirous to commend his whole army, on account of the great exploits they had performed, and to bestow proper rewards on such as had signalized themselves therein. (6) He had therefore a great tribunal made for him in the midst of the place where he had formerly encamped, and stood upon it with his principal commanders about him, and spake so as to be heard by the whole arrmy in the manner following: (7) That he returned them abundance of thanks for their goodwill which they had showed to him: he commended them for that ready obedience they had exhibited in this whole war, which obedience had appeared in the many and great dangers which they had courageously undergone; as also for that courage they had shown, and had thereby augmented of themselves their country's power, and had made it evident to all men, that neither the multitude of their enemies, nor the strength of their places, nor the largeness of their cities, nor the rash boldness and brutish rage of their antagonists, were sufficient at any time to get clear of the Roman valor, although some of them may have fortune in many respects on their side. (8) He said further, that it was but reasonable for them to put an end to this war, now it had lasted so long, for that they had nothing better to wish for when they entered into it; (9) and that this happened more favorably for them, and more for their glory, that all the Romans had willingly accepted of those for their governors, and the curators of their dominions, whom they had chosen for them, and had sent into their own country for that purpose, which still continued under the management of those whom they had pitched on, and were thankful to them for pitching upon them. (10) That accordingly, although he did both admire and tenderly regard them all, because he knew that every one of them had gone as cheerfully about their work as their abilities and opportunities would give them leave; (11) yet, he said, that he would immediately bestow rewards and dignities on those that had fought the most bravely, and with greater force, and had signalized their conduct in the most glorious manner, and had made his army more famous by their noble exploits; and that no one who had been willing to take more pains than another should miss of a just retribution for the same; (12) for that he had been exceedingly careful about this matter, and that the more, because he had much rather reward the virtues of his fellow soldiers than punish such as had offended.

3. (13) Hereupon Titus ordered those whose business it was to read the list of all that had performed great exploits in this war, (14) whom he called to him by their names, and commended them before the company, and rejoiced in them in the same manner as a man would have rejoiced in his own exploits. He also put on their heads crowns of gold, and golden ornaments about their necks, and gave them long spears of gold, and ensigns that were made of silver, (15) and removed every one of them to a higher rank; and besides this, he plentifully distributed among them, out of the spoils, and the other prey they had taken, silver, and gold, and garments. (16) So when they had all these honors bestowed on them, according to his own appointment made to every one, and he had wished all sorts of happiness to the whole army, he came down, among the great acclamations which were made to him, and then betook himself to offer thank-offerings [to the gods], and at once sacrificed a vast number of oxen, that stood ready at the altars, and distributed them among the army to feast on. (17) And when he had staid three days among the principal commanders, and so long feasted with them, he sent away the rest of his army to the several places where they would be every one best situated; but permitted the tenth legion to stay, as a guard at Jerusalem, and

Emblem of the Tenth Roman Legion—stamp impression on a roof tile found in Jerusalem. (Carta collection)

General view of Cesarea Philippi (modern Banias). (photo Samuel Magal)

did not send them away beyond Euphrates, where they had been before. (18) And as he remembered that the twelfth legion had given way to the Jews, under Cestius their general, he expelled them out of all Syria, for they had lain formerly at Raphanea, and sent them away to a place called Meletine, near Euphrates, which is in the limits of Armenia and Cappadocia; (19) he also thought fit that two of the legions should stay with him till he should go to Egypt. (20) He then went down with his army to that Cesarea which lay by the sea-side, and there laid up the rest of his spoils in great quantities, and gave order that the captives should he kept there; for the winter season hindered him then from sailing into Italy.

CHAPTER 2.

HOW TITUS EXHIBITED ALL SORTS OF SHOWS AT CESAREA PHILIPPI. CONCERNING SIMON THE TYRANT HOW HE WAS TAKEN, AND RESERVED FOR THE TRIUMPH.

1. (21) NOW at the same time that Titus Caesar lay at the siege of Jerusalem, did Vespasian go on board a merchantship and sailed from Alexandria to Rhodes; (22) whence he sailed away ,in ships with three rows of oars; and as he touched at several cities that lay in his road, he was joyfully received by them all, and so passed over from Ionia into Greece; whence he set sail from Corcyra to the promontory of Iapyx, whence he took his journey by land. (23) But as for Titus, he marched from that Cesarea which lay by the sea-side, and came to that which is named Cesarea Philippi, and staid there a considerable time, and exhibited all sorts of shows there. (24) And here a great number of the captives were destroyed, some being thrown to wild beasts, and others in multitudes forced to kill one another, as if they were their enemies. (25) And here it was that Titus was informed of the seizure of Simon the son of Gioras, which was made after the manner following: (26) This Simon, during the siege of Jerusalem, was in the upper city; but when the Roman army was gotten within the walls, and were laying the city waste, he then took the most faithful of his friends with him, and among them some that were stone-cutters, with those iron tools which belonged to their occupation, and as great a quantity of provisions as would suffice them for a long time, and let himself and all them down into a certain subterraneous cavern that was not visible above ground. (27) Now, so far as had been digged of old, they went onward along it without disturbance; but where they met with solid earth, they dug a mine under ground, and this in hopes that they should be able to proceed so far as to rise from under ground in a safe place, and by that means escape. (28) But when they came to make the experiment, they were disappointed of their hope; for the miners could make but small progress, and that with difficulty also; insomuch that their provisions, though they distributed them by measure, began to fail them. (29) And now Simon, thinking he might be able to astonish and elude the Romans, put on a white frock, and buttoned upon him a purple cloak, and appeared out of the ground in the place where the temple had formerly been. (30) At the first, indeed, those that saw him were greatly astonished, and stood still where they were; but afterward they came nearer to him, and asked him who he was. (31) Now Simon would not tell them, but bid them call for their captain; and when they ran to call him, Terentius Rufus (**cf. Micah 3:12; Jeremiah 26:18**) who was left to command the army there, came to Simon, and learned of him the whole truth, and kept him in bonds, and let Caesar know that he was taken. (32) Thus did God bring this man to be punished for what bitter and savage tyranny

he had exercised against his countrymen by those who were his worst enemies; (33) and this while he was not subdued by violence, but voluntarily delivered himself up to them to be punished, and that on the very same account that he had laid false accusations against many Jews, as if they were falling away to the Romans, and had barbarously slain them, (34) for wicked actions do not escape the Divine anger, nor is justice too weak to punish offenders, but in time overtakes those that transgress its laws, and inflicts its punishments upon the wicked in a manner, so much more severe, as they expected to escape it on account of their not being punished immediately. (see Ecclesiastes 8:11) Simon was made sensible of this by falling under the indignation of the Romans. (35) This rise of his out of the ground did also occasion the discovery of a great number of others of the seditious at that time, who had hidden themselves under ground. (36) But for Simon, he was brought to Caesar in bonds, when he was come back to that Cesarea which was on the seaside, who gave orders that he should be kept against that triumph which he was to celebrate at Rome upon this occasion.

CHAPTER 3.

HOW TITUS UPON THE CELEBRATION OF HIS BROTHERS AND FATHERS BIRTHDAYS HAD MANY OF THE JEWS SLAIN. CONCERNING THE DANGER THE JEWS WERE IN AT ANTIOCH, BY MEANS OF THE TRANSGRESSION AND IMPIETY OF ONE ANTIOCHUS, A JEW.

1. (37) WHILE Titus was at Cesarea, he solemnized the birthday of his brother Domitian] after a splendid manner, and inflicted a great deal of the punishment intended for the Jews in honor of him; (38) for the number of those that were now slain in fighting with the beasts, and were burnt, and fought with one another, exceeded two thousand five hundred. Yet did all this seem to the Romans, when they were thus destroyed ten thousand several ways, to be a punishment beneath their deserts. (39) After this Caesar came to Berytus, which is a city of Phoenicia, and a Roman colony, and staid there a longer time, and exhibited a still more pompous solemnity about his father's birthday, both in the magnificence of the shows, and in the other vast expenses he was at in his devices thereto belonging; (40) so that a great multitude of the captives were here destroyed after the same manner as before.

2. (41) It happened also about this time, that the Jews who remained at Antioch were under accusations, and in danger of perishing, from the disturbances that were raised against them by the Antiochians; and this both on account of the slanders spread abroad at this time against them, and on account of what pranks they had played not long before; (42) which I am obliged to describe without fail, though briefly, that I may the better connect my narration of future actions with those that went before.

3. (43) For as the Jewish nation is widely dispersed over all the habitable earth among its inhabitants, so it is very much intermingled with Syria by reason of its neighborhood, and had the greatest multitudes in Antioch by reason of the largeness of the city, wherein the kings, after Antiochus, had afforded them a habitation with the most undisturbed tranquillity; (44) for though Antiochus, who was called Epiphanes, laid Jerusalem waste, and spoiled the temple, yet did those that succeeded him in the kingdom restore all the donations that were made of brass to the Jews of Antioch, and dedicated them to their synagogue, and granted them the enjoyment of equal privileges of citizens with the Greeks themselves; (45) and as the succeeding kings treated them after the same manner, they both multiplied to a great number, and adorned their temple gloriously by fine ornaments, and with great magnificence, in the use of what had been given them. They also made proselytes of a great many of the Greeks perpetually, and thereby after a sort brought them to be a portion of their own body. (46) But about this time when the present war began, and Vespasian was newly sailed to Syria, (47) and all men had taken up a great hatred against the Jews, then it was that a certain person, whose name was Antiochus, being one of the Jewish nation, and greatly respected on account of his father, who was governor of the Jews at Antioch came upon the theater at a time when the people of Antioch were assembled together, and became an informer against his father, and accused both him and others that they had resolved to burn the whole city in one night; he also delivered up to them some Jews that were foreigners, as partners in their resolutions. (48) When the people heard this, they could not refrain their passion, but commanded that those who were delivered up to them should have fire brought to burn them, who were accordingly all burnt upon the theater immediately. (49) They did also fall violently upon the multitude of the Jews, as supposing that by punishing them suddenly they should save their own city. (50) As for Antiochus, he aggravated the rage they were in, and thought to give them a demonstration of his own conversion, arm of his hatred of the Jewish customs, by sacrificing after the manner of the Greeks; (51) he persuaded the rest also to compel them to do the same, because they would by that means discover who they were that had plotted against them, since they would not do so; and when the people of Antioch tried the experiment, some few complied, but those that would not do so were slain. (52) As for Antiochus himself, he obtained soldiers from the Roman commander, and became a severe master over his own citizens, not permitting them to rest on the seventh day, but forc-

Antioch-on-the-Orontes. (photo Zachary Wong)

ing them to do all that they usually did on other days; (53) and to that degree of distress did he reduce them in this matter, that the rest of the seventh day was dissolved not only at Antioch, but the same thing which took thence its rise was done in other cities also, in like manner, for some small time.

4. (54) Now, after these misfortunes had happened to the Jews at Antioch, a second calamity befell them, the description of which when we were going about we premised the account foregoing; (55) for upon this accident, whereby the four-square market-place was burnt down, as well as the archives, and the place where the public records were preserved, and the royal palaces, (and it was not without difficulty that the fire was then put a stop to, which was likely, by the fury wherewith it was carried along, to have gone over the whole city,) Antiochus accused the Jews as the occasion of all the mischief that was done. (56) Now this induced the people of Antioch, who were now under the immediate persuasion, by reason of the disorder they were in, that this calumny was true, and would have been under the same persuasion, even though they had not borne an ill-will at the Jews before, to believe this man's accusation, especially when they considered what had been done before, and this to such a degree, that they all fell violently upon those that were accused, (57) and this, like madmen, in a very furious rage also, even as if they had seen the Jews in a manner setting fire themselves to the city; (58) nor was it without difficulty that one Cneius Collegas, the legate, could prevail with them to permit the affairs to be laid before Caesar; (59) for as to Cesennius Petus, the president of Syria, Vespasian had already sent him away; and so it happened that he was not yet come back thither. (60) But when Collegas had made a careful inquiry into the matter, he found out the truth, and that not one of those Jews that were accused by Antiochus had any hand in it, (61) but that all was done by some vile persons greatly in debt, who supposed that if they could once set fire to the market-place, and burn the public records, they should have no further demands made upon them. (62) So the Jews were under great disorder and terror, in the uncertain expectations of what would be the upshot of these accusations against them.

CHAPTER 4.

HOW VESPASIAN WAS RECEIVED AT ROME; AS ALSO HOW THE GERMANS REVOLTED FROM THE ROMANS, BUT WERE SUBDUED. THAT THE SARMATIANS OVERRAN MYSIA, BUT WERE COMPELLED TO RETIRE TO THEIR OWN COUNTRY AGAIN.

1. (63) AND now Titus Caesar, upon the news that was brought him concerning his father, that his coming was much desired by all the Italian cities, and that Rome especially received him with great alacrity and splendor, betook himself to rejoicing and pleasures to a great degree, as now freed from the solicitude he had been under, after the most agreeable manner. (64) For all men that were in Italy showed their respects to him in their minds before he came thither, as if he were already come, as esteeming the very expectation they had of him to be his real presence, on account of the great desires they had to see him, and because the good-will they bore him was entirely free and unconstrained; (65) for it was, desirable thing to the senate, who well remembered the calamities they had undergone in the late changes of their governors, to receive a governor who was adorned with the gravity of old age, and with the highest skill in the actions of war, whose advancement would be, as they knew, for nothing else but for the preservation of those that were to be governed. (66) Moreover, the people had been so harassed by their civil miseries, that they were still more earnest for his coming immediately, as supposing they should then be firmly delivered from their calamities, and believed they should then recover their secure tranquillity and prosperity; (67) and for the soldiery, they had the principal regard to him, for they were chiefly apprized of his great exploits in war; and since they had experienced the want of skill and want of courage in other commanders, they were very desirous to be free from that great shame they had undergone by their means, and heartily wished to receive such a prince as might be a security and an ornament to them. (68) And as this good-will to Vespasian was universal, those that enjoyed any remarkable dignities could not have patience enough to stay in Rome, but made haste to meet him at a very great distance from it; (69) nay, indeed, none of the rest could endure the delay of seeing him, but did all pour out of the city in such crowds, and were so universally possessed with the opinion that it was easier and better for them to go out than to stay there, that this was the very first time that the city joyfully perceived itself almost empty of its citizens; for those that staid within were fewer than those that went out. (70) But as soon as the news was come that he was hard by, and those that had met him at first related with what good humor he received every one that came to him, then it was that the whole multitude that had remained in the city, with their wives and children, came into the road, and waited for him there; (71) and for those whom he passed by, they made all sorts of acclamations, on account of the joy they had to see him, and the pleasantness of his countenance, and styled him their Benefactor and Savior, and the only person who was worthy to be ruler of the city of Rome. (72) And now the city was like a temple, full of garlands and sweet odors; nor was it easy for him to come to the royal palace, for the multitude of the people that stood about him, where yet at last he performed his sacrifices of thanksgiving to his household gods for his safe return to the city. (73) The multitude did also betake themselves to feasting; which feasts and drink-offerings they celebrated by their tribes, and their families, and their neighborhoods, and still prayed God to grant that Vespasian, his sons, and all their posterity, might continue in the Roman government for a very long time, and that his dominion might be preserved from all opposition. (74) And this was the manner in which Rome so joyfully received Vespasian, and thence grew immediately into a state of great prosperity.

Cavalry battle against the Sarmatians; detail on Trajan's Column. (attributed to Apollodorus of Damascus; graphics Conrad Cichorius [1863–1932])

Remains of the theater and altar of Zeus at Pergamon, the largest city in Mysia. (photo R. Steven Notley)

2. (75) But before this time, and while Vespasian was about Alexandria, and Titus was lying at the siege of Jerusalem, (76) a great multitude of the Germans were in commotion, and tended to rebellion; and as the Gauls in their neighborhood joined with them, they conspired together, and had thereby great hopes of success, and that they should free themselves from the dominion of the Romans. (77) The motives that induced the Germans to this attempt for a revolt, and for beginning the war, were these: In the first place, the nature [of the people], which was destitute of just reasonings, and ready to throw themselves rashly into danger, upon small hopes; (78) in the next place, the hatred they bore to those that were their governors, while their nation had never been conscious of subjection to any but to the Romans, and that by compulsion only. Besides these motives, it was the opportunity that now offered itself, which above all the rest prevailed with them so to do; (79) for when they saw the Roman government in a great internal disorder, by the continual changes of its rulers, and understood that every part of the habitable earth under them was in an unsettled and tottering condition, they thought this was the best opportunity that couldd afford itself for themselves to make a sedition, when the state of the Romans was so ill. (80) Classicus also, and Vitellius, two of their commanders, puffed them up with such hopes. (81) These had for a long time been openly desirous of such an innovation, and were induced by the present opportunity to venture upon the declaration of their sentiments; the multitude was also ready; and when these men told them of what they intended to attempt, that news was gladly received by them. (82) So when a great part of the Germans had agreed to rebel, and the rest were no better disposed, Vespasian, as guided by Divine Providence, sent letters to Petilius Cerealis, who had formerly had the command of Germany, whereby he declared him to have the dignity of consul, and commanded him to take upon him the government of Britain; (83) so he went whither he was ordered to go, and when he was informed of the revolt of the Germans, he fell upon them as soon as they were gotten together, and put his army in battle-array, and slew a great number of them in the fight, and forced them to leave off their madness, and to grow wiser; (84) nay, had he not fallen thus suddenly upon them on the place, it had not been long ere they would however have been brought to punishment; (85) for as soon as ever the news of their revolt was come to Rome, and Caesar Domitian was made acquainted with it, he made no delay, even at that his age, when he was exceeding young, but undertook this weighty affair. (86) He had a courageous mind from his father, and had made greater improvements than belonged to such an age: accordingly he marched against the barbarians immediately; (87) whereupon their hearts failed them at the very rumor of his approach, and they submitted themselves to him with fear, and thought it a happy thing that they were brought under their old yoke again without suffering any further mischiefs. (88) When therefore Domitian had settled all the affairs of Gaul in such good order, that it would not be easily put into disorder any more, he returned to Rome with honor and glory, as having performed such exploits as were above his own age, but worthy of so great a father.

3. (89) At the very same time with the forementioned revolt of the Germans did the bold attempt of the Scythians against the Romans occur; (90) for those Scythians who are called Sarmatians, being a very numerous people, transported themselves over the Danube into Mysia, without being perceived; after which, by their violence, and entirely unexpected assault, they slew a great many of the Romans that guarded the frontiers; (91) and as the consular legate Fonteius Agrippa came to meet them, and fought courageously against them, he was slain by them. They then overran all the region that had been subject to him, tearing and rending every thing that fell in their way. (92) But when Vespasian was informed of what had happened, and how Mysia was laid waste, he sent away Rubrius Gallus to punish these Sarmatians; (93) by whose means many of them perished in the battles he fought against them, and that part which escaped fled with fear to their own country. (94) So when this general had put an end to the war, he provided for the future security of the country also; for he placed more and more numerous garrisons in the place, till he made it altogether impossible for the barbarians to pass over the river any more. (95) And thus had this war in Mysia a sudden conclusion.

CHAPTER 5.

CONCERNING THE SABBATIC RIVER WHICH TITUS SAW AS HE WAS JOURNEYING THROUGH SYRIA; AND HOW THE PEOPLE OF ANTIOCH CAME WITH A PETITION TO TITUS AGAINST THE JEWS BUT WERE REJECTED BY HIM; AS ALSO CONCERNING TITUS'S AND VESPASIAN'S TRIUMPH.

1. (96) NOW Titus Caesar tarried some time at Berytus, as we told

you before. He thence removed, and exhibited magnificent shows in all those cities of Syria through which he went, and made use of the captive Jews as public instances of the destruction of that nation. He then saw a river as he went along, of such a nature as deserves to be recorded in history; (97) it runs in the middle between Arcea, belonging to Agrippa's kingdom, and Raphanea. It hath somewhat very peculiar in it; (98) for when it runs, its current is strong, and has plenty of water; (99) after which its springs fail for six days together, and leave its channel dry, as any one may see; after which days it runs on the seventh day as it did before, and as though it had undergone no change at all; it hath also been observed to keep this order perpetually and exactly; whence it is that they call it the Sabbatic River that name being taken from the sacred seventh day among the Jews.

2. (100) But when the people of Antioch were informed that Titus was approaching, they were so glad at it, that they could not keep within their walls, but hasted away to give him the meeting; (101) nay, they proceeded as far as thirty furlongs, and more, with that intention. These were not the men only, but a multitude of women also with their children did the same; (102) and when they saw him coming up to them, they stood on both sides of the way, and stretched out their right hands, saluting him, and making all sorts of acclamations to him, and turned back together with him. (103) They also, among all the acclamations they made to him, besought him all the way they went to eject the Jews out of their city; (104) yet did not Titus at all yield to this their petition, but gave them the bare hearing of it quietly. However, the Jews were in a great deal of terrible fear, under the uncertainty they were in what his opinion was, and what he would do to them. (105) For Titus did not stay at Antioch, but continued his progress immediately to Zeugma, which lies upon the Euphrates, whither came to him messengers from Vologeses king of Parthia, and brought him a crown of gold upon the victory he had gained over the Jews; (106) which he accepted of, and feasted the king's messengers, and then came back to Antioch. (107) And when the senate and people of Antioch earnestly entreated him to come upon their theater, where their whole multitude was assembled, and expected him, he complied with great humanity; (108) but when they pressed him with much earnestness, and continually begged of him that he would eject the Jews out of their city, he gave them this very pertinent answer: (109) "How can this be done, since that country of theirs, whither the Jews must be obliged then to retire, is destroyed, and no place will receive them besides?" (110) Whereupon the people of Antioch, when they had failed of success in this their first request, made him a second; for they desired that he would order those tables of brass to be removed on which the Jews' privileges were engraven. (111) However, Titus would not grant that neither, but permitted the Jews of Antioch to continue to enjoy the very same privileges in that city which they had before, and then departed for Egypt; (112) and as he came to Jerusalem in his progress, and compared the melancholy condition he saw it then in, with the ancient glory of the city, and called to mind the greatness of its present ruins, as well as its ancient splendor, he could not but pity the destruction of the city, (113) so far was he from boasting that so great and goodly a city as that was had been by him taken by force; nay, he frequently cursed those that had been the authors of their revolt, and had brought such a punishment upon the city; insomuch that it openly appeared that he did not desire that such a calamity as this punishment of theirs amounted to should be a demonstration of his courage. (114) Yet was there no small quantity of the riches that had been in that city still found among its ruins, (115) a great deal of which the Romans dug up; but the greatest part was discovered by those who were captives, and so they carried it away; I mean the gold and the silver, and the rest of that most precious furniture which the Jews had, and which the owners had treasured up under ground, against the uncertain fortunes of war.

3. (116) So Titus took the journey he intended into Egypt, and passed over the desert very suddenly, and came to Alexandria, (117) and took up a resolution to go to Rome by sea. And as he was accompanied by two legions, he sent each of them again to the places whence they had before come; the fifth he sent to Mysia, and the fifteenth to Pannonia: (118) as for the leaders of the captives, Simon and John, with the other seven hundred men, whom he had selected out of the rest as being eminently tall and handsome of body, he gave order that they should be soon carried to Italy, as resolving to produce them in his triumph. (119) So when he had had a prosperous voyage to his mind, the city of Rome behaved itself in his reception, and their meeting him at a distance, as it did in the case of his father. But what made the most splendid appearance in Titus's opinion was, when his father met him, and received him; (120) but still the multitude of the citizens conceived the greatest joy when they saw them all three together, as they did at this time; (121) nor were many days overpast when they determined to have but one triumph, that should be common to both of them, on account of the glorious exploits they had performed, although the senate had decreed each of them a separate triumph by himself. (122) So when notice had been given beforehand of the day appointed for this pompous solemnity to be made, on account of their victories, not one of the immense multitude was left in the city, but every body went out so far as to gain only a station where they might stand, and left only such a passage as was necessary for those that were to be seen to go along it.

4. (123) Now all the soldiery marched out beforehand by companies, and in their several ranks, under their several commanders, in the night time, and were about the gates, not of the upper palaces, but those near the temple of Isis; for there it was that the emperors had rested the foregoing night. (124) And as soon as ever it was day, Vespasian and Titus came out crowned with laurel, and clothed in those ancient purple habits which were proper to their family, and then went as far as Octavian's Walks; (125) for there it was that the senate, and the principal rulers, and those that had been recorded as of the equestrian order, waited for them. (126) Now a tribunal had been erected before the cloisters, and ivory chairs had been set upon it, when they came and sat down upon them. Whereupon the soldiery made an acclamation of joy to them immediately, and all gave them attestations of their valor; while they were themselves without their arms, and only in their silken garments, and crowned with laurel: (127) then Vespasian accepted of these shouts of theirs; but while they were still disposed to go on in such acclamations, he gave them a signal of silence. (128) And when everybody entirely held their peace, he stood up, and covering the greatest part of his head with his cloak, he put up the accustomed solemn prayers; the like prayers did Titus put up also; (129) after which prayers Vespasian made a short speech to all the people, and then sent away the soldiers to a dinner prepared for them by the emperors. (130) Then did he retire to that gate which was called the Gate of the Pomp, because pompous shows do always go through that gate; (131) there it was that they tasted some food, and when they had put on their triumphal garments, and had offered sacrifices to the gods that were placed at the gate, they sent the triumph forward, and marched through the theatres, that they might be the more easily seen by the multitudes.

Scale model of ancient Rome. (Museo Della Civita Romano; photo Samuel Magal)

5. (132) Now it is impossible to describe the multitude of the shows as they deserve, and the magnificence of them all; such indeed as a man could not easily think of as performed, either by the labor of workmen, or the variety of riches, or the rarities of nature; (133) for almost all such curiosities as the most happy men ever get by piece-meal were here one heaped on another, and those both admirable and costly in their nature; and all brought together on that day demonstrated the vastness of the dominions of the Romans; (134) for there was here to be seen a mighty quantity of silver, and gold, and ivory, contrived into all sorts of things, and did not appear as carried along in pompous show only, but, as a man may say, running along like a river. Some parts were composed of the rarest purple hangings, and so carried along; and others accurately represented to the life what was embroidered by the arts of the Babylonians. (135) There were also precious stones that were transparent, some set in crowns of gold, and some in other ouches, as the workmen pleased; and of these such a vast number were brought, that we could not but thence learn how vainly we imagined any of them to be rarities. (136) The images of the gods were also carried, being as well wonderful for their largeness, as made very artificially, and with great skill of the workmen; nor were any of these images of any other than very costly materials; and many species of animals were brought, every one in their own natural ornaments. (137) The men also who brought every one of these shows were great multitudes, and adorned with purple garments, all over interwoven with gold; those that were chosen for carrying these pompous shows having also about them such magnificent ornaments as were both extraordinary and surprising. (138) Besides these, one might see that even the great number of the captives was not unadorned, while the variety that was in their garments, and their fine texture, concealed from the sight the deformity of their bodies. (139) But what afforded the greatest surprise of all was the structure of the pageants that were borne along; for indeed he that met them could not but be afraid that the bearers would not be able firmly enough to support them, such was their magnitude; (140) for many of them were so made, that they were on three or even four stories, one above another. The magnificence also of their structure afforded one both pleasure and surprise; (141) for upon many of them were laid carpets of gold. There was also wrought gold and ivory fastened about them all; (142) and many resemblances of the war, and those in several ways, and variety of contrivances, affording a most lively portraiture of itself. (143) For there was to be seen a happy country laid waste, and entire squadrons of enemies slain; while some of them ran away, and some were carried into captivity; with walls of great altitude and magnitude overthrown and ruined by machines; with the strongest fortifications taken, and the walls of most populous cities upon the tops of hills seized on, (144) and an army pouring itself within the walls; as also every place full of slaughter, and supplications of the enemies, when they were no longer able to lift up their hands in way of opposition. Fire also sent upon temples was here represented, and houses overthrown, and falling upon their owners: (145) rivers also, after they came out of a large and melancholy desert, ran down, not into a land cultivated, nor as drink for

The triumphal Arch of Titus in Rome. (photo Samuel Magal)

men, or for cattle, but through a land still on fire upon every side; for the Jews related that such a thing they had undergone during this war. (146) Now the workmanship of these representations was so magnificent and lively in the construction of the things, that it exhibited what had been done to such as did not see it, as if they had been there really present. (147) On the top of every one of these pageants was placed the commander of the city that was taken, and the manner wherein he was taken. Moreover, there followed those pageants a great number of ships; (148) and for the other spoils, they were carried in great plenty. But for those that were taken in the temple of Jerusalem, they made the greatest figure of them all; that is, the golden table, of the weight of many talents; the candlestick also, that was made of gold, though its construction were now changed from that which we made use of; (149) for its middle shaft was fixed upon a basis, and the small branches were produced out of it to a great length, having the likeness of a trident in their position, and had every one a socket made of brass for a lamp at the tops of them. These lamps were in number seven, and represented the dignity of the number seven among the Jews; (150) and the last of all the spoils, was carried the Law of the Jews. (151) After these spoils passed by a great many men, carrying the images of Victory, whose structure was entirely either of ivory or of gold. (152) After which Vespasian marched in the first place, and Titus followed him; Domitian also rode along with them, and made a glorious appearance, and rode on a horse that was worthy of admiration.

6. (153) Now the last part of this pompous show was at the temple of Jupiter Capitolinus, whither when they were come, they stood still; for it was the Romans' ancient custom to stay till somebody brought the news that the general of the enemy was slain. (154) This general was Simon, the son of Gioras, who had then been led in this triumph among the captives; a rope had also been put upon his head, and he had been drawn into a proper place in the forum, and had withal been tormented by those that drew him along; and the law of the Romans required that malefactors condemned to die should be slain there. (155) Accordingly, when it was related that there was an end of him, and all the people had set up a shout for joy, they then began to offer those sacrifices which they had consecrated, in the prayers used in such solemnities; which when they had finished, they went away to the palace. (156) And as for some of the spectators, the emperors entertained them at their own feast; and for all the rest there were noble preparations made for feasting at home; (157) for this was a festival day to the city of Rome, as celebrated for the victory obtained by their army over their enemies, for the end that was now put to their civil miseries, and for the commencement of their hopes of future prosperity and happiness.

7. (158) After these triumphs were over, and after the affairs of the Romans were settled on the surest foundations, Vespasian resolved to build a temple to Peace, which was finished in so short a time, and in so glorious a manner, as was beyond all human expectation and opinion: (159) for he having now by Providence a vast quantity of wealth, besides what he had formerly gained in his other exploits, he had this temple adorned with pictures and statues; (160) for in this temple were collected and deposited all such rarities as men aforetime used to wander all over the habitable world to see, when they had a desire to see one of them after another; (161) he also laid up therein those golden vessels and instruments that were taken out of the Jewish temple, as ensigns of his glory. (162) But still he gave order that they should lay up their Law, and the purple veils of the holy place, in the royal palace itself, and keep them there.

CHAPTER 6.

CONCERNING MACHERUS, AND HOW LUCILIUS BASSUS TOOK THAT CITADEL, AND OTHER PLACES.

1. (163) NOW Lucilius Bassus was sent as legate into Judea, and there he received the army from Cerealis Vitellianus, and took that citadel which was in Herodium, together with the garrison that was in it; (164) after which he got together all the soldiery that was there, (which was a large body, but dispersed into several parties,) with the tenth legion, and resolved to make war upon Macherus; for it was highly necessary that this citadel should be demolished, lest it might be a means of drawing away many into a rebellion, by reason of its strength; (165) for the nature of the place was very

capable of affording the surest hopes of safety to those that possessed it, as well as delay and fear to those that should attack it; (166) for what was walled in was itself a very rocky hill, elevated to a very great height; which circumstance alone made it very hard to he subdued. It was also so contrived by nature, that it could not be easily ascended; (167) for it is, as it were, ditched about with such valleys on all sides, and to such a depth, that the eye cannot reach their bottoms, and such as are not easily to be passed over, and even such as it is impossible to fill up with earth. (168) For that valley which cuts it on the west extends to threescore furlongs, and did not end till it came to the lake Asphaltitis; on the same side it was also that Macherus had the tallest top of its hill elevated above the rest. (169) But then for the valleys that lay on the north and south sides, although they be not so large as that already described, yet it is in like manner an impracticable thing to think of getting over them; (170) and for the valley that lies on the east side, its depth is found to be no less than a hundred cubits. It extends as far as a mountain that lies over against Macherus, with which it is bounded.

2. (171) Now when Alexander [Janneus], the king of the Jews, observed the nature of this place, he was the first who built a citadel here, which afterwards was demolished by Gabinius, when he made war against Aristobulus. (172) But when Herod came to be king, he thought the place to be worthy of the utmost regard, and of being built upon in the firmest manner, and this especially because it lay so near to Arabia; for it is seated in a convenient place on that account, and hath a prospect toward that country; (173) he therefore surrounded a large space of ground with walls and towers, and built a city there, out of which city there was a way that led up to the very citadel itself on the top of the mountain; (174) nay, more than this, he built a wall round that top of the hill, and erected towers at the corners, of a hundred and sixty cubits high; (175) in the middle of which place he built a palace, after a magnificent manner, wherein were large and beautiful edifices. (176) He also made a great many reservoirs for the reception of water, that there might be plenty of it ready for all uses, and those in the properest places that were afforded him there. Thus did he, as it were, contend with the nature of the place, that he might exceed its natural strength and security (which yet itself rendered it hard to be taken) by those fortifications which were made by the hands of men. (177) Moreover, he put a large quantity of darts and other machines of war into it, and contrived to get every thing thither that might any way contribute to its inhabitants' security, under the longest siege possible.

3. (178) Now within this place there grew a sort of rue that deserves our wonder on account of its largeness, for it was no way inferior to any fig tree whatsoever, either in height or in thickness; (179) and the report is, that it had lasted ever since the times of Herod, and would probably have lasted much longer, had it not been cut down by those Jews who took possession of the place afterward. (180) But still in that valley which encompasses the city on the north side there is a certain place called Baaras, which produces a root of the same name with itself; (181) its color is like to that of flame, and towards the evenings it sends out a certain ray like lightning. It is not easily taken by such as would do it, but recedes from their hands, nor will yield itself to be taken quietly, until either the urine of a woman, or her menstrual blood, be poured upon it; (182) nay, even then it is certain death to those that touch it, unless any one take and hang the root itself down from his hand, and so carry it away. (183) It may also be taken another way, without danger, which is this: they dig a trench quite round about it, till the hidden part of the root be very small, (184) they then tie a dog to it, and when the dog tries hard to follow him that tied him, this root is easily plucked up, but the dog dies immediately, as if it were instead of the man that would take the plant away; nor after this need any one be afraid of taking it into their hands. (185) Yet, after all this pains in getting, it is only valuable on account of one virtue it hath, that if it be only brought to sick persons, it quickly drives away those called demons, which are no other than the spirits of the wicked, that enter into men that are alive and kill them, unless they can obtain some help against them. (186) Here are also fountains of hot water, that flow out of this place, which have a very different taste one from the other; for some of them are bitter, and others of them are plainly sweet. (187) Here are also many eruptions of cold waters, and this not only in the places that lie lower, and have their fountains near one another, (188) but, what is still more wonderful, here is to be seen a certain cave hard by, whose cavity is not deep, but it is covered over by a rock that is prominent; (189) above this rock there stand up two [hills or] breasts, as it were, but a little distant one from another, the one of which sends out a fountain that is very cold, and the other sends out one that is very hot; which waters, when they are mingled together, compose a most pleasant bath; they are medicinal indeed for other maladies, but especially good for strengthening the nerves. This place has in it also mines of sulfur and alum.

4. (190) Now when Bassus had taken a full view of this place, he resolved to besiege it, by filling up the valley that lay on the east side; so he fell hard to work, and took great pains to raise his banks as soon as possible, and by that means to render the siege easy. (191) As for the Jews that were caught in this place, they separated themselves from the strangers that were with them, and they forced those strangers, as an otherwise useless multitude, to stay in the lower part of the city, and undergo the principal dangers, (192) while they themselves seized on the upper citadel, and held it, and this both on account of its strength, and to provide for their

MACHERUS—PLAN

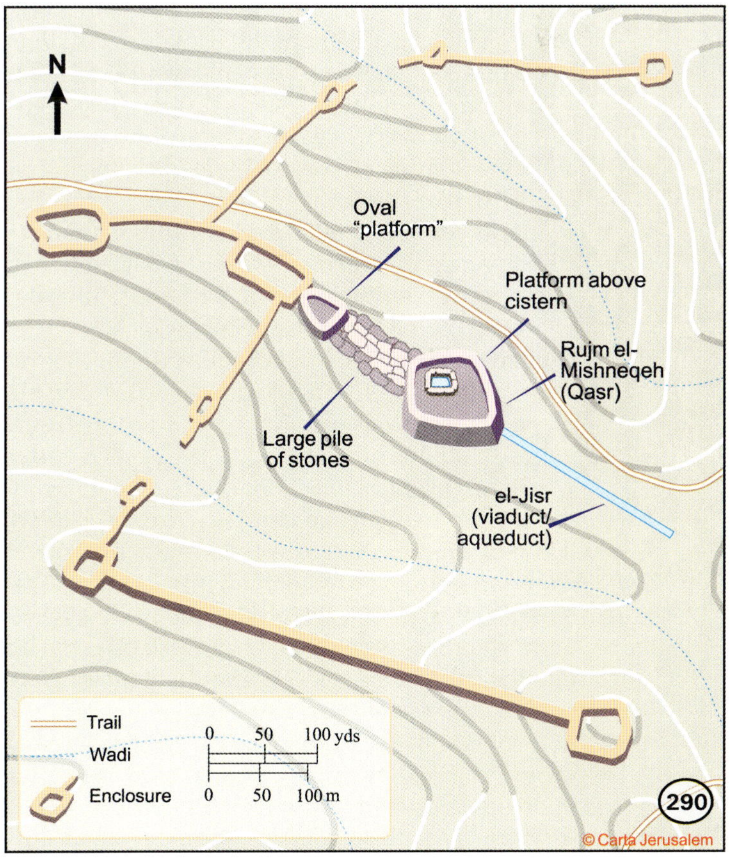

The stronghold of Macherus. (photo Samir I. Sharbaty, via Wikimedia Commons)

own safety. They also supposed they might obtain their pardon, in case they should [at last] surrender the citadel. (193) However, they were willing to make trial, in the first place, whether the hopes they had of avoiding a siege would come to any thing; with which intention they made sallies every day, and fought with those that met them; in which conflicts they were many of them slain, as they therein slew many of the Romans. (194) But still it was the opportunities that presented themselves which chiefly gained both sides their victories; these were gained by the Jews, when they fell upon the Romans as they were off their guard; but by the Romans, when, upon the others' sallies against their banks, they foresaw their coming, and were upon their lard when they received them. (195) But the conclusion of this siege did not depend upon these bickerings; but a certain surprising accident, relating to what was done in this siege, forced the Jews to surrender the citadel. (196) There was a certain young man among the besieged, of great boldness, and very active of his hand, his name was Eleazar; (197) he greatly signalized himself in those sallies, and encouraged the Jews to go out in great numbers, in order to hinder the raising of the banks, and did the Romans a vast deal of mischief when they came to fighting; he so managed matters, that those who sallied out made their attacks easily, and returned back without danger, and this by still bringing up the rear himself. (198) Now it happened that, on a certain time, when the fight was over, and both sides were parted, and retired home, he, in way of contempt of the enemy, and thinking that none of them would begin the fight again at that time, staid without the gates, and talked with those that were upon the wall, and his mind was wholly intent upon what they said. (199) Now a certain person belonging to the Roman camp, whose name was Rufus, by birth an Egyptian, ran upon him suddenly, when nobody expected such a thing, and carried him off, with his armor itself; while, in the mean time, those that saw it from the wall were under such an amazement, that Rufus prevented their assistance, and carried Eleazar to the Roman camp. (200) So the general of the Romans ordered that he should be taken up naked, set before the city to be seen, and sorely whipped before their eyes. Upon this sad accident that befell the young man, the Jews were terribly confounded, and the city, with one voice, sorely lamented him, and the mourning proved greater than could well be supposed upon the calamity of a single person. (201) When Bassus perceived that, he began to think of using a stratagem against the enemy, and was desirous to aggravate their grief, in order to prevail with them to surrender the city for the preservation of that man. Nor did he fail of his hope; (202) for he commanded them to set up a cross, as if he were just going to hang Eleazar upon it immediately; the sight of this occasioned a sore grief among those that were in the citadel, and they groaned vehemently, and cried out that they could not bear to see him thus destroyed. (203) Whereupon Eleazar besought them not to disregard him, now he was going to suffer a most miserable death, and exhorted them to save themselves, by yielding to the Roman power and good fortune, since all other people were now conquered by them. (204) These men were greatly moved with what he said, there being also many within the city that interceded for him, because he was of an eminent and very numerous family; (205) so they now yielded to their passion of commiseration, contrary to their usual custom. Accordingly, they sent out immediately certain messengers, and treated with the Romans, in order to a surrender of the citadel to them, and desired that they might be permitted to go away, and take Eleazar along with them. (206) Then did the Romans and their general accept of these terms; while the multitude of strangers that were in the lower part of the city, hearing of the agreement that was made by the Jews for themselves alone, were resolved to fly away privately in the night time; (207) but as soon as they had opened their gates, those that had come to terms with Bassus told him of it; whether it were that they envied the others' deliverance, or whether it were done out of fear, lest an occasion should be taken against them upon their escape, is uncertain. (208) The most courageous, therefore, of those men that went out prevented the enemy, and got away, and fled for it; but for those men that were caught within, they were slain, to the number of seventeen hundred; the women and children were enslaved. (209) Bassus, holding himself bound to observe his agreement with those who had surrendered the fortress, let them depart and restored Eleazar.

5. (210) When Bassus had settled these affairs, he marched hastily to the forest of Jarden, as it is called; for he had heard that a great many of those that had fled from Jerusalem and Macherus formerly were there gotten together. (211) When he was therefore come to the place, and understood that the former news was no mistake, he, in the first place, surrounded the whole place with his horsemen, that such of the Jews as had boldness enough to try to break through might have no way possible for escaping, by reason of the situation of these horsemen; and for the footmen, he ordered them to cut down the trees that were in the wood whither they were fled. (212) So the Jews were under a necessity of performing some glorious exploit, and of greatly exposing themselves in a battle, since they might perhaps thereby escape. So they made a general attack, and with a great shout fell upon those that surrounded them, (213) who received them with great courage; and so while the one side fought desperately, and the others would not yield, the fight was prolonged on that account. But the event of the battle did not answer the expectation of the assailants; (214) for so it happened, that no more than twelve fell on the Roman side, with a few that were wounded; but not one of the Jews escaped out of this battle, but they were all killed, being in

the whole not fewer in number than three thousand, (215) together with Judas, the son of Jairus, their general, concerning whom we have before spoken, that he had been a captain of a certain band at the siege of Jerusalem, and by going down into a certain vault under ground, had privately made his escape.

6. (216) About the same time it was that Caesar sent a letter to Bassus, and to Liberius Maximus, who was the procurator [of Judea], and gave order that all Judea should be exposed to sale (217) for he did not found any city there, but reserved the country for himself. However, he assigned a place for eight hundred men only, whom he had dismissed from his army, which he gave them for their habitation; it is called Emmaus, and is distant from Jerusalem threescore furlongs. (218) He also laid a tribute upon the Jews wheresoever they were, and enjoined every one of them to bring two drachmae every year into the Capitol, as they used to pay the same to the temple at Jerusalem. And this was the state of the Jewish affairs at this time.

CHAPTER 7.

CONCERNING THE CALAMITY THAT BEFELL ANTIOCHUS, KING OF COMMAGENE. AS ALSO CONCERNING THE ALANS AND WHAT GREAT MISCHIEFS THEY DID TO THE MEDES AND ARMENIANS.

1. (219) AND now, in the fourth year of the reign of Vespasian, it came to pass that Antiochus, the king of Commagene, with all his family, fell into very great calamities. The occasion was this: (220) Cesennius Petus, who was president of Syria at this time, whether it were done out of regard to truth, or whether out of hatred to Antiochus, (for which was the real motive was never thoroughly discovered,) sent an epistle to Caesar, (221) and therein told him that Antiochus, with his son Epiphanes, had resolved to rebel against the Romans, and had made a league with the king of Parthia to that purpose; (222) that it was therefore fit to prevent them, lest they prevent us, and begin such a war as may cause a general disturbance in the Roman empire. (223) Now Caesar was disposed to take some care about the matter, since this discovery was made; for the neighborhood of the kingdoms made this affair worthy of greater regard; (224) for Samosata, the capital of Commagene, lies upon Euphrates, and upon any such design could afford an easy passage over it to the Parthians, and could also afford them a secure reception. (225) Petus was accordingly believed, and had authority given him of doing what he should think proper in the case; so he set about it without delay, and fell upon Commagene before Antiochus and his people had the least expectation of his coming: he had with him the tenth legion, as also some cohorts and troops of horsemen. (226) These kings also came to his assistance: Aristobulus, king of the country called Chalcidene, and Sohemus, who was called king of Emesa. (227) Nor was there any opposition made to his forces when they entered the kingdom; for no one of that country would so much as lift up his hand against them. (228) When Antiochus heard this unexpected news, he could not think in the least of making war with the Romans, but determined to leave his whole kingdom in the state wherein it now was, and to retire privately, with his wife and children, as thinking thereby to demonstrate himself to the Romans to be innocent as to the accusation laid against him. (229) So he went away from that city as far as a hundred and twenty furlongs, into a plain, and there pitched his tents.

2. (230) Petus then sent some of his men to seize upon Samosata, and by their means took possession of that city, while he went himself to attack Antiochus with the rest of his army. (231) However, the king was not prevailed upon by the distress he was in to do any thing in the way of war against the Romans, but bemoaned his own hard fate, and endured with patience what he was not able to prevent. (232) But his sons, who were young, and unexperienced in war, but of strong bodies, were not easily induced to bear this calamity without fighting. Epiphanes, therefore, and Callinicus, betook themselves to military force; (233) and as the battle was a sore one, and lasted all the day long, they showed their own valor in a remarkable manner, and nothing but the approach of night put a period thereto, and that without any diminution of their forces; (234) yet would not Antiochus, upon this conclusion of the fight, continue there by any means, but took his wife and his daughters, and fled away with them to Cilicia, and by so doing quite discouraged the minds of his own soldiers. (235) Accordingly, they revolted, and went over to the Romans, out of the despair they were in of his keeping the kingdom; and his case was looked upon by all as quite desperate. (236) It was therefore necessary that Epiphanes and his soldiers should get clear of their enemies before they became entirely destitute of any confederates; nor were there any more than ten horsemen with him, who passed with him over Euphrates, (237) whence they went undisturbed to Vologeses, the king of Parthia, where they were not disregarded as fugitives, but had the same respect paid them as if they had retained their ancient prosperity.

3. (238) Now when Antiochus was come to Tarsus in Cilicia, Petus ordered a centurion to go to him, and send him in bonds to Rome. (239) However, Vespasian could not endure to have a king brought to him in that manner, but thought it fit rather to have a regard to the ancient friendship that had been between them, than to preserve an inexorable anger upon pretense of this war. (240) Accordingly, he gave orders that they should take off his bonds, while he was still upon the road, and that he should not come to Rome, but should now go and live at Lacedemon; he also gave him large revenues, that he might not only live in plenty, but like

Cleopatra's Gate in Tarsus. (CeeGee, via Wikimedia Commons)

a king also. (241) When Epiphanes, who before was in great fear for his father, was informed of this, their minds were freed from that great and almost incurable concern they had been under. (242) He also hoped that Caesar would be reconciled to them, upon the intercession of Vologeses; for although he lived in plenty, he knew not how to bear living out of the Roman empire. (243) So Caesar gave him leave, after an obliging manner, and he came to Rome; and as his father came quickly to him from Lacedemon, he had all sorts of respect paid him there, and there he remained.

4. (244) Now there was a nation of the Alans, which we have formerly mentioned some where as being Scythians and inhabiting at the lake Meotis. (245) This nation about this time laid a design of falling upon Media, and the parts beyond it, in order to plunder them; with which intention they treated with the king of Hyrcania; for he was master of that passage which king Alexander [the Great] shut up with iron gates. (246) This king gave them leave to come through them; so they came in great multitudes, and fell upon the Medes unexpectedly, and plundered their country, which they found full of people, and replenished with abundance of cattle, while nobody durst make any resistance against them; (247) for Paeorus, the king of the country, had fled away for fear into places where they could not easily come at him, and had yielded up every thing he had to them, and had only saved his wife and his concubines from them, and that with difficulty also, after they had been made captives, by giving them a hundred talents for their ransom. (248) These Alans therefore plundered the country without opposition, and with great ease, and proceeded as far as Armenia, laying all waste before them. (249) Now Tiridates was king of that country, who met them, and fought them, but had like to have been taken alive in the battle; (250) for a certain man threw a net over him from a great distance, and had soon drawn him to him, unless he had immediately cut the cord with his sword, and ran away, and prevented it. (251) So the Alans, being still more provoked by this sight, laid waste the country, and drove a great multitude of the men, and a great quantity of the other prey they had gotten out of both kingdoms, along with them, and then retreated back to their own country.

CHAPTER 8.

CONCERNING MASADA AND THOSE SICARII WHO KEPT IT; AND HOW SILVA BETOOK HIMSELF TO FORM THE SIEGE OF THAT CITADEL. ELEAZAR'S SPEECHES TO THE BESIEGED.

1. (252) WHEN Bassus was dead in Judea, Flavius Silva succeeded him as procurator there; who, when he saw that all the rest of the country was subdued in this war, and that there was but one only strong hold that was still in rebellion, he got all his army together that lay in different places, and made an expedition against it. This fortress was called Masada. (253) It was one Eleazar, a potent man, and the commander of these Sicarii, that had seized upon it. He was a descendant from that Judas who had persuaded abundance of the Jews, as we have formerly related, not to submit to the taxation when Cyrenius was sent into Judea to make one; (254) for then it was that the Sicarii got together against those that were willing to submit to the Romans, and treated them in all respects as if they had been their enemies, both by plundering them of what they had, by driving away their cattle, and by setting fire to their houses; (255) for they said that they differed not at all from foreigners, by betraying, in so cowardly a manner, that freedom which Jews thought worthy to be contended for to the utmost, and by owning that they preferred slavery under the Romans before such a contention. (256) Now this was in reality no better than a pretense and a cloak for the barbarity which was made use of by them, and to color over their own avarice, which they afterwards made evident by their own actions; (257) for those that were partners with them in their rebellion joined also with them in the war against the Romans, and went further lengths with them in their impudent undertakings against them; (258) and when they were again convicted of dissembling in such their pretenses, they still more abused those that justly reproached them for their wickedness. (259) And indeed that was a time most fertile in all manner of wicked practices, insomuch that no kind of evil deeds were then left undone; nor could any one so much as devise any bad thing that was new, (260) so deeply were they all infected, and strove

Aerial view of Masada, looking southeast; note the Serpent path (left) leading up to the mountain-fortress. (photo Samuel Magal)

with one another in their single capacity, and in their communities, who should run the greatest lengths in impiety towards God, and in unjust actions towards their neighbors; the men of power oppressing the multitude, and the multitude earnestly laboring to destroy the men of power. (261) The one part were desirous of tyrannizing over others, and the rest of offering violence to others, and of plundering such as were richer than themselves. (262) They were the Sicarii who first began these transgressions, and first became barbarous towards those allied to them, and left no words of reproach unsaid, and no works of perdition untried, in order to destroy those whom their contrivances affected. (263) Yet did John demonstrate by his actions that these Sicarii were more moderate than he was himself, for he not only slew all such as gave him good counsel to do what was right, but treated them worst of all, as the most bitter enemies that he had among all the Citizens; nay, he filled his entire country with ten thousand instances of wickedness, such as a man who was already hardened sufficiently in his impiety towards God would naturally do; (264) for the food was unlawful that was set upon his table, and he rejected those purifications that the law of his country had ordained; so that it was no longer a wonder if he, who was so mad in his impiety towards God, did not observe any rules of gentleness and common

MASADA—PLAN

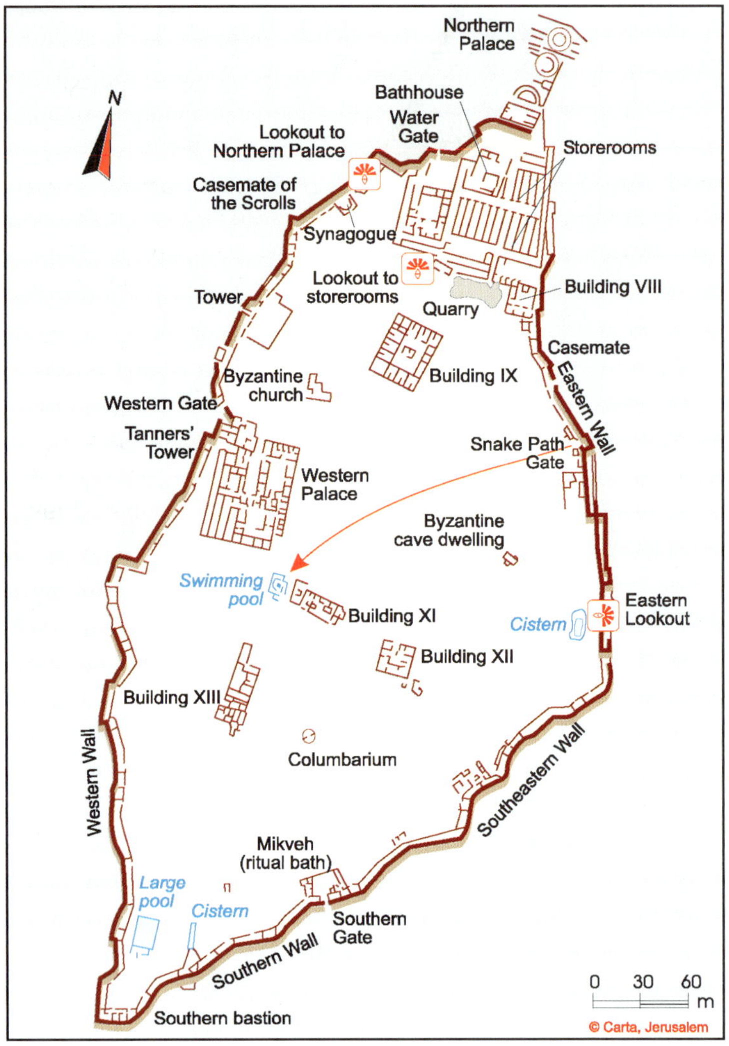

(from *Masada: A Carta Field Guide* / Hanan Eshel)

affection towards men. (265) Again, therefore, what mischief was there which Simon the son of Gioras did not do? or what kind of abuses did he abstain from as to those very free-men who had set him up for a tyrant? (266) What friendship or kindred were there that did not make him more bold in his daily murders? for they looked upon the doing of mischief to strangers only as a work beneath their courage, but thought their barbarity towards their nearest relations would be a glorious demonstration thereof. (267) The Idumeans also strove with these men who should be guilty of the greatest madness! for they [all], vile wretches as they were, cut the throats of the high priests, that so no part of a religious regard to God. might be preserved; they thence proceeded to destroy utterly the least remains of a political government, (268) and introduced the most complete scene of iniquity in all instances that were practicable; under which scene that sort of people that were called zealots grew up, and who indeed corresponded to the name; (269) for they imitated every wicked work; nor, if their memory suggested any evil thing that had formerly been done, did they avoid zealously to pursue the same; (270) and although they gave themselves that name from their zeal for what was good, yet did it agree to them only by way of irony, on account of those they had unjustly treated by their wild and brutish disposition, or as thinking the greatest mischiefs to be the greatest good. (271) Accordingly, they all met with such ends as God deservedly brought upon them in way of punishment; (272) for all such miseries have been sent upon them as man's nature is capable of undergoing, till the utmost period of their lives, and till death came upon them in various ways of torment; (273) yet might one say justly that they suffered less than they had done, because it was impossible they could be punished according to their deserving. (274) But to make a lamentation according to the deserts of those who fell under these men's barbarity, this is not a proper place for it;—I therefore now return again to the remaining part of the present narration.

2. (275) For now it was that the Roman general came, and led his army against Eleazar and those Sicarii who held the fortress Masada together with him; and for the whole country adjoining, he presently gained it, and put garrisons into the most proper places of it; (276) he also built a wall quite round the entire fortress, that none of the besieged might easily escape; he also set his men to guard the several parts of it; (277) he also pitched his camp in such an agreeable place as he had chosen for the siege, and at which place the rock belonging to the fortress did make the nearest approach to the neighboring mountain, which yet was a place of difficulty for getting plenty of provisions; (278) for it was not only food that was to be brought from a great distance [to the army], and this with a great deal of pain to those Jews who were appointed for that purpose, but water was also to be brought to the camp, because the place afforded no fountain that was near it. (279) When therefore Silva had ordered these affairs beforehand, he fell to besieging the place; which siege was likely to stand in need of a great deal of skill and pains, by reason of the strength of the fortress, the nature of which I will now describe.

3. (280) There was a rock, not small in circumference, and very high. It was encompassed with valleys of such vast depth downward, that the eye could not reach their bottoms; they were abrupt, and such as no animal could walk upon, excepting at two places of the rock, where it subsides, in order to afford a passage for ascent, though not without difficulty. (281) Now, of the ways that lead to it, one is that from the lake Asphaltitis, towards the sun-rising, and another on the west, where the ascent is easier: (282) the one of these ways is called the Serpent, as resembling that animal in its narrowness and its perpetual windings; for it is broken off at the prominent precipices of the rock, and returns frequently into itself, and lengthening again by little and little, hath much ado to proceed forward; (283) and he that would walk along it must first go on one leg, and then on the other; there is also nothing but destruction, in case your feet slip; for on each side there is a vastly deep chasm and precipice, sufficient to quell the courage of every body by the terror it infuses into the mind. (284) When, therefore, a man hath gone along this way for thirty furlongs, the rest is the top of the hill—not ending at a small point, but is no other than a plain upon the highest part of the mountain. (285) Upon this top of the hill, Jonathan the high priest first of all built a fortress, and called it Masada: after which the rebuilding of this place employed the care of king Herod to a great degree; (286) he also built a wall round about the entire top of the hill, seven furlongs long; it was composed of white stone; its height was twelve, and its breadth eight cubits; (287) there were also erected upon that wall thirty-eight towers, each of them fifty cubits high; out of which you might pass into lesser edifices, which were built on the inside, round the entire wall; (288) for the king reserved the top of the hill, which was of a fat soil, and better mould than any valley for agriculture, that such as committed themselves to this fortress for their preservation might not even there be quite destitute of food, in case they should ever be in want of it from abroad. (289) Moreover, he built a palace therein at the western ascent; it was within and beneath the walls of the citadel, but inclined to its north side. Now the wall of this palace was very high and strong, and had at

its four corners towers sixty cubits high. (290) The furniture also of the edifices, and of the cloisters, and of the baths, was of great variety, and very costly; and these buildings were supported by pillars of single stones on every side; the walls and also the floors of the edifices were paved with stones of several colors. He also had cut many and great pits, as reservoirs for water, out of the rocks, (291) at every one of the places that were inhabited, both above and round about the palace, and before the wall; and by this contrivance he endeavored to have water for several uses, as if there had been fountains there. (292) Here was also a road digged from the palace, and leading to the very top of the mountain, which yet could not be seen by such as were without [the walls]; nor indeed could enemies easily make use of the plain roads; (293) for the road on the east side, as we have already taken notice, could not be walked upon, by reason of its nature; and for the western road, he built a large tower at its narrowest place, at no less a distance from the top of the hill than a thousand cubits; which tower could not possibly be passed by, nor could it be easily taken; nor indeed could those that walked along it without any fear (such was its contrivance) easily get to the end of it; (294) and after such a manner was this citadel fortified, both by nature and by the hands of men, in order to frustrate the attacks of enemies.

4. (295) As for the furniture that was within this fortress, it was still more wonderful on account of its splendor and long continuance; (296) for here was laid up corn in large quantities, and such as would subsist men for a long time; here was also wine and oil in abundance, with all kinds of pulse and dates heaped up together; (297) all which Eleazar found there, when he and his Sicarii got possession of the fortress by treachery. These fruits were also fresh and full ripe, and no way inferior to such fruits newly laid in, although they were little short of a hundred years from the laying in these provisions [by Herod], till the place was taken by the Romans; nay, indeed, when the Romans got possession of those fruits that were left, they found them not corrupted all that while; (298) nor should we be mistaken, if we supposed that the air was here the cause of their enduring so long; this fortress being so high, and so free from the mixture of all terrain and muddy particles of matter. (299) There was also found here a large quantity of all sorts of weapons of war, which had been treasured up by that king, and were sufficient for ten thousand men; there was east iron, and brass, and tin, which show that he had taken much pains to have all things here ready for the greatest occasions; (300) for the report goes how Herod thus prepared this fortress on his own account, as a refuge against two kinds of danger; the one for fear of the multitude of the Jews, lest they should depose him, and restore their former kings to the government; the other danger was greater and more terrible, which arose from Cleopatra queen of Egypt, (301) who did not conceal her intentions, but spoke often to Antony, and desired him to cut off Herod, and entreated him to bestow the kingdom of Judea upon her. (302) And certainly it is a great wonder that Antony did never comply with her commands in this point, as he was so miserably enslaved to his passion for her; nor should any one have been surprised if she had been gratified in such her request.

The summit of Masada, looking southwest, showing the Herodian remains, with the Dead Sea (the lake Asphaltitis) in the background. (photo Samuel Magal)

(303) So the fear of these dangers made Herod rebuild Masada, and thereby leave it for the finishing stroke of the Romans in this Jewish war.

5. (304) Since therefore the Roman commander Silva had now built a wall on the outside, round about this whole place, as we have said already, and had thereby made a most accurate provision to prevent any one of the besieged running away, he undertook the siege itself, though he found but one single place that would admit of the banks he was to raise; (305) for behind that tower which secured the road that led to the palace, and to the top of the hill from the west; there was a certain eminency of the rock, very broad and very prominent, but three hundred cubits beneath the highest part of Masada; it was called the White Promontory. (306) Accordingly, he got upon that part of the rock, and ordered the army to bring earth; and when they fell to that work with alacrity, and abundance of them together, the bank was raised, and became solid for two hundred cubits in height. (307) Yet was not this bank thought sufficiently high for the use of the engines that were to be set upon it; but still another elevated work of great stones compacted together was raised upon that bank; this was fifty cubits, both in breadth and height. (308) The other machines that were now got ready were like to those that had been first devised by Vespasian, and afterwards by Titus, for sieges. (309) There was also a tower made of the height of sixty cubits, and all over plated with iron, out of which the Romans threw darts and stones from the engines, and soon made those that fought from the walls of the place to retire, and would not let them lift up their heads above the works. (310) At the same time Silva ordered that great battering ram which he had made to be brought thither, and to be set against the wall, and to make frequent batteries against it, which with some difficulty broke down a part of the wall, and quite overthrew it. (311) However, the Sicarii made haste, and presently built another wall within that, which should not be liable to the same misfortune from the machines with the other; it was made soft and yielding, and so was capable of avoiding the terrible blows that affected the other. It was framed after the following manner: (312) They laid together great beams of wood lengthways, one close to the end of another, and the same way in which they were cut: there were two of these rows parallel to one another, and laid at such a distance from each other as the breadth of the wall required, and earth was put into the space between those rows. (313) Now, that the earth might not fall away upon the elevation of this bank to a greater height, they further laid other beams over cross them, and thereby bound those beams together that lay lengthways. (314) This work of theirs was like a real edifice; and when the machines were applied, the blows were weakened by its yielding; and as the materials by such concussion were shaken closer together, the pile by that means became firmer than before. (315) When Silva saw this, he thought it best to endeavor the taking of this wall by setting fire to it; so he gave order that the soldiers should throw a great number of burning torches upon it: (316) accordingly, as it was chiefly made of wood, it soon took fire; and when it was once set on fire, its hollowness made that fire spread to a mighty flame. (317) Now, at the very beginning of this fire, a north wind that then blew proved terrible to the Romans; for by bringing the flame downward, it drove it upon them, and they were almost in despair of success, as fearing their machines would be burnt: (318) but after this, on a sudden the wind changed into the south, as if it were done by Divine Providence, and blew strongly the contrary way, and carried the flame, and drove it against the wall, which was now on fire through its entire thickness. (319) So the Romans, having now assistance from God, returned to their camp with joy, and resolved to attack their enemies the very next day; on which occasion they set their watch more carefully that night, lest any of the Jews should run away from them without being discovered.

Masada, with the northern complex and three-tiered palace of Herod the Great in foreground. (photo Samuel Magal)

6. (320) However, neither did Eleazar once think of flying away, nor would he permit any one else to do so; (321) but when he saw their wall burned down by the fire, and could devise no other way of escaping, or room for their further courage, and setting before their eyes what the Romans would do to them, their children, and their wives, if they got them into their power, he consulted about having them all slain. (322) Now as he judged this to be the best thing they could do in their present circumstances, he gathered the most courageous of his companions together, and encouraged them to take that course by a speech which he made to them in the manner following: (323) "Since we, long ago, my gener-

Camp F, the headquarters of the Roman commander Flavius Silva, at the western foot of Masada. (photo Samuel Magal)

ous friends, resolved never to be servants to the Romans, nor to any other than to God himself, who alone is the true and just Lord of mankind, the time is now come that obliges us to make that resolution true in practice. (324) And let us not at this time bring a reproach upon ourselves for self-contradiction, while we formerly would not undergo slavery, though it were then without danger, but must now, together with slavery, choose such punishments also as are intolerable; I mean this, upon the supposition that the Romans once reduce us under their power while we are alive. We were the very first that revolted from them, and we are the last that fight against them; (325) and I cannot but esteem it as a favor that God hath granted us, that it is still in our power to die bravely, and in a state of freedom, which hath not been the case of others, who were conquered unexpectedly. (326) It is very plain that we shall be taken within a day's time; but it is still an eligible thing to die after a glorious manner, together with our dearest friends. This is what our enemies themselves cannot by any means hinder, although they be very desirous to take us alive. Nor can we propose to ourselves any more to fight them, and beat them. (327) It had been proper indeed for us to have conjectured at the purpose of God much sooner, and at the very first, when we were so desirous of defending our liberty, and when we received such sore treatment from one another, and worse treatment from our enemies, and to have been sensible that the same God, who had of old taken the Jewish nation into his favor, had now condemned them to destruction; (328) for had he either continued favorable, or been but in a lesser degree displeased with us, he had not overlooked the destruction of so many men, or delivered his most holy city to be burnt and demolished by our enemies. (329) To be sure we weakly hoped to have preserved ourselves, and ourselves alone, still in a state of freedom, as if we had been guilty of no sins ourselves against God, nor been partners with those of others; we also taught other men to preserve their liberty. (330) Wherefore, consider how God hath convinced us that our hopes were in vain, by bringing such distress upon us in the desperate state we are now in, and which is beyond all our expectations; (331) for the nature of this fortress which was in itself unconquerable, hath not proved a means of our deliverance; and even while we have still great abundance of food, and a great quantity of arms, and other necessaries more than we want, we are openly deprived by God himself of all hope of deliverance; (332) for that fire which was driven upon our enemies did not of its own accord turn back upon the wall which we had built; this was the effect of God's anger against us for our manifold sins, which we have been guilty of in a most insolent and extravagant manner with regard to our own countrymen; (333) the punishments of which let us not receive from the Romans, but from God himself, as executed by our own hands; for these will be more moderate than the other. (334) Let our wives die before they are abused, and our children before they have tasted of slavery; and after we have slain them, let us bestow that glorious benefit upon one another mutually, and preserve ourselves in freedom, as an excellent funeral monument for us. (335) But first let us destroy our money and the fortress by fire; for I am well assured that this will be a great grief to the Romans, that they shall not be able to seize upon our bodies, and shall fall of our wealth also; (336) and let us spare nothing but our provisions; for they will be a testimonial when we are dead that we were not subdued for want of necessaries, but that, according to our original resolution, we have preferred death before slavery."

7. (337) This was Eleazar's speech to them. Yet did not the opinions of all the auditors acquiesce therein; but although some of them were very zealous to put his advice in practice, and were in a manner filled with pleasure at it, and thought death to be a good thing, (338) yet had those that were most effeminate a commiseration for their wives and families; and when these men were especially moved by the prospect of their own certain death, they looked wistfully at one another, and by the tears that were in their eyes declared their dissent from his opinion. (339) When Eleazar saw these people in such fear, and that their souls were dejected at so prodigious a proposal, he was afraid lest perhaps these effeminate persons should, by their lamentations and tears, enfeeble those that heard what he had said courageously; (340) so he did not leave off exhorting them, but stirred up himself, and

recollecting proper arguments for raising their courage, he undertook to speak more briskly and fully to them, and that concerning the immortality of the soul. (341) So he made a lamentable groan, and fixing his eyes intently on those that wept, he spake thus: "Truly, I was greatly mistaken when I thought to be assisting to brave men who struggled hard for their liberty, and to such as were resolved either to live with honor, or else to die; (342) but I find that you are such people as are no better than others, either in virtue or in courage, and are afraid of dying, though you be delivered thereby from the greatest miseries, while you ought to make no delay in this matter, nor to await any one to give you good advice; (343) for the laws of our country, and of God himself, have from ancient times, and as soon as ever we could use our reason, continually taught us, and our forefathers have corroborated the same doctrine by their actions, and by their bravery of mind, that it is life that is a calamity to men, and not death; (344) for this last affords our souls their liberty, and sends them by a removal into their own place of purity, where they are to be insensible of all sorts of misery; for while souls are tied clown to a mortal body, they are partakers of its miseries; and really, to speak the truth, they are themselves dead; for the union of what is divine to what is mortal is disagreeable. (345) It is true, the power of the soul is great, even when it is imprisoned in a mortal body; for by moving it after a way that is invisible, it makes the body a sensible instrument, and causes it to advance further in its actions than mortal nature could otherwise do. (346) However, when it is freed from that weight which draws it down to the earth and is connected with it, it obtains its own proper place, and does then become a partaker of that blessed power, and those abilities, which are then every way incapable of being hindered in their operations. It continues invisible, indeed, to the eyes of men, as does God himself; (347) for certainly it is not itself seen while it is in the body; for it is there after an invisible manner, and when it is freed from it, it is still not seen. It is this soul which hath one nature, and that an incorruptible one also; but yet it is the cause of the change that is made in the body; (348) for whatsoever it be which the soul touches, that lives and flourishes; and from whatsoever it is removed, that withers away and dies; such a degree is there in it of immortality. (349) Let me produce the state of sleep as a most evident demonstration of the truth of what I say; wherein souls, when the body does not distract them, have the sweetest rest depending on themselves, and conversing with God, by their alliance to him; they then go every where, and foretell many futurities beforehand. (350) And why are we afraid of death, while we are pleased with the rest that we have in sleep? And how absurd a thing is it to pursue after liberty while we are alive, and yet to envy it to ourselves where it will be eternal! (351) We, therefore, who have been brought up in a discipline of our own, ought to become an example to others of our readiness to die. Yet, if we do stand in need of foreigners to support us in this matter, let us

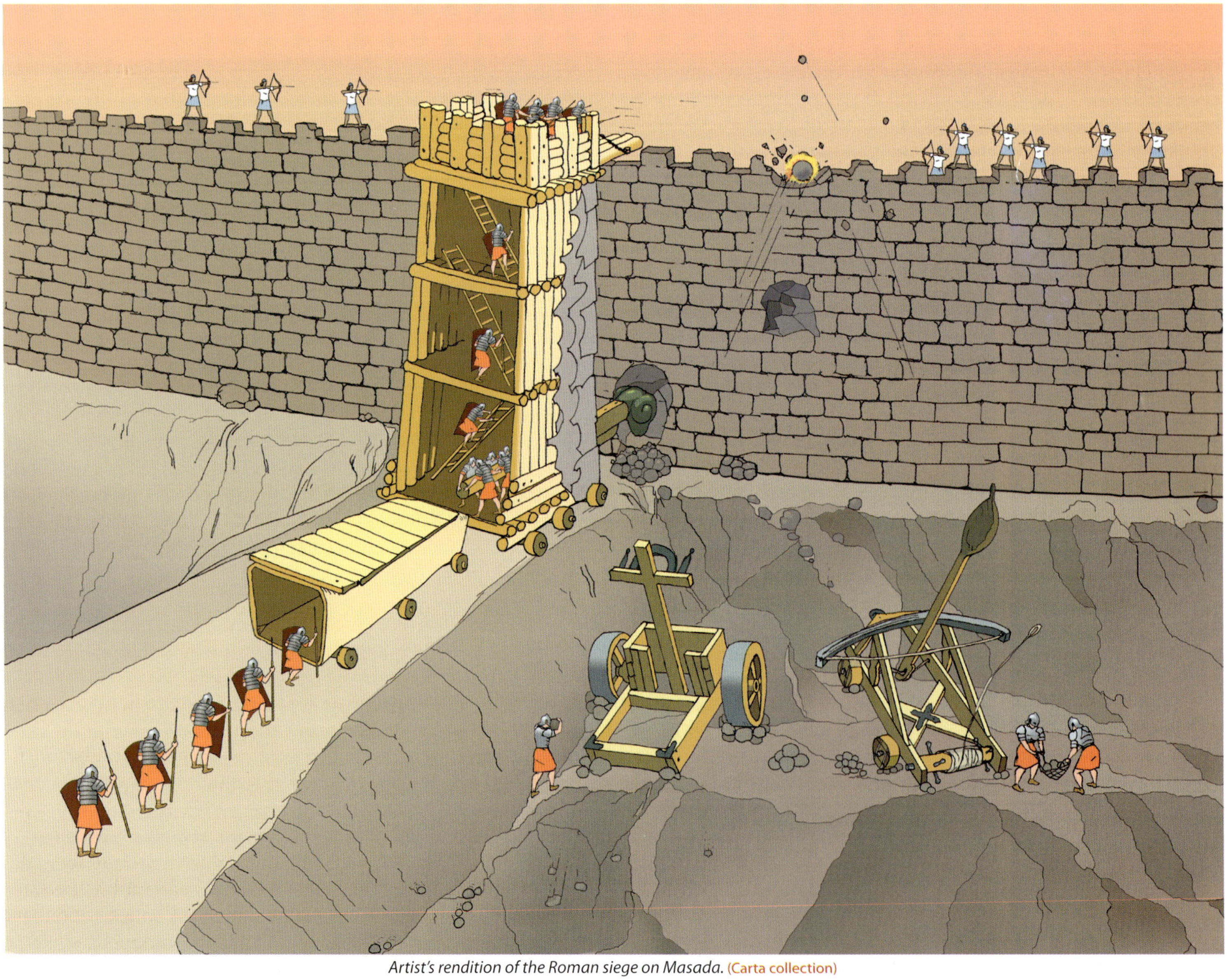

Artist's rendition of the Roman siege on Masada. (Carta collection)

regard those Indians who profess the exercise of philosophy; (352) for these good men do but unwillingly undergo the time of life, and look upon it as a necessary servitude, (353) and make haste to let their souls loose from their bodies; nay, when no misfortune presses them to it, nor drives them upon it, these have such a desire of a life of immortality, that they tell other men beforehand that they are about to depart; and nobody hinders them, but every one thinks them happy men, and gives them letters to be carried to their familiar friends [that are dead], (354) so firmly and certainly do they believe that souls converse with one another [in the other world]. (355) So when these men have heard all such commands that were to be given them, they deliver their body to the fire; and, in order to their getting their soul a separation from the body in the greatest purity, they die in the midst of hymns of commendations made to them; (356) for their dearest friends conduct them to their death more readily than do any of the rest of mankind conduct their fellow-citizens when they are going a very long journey, who at the same time weep on their own account, but look upon the others as happy persons, as so soon to be made partakers of the immortal order of beings. (357) Are not we, therefore, ashamed to have lower notions than the Indians? and by our own cowardice to lay a base reproach upon the laws of our country, which are so much desired and imitated by all mankind? (358) But put the case that we had been brought up under another persuasion, and taught that life is the greatest good which men are capable of, and that death is a calamity; however, the circumstances we are now in ought to he an inducement to us to bear such calamity courageously, since it is by the will of God, and by necessity, that we are to die; (359) for it now appears that God hath made such a decree against the whole Jewish nation, that we are to be deprived of this life which [he knew] we would not make a due use of. (360) For do not you ascribe the occasion of our present condition to yourselves, nor think the Romans are the true occasion that this war we have had with them is become so destructive to us all: these things have not come to pass by their power, but a more powerful cause hath intervened, and made us afford them an occasion of their appearing to be conquerors over us. (361) What Roman weapons, I pray you, were those by which the Jews at Cesarea were slain? (362) On the contrary, when they were no way disposed to rebel, but were all the while keeping their seventh day festival, and did not so much as lift up their hands against the citizens of Cesarea, yet did those citizens run upon them in great crowds, and cut their throats, and the throats of their wives and children, and this without any regard to the Romans themselves, who never took us for their enemies till we revolted from them. (363) But some may be ready to say, that truly the people of Cesarea had always a quarrel against those that lived among them, and that when an opportunity offered itself, they only satisfied the old rancor they had against them. (364) What then shall we say to those of Scythopolis, who ventured to wage war with us on account of the Greeks? Nor did they do it by way of revenge upon the Romans, when they acted in concert with our countrymen. (365) Wherefore you see how little our good-will and fidelity to them profiled us, while they were slain, they and their whole families, after the most inhuman manner, which was all the requital that was made them for the assistance they had afforded the others; (366) for that very same destruction which they had prevented from falling upon the others did they suffer themselves from them, as if they had been ready to be the actors against them. It would be too long for me to speak at this time of every destruction brought upon us; (367) for you cannot but know that there was not any one Syrian city which did not slay their Jewish inhabitants, and were not more bitter enemies to us than were the Romans themselves; (368) nay, even those of Damascus, when they were able to allege no tolerable pretense against us, filled their city with the most barbarous slaughters of our people, and cut the throats of eighteen thousand Jews, with their wives and children. (369) And as to the multitude of those that were slain in Egypt, and that with torments also, we have been informed they were more than sixty thousand; those indeed being in a foreign country, and so naturally meeting with nothing to oppose against their enemies, were killed in the manner forementioned. As for all those of us who have waged war against the Romans in our own country, had we not sufficient reason to have sure hopes of victory? (370) For we had arms, and walls, and fortresses so prepared as not to be easily taken, and courage not to be moved by any dangers in the cause of liberty, which encouraged us all to revolt from the Romans. (371) But then these advantages sufficed us but for a short time, and only raised our hopes, while they really appeared to be the origin of our miseries; for all we had hath been taken from us, and all hath fallen under our enemies, as if these advantages were only to render their victory over us the more glorious, and were not disposed for the preservation of those by whom these preparations were made. (372) And as for those that are already dead in the war, it is reasonable we should esteem them blessed, for they are dead in defending, and not in betraying their liberty; but as to the multitude of those that are now under the Romans, who would not pity their condition? and who would not make haste to die, before he would suffer the same miseries with them? (373) Some of them have been put upon the rack, and tortured with fire and whippings, and so died. Some have been half devoured by wild beasts, and yet have been reserved alive to be devoured by them a second time, in order to afford laughter and sport to our enemies; (374) and such of those as are alive still are to be looked on as the most miserable, who, being so desirous of death, could not come at it. (375) And where is now that great city, the metropolis of the Jewish nation, which vas fortified by so many walls round about, which had so many fortresses and large towers to defend it, which could hardly contain the instruments prepared for the war, and which had so many ten thousands of men to fight for it? (376) Where is this city that was believed to have God himself inhabiting therein? It is now demolished to the very foundations, and hath nothing but that monument of it preserved, I mean the camp of those that hath destroyed it, which still dwells upon its ruins; (377) some unfortunate old men also lie upon the ashes of the temple, and a few women are there preserved alive by the enemy, for our bitter shame and reproach. (378) Now who is there that revolves these things in his mind, and yet is able to bear the sight of the sun, though he might live out of danger? Who is there so much his country's enemy, or so unmanly, and so desirous of living, as not to repent that he is still alive? (379) And I cannot but wish that we had all died before we had seen that holy city demolished by the hands of our enemies, or the foundations of our holy temple dug up after so profane a manner. (380) But since we had a generous hope that deluded us, as if we might perhaps have been able to avenge ourselves on our enemies on that account, though it be now become vanity, and hath left us alone in this distress, let us make haste to die bravely. Let us pity ourselves, our children, and our wives while it is in our own power to show pity to them; (381) for we were born to die, as well as those were whom we have begotten; nor is it in the power of the most happy of our race to avoid it. (382) But for abuses, and slavery, and the sight of our wives led away after an ignominious manner, with their children, these are not such evils as are natural and necessary among men; although such as do not prefer death

THE FALL OF MASADA, A.D. 73

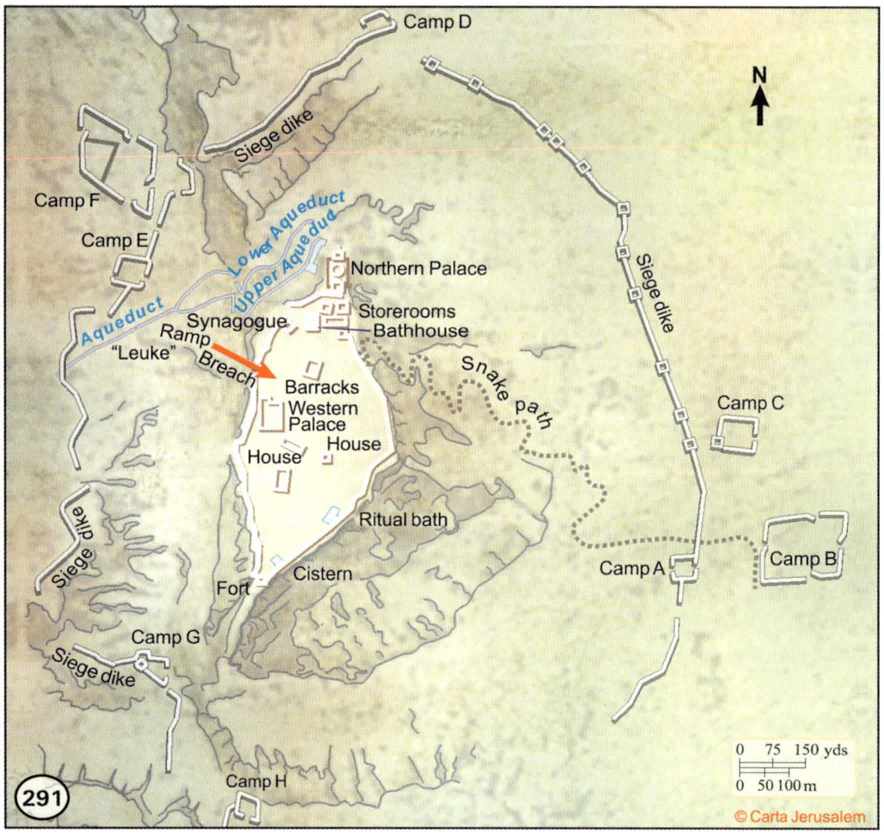

before those miseries, when it is in their power so to do, must undergo even them, on account of their own cowardice. (383) We revolted from the Romans with great pretensions to courage; and when, at the very last, they invited us to preserve ourselves, we would not comply with them. (384) Who will not, therefore, believe that they will certainly be in a rage at us, in case they can take us alive? Miserable will then be the young men who will be strong enough in their bodies to sustain many torments! miserable also will be those of elder years, who will not be able to bear those calamities which young men might sustain! (385) One man will be obliged to hear the voice of his son implore help of his father, when his hands are bound. (386) But certainly our hands are still at liberty, and have a sword in them; let them then be subservient to us in our glorious design; let us die before we become slaves under our eneimies, and let us go out of the world, together with our children and our wives, in a state of freedom. (387) This it is that our laws command us to do this it is that our wives and children crave at our hands; nay, God himself hath brought this necessity upon us; while the Romans desire the contrary, and are afraid lest any of us should die before we are taken. (388) Let us therefore make haste, and instead of affording them so much pleasure, as they hope for in getting us under their power, let us leave them an example which shall at once cause their astonishment at our death, and their admiration of our hardiness therein."

CHAPTER 9.

HOW THE PEOPLE THAT WERE IN THE FORTRESS WERE PREVAILED ON BY THE WORDS OF ELEAZAR, TWO WOMEN AND FIVE CHILDREN ONLY EXCEPTED AND ALL SUBMITTED TO BE KILLED BY ONE ANOTHER.

1. (389) NOW as Eleazar was proceeding on in this exhortation, they all cut him off short, and made haste to do the work, as full of an unconquerable ardor of mind, and moved with a demoniacal fury. So they went their ways, as one still endeavoring to be before another, and as thinking that this eagerness would be a demonstration of their courage and good conduct, if they could avoid appearing in the last class; so great was the zeal they were in to slay their wives and children, and themselves also! (390) Nor indeed, when they came to the work itself, did their courage fail them, as one might imagine it would have done, but they then held fast the same resolution, without wavering, which they had upon the hearing of Eleazar's speech, while yet every one of them still retained the natural passion of love to themselves and their families, because the reasoning they went upon appeared to them to be very just, even with regard to those that were dearest to them; (391) for the husbands tenderly embraced their wives, and took their children into their arms, and gave the longest parting kisses to them, with tears in their eyes. (392) Yet at the same time did they complete what they had resolved on, as if they had been executed by the hands of strangers; and they had nothing else for their comfort but the necessity they were in of doing this execution, to avoid that prospect they had of the miseries they were to suffer from their enemies. (393) Nor was there at length any one of these men found that scrupled to act their part in this terrible execution, but every one of them despatched his dearest relations. Miserable men indeed were they! whose distress forced them to slay their own wives and children with their own hands, as the lightest of those evils that were before them. (394) So they being not able to bear the grief they were under for what they had done any longer, and esteeming it an injury to those they had slain, to live even the shortest space of time after them, they presently laid all they had upon a heap, and set fire to it. (395) They then chose ten men by lot out of them to slay all the rest; every one of whom laid himself down by his wife and children on the ground, and threw his arms about them, and they offered their necks to the stroke of those who by lot executed that melancholy office; (396) and when these ten had, without fear, slain them all, they made the same rule for casting lots for themselves, that he whose lot it was should first kill the other nine, and after all should kill himself. Accordingly, all these had courage sufficient to be no way behind one another in doing or suffering; (397) so, for a conclusion, the nine offered their necks to the executioner, and he who was the last of all took a view of all the other bodies, lest perchance some or other among so many that were slain should want his assistance to be quite despatched, and when he perceived that they were all slain, he set fire to the palace, and with the great force of his hand ran his sword entirely through himself, and fell down dead near to his own relations. (398) So these people died with this intention, that they would not leave so much as one soul among them all alive to be subject to the Romans. (399) Yet was there an ancient woman, and another who was of kin to Eleazar, and superior to most women in prudence and learning, with five children, who had concealed themselves in caverns under ground, and had carried water thither for their drink, and were hidden there when the rest were intent upon the slaughter of one another. (400) Those others were nine hundred and sixty in number, the women and children being withal included in that computation. (401) This calamitous slaughter was made on the fifteenth day of the month Xanthicus [Nisan].

2. (402) Now for the Romans, they expected that they should be fought in the morning, when, accordingly, they put on their armor,

Ostracon inscribed "son of Ya'ir," one of the "lots" used by the last defenders of Masada. (Y. Yadin 1989, Pl. 25, No. 437)

and laid bridges of planks upon their ladders from their banks, to make an assault upon the fortress, which they did; (403) but saw nobody as an enemy, but a terrible solitude on every side, with a fire within the place, as well as a perfect silence. So they were at a loss to guess at what had happened. At length they made a shout, as if it had been at a blow given by the battering ram, to try whether they could bring any one out that was within; (404) the women heard this noise, and came out of their under-ground cavern, and informed the Romans what had been done, as it was done; and the second of them clearly described all both what was said and what was done, and this manner of it; (405) yet did they not easily give their attention to such a desperate undertaking, and did not believe it could be as they said; they also attempted to put the fire out, and quickly cutting themselves a way through it, they came within the palace, (406) and so met with the multitude of the slain, but could take no pleasure in the fact, though it were done to their enemies. Nor could they do other than wonder at the courage of their resolution, and the immovable contempt of death which so great a number of them had shown, when they went through with such an action as that was.

CHAPTER 10.

THAT MANY OF THE SICARII FLED TO ALEXANDRIA ALSO AND WHAT DANGERS THEY WERE IN THERE; ON WHICH ACCOUNT THAT TEMPLE WHICH HAD FORMERLY BEEN BUILT BY ONIAS THE HIGH PRIEST WAS DESTROYED.

1. (407) WHEN Masada was thus taken, the general left a garrison in the fortress to keep it, and he himself went away to Cesarea; (408) for there were now no enemies left in the country, but it was all overthrown by so long a war. Yet did this war afford disturbances and dangerous disorders even in places very far remote from Judea; (409) for still it came to pass that many Jews were slain at Alexandria in Egypt; (410) for as many of the Sicarii as were able to fly thither, out of the seditious wars in Judea, were not content to have saved themselves, but must needs be undertaking to make new disturbances, and persuaded many of those that entertained them to assert their liberty, to esteem the Romans to be no better than themselves, and to look upon God as their only Lord and Master. (411) But when part of the Jews of reputation opposed them, they slew some of them, and with the others they were very pressing in their exhortations to revolt from the Romans; (412) but when the principal men of the senate saw what madness they were come to, they thought it no longer safe for themselves to overlook them. So they got all the Jews together to an assembly, and accused the madness of the Sicarii, and demonstrated that they had been the authors of all the evils that had come upon them. (413) They said also that "these men, now they were run away from Judea, having no sure hope of escaping, because as soon as ever they shall be known, they will be soon destroyed by the Romans, they come hither and fill us full of those calamities which belong to them, while we have not been partakers with them in any of their sins." (414) Accordingly, they exhorted the multitude to have a care, lest they should be brought to destruction by their means, and to make their apology to the Romans for what had been done, by delivering these men up to them; (415) who being thus apprized of the greatness of the danger they were in, complied with what was proposed, and ran with great violence upon the Sicarii, and seized upon them; (416) and indeed six hundred of them were caught immediately: but as to all those that fled into Egypt and to the Egyptian Thebes, it was not long ere they were caught also, and brought back, (417) whose courage, or whether we ought to call it madness, or hardiness in their opinions, every body was amazed at. (418) For when all sorts of torments and vexations of their bodies that could be devised were made use of to them, they could not get any one of them to comply so far as to confess, or seem to confess, that Caesar was their lord; but they preserved their own opinion, in spite of all the distress they were brought to, as if they received these torments and the fire itself with bodies insensible of pain, and with a soul that in a manner rejoiced under them. (419) But what was most of all astonishing to the beholders was the courage of the children; for not one of these children was so far overcome by these torments, as to name Caesar for their lord. So far does the strength of the courage [of the soul] prevail over the weakness of the body.

2. (420) Now Lupus did then govern Alexandria, who presently sent Caesar word of this commotion; (421) who having in suspicion the restless temper of the Jews for innovation, and being afraid lest they should get together again, and persuade some others to join with them, gave orders to Lupus to demolish that Jewish temple which was in the region called Onion, (422) and was in Egypt, which was built and had its denomination from the occasion following: (423) Onias, the son of Simon, one of the Jewish high priests fled from Antiochus the king of Syria, when he made war with the Jews, and came to Alexandria; and as Ptolemy received him very kindly, on account of hatred to Antiochus, he assured him, that if he would comply with his proposal, he would bring all the Jews to his assistance; (424) and when the king agreed to do it so far as he was able, he desired him to give him leave to build a temple some where in Egypt, and to worship God according to the customs of his own country; (425) for that the Jews would then be so much readier to fight against Antiochus who had laid waste the temple at Jerusalem, and that they would then come to him with greater good-will; and that, by granting them liberty of conscience, very many of them would come over to him.

3. (426) So Ptolemy complied with his proposals, and gave him a place one hundred and eighty furlongs distant from Memphis. That Nomos was called the Nomos of Hellopolls [Heliopolis], (427) where Onias built a fortress and a temple, not like to that at Jerusalem, but such as resembled a tower. He built it of large stones to the height of sixty cubits; (428) he made the structure of the altar in imitation of that in our own country, and in like manner adorned with gifts, excepting the make of the candlestick, (429) for he did not make a candlestick, but had a [single] lamp hammered out of a piece of gold, which illuminated the place with its rays, and which he hung by a chain of gold; (430) but the entire temple was encompassed with a wall of burnt brick, though it had gates of stone. The king also gave him a large country for a revenue in money, that both the priests might have a plentiful provision made for them, and that God might have great abundance of what things were

Leontopolis (Tell el-Yahudiyeh): plan of the city and the temple built by Onias.

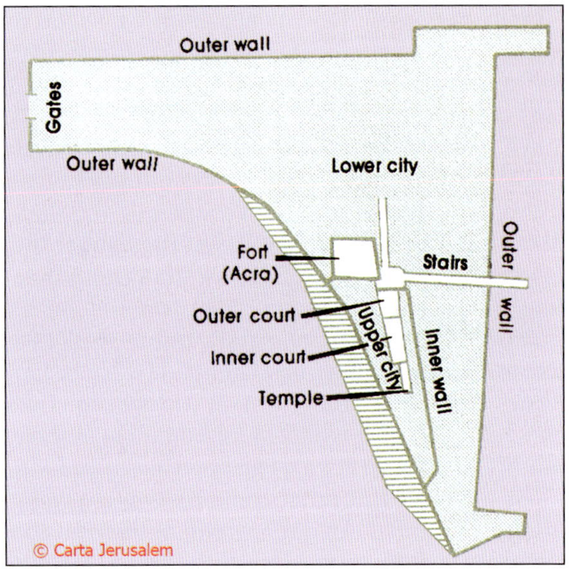

necessary for his worship. (431) Yet did not Onias do this out of a sober disposition, but he had a mind to contend with the Jews at Jerusalem, and could not forget the indignation he had for being banished thence. Accordingly, he thought that by building this temple he should draw away a great number from them to himself. (432) There had been also a certain ancient prediction made by [a prophet] whose name was Isaiah, about six hundred years before, that this temple should be built by a man that was a Jew in Egypt. And this is the history of the building of that temple.

4. (433) And now Lupus, the governor of Alexandria, upon the receipt of Caesar's letter, came to the temple, and carried out of it some of the donations dedicated thereto, and shut up the temple itself. (434) And as Lupus died a little afterward, Paulinus succeeded him. This man left none of those donations there, and threatened the priests severely if they did not bring them all out; nor did he permit any who were desirous of worshipping God there so much as to come near the whole sacred place; (435) but when he had shut up the gates, he made it entirely inaccessible, insomuch that there remained no longer the least footsteps of any Divine worship that had been in that place. (436) Now the duration of the time from the building of this temple till it was shut up again was three hundred and forty-three years.

CHAPTER 11.

CONCERNING JONATHAN, ONE OF THE SICARII, THAT STIRRED UP A SEDITION IN CYRENE, AND WAS A FALSE ACCUSER [OF THE INNOCENT].

1. (437) AND now did the madness of the Sicarii, like a disease, reach as far as the cities of Cyrene; (438) for one Jonathan, a vile person, and by trade a weaver, came thither and prevailed with no small number of the poorer sort to give ear to him; he also led them into the desert, upon promising them that he would show them signs and apparitions. (439) And as for the other Jews of Cyrene, he concealed his knavery from them, and put tricks upon them; but those of the greatest dignity among them informed Catullus, the governor of the Libyan Pentapolis, of his march into the desert, and of the preparations he had made for it. (440) So he sent out after him both horsemen and footmen, and easily overcame them, because they were unarmed men; of these many were slain in the fight, but some were taken alive, and brought to Catullus. (441) As for Jonathan, the head of this plot, he fled away at that time; but upon a great and very diligent search, which was made all the country over for him, he was at last taken. And when he was brought to Catullus, he devised a way whereby he both escaped punishment himself, and afforded an occasion to Catullus of doing much mischief; (442) for he falsely accused the richest men among the Jews, and said that they had put him upon what he did.

2. (443) Now Catullus easily admitted of these his calumnies, and aggravated matters greatly, and made tragical exclamations, that he might also be supposed to have had a hand in the finishing of the Jewish war. (444) But what was still harder, he did not only give a too easy belief to his stories, but he taught the Sicarii to accuse men falsely. (445) He bid this Jonathan, therefore, to name one Alexander, a Jew (with whom he had formerly had a quarrel, and openly professed that he hated him); he also got him to name his wife Bernice, as concerned with him. These two Catullus ordered to be slain in the first place; nay, after them he caused all the rich and wealthy Jews to be slain, being no fewer in all than three thousand. (446) This he thought he might do safely, because he confiscated their effects, and added them to Caesar's revenues.

3. (447) Nay, indeed, lest any Jews that lived elsewhere should convict him of his villainy, he extended his false accusations further, and persuaded Jonathan, and certain others that were caught with him, to bring an accusation of attempts for innovation against the Jews that were of the best character both at Alexandria and at Rome. (448) One of these, against whom this treacherous accusation was laid, was Josephus, the writer of these books. (449) However, this plot, thus contrived by Catullus, did not succeed according to his hopes; for though he came himself to Rome, and brought Jonathan and his companions along with him in bonds, and thought he should have had no further inquisition made as to those lies that were forged under his government, or by his means; (450) yet did Vespasian suspect the matter and made an inquiry how far it was true. And when he understood that the accusation laid against the Jews was an unjust one, he cleared them of the crimes charged upon them, and this on account of Titus's concern about the matter, and brought a deserved punishment upon Jonathan; for he was first tormented, and then burnt alive.

4. (451) But as to Catullus, the emperors were so gentle to him, that he underwent no severe condemnation at this time; yet was it not long before he fell into a complicated and almost incurable distemper, and died miserably. He was not only afflicted in body, but the distemper in his mind was more heavy upon him than the other; (452) for he was terribly disturbed, and continually cried out that he saw the ghosts of those whom he had slain standing before him. Whereupon he was not able to contain himself, but leaped out of his bed, as if both torments and fire were brought to him. (453) This his distemper grew still a great deal worse and worse continually, and his very entrails were so corroded, that they fell out of his body, and in that condition he died. Thus he became as great an instance of Divine Providence as ever was, and demonstrated that God punishes wicked men.

5. (454) And here we shall put an end to this our history; wherein we formerly promised to deliver the same with all accuracy, to such as should be desirous of understanding after what manner this war of the Romans with the Jews was managed. (455) Of which history, how good the style is, must be left to the determination of the readers; but as for its agreement with the facts, I shall not scruple to say, and that boldly, that truth hath been what I have alone aimed at through its entire composition.

INDEX TO PERSONS

Page numbers in italics refer to maps.

INDEX TO PLACES

Page numbers in italics refer to maps.